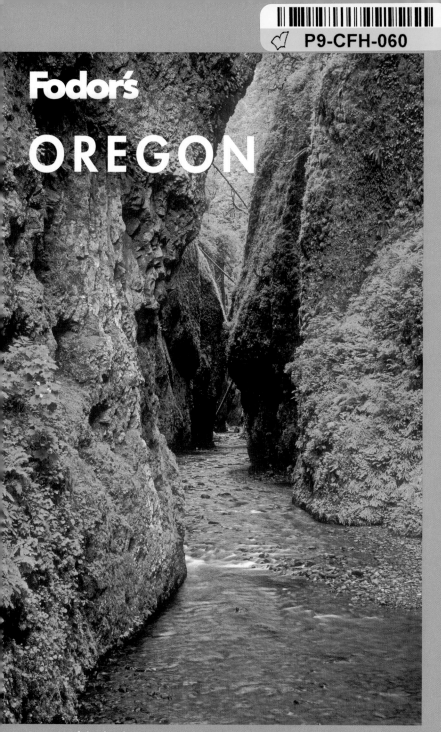

P9-CFH-060

Fodor's

OREGON

WELCOME TO OREGON

Rugged beauty, locavore cuisine, and indie spirit are just some of Oregon's charms. The Pacific Northwest darling is home to hip Portland, whose happening foodie and arts scenes are anchored by an eco-friendly lifestyle. Smaller cities draw you in, too: you can sample microbrews in Bend, see top-notch theater in Ashland, and explore maritime history in Astoria. Miles of bike paths, hikes up Mt. Hood, and rafting in the Columbia River Gorge thrill outdoor enthusiasts. For pure relaxation, taste award-winning Willamette Valley wines and walk windswept Pacific beaches.

TOP REASONS TO GO

★ **Portland:** Terrific food, eclectic music, boutique hotels, and culture galore.

★ **Seafood:** Fresh crab, sea scallops, razor clams, oysters, and salmon.

★ **Wine:** Perfect Pinot Noir, Pinot Gris, and more in the Willamette Valley and beyond.

★ **The Coast:** Scenic strands, tidal pools, whale sightings, headland walks.

★ **Mountains:** From majestic Mt. Hood to the mighty cliffs surrounding Crater Lake.

★ **Scenic Drives:** In the Cascade Range, along the Pacific, through evergreen forests.

Fodor's OREGON

Publisher: Amanda D'Acierno, *Senior Vice President*

Editorial: Arabella Bowen, *Editor in Chief*; Linda Cabasin, *Editorial Director*

Design: Tina Malaney, *Associate Art Director*; Chie Ushio, *Senior Designer*; Ann McBride, *Production Designer*

Photography: Jennifer Arnow, *Senior Photo Editor*; Mary Robnett, *Photo Researcher*

Production: Linda Schmidt, *Managing Editor*; Evangelos Vasilakis, *Associate Managing Editor*; Angela L. McLean, *Senior Production Manager*

Maps: Rebecca Baer, *Senior Map Editor*; Mark Stroud (Moon Street Cartography), David Lindroth, *Cartographers*

Sales: Jacqueline Lebow, *Sales Director*

Marketing & Publicity: Heather Dalton, *Marketing Director*; Katherine Punia, *Publicity Director*

Business & Operations: Susan Livingston, *Vice President, Strategic Business Planning*; Sue Daulton, *Vice President, Operations*

Fodors.com: Megan Bell, *Executive Director, Revenue & Business Development*; Yasmin Marinaro, *Senior Director, Marketing & Partnerships*

Copyright © 2015 by Fodor's Travel, a division of Random House LLC

Writers: Kimberly Bowker, Andrew Collins, Dave Sandage, Christine Vovakes

Editor: Amanda Sadlowski

Editorial Contributors: Caroline Trefler (*Portland editor*), Stephen Brewer, Jacinta O'Halloran

Production Editor: Teddy Minford

6th Edition

ISBN 978-1-101-87923-8

ISSN 1523-8776

All details in this book are based on information supplied to us at press time. Always confirm information when it matters, especially if you're making a detour to visit a specific place. Fodor's expressly disclaims any liability, loss, or risk, personal or otherwise, that is incurred as a consequence of the use of any of the contents of this book.

SPECIAL SALES

This book is available at special discounts for bulk purchases for sales promotions or premiums. For more information, e-mail specialmarkets@penguinrandomhouse.com

PRINTED IN THE UNITED STATES OF AMERICA

10 9 8 7 6 5 4 3 2 1

CONTENTS

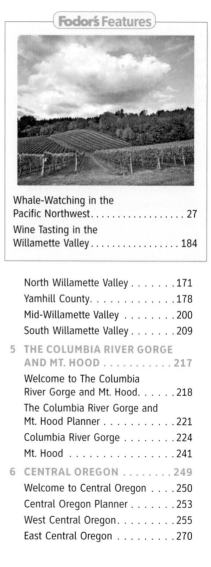

CONTENTS

MAPS

ABOUT THIS GUIDE

Fodor's Recommendations

Everything in this guide is worth doing—we don't cover what isn't—but exceptional sights, hotels, and restaurants are recognized with additional accolades. **Fodor's Choice ★** indicates our top recommendations; and **Best Bets** call attention to notable hotels and restaurants in various categories. Care to nominate a new place? Visit Fodors.com/contact-us.

Trip Costs

We list prices wherever possible to help you budget well. Hotel and restaurant price categories from **$** to **$$$$** are noted alongside each recommendation. For hotels, we include the lowest cost of a standard double room in high season. For restaurants, we cite the average price of a main course at dinner or, if dinner isn't served, at lunch. For attractions, we always list adult admission fees; discounts are usually available for children, students, and senior citizens.

Hotels

Our local writers vet every hotel to recommend the best overnights in each price category, from budget to expensive. Unless otherwise specified, you can expect private bath, phone, and TV in your room. For expanded hotel reviews, facilities, and deals, visit Fodors.com.

Top Picks	Hotels & Restaurants
★ Fodor's Choice	
	⌂ Hotel
Listings	⤴ Number of rooms
⊠ Address	
⊠ Branch address	⦿| Meal plans
☏ Telephone	✕ Restaurant
🖷 Fax	⇴ Reservations
⊕ Website	🏛 Dress code
✉ E-mail	▭ No credit cards
⌑ Admission fee	$ Price
☉ Open/closed times	**Other**
Ⓜ Subway	⇨ See also
✛ Directions or Map coordinates	☞ Take note
	🏌 Golf facilities

Restaurants

Unless we state otherwise, restaurants are open for lunch and dinner daily. We mention dress code only when there's a specific requirement and reservations only when they're essential or not accepted. To make restaurant reservations, visit Fodors.com.

Credit Cards

The hotels and restaurants in this guide typically accept credit cards. If not, we'll say so.

EUGENE FODOR

Hungarian-born Eugene Fodor (1905–91) began his travel career as an interpreter on a French cruise ship. The experience inspired him to write *On the Continent* (1936), the first guidebook to receive annual updates and discuss a country's way of life as well as its sights. Fodor later joined the U.S. Army and worked for the OSS in World War II. After the war, he kept up his intelligence work while expanding his guidebook series. During the Cold War, many guides were written by fellow agents who understood the value of insider information. Today's guides continue Fodor's legacy by providing travelers with timely coverage, insider tips, and cultural context.

EXPERIENCE OREGON

WHAT'S WHERE

Numbers refer to chapters.

2 Portland. With its pedestrian-friendly Downtown and great public transit, Portland is easy to explore. The city has become a magnet for fans of artisanal food, beer, wine, and spirits, and its leafy parks and miles of bike lanes make it a prime spot for outdoors enthusiasts.

3 The Oregon Coast. Oregon's roughly 300 miles of rugged shoreline are every bit as scenic as the more crowded and famous California coast. Oregon Dunes National Recreation Area, the Oregon Coast Aquarium, Cannon Beach, and the Columbia River Maritime Museum are key highlights.

4 The Willamette Valley and Wine Country. Just beyond the Portland city limits and extending south for 120 miles to Eugene, the Willamette Valley is synonymous with exceptional wine-making.

5 The Columbia River Gorge and Mt. Hood. Less than an hour east of Portland, the Columbia Gorge extends for about 160 miles along the Oregon-Washington border. Sailboarding, kitesurfing, hiking, and white-water rafting abound. Just 35 miles south of Hood River, iconic Mt. Hood is renowned for hiking and skiing.

6 Central Oregon. The swatch of Oregon immediately east of the Cascade Range takes in a varied landscape, with the outdoorsy city of Bend as the regional hub. Make time for the funky mountain town of Sisters and the world-famous rock climbing of Smith Rock State Park.

7 Crater Lake National Park. The 21-square-mile sapphire-blue expanse is the nation's deepest lake and a scenic wonder. You can drive the loop road around the lake, hike, or take a guided boat tour.

8 Southern Oregon. Artsy Ashland and Old West–looking Jacksonville have sophisticated restaurants, shops, and wineries. Nearby, Oregon Caves National Monument is a fascinating natural attraction while the Klamath Falls region has some of the best birding and wildlife-viewing in the state.

9 Eastern Oregon. The vast and sparsely populated eastern reaches of the state promise plenty of memorable sights and recreational opportunities for those who make the effort. The Wild West town of Pendleton (famed for its annual rodeo), the picturesque mountain town of Joseph, and historic Baker City are among the top destinations here.

WASHINGTON

Walla Walla

82

11

30   Umatilla   Milton-Freewater

Hells Canyon
National
Recreation
Area

Columbia River Gorge

84

Pendleton   **82**

Enterprise   **3**

Hood
River

The
Dalles

26   Crown Point
State Park

206

74

Heppner   74

La Grande   **204**

395

Joseph

Wallowa–
Whitman
National
Forest

WALLOWA MOUNTAINS

5   Mt. Hood

Mt. Hood
National
Forest

197

Maupin   **97**

Condon

206

9

Baker City

Kent

Antelope   19   Fossil

218   19

207

BLUE MOUNTAINS

Umatilla National
Forest

26

19   Long Creek

7

245

30

84

Madras

Mitchell

John Day Fossil Beds
National Monument

Deschutes

CASCADE RANGE

Sisters

26   Dayville

Mt. Vernon   John Day

IDAHO

Snake River

Ochoco National
Forest

Malheur National
Forest

26

Ontario

20

Redmond

Prineville

Deschutes
National
Forest

6   Bend

Paulina

Vale

Mt. Bachelor   **395**

20

Willamette
National
Forest

La Pine

Burns

Owyhee
Lake

97   31

Riley   **20**

Crater Lake
National Park

Silver Lake

Malheur
Lake   Crane

Harney
Lake   Malheur National
Wildlife Refuge

Jordan
Valley

Crater
Lake

7

395

Crater
Lake   Mt. Scott

Summer
Lake

Frenchglen

Diamond

78

Burns
Junction

95

Crooked R.

Fremont
National
Forest

Lake
Abert

Steens
Mountain

Owyhee R.

Upper
Klamath
Lake

Beatty

Valley Falls

205

Alvord Desert

66   **8**   Klamath
Falls

Lakeview   **140**

95

CALIFORNIA   NEVADA

0   60 miles

0   60 kilometers

OREGON PLANNER

Fast Facts	Getting Here and Around

Fast Facts

Packing It's all about the layers here, as the weather can morph from cold and overcast to warm and sunny and back again in the course of a few hours, especially in spring and fall. The climate also varies tremendously within relatively short distances, such as between the coast and the Willamette Valley, or between the mostly dry and sunny eastern half of the state and the cold and frequently snowy Cascade Range.

Safety The most dangerous element of Oregon is the great outdoors. Don't hike alone, and make sure you bring enough water plus basic first-aid items. If you're not an experienced hiker, stick to tourist-friendly spots like the more accessible parts of the designated parks. When driving, take care to use only designated and maintained roads and check road conditions ahead of time when planning to pass through mountainous terrain from fall through spring—many roads over the Coast and Cascades Ranges are closed in winter.

Taxes Oregon has no sales tax—even in restaurants—making it a popular destination for shoppers, although many cities and counties levy a tax on lodging and services. Room taxes, for example, vary from 6% to 10.4%.

Getting Here and Around

Most visitors arriving by plane fly into Portland, home of the state's largest airport. There are smaller regional airports in Bend, Coos Bay, Eugene, Medford, and Pendleton. A smaller number of visitors arrive by Amtrak, which has major service connecting Portland, Salem, Eugene, and Klamath Falls with San Francisco, Seattle, and Spokane, or by Greyhound bus, with stops in most major cities and towns.

Major interstate highways connect Oregon with neighboring Washington, Idaho, and Northern California, making it easy to include the state as part of a regional Pacific Northwest road trip to Seattle, Vancouver, and environs. Interstate 5 is Oregon's major north–south freeway, and Interstate 84 cuts east–west across the northern part of the state from Portland through the Columbia Gorge and then southeast toward Boise, Idaho. Other major roads through the state, all of them offering plenty of beautiful scenery, include U.S. 101 up and down the coast, U.S. 97 north–south along the eastern edge of the Cascade Range, and U.S. 20 and U.S. 26, both of which run east–west from the coast through the Willamette Valley, over the Cascades, and across the state's vast eastern interior.

The only destination within Oregon that's genuinely easy to visit without a car is Portland, which is served by a superb public transportation system that includes buses, streetcars, and light rail. The city's attractive, safe Downtown is also easy to navigate on foot. If you do bring a car to Portland, you'll find the driving relatively easy—parking can be pricey at Downtown hotels but is otherwise cheap and easy to find outside the immediate city center. However, a car is necessary for exploring nearby points of interest or making day trips to the Willamette wine country, Columbia Gorge, Mt. Hood, and the coast.

Beyond Portland, it's possible (but not especially practical) to get by without a car in compact cities and larger towns like Ashland, Bend, Eugene, and Salem, but many key attractions in these areas lie farther afield, and a car is ideal for exploring. To reach and explore most of the state, including the beautiful coastline and the rugged, sparsely populated central and eastern portions, a car is a necessity.

Top Festivals

Portland is the state's festivals hub, with many events taking place Downtown on the city's scenic Willamette riverfront, but you'll find plenty of engaging festivals elsewhere. Also keep in mind that Oregon is wild about farmers' markets—most towns in the state have one from spring through fall, and Portland has dozens. There's often live entertainment, arts and crafts, and prepared food at these bustling outdoor markets.

Spring Portland's **Cinco de Mayo** festival celebrates its sister-city relationship with Guadalajara, Mexico, and runs a full weekend in early May. Arguably the most famous event in the state, the **Portland Rose Festival** consists of numerous events and parties throughout late May and early June, culminating in a huge parade.

Summer Among the many big waterfront gatherings in Portland each summer, check out **Portland Gay Pride** in mid-June, the **Waterfront Blues Festival** over Fourth of July weekend, the **Oregon Brewers Festival** in late July, and the **Bite of Oregon** food festival in early August.

Wine lovers flock to McMinnville, in the Willamette Valley, to sample fine regional vintages in late July during the **International Pinot Noir Celebration**. Autumn is just around the corner with the arrival of the **Oregon State Fair** in Salem in late August and early September.

Fall Since 2012, Portland's **Feast** has rapidly earned kudos as one of the most talked-about international culinary festivals in the country, with events and meals prepared by both local and national star chefs. The **Pendleton Round-Up** is one of the most prestigious and downright fun rodeos in the country, drawing more than 50,000 participants and spectators in September. In coastal Bandon each September, the **Cranberry Festival** comprises a fair and parade. The **Sisters Folk Festival** brings top-name artists to this scenic mountain town near Bend, which hosts its bustling **Bend Fall Festival** in mid-September.

Winter Although it sounds like a short-term seasonal event, Ashland's famed **Oregon Shakespeare Festival** actually runs from late February through early November. In mid-February, **Oregon WinterFest** in Bend celebrates the region's winter sports with a mix of outdoors activities and indoor concerts. Late February's **Newport Seafood and Wine Festival** is a tasty time to visit the coast. Film lovers will enjoy the **Portland International Film Festival**, featuring works from throughout the world each February, which coincides with the acclaimed **Portland Jazz Festival**.

When to Go

There's no more scenic and enjoyable time to visit just about any part of Oregon than summer, which promises the driest, sunniest weather and mild temperatures, as well as lush, verdant terrain and the majority of the state's key festivals and gatherings—it's also the only time the road encircling Crater Lake is open. You should plan for occasionally intense (but dry) heat waves in the valleys, from Ashland clear north to Portland as well as east through the Columbia Gorge. Even in summer, fog and rain can sometimes overpower the coast for a few days at a time.

Spring and fall, however, can be just as beautiful, with blooming flowers and fall foliage, and with fewer crowds in popular spots at the coast, Columbia Gorge, and Willamette wine country.

During the winter months, from the coast to the Cascades (including Portland and the Willamette Valley), rain and gray skies are the norm and quite common in spring and fall. On the balance, temperatures in the Willamette Valley rarely dip below freezing. Although inclement weather dominates the western third of the state, eastern Oregon is typically dry and pleasant, and there's great skiing in the Cascades. Winter is also the best time for whale- and storm-watching along the coast and bird-watching in southeastern Oregon.

OREGON TODAY

Politics

After years as one of the country's "battleground" states, Oregon has steadily become more Democrat: nearly all of the state's major officeholders are Dems, and Portland and Eugene are considered two of the most progressive cities in America. In 2014, the state legalized same-sex marriage and passed a ballot initiative making Oregon the third state in the country to legalize marijuana for personal consumption (as opposed to medical use). However, in rural areas, especially the eastern two-thirds of Oregon and southern sections of the coast, you will encounter decidedly more conservative attitudes, but Republicans here are a mix of socially right and libertarian types. A fair share of self-described Oregon conservatives favor same-sex marriage and marijuana legalization, but retain a strong distrust of what they perceive as big-government regulation—this is especially true among Oregon farmers and ranchers. On the other hand, the Republican Party seldom fields candidates for mayoral and city council elections in the state's largest city, which has half-jokingly been dubbed the "People's Republic of Portland" for its decidedly left-of-center vibe.

Eating

It's hard to think of another part of the country with a culinary scene that's both incredibly inventive and sustainable while still eschewing high prices and formality. Oregon chefs have been at the forefront of the locally sourced and seasonal dining movement, especially those in Portland, Eugene, Ashland, and stretches of the northern coast and Columbia Gorge. Farmers' markets thrive all over the state, and restaurants flock to them for local produce such as hazelnuts, marionberries, pears, and chanterelle mushrooms as well as for artisan products ranging from aged goat cheese to spicy kimchi. Even in small towns like Joseph, Grants Pass, and Depoe Bay, you'll find stellar eateries with oft-changing menus featuring sophisticated Northwestern fare. But the best part is that most of the hottest chef-driven spots around the state offer meals that cost a fraction of what you'd pay for comparable cuisine in San Francisco or even Seattle.

Drinking

Oregon is beyond merely beer-obsessed, although craft ales are clearly at the forefront of the state's assiduous attention to beverages. Portland is well regarded for long-time breweries like Bridgeport and Widmer, but you're more likely to find serious fans hanging out at newer, smaller spots like Commons Brewery and Hopworks. Many of the most acclaimed beer-makers are outside the Portland area—consider Rogue in Newport, Pfriem in Hood River, Deschutes in Bend, and Terminal Gravity in Enterprise. Beyond beer, the state ranks third in the nation in wine production, and plenty of *vino* aficionados consider Oregon Pinot Noirs among the world's best, with Pinot Gris and Chardonnay also earning a great deal of praise. The Willamette Valley, just south of Portland, has been producing top wines for a few decades now; new wineries are also popping up increasingly in the Columbia Gorge and southern Oregon's Rogue Valley. You'll also find coffeehouses sourcing and house-roasting high-caliber, single-origin beans in virtually every neighborhood in Portland, in every good-size town elsewhere in the state, and even in a few small villages (like Sleepy Monk in Cannon Beach and Red Horse in Joseph). Finally, there's Oregon's fast-growing bounty of microdistilleries, with Portland once again at the forefront but with towns as varied as outdoorsy Bend and remote Brookings also joining the action.

Environmentalism

Oregon's embrace of eco-friendly practices permeates just about every aspect of the state. Sustainable design plays an increasing role in real-estate projects—according to the U.S. Green Building Council, the state ranks sixth in the country for LEED-certified "green" construction. Oregon's most populous city, Portland, has become a prime example in promoting high-density development and reining in suburban sprawl; the city maintains a strict urban growth boundary, which was instituted in the early 1970s as part of a then-novel statewide policy. The state is home to thousands of square miles of undeveloped wilderness—Oregon ranks behind only Alaska, Nevada, Utah, and Idaho in its percentage (60.4%) of public lands. As you travel around, it's easy to encounter examples of this eco-conscious ethic, especially in terms of the fast-growing number of hotels, farms, restaurants, coffee roasters, breweries, and wineries that adhere strictly to environmentally friendly practices.

The Outdoors

Oregon offers plenty of activities for outdoor enthusiasts. Just 60 miles east of Portland, Mt. Hood (the state's highest mountain) is the only place in the Lower 48 where you can ski year-round (although trails are limited in summer). There are three different facilities on this mammoth, snowcapped mountain. Timberline Lodge Ski Area is the one that remains open year-round, and its runs pass beside the venerable 1930s Timberline Lodge. Nearby Mt. Hood Skibowl

has less interesting terrain but the most night-skiing acreage in the country. Around the north side of the mountain, you'll find the most challenging, extensive, and interesting terrain at Mt. Hood Meadows Ski Resort, which offers some 2,000 acres of winter snowboarding and ski fun. Of the many excellent places for white-water rafting in Oregon, the Rogue River offers some of the most thrilling rides. Several outfitters offer trips along this frothy, 215-mile river in the southwestern part of the state, from half-day adventures well suited to beginners to multiday trips that include camping or overnights in local lodges. The lush Silver Falls State Park, about 25 miles east of Salem, is so impressive that serious campaigns to admit it to the national park system have taken place recently. In the meantime, it's something of a secret treasure. The 8,700-acre swath of skyscraping old-growth Douglas firs climbs into the foothills of the Cascade Range, where rain and melting snow supply the torrent that roars through 14 different waterfalls, several of them more than 100 feet tall.

OREGON
TOP ATTRACTIONS

Cannon Beach

(A) The nearest town on the dramatically rocky, windswept Oregon Coast from Portland also happens to be one of the most idyllic communities in the coastal Northwest. This town, anchored by 235-foot-tall Haystack Rock, is rife with beachside hiking trails, fine-art galleries, and cafés specializing in organic coffee, Oregon wines, and fresh-caught seafood. Nearby Oswald West and Ecola State Parks have some of the most stunning beaches and hiking trails in the state.

Columbia River Gorge

(B) The 110-mile section of the breath-taking Columbia River provides some of the Pacific Northwest's most spectacular vistas. Towering cliffs on both the Washington and Oregon sides of the river form a dramatic backdrop, and meandering highways line both banks. Water and wind sports abound, and a growing wine-making, craft-brewing, and culinary scene has flourished in recent years.

Columbia River Maritime Museum, Astoria

(C) At this dazzling, contemporary facility in the steadily gentrifying town of Astoria, where the northern Oregon Coast meets the Columbia River, you can tour a fully operational U.S. Coast Guard lightship, and check out engaging exhibits on local shipwrecks, marine life, and how the mighty Columbia has driven the economic and cultural development of the Pacific Northwest.

Crater Lake National Park

(D) The deepest lake in the United States is also the clearest, a fact readily grasped as soon as you behold this searing-blue body of water. It's closed much of the year due to snow, but in summer this 21-square-mile lake is southern Oregon's foremost attraction—the nearly century-old Crater Lake Lodge, perched on the southern shore, makes a memorable overnight and dinner venue.

High Desert Museum, Bend

(E) Evocative and intricate walk-through dioramas and an indoor-outdoor zoo with creatures great and tiny convey the high desert's past and present in a delightfully airy and family-friendly space just south of Bend.

Mt. Hood

(F) Just 60 miles east of Portland, the state's highest mountain is the only place in the Lower 48 where you can ski year-round. There are five different facilities, Timberline Lodge Ski Area being the most scenic.

Oregon Sand Dunes

(G) The 41 miles of rolling bluffs that make up Oregon Dunes National Recreation Area bring out the kid in visitors of all ages—there's something inherently happy about frolicking amid these massive mountains of sand, some of them climbing nearly 500 feet higher than the surf. Here you can hike, ride horseback, and race on a dune buggy, and there's great boating and fishing (plus several excellent seafood restaurants) in the nearby town of Florence.

Powell's Bookstore, Portland

(H) The Downtown Portland legend is the world's largest bookstore carrying both new and used titles, and with its coffee-house, late hours, and endless aisles of reading, it's also a prime spot for literary-minded people-watching.

Willamette Valley Wine Country

(I) Within easy day-tripping of Portland, this swath of fertile, hilly countryside is home to more than 200 wineries and has earned a reputation as one of the finest producers of Pinot Noir in the world—some say the best outside Burgundy. Winemakers in these parts also produce first-rate Pinot Gris and Chardonnay.

IF YOU LIKE

Hidden Food and Wine Finds

As the state—and especially greater Portland—continues to develop cachet for its superb restaurants, farmers' markets, wineries, and microbreweries, it's worth making the effort to venture a bit off the beaten path to find some genuine only-in-Oregon culinary treats.

Clear Creek Distillery, Portland. Clear Creek paved the distillery way with its unique spirits—the pear brandy or cherry Kirschwasser make a perfect nightcap, and a sip of Douglas fir eau de vie will deliver you right to the heart of an Oregon forest.

Josephson's Smokehouse, Astoria. Once the heart of Oregon's salmon-canning industry, the endearingly raffish town of Astoria is still a prime destination for seafood lovers. Drop by Josephson's for hot- and cold-smoked salmon, prawns, halibut, and albacore.

Pfriem Family Brewers, Hood River. This up-and-coming craft brewery offers a Belgian-inspired take on Oregon's hoppy brewing style by creating some of the most distinctive and well-respected beers in the state. The modern tasting room on the Columbia River also serves tasty contemporary pub fare.

Rogue Creamery, Central Point. This small dairy in an otherwise nondescript town near Medford produces phenomenal blue cheeses in several varieties (from Smokey Blue to Oregonzola) plus a delectable lavender-infused cheddar.

Sleepy Monk, Cannon Beach. Portland's Stumptown Coffee is Oregon's most famous coffee roaster, but true aficionados rave about this tiny, organic coffeehouse in Cannon Beach—the dark, bold Bogsman Brew blend is heaven in a cup.

Offbeat Museums

Although you'll discover a plethora of art and history museums, Oregon fascinates visitors with its diverse selection of lesser-known, quirky museums.

Columbia River Maritime Museum, Astoria. The observation tower of a World War II submarine and the personal belongings of the passengers of area shipwrecks are among the exhibits inside, while outdoors on the riverside dock you can tour the lightship *Columbia*, which formerly plied the region's waters as a floating lighthouse.

Evergreen Aviation & Space Museum, McMinnville. Engrossing facts about aviation complement an awesome assortment of flying machines at this expansive repository best known as the home of Howard Hughes's "flying boat," the *Spruce Goose*, which has a wingspan longer than a football field and its end zones.

High Desert Museum, Bend. Evocative and intricate walk-through dioramas and an indoor-outdoor zoo with creatures great and tiny convey the high desert's past and present in a delightfully airy and family-friendly space.

National Historic Oregon Trail Interpretive Center, Baker City. With a simulated span of the legendary Oregon Trail, this well-designed museum offers a thorough and vivid look at life for the some 300,000 pioneers who entered Oregon from the Midwest during the 19th century.

Western Antique Aeroplane & Automobile Museum, Hood River. Two massive hangars make up this museum filled with beautifully restored and still working vintage planes and cars dating back as far as the 1910s.

© 2008 Richard Hallman / Freelanceimaging.com

Distinctive Lodging

In Oregon you can stay in hip, urban neighborhoods, along the beach, in the woods, or atop snow-covered mountains. Accommodations include elegant, full-service boutique hotels, luxury alpine retreats, historic bed-and-breakfasts, cozy ski chalets, rustic national park cabins, and funky local motels.

The Allison Inn & Spa, Newberg. Elegant yet refreshingly contemporary, this 80-room boutique resort and spa has finally given Oregon's scenic Willamette Valley accommodations worthy of the region's ethereal Pinot Noirs.

Caravan–The Tiny House Hotel, Portland. A complex of about a half-dozen ingeniously designed and truly minuscule (80 to 160 square feet) houses, Caravan is situated along hip and artsy Northeast Alberta Street. Each of these bungalows-on-wheels has a kitchenette.

Heceta Head Lighthouse, Florence. Occupying the same dramatic promontory as a working lighthouse, this Queen Anne–style bed-and-breakfast has views of the Pacific that inspire many a marriage proposal.

McMenamins Kennedy School, Portland. The quirky McMenimans company has readapted dozens of buildings around Oregon as pubs, restaurants, and hotels—from a former asylum to this cleverly designed property in a funky northeast Portland neighborhood, a 1915 elementary school.

Timberline Lodge, Mt. Hood. This iconic 60-room lodge on the upper slopes of Oregon's highest peak is buried beneath many feet of snow for much of the year. Admire the 96-foot stone chimney in the lobby.

Majestic Mountaintops

Oregon is studded with mostly conical mountain peaks, which are strung along its Cascade Range from the Columbia River right down to the California border. The lofty summits, most of them topped with a full cover of snow all year-round, make for memorable photography subjects. Those who venture closer, however, will discover some of the state's best opportunities for recreation.

Mt. Ashland. The first soaring peak you encounter upon crossing into southern Oregon on Interstate 5, this 7,533-foot peak has great skiing much of the year, and also rewards visitors with fantastic views of the Rogue Valley.

Mt. Bachelor. This 9,065-foot peak offers some of the best downhill skiing and snowboarding in the West—consider the impressive 3,265-foot vertical drop. In summer, you can ride a chairlift to the Pine Marten Lodge for panoramic vistas across the shimmering Cascade Lakes.

Mt. Hood. One of Oregon's most recognizable land features, the snowy, conical Mt. Hood rises to some 11,245 feet (the tallest in the state).

Neahkahnie Mountain. Although it tops out at just 1,680 feet, this craggy peak is one of the most dramatic along the state's winding coastline. Trails leading to the top draw plenty of hikers from nearby Manzanita and Cannon Beach.

Steens Mountain. A striking sight in eastern Oregon's otherwise rather level high desert, this 9,700-foot peak was created from a massive block of fractured lava and is largely devoid of vegetation. Hikers here have been known to spot golden eagles and bighorn sheep.

FLAVORS OF OREGON

Short of tropical fruit, there aren't too many types of food that don't grow somewhere in Oregon. Myriad fish and shellfish species dwell off the coast, while tree fruits line the windswept Columbia Gorge, and berries grow wild and on farms in the fertile Willamette Valley. A host of other fruits, vegetables, greens, and produce thrive in the temperate climate. Ranch lands, dairy farms, and acres of wheat and other crops round out an abundance that changes with the seasons.

Natural Bounty

Few states can match Oregon's agricultural diversity, which is good news for both chefs and food-crazy locals.

Nuts: There's a reason why hazelnuts—also known as filberts—are the official state nut. Oregon produces 99 percent of the country's hazelnuts, which add a toasty-sweet flavor to meat, salads, desserts, coffee drinks, and more.

Berries: Blueberries, blackberries, and strawberries thrive in the lush Willamette Valley. But the state is home to lesser-known berries highlighted in local preserves, baked goods, and sweet sauces. Subtly tart loganberries are a cross between blackberries and red raspberries. Marionberries have a slightly earthy flavor, and are sometimes dubbed "the Cabernet of blackberries."

Produce: Farmers' markets and restaurant menus are filled with locally grown staples like chanterelle mushrooms, rhubarb, kale, spinach, onions, lemon cucumbers, green beans, potatoes, peaches, cherries, apples, and pears.

Cheese: Open an Oregonian's refrigerator and you're likely to find a fat yellow brick (or a diminutive "baby loaf") of Tillamook cheddar from the century-old collective of coastal creameries. The state's broad swaths of grazing lands generate milk that fuels dozens of artisanal cheese producers. Some of the country's best blue cheese comes from the Rogue Creamery in southern Oregon.

Seafood

With 362 miles of coastline, bays, tide flats, and estuaries, Oregon has a stunning variety of fish and shellfish off its shores. Restaurants and locals are attuned to the seasons, from the start of Dungeness season to the best months for oysters.

Salmon: Oregonians know king salmon as chinook salmon, but make no mistake—the largest Pacific salmon reigns as the prize catch of the state's native cuisine. Silvery coho salmon also swim in the state's coastal rivers. Oregon salmon is phenomenal simply grilled or roasted. Perhaps the most indigenous way to cook salmon is to smoke it, a practice that dates back to Native American dwellers.

Crab: Dungeness crab may be named for a town in Washington, but Oregon harvests more of these prized crustaceans than any other state. They are a delicacy simply boiled and served whole, but picked meat often appears in crab cakes or as a focal point in modern regional dishes.

Shellfish: Low tide on Oregon's beaches can yield thin razor clams or a variety of bay clams. Mussels also grow in clusters along rocky costal stretches while oysters are harvested in several spots. Mussels and clams are delicious steamed (perhaps in an Oregon wine or beer) or in a creamy chowder. Oysters are enjoyed raw on the half shell or lightly battered and fried.

Ocean fish: Pacific halibut, sole, rockfish, hake, lingcod, and the prized albacore tuna are all fished off the Oregon coast. The Columbia River also offers up freshwater favorites like steelhead trout and Columbia River sturgeon.

Pacific Northwest Restaurants

Chefs across the country are in the throes of the farm-to-table movement, but in Oregon the close connection between chef and producer has long bypassed trend status. It's simply how things are done. Restaurants like **Clyde Common, Higgins,** and **Paley's Place** have been producing organic, locally sourced dishes since well before these approaches became national ideals.

Cuisine here tends to be modern and unfussy—a simple, slightly edgy celebration of what grows nearby. Dishes can have Asian, French, or other global influences, but the ingredients ground them solidly in the Northwest. But there is perhaps no more authentically Oregon preparation of meat or fish than cooking it with a crust of hazelnuts.

Portland is assuredly the epicenter of the state's restaurant scene, but wine-country tourism has helped spread noteworthy cuisine to the Willamette Valley, Hood River and the Columbia Gorge, Bend, the Rogue Valley, and the coastal wine region.

Since it was first inhabited, Oregon has looked to the ocean to feed its population. Nevertheless, eastern Oregon cattle ranches provide a ready supply of sustainably raised beef that chefs love to showcase. The recent nose-to-tail dining trend has generated interest in other meats, including rabbit, pork, goat, and lamb, sourced from Oregon farms.

Wine

Pinot Noir grapes have been the central force of Oregon wine-making since the industry took root in the 1960s. Frustrated by Pinot's poor performance in California, a few intrepid winemakers headed north to test out Oregon's cooler climate. Since then, the state has built an international reputation as a paradise of Pinot Noir.

The Willamette Valley's climate is similar to that of France's Burgundy region, where Pinot Noir grapes have reigned for centuries. The rich farmland on the valley floor isn't optimal for grape growing; most vineyards spread across the hillsides that ring the valley, taking advantage of higher elevation, thinner soil, and cool ocean breezes.

Oregon played a central role in America's rediscovery of this famously finicky grape. Today the state is the country's top producer of Pinot Noir. Oregon has 16 official wine-growing regions, though the vast majority of wineries are clustered in the Willamette Valley. Grapes also flourish in parts of southern Oregon and the Columbia Valley along the Washington border.

After Pinot Noir, Pinot Gris is the second most prevalent wine varietal in the state. The delicate and dry yet fruity white wine is somewhat of an unsung hero, since its darker Pinot cousin earns so much acclaim. Chardonnay, Merlot, and Riesling round out the state's top wines. Oregon wines are generally highly affordable, and deliver a great value for the money, although top Pinot Noirs can cost a pretty penny.

Unencumbered by the wine-making traditions of France, or even California, Oregon vintners have taken the lead in growing organic grapes and producing wines using sustainable methods.

PORTLAND WITH KIDS

Many of Oregon's best kids-oriented attractions and activities are in greater Portland. Just getting around the Rose City—via streetcars and light-rail trains on city streets and kayaks, excursion cruises, and jet boats on the Willamette River—is fun. For listings of family-oriented concerts, performances by the Oregon Children's Theatre, and the like, check the free *Willamette Weekly* newspaper.

Museums and Attractions

On the east bank of the Willamette River, the **Oregon Museum of Science and Industry** (OMSI) is a leading interactive museum, with touch-friendly exhibits, an Omnimax theater, the state's biggest planetarium, and a 240-foot submarine moored just outside in the river. Along Portland's leafy Park Blocks, both the **Oregon History Museum** and the **Portland Art Museum** have exhibits and programming geared toward kids.

In Old Town, kids enjoy walking amid the ornate pagodas and dramatic foliage of the **Lan Su Chinese Garden**. This is a good spot for a weekend morning, followed by a visit to the **Portland Saturday Market**, where food stalls and musicians keep younger kids entertained, and the cool jewelry, toys, and gifts handcrafted by local artisans appeal to teens. Steps from the market is the **Oregon Maritime Museum**, set within a vintage stern-wheeler docked on the river. And just up Burnside Street from the market, **Powell's City of Books** contains enormous sections of kids' and young adults' literature.

Parks

Portland is dotted with densely wooded parks—many of the larger ones have ball fields, playgrounds, and picnic areas. The most famous urban oasis in the city, **Forest Park** (along with adjoining **Washington Park**) offers a wealth of engaging activities. You can ride the MAX light rail right to the park's main hub of culture, a complex comprising the **Oregon Zoo, Portland Children's Museum**, and **World Forestry Discovery Center Museum**. Ride the narrow-gauge railroad from the zoo for 2 miles to reach the **International Rose Test Garden** and **Japanese Garden**. From here it's an easy downhill stroll to **Northwest 23rd and 21st Avenues'** pizza parlors, ice-cream shops, and bakeries.

Outdoor Adventures

Tour boats ply the **Willamette River,** and a couple of marinas near OMSI rent **kayaks** and conduct **drag-boat races** out on the water. There are also several shops in town that rent **bikes** for use on the city's many miles of dedicated bike lanes and trails. There's outstanding **white-water rafting** just southeast of Portland, along the Clackamas River. On your way toward the Clackamas, check out **North Clackamas Aquatic Park** and **Oaks Amusement Park**, which have rides and wave pools galore.

Nearby **Mt. Hood** has camping, hiking, and biking all summer, and three of the most family-friendly ski resorts in the Northwest—**Timberline** is especially popular for younger and less experienced boarders and skiers. From summer through fall, the pick-your-own berry farms and pumpkin patches on **Sauvie Island** make for an engaging afternoon getaway—for an all-day outing, continue up U.S. 30 all the way to **Astoria,** at the mouth of the Columbia River, to visit the **Columbia River Maritime Museum** and **Fort Stevens State Park,** where kids love to scamper about the remains of an early-20th-century shipwreck.

ECOTOURISM IN OREGON

The word *ecotourism* is believed to have been coined by Mexican environmentalist Héctor Ceballos-Lascuráin in 1983. According to Ceballos-Lascuráin, ecotourism "involves traveling to relatively undisturbed natural areas with the specific object of studying, admiring, and enjoying the scenery and its wild plants and animals." His original definition seemed a bit too general, so in 1993 he amended it with a line that stressed that "ecotourism is environmentally responsible travel."

Natural beauty abounds in Oregon, which has been a pioneer in sustainability and conservation. Famously "green" Portland is a model of eco-friendly urban planning, with its superb public transit, network of urban-growth boundaries, multitude of bike lanes, and abundance of LEED-certified buildings. Outside the city, six of the state's ski areas (Mt. Ashland, Mt. Bachelor, Mt. Hood Meadows, Timberline, and Anthony Lakes) are members of the **Bonneville Environmental Foundation's Ski Green Program** (⊕ *www.skigreen.org*).

Travel-related businesses that embrace the principles of environmental sustainability are common throughout Oregon. The state's tremendous stock of forests, parks, and preserves is a big reason there's been such a push here to balance growth with preservation.

Travel Portland is one of the only tourism organizations in the country with its own public relations manager dedicated solely to promoting environmentally responsible travel.

Accommodations

Oregon has dozens of accommodations committed to sustainable design and operating practices. Many smaller properties are members of **OBBG Green** (⊕ *www.obbg.org/oregon-green-travel.php*), which is made up of about 15 bed-and-breakfasts that qualify as eco-friendly.

Food and Beverages

Oregon has been a leader in the movement toward producing food, beer, and wine using sustainable practices and emphasizing local and organic ingredients. One excellent resource for learning about organic and sustainable pick-your-own farms and farmers' markets around the state is **Oregon Tilth** (⊕ *www.tilth.org*).

Two statewide organizations dedicated to sustainability in wine-making are **Low Input Viticulture & Enology** (⊕ *www.liveinc.org*) and **Oregon Certified Sustainable Wine** (⊕ *www.ocsw.org*). Dozens of wineries around the state have been recognized for their environmentally friendly practices. Additionally, local breweries with eco-friendly reputations include **Deschutes, Hopworks, Ninkasi, Pfriem,** and **Full Sail.**

Tours

EcoShuttle (⊕ *www.ecoshuttle.net*) is an environmentally oriented charter tour company that arranges winery, brewery, and ecotours. The popular Willamette River boat-tour company **Portland Spirit River Cruises** (⊕ *www.portlandspirit.com*) is a recognized member of Travel Portland's green resources program, as is **Portland Walking Tours** (⊕ *www.portlandwalkingtours.com*). To gain a better sense of the progress Oregon's logging industry has made toward sustainable practices, be sure to visit the **World Forestry Center Discovery Museum** in Portland's Washington Park.

GREAT ITINERARIES

BEST OF OREGON TOUR

With 10 days, you can get a taste of Oregon's largest city, eco-conscious Portland, while also getting a nice sense of the state's geographical diversity—the mountainous and sweeping coast, gorgeous Crater Lake, the rugged Cascade Mountains, and the eastern high-desert regions.

Days 1 and 2: Portland

Start by spending a couple of days in Portland, where you can tour the museums and attractions that make up **Washington Park**, as well as the **Lan Su Chinese Garden** in Old Town, and the excellent museums and cultural institutions along Downtown's leafy **Park Blocks**. This city of vibrant, distinctive neighborhoods offers plenty of great urban exploring, with Nob Hill, Hawthorne, and the Mississippi Avenue Arts District among the best areas for shopping, café-hopping, and people-watching. If you have a little extra time, consider spending a couple of hours just south of the city in the **Willamette Valley Wine Country**—it's an easy jaunt from Portland.

Days 3 and 4: Oregon Coast

(1½ hours by car from Portland to Cannon Beach)

Leave Portland early on Day 3 for the drive west about 100 miles on U.S. 30 to the small city of **Astoria**, which has several excellent spots for lunch and the **Columbia River Maritime Museum**. Pick the main scenic highway down the Oregon Coast, U.S. 101, and continue south, stopping at **Fort Stevens State Park** and the **Fort Clatsop National Memorial**. End the day in charming **Cannon Beach** (26 miles south of Astoria), which has a wealth of oceanfront hotels and inns, many with views of one of the region's seminal features,

235-foot-tall **Haystack Rock**. Be sure to check out the stunning beach scenery at nearby **Ecola State Park** and **Oswald West State Park**.

The following morning, continue south down U.S. 101. In **Tillamook** (famous for its cheese), take a detour onto the **Three Capes Loop**, a stunning 35-mile byway. Stop in small and scenic **Pacific City** (at the south end of the loop) for lunch. Once you're back on U.S. 101, continue south to **Newport**, spending some time at the excellent **Oregon Coast Aquarium** as well as Oregon State University's fascinating **Hatfield Marine Science Center**. Your final stop is the charming village of **Florence**, 160 miles (four to six hours) from Cannon Beach.

Day 5: Eugene

(2½ hours by car from Florence to Eugene with detour at Oregon Dunes)

Spend the morning driving 20 miles south of Florence along U.S. 101 to scamper about the sandy bluffs at **Oregon Dunes National Recreation Area** near Reedsport. Then backtrack to Florence for lunch in Old Town before taking Highway 126 east for 60 miles to the attractive college city of **Eugene**, staying at one of the charming inns or bed-and-breakfasts near the leafy campus of the University of Oregon. Take a walk to the summit of **Skinner Butte**, which affords fine views of the city, and plan to have dinner at one of the top-notch restaurants at the **5th Street Public Market**. Budget some additional time in Eugene the following morning to visit two excellent University of Oregon museums, the **Jordan Schnitzer Museum of Art** and the **Oregon Museum of Natural History**.

Days 6 and 7: Crater Lake and Ashland

(3 hours by car from Eugene to Crater Lake National Park or Prospect)

From Eugene, take Interstate 5 south for 75 miles to Roseburg, and then head east along Highway 138 (the Umpqua River Scenic Byway), which twists and turns over the Cascade Range for 85 miles to the northern entrance of **Crater Lake National Park**. Once inside the park, you can continue along Rim Drive for another half hour for excellent views of the lake. Overnight in the park or in nearby **Prospect.**

The following morning, take the lake boat tour to **Wizard Island** and hike through the surrounding forest. In the afternoon, head southwest on Highway 62 to Interstate 5, and then on to **Ashland**, 95 miles (about two hours) from Crater Lake. Plan to stay the night in one of Ashland's many superb bed-and-breakfasts. Have dinner and attend one of the **Oregon Shakespeare Festival** productions (mid-February through early November).

Days 8 and 9: Bend
(3½ hours by car from Ashland)

Get an early start out of Ashland, driving east along scenic Highway 140, which skirts picturesque **Upper Klamath Lake**, and then north on U.S. 97, stopping if you have time at **Collier Memorial State Park,** to reach the outdoorsy resort town of **Bend**. Here you can spend two nights checking out the parks, mountain hikes, microbreweries, and restaurants of the state's largest city east of the Cascades. Be sure to visit the outstanding **High Desert Museum**, the **Old Mill District**, and **Mt. Bachelor Ski Area.**

Day 10: Hood River
(3 hours by car from Bend)

From Bend, continue north up U.S. 97, and then northwest up U.S. 26 to **Mt. Hood**, 105 miles total. Have lunch at the historic **Timberline Lodge**, admiring the stunning views south down the Cascade

Range. Pick up Highway 35 and drive around the east side of Mt. Hood and then north 40 miles up to the dapper town of **Hood River,** in the heart of the picturesque Columbia Gorge. Spend the night at one of the attractive inns, and try one of this town's stellar restaurants for dinner. From here it's just a 60-mile drive west along a scenic stretch of Interstate 84 to reach Portland.

FIVE SCENIC OREGON DRIVES

Cascades Lakes Scenic Byway
2 to 4 Hours This mountainous 66-mile tour, which is closed in winter due to snow, passes shimmering mountain lakes and prime geological examples of how glaciers and volcanoes have contributed to Oregon's rugged landscape. The route

begins just west of **Bend** on Forest Road 46, which climbs up into the Cascades and through the towering evergreens of **Deschutes National Forest** before turning south by **Devil's Lake**. The road ends at Highway 58, about 80 miles southeast of **Eugene**.

The High Desert: Bend to Baker City

5 to 8 Hours This 230-mile drive from **Bend** across the state's consistently sunny high desert is popular year-round for its stunning big-sky panoramas. Follow U.S. 97 north to **Redmond** (from which you could easily detour to **Cline Falls State Park** for a picnic, or up to the rugged hiking of **Smith Rock State Park**). Next turn east on U.S. 26 and follow the road through verdant ranch lands around **Prineville** and into the pine-forested ridges of **Ochoco National Forest**. Continue into eastern Oregon through the **Painted Hills** unit of **John Day Fossil Beds National Monument**, with its fascinating geological formations, and on through such historic gold-mining centers as **John Day**, and—via scenic U.S. 26 and Highway 7—**Baker City**.

Historic Columbia River Highway

1 to 3 Hours Several sections still exist of this 75-mile road through the magnificent Columbia Gorge. The **Historic Columbia River Highway** (U.S. 30) opened in 1922 and is considered a masterful feat of highway engineering, as it climbs over verdant riverside bluffs and passes beside several massive waterfalls. The longest continuous stretch of road extends from **Troutdale**, just east of Portland, and climbs and dips for 22 miles parallel to the Columbia River, ending just west of **Bonneville Dam**. Be sure to stop by **Vista House at Crown Point**, with its 30-mile views up and down the gorge.

The Southern Coast: U.S. 101 from Brookings to Florence

4 to 6 Hours You'll spy some of the most majestic maritime scenery in the West on the stretch of U.S. 101 that extends north from the Oregon/California border for 160 miles to Florence. You'll first arrive in the pretty fishing village of **Brookings**, through panoramic views from **Samuel H. Boardman State Park**, quaint **Port Orford**, and **Oregon Dunes National Recreation Area** in **Reedsport**. Finish just north in picturesque Florence, which lies on the Siuslaw River and has a charming Old Town with several fine restaurants.

Washington County's Vineyard and Valley Scenic Tour

3 to 6 Hours This meandering series of country roads passes through the heart of Washington County, the nearest patch of the Willamette wine country to Portland, which makes it perfect for an afternoon drive—interspersed with some first-rate wine tasting. The 50-mile route (⊕ *www. oregonswashingtoncounty.com/discover-wine-country/scenic-tour-route*) begins just off U.S. 26, Exit 61, in Swiss-settled **Helvetia**, turns south through **Forest Grove's** pastoral wine country, and then finishes with a turn through the fertile **Tualatin Valley**, passing by vintage general stores and historic taverns.

WHALE-WATCHING
IN THE PACIFIC NORTHWEST

The thrill of seeing whales in the wild is, for many, one of the most enduring memories of a trip to the Pacific Northwest. In this part of the world, you'll generally spot two species—gray whales and killer "orca" whales.

About 20,000 grays migrate up the West Coast in spring and back down again in early winter (a smaller group of gray whales live off the Oregon coast all summer). From late spring through early autumn about 80 orcas inhabit Washington's Puget Sound and BC's Georgia Strait. Although far fewer in number, the orcas live in pods and travel in predictable patterns; therefore chances are high that you will see a pod on any given trip. Some operators claim sighting rates of 90 percent; others offer guaranteed sightings, meaning that you can repeat the tour free of charge until you spot a whale.

COMMON PACIFIC NORTHWEST SPECIES

0   20   40   60   80   100 (ft)

Killer (orca) whale. The killer whale is actually a member of the dolphin family. These white-breasted whales with shiny black dorsal fins live in family-like pods with complex social hierarchies.

Minke whale. The smallest of the great whales, minkes generally feed near the coast and are often spotted around the San Juan Islands and off the coast of Victoria.

Humpback whale. The humpback can leap entirely from the water (known as a full breach). Comparable to gray whales in size, humpbacks are seen most often during spring and fall migrations.

Gray whale. This magnificent creature—noted for its double blowhole—migrates annually between Mexico and the Arctic, making it by far the most common species sighted along the Oregon and Washington coast.

Sperm whale. The only toothed (rather than baleen) great whale, this prodigious animal is observed infrequently because it generally inhabits very deep waters.

Blue whale. Considered the largest animal ever to have lived, the blue whale can weigh up to 200 tons and primarily dwells several miles off-coast, but sightings do occur throughout the Northwest. The whales can blow up to 30 feet in the air.

TAKING A TOUR

Spotting an orca in the Haro Strait between British Columbia and Washington

CHOOSING YOUR BOAT

The type of boat you choose does not affect how close you can get to the whales. For the safety of whales and humans, government regulations require boats to stay at least 100 meters (328 feet) from the pods, though closer encounters are possible if whales approach a boat when its engine is off.

Motor Launches. These cruisers carry from 30 to more than 80 passengers. They are comfortable, with washrooms, protection from the elements, and even snack-and-drink concessions. They can be either glass-enclosed or open-air.

Zodiacs. Open inflatable boats, Zodiacs carry about 12 passengers. They are smaller and more agile than cruisers and offer both an exciting ride bouncing over the waves and an eye-level view of the whales. Passengers are supplied with warm, waterproof survival suits. Note: Zodiac tours are not recommended for people with back or neck problems, pregnant women, or small children.

Most companies have naturalists on board as guides, as well as hydrophones that, if you get close enough, allow you to listen to the whales singing and vocalizing. Although the focus is on whales, you also have a good chance of spotting marine birds, Dall's porpoises, dolphins, seals, and sea lions, as well as other marine life. And, naturally, there's the scenery of forested islands, distant mountains, and craggy coastline.

MOTION SICKNESS

Seasickness isn't usually a problem in the sheltered waters of Puget Sound and the Georgia Strait, but seas can get choppy off the Washington and Oregon coasts. If you're not a good sailor, it's wise to wear a seasickness band or take anti-nausea medication. Ginger candy often works, too.

THE OREGON AND WASHINGTON COAST

A full breach in open waters is a thrilling sight

WHEN TO GO

Mid-December through mid-January is the best time for viewing the southbound migration, with April through mid-June the peak period for the northbound return (when whales swim closer to shore). Throughout summer, several hundred gray whales remain in Oregon waters, often feeding within close view of land. Mornings are often the best time for viewing, as it's more commonly overcast at this time, which means less glare and calmer seas. Try to watch for vapor or water expelled from whales' spouts on the horizon.

WHAT IT COSTS

Trips are generally 2 hours and prices for adults range from about $25 to $40.

RECOMMENDED OUTFITTERS

Depoe Bay, with its sheltered, deepwater harbor, is Oregon's whale-watching capital, and here you'll find several outfitters.

Dockside Charters (☎ 800/733–8915 ⊕ www. docksidedepoebay.com) and **Tradewind Charters** (☎ 800/445–8730 ⊕ www. tradewindscharters.com) have excellent reputations. Green-oriented **Eco Tours of Oregon** (☎ 888/868–7733, ⊕ www.ecotours-of-oregon. com) offers full day tours that depart from Portland hotels and include a stop along the coast at Siletz Bay, a 75-minute charter boat tour, lunch, and stops at state parks near Newport and Lincoln City.

Along the Washington coast, several of the fishing-charter companies in Westport offer seasonal whale-watching cruises, including **Deep Sea Charters** (☎ 800/562–0151 ⊕ www.deepseacharters.net) and **Ocean Sportfishing Charters** (☎ 800/562–0105, ⊕ www.oceansportfishing. com).

BEST VIEWING FROM SHORE

Washington: On Long Beach Peninsula, the North Head Lighthouse at the mouth of the Columbia River, makes an excellent perch for whale sightings. Westport, farther up the coast at the mouth of Grays Harbor, is another great spot.

Oregon Coast: You can spot gray whales all summer long and especially during the spring migration—excellent locales include Neahkanie Mountain Overlook near Manzanita, Cape Lookout State Park, the Whale Watching Center in Depoe Bay, Cape Perpetua Interpretive Center in Yachats, and Cape Blanco Lighthouse near Port Orford.

PORTLAND

2

Visit Fodors.com for advice, updates, and bookings

WELCOME TO PORTLAND

TOP REASONS TO GO

★ **Appreciate the parks:** Head to Washington Park's Japanese Garden and International Rose Test Garden; stroll along the Willamette in Tom McCall Riverfront Park, or ramble amid the evergreens atop Mt. Tabor.

★ **View works of art:** Take part in either the First Thursday Pearl District or Last Thursday Alberta Street art walks if you can. Galleries stay open late, often with receptions and openings.

★ **Float on:** Gaze at Portland's gorgeous skyline in the afternoon light, while gently gliding down the Willamette River aboard the *Portland Spirit.*

★ **Sample the liquid assets:** Visit a few of the dozens of superb local producers of craft spirits and beer, artisanal coffee and tea, and fine wine.

★ **Eat locally:** Plenty of visitors to Portland build their entire daily itineraries around eating; food trucks, cafés, and restaurants showcase the city's farm-to-table, locavore ethic.

1 Downtown. At the center of it all, Portland's Downtown boasts the Portland Art Museum, Pioneer Courthouse Square, and the Portland Farmers' Market along with notable restaurants.

2 Old Town/China-town. This is the area for Asian-inspired public art and the Lan Su Chinese Garden. It's also home to the Portland Saturday Market, North America's largest open-air handicraft market.

3 Pearl District. Bordering Old Town to the northwest is Portland's trendy and posh and bars draw a younger but still sophisticated crowd.

5 Forest Park. Forest Park is the largest forested area within city limits in the nation. Trailheads are easily accessible from Nob Hill.

6 North. The "fifth quadrant," North Portland sits on the peninsula formed by the joining of the Willamette River and the Columbia River. Part working-class, part trendy, North Mississippi Avenue and North Williams Street are hip dining and drinking destinations.

7 Northeast. Containing the Rose Garden basketball arena, the Lloyd Center Mall, the Alberta Arts District, and some of the city's poorest and most affluent neighborhoods, Portland's Northeast quadrant is diverse.

8 Southeast. The vibrant pockets of foodie-approved restaurants make the Southeast a Portland cultural must-see. This neighborhood is also kid-friendly with the OMSI science museum and Mount Tabor Park.

9 West Hills and Southwest. This neighborhood is home to Washington Park, which contains the Hoyt Arboretum, International Rose Test Garden, Japanese Garden, and Portland Children's Museum.

GETTING ORIENTED

Geographically speaking, Portland is relatively easy to navigate. The city's 200-foot-long blocks are highly walkable, and mapped out into quadrants. The Willamette River divides east and west and Burnside Street separates north from south. "Northwest" refers to the area north of Burnside and west of the river; "Southwest" refers to the area south of Burnside and west of the river; "Northeast" refers to the area north of Burnside and east of the river; "Southeast" refers to the area south of Burnside and east of the river. As you travel around the Portland metropolitan area, keep in mind that named east and west streets intersect numbered avenues, run north to south, and begin at each side of the river. For instance, Southwest 12th Avenue is 12 blocks west of the Willamette. Most of Downtown's streets are one-way.

neighborhood teaming with upscale restaurants, bars, and shopping, along with pricey condos and artists' lofts. Don't leave Portland without visiting Powell's City of Books here.

4 Nob Hill. From funky to fabulous, this neighborhood's exciting shopping, restaurants,

Updated
by Andrew
Collins

What distinguishes Portland, Oregon, from the rest of America's cityscapes? Or from the rest of the world's urban destinations for that matter? In a Northwest nutshell: everything. For some, it's the wealth of cultural offerings and never-ending culinary choices; for others, it's Portland's proximity to the ocean and mountains, or simply the beauty of having all these attributes in one place.

Strolling through Downtown or within one of Portland's numerous neighborhoods, there's an unmistakable vibrancy to this city—one that is encouraged by clean air, infinite trees, and a blend of historic and modern architecture. Portland's various nicknames—Rose City, Bridgetown, Beervana, Brewtopia—tell its story in a nutshell.

Rich cultural offerings, prime historic and modern architecture, endless recreational activities, and a friendly feel make Portland alluring for just about everyone. But it seems that Portland's food scene is one of its biggest attractions these days. It's true that Portland's filled with amazing restaurants—though it's not necessarily the recipes that are causing all the commotion. Rather, it's the "locavore" movement—using ingredients that are raised, grown, or foraged within a reasonable distance—that's got diners and chefs excited. Often, diners experience savory fish, fowl, or pasta dishes made with seasonal fruit and vegetable accompaniments that have just been plucked from the vine or ground.

PORTLAND PLANNER

WHEN TO GO

Portland's mild climate is best from June through September. Hotels are often filled in July and August, so it's important to book reservations in advance. Spring and fall are also excellent times to visit. The weather usually remains quite good, and the prices for accommodations, transportation, and tours can be lower (and the crowds much smaller) in the most popular destinations. In winter, snow is uncommon in the city but abundant in the nearby mountains, making the region a skier's dream.

Average daytime summer highs are in the 70s; winter temperatures are generally in the 40s. Rainfall varies greatly from one locale to another. In the coastal mountains, for example, 160 inches of rain fall annually, creating temperate rain forests. Portland has an average of only 36 inches of rainfall a year—less than New York, Chicago, or Miami. In winter, however, the rain may never seem to end. More than 75% of Portland's annual precipitation occurs from October through March.

GETTING HERE AND AROUND

AIR TRAVEL

It takes about five hours to fly nonstop to Portland from New York, four hours from Chicago and Atlanta, and 2½ hours from Los Angeles. Flying to Seattle takes just under an hour, and flying to Vancouver takes just over an hour.

Portland International Airport (PDX) is an efficient, modern airport with service to most major national and a handful of international destinations. It's a relatively uncrowded facility, and both check-in and security lines tend to proceed quickly. It's also easily accessible from Downtown Portland, both by car and public transit.

Portland International Airport (*PDX*). This is the city's—and the region's—major airport. You'll find a pretty good selection of local restaurants and shops inside the terminal. ⊠ *7000 N.E. Airport Way, Portland* ☎ *877/739–4636* ⊕ *www.pdx.com.*

GROUND TRANSPORTATION

Taking the MAX, Portland's light rail train, to and from Portland International Airport is straightforward. The Red Line MAX stops right at the terminal, and the approximately 35- to 45-minute ride to Downtown costs $2.50. Trains run daily from early morning until around midnight—MAX won't be available to some very late-arriving passengers, but it generally runs early enough to catch even the first flights of the day out of Portland, which typically depart around 6 am. You purchase your ticket before boarding at one of the vending machines located in the terminal and at every MAX stop; tickets are also good on TriMet buses and the Portland Streetcar, and transfers within two hours of the time of purchase are free.

Contacts TriMet/MAX ☎ *503/238–7433* ⊕ *www.trimet.org.*

CAR TRAVEL

Portland is a fairly easy city to navigate by car, and if you're planning to explore neighboring regions—such as the coast, Willamette Wine Country, and Columbia Gorge—it's best to do so by car, as public transportation options to these areas, especially the coast, is limited. That said, parking Downtown can get expensive and a car isn't necessary for getting around the city itself. One practical strategy is going without a car during the days you plan to spend in the city center, and then renting a car just for those days when you're venturing outside of the city or exploring some of the East Side neighborhoods, which have ample free parking. Most major rental agencies have Downtown offices, and renting Downtown can save you plenty of money, as you avoid paying the hefty taxes and surcharges that airport agencies charge.

Portland is easily reached via the West Coast's major interstate highway, Interstate 5, which connects Portland to Seattle (which is a three hours' drive north) and Eugene (a little over two hours' drive south). Interstate 84 begins in Downtown Portland and runs east into the Columbia Gorge and eventually to Idaho. U.S. 26 is the main route to the Oregon Coast west from Downtown, and to Mt. Hood going east. Bypass freeways are Interstate 205, which links Interstate 5 and Interstate 84 before crossing the Columbia River north into Washington, and Interstate 405, which arcs around western Downtown. Most city-center streets are one way, and some Downtown streets—including 5th and 6th avenues—are limited primarily to bus and MAX traffic (with just one lane for cars, and limited turns).

PARKING   Compared with other major U.S. cities, Portland has ample parking, even Downtown, both metered and in garages. The most affordable and accessible option is to park in one of several city-owned "Smart Park" lots. Rates start at $1.60 per hour (short-term parking, four hours or less) to $5 per hour (long-term parking, weekdays 5 am–6 pm), with a $15 daily maximum; weekends and evenings have lower rates. The best part about Smart Park is that hundreds of participating merchants validate tickets, covering the first two hours of parking when you spend at least $25 in their establishments.

There are numerous privately owned lots around the city as well; fees for these vary and can be quite pricey, and Downtown hotels also charge significantly (as much as $30 to $40 nightly).

Downtown street parking is metered only, and enforcement is vigilant. You can use cash or a credit card to pay ($1.60 per hour) at machines located on each block; display your receipt on the inside of your curbside window. Metered spaces are mostly available for one to three hours, with a few longer-term spaces available on certain streets.

Outside of the Downtown core, you'll find plenty of free street parking, although time limits (usually an hour to three hours) are enforced in some busier, commercial parts of town. You can find a number of streets with unmetered parking relatively close to Downtown, by heading west of the Pearl District and north of Burnside Street, in Nob Hill and environs. On the east side of the river, unmetered parking is the norm.

TAXI TRAVEL

Taxi fare is $2.50 at flag drop plus $2.60 per mile; each additional passenger is charged $1. Cabs sometimes cruise Downtown streets, but it's far more reliable to phone for one. The major companies are Broadway Cab, New Rose City Cab, Portland Taxi Company, and Radio Cab. The trip between Downtown Portland and the airport takes about 30 minutes by taxi, and the fare averages $35–$40.

Taxi Contacts Broadway Cab ☎ *503/333-3333* ⊕ *www.broadwaycab. com* **New Rose City Cab** ☎ *503/282-7707* ⊕ *www.newrosecitycabco.biz* **Portland Taxi Company** ☎ *503/256-5400* ⊕ *www.portlandtaxi.net.* **Radio Cab** ☎ *503/227-1212* ⊕ *www.radiocab.net.*

TRIMET/MAX TRAVEL

TriMet operates an extensive system of buses, streetcars, and light-rail trains. The Central City streetcar line runs from Nob Hill through the Pearl District, Downtown, and Portland State University campus to South Waterfront. From the Pearl District, the Central Loop streetcar line crosses the Willamette River to the East Side, stopping at the Oregon Convention Center and continuing south to the Oregon Museum of Science and Industry (OMSI). Eventually, the streetcar will cross back to the West Side from just south of OMSI to South Waterfront via the new Tilikum Crossing transit-pedestrian bridge, which is expected to open in September 2015. At first, the bridge will be open only to buses and MAX light rail, but eventual plans call for the streetcar to use the bridge, too.

Metropolitan Area Express, which everybody simply calls MAX, links the eastern and western Portland suburbs with Downtown, Washington Park and the Oregon Zoo, the Lloyd Center district, the Convention Center, and the Rose Quarter. Once the new Tilikum Crossing Bridge opens in fall 2015, an extension of Downtown's MAX Green line will bring service to Southeast Division Street, Sellwood, and the suburbs south of the city. From Downtown, trains operate daily from about 5 am–1 am, with a fare of $2.50 for up to two hours of travel (transfers to other MAX trains, buses, and streetcars are free within this time period), and $5 for an unlimited all-day ticket, which is also good system-wide. A seven-day visitor pass is also available for $26. The ticket for riding without a fare is stiff.

Upon boarding TriMet buses, the driver will hand you a transfer ticket that's good for up to two hours, on all buses, MAX trains, and streetcars. Be sure to hold onto it whether you're transferring or not; it also serves as proof that you have paid your fare. The most central bus routes operate every 10 to 15 minutes throughout the day. Bikes are allowed in designated areas of MAX trains, and there are bike racks on the front of all buses that everyone is free to use.

Contacts TriMet/MAX ⊠ *Ticket Office at Pioneer Courthouse Square, 701 S.W. 6th Ave., Downtown* ☎ *503/238–7433* ⊕ *www.trimet.org.*

TOURS

BIKE TOURS

Portland is famously bike-friendly, with miles of dedicated bike lanes and numerous rental shops *(see the Sports and the Outdoors chapter for more details)*. There are also a couple of great companies that offer guided rides around the city, covering everything from eating and brewpub-hopping to checking out local parks and historic neighborhoods.

Cycle Portland Bike Tours and Rentals. Trust your guide at Cycle Portland to know Portland's popular and lesser-known spots. Tour themes include Essential Portland, Taste of Portland, Breweries by Bike, and several others. A well-stocked bike shop is on-site and serves beer on tap. Bike and helmet are included with tours. ⊠ *117 N.W. 2nd Ave., Old Town/Chinatown* ☎ *503/902–5035, 844/739–2453* ⊕ *www. portlandbicycletours.com* 🔄 *From $40.*

FAMILY **Pedal Bike Tours.** This reliable company takes riders into the heart of the city and out to the beauty that surrounds it, from the Columbia Gorge to the Willamette wine country. If one of the many tours offered here doesn't meet your criteria, custom tours are available, too. Bikes and helmets are included with each tour. ✉ *133 S.W. 2nd Ave., Downtown* ☎ *503/243–2453* ⊕ *www.pedalbiketours.com* ✆ *From $49.*

BOAT TOURS

Portland Spirit River Cruises. Two major rivers lined with pleasant scenery make Portland Spirit River Cruises an engaging tour option. There are brunch, lunch, and dinner cruises, as well as those centered on themes like holidays, tea parties, or live music. Some cruises have a sightseeing option that doesn't include the meal and are less expensive. The company also offers high-speed Explorer Cruises from June through September, which take in about 120 miles of sights along both the Willamette and Columbia rivers; these depart and return to Downtown Portland. Additionally, departing from the town of Cascade Locks (a one-hour drive east of Portland), the stern-wheeler *Columbia Gorge* cruises the Columbia Gorge. ✉ *Foot of S.W. Salmon St., at Tom McCall Waterfront Park, Downtown* ☎ *503/224–3900, 800/224–3901* ⊕ *www. portlandspirit.com* ✆ *From $28.*

WALKING TOURS

Walk the Portland beat with guides who share their personal Portland knowledge, including history, food, brews, arts, and sights.

Food Carts Portland. Get to know the city's famed food-cart scene by tagging along with Brett Burmeister, a true expert on the subject. This 90-minute tour is not just a great way to sample bites from some favorite carts, but also an opportunity to learn more about the culture behind the carts. The tour starts at a predetermined Downtown food cart. ✉ *tours@foodcartsportland.com* ⊕ *www.foodcartsportland.com/tours* ✆ *From $37.50.*

Portland Walking Tours. A slew of tours are offered by this well-established company, but it's the Beyond Bizarre tour that generates the most buzz. Ghost-hunter wannabes and paranormal junkies make this a popular tour that often sells out during the peak season. If it's unavailable, there's also the Underground Portland tour, which highlights the sinister history of Portland, along with a few other options, including tours that focus on the local food scene. Departure points vary depending on the tour. ☎ *503/774–4522* ⊕ *www.portlandwalkingtours.com* ✆ *From $20.*

VISITOR INFORMATION

Travel Portland Information Center ✉ *Pioneer Courthouse Square, 701 S.W. 6th Ave., Downtown* ☎ *503/275–8355, 877/678–5263* ⊕ *www. travelportland.com* ☽ *May–Oct., weekdays 8:30–5:30, Sat. 10–4, Sun. 10–2; Nov.–Apr., weekdays 8:30–5:30, Sat. 10–4.*

EXPLORING

One of the greatest things about Portland is that there's so much to explore. This city rightfully boasts that there's something for everyone. What makes discovering Portland's treasures even more enticing is that its attractions, transportation options, and events are all relatively accessible and affordable.

DOWNTOWN

Portland has one of the most attractive, inviting Downtown centers in the United States. It's clean, compact, and filled with parks, plazas, and fountains. Architecture fans find plenty to admire in its mix of old and new. Whereas many urban U.S. business districts clear out at night and on weekends, Portland's Downtown is decidedly mixed-use, with plenty of residential and commercial buildings, and an appealing mix of hotels, shops, museums, restaurants, and bars. You can easily walk from one end of Downtown to the other, and the city's superb public transportation system—which includes MAX light rail, buses, and the streetcar—makes it easy to get here from other parts of the city. A day pass is recommended.

TOP ATTRACTIONS

FAMILY
Fodor's Choice
★

Governor Tom McCall Waterfront Park. Named for a former governor revered for his statewide land-use planning initiatives, this park stretches north along the Willamette River for about a mile from near the historic Hawthorne Bridge to Steel Bridge. Broad and grassy, Waterfront Park affords a fine ground-level view of Downtown Portland's bridges and skyline. Once an expressway, it's now the site for many annual celebrations, among them the Rose Festival, classical and blues concerts, Gay Pride, Cinco de Mayo, and the Oregon Brewers Festival. The arching jets of water at the **Salmon Street Fountain** change configuration every few hours, and are a favorite cooling-off spot during the dog days of summer. ■ TIP→ Both the Hawthorne Bridge and Steel Bridge offer dedicated pedestrian lanes, allowing joggers, cyclists, and strollers to make a full loop along both banks of the river, via Vera Katz Eastside Esplanade. ⊠ *S. W. Naito Pkwy. (Front Ave.), from south of Steel Bridge to south of Hawthorne Bridge, Downtown* ⊕ *www. portlandoregon.gov/parks.*

Oregon History Museum. Impressive eight-story-high trompe l'oeil murals of Lewis and Clark and the Oregon Trail invite history lovers into this Downtown museum that is operated by the Oregon Historical Society and relates the state's story from prehistoric times to the present. A pair of 9,000-year-old sagebrush sandals, a covered wagon, and an early chainsaw are displayed in "Oregon My Oregon," a permanent exhibit that provides a comprehensive overview of the state's past. Other spaces host large traveling exhibits and changing regional shows. The center's research library is open to the public Tuesday through Saturday; its bookstore is a good source for maps and publications on Pacific Northwest history. ⊠ *1200 S.W. Park Ave., Downtown* ☎ *503/222–1741* ⊕ *www.ohs.org* ☑ *$11* ☉ *Mon.–Sat. 10–5, Sun. noon–5.*

Downtown

← TO JELD-WEN FIELD

First Congregationalist Church

GOVERNOR TOM McCALL WATERFRONT PARK

Willamette River

Hawthorne Bridge

KEY

- ─○─ Max Light Rail
- ←- Streetcar
- ⋯⋯ Bus
- 🚲 Bike only

0   1/4 mile

0   1/4 kilometer

Pioneer Square, Downtown

Pioneer Courthouse Square. Often billed as the living room, public heart, and commercial soul of Downtown, Pioneer Square is not entirely square, but rather an amphitheater-like brick piazza. Special seasonal, charitable, and festival-oriented events often take place in this premier people-watching venue, although over the years, as other parts of Downtown (the Park Blocks, the Pearl District) have become more trendy, the square has lost a bit of its prominence. Directly across the street is one of Downtown Portland's most familiar landmarks, the classically sedate **Pioneer Courthouse**; built in 1869, it's the oldest public building in the Pacific Northwest. A couple of blocks east of the square, you'll find **Pioneer Place Mall**, an upscale retail center that spans four city blocks. ⊠ *701 S.W. 6th Ave., Downtown* ⊕ *www.thesquarepdx.org*

Fodor'sChoice ★ **Portland Art Museum.** The treasures at the Pacific Northwest's oldest arts facility span 35 centuries of Asian, European, and American art—it's an impressive collection for a midsize city. A high point is the Center for Native American Art, with regional and contemporary art from more than 200 tribes. The **Jubitz Center for Modern and Contemporary Art** contains six floors devoted entirely to modern art, including a small but superb photography gallery, with the changing selection chosen from more than 400 pieces in the museum's permanent collection. The film center presents the annual Portland International Film Festival in February and the Northwest Filmmakers' Festival in early November. Also, take a moment to linger in the peaceful outdoor sculpture garden. Kids under 17 are admitted free. ⊠ *1219 S.W. Park Ave., Downtown* ☎ *503/226–2811, 503/221–1156 film schedule* ⊕ *www.*

portlandartmuseum.org ✉ *$15* ⊘ *Tues., Wed., and Sat. 10–5, Thurs. and Fri. 10–8, Sun. noon–5.*

Portland Farmers' Market. On Saturday from mid-March through mid-December, local farmers, bakers, chefs, and entertainers converge at the South Park Blocks near the PSU campus for Oregon's largest open-air farmers' market—it's one of the most impressive in the country. It's a great place to sample the regional bounty and to witness the local-food obsession that's revolutionized Portland's culinary scene. There's plenty of food you can eat on the spot, plus nonperishable local items (wine, hazelnuts, chocolates, vinegars) you can take home with you. There's a smaller Wednesday market, May through November, on a different section of the Park blocks (between Southwest Salmon and Southwest Main). On Monday, June through August, the market is held at Pioneer Courthouse Square, and at other times the Portland Farmers' Market is held in different locations around town (check the website for details). ✉ *South Park Blocks at S.W. Park Ave. and Montgomery St., Downtown* ☎ *503/241–0032* ⊕ *www.portlandfarmersmarket.org* ⊘ *Mid-Mar.–mid-Dec., Sat. 8:30–2; May–Oct., Mon. and Wed. 10–2.*

West End. A formerly rough-around-the-edges section of Downtown, sandwiched between the Pioneer Square area and the swanky Pearl District, this triangular patch of vintage buildings—interspersed with a handful of contemporary ones—has evolved since the early 2000s into one of the city's most vibrant and eclectic hubs of retail, nightlife, and dining. Hip boutique hotels like the Ace, McMenamins Crystal, and Sentinel rank among the city's trendiest addresses. Along Stark Street, formerly the heart of Portland's LGBT scene, there are still a couple of gay bars, but now you'll also find noteworthy restaurants and lounges. ✉ *S.W. 13th to S.W. 9th Aves., between W. Burnside St. and S.W. Alder St., Downtown* ⊕ *www.wepdx.com.*

WORTH NOTING

Portland State University. The only public university in the city takes advantage of Downtown's South Park Blocks to provide trees and greenery for its 29,500 students. The attractive, compact, but steadily growing campus, between Market Street and Interstate 405, spreads west from the Park Blocks to 12th Avenue and east to 5th Avenue. Seven schools offer undergraduate, master's, and doctoral degrees. Close to the Portland Art Museum and Oregon History Museum at the Oregon Historical Society, PSU doesn't have any major attractions of its own, but the campus blends almost imperceptibly with a pretty part of Downtown, and it's the site—along the leafy South Park Blocks—of the city's largest farmers' market on Saturday mornings. ✉ *Park Ave. and Market St., Downtown* ☎ *503/725–3000* ⊕ *www.pdx.edu.*

OLD TOWN/CHINATOWN

The Skidmore Old Town National Historic District, commonly called Old Town/Chinatown, is where Portland was born. The 20-square-block section, bounded by Oak Street to the south and Hoyt Street to the north, includes buildings of varying ages and architectural designs. Before it was renovated, this was skid row. Vestiges of it remain in parts of Chinatown; older buildings are gradually being remodeled, and lately the immediate area has experienced a small surge in development. Portland doesn't have a gay district per se—the scene permeates just about every neighborhood of this extremely LGBT-welcoming city. But you will find many of Portland's gay nightspots in Old Town (and a few others close by in Downtown's West End). MAX serves the area with a stop at the Old Town/Chinatown station.

Fodor'sChoice ★ **Lan Su Chinese Garden.** In a twist on the Joni Mitchell song, the city of Portland and private donors took down a parking lot and unpaved paradise when they created this wonderland near the Pearl District and Old Town/Chinatown. It's the largest Suzhou-style garden outside China, with a large lake, bridged and covered walkways, koi- and water lily–filled ponds, rocks, bamboo, statues, waterfalls, and courtyards. A team of 60 artisans and designers from China literally left no stone unturned—500 tons of stone were brought here from Suzhou—in their efforts to give the windows, roof tiles, gateways, including a "moongate," and other architectural aspects of the garden some specific meaning or purpose. Also on the premises are a gift shop and a two-story teahouse, operated by Portland's esteemed Tao of Tea company, overlooking the lake and garden. ✉ *239 N.W. Everett St., Old Town/ Chinatown* ☎ *503/228–8131* ⊕ *www.lansugarden.org* ⌨ *$9.50* ☉ *mid- Oct.–mid-Apr., daily 10–5; mid-Apr.–mid-Oct., daily 10–6.*

FAMILY **Oregon Maritime Museum.** Local model makers created most of this museum's models of ships that once plied the Columbia River. Contained within the stern-wheeler steamship *Portland,* this small museum provides an excellent overview of Oregon's maritime history with artifacts and memorabilia. The Children's Room has nautical items that can be touched and operated. The *Portland* was the last steam-powered stern-wheel tugboat operating in the United States, and volunteer-guided tours include the pilothouse and engine room. ✉ *Portland steamship, end of S.W. Pine St., in Tom McCall Waterfront Park, Old Town/Chinatown* ☎ *503/224–7724* ⊕ *www.oregonmaritimemuseum.org* ⌨ *$7* ☉ *Wed., Fri., and Sat. 11–4.*

FAMILY Fodor'sChoice ★ **Portland Saturday Market.** On weekends from March to Christmas, the west side of the Burnside Bridge and the Skidmore Fountain area hosts North America's largest ongoing open-air handicraft market. If you're looking for jewelry, yard art, housewares, and decorative goods made from every material under the sun, then there's an amazing collection of works by talented artisans on display here. Entertainers and food booths add to the festive feel (although be careful not to mistake this market for the food-centric PSU Portland Farmers' Market, which also takes place on Saturday, on the other side of Downtown). If taking the MAX train to the market, get off at the Skidmore Fountain stop. ✉ *2 S.W. Naito Pkwy. at foot of S.W. Ankeny, in Tom McCall Waterfront Park, Old Town/Chinatown* ☎ *503/222–6072* ⊕ *www.portlandsaturdaymarket. com* ☉ *Mar.–Dec., Sat. 10–5, Sun. 11–4:30.*

PEARL DISTRICT

Bordering Old Town to the west and Downtown and the West End to the north, the Pearl District comprises a formerly rough-and-tumble warren of warehouses and railroad yards. Much of the Pearl is new construction, but dozens of the district's handsome, historic industrial buildings have been converted into trendy, loft-style housing and commercial concerns, too. You'll find some of the city's most buzzed-about restaurants, galleries, and shops in this neighborhood. The Portland streetcar line passes through here on its way from Nob Hill to Downtown and Portland State University, with stops at ecologically themed Jamison Square and Tanner Springs parks.

Jamison Square Park. This gently terraced park surrounded by tony Pearl District lofts contains a soothing fountain that mimics nature. Rising water gushes over a stack of basalt blocks, gradually fills the open plaza, and then subsides. Colorful 30-foot tiki totems by pop artist Kenny Scharf stand along the park's west edge. There are tables and chairs in the park and wading in the fountain is encouraged. The streetcar stops right at the park. ⊠ *N.W. 10th Ave. and Lovejoy St., Pearl District* ⊕ *www.portlandoregon.gov/parks.*

Lan Su Chinese Garden, Old Town/Chinatown

NEED A BREAK? **Nuvrei.** You'll find some of the tastiest sweets in town at this cozy patisserie and café a few blocks south of Jamison Square. Try the bacon-cheddar biscuit topped with smoked bacon, fried egg, and raspberry jam, and don't miss the little *macaron* bar downstairs. ✉ *404 N.W. 10th Ave., Pearl District* ☎ *503/972–1700* ⊕ *www.nuvrei.com.*

NOB HILL

Fashionable since the 1880s and still filled with Victorian houses, Nob Hill is a mixed-use cornucopia of old Portland charm and new Portland retail and dining. With its cafés, restaurants, galleries, and boutiques, it's a great place to stroll, shop, and people-watch. A quite trendy neighborhood in the 1980s and '90s, Nob Hill feels more established but no less inviting today. At the southern end of 23rd, on the blocks nearest Burnside, you'll mostly encounter upscale chain shops, whereas more independent and generally less spendy retail proliferates farther north. More restaurants and nightspots, along with a handful of shops, line Northwest 21st Avenue, two blocks east of 23rd. The Portland Streetcar runs from Legacy Good Samaritan Hospital on 23rd, connecting with the Pearl District and Downtown.

Bull Run Distilling. Opened in 2011, this exceptional small-batch spirits producer joined long-established Clear Creek as yet another highly quaffable reason to explore Nob Hill. In Bull Run's cozy tasting room, sample such acclaimed spirits as Medoyeff Vodka, Temperance Straight Bourbon Whiskey, Hawaiian cane-sugar-distilled Pacific Rum, and—arguably the prize of the pack—Aria Portland Dry Gin. ✉ *2259 N.W.*

Pearl District and
Nob Hill

Quimby St., Nob Hill ☎ 503/224–3483 ⊕ www.bullrundistillery.com/
☉ Wed.–Sun. noon–6.

Fodor'sChoice
★
Clear Creek Distillery. A pioneer in what has become an internationally
acclaimed local distillery scene, this producer of high-quality spirits is
tucked down a quiet street in an industrial area just north of Nob Hill.
Just ring the bell and someone will unlock the wrought-iron gate and
let you into a cozy tasting room where you can sample Clear Creek's
world-famous Oregon apple and pear brandies, distinctive Douglas Fir
Eau de Vie, and other liqueurs and grappas. ■ TIP➜ **If the peaty, highly
prized McCarthy's Oregon Single Malt Whiskey is available, grab a bottle—they sell out fast.** ⊠ 2389 N.W. Wilson St., Nob Hill ☎ 503/248–
9470 ⊕ www.clearcreekdistillery.com ☉ Mon.–Sat. 9–5.

FOREST PARK

One of the largest city parks in the country, Forest Park stretches eight
miles along the hills overlooking the Willamette River west of Downtown. More than 70 miles of trails through forests of Douglas fir, hemlock, and cedar (including a few patches of old growth) offer numerous
options for those looking to log some miles or spend some time outside.

FodorśChoice **Forest Park.** One of the nation's largest urban wildernesses (5,170 acres),
★ this city-owned, car-free park has more than 50 species of birds and
mammals and more than 80 miles of trails through forests of Douglas
fir, hemlock, and cedar. Running the length of the park is the 30-mile
Wildwood Trail, which extends into adjoining Washington Park (and
is a handy point for accessing Forest Park), starting at the Vietnam
Veteran's Memorial in Hoyt Arboretum. You can access a number of
spur trails from the Wildwood Trail, including the 11-mile Leif Erikson Drive, which picks up from the end of Northwest Thurman Street
and is a popular route for jogging and mountain biking. ■TIP→ **You
can find information and maps at the Forest Park Conservancy office
and website.** ⊠ *Forest Park Conservancy, 1505 N.W. 23rd Ave., West
Hills* ☎ *503/223–5449* ⊕ *www.forestparkconservancy.org* ☉ *Daily
5 am–10 pm*

NORTH

Long dismissed as the city's "fifth quadrant," North Portland has come
into its own in recent years, as the comparatively low cost of real estate
has made it popular with young entrepreneurs, students, and other
urban pioneers. Marked by a 31-foot-tall roadside statue of the strap-
ping lumberman Paul Bunyan (on the National Register of Historic
Places), the neighborhood occupies the peninsula formed by the confluence of the Willamette River (to the west) and the Columbia River (to
the north). In the working-class, portside neighborhood of St. Johns,
old-school barbershops and hardware stores sit alongside a steadily
growing mix of hipster-favored shops, restaurants, and cafés. Farther
south (and closer to Downtown), North Mississippi and North Williams avenues, which are about 10 short blocks apart, have become
home to some of the hottest food, drink, and music venues in the city.

FodorśChoice **North Mississippi Avenue.** One of North Portland's strips of indie retailers,
★ the liveliest section of North Mississippi Avenue stretches for several
blocks and includes a mix of old storefronts and sleek new buildings
that house cafés, collectives, shops, music venues, and an excellent
food-cart pod, Mississippi Marketplace. Bioswale planter boxes, found-
object fences, and café tables built from old doors are some of the
innovations you'll see along this eclectic thoroughfare. At the southern
end of the strip, stop by the ReBuilding Center, an outlet for recycled
building supplies that has cob (clay-and-straw) trees and benches built
into the facade. About a 10-minute walk east and running parallel to
North Mississippi, the bike-friendly North Williams corridor is an even
newer thoroughfare of almost entirely new, eco-friendly buildings rife
with trendy restaurants, nightspots, and boutiques. To get here on MAX
light rail, get off at the Albina/Mississippi station. ⊠ *N. Mississippi Ave.
between N. Fremont and N. Skidmore Sts., Boise, North.*

NORTHEAST

Containing the Rose Garden basketball arena, the Oregon Convention
Center, Lloyd Center Mall, the Alberta Arts District, and some of the
city's poorest and most affluent neighborhoods, Portland's Northeast

Northeast and Southeast

N. E. Killingsworth St.

N. E. Alberta St.

TO AIRPORT →

N. E. Cully Blvd.

N. E. Prescott St.

1

2

N. Mississippi Ave.

Martin Luther King Jr. Blvd.

N. E. 33rd Ave.

N. E. 42nd Ave.

N. E. 57th Ave.

N. E. Sandy Blvd.

N. E. Fremont St.

N. E. Knott St.

N. E. Russell St.

99E

N. E. Broadway
Weidler St.

HOLLYWOOD

TO I-205
→

Memorial
Coliseum

Rose
Garden
Arena

♦ Lloyd Center

Halsey St.

N. W. Naito Pkwy. (Front Ave.)

Oregon
Convention
Center

30

84

N.E. Glisan St.

N. E. 60th Ave.

5

4

3

E. Burnside St.

S. E. Stark St.

S. E. Belmont St.

S. E. Yamill St.

M. L. King Jr. Blvd.

S. E. Grand Ave.

S. E. 20th Ave.

S. E. 28th Ave.

S. E. 39th Ave.

6

S. E. Madison St.

7

S. E. Division St.

8

10

9

11

Mt. Tabor
Park

S. E. 50th Ave.

405

S. W. Naito Pkwy. (Front Ave.)

26

S. E. Powell Blvd.

26

0   1 miles

0   1 kilometers

99E

S. E. Milwaukie Ave.

S. E. Holgate Blvd.

Ross
Island

43

Eastmoreland
General
Hospital ♦

S. E. 72nd Ave.

S. E. 82nd Ave.

Lents
Park

♦ Reed
College

S. E. Woodstock Blvd.

205

S. W. Macadam Ave.

Willamette River

5

Oaks Bottom
Wildlife
Refuge

S. E. McLoughlin Blvd.

S. E. Bybee
Blvd.

S. E. 13th Ave.

EASTMORELAND

S. E. 52nd Ave.

S. E. Tacoma St.

quadrant is diverse to say the least. Still the epicenter of the city's relatively small—compared with other U.S. cities the size of Portland—
African American community, the inner parts of Northeast have slowly
gentrified over the last half century. In the Irvington, Laurelhurst, and
Alameda neighborhoods, you'll find some of the largest, most historic
homes in town.

Lined with many excellent—and generally quite affordable—restaurants, bars, galleries, and boutiques, Alberta Street has become one of
the city's trendiest neighborhoods. It also hosts a bustling street art fair
the last Thursday of every month during summer (primarily between
12th and 31st avenues). Nearer to Downtown, the Lloyd Center—both
the name of a rather prosaic shopping mall and the surrounding neighborhood (containing the Oregon Convention Center and Rose Garden)
is an unfortunately drab example of late-20th-century urban renewal.
The area serves a purpose, as it's home to the bulk of the East Side's
hotels, but it lacks the historic charm and indie spirit of other neighborhoods on this side of the river.

EXPLORING

East Burnside and 28th Avenue. A roughly T-shaped dining and retail district that's less defined but no less popular and impressive than some
of the East Side's other culinary and shopping hot spots (like N.E.
Alberta and Division Streets), this diverse neighborhood comprises a
slew of mostly food-related ventures along East Burnside Street from
about 22nd to 28th avenues. Then, where Burnside meets 28th Avenue,
you'll find several blocks of first-rate eateries as well as a handful of
boutiques in either direction, heading north up to about Glisan Street
and south down to about Stark Street. The neighborhood isn't close
to any light-rail stops, but you can get here easily from Downtown via
Bus 20, and street parking is free and abundant. ⊠ *E. Burnside St. from
22nd to 28th Aves., and 28th Ave. from N.E. Glisan to S.E. Stark Sts.,
Kerns, Northeast.*

The Grotto. Owned by the Catholic Church, the National Sanctuary of
Our Sorrowful Mother, as it's officially known, displays more than 100
statues and shrines in 62 acres of woods. The grotto was carved into the
base of a 110-foot cliff, and has a replica of Michelangelo's *Pietà*. The
real treat is found after ascending the cliff face via elevator, as you enter
a wonderland of gardens, sculptures, and shrines, and a glass-walled
cathedral with an awe-inspiring view of the Columbia River and the
Cascades. There's a dazzling Festival of Lights at Christmastime (late
November and December), with 500,000 lights and more than 150
holiday concerts in the 600-seat chapel. Daily masses are held here,
too. ■TIP→ **Hours can vary seasonally so call ahead if visiting late in
the day.** ⊠ *8840 N.E. Skidmore St. Main entrance: N.E. Sandy Blvd.
at N.E. 85th Ave., Northeast* ☎ *503/254–7371* ⊕ *www.thegrotto.org*
🎫 *Plaza level free; elevator to upper level $4.50* ⊙ *Daily 9–sunset.*

**NEED A
BREAK?**

Pix Patisserie. In a handsome café and bar with a small patio along East
Burnside Street, Pix is famous for its sweet treats, including passion-fruit
macarons and dark-chocolate truffles. The adjoining Bar Vivant serves
authentic Spanish tapas and has one of the most impressive selections

of champagne in the country. ✉ *2225 E. Burnside St., Kerns, Northeast* ☎ *971/271-7166* ⊕ *www.pixpatisserie.com.*

Fodor's Choice ★   **Northeast Alberta Street.** Few of Portland's several hipster-favored East Side neighborhoods have developed as quickly and as interestingly as Northeast Alberta Street, aka Northeast Alberta, aka the Alberta Arts District, which has morphed from a downcast area into a funky strip of hippie-driven counterculture into a considerably more eclectic stretch of both indie arts spaces and downright sophisticated bistros and galleries. Extending a little more than a mile, Northeast Alberta offers plenty of one-of-a-kind dining and shopping; you'll find virtually no national chains along here. The area is also home to some of the best people-watching in Portland, especially during the Last Thursday (of the month) art walks, held May–September from 6 pm until 9:30 pm. The Alberta Street Fair in August showcases the neighborhood's offerings with arts-and-crafts displays and street performances. ■TIP→ Northeast Alberta is about a mile from the smaller but similarly intriguing North Mississippi and North Williams corridors; fans of indie dining and shopping could easily spend a full day strolling or biking among both areas. ✉ *N.E. Alberta St. between N.E. Martin Luther King Jr. Blvd. and N.E. 30th Ave., Alberta Arts District, Northeast* ⊕ *www. albertamainst.org.*

SOUTHEAST

Bounded on the west by the Willamette River and on the north by Burnside Avenue, the city's Southeast quadrant comprises several of Portland's hottest and hippest neighborhoods. Packed with shade trees, Craftsman-style houses, and backyard chicken coops, this neighborhood is industrial close in (the river to 7th)—an increasingly trendy food and retail district known as the Central Eastside, which has also lately blossomed with top-quality artisanal distilleries and urban wineries—and middle- to upper-middle-class residential farther out (8th to 82nd). You'll encounter vibrant pockets of foodie-driven restaurants—as well as bars, coffeehouses, markets, food-cart pods, and boutiques—along east–west running Division, Hawthorne, Belmont, Stark, and Burnside streets, making Southeast a Portland cultural must-see. Other Southeast highlights include the Eastbank Esplanade on the Willamette River (which connects with Downtown via several historic bridges), the kid-focused science museum Oregon Museum of Science and Industry (OMSI), and the beautiful park at Mt. Tabor, an inactive volcanic cinder cone.

TOP ATTRACTIONS

Fodor's Choice ★   **Division Street.** Back in the early 1970s, Division Street (or "Southeast Division," as many locals call it) was earmarked for condemnation as part of a proposed—and thankfully never built—freeway that would have connected Downtown to Mt. Hood. For many years, this street sat forlornly, just a long stretch of modest buildings and empty lots. These days, Southeast Division—no longer threatened with condemnation—is one of the hottest restaurant rows in the city, perhaps even the Western United States, and sleek three- and four-story contemporary condos and apartments are popping up like dandelions. Bus 4 crosses the Hawthorne Bridge from Downtown and continues along Division Street; there's also plenty of free street parking in the neighborhood. ⊠ *S.E. Division St. from 30th to 39th Aves., Southeast.*

Fodor's Choice
★
Hawthorne District. Stretching from the foot of Mt. Tabor to Southeast 12th Avenue, with some blocks far livelier than others, this eclectic commercial thoroughfare was at the forefront of Portland's hippie and LGBT scenes in the '60s and '70s. As the rest of Portland's East Side has become more urbane and popular among hipsters, young families, students, and the so-called creative class over the years, Hawthorne has retained an arty, homegrown flavor. An influx of trendy eateries and shops opening alongside the still-colorful and decidedly low-frills thrift shops and old-school taverns and cafés make for a hodgepodge of styles and personalities—you could easily spend an afternoon popping in and out of boutiques, and then stay for happy hour at a local nightspot or even later for dinner. ■ TIP→ Bus 14 runs from Downtown along the length of Hawthorne, and there's plenty of free street parking, too. ⊠ *S.E. Hawthorne Blvd., between S.E. 12th and S.E. 50th Aves., Buckman, Southeast* ⊕ *www.thinkhawthorne.com.*

Fodor's Choice
★
House Spirits Distillery. One of the stalwarts of Distillery Row—a group of seven craft spirits producers mostly clustered together in the Central Eastside—this highly respected outfit opened in 2004, moved into a spacious 14,000-square-foot facility in fall 2014, and has earned international acclaim for its Aviation American Gin and Krogstad Festlig Aquavit. Other favorites include Westward Oregon Straight Malt Whiskey made with locally sourced barley, and—apt in java-loving Portland—coffee liqueur produced using pot-distilled rum and the city's fine Stumptown Coffee beans. In the cozy tasting room, you can also browse a fine selection of barware, books, and other booze-related gifts. Tours are offered Saturdays at 1 and 3 pm. ■ TIP→ Check out the Distillery Row website (⊕ www.distilleryrowpdx.com), where you can view a map of other nearby distilleries and order a Distillery Row Passport, which costs $20 but includes a $5 gift card, complimentary tastings and tours, and discounts at a number of restaurants, hotels, and shops around the city. ⊠ *68 S.E. Stark St., Southeast* ☎ *503/235–3174* ⊕ *www.housespirits.com* ☉ *Sun.–Wed. noon–5, Fri.–Sat. noon–6.*

FAMILY
Fodor's Choice
★
Mt. Tabor Park. A playground on top of a volcano cinder cone? Yup, that's here. The cinders, or glassy rock fragments, unearthed in the park's construction, were used to surface the respite's roads; the ones leading to the top are closed to cars, but popular with cyclists. They're also popular with cruisers—each August there's an old-fashioned soapbox derby. Picnic tables and tennis, basketball, and volleyball courts make Mt. Tabor Park a popular spot for outdoor recreation, but plenty of quiet, shaded trails and wide-open grassy lawns with panoramic views of the Downtown skyline appeal to sunbathers, hikers, and nature lovers. The whole park is closed to cars every Wednesday. ■ TIP→ Just down the hill on the west side of Mt. Tabor, you'll find the lively cafés and restaurants of the hip Hawthorne District. ⊠ *S.E. 60th Ave. and S.E. Salmon St., Mt. Tabor, Southeast* ⊕ *www.portlandoregon.gov/parks* ☉ *Daily dawn–dusk.*

FAMILY **Oregon Museum of Science and Industry** (*OMSI*). Hundreds of engaging
Fodor'sChoice exhibits draw families to this outstanding interactive science museum,
★ which also has an Omnimax theater and the Northwest's largest planetarium. The many permanent and touring exhibits are loaded with enough hands-on play for kids to fill a whole day exploring robotics, ecology, rockets, animation, and outer space. Moored in the Willamette River as part of the museum is a 240-foot submarine, the USS *Blueback*, which can be toured for an extra charge. OMSI also offers some very cool event programming for adults, including the hugely popular monthly OMSI After Dark nights, where "science nerds" can enjoy food, drink, and science fun, and the twice-monthly OMSI Science Pub nights, where local and national experts lecture on a wide range of topics at theater-pubs in Portland. ■TIP➔ OMSI's excellent restaurant, Theory, open for lunch, offers great views of the Willamette River and Downtown skyline. ✉ *1945 S.E. Water Ave., Central East Side, Southeast* ☎ *503/797–4000, 800/955–6674* ⊕ *www.omsi.edu* ✉ *Museum $13, planetarium $7.50, Omnimax $8.50, submarine $6.75; combined ticket $23* ⊘ *Mid-June–early Sept., daily 9:30–7; early Sept.–mid-June, daily 9:30–5:30.*

Fodor'sChoice **SE Wine Collective.** Opened in 2012 along Division Street's white-hot
★ restaurant row, this growing collective houses nine small wineries and has quickly become the city's leading incubator for *vino* entrepreneurs. The spacious facility includes a large, light-filled tasting bar with glass roll-up doors (offering a peek at the vinification process) and a main wall and bench seating made from old wine barrels. The tasting bar is also a wine bar, so you can sample the artisanal wines produced on-site, or order a flight, glass, or bottle (to go or to enjoy on-site) as well as tasty small plates from an extensive menu. Although Oregon is chiefly known for Pinot Noir, Pinot Gris, and Chardonnay, the wineries at the collective produce a richly varied assortment of varietals, including a heady Syrah from Helioterra, a supple Viognier from Jackalope Wine Cellars, and a peppery Cabernet Franc from Willful Wines. ■TIP➔ Here, and at several other wineries in the city, you can by a PDX Urban Wineries Passport for $20; it comes with a $5 gift card, free tastings, and discounts at a number of local eateries and other businesses. ✉ *2425 S.E. 35th Pl., Richmond, Southeast* ☎ *503/208–2061* ⊕ *www.sewinecollective.com* ⊘ *Mon. and Wed.–Fri. 4 pm–10 pm, Sat. 1 pm–10 pm, Sun. 1 pm–8 pm.*

WORTH NOTING

Central Eastside. This expansive 681-acre tract of mostly industrial and commercial buildings was largely ignored by all but local workers until shops, galleries, and restaurants began opening in some of the neighborhood's handsome, high-ceilinged buildings beginning in the '90s. These days, it's a legitimately hot neighborhood for shopping and coffeehouse-hopping by day, and dining and clubbing at night. Businesses of particular note in these parts include urban-chic coffeehouses (Water Avenue, Coava), breweries (Base Camp Brewing, Cascade Brewing Barrel House, Commons Brewery), shops and galleries, and restaurants (ClarkLewis, Le Pigeon, Biwa, Bunk Sandwiches). In the past few years, a number of acclaimed craft distilleries and urban wineries have joined the mix, including House Spirits and New Deal Distillery among the former, and Clay Pigeon and Coopers Hall among the latter. This is a large neighborhood, and some streets are a bit desolate (though still quite safe), but you can reach it via the East Side Streetcar, and walking from Downtown across the Hawthorne or Burnside bridges. If you're coming by car, street parking is relatively easy to find. ⊠ *Willamette River to S.E. 12th Avenue from Burnside to Division Sts., Southeast* ⊕ *www.ceic.cc.*

Laurelhurst Park. Completed in 1914 by Emanuel Mische, who trained with the iconic Olmsted Brothers landscaping design firm, resplendent Laurelhurst Park's hundred-year-old trees and winding, elegant paths are evocative of another time, and may trigger an urge to don a parasol. Listed on the National Register of Historic Places, Laurelhurst offers plentiful trails, playgrounds, tennis courts, soccer fields, horseshoe pits, an off-leash area for dogs, a serene pond with ducks, and many sunny and shady picnic areas. Take a stroll around the large spring-fed pond and keep an eye out for blue heron, the city's official bird. On the south side of this 31-acre park is one of the busiest basketball courts in town. Though the park is always beautiful, it is especially so in fall. The trendy dining and café culture of East Burnside and 28th and Belmont Street are within walking distance. ⊠ *S.E. 39th Ave. and S.E. Stark St., Laurelhurst, Southeast* ⊕ *www.portlandoregon.gov/parks.*

WEST HILLS AND SOUTHWEST

Forming a natural western border of Downtown and Nob Hill, the West Hills extend as a high (up to around 1,000 feet in elevation) ridgeline from Southwest to Northwest Portland. Part of this lofty neighborhood is residential, containing some of the largest and finest homes in the city, many of them with knockout views of the Downtown skyline and Mt. St. Helens and Mt. Hood in the distance. Technically, Downtown Portland is in the city's Southwest quadrant, as are most of the attractions included in the aforementioned West Hills section of town. But when locals mention Southwest, they're generally referring to the area south and southwest of Downtown, a mostly middle- to upper-middle-class residential district with a few commercial pockets. The most interesting section is the RiverPlace and, a bit farther south, South Waterfront development along the Willamette River. A formerly industrial tract, this area has been rapidly developed since the early 2000s into a contemporary mixed-use neighborhood of both mid- and high-rise glass-and-steel condos, office buildings, a huge expansion of prestigious Oregon Health and Science University, and a growing but still limited number of restaurants, hotels, and shops. RiverPlace begins just south of Hawthorne Bridge and is easily accessed from Tom McCall Waterfront Park—there's a pretty pedestrian promenade along the river, with a handful of sidewalk cafés and boutiques.

TOP ATTRACTIONS

Hoyt Arboretum. Twelve miles of trails, which connect with others in Washington Park and Forest Park, wind through the arboretum, which has more than 1,400 species of plants and one of the nation's largest collections of coniferous trees; pick up trail maps at the visitor center.

Guided 90-minute tours ($3 suggested donation) are offered most Saturdays at noon from May through September. Also here are the Winter Garden and a memorial to veterans of the Vietnam War. The visitor center is a half mile from the Washington Park MAX station. ✉ *4000 S.W. Fairview Blvd., Arlington Heights, West Hills* ☎ *503/865–8733* ⊕ *www.hoytarboretum.org* ☜ *Free* ⊘ *Arboretum daily 5 am–10 pm; visitor center weekdays 9–4, weekends 11–3.*

Fodor'sChoice
★

International Rose Test Garden. Despite the name, these grounds are not an experimental greenhouse laboratory, but rather three terraced gardens, set on 4½ acres, where more than 10,000 bushes and some 550 varieties of roses grow. The flowers, many of them new varieties, are at their peak in June, July, September, and October. From the gardens you can take in highly photogenic views of the Downtown skyline and, on fine days, the Fuji-shaped slopes of Mt. Hood, 50 miles to the east. Summer concerts take place in the garden's amphitheater. It's a pretty but hilly 30- to 40-minute walk from Downtown, or you can get here via MAX light rail (either to Washington Park or Kings Hill/S.W. Salmon Street stations); then transfer to Bus No. 63 (no weekend service) or Washington Park shuttle (late May–early September only). ✉ *400 S.W. Kingston Ave., Arlington Heights, West Hills* ☎ *503/227–7033* ⊕ *www. rosegardenstore.org* ☜ *Free* ⊘ *Daily 7:30 am–9 pm.*

Portland Rose Festival parade

Fodor's Choice
★ **Japanese Garden.** One of the most authentic Japanese gardens outside Japan, this serene landscape unfolds over 5½ acres of Washington Park, just a short stroll up the hill from the International Rose Test Garden. This serene spot, designed by a Japanese landscape master, represents five separate garden styles: Strolling Pond Garden, Tea Garden, Natural Garden, Sand and Stone Garden, and Flat Garden. The Tea House was built in Japan and reconstructed here. The east side of the Pavilion has a majestic view of Portland and Mt. Hood. Take MAX light rail to Washington Park station, and transfer to Bus No. 63 (no weekend service) or the Washington Park Shuttle (May–Aug. only). ■ TIP→ The public tours are given by knowledgeable volunteers. Check for tour times at the admission gate. ⊠ *611 S.W. Kingston Ave., Arlington Heights, West Hills* ☎ *503/223–1321* ⊕ *www.japanesegarden.com* 🎟 *$9.50* ⊘ *Oct.–Mar., Mon. noon–4, Tues.–Sun. 10–4; Apr.–Sept., Mon. noon–7, Tues.–Sun. 10–7.*

FAMILY **Oregon Zoo.** This beautiful animal park in the West Hills, famous for its Asian elephants, is undergoing a two-decade-long series of major improvements and expansions to make the zoo more sustainable and provide more stimulating spaces, education and conservation opportunities, as well as improved guest amenities and event spaces. Major draws include an African Savanna with rhinos, hippos, zebras, and giraffes. Steller Cove, a state-of-the-art aquatic exhibit, has Steller sea lions and a family of sea otters. Take the MAX light rail to the Washington Park station. ⊠ *4001 S.W. Canyon Rd., Arlington Heights, West Hills* ☎ *503/226–1561* ⊕ *www.oregonzoo.org* 🎟 *$11.50* ⊘ *Late May–Aug.,* *daily 9–6; Mar.–mid-May and Sept.–Dec., daily 9–4; Jan. and Feb., daily 10–4.*

WORTH NOTING

Oregon Holocaust Memorial. This memorial to those who perished during the Holocaust bears the names of surviving families who live in Oregon and southwest Washington. A bronzed baby shoe, a doll, broken spectacles, and other strewn possessions await notice on the cobbled courtyard. Soil and ash from six Nazi concentration camps is interred beneath the black granite wall. The memorial is operated by the nearby Oregon Jewish Museum and Center for Holocaust Education, on the edge of Nob Hill at 1953 N.W. Kearney Street, and hosts rotating history and art exhibits, films, concerts, and lectures. ⊠ *S.W. Wright Ave. and S.W. Park Pl., Arlington Heights, West Hills* ☎ *503/226–3600* ⊕ *www.ojmche.org* ✉ *Free* ☉ *Daily dawn–dusk.*

Pittock Mansion. Henry Pittock, the founder and publisher of the *Oregonian* newspaper, built this 22-room, castlelike mansion, which combines French Renaissance and Victorian styles. The opulent manor, built in 1914, is filled with art and antiques. The 46-acre grounds, north of Washington Park and 1,000 feet above the city, have superb views of the skyline, rivers, and the Cascade Range, including Mt. Hood and Mt. St. Helens. The mansion is a half-mile uphill trek from the nearest bus stop. The mansion is also a highly popular destination among hikers using Forest Park's and Washington Park's well-utilized Wildwood Trail. ⊠ *3229 N.W. Pittock Dr., Hillside, West Hills* ☎ *503/823–3623* ⊕ *www.pittockmansion.com* ✉ *$9.50* ☉ *July and Aug., daily 10–5; Sept.–Dec. and Feb.–June, daily 11–4.*

FAMILY **Portland Children's Museum.** Colorful sights and sounds offer a feast of sensations for kids of all ages where hands-on play is the order of the day. Visit nationally touring exhibits, catch a story time, a sing-along, or a puppet show in the Play It Again theater, create sculptures in the clay studio, splash hands in the waterworks display, or make a creation from junk in the Garage. The museum shares the same parking lot as the zoo and can also be reached via the MAX light rail Washington Park stop. ⊠ *4015 S.W. Canyon Rd., Arlington Heights, West Hills, Portland* ☎ *503/223–6500* ⊕ *www.portlandcm.org* ✉ *$10* ☉ *Mar.–Aug., daily 9–5; Sept.–Feb., Tues.–Sun. 9–5.*

FAMILY **World Forestry Center Discovery Museum.** This handsomely designed, contemporary museum across from the zoo contains interactive and multimedia exhibits about forest sustainability. A white-water raft ride, smokejumper training simulator, and Timberjack tree harvester all provide different perspectives on Pacific Northwest forests. On the second floor the forests of the world are explored in various travel settings. A canopy lift ride hoists visitors to the 50-foot ceiling to look at a Douglas fir. ⊠ *4033 S.W. Canyon Rd., Arlington Heights, West Hills, Portland* ☎ *503/228–1367* ⊕ *www.worldforestry.org* ✉ *$9* ☉ *Daily 10–5.*

WHERE TO EAT

These days, rising-star chefs and the foodies who adore them are flocking to Portland. In this playground of sustainability and creativity, many of the city's hottest restaurants change menus weekly—sometimes even daily—depending upon the ingredients they have delivered to their door that morning from local farms. The combination of fertile soils, temperate weather, and nearby waters contributes to a year-round bountiful harvest (be it lettuces or hazelnuts, mushrooms or salmon) that is within any chef's reach.

And these chefs are not shy about putting new twists on old favorites. Restaurants like Le Pigeon, Beast, Ox, Ned Ludd, Natural Selection, and Aviary have all taken culinary risks by presenting imaginatively executed, often globally inspired fare while utilizing sustainable ingredients. There's a strong willingness in and around Portland for chefs to explore their creative boundaries.

Menus frequently extend across nations and continents. First-time visitors to Portland always seem to be impressed by the culinary scene's international diversity, especially when it comes to Asian and Mediterranean fare, but you'll also find outstanding examples of Peruvian, Russian, regional Mexican, and dozens of other ethnic restaurants. Of course, seafood is prevalent, with chefs regularly taking advantage of the availability of fresh salmon, albacore, halibut, crab, oysters, and mussels from the rivers and the Pacific Ocean.

Most of the city's longtime favorites are concentrated in Nob Hill, the Pearl District, and Downtown. But many of the city's most exciting food scenes are on the East Side, along Alberta Street, Mississippi Avenue, Williams Avenue, Fremont Street, Martin Luther King Jr. Boulevard, Burnside Street, 28th Avenue, Belmont Street, Hawthorne Boulevard, and Division Street, and tucked away in many neighborhoods in between. Serious food enthusiasts will definitely want to make some trips to some of these vibrant, if out-of-the-way neighborhoods.

HOURS, PRICES, AND DRESS

Compared to many other major cities, Portland restaurants aren't open quite as late, and it's unusual to see many diners after 11 pm even on weekends, though there are a handful of restaurants and popular bars that do serve late, albeit often with limited bar menus.

One aspect to Portland's dining scene that many locals and out-of-towners find appealing is how reasonably priced top-notch restaurants are. Particularly welcome in Portland is happy hour, when both inventive cocktails as well as small plates of food can be a good value; you can easily put together a fine early—or in some cases late-night—dinner by grazing from the happy-hour menu at a restaurant that also has a bar scene.

In Portland, many diners dress casually for even higher-end establishments—a proclivity that's refreshing to some and annoying to others. In any case, jeans are acceptable almost everywhere.

In alphabetical order by neighborhood. Use the coordinate (✛ B2) at the end of each listing to locate a site on the corresponding map.

WHAT IT COSTS IN U.S. DOLLARS			
$	$$	$$$	$$$$
At Dinner	Under $16	$16–$22	$23–$30	Over $30

Restaurant prices are the average cost of a main course at dinner, or if dinner is not served, at lunch.

DOWNTOWN

$ ✕ **Blue Star Donuts.** The lines outside much-hyped competitor Voodoo

BAKERY   Doughnut are longer, but that doesn't mean you should bypass a chance

FAMILY   to sample the creative confections at this handsome, light-filled dough-

Fodor's Choice   nut shop on the street level of a glassy condo tower in the West End.

★   Part of Micah Camden's nouvelle–fast-food empire (that includes Little Big Burger, Boxer Ramen, and Son of a Biscuit), Blue Star opens at 7 or 8 each morning and remains open until that day's fresh-baked stock of delicious doughnuts is sold out. Flavors change regularly, but often include blueberry-bourbon-basil, bacon-maple, and Valrhona chocolate crunch with a Boston-cream-style filling. Stumptown coffee is served, too. If you have time for just one Portland doughnut shop, choose this one; if possible, though, try them both. Additional locations can be found in Hawthorne and North Mississippi. $ *Average main: $4* ✉ *1237 S.W. Washington St., West End, Downtown* ☎ *503/265–8410* ⊕ *www.bluestardonuts.com* $ *Average main: $4* ✉ *3753 N. Mississippi Ave., Mississippi, Downtown* ☎ *503/265–8410* ⊕ *www.bluestardonuts. com* $ *Average main: $4* ✉ *3549 S.E. Hawthorne Blvd., Hawthorne, Southeast* ☎ *503/477–9635* ⊕ *www.bluestardonuts.com* ✛ *D4.*

$$$ ✕ **Clyde Common.** Gourmands from all walks of life—politicians, rock

PACIFIC   stars, socialites, and hipsters—eat and drink at this bustling bistro and

NORTHWEST   bar in the Ace Hotel. Long, communal tables dominate the space, which

Fodor's Choice   means you never know who you'll end up sitting next to. With wood-

★   and-canvas decor, expansive front windows, and an open kitchen, the restaurant has a warm, airy feel, although it can get loud. The seasonally driven menu showcases the region's bounty; you might start with quail stuffed with maple-bourbon sausage, before tucking into a plate of black-truffle tagliatelle pasta with chicken-heart ragout, *chicharrons*, pears, and egg yolk. The cocktail list is one of the best in the city; try the barrel-aged Negroni made with Beefeater gin, Cinzano sweet vermouth, Campari, and orange peel, or the bartender's daily punch. Weekend brunch is memorable and there are great happy-hour deals, too. $ *Average main: $27* ✉ *Ace Hotel, 1014 S.W. Stark St., West End* ☎ *503/228–3333* ⊕ *www.clydecommon.com* ✛ *D4.*

$$$ ✕ **Departure Restaurant + Lounge.** This swanky rooftop restaurant and

ASIAN FUSION   lounge on the top floor of The Nines hotel looks fresh out of L.A.—a look and feel that is, indeed, a departure from Portland's usual no-fuss vibe. The retro-chic interior has an extravagant, space-age, airport-lounge feel, and the outdoor patio—furnished with low, white couches and bright-orange tables and chairs—offers panoramic views of the Downtown skyline. It's not just about the view here at this see-and-be-seen

BEST BETS FOR PORTLAND DINING

Fodor's writers and editors have selected their favorite restaurants by price, cuisine, and experience in the lists below. In the first column, Fodor's Choice properties represent the "best of the best" in every price category. You can also search by neighborhood for excellent eats—just peruse our reviews on the following pages.

Fodor's Choice ★

Andina, $$$, p. 66
Apizza Scholls, $, p. 72
Ava Gene's, $$$, p. 72
Block + Tackle, $$, p. 73
Blue Star Donuts, $, p. 58
Broder, $, p. 74
Castagna Restaurant, $$$$, p. 74
Clyde Common, $$$, p. 58
Country Cat, $$, p. 74
Higgins, $$$, p. 61
Imperial, $$$, p. 61
Interurban, $, p. 68
Irving Street Kitchen, $$$, p. 66
Kachka, $$, p. 75
Langbaan, $$$$, p. 75
Lardo, $, p. 76
Laurelhurst Market, $$$, p. 76
Lauretta Jean's, $, p. 76
Le Pigeon, $$$, p. 77
Natural Selection, $$$$, p. 69
Ned Ludd, $$$, p. 69
Olympic Provisions, $$, p. 77
Ox Restaurant, $$$$, p. 69
PaaDee, $, p. 77
Pazzo Ristorante, $$$, p. 62
Pok Pok, $, p. 78
Ración, $$$, p. 63
Roe, $$$$, p. 78
Salt & Straw Ice Cream, $, p. 67
Screen Door, $$, p. 70
Tamale Boy, $, p. 71
Toro Bravo, $$, p. 72
Trifecta Tavern, $$, p. 78

By Price

$

Apizza Scholls, p. 72
Bollywood Theater, p. 73
Broder, p. 74
Interurban, p. 68
Ken's Artisan Pizza, p. 75
Lardo, p. 76
Lauretta Jean's, p. 76
Mi Mero Mole, p. 63
Pine State Biscuits, p. 70
Pok Pok, p. 78
Salt & Straw Ice Cream, p. 67
Tamale Boy, p. 71

$$

Aviary, p. 68
Block + Tackle, p. 73
Country Cat, p. 74
Kachka, p. 75
Olympic Provisions, p. 77
Toro Bravo, p. 72

$$$

Andina, p. 66
Clarklewis, p. 74
Clyde Common, p. 58
Grüner, p. 61
Higgins, p. 61
Imperial, p. 61
Le Pigeon, p. 77
Meriwether's Restaurant, p. 67
Pazzo Ristorante, p. 62
Ración, p. 63

$$$$

Beast, p. 68
Castagna Restaurant, p. 74
Langbaan, p. 75
Natural Selection, p. 69
Ox Restaurant, p. 69
Roe, p. 78

By Cuisine

ASIAN

Aviary, $$, p. 68
Bamboo Sushi, $$, p. 72
Bollywood Theater, $, p. 73
Departure, $$$, p. 58
Langbaan, $$$$, p. 75
PaaDee, $, p. 77
Pok Pok, $, p. 78
Smallwares, $$, p. 71

BRUNCH

Broder, $, p. 74
Country Cat, $$, p. 74
Irving Street Kitchen, $$$, p. 66
Meriwether's Restaurant, $$$, p. 67
Pine State Biscuits, $, p. 70
Screen Door, $$, p. 70
Tasty n Alder, $$$, p. 63
Tin Shed Garden Cafe, $, p. 71
Veritable Quandary, $$$, p. 63

2

Portland's Food Carts

Throughout Portland at any given mealtime, around 600 food carts are dishing up steaming plates of everything from Korean tacos to shawarma to artisanal cupcakes. While food carts have seen a rise in popularity throughout the country, the culture is especially strong in Portland.

Brightly colored and mostly stationary, the carts tend to cluster in former parking lots in pods ranging from three to nearly 60 establishments, oftentimes ringing a cluster of picnic tables or a covered awning.

With plate prices averaging $6 to $9, cart fare provides a quick, inexpensive, and delicious alternative to traditional sit-down restaurants if you don't mind sitting outside. Cart dining is also an easy way to sample Portland's many ethnic food offerings.

For up-to-date information on hours and locations, check out the extensive local blog **Food Carts Portland** (⊕ www.foodcartsportland.com), the corresponding FoodCartsPDX iPhone and Droid apps FoodCartsPDX, and the Twitter thread @pdxfoodcarts.com.

TOP PODS

Downtown, S.W. 9th (and 10th) and Alder: Covering more than an entire city block, this Downtown pod, home to nearly 60 carts, is the largest in the city. The spot is lively during the workweek but slower on the weekends. We recommend the signature Thai chicken dish at **Nong's Khao Man Gai**; battered fish-and-chips at **The Frying Scotsman**; kielbasa and other Polish classics at **EuroDish**; the porchetta-and-arugula sandwich at the **People's Pig Wood-Fired Grill**; and kalua pig at the Hawaiian cart **808 Grinds.**

Downtown, S.W. 3rd and Washington: This pod has an international bent, with some of the city's oldest Mexican carts on-site, plus Egyptian, Greek, Indonesian, Lebanese, and Vietnamese establishments. We recommend the spicy Southwest mac and cheese and pulled-pork sliders at **I Heart This Cart**; falafel or chicken shawarma at **El Masry Egyptian** cart; and vegan cheesesteak at **DC Vegetarian.**

Southeast, Tidbit Food Farm and Garden (S.E. Division and 28th): Southeast Portlanders were saddened to see the Good Food Here (on Belmont) and Cartopia (on Hawthorne) carts close in 2014 to make way for new construction projects, but this new, beautifully designed cart colony with a large central dining area and a fire pit has given cart hounds a reason to rejoice. Try the Heartbreak Hotel hot dog topped with bacon, cheddar, ketchup, and a fried egg at **Timber's DogHouse PDX**; the blistered-crust wood-fired pizzas (the one with fennel sausage is killer) at **Pyro Pizza**; and the stick-to-your-ribs braised tri-tip plate, with roasted red peppers and onions, followed by a slice of pineapple upside-down cake, at **Love Belizean.** You can also grab a pint of local IPA or porter to accompany your meal at Scout Beer Garden.

late-night lounge. The seafood-focused Pan-Asian dishes, which include big-eye tuna *poke* (salad), crispy squid with spicy miso, scallop skewers with asparagus, and wok-fried chili prawns with candied walnuts, are served in small portions and are consistently excellent, thanks to charismatic chef Gregory Gourdet's dedication to quality and creativity. $ *Average main: $25* ✉ *Nines Hotel, 525 S.W. Morrison St., Downtown* ☎ *503/802–5370* ⊕ *www.departureportland.com* ☾ *No lunch* ✛ *D4.*

$$$
MODERN
EUROPEAN

✕**Grüner.** Grüner means "greener" in German, and this sleek West End restaurant with angular furniture and blond-wood tables and chairs focuses strongly on seasonal Northwest produce and modern interpretations of recipes culled from throughout verdant Germany's Alps, forests, and river valleys. Start, perhaps, with the Swabian *maultaschen,* a hearty ravioli in a fragrant beef broth filled with beef, pork, spinach, and onion. Then consider traditional *choucroute garnie* with housemade meats, or quark spaetzle served with Black Forest ham, leeks, zucchini, hen-of-the-woods mushrooms, and crème fraîche. Available only at Grüner's bar, the burger topped with smoked bacon, fontina, pickled red onions, aioli, and house-made ketchup is one of the best in town. Be sure to check out the terrific wine list with its emphasis on German, Austrian, and northern Italian wines; Grüner Veltliner is well represented, of course. Sister establishment Kask, next door, is a hip and cozy craft-cocktail lounge featuring simpler bar snacks. $ *Average main: $25* ✉ *527 S.W. 12th Ave., West End, Downtown* ☎ *503/241–7163* ⊕ *www. grunerpdx.com* ☾ *Closed Sun. No lunch Sat.* ✛ *D4.*

$$$
PACIFIC
NORTHWEST
Fodor's Choice
★

✕**Higgins.** One of Portland's original farm-to-table restaurants, this classic eatery, opened in 1994 by renowned namesake chef Greg Higgins, has built its menu—and its reputation—on its dedication to local, seasonal, organic ingredients. Higgins' dishes display the diverse bounty of the Pacific Northwest, incorporating ingredients like heirloom tomatoes, forest mushrooms, mountain huckleberries, Pacific oysters, Oregon Dungeness crab, and locally raised pork. A reasonably priced bistro menu is available in the adjoining bar, where comfortable leather booths and tables provide an alternative to the formal, white-tableclothed main dining room. Don't miss the house-made charcuterie plate with Higgins pickles or the tender duck confit entrée. $ *Average main: $28* ✉ *1239 S.W. Broadway, Downtown* ☎ *503/222–9070* ⊕ *higginsportland.com* ☾ *No lunch weekends* ✛ *D5.*

$$$
PACIFIC
NORTHWEST
Fodor's Choice
★

✕**Imperial.** Tall concrete pillars, exposed brick and ductwork, soft overhead lighting, and rustic wood tables and floors create an industrialchic vibe at acclaimed chef Vitaly Paley's buzzy restaurant inside the hip Hotel Lucia. Open for breakfast, lunch, and dinner, and serving up exemplary contemporary Pacific Northwest fare from a wood-fired grill and rotisserie in the open kitchen, Paley draws inspiration—and ingredients—from the surrounding area. Menu highlights include Dungeness crab omelet, duck meatballs, grilled king salmon with corn purée and chanterelles, and a mixed grill of Oregon lamb (T-bone, leg, shoulder, and merguez sausage). Imperial has one of the best Downtown happy hours, and a stellar cocktail program to match; try the Konami Code with cognac, vermouth, Becherovka liqueur, framboise, and orange bitters. Paley also operates the hip and casual Portland Penny Diner, also inside the Lucia. $ *Average main: $25* ⊠ *Hotel Lucia, 410 S.W. Broadway, Downtown* ☎ *503/228–7222* ⊕ *www.imperialpdx.com* ✛ *D4.*

$ ✕**Kenny & Zuke's Delicatessen.** The reputation of this Jewish deli beside
DELI   the hip Ace Hotel is based largely on its much-prized pastrami. Cured
FAMILY   for seven days, then smoked for 10 hours and steamed for three, the
rich and flavorful meat is best tasted on a rye bread sandwich or, if
your appetite is heartier, the warm, sauerkraut-packed Reuben. Kenny
& Zuke's makes its own pickles and produces its own bagels, proofing the dough for 36 hours before hand-forming the circles then boiling and baking them in small batches. The open and airy Downtown
space serves omelets, Benedicts, biscuits, and breakfast sandwiches all
day (it's open until 8 or 9, depending on the day), along with a wide
selection of soups, salads, and meaty sandwiches. The Thurman Street
location, in a no-frills space furnished with picnic tables, specializes in
the bagels, and the North Williams location, which bills itself as a deli-bar, stays open late serving food and cocktails. $ *Average main: $14*
⊠ *1038 S.W. Stark St., West End, Downtown* ☎ *503/222–3354* ⊕ *www.
kennyandzukes.com* $ *Average main: $14* ⊠ *3901 N. Williams Ave.,
Boise, North* ☎ *503/287–0782* ⊕ *www.kennyandzukes.com* $ *Average main: $14* ⊠ *2376 N.W. Thurman St., Nob Hill* ☎ *503/954–1737*
⊕ *www.kennyandzukes.com* ☽ *No dinner* ✛ *D4.*

$$$ ✕**Little Bird Bistro.** Celeb-chef Gabriel Rucker of Le Pigeon fame opened
BISTRO   this lively Downtown sister restaurant which has gained a following
for its deliciously curated charcuterie board and a certain notoriety for
its decadent $32 burger, which is topped with a large serving of seared
foie gras (it's available sans foie for $12). This classic but casual bistro
is highly popular with the business-lunch set, but open until midnight
(with a limited but still extensive menu after 10), it also pulls pretheater
diners and postdrinks noshers. Other notable dishes include a classic
cassoulet of duck leg and pork belly, smoked-salmon belly with Brussels sprouts and porcini butter, and crispy rabbit with bacon, caramelized apples, turnips, and mustard. There are a couple of prix-fixe
options, too, and a commendable dessert list that includes a knockout
passion-fruit pudding cake with coconut-Graham crumble, huckleberries, passion-fruit curd, and mint. $ *Average main: $26* ⊠ *219 S.W. 6th
Ave., Downtown* ☎ *503/688–5952* ⊕ *www.littlebirdbistro.com* ☽ *No
lunch weekends* ✛ *E4.*

$$$ ✕**Pazzo Ristorante.** The aromas of roasted garlic and wood smoke greet
ITALIAN   patrons of the bustling, street-level dining room of the Hotel Vintage
Fodor's Choice   Plaza. The unprepossessing decor of dark wood and terra cotta and
★   the menu of deceptively simple contemporary Italian cuisine belie the
fact that Pazzo serves some of the most beautifully prepared, flavorful
food in Downtown: consider the thinly pounded beef carpaccio with
pickled shimeji mushrooms and edible chrysanthemums, and ravioli
filled with fennel and topped with Dungeness crab and a chive-butter
sauce. All the baked goods are made in the adjacent Pazzoria Bakery &
Cafe. Breakfast is served daily. $ *Average main: $26* ⊠ *Hotel Vintage
Plaza, 627 S.W. Washington St., Downtown* ☎ *503/228–1515* ⊕ *www.
pazzo.com* ✛ *E4.*

$$$
TAPAS
Fodor's Choice
★

✕ Ración. In the same shiny West End condo tower that's home to the Downtown branches of Blue Star Donuts and Lardo, this sleek space specializing in gorgeously complex and playful modern Spanish small plates presents a true feast for the senses. Most of the seating is around a polished-wood L-shape counter that faces the open kitchen—a great spot for mingling with fellow diners and watching chef Anthony Cafiero work his molecular magic. Specialties from the small menu include Serrano ham with walnut purée, dandelion greens, and mushroom caramel, and an egg poached sous vide with Brussels sprouts, oyster cream, and smoked oil. The best approach here, especially if it's a special occasion, is ordering the five-course $55 chef's tasting menu. The cocktails here are every bit as interesting as the food, using such cockeyed ingredients as Serrano ham–infused gin and ginger-habanero syrup. $ *Average main: $25* ✉ *1205 S.W. Washington St., West End, Downtown* ☎ *971/276–8008* ⊕ *www.racionpdx.com* ⊗ *Closed Sun. and Mon. No lunch* ✛ *D4.*

$$$
ECLECTIC

✕ Tasty n Alder. The first Downtown venture of celebrated Portland chef John Gorham, this all-day brunch and evening dinner spot serves some of the most interesting food in the city. Designed for sharing, the tapas-style menu draws on global influences and delivers bold, delicious flavors. Try the *patatas bravas*, potatoes served with fried egg on top and aioli on the side, and the Korean fried chicken (yes, for breakfast), served with rice, house kimchi, and eggs cooked two ways (pickled and over-easy). At dinnertime, Tasty n Alder turns up the class, offering a selection of top-notch steaks from family-run ranches, along with well-crafted original cocktails. The atmosphere is modern, clean, and inviting. $ *Average main: $24* ✉ *580 S.W. 12th Ave., West End, Downtown* ☎ *503/621–9251* ⊕ *www.tastyntasty.com* ✛ *D4.*

$$$
AMERICAN

✕ Veritable Quandary. As trendy eateries have come and gone in Downtown Portland over the years, this long-standing local favorite has continued to excel as both a charming weekend brunch option and a lively, see-and-be-seen dinner spot. The beautiful outdoor patio overlooking the Hawthorne Bridge is an oasis of roses, fuchsias, and hanging begonia baskets. The menu emphasizes fresh, flavorful produce and seafood, and the 200-plus-wine list is one of the best in town. The convivial bar, with its deep wooden booths, is a laid-back spot for drinks and lighter fare, including outstanding beef and veggie burgers. $ *Average main: $27* ✉ *1220 S.W. 1st Ave., Downtown* ☎ *503/227–7342* ⊕ *www.veritablequandary.com* ✛ *E5.*

OLD TOWN/CHINATOWN

$
MEXICAN

✕ Mi Mero Mole. Graffiti and murals decorate one concrete wall of this colorful Old Town–Chinatown eatery dedicated to Mexico City–style street food, proof that superb ethnic food still exists in the Chinatown neighborhood (even if none of it, at the moment, is Chinese). This is some of the most flavorful, authentic Mexican food in town. You pick as many items as you'd like from the list of perfectly seasoned fillings, including pork *mole verde* with tomatillo and green chili, smoked tongue with potatoes and cactus in salsa verde, and butternut squash cooked in a rich chocolate mole sauce. Then choose your format for eating these delicacies: a combo platter, quesadillas, burritos, tacos,

Where to Eat and Stay in Portland

E

Viking Motel

5 (I-5 shield) N.E. Vancouver Ave.

Interurban

N.E. Wheeler Ave.

N.E. Interstate Ave.

Broadway Bridge

◆ AMTRAK STATION

OLD TOWN

N.W. Hoyt St.

N.W. 6th Ave.
N.W. 5th Ave.
N.W. 4th Ave.
N.W. 3rd Ave.

N.W. Davis St.

Mi Mero More
Little Bird Bistro   **CHINATOWN GATE**
Voodoo Doughnut
W. Burnside St.
S.W. Ankeny St.
Courtyard by Marriott Portland City Center
Bijou Café
S.W. Pine St.
The Original Pazzo Pistorante
S.W. Oak St.
Embassy Suites Portland-Downtown
S.W. Stark St.
S.W. Washington St.
Hotel Monaco

Hotel Rose

S.W. 3rd Ave.
S.W. 2nd Ave.
S.W. 1st Ave.
S.W. Naito Parkway (Front Ave.)

Tom McCall Waterfront Park

Morrison Bridge

Veritable Quandary

Hawthorne Bridge

RiverPlace Hotel

River's Edge Hotel & Spa

F

5 (I-5 shield) N.E. Vancouver Ave.

Ned Ludd
Ox Restaurant
Tamale Boy
Toro Bravo
Caravan —
The Tiny House Hotel

N.E. Williams Ave.

N.E. Broadway

N.E. 2nd Ave.

MEMORIAL COLISEUM ◆

ROSE GARDEN ARENA ◆

Steel Bridge

Burnside Bridge

N.E. 1st Ave.

5 (I-5 shield)
S.E. 1st Ave.
S.E. 2nd Ave.

Olympic Provisions

S.E. Martin Luther King Jr. Blvd.
S.E. Grand Ave.

Clarklewis

S.E. Water Ave.

S.E. 3rd Ave.

S.E. Madison St.

S.E. Hawthorne Blvd.

S.E. Clay St.

S.E. Market St.

0   1/4 mile
0   1/4 kilometer

G

Smallwares
Tin Shed Garden Cafe
Podnah's Pit BBQ
Pine State Biscuits
Aviary
Beast
Natural Selection
Lion and the Rose
McMenamins Kennedy School
Aloft Portland Airport at Cascade Station
Embassy Suites Portland Airport

N.E. Martin Luther King Jr. Blvd.

N.E. Wasco St.

N.E. Multnomah St.

OREGON CONVENTION CENTER

N.E. Holladay St.

N.E. Lloyd Blvd.

84 (I-84 shield)

N.E. Glisan St.

N.E. Everett St.

N.E. Davis St.

N.E. Couch St.

E. Burnside St.

S.E. 7th Ave.
S.E. 8th Ave.
S.E. 9th Ave.
S.E. 10th Ave.

Le Pigeon

S.W. Ankeny St.

S.E. Ash St.

99E

S.E. Pine St.

S.E. Oak St.

S.E. Stark St.

S.E. Washington St.

Trifecta Tavern
S.E. Morrison St.

Kachka

S.E. Belmont St.

BUCKMAN DISTRICT

S.E. Main St.

S.E. 11th Ave.
S.E. 12th Ave.

Ava Gene's
Block + Tackle
Bollywood Theater
Broder
Lauretta Jean's
Pok Pok
Roe
Evermore Guesthouse

H

N.E. Hancock St.
N.E. Schuyler St.
Portland's White House

N.E. Halsey St.

LLOYD DISTRICT

◆ LLOYD CENTER

Doubletree by Hilton–Portland

N.E. Weidler St.

Everett Street Guesthouse

Voodoo Doughnuts

Screen Door

Jupiter Hotel

Langbaan
Laurelhurst Market

Sandy Blvd.

PaaDee

Bamboo Sushi

Ken's Artisan Pizza

Country Cat

Lardo

Apizza Schools

Castagna Restaurant

TO HAWTHORNE DISTRICT

and so on. There's an extensive list of fine tequilas and mezcals, plus several handcrafted margaritas. There's a smaller, original branch on Division Street in Southeast. $[S]$ *Average main: $10* ⊠ *32 N.W. 5th Ave., Old Town/Chinatown* ☎ *971/266–8575* ⊕ *www.mmmtacospdx.com* ⊙ *Closed Sun.* $[S]$ *Average main: $10* ⊠ *5026 S.E. Division St., Clinton, Old Town/Chinatown* ☎ *503/232–8226* ⊕ *www.mmmtacospdx.com* ⊙ *Closed Mon. No lunch Tues.–Thurs.* ✛ *E4.*

$ **✕ Voodoo Doughnut.** The long lines outside this Old Town 24/7 doughnut
BAKERY shop, marked by its distinctive pink-neon sign, attest to the fact that this irreverent bakery is almost as famous a Portland landmark as Powell's Books. The aforementioned sign depicts one of the shop's biggest sellers, a raspberry-jelly-topped chocolate voodoo-doll doughnut, but all the creations here, some of them witty, some ribald, bring smiles to the faces of customers—even those who have waited 30 minutes in the rain. The Loop (covered in Fruit Loops cereal), Grape Ape (vanilla frosting, grape dust, and lavender sprinkles), and Dirty Snowballs (marshmallow topping, dipped in coconut, with peanut butter center) are other faves. The location, sandwiched between an adult theater and a beer garden in a slightly seedy section of Old Town, makes this a not-quite-appropriate venue for very young kids—plus some of the more amusing doughnuts are adult themed. ■ TIP➔ **A second location in Northeast tends to be a bit less crowded.** $[S]$ *Average main: $4* ⊠ *22 S.W. 3rd Ave., Old Town/ Chinatown* ☎ *503/241–4704* ⊕ *www.voodoodoughnut.com* ▭ *No credit cards* $[S]$ *Average main: $4* ⊠ *1501 N.E. Davis St., Old Town/ Chinatown* ☎ *503/235–2666* ⊕ *www.voodoodoughnut.com* ✛ *E4.*

PEARL DISTRICT

$$$ **✕ Andina.** This popular upscale Pearl District restaurant offers an inven-
PERUVIAN tive menu—a combination of traditional Peruvian and contemporary
Fodor's Choice "Novoandina" cuisines—served in a large but nook-filled space. The
★ extensive seafood offerings include four kinds of ceviche, grilled octopus, and pan-seared scallops with white and black quinoa. There are also entrées with chicken, duck, beef, and lamb. A late-night bar offers sangria, small plates, and cocktails. Don't miss the traditional Peruvian pisco sour, a lemon and pisco liqueur cocktail topped with a froth of egg whites and bitters. There's live music most evenings. $[S]$ *Average main: $27* ⊠ *1314 N.W. Glisan St., Pearl District* ☎ *503/228–9535* ⊕ *www. andinarestaurant.com* ✛ *C3.*

$$$ **✕ Irving Street Kitchen.** You might come to this hip Pearl District res-
MODERN taurant set inside a gorgeously transformed warehouse building just
AMERICAN because you heard about the rich butterscotch pudding with roasted-
Fodor's Choice banana caramel and peanut butter bonbons (it's available to go, sold
★ in its own adorable canning jar); but chances are, once you see the exposed-brick-and-wood-beam walls, striking Edison bulb chandeliers, inviting central bar, and patio seats on a converted loading dock, you'll want to stay. And you'll be glad you did. The well-executed contemporary American dinner and brunch fare includes duck-fat-poached halibut with baby artichokes and sour-pickle aioli and a smoked-brisket-and-fried-egg sandwich with pepper pickles and cheesy Cajun fries which reflect chef Sarah Schafer's creative, if rather decadent, hand

in the kitchen. Wines by the glass are dispensed from state-of-the-art taps, ensuring freshness. ⑤ *Average main: $26* ✉ *701 N.W. 13th Ave., Pearl District* ☎ *503/343–9440* ⊕ *www.irvingstreetkitchen.com* ⊗ *No lunch weekdays* ✣ *C3.*

$$ ✕ **Mediterranean Exploration Company.** The latest venture by cookbook
MEDITERRANEAN author and celeb-chef John Gorham, this tribute to Mediterranean cuisine occupies a handsome former warehouse on historic 13th Avenue in the Pearl. MEC (for short) is an energy-filled, open space with a mix of communal and individual tables—it's surprisingly affordable considering the quality and portions, particularly if you opt for the $40 tasting menu. Food is served family style, and highlights include house-made *labneh* (strained yogurt) with olive oil and fried cauliflower; Lebanese lamb tartare kibbeh; Nazareth kebabs with beef and lamb; and *chreime*, a traditional Jewish fish stew from Tripoli. There are plenty of veggie options, too. Save room for cardamom ice cream, over which your server ladles robust Turkish coffee. Many drinks from the cocktail menu also touch on the region, such as the Casablanca, with three types of rum, lime, date sugar, and rose water. ⑤ *Average main: $22* ✉ *333 N.W. 13th Ave., Pearl District* ☎ *503/222–0906* ⊕ *www. mediterraneanexplorationcompany.com* ⊗ *No lunch* ✣ *D3.*

$ ✕ **Pearl Bakery.** Known for its excellent pastries and fresh baked breads
BAKERY (which are served at many top restaurants around town), this superb café was the first of the city's true artisan bakeries. It offers light breakfasts and delicious sandwiches (the tomato-basil-mozzarella on a puffy *pistolet* roll is particularly good) for lunch. The cakes, cookies, and croissants are among the best in the city. ⑤ *Average main: $7* ✉ *102 N.W. 9th Ave., Pearl District* ☎ *503/827–0910* ⊕ *www.pearlbakery. com* ⊗ *No dinner* ✣ *C3.*

NOB HILL

$$$ ✕ **Meriwether's Restaurant.** The 5-acre Skyline Farm just 12 miles away
PACIFIC grows all the produce for this high-end, yet quaint and unpretentious
NORTHWEST restaurant on the edge of the north end of the Northwest 23rd shopping district. A lush covered and heated garden patio allow diners to eat alfresco even during cooler months. The farm-to-table offerings include the Skyline Farm beet salad with spiced coconut, feta, and almonds and Dungeness crab risotto. The dessert menu features tasty seasonal treats like pumpkin pots de creme. The weekend brunch, where the omelets, scrambles, and Benedicts are made with farm-fresh eggs, is wildly popular—and for good reason. ⑤ *Average main: $26* ✉ *2601 N.W. Vaughn St., Nob Hill* ☎ *503/228–1250* ⊕ *www.meriwethersnw.com* ✣ *A1.*

$ ✕ **Salt & Straw Ice Cream.** In 2011, cousins Kim and Tyler Malek started
CAFÉ a business with a small pushcart and a humble idea—to create unique
FAMILY ice-cream flavors with quality, local ingredients. Today, Salt & Straw Ice
Fodor's Choice Cream has grown into three brick-and-mortar ice-cream parlors around
★ town, with lines out the door at each location, and it is recognized as one of the best ice-cream makers in the nation. Seasonal, local ingredients drive the flavors here, and constant experimentation keeps ice-cream lovers coming back. Ongoing favorites include almond brittle with salted ganache, pear and blue cheese, and honey-balsamic strawberry

with black pepper, but each month five special concoctions are featured. Locally produced Woodblock chocolate bars and house-made salted-caramel sauce are among the toppings. The location in Nob Hill is handiest if you're staying at a Downtown hotel, but the original on Alberta and newest branch on S.E. Division Street are just as popular; expect a long line, but take heart in knowing that the patient staff works fast, even while encouraging patrons to sample the wildly imaginative flavors. ⑤ *Average main: $5* ⊠ *838 N.W. 23rd Ave., Nob Hill* ☎ *971/271–8168* ⊕ *www.saltandstraw.com* ⑤ *Average main: $5* ⊠ *3345 S.E. Division St., Richmond, Southeast* ☎ *503/208–2054* ⊕ *www.saltandstraw.com* ⑤ *Average main: $5* ⊠ *2035 N.E. Alberta St., Alberta District, Nob Hill* ☎ *503/208–3867* ⊕ *www.saltandstraw.com* ✛ *A2.*

NORTH

$ ✕ **Interurban.** A laid-back North Mississippi gastropub with an L-shape indoor bar and a bi-level back patio with lush landscaping and a shaded pergola, Interurban is both a convivial drinkery and a fine spot for affordable, well-crafted American fare served from midafternoon until 2:30 (hours are earlier on weekends, with brunch kicking off at 10 am). The kitchen creates consistently good and creative food, with starters like venison tartare with house-made potato chips and whiskey-infused chicken-liver mousse with bacon and foie gras. More substantial but still bargain-priced items include a rotisserie lamb sandwich with local Mama Lil's hot peppers, *fromage blanc,* and Dijon aioli, and brined and roasted game hen cooked on a rotisserie. A big part of Interurban's success is the extensive selection of cocktails and microbrews. ⑤ *Average main: $13* ⊠ *4057 N. Mississippi Ave., North Mississippi, North* ☎ *503/284–6669* ⊕ *www.interurbanpdx.com* ⊗ *No lunch weekdays* ✛ *F1.*

MODERN
AMERICAN
Fodor'sChoice
★

NORTHEAST

$$ ✕ **Aviary.** Eschewing many culinary conventions, this visionary Alberta Street eatery serves up innovative dishes that sometimes push boundaries but consistently succeed in flavor and execution. The simple menu of small plates (order two to three per person) is influenced by Asian flavors and uses European cooking techniques, combining unusual ingredients that offer pleasing contrasts in flavor and texture. For example, the charred octopus, cooked to the perfect tenderness, is served with scallion pancakes and a salad of papaya, beans, and cashews. The signature dish, a mini wok containing crispy pig ears over mildly sweet coconut rice, is served with Chinese sausage, avocado, mint, and cilantro. The dining room is warm yet simple with white walls and concrete floors—a nice contrast to the boldness of the plates. The helpful waitstaff is available to guide and explain, easing adventurous eaters outside their comfort zones, where the payoff is big. ⑤ *Average main: $18* ⊠ *1733 N.E. Alberta St., Alberta District, Northeast* ☎ *503/287–2400* ⊕ *aviarypdx.com* ⊗ *Closed Sun. No lunch* ✛ *H1.*

ASIAN FUSION

$$$$ ✕ **Beast.** This meat-centric examplar of Portland's cutting-edge culinary scene occupies a nondescript red building with subtle signage. Chef-owner Naomi Pomeroy, who also operates the trendy Expatriate bar

PACIFIC
NORTHWEST

across the street, has appeared on TV's *Top Chef Masters* and garnered countless accolades. Inside her surprisingly casual restaurant, the seating is communal, at two large tables that seat 8 and 16. The six-course prix-fixe dinner (and four-course brunch on Sunday) changes weekly, depending on the meat at the market—substitutions are declined, so vegetarians won't find Beast a good fit. Most dishes are prepared right before your eyes in the open kitchen: there might be chicken and duck-liver mousse, wine- and truffle-braised beef, foie-gras bon bons, or steak tartare with quail-egg toast. There are two seatings per night at 6 and 8:45; view the week's menu online starting Tuesday afternoon. $ *Average main: $75* ⊠ *5425 N.E. 30th Ave., Concordia, Northeast* ☎ *503/841–6968* ⊕ *www.beastpdx.com* ⌲ *Reservations essential* ⊗ *Closed Mon. and Tues.* ✣ *H1.*

$$$$ ✕ **Natural Selection.** With a full two hours of table time from the start of
VEGETARIAN your reservation, this modern-rustic European-style café encourages you
Fodor'sChoice to slow down and savor your meal—and there's so much to savor. A small
★ vegetarian restaurant with cocoa-colored walls and exposed-filament Edison bulbs over each table, Natural Selection serves a four-course, fixed-price menu (available with or without wine pairings) whose brilliance rests in the pure and natural flavors of its ingredients. Assembled in new combinations—tomato-almond soup with fennel, parsnip, and watercress, for example, or chard gnocchi with winter squash, apple, basil, and balsamic vinegar—the ingredients, which change by season, send your taste buds on lovely explorations with each bite. $ *Average main: $45* ⊠ *3033 N.E. Alberta St., Concordia, Northeast* ☎ *503/288–5883* ⊕ *www.naturalselectionpdx.com* ⊗ *Closed Sun.–Tues.* ✣ *H1.*

$$$ ✕ **Ned Ludd.** Named for the founder of the Luddites, the group that
PACIFIC resisted the technological advances of the Industrial Revolution, this
NORTHWEST Northwest-inspired kitchen prepares its food the most low-tech way
Fodor'sChoice possible: in a wood-burning brick oven, over an open flame. Sourcing
★ most of its ingredients locally (or carefully, if they come from afar), Ned Ludd's menu varies completely depending on the season and weather. The whole roasted trout, a delicious constant on the menu, has a crisp, charred exterior and a moist, flavorful interior and comes with charred leeks and carrot-and-fennel salad. Consider the house-made pickle plate and any one of the salads or roasted vegetable dishes to accompany the meal. Fitting the simple, from-the-earth theme, the decor incorporates salvaged wood, dried flowers, and small succulent plants under glass domes. On Monday nights, the kitchen is turned over to two talented staff members—line cook Nicholas Ford and server Brandon Gomez—for pizza night, served up with Oregon microbrews and a healthy dose of old-school rap. ■TIP➔ **If you visit on a Monday, order the always-changing special pie for a taste of both what's in season and in play with chef Ford.** $ *Average main: $23* ⊠ *3925 N.E. Martin Luther King Blvd., King, Northeast* ⊕ *www.nedluddpdx.com* ⊗ *No lunch* ✣ *G1.*

$$$$ ✕ **Ox Restaurant.** Specializing in "Argentine-inspired Portland food," Ox
ARGENTINE is all about prime cuts of meat prepared well. In a dimly lit dining room
Fodor'sChoice with hardwood floors, exposed brick walls, and a bar against the front
★ window, the flannel-shirt-and-white-apron clad waitstaff serves beef, lamb, pork, and fish dishes cooked over flames in a large, hand-cranked

grill. The *asado Argentino,* a platter of short ribs, chorizo, *morcilla* (blood sausage), and skirt steak with a few sides, is an ideal choice for two. Or try the grass-fed Uruguayan rib eye for one, which is a better choice than the skirt steak. The vegetable-based sides provide cool complements to the rich asados: try the chopped endive salad with pear, Gruyère, arugula, pecans, and Dijon vinaigrette, or the buttered beet salad with sweet onion, blue cheese, and walnuts. Save room for the chef's dessert specialty, a vanilla bean *tres leches* cake accompanied by banana pudding, dulce de leche, and a traditional *alfajor* cookie. $ *Average main: $34* ⊠ *2225 N.E. Martin Luther King Blvd., Eliot, Northeast* ☎ *503/284–3366* ⊕ *oxpdx.com* ⊗ *Closed Mon. No lunch* ✛ *G1.*

$ ✕ **Pine State Biscuits.** Loosen your belt a notch or two before venturing
SOUTHERN inside this down-home Southern restaurant that's especially beloved for its over-the-top breakfast biscuit fare. Pat yourself on the back, or belly, if you can polish off the Reggie Deluxe (a fluffy house-baked biscuit topped with fried chicken, bacon, cheese, an egg, and sage gravy), a masterful mélange of calorie-laden ingredients. Other gut-busting favorites include the steak-club biscuit sandwich, shrimp and grits, and andouille corn dog featuring locally made Otto's sausage. Pine State began at the Saturday Portland Farmers' Market and continues to excel there. The Alberta location, which has both counter and booth seating, keeps the longest hours, serving hungry bar goers into the wee hours. A sleek branch on S.E. Division opened in summer 2014. $ *Average main: $7* ⊠ *2204 N.E. Alberta St., Alberta District, Northeast* ☎ *503/477–6605* ⊕ *www.pinestatebiscuits.com* ⊗ *No dinner Mon.–Wed.* $ *Average main: $7* ⊠ *1100 S.E. Division St., Central East Side, Southeast* ☎ *503/236–3346* ⊕ *www.pinestatebiscuits.com* ✛ *H1.*

$ ✕ **Podnah's Pit BBQ.** Firing up the smoker at 5 every morning, the pit crew
BARBECUE at Podnah's spends the day slow cooking some of the best Texas- and Carolina-style barbecue in the Northwest. Melt-in-your-mouth, oak-smoked brisket, ribs, pulled pork, chicken, and lamb are all served up in a sassy vinegar-based sauce. Some sides, like the delicious green-chili mac and cheese, rotate on and off the menu, but the collard greens, barbecue baked beans, and the iceberg wedge, topped with blue cheese and a punchy Thousand Island dressing, are excellent mainstays. Delicious Southwestern and Tex-Mex fare is served at breakfast on weekend mornings. $ *Average main: $15* ⊠ *1625 N.E. Killingsworth St., Vernon, Northeast* ☎ *503/281–3700* ⊕ *podnahspit.com* ✛ *H1.*

$$ ✕ **Screen Door.** The line that forms outside this Southern cooking res-
SOUTHERN taurant at brunch and dinner is as epic as the food itself. But think of
Fodor'sChoice the wait that precedes the meal—which you can spice up with cocktails
★ from the bar—as a chance to ramp up your appetite and fully anticipate the experience to come. A large, packed dining room with canned pickles and peppers along the walls, this Portland hot spot does justice to authentic Southern cooking. Try the fried chicken plate—two moist pieces of meat in crisp and peppery buttermilk batter, accompanied by creamy mashed potatoes and collard greens cooked in bacon fat—or the Screen Door plate with your choice of four sides (consider the mac and cheese, creamy grits, and most any of the salads on the rotating seasonal menu). $ *Average main: $16* ⊠ *2337 E. Burnside St., Kerns,*

Northeast ☎ *503/542–0880* ⊕ *www.screendoorrestaurant.com* ⊗ *No lunch weekdays* ⊹ *H3.*

$$ ✕ **Smallwares.** Chef-owner Johanna Ware happily admits to taking cre-
ASIAN FUSION   ative liberties in the kitchen of her colorful, contemporary bistro in Northeast Portland's somewhat under-the-radar Beaumont neighborhood, describing her restaurant concept as "small plates of inauthentic Asian cuisine meant to be shared." The name of the place, as well as the drinks-centric Barwares lounge in back, is a play on her last name, and the intimate space decorated in a bold black, red, and white color scheme provides the perfect, vibrant milieu for sampling such creatively flavorful treats as rice cakes topped with sea urchin, turmeric chutney, and poppy seed; hanger steak with red miso, chanterelles, balsamic vinegar, and *hijiki* seaweed; and fried kale with candied bacon, fish sauce, and mint. A short menu is served in Barwares until 1 am, and there's an extensive selection of sakes and Asian-inspired cocktails. $ *Average main: $20* ✉ *4605 N.E. Fremont St., Beaumont, Northeast* ☎ *971/229–0995* ⊕ *www.smallwarespdx.com* ⊗ *No lunch* ⊹ *H1.*

$ ✕ **Tamale Boy.** Chef Abel Hernandez hails from Veracruz by way of
MEXICAN   Mexico City, and while he's adept at preparing tamales—both the Oax-
Fodor'sChoice   acan style wrapped in banana leaves and the more conventional style
★   wrapped in corn husks (try the version filled with roasted pasilla peppers, onions, corn kernels, and *queso fresco*), he also turns out fabulous ceviche and *alambre de camarones* (adobe shrimp with bacon and Oaxacan cheese over flat corn tortillas). Be sure to start with an order of table-side guacamole, and the El Diablo margarita with roasted-habanero-infused tequila and mango purée. Order at the counter in the simple dining room that's brightened with a colorful mural by L.A.-based artist Steven Lopez. When the weather cooperates, take your seat in the expansive side patio. $ *Average main: $7* ✉ *1764 N.E. Dekum St., Woodlawn, Northeast* ☎ *503/206–8022* ⊕ *www.tamaleboy.com* ⊗ *Closed Mon.* ⊹ *G1.*

$ ✕ **Tin Shed Garden Cafe.** Sided in metal, this busy restaurant on Alberta
CAFÉ   Street is known for its hearty breakfasts—namely, its biscuits and gravy,
FAMILY   shredded-potato cakes, egg and tofu scrambles, and breakfast burritos; in fact, it's so well-known that there can be a long wait for a table for breakfast on weekends. The lunch and dinner menus have creative choices as well, like a creamy artichoke sandwich and a mac and cheese of the day. There's a kid's menu containing simple scrambles, sandwiches, and noodles (in the $2–$4 range). Dogs are allowed on the comfortable outdoor patio; there's even a dog menu with a variety of free-range meat dishes (in the $6–$7 range). With a large stone fireplace and chimney, the covered, comfortable outdoor area doubles as a beer garden on warm spring and summer evenings, and the adjacent garden rounds off the property with a peaceful sitting area. $ *Average main: $12* ✉ *1438 N.E. Alberta St., Alberta District, Northeast* ☎ *503/288–6966* ⊕ *www.tinshedgardencafe.com* ⌧ *Reservations not accepted* ⊹ *H1.*

$$ ✕**Toro Bravo.** The success of this wildly popular and impressively authentic Spanish tapas bar has spawned a popular cookbook and helped spur chef-owner John Gorham to create something of a restaurant empire in Portland: he operates three other superb eateries around town. This bustling spot with closely spaced tables and a lively vibe caters heavily to groups, as the small-plates format is perfect for sharing. Best bets include marinated sheep's cheese with rose-petal harissa and mint, griddled bacon-wrapped dates with honey, Basque-style pipérade with a duck egg and grilled bread, duck-liver-mousse terrine with morel mushrooms and mustard, and oxtail croquettes topped with chili mayo. There's a long dessert list that includes a richly delicious olive-oil cake topped with apple-caramel sauce. If you're feeling indecisive, order the "chef's choice for the table," which at $40 is a good value for a remarkable variety of dishes. $ *Average main: $20* ⊠ *120 N.E. Russell St., Northeast* ☎ *503/281–4464* ⊕ *www.torobravopdx.com* ⊘ *No lunch* ✛ *G1.*

TAPAS

Fodor's Choice

★

SOUTHEAST

$$$ ✕**Ava Gene's.** Stumptown Coffee founder Duane Sorenson has steadily shifted from cafés to full-service restaurants in recent years, having scored considerable acclaim with his Northwest hunter-gatherer–inspired restaurant Woodsman Tavern and, in 2013, the fantastic rustic Italian eatery Ava Gene's, which ranks among the top tables in town both in popularity and quality. Capsule-shape lamps dangle from the vaulted ceiling of this buzzy dining room with two long rows of banquette seating and several more closely spaced tables. Chef Joshua McFadden draws on regional, home-style recipes from throughout Italy, but focuses on local produce. You could make an impressive feast of three or four *giardini* (gardens) sides, such as pumpkin with brown butter, currants, and pecans. Satisfyingly hearty mains include spaghetti with artichokes, *bottarga* (cured fish roe), and lemon, and the tender culotte steak with radishes and anchovy butter. The cocktail and wine programs are also top-notch. Next door, Sorenson's Roman Candle Baking Co. produces delicious wood-baked Roman-style flatbread pizzas, artisanal breads, and light brunch and lunch fare. $ *Average main: $27* ⊠ *3377 S.E. Division St., Richmond, Southeast* ☎ *971/229–0571* ⊕ *www.avagenes.com* ⊘ *No lunch* ✛ *G6.*

ITALIAN

Fodor's Choice

★

$ ✕**Apizza Scholls.** The pies at Apizza Scholls, lauded by Anthony Bourdain, Rachael Ray, and most any pizza lover who visits, deserve the first-class reputation they enjoy. The greatness of the pies rests not in innovation or complexity, but in the simple quality of the ingredients. The dough is made by hand in small batches and baked to crispy-outside, tender-inside perfection. The toppings—including basil, pecorino romano, and house-cured bacon—are fresh and delicious and served no more than three per pie. While the decor is rather plain and you'll likely have to wait for a table (reservations are recommended), you'll forget all once you take your first bite and start basking in the glory of some of the best pizza in the city. $ *Average main: $13* ⊠ *4741 S.E. Hawthorne Blvd., Hawthorne, Southeast* ☎ *503/233–1286* ⊕ *www.apizzascholls.com* ⊘ *No lunch* ✛ *G6.*

PIZZA

Fodor's Choice

★

$$ ✕**Bamboo Sushi.** The best sushi spot in Portland is also the most environmentally sustainable, sourcing its fish conscientiously from fishing

SUSHI

operations that follow guidelines set by the Monterey Bay Aquarium and Blue Ocean Institute. Try the black cod with smoked soy and roasted garlic glaze or the house-smoked wild ivory salmon *nigiri*. Or, opt for a couple of the signature rolls, like the Lucky 13, an albacore tuna, cucumber, and avocado roll topped with red crab, scallops, *yuzu tobiko* (flying fish roe), and cilantro, or the vegetarian Green Machine, with tempura fried asparagus and green onion topped with avocado and cilantro sweet chili aioli. The sleek, modern interior gives the place a polished, classy feel, and although no item is priced over $20, a meal of several small plates can quickly become spendy. Sidewalk tables allow you to bask in the sunshine while enjoying your meal. There's a second location on 23rd Avenue in Nob Hill, and the owners opened Bamboo Izakaya, with a focus on tasty and sophisticated Japanese bar fare, in Alberta in fall 2014. Ⓢ *Average main: $18* ⊠ *310 S.E. 28th Ave., Kerns, Southeast* ☎ *503/232–5255* ⊕ *www.bamboosushi.com* ☽ *No lunch* Ⓢ *Average main: $18* ⊠ *1409 N.E. Alberta St., Alberta District, Southeast* ☎ *503/889–0336* ⊕ *www.bambooizakaya.com* ☽ *No lunch.* Ⓢ *Average main: $18* ⊠ *836 N.W. 23rd Ave., Nob Hill* ☎ *971/229–1925* ⊕ *bamboosushi.com* ☽ *No lunch.* ✛ *H4.*

$$
SEAFOOD
Fodor'sChoice
★

✕ **Block + Tackle.** This airy, high-ceiling space on trendy Division Street showcases the inventive techniques and dedication to freshness of chef Trent Pierce, who also operates a stellar reservations-only prix-fixe restaurant, Roe, in a small space reached through Block + Tackle's dining room. Offering a conventional à la carte approach, this scene-y seafood spot has a large central communal table, several tables to one side, a long bar, and a large chalkboard menu listing the day's specials and local oysters. Try Dungeness crab Louie with deviled egg and avocado, or the grilled-mackerel sandwich with honey mustard, caraway butter, pickles, and capers. The small-plates portions are designed for sharing. Ⓢ *Average main: $22* ⊠ *3113 S.E. Division St., Southeast* ☎ *503/236–0205* ⊕ *www. blockandtacklepdx.com* ☽ *Closed Mon. and Tues. No lunch* ✛ *H6.*

$
INDIAN

✕ **Bollywood Theater.** Set beneath a soaring beamed ceiling, and with a welcoming mix of worn wooden seating, kitschy decor, bright fabrics, and intoxicating smells, this lively restaurant along Division Street's hoppin' restaurant row specializes in Indian street food and reflects chef-owner Troy MacLarty's colorful, delicious, authentic vision of India as experienced on several trips. Order at the counter, and your food will be brought to you—there's a mix of two-tops and communal tables, with additional seating on a spacious patio. Nosh on *vada pav* (spicy potato dumplings with chutney), *gobi* Manchurian (Indo-Chinese fried cauliflower with lemon, curry leaves, and sweet-and-sour sauce), and beets roasted in coconut milk, before moving on to one of the larger plates, such as Goan-style shrimp served with a full complement of chutneys, paratha bread, and dal. There's even a market to one side of the open-plan dining room selling spices, curries, and other edibles and gifts from India.The original location in the Alberta Arts District is cute but small, and often crowded. Ⓢ *Average main: $12* ⊠ *3010 S.E. Division St., Richmond, Southeast* ☎ *503/477–6699* ⊕ *www.bollywoodtheaterpdx. com* Ⓢ *Average main: $12* ⊠ *2039 N.E. Alberta St., Alberta District, Northeast* ☎ *971/200–4711* ⊕ *www.bollywoodtheaterpdx.com* ✛ *H6.*

$ ✕ **Broder.** This delightful neighborhood café—one of the most outstand-
SCANDINAVIAN   ing brunch spots in town—serves fresh and delicious Scandinavian food
Fodor'sChoice   with fun-to-pronounce names like *friterade applen* (apple fritter) and
★   *aebleskivers* (Danish pancakes). All the food—the hashes, the baked
egg scrambles, the Swedish breakfast boards—is delicious. The Swedish
meatballs and egg, shrimp, and chicken salads are also excellent mid-
day choices. The light and narrow space, decorated with rustic modern
furniture and accented with white tile and mirrors, has a laid-back and
friendly vibe. Though you'll likely have to wait for a table at breakfast,
the café serves complimentary coffee and borrows seating from adjacent
sister restaurant, Savoy, which opens later in the day. Owner Peter Bro
opened a second location, Broder Nord, in North Portland in 2014;
that branch also has dinner service. ⑤ *Average main: $11* ✉ *2508 S.E.
Clinton St., Hosford-Abernethy, Southeast* ☎ *503/736–3333* ⊕ *www.
broderpdx.com* ⊗ *No dinner* ⑤ *Average main: $11* ✉ *2240 N. Interstate
Ave., Eliot, North* ☎ *503/282–5555* ⊕ *www.broderpdx.com* ⊗ *No lunch
Sun.–Tues.* ✛ *H6.*

$$$$ ✕ **Castagna Restaurant.** Enjoy artful Pacific Northwest cuisine—like
PACIFIC   grilled halibut, kohlrabi, and mussels, or summer beans, chanterelles,
NORTHWEST   wilted sorrel, and roasted-duck jus—at this tranquil Hawthorne restau-
Fodor'sChoice   rant. Dinner options from chef Justin Woodward's monthly changing
★   menu include either a classic three-course prix fixe for $75 or a lavish
10-course tasting menu that runs $125; opt for the superb wine pair-
ings for an additional $40 or $60 (with the tasting menu). Next door is
the more casual Cafe Castagna, a bistro and bar open nightly, serving
simple but still superb burgers, pastas, salads, seafood grills, and other
less expensive fare. ⑤ *Average main: $75* ✉ *1752 S.E. Hawthorne Blvd.,
Hawthorne, Southeast* ☎ *503/231–7373* ⊕ *www.castagnarestaurant.
com* ⊗ *Restaurant: Closed Sun.–Tues. No lunch. Cafe: No lunch* ✛ *H6.*

$$$ ✕ **Clarklewis.** Located in a former warehouse between the Willamette
PACIFIC   River and the train tracks in the industrial Central East Side, this upscale
NORTHWEST   restaurant serves up inventive, farm-fresh, modern American cuisine
and has an excellent happy hour. The daily changing menu features
entrées like fire-grilled lamb with harissa, ratatouille, raisin-and-pine-
nut gremolata, and a balsamic glaze, and agnolotti pasta with shishito
peppers, Dungeness crab, and mascarpone. If you're feeling indecisive
or adventurous, let the chef bring you a four-course prix-fixe ($55)
meal, which is served family style and spans the menu. The glass-paned
garage doors that run along the front wall let in natural light and
refreshing breezes when open in summer. ⑤ *Average main: $23* ✉ *1001
S.E. Water Ave., Central East Side, Southeast* ☎ *503/235–2294* ⊕ *www.
clarklewispdx.com* ⊗ *Closed Sun. No lunch Sat.* ✛ *F5.*

$$ ✕ **Country Cat.** Pork lovers rejoice: you've found hog heaven. House-
SOUTHERN   cured, slow-cooked country ham and bacon and samplers of pork
   shoulders, head, and belly await you at this neighborhood craft eatery
★   run by James Beard–nominated chef and in-house butcher Adam Sap-
pington. The menu emphasizes Southern dishes with a Northwest twist,
such a fish fry with beer-battered Pacific rockfish, hickory-smoked duck
leg with chanterelles and pickled plums, and skillet fried chicken. This
is one of the tastiest brunch experiences in town—standouts include

pumpkin pancakes with roasted apples and salted-caramel butter, and eggs Benedict with smoked steelhead over a sweet-cream biscuit. There's also a bar here where the Bloody Mary comes garnished with beef jerky, pickled vegetables, and a giant olive. ⑤ *Average main: $18* ⌧ *7937 S.E. Stark St., Montavilla, Southeast* ☎ *503/408–1414* ⊕ *www. thecountrycat.net* ⊹ *H4.*

$ ✕**Ken's Artisan Pizza.** Doug-fir beams, old wine barrels, and hungry
PIZZA crowds surround the glowing, beehive-shaped wood oven in the open-kitchen of this thin-crust pizza joint. Ken Forkish, also of Ken's Artisan Bakery and Trifecta Tavern, uses fresh, organic ingredients for the dough, sauces, and toppings of his pies. Fans rave about the margherita with arugula, the handpressed fennel sausage with onion, and the soppressata with basil. While the roasted vegetable plate and Caeser salad are delicious and the wine selection is solid, pizza is the real star. Be prepared for a wait. ⑤ *Average main: $14* ⌧ *304 S.E. 28th Ave., Kerns, Southeast* ☎ *503/517–9951* ⊕ *www.kensartisan.com* ⌔ *Reservations not accepted* ⊘ *No lunch* ⊹ *H4.*

$$ ✕**Kachka.** In a city with a sizable population of Russian immigrants,
RUSSIAN the success of this new Central East Side establishment decorated to
Fodor's Choice resemble a *dasha* is hardly surprising, although it's really the devotion
★ of the city's foodies that resulted in Kachka's white-hot popularity; reservations here a good idea here. If you are expecting heavy cuisine, you'll be surprised by the wonderfully creative and often quite light fare, including plenty of shareable small plates, like crispy beef tongue with sweet onion sauce, orange, and pomegranate; panfried sour-cherry *vareniki* (Ukranian dumplings), and—of course—caviar with blini and all the usual accompaniments. Another crowd-pleaser on the menu is the classic chicken Kiev, prepared the old-fashioned way, oozing with butter. And, yes, there's an extensive vodka selection, plus several Russian beers (the wines are mostly from Oregon and France, but there are some notable Slovenian and Hungarian selections). ⑤ *Average main: $19* ⌧ *720 S.E. Grand Ave., Central East Side, Southeast* ☎ *503/235–0059* ⊕ *www.kachkapdx.com* ⊘ *No lunch* ⊹ *G5.*

$$$$ ✕**Langbaan.** Guests reach this tiny, wood-paneled, 24-seat gem with
THAI an open kitchen by walking through the adjoining PaaDee restaurant
Fodor's Choice and pushing open a faux bookshelf that's actually a door. Of course,
★ you won't even get this far unless you've called ahead to reserve a table: this very special prix-fixe restaurant, serving the most interesting and consistently delicious Asian food in Portland, is only open Thursday–Saturday, with a 6 pm seating each night and an additional 8:30 seating Friday and Saturday. Owner Earl Ninsom and chef Rassamee Ruaysuntia present a weekly changing 10-course, $65 tasting menu that often features exquisite recipes and even some ingredients you'll rarely find outside Thailand. Expect boldly flavorful fare like lobster with fish-sauce-cured pork, mint, shallots, tropical *lambutan* fruit, peanuts, and coconut; or roast duck breast with monkey apple, heart of palm, cherry tomatoes, and a fragrant red curry. There's a $30 wine-pairing option, too—a great deal, all in all, considering the caliber of food and service. ⑤ *Average main: $65* ⌧ *6 S.E. 28th Ave., Southeast* ☎ *971/344–2564* ⊕ *www.langbaanpdx.com* ⌔ *Reservations essential* ⊘ *Closed Sun.–Wed. No lunch* ⊹ *H4.*

$ ✕ **Lardo.** One of several spots around Portland that has become known
AMERICAN   for advancing the art of sandwich making, Lardo offers a steady roster of
Fodor's Choice   about a dozen wonderfully inventive variations, plus one or two weekly
★   specials, along with no-less-impressive sides like maple carrots, escarole
Caesar salads, and "dirty fries" topped with pork scraps, marinated peppers, fried herbs, and Parmesan. Sandwiches of particular note include
the tender Korean-style braised pork shoulder with kimchi, chili mayo,
cilantro, and lime, and grilled mortadella with provolone, marinated peppers, and mustard aioli. Wash it all down with a drink from the terrific
craft-beer and cocktail selection. ■ TIP➜ The Hawthorne branch is especially inviting for its large, covered, outdoor seating area, which it shares
with the dessert-themed food cart, Hungry Heart Cupcakes. ⑤ *Average
main: $10* ⊠ *1212 S.E. Hawthorne Blvd., Southeast* ☎ *503/234–7786*
⊕ *www.lardosandwiches.com* ⑤ *Average main: $10* ⊠ *4090 N. Williams
Ave., Boise, North* ☎ *503/841–5373* ⊕ *www.lardosandwiches.com* ⑤ *Average main: $10* ⊠ *1205 S.W. Washington St., West End, Downtown*
☎ *503/241–2490* ⊕ *www.lardosandwiches.com* ✛ *H6.*

$$$ ✕ **Laurelhurst Market.** With an artisanal butcher shop anchoring the right
PACIFIC   side of the building, Laurelhurst Market offers some of the best meaty
NORTHWEST   fare in Portland. Case in point: the Wagyu brisket smoked for 12 hours
Fodor's Choice   and marinated in Ozark barbecue sauce, and the beef short ribs braised
★   with red wine and prunes. Despite the meat-centric focus, Laurelhurst
delivers when it comes to veggies, too: the reasonably priced seasonal
salads and sides can serve as interesting, flavorful complements to the
meaty main courses or, mixed and matched, as meals themselves. The
candlelit dining room is comfortable and sophisticated and the stain-
less steel kitchen along the back wall underneath the beef cuts diagram
illustrates what this place is all about: the preparation and serving
of outstanding meat. The butcher shop sells fantastic sandwiches at
lunchtime; you can take your purchase to go or eat at one of the res-
taurant tables, though there's no waitstaff on duty. ⑤ *Average main:
$27* ⊠ *3155 E. Burnside St., Laurelhurst, Southeast* ☎ *503/206–3097*
⊕ *www.laurelhurstmarket.com* ✛ *H4.*

$ ✕ **Lauretta Jean's.** Kate McMillen and Noah Cable's pie-focused opera-
CAFÉ   tion began as a stall at Portland's Saturday farmers' market at PSU and
Fodor's Choice   now comprises a couple of charming, homey, brick-and-mortar cafés,
★   with the most atmospheric along Division Street in Southeast. While
it's the delicious pies—with feathery-light crusts and delicious fillings
like tart cherry, salted pecan, and chocolate-banana cream—that have
made Lauretta Jean's a foodie icon in Portland, these cheerful eateries
also serve exceptional brunch fare, including the LJ Classic, a fluffy bis-
cuit topped with an over-easy egg, Jack cheese, bacon, and strawberry
jam. In the evening, it's a popular spot for desserts and coffee, or even
cocktails—the Peppermint Fancy with housemade schnapps and marsh-
mallows along with hot cocoa pairs nicely with the sea-salt brownie.
⑤ *Average main: $6* ⊠ *3402 S.E. Division St., Richmond, Southeast*
☎ *503/235–3119* ⊕ *www.laurettajean.com* ☾ *No dinner* ⑤ *Average
main: $6* ⊠ *600 S.W. Pine St., Southeast* ☎ *503/224–9236* ⊕ *www.
laurettajean.com* ☾ *Closed weekends. No dinner* ✛ *H6.*

$$$ ✕ **Le Pigeon.** Specializing in adventurous Northwest-influenced French
FRENCH dishes of extraordinary quality, this cozy and unassuming restaurant
Fodor'sChoice consistently ranks among the city's most acclaimed dining venues.
★ The menu changes regularly but often features items like beef-cheek
bourguignon, chicken and oxtail with semolina gnocchi, and seared
foie gras with chestnut, raisins, bacon, and cinnamon toast (especially
exceptional). And, yes, pigeon is served, too. Everything is prepared
with balance, nuance, and attention to detail. Less adventurous eaters
might opt for the burger, delicious in its own right, and there's always
a vegetarian option as well. With exposed brick, mismatched antique
china, communal tables, and a counter overlooking the open kitchen
that allows diners to interact with the chefs, the atmosphere at this
42-seat restaurant is trendy yet casual. While not required, reservations
are a good idea, especially on weekends. James Beard–winning chef
Gabriel Rucker also operates an excellent sister restaurant in Down-
town, Little Bird Bistro. $ *Average main: $26* ⊠ *738 E. Burnside St.,
Central East Side, Southeast* ☎ *503/546–8796* ⊕ *www.lepigeon.com*
⊘ *No lunch* $ *Average main: $26* ⊠ *219 S.W. 6th Ave., Downtown*
☎ *503/688–5952* ⊕ *littlebirdbistro.com* ⊘ *No lunch weekends* ✛ *H4.*

$$ ✕ **Olympic Provisions.** Salumist Elias Cairo made a name for himself
MODERN throughout the country with his artisanal charcuterie, such as smoked
AMERICAN chorizo, pepper-coated capicola, and pork-pistachio pâté, which is sold
Fodor'sChoice in fine grocery stores nationally as well as at numerous Portland farmers'
★ markets and gourmet shops. Now Cairo, alongside chef Alex Yoder, is
gaining recognition for a pair of stellar, meat-centric restaurants—Olympic Provisions Northwest and Olympic Provisions Southeast—in which
you can order platters of charcuterie and cheeses along with more eclectic
seasonal American fare. Consider the starter of olive-oil-poached albacore with corona beans, and main dishes that include braised short ribs,
roasted French garlic sausage with white beans and tarragon mustard,
and roasted chicken thighs with eggplant caponata and garlic-yogurt
sauce. The original Central East Side location is in a smartly designed
warehouse space and features a glowing "Meat" sign which quite simply
says it all. The Northwest branch is in an airy storefront space on the
northern edge of the Pearl District. Both spots are popular for brunch
and happy hour, and carry extensive cocktail and wine lists. $ *Aver-
age main: $22* ⊠ *107 S.E. Washington St., Central East Side, Southeast*
☎ *503/954–3663* ⊕ *www.olympicprovisions.com* ⊘ *No dinner Mon.*
$ *Average main: $22* ⊠ *1632 N.W. Thurman St., Southeast* ☎ *503/894–
8136* ⊕ *www.olympicprovisions.com* ⊘ *No dinner Mon.* ✛ *G5.*

$ ✕ **PaaDee.** Hiding in the shadow of adjoining, attention-hogging, res-
THAI ervations-only sister restaurant Langbaan, PaaDee serves some of the
Fodor'sChoice freshest, most flavorful Thai food in town, and at remarkably fair prices
★ given the complexity of the cooking, the warmth of the staff, and the
attractiveness of the dining room, which is on the ground floor of a
contemporary condo building at the restaurant-blessed intersection of
28th and Burnside. The kitchen here specializes in traditional Thai
comfort fare: grilled squid skewers with chili-lime sauce; wild-caught
prawns with lemongrass, scallions, ground rice, and a spicy lime dressing; and sautéed pork belly with basil, chili, green beans, and a fried egg

rank among the most popular dishes. The bar pours some interesting cocktails and well-chosen local wines and beers, too. ⑤ *Average main: $14* ⊠ *6 S.E. 28th Ave., Kerns, Southeast* ☎ *503/360–1453* ⊕ *www. paadeepdx.com* ✛ *H4.*

$ ✕ **Pok Pok.** Andy Ricker, the owner of one of Portland's most talked-
ASIAN   about restaurants, regularly travels to Southeast Asia to research street
Fodor'sChoice   food and home-style recipes to include on the menu of this always-
★   hopping spot. Ike's Vietnamese chicken wings, deep-fried in caramel-
ized fish sauce and garlic, are legendary. Other favorites include the namesake green papaya salad and the charcoal-roasted game hen. The menu is designed for sharing, and some dishes are quite fiery—discuss your preferences with the knowledgeable staff before ordering. Diners have the option of sitting outside under tents, or in the funky, cavelike interior. Across the street, sister space Whiskey Soda Lounge is both a Pok Pok waiting area and restaurant in its own right, with a full bar and a limited Pok Pok menu. The Pok Pok mini empire includes Pok Pok Noi in the funky Alberta District and Sen Yai noodle house, a few blocks east of the original Pok Pok on Division. ⑤ *Average main: $14* ⊠ *3226 S.E. Division St., Richmond, Southeast* ☎ *503/232–1387* ⊕ *www.pokpokpdx.com* ✛ *H6.*

$$$$ ✕ **Roe.** With its unmarked entrance in the back of lively restaurant Block
SEAFOOD   + Tackle, and just a handful of tables and a few counter seats overlook-
Fodor'sChoice   ing the open kitchen, this intimate spot feels a little under the radar—
★   but it isn't. Roe is regularly lauded by the national restaurant press, and with good reason. The menu changes often and always features a mix of raw and cooked fare, perhaps silver-snapper ceviche with corn, tomato "caviar," smoked-citrus *nuoc mam*, and edamame mousse; and butter-poached blue prawns with buttered-popcorn emulsion and piquillo and padron peppers. Chef Trent Pierce runs both Block + Tackle and Roe, but saves his most complex, inventive creations for Roe, which is open just four nights a week and offers either four- or seven-course prix-fixe menus ($75 or $115 per person), with different wine- and beverage-pairing options available for an additional charge. ⑤ *Average main: $75* ⊠ *3113 S.E. Division St., Southeast* ☎ *503/232–1566* ⊕ *www.roepdx. rest* ⌢ *Reservations essential* ⊘ *Closed Sun.–Tues. No lunch* ✛ *H6.*

$$ ✕ **Trifecta Tavern.** Baker extraordinaire Ken Forkish (of Ken's Artisan
MODERN   Bakery and Artisan Pizza fame) opened this extremely well-received
AMERICAN   tavern in 2014 inside a converted garage in the industrial Central East
Fodor'sChoice   Side. The menu still reflects the owner's devotion to wood-fired ovens—
★   there's even a Negroni cocktail infused with charred maple wood on the menu—but you'll also discover an exhaustive selection of snacks and larger plates that have never met with an open flame, such as the compressed-watermelon salad with sheep's milk vinaigrette and spiced almonds. You could make a meal of several bar snacks (Oregon bay shrimp rolls, deviled eggs), or dive into more substantial fare like pork shank with miso broth, or the 18-ounce "Big-Ass Steak," served with wood-fired marrow bones. The airy dining room, with red-leather booths and glass garage-door windows, is festive, if a bit loud. ⑤ *Average main: $20* ⊠ *726 S.E. 6th Ave., Central East Side, Southeast* ☎ *503/841–6675* ⊕ *www.trifectapdx.com* ⊘ *No lunch* ✛ *G5.*

WHERE TO STAY

Portland has an unusually rich variety of distinctive, design-driven boutique hotels, historic properties, and charming B&Bs, and while you'll find the usual mix of budget-oriented, midrange, and upscale chains here, if you'd rather avoid cookie-cutter brand-name properties, you're in the right city.

Although you won't find ultraluxury brands like Four Seasons or W Hotels, the vast majority of Downtown properties are high-end, with the rates to prove it, especially during the week when conventions are in town, and during the summer high season, when many properties command at least double what they can during the slower, wetter winter months.

A B&B might make a better option than a larger hotel if you're looking for a more personal and authentic Portland experience. Most of Portland's smaller accommodations are in lively neighborhoods abundant with distinctive shopping and dining, and most often, an inn will offer unique guest rooms, deluxe home-cooked breakfasts, and friendly and knowledgeable innkeepers.

HOTEL PRICES

Although rates have risen considerably in Portland in recent years as the city's popularity has soared, rates even at upscale Downtown hotels are usually a notch or two lower than what you'd pay in other West Coast cities, such as Seattle and San Francisco. In summer, when the city is abuzz with festivals and festival goers, it can be difficult to find a room in Downtown for under $300 nightly. Most of the time, however, even the more luxurious hotels will run you under $250 per night, and there are a lot of options around $175 or less. Outside Downtown, but still within city limits, it is much easier to find rooms in midrange chains and B&Bs for a little over $100 nightly, and at a handful of reliable budget properties around town (we've included several in this chapter), for under $100 nightly.

If you don't mind a dull but pleasant suburban location, the surrounding towns of Beaverton, Lake Oswego, Gresham, and Vancouver, Washington, abound with chain hotels with rates typically 25% to 50% lower than what you'd pay in Portland, and nearly always with free parking. *Hotel reviews have been shortened. For full information, visit Fodors.com.*

WHAT IT COSTS IN U.S. DOLLARS				
	$	$$	$$$	$$$$
Hotels	Under $110	$110–$175	$176–$250	Over $250

Hotel prices are the lowest cost of a standard double room in high season.

In alphabetical order by neighborhood. Use the coordinate (✛ B2) at the end of each listing to locate a site on the corresponding map.

DOWNTOWN

$$
HOTEL
Fodor'sChoice
★
Ace Hotel. The quintessential Portland hipster hotel, the Ace is sandwiched between Stumptown Coffee and Clyde Common restaurant, a block from Powell's Books and the Pearl District, and right in the heart of Downtown's ever-trendy West End neighborhood. **Pros:** prime Downtown location; unique design and artwork in each room; free city bicycles available for guests. **Cons:** water pressure can be weak; some shared baths. *$ Rooms from: $155 ⊠ 1022 S.W. Stark St., Downtown ☎ 503/228–2277 ⊕ www.acehotel.com ⤳ 78 rooms ⊙ No meals ✛ D4.*

$$$
HOTEL
Benson Hotel. Portland's venerable grande dame may now be overshadowed by several other upscale properties in town in terms of luxury, especially given the steep rates, but the Benson has hosted most every president since it opened in 1913. **Pros:** historic building; beautiful lobby; excellent location; excellent service. **Cons:** rooms and hallways are a bit dark; many bathrooms are quite small. *$ Rooms from: $249 ⊠ 309 S.W. Broadway, Downtown ☎ 503/228–2000, 800/716–6199 ⊕ www.bensonhotel.com ⤳ 230 rooms, 57 suites ⊙ No meals ✛ D4.*

$$$
HOTEL
Courtyard by Marriott–Portland City Center. More boutique feeling than typical Courtyards, this LEED-certified hotel has individual check-in kiosks in its lobby rather than one big reception desk, and the spacious, tasteful rooms showcase local art and photography. **Pros:** environmental consciousness; in the heart of Downtown; good on-site restaurant. **Cons:** only some rooms have tubs; rates are not much lower than some significantly fancier competitors. *$ Rooms from: $179 ⊠ 550 S.W. Oak St., Downtown ☎ 503/505–5000 ⊕ www.marriott.com ⤳ 253 rooms, 3 suites ⊙ No meals ✛ E4.*

$$$
HOTEL
FAMILY
Embassy Suites Portland–Downtown. The grand lobby of the former Multnomah Hotel, built in 1912, offers an extravagant welcome to this all-suites hotel located close to both the riverfront and Old Town. **Pros:** central location; atmospheric old building; breakfast and evening drinks and snacks included. **Cons:** surrounding blocks can feel a bit seedy (though still quite safe) at night; no in-and-out privileges in $27 self-park garage across the street. *$ Rooms from: $189 ⊠ 319 S.W. Pine St., Downtown ☎ 503/279–9000, 800/643–7892 ⊕ www.embassyportland.com ⤳ 276 suites ⊙ Breakfast ✛ E4.*

$$$$
HOTEL
Fodor'sChoice
★
Heathman Hotel. From the teak-paneled lobby to the marble fireplaces to the rosewood elevators with Warhol prints at each landing, this wonderfully atmospheric, art-filled 1927 hotel exudes refinement. **Pros:** superior service; central location adjoining Portland Center for the Performing Arts, and a block from Portland Art Museum; outstanding art collection. **Cons:** some rooms are small; expensive parking. *$ Rooms from: $269 ⊠ 1001 S.W. Broadway, Downtown ☎ 503/241–4100, 800/551–0011 ⊕ portland.heathmanhotel.com ⤳ 110 rooms, 40 suites ⊙ No meals ✛ D5.*

$$$
HOTEL
Fodor'sChoice
★
Hotel deLuxe. This retro-glam 1912 boutique hotel with its original chandeliers, gilded ceilings, black-and-white photography (arranged by movie themes), heavy drapes, and hip cocktail lounge evokes Hollywood's golden age, but with welcome modern touches like flat-screen TVs, free Wi-Fi, and iPod docks. **Pros:** fun and artistic vibe; friendly and helpful staff; nice touches like pillow menu, preprogrammed iPods,

BEST BETS FOR PORTLAND LODGING

Fodor's offers a selective listing of fine lodging experiences in every price range, from the city's best budget beds to its most sophisticated luxury hotels. Here we've compiled our top recommendations by price and experience. The very best properties—in other words, those that provide a particularly remarkable experience in their price range—are designated in the listings with the Fodor's Choice logo.

Fodor's Choice ★

Ace Hotel, $$ p. 80

Evermore Guesthouse, $$ p. 87

Heathman Hotel, $$$$ p. 80

Hotel deLuxe, $$$ p. 80

Hotel Monaco, $$$$ p. 82

Inn @ Northrup Station, $$$ p. 84

Lion and the Rose Victorian B&B, $$ p. 86

McMenamins Kennedy School, $$ p. 86

The Nines, $$$$ p. 83

Residence Inn–Pearl District, $$$ p. 84

Sentinel Hotel, $$$ p. 84

Viking Motel, $, p. 85

By Price

$

Everett Street Guesthouse, p. 85

McMenamins Crystal Hotel, p. 83

Viking Motel, p. 85

$$

Ace Hotel, p. 80

Caravan–The Tiny House Hotel, p. 85

Evermore Guesthouse, p. 87

Heron Haus, p. 84

Jupiter Hotel, p. 87

Lion and the Rose Victorian B&B, p. 86

McMenamins Kennedy School, p. 86

Portland's White House Bed and Breakfast, p. 86

Silver Cloud Inn–Portland, p. 85

$$$

Hotel deLuxe, p. 80

Hotel Lucia, p. 82

Hotel Modera, p. 82

Inn @ Northrup Station, p. 84

The Paramount Hotel, p. 83

Residence Inn–Pearl District, p. 84

Sentinel Hotel, p. 84

$$$$

Heathman Hotel, p. 80

Hotel Monaco, p. 82

The Nines, p. 83

RiverPlace Hotel, p. 83

By Experience

BEST FOR FAMILIES

Embassy Suites Portland–Downtown, $$$, p. 80

Silver Cloud Inn–Portland, $$, p. 85

BEST FOR ROMANCE

Hotel deLuxe, $$$, p. 80

Hotel Monaco, $$$$, p. 82

Lion and the Rose Victorian B&B, $$, p. 86

The Nines, $$$$, p. 83

Portland's White House Bed and Breakfast, $$, p. 86

RiverPlace Hotel, $$$$, p. 83

Sentinel Hotel, $$$, p. 84

BEST B&BS

Evermore Guesthouse, $$, p. 87

Heron Haus, $$, p. 84

Lion and the Rose Victorian B&B, $$, p. 86

Portland's White House Bed and Breakfast, $$, p. 86

BEST SERVICE

Benson Hotel, $$$, p. 80

Heathman Hotel, $$$$, p. 80

Hotel Lucia, $$$, p. 82

Hotel Monaco, $$$$, p. 82

Residence Inn–Pearl District, $$$, p. 84

RiverPlace Hotel, $$$$, p. 83

spiritual book library, and classic movies. **Cons:** standard rooms are a bit compact; location is less central than competitors. ⑤ *Rooms from: $189* ✉ *729 S.W. 15th Ave., Downtown* ☎ *503/219–2094, 866/986–8085* ⊕ *www.hoteldeluxeportland.com* ⮑ *97 rooms, 33 suites* ⦿ *No meals* ✛ *C4.*

$$$ ⛶ **Hotel Lucia.** Black-and-white celebrity photos from Pulitzer Prize–win-
HOTEL   ner and native Oregonian David Hume Kennerly, comfy leather chairs, and stylish low-slung furniture adorn the rooms of this nine-story, 1909 European-style boutique hotel in the heart of Downtown. **Pros:** prime location; luxurious amenities; two outstanding restaurants. **Cons:** lim-ited shelf and storage space in the small bathrooms; steep rates during busy times. ⑤ *Rooms from: $229* ✉ *400 S.W. Broadway, Downtown* ☎ *503/225–1717, 866/986–8086* ⊕ *www.hotellucia.com* ⮑ *127 rooms, 33 suites* ⦿ *No meals* ✛ *D4.*

$$$ ⛶ **Hotel Modera.** Decorated with local artwork, sleek, contemporary
HOTEL   furnishings, and wood-and-marble accents, this boutique property is both upscale and accessible, and offers a location convenient to the Southwest Park Blocks and Portland State University. **Pros:** friendly staff; nice courtyard; great bar-restaurant; individually bagged ice in hand-carved chests in every hall. **Cons:** rooms on the small side; no on-site gym; a 10- to 15-minute walk from West End and Pearl Dis-trict dining and nightlife. ⑤ *Rooms from: $209* ✉ *515 S.W. Clay St., Downtown* ☎ *503/484–1084, 877/484–1084* ⊕ *www.hotelmodera.com* ⮑ *167 rooms, 7 suites* ⦿ *No meals* ✛ *D6.*

$$$$ ⛶ **Hotel Monaco.** This artsy Downtown Portland outpost of the Kimpton-
HOTEL   operated Monaco boutique-hotel brand offers eclectic textiles and
Fodor'sChoice   patterns, bright spaces and bold colors, quirky amenities like compli-
★   mentary companion goldfish for your room, and the overall sense that staying here is a lot of fun. **Pros:** sumptuous interior; interesting decor; impeccable service; well-equipped fitness center; excellent on-site res-taurant and bar. **Cons:** design style may not suit all; pricey. ⑤ *Rooms from: $289* ✉ *506 S.W. Washington St., Downtown* ☎ *503/222–0001, 888/207–2201* ⊕ *www.portland-monaco.com* ⮑ *86 rooms, 135 suites* ⦿ *No meals* ✛ *E4.*

$$$ ⛶ **Hotel Rose.** This recently renovated and rebranded boutique property
HOTEL   overlooking the Willamette River affords stellar views of the water, easy access to the waterfront park and the events that take place there (Rose Festival, Blues Festival, Gay Pride, and so on), and—as part of the Pineapple Hospitality chain—a pineapple-cupcake welcome at recep-tion. **Pros:** central location on the riverfront; typically lower rates than many comparable Downtown hotels; complimentary bike rentals; easy access to the MAX. **Cons:** rooms not facing the river have dull views; no on-site fitness facility. ⑤ *Rooms from: $219* ✉ *50 S.W. Morrison St., Downtown* ☎ *503/221–0711, 866/866–7977* ⊕ *www.hotelfifty.com* ⮑ *140 rooms, 1 suite* ⦿ *No meals* ✛ *E5.*

$$$ ⛶ **Hotel Vintage Plaza.** This historic landmark takes its theme from Ore-
HOTEL   gon vineyards, with rooms named after local wineries, complimentary wine served every evening, and an extensive collection of Oregon vin-tages displayed in the tasting room. **Pros:** terrific on-site Italian restau-rant, Pazzo; friendly staff; several distinctive and romantic specialty

2

suites. **Cons:** pricey parking; some street noise on the lower levels on the Washington Street side. $ *Rooms from: $249* ⊠ *422 S.W. Broadway, Downtown* ☎ *503/228–1212, 800/263–2305* ⊕ *www.vintageplaza.com* ⇨ *96 rooms, 21 suites* ¶◯| *No meals* ✛ *D4.*

$$$
HOTEL
Mark Spencer Hotel. This family-owned hotel, with a prime location in the hip West End near Powell's Books and the Pearl District, is one of the better values in town, with most of its warmly decorated rooms containing well-equipped kitchenettes. **Pros:** commitment to the arts; afternoon tea and cookies and evening local wine tasting; most rooms have kitchenettes. **Cons:** some rooms are small and dark; street noise can be a problem. $ *Rooms from: $219* ⊠ *409 S.W. 11th Ave., Downtown* ☎ *503/224–3293, 800/548–3934* ⊕ *www.markspencer.com* ⇨ *36 rooms, 66 suites* ¶◯| *Breakfast* ✛ *D4.*

$
HOTEL
McMenamins Crystal Hotel. Travelers who appreciate good music and good beer—especially together—love this West End branch of the McMenamin brothers' unorthodox empire, which is home to three bars and a restaurant and is affiliated with the Crystal Ballroom concert venue a block away. **Pros:** historic building with eccentric, rock-star vibe and decor; lots of bars and dining both on-site and on surrounding blocks; shared-bath rooms are extremely affordable. **Cons:** quirky vibe isn't for everyone; shared bath down the hall in most rooms; no TVs. $ *Rooms from: $105* ⊠ *303 S.W. 12th Ave., Downtown* ☎ *503/972–2670, 855/205–3930* ⊕ *www.mcmenamins.com/crystalhotel* ⇨ *51 rooms, 9 with bath* ¶◯| *No meals* ✛ *C4.*

$$$$
HOTEL
Fodor's Choice
★
The Nines. On the top nine floors of a former landmark department store, this swanky hotel, part of the Starwood Luxury Collection, has the city's poshest accommodations, with luxe decor, great views, and two see-and-be-seen restaurants. **Pros:** stunning views; swanky vibe and cool design; two scene-y restaurants. **Cons:** rooms facing the atrium and overlooking the bar and restaurant can be noisy; expensive valet-only parking. $ *Rooms from: $329* ⊠ *525 S.W. Morrison St., Downtown* ☎ *503/222–9996, 877/229–9995* ⊕ *www.thenines.com* ⇨ *318 rooms, 13 suites* ¶◯| *No meals* ✛ *D4.*

$$$
HOTEL
The Paramount Hotel. This pale-stone, 15-story hotel overlooking Director Park is a few blocks from Pioneer Square, the Arlene Schnitzer Concert Hall, the Portland Art Museum, the MAX, and the streetcar. **Pros:** central location; beautiful granite bathrooms; excellent bar and restaurant off lobby. **Cons:** small fitness facility; parking is expensive. $ *Rooms from: $219* ⊠ *808 S.W. Taylor St., Downtown* ☎ *503/223–9900* ⊕ *www.portlandparamount.com* ⇨ *152 rooms, 2 suites* ¶◯| *No meals* ✛ *D5.*

$$$$
HOTEL
RiverPlace Hotel. With textured wall coverings, pillows made of Pendleton wool, and a color palette of slate blue, mustard yellow, and a variety of browns, this Kimpton-operated boutique hotel on the banks of the Willamette River captures the look and feel of the Pacific Northwest. **Pros:** stellar views and park-side riverfront location; rooms are spacious and airy; some suites have wood-burning fireplaces. **Cons:** location on south edge of Downtown is a bit of a walk from bars, restaurants, and shopping. $ *Rooms from: $309* ⊠ *1510 S.W. Harbor Way, Downtown* ☎ *503/228–3233, 888/869–3108* ⊕ *www.riverplacehotel.com* ⇨ *39 rooms, 45 suites* ¶◯| *No meals* ✛ *E6.*

$$$ **Sentinel Hotel.** Formerly known as the Governor Hotel, the grand
HOTEL Sentinel Hotel underwent a $6 million renovation and rebranding in
Fodor'sChoice 2014 to take it from historic to hip-historic; all guest rooms and public
★ spaces in the landmark, early-20th-century buildings were brought up-
to-date, and the hotel now reflects a very Portland vibe, with locally
sourced textiles, furnishings, and goods. **Pros:** indie style meets luxury;
central location; spacious, well-designed rooms; well-equipped gym.
Cons: pricey valet parking. $ *Rooms from: $199* ⊠ *614 S.W. 10th Ave.,
Downtown* ☎ *503/224–3400, 888/246–5631* ⊕ *www.sentinelhotel.com*
⤵ *76 rooms, 24 suites* ⫶⊙⫶ *No meals* ✛ *D4.*

$$$ **The Westin Portland.** This pale-stone, upscale hotel combines luxury
HOTEL with convenience, with Pioneer Square and the MAX just two blocks
away, and West End and Pearl District dining within a 10-minute walk.
Pros: prime Downtown location (a stone's throw from one of the city's
largest, most established food-cart pods); handsome rooms; plush bed-
ding. **Cons:** pricey overnight parking; attractive but not especially distinctive rooms. $ *Rooms from: $209* ⊠ *750 S.W. Alder St., Downtown*
☎ *503/294–9000, 888/625–5144* ⊕ *www.westinportland.com* ⤵ *189
rooms, 16 suites* ⫶⊙⫶ *No meals* ✛ *D4.*

PEARL DISTRICT

$$$ **Residence Inn–Pearl District.** Opened in spring 2014, this sleek, six-
HOTEL floor, all-suites hotel is the trendy Pearl District's first hotel. **Pros:** new,
Fodor'sChoice modern design both inside and out; best location for proximity to Pearl
★ District businesses; in-room kitchens; many rooms can sleep four to six
guests. **Cons:** a little far from Downtown attractions; parking costs $32
nightly. $ *Rooms from: $179* ⊠ *1150 N.W. 9th Ave., Pearl District*
☎ *503/220–1339, 888/236–2427* ⊕ *www.marriott.com* ⤵ *224 suites*
⫶⊙⫶ *Breakfast* ✛ *D2.*

NOB HILL

$$ **Heron Haus.** In a stately, ivy-covered mansion built in 1904, this bright
B&B/INN and lovely Tudor Revival home sets you on a lush, fern-covered hillside
within walking distance of Forest Park, overlooking the trendy Nob Hill
shopping and dining area, and just a 10-minute walk to the streetcar.
Pros: serene environment; discerning owners have great local knowledge. **Cons:** the residential neighborhood is a bit
inconvenient to the Downtown core; no tubs in bathrooms. $ *Rooms
from: $175* ⊠ *2545 N.W. Westover Rd., Nob Hill* ☎ *503/274–1846*
⊕ *www.heronhaus.com* ⤵ *6 rooms* ⫶⊙⫶ *Breakfast* ✛ *A2.*

$$$ **Inn @ Northrup Station.** Bright colors, bold patterns, and retro designs
HOTEL characterize this Nob Hill hotel containing luxurious suites with full
FAMILY kitchens or kitchenettes. **Pros:** roomy suites have kitchens and feel like
Fodor'sChoice home; steps from Nob Hill shopping, dining, and the streetcar; free
★ parking. **Cons:** the bold color scheme isn't for everyone; a 15-minute
walk, or slightly shorter streetcar ride, from Downtown core; in demand
so it can be hard to get a reservation. $ *Rooms from: $199* ⊠ *2025
N.W. Northrup St., Nob Hill* ☎ *503/224–0543, 800/224–1180* ⊕ *www.
northrupstation.com* ⤵ *70 suites* ⫶⊙⫶ *Breakfast* ✛ *B2.*

$$ ⬚ **Silver Cloud Inn–Portland.** The sole Portland branch of a small, Seattle-
HOTEL   area, midprice hotel chain is just a block from the lively upper end of
N.W. 23rd Avenue and a great alternative to the bustle Downtown.
Pros: free parking; close to Nob Hill boutiques and dining as well as
Forest Park hiking trails; easy access to bus and streetcar. **Cons:** gym
but no pool; not especially close to Downtown; front rooms face a
busy street. ⑤ *Rooms from: $159* ✉ *2426 N.W. Vaughn St., Nob Hill*
☎ *503/242–2400, 800/205–6939* ⊕ *www.silvercloud.com* ⟳ *75 rooms,*
6 suites ⦿ *Breakfast* ✛ *A1.*

NORTH

$$ ⬚ **Caravan–The Tiny House Hotel.** In keeping with the artsy, idiosyncratic
B&B/INN   vibe of the surrounding Alberta Arts District, this cluster of itty-bitty
custom-built houses-on-wheels offers visitors the chance to experience
Portland's unabashed quirky side. **Pros:** a quirky, only-in-Portland experience; in the heart of Alberta's hip retail-dining district; all units have
kitchenettes. **Cons:** these houses really are tiny; 15-minute drive or
35-minute bus ride from Downtown; often books up weeks in advance
(especially weekends). ⑤ *Rooms from: $125* ✉ *5009 N.E. 11th Ave.,*
Alberta Arts District, North ☎ *503/288–5225* ⊕ *www.tinyhousehotel.*
com ⟳ *6 cottages* ⦿ *No meals* ✛ *G1.*

$ ⬚ **Viking Motel.** When this clean, family-run, midcentury motel opened
HOTEL   in the late 1970s, it served the nearby shipyard; today, this eco-friendly
Fodor's Choice   property is arguably Portland's best bargain lodging, catering to savvy
★   visitors who take the nearby MAX to Downtown Portland. **Pros:** rock-
bottom rates (and free parking and Wi-Fi); friendly owners who take
great pride in the property's upkeep; just off Interstate 5 and a block from
MAX light-rail station. **Cons:** North Portland neighborhood is 15-minute
drive north of Downtown; few frills. ⑤ *Rooms from: $65* ✉ *6701 N.*
Interstate Ave., Arbor Lodge, North ☎ *503/285–4896, 800/308–5097*
⊕ *www.vikingmotelportland.com* ⟳ *26 rooms* ⦿ *No meals* ✛ *E1.*

NORTHEAST

$$ ⬚ **DoubleTree by Hilton–Portland.** This bustling, business hotel maintains
HOTEL   a steady customer base in meetings and special events, so you will
find all the usual business-friendly perks and luxuries, and—as a lei-
sure traveler—the best rates on weekends. **Pros:** convenient location
for light rail, conventions, and concerts and Trail Blazers basketball
games; nice views from upper floors. **Cons:** pool is outdoors; hotel
can be crowded with conventioneers; surrounding Lloyd District has
chain shops and movie theaters but lacks charm. ⑤ *Rooms from: $149*
✉ *1000 N.E. Multnomah St., Lloyd District, Northeast* ☎ *503/281–*
6111, 800/222–8733 ⊕ *www.doubletree.com* ⟳ *458 rooms, 18 suites*
⦿ *No meals* ✛ *H2.*

$ ⬚ **Everett Street Guesthouse.** Innkeeper Terry Rusinow proudly assures
B&B/INN   guests who stay in her 1907 Craftsman-style bed-and-breakfast that
they won't encounter any "frilly curtains, teddy bears, or potpourri"—
indeed, the two cozy rooms and adjacent cottage are tastefully appointed
with well-chosen artwork and crafts. **Pros:** affordable; simple, tasteful

rooms; short walk from the terrific restaurants and bars of 28th and Burnside. **Cons:** with so few rooms and great rates, it can book up fast; 10-minute drive or 20-minute bus ride from Downtown. ⑤ *Rooms from: $90* ⊠ *2306 N.E. Everett St., Kerns, Northeast* ☎ *503/230–0211* ⊕ *www.everettstreetguesthouse.com* ⇄ *2 rooms with shared bath, 1 cottage* ✶◎✶ *Breakfast* ✛ *H3.*

$$ ⬚ **Lion and the Rose Victorian B&B.** Oak and mahogany floors, original light fixtures, and a coffered dining-room ceiling set a tone of formal elegance in this 1906 mansion, while the wonderfully friendly, accommodating, and knowledgeable innkeepers—Dusty and Steve—make sure that you feel perfectly at home. **Pros:** gorgeous house; top-notch service; home-cooked meals. **Cons:** young children not allowed in main house; nearest commercial neighborhood, the Lloyd District, is pretty bland. ⑤ *Rooms from: $155* ⊠ *1810 N.E. 15th Ave., Irvington, Northeast* ☎ *503/287–9245, 800/955–1647* ⊕ *www.lionrose.com* ⇄ *7 rooms, 1 apartment* ✶◎✶ *Breakfast* ✛ *H1.*

B&B/INN
Fodor'sChoice
★

$$ ⬚ **McMenamins Kennedy School.** In a renovated elementary school on the edge of a trendy Northeast Portland neighborhood, Oregon's famously creative McMenamin brothers hoteliers have created a quirky and fantastical multiuse facility with rooms that feature original schoolhouse touches like chalkboards and cloakrooms and literature-inspired themes, a movie theater, a restaurant, a warm outdoor soaking pool, a brewery, and several small bars. **Pros:** funky and authentic Portland experience; room rates include movies and use of year-round soaking pool; free parking; close to trendy Alberta Arts District. **Cons:** rooms have showers but no tubs; no TVs in rooms; 20-minute drive or 40-minute bus ride from Downtown. ⑤ *Rooms from: $139* ⊠ *5736 N.E. 33rd Ave., Concordia, Northeast* ☎ *503/249–3983* ⊕ *www.kennedyschool.com* ⇄ *57 rooms* ✶◎✶ *No meals* ✛ *G1.*

HOTEL
FAMILY
Fodor'sChoice
★

$$ ⬚ **Portland's White House Bed and Breakfast.** Hardwood floors with Oriental rugs, chandeliers, antiques, and fountains create a warm and romantic mood at this lavish 1910 Greek Revival mansion in the historic Irvington District. **Pros:** over-the-top romantic; excellent service; a short drive or bus ride to several hip East Side restaurant and retail districts. **Cons:** in residential neighborhood a few miles from Downtown; nearest commercial neighborhood is the rather bland Lloyd District. ⑤ *Rooms from: $135* ⊠ *1914 N.E. 22nd Ave., Irvington, Northeast* ☎ *503/287–7131, 800/272–7131* ⊕ *www.portlandswhitehouse.com* ⇄ *8 suites* ✶◎✶ *Breakfast* ✛ *H1.*

B&B/INN

AIRPORT

The airport is about a 20- to 25-minute drive away from Downtown Portland, and as expected you can find a number of chain properties here, all offering much lower rates than comparable Downtown hotels.

$$ ⬚ **Aloft Portland Airport at Cascade Station.** High-end vibrant design, sophisticated amenities, and close proximity to the Cascade Station MAX station make the first Aloft in Oregon a standout amid the generally mediocre hotels near the airport. **Pros:** lots of high-tech amenities; welcoming social areas; stylish, spacious rooms. **Cons:** airport location; no sit-down restaurant; no complimentary breakfast. ⑤ *Rooms from: $159* ⊠ *9920 N.E. Cascades Pkwy., Airport, Northeast*

HOTEL

☎ *503/200–5678* ⊕ *www.aloftportlandairport.com* ⟿ *136 rooms* ◯| *No meals* ✛ *H1.*

$$ 🛏 **Embassy Suites Portland Airport.** Suites in this eight-story atrium hotel,
HOTEL within view of the airport, come with separate bedrooms, living areas
with sleeper sofas, and flat-screen TVs. **Pros:** spacious suites; full break-
fast and happy-hour cocktails included; walking distance from Cascade
Station chain shops and restaurants. **Cons:** airport location; parking is
$10. ⑤ *Rooms from: $149* ⊠ *7900 N.E. 82nd Ave., Airport, Northeast*
☎ *503/460–3000* ⊕ *www.portlandairport.embassysuites.com* ⟿ *251
suites* ◯| *Breakfast* ✛ *H1.*

SOUTHEAST

$$ 🛏 **Evermore Guesthouse.** Just a block from the trendy dining along South-
B&B/INN east Portland's hip Division Street, this beautifully restored, 1909 Arts
Fodor'sChoice and Crafts–style mansion contains spacious, light-filled rooms, some
★ with private balconies, claw-foot soaking tubs, and good-size sitting
areas; one detached suite has a full kitchen, and a cozy and romantic
third-floor room has skylights and pitched ceilings. **Pros:** located in
hip, charming neighborhood with many bars and restaurants; reasonably priced with free off-street parking; free laundry and breakfast;
distinctive, charming decor. **Cons:** some rooms face busy Cesar Chavez
Boulevard; a 15-minute drive or 30-minute bus ride from Downtown.
⑤ *Rooms from: $120* ⊠ *3860 S.E. Clinton St., Richmond, Southeast*
☎ *503/206–6509, 877/600–6509* ⊕ *www.evermoreguesthouse.com*
⟿ *3 rooms, 3 suites* ◯| *Breakfast* ✛ *H6.*

$$ 🛏 **Jupiter Hotel.** The hip, creative, and adventurous flock to this contem-
HOTEL porary boutique hotel, formerly a motor inn, adjacent to the Doug Fir
Lounge, a bar and restaurant that's also one of the city's most popular
concert venues. **Pros:** funky decor and vibe; trendy bar and music club
attached; easy access to Downtown. **Cons:** youthful, hipster personal-
ity isn't to everyone's taste; request a room on the "chill side" if you
want distance from the noisy patio/bar scene; thin walls between rooms.
⑤ *Rooms from: $164* ⊠ *800 E. Burnside St., Central East Side, South-
east* ☎ *503/230–9200, 877/800–0004* ⊕ *www.jupiterhotel.com* ⟿ *80
rooms, 1 suite* ◯| *No meals* ✛ *H4.*

SOUTHWEST

$$$ 🛏 **River's Edge Hotel & Spa.** On the edge of Portland's recently developed
HOTEL South Waterfront District and just a 10- to 15-minute drive or bus ride
from Downtown, this tranquil boutique property is nestled among trees
along the meandering Willamette River. **Pros:** expansive river views;
most rooms have balconies; trails nearby for walking and jogging; full-
service spa on-site. **Cons:** few restaurants or businesses within walking distance; need a car or bus to get to Downtown; only valet ($25)
parking is available. ⑤ *Rooms from: $219* ⊠ *0455 S.W. Hamilton Ct.,
South Waterfront, Southwest* ☎ *503/802–5800, 888/556–4402* ⊕ *www.
riversedgehotel.com* ⟿ *81 rooms, 18 suites* ◯| *Breakfast* ✛ *E6.*

NIGHTLIFE AND PERFORMING ARTS

Portland is quite the creative town. Every night top-ranked dance, theater, and musical performers take the stage somewhere in the city. Expect to find never-ending choices for things to do, from taking in true independent films, performance art, and plays, to checking out some of the Northwest's (and the country's) hottest bands at one of the city's many nightclubs or concert venues.

Given the city's unabashed passion for craft cocktails and beer, local wines, and artisanal coffee, it makes sense that Portland abounds with cool lounges, coffeehouses, and bars. Hard-core clubbing and dancing has a bit less of a following here than more casual barhopping, and Portlanders do like to combine noshing and sipping—you'll find an abundance of nightspots serving exceptional food (and often offering great happy-hour deals on victuals and drinks), and quite a few full-service restaurants with popular side bars and lounges. Nightlife and dining really overlap in the Rose City.

EVENT LISTINGS

"A&E, The Arts and Entertainment Guide," published each Friday in the *Oregonian* (⊕ *www.oregonlive.com*), contains listings of performers, productions, events, and club entertainment. *Willamette Week* (⊕ *wweek.com*), published free each Wednesday and widely available throughout the metropolitan area, contains similar, but hipper, listings. The *Portland Mercury* (⊕ *www.portlandmercury.com*), also free, is an even edgier entertainment publication distributed each Wednesday. The glossy newsstand magazine *Portland Monthly* (⊕ *www.portlandmonthlymag.com*) covers Portland culture and lifestyle and provides great nightlife, entertainment, and dining coverage for the city. The free monthly publication *Portland Family Magazine* (⊕ *www.portlandfamily.com*) has an excellent calendar of events for recreational and educational opportunities for families. PQ Monthly (⊕ *www.pqmonthly.com*) is the city's gay publication.

NIGHTLIFE

Portland has become something of a base for up-and-coming alternative-rock bands, which perform in clubs scattered throughout the city. Good jazz groups perform nightly in a handful of bars as well.

Portland's most diverting neighborhoods for barhopping are, not surprisingly, its favored dining districts, too—the West End, Pearl District, and Nob Hill on the west side of the Willamette River, within walking distance (or a streetcar ride) of Downtown hotels; Alberta Street, North Mississippi Avenue, East Burnside Street in the 20s, the Central East Side, Belmont Street, Hawthorne Boulevard, and Division Street on the East Side. Note that many of the restaurants listed in Where to Eat also double as highly popular nightspots; especially notable for sipping and socializing are Bluehour, Clyde Common, Departure, Interurban, Irving Street Kitchen, RingSide Steakhouse, Smallwares, and Veritable Quandary.

DOWNTOWN

BARS AND LOUNGES

Fodor'sChoice **Driftwood Room.** Once your eyes adjust to the romantically dim lighting,
★ you'll find a curved bar, leather banquette seating, and polished-wood ceilings and walls in this retro-chic bar in the Old Hollywood–themed Hotel deLuxe. The trendy cocktails are garnished with herbs culled from the hotel's garden. ■ TIP→ The happy-hour food menu is one of the best in the city. ⊠ *Hotel deLuxe, 729 S.W. 15th Ave., Downtown* ☎ *503/820–2076* ⊕ *www.hoteldeluxeportland.com.*

Fodor'sChoice **The Heathman Restaurant & Bar.** At the elegant Heathman Hotel, you can
★ sip tea in the eucalyptus-paneled Tea Court or beer, wine, and cocktails in the marble bar. This is one of the city's most popular see-and-be-seen venues, especially before or after shows at nearby theaters and concert halls. ⊠ *1001 S.W. Broadway, Downtown* ☎ *503/790–7752* ⊕ *www. heathmanrestaurantandbar.com.*

Huber's Cafe. The city's oldest restaurant (est. 1879) is notable for its old-fashioned feel and iconic Spanish coffee cocktail, which is set aflame at your table. The old bar in the back has great character. Huber's is on the ground floor of the historic Oregon Pioneer Building, which is being converted into an upscale boutique hotel with a planned 2015 opening, but Huber's will remain open during construction. ⊠ *411 S.W. 3rd Ave., Downtown* ☎ *503/228–5686* ⊕ *www.hubers.com.*

Fodor'sChoice **Multnomah Whiskey Library.** Smartly dressed mixologists roll drink
★ carts around the seductively clubby room—with beam ceilings, wood panelling, leather club chairs, a wood-burning fireplace, and crystal chandeliers—pouring cocktails table-side. The emphasis, of course, is whiskey and bourbon—Multnomah has such an extensive collection in its "library" that bartenders need rolling ladders to access the bottles perched on the tall shelves lining the exposed-brick walls—but don't overlook the impressive food menu. ⊠ *1124 S.W. Alder St., West End, Downtown* ☎ *503/954–1381* ⊕ *www.multnomahwhiskeylibrary.com.*

Raven & Rose. Popular with the after-work set as well as guests of Downtown hotels, this ornate Victorian two-level carriage house amid Downtown's office towers serves English-style pub fare and a worldly list of beers, wines, and cocktails in the Rookery Bar upstairs. Downstairs, you'll find a main dining room and a small lounge area. There's live music some evenings. ⊠ *1331 S.W. Broadway, Downtown* ☎ *503/222–7673* ⊕ *www.ravenandrosepdx.com.*

Saucebox. A sophisticated crowd flocks here to enjoy colorful cocktails and trendy DJ music many evenings a week. The kitchen turns out consistently good pan-Asian fare. ⊠ *214 S.W. Broadway, Downtown* ☎ *503/241–3393* ⊕ *www.saucebox.com.*

BREWPUBS AND MICROBREWERIES

First National Taphouse. Opened in fall 2014 near Portland State University—a section of Downtown surprisingly bereft of noteworthy bars—this outpost of a Eugene brewpub carries an exhaustive selection of some 30 beers on tap, plus another 400 or so by the bottle, along with wines, hard ciders, and spirits. Upscale pub fare is served, too, and the weekend brunch has quickly become popular. ✉ *1962 S.W. 5th Ave., Downtown* ☎ *971/703–4579* ⊕ *www.firstnationaltaphouse.com.*

COFFEEHOUSES

Case Study Coffee. A first-rate indie alternative to the scads of chain coffeehouses in Downtown, Case Study serves exceptional, house-roasted coffee in a variety of formats, from Chemex to Aeropress; they also make their own syrups and serve delicious drinking chocolates. Nibble delectable sweets from local bakeries Nuvrei and Petunia's (the latter is gluten-free). There are two additional locations in Northeast, as well as one in Hollywood and a newer one in Alberta. Other locations include 5347 N.E. Sandy Blvd. (Northeast) and 1422 N. E. Alberta St. (Northeast). ✉ *802 S.W. 10th Ave., Downtown* ☎ *503/475–3979* ⊕ *www.casestudycoffee.com* ✉ *5347 N.E. Sandy Blvd., Hollywood, Northeast* ☎ *503/477–8221* ⊕ *www.casestudycoffee.com.* ✉ *1422 N.E. Alberta St., Alberta District, Northeast* ☎ *503/477–8221* ⊕ *www. casestudycoffee.com*

Fodor'sChoice
★
Heart Coffee. Inside this sleek East Burnside coffeehouse, patrons sip coffees from Central America, South America, and Africa, and feast on *affogato* (homemade coconut ice cream topped with a shot of espresso) while admiring the rather elegant roasting equipment, which looks like a large-scale art installation. Finnish owner Wille Yli-Luoma brings a modern, minimalist aesthetic to this fiercely popular café. There's another location at 537 S.W. 12th Ave. (Downtown). ✉ *2211 E. Burnside St., Downtown* ☎ *503/206–6602* ⊕ *www.heartroasters.com* ✉ *537 S.W. 12th Ave., West End, Downtown* ☎ *503/224–0036* ⊕ *www. heartroasters.com.*

GAY AND LESBIAN

Casey's. Having moved from Old Town to a large, rather snazzy two-level space in Downtown, just a block or so from another popular LGBT hangout, the Silverado strip club, this festive gay video bar draws a mixed-age crowd for tempting happy-hour deals (daily 3–7 pm), karaoke, and assorted drinking games. ✉ *412 S.W. 4th Ave., Downtown* ☎ *503/505–9468* ⊕ *www.caseyspdx.net.*

Scandals. This low-key bar is the lone remaining LGBT hangout in the West End, which used to be the city's gay nightlife district (it's still a diverse, progressive neighborhood with plenty of mixed hangouts, but the city's gay bars are now mostly in Old Town). There's a small dance floor, a pool table, and light food service noon to closing. The plate-glass windows offer a view of Stark Street, and there's also seating along the sidewalk. ✉ *1125 S.W. Stark St., Downtown* ☎ *503/227–5887* ⊕ *www. scandalspdx.com.*

LIVE MUSIC

McMenamins Crystal Ballroom. With a 7,500-square-foot springy dance floor built on ball bearings to ramp up the energy, this historic former dance hall draws local, regional, and national acts every night but Monday. Past performers include Billy Idol, Jefferson Airplane, Emylou Harris, Death Cab for Cutie, and the Shins. ✉ *1332 W. Burnside St., Downtown* ☎ *503/225–0047* ⊕ *www.mcmenamins.com.*

PEARL DISTRICT

BARS AND LOUNGES

Fodor's Choice ★ **Teardrop Cocktail Lounge.** A swanky, see-and-be-seen bar in the heart of the trendy Pearl District, Teardrop has earned a loyal following for its creative cocktail menu. ⊠ *1015 N.W. Everett St., Pearl District* ☎ *503/445–8109* ⊕ *www.teardroplounge.com.*

BREW PUBS AND MICROBREWERIES

Fodor's Choice ★ **BridgePort BrewPub & Restaurant.** Sample consistently good craft beers at the oldest microbrewery in Portland, a beautiful brick-and-ivy building that's long been a cornerstone of the Pearl Distirct. Free brewery tours are given on Saturday; call for hours. ⊠ *1313 N.W. Marshall St., Pearl District* ☎ *503/241–3612* ⊕ *www.bridgeportbrew.com.*

Deschutes Brewery & Public House. The Portland branch of the Bend-based Deschutes Brewery typically has more than 20 beers on tap, including nationally acclaimed mainstays Mirror Pond Pale Ale, Inversion IPA, and Black Butte Porter, plus seasonal and experimental brews. There's an extensive menu of well-prepared pub fare, too. ⊠ *210 N.W. 11th Ave., Pearl District* ☎ *503/296–4906* ⊕ *www.deschutesbrewery.com.*

LIVE MUSIC

Fodor's Choice ★ **Jimmy Mak's.** Dubbed one of the world's "top 100 places to hear jazz" by *DownBeat Magazine,* this old-school music club also serves Greek and Middle Eastern dishes. ⊠ *221 N.W. 10th Ave., Pearl District* ☎ *503/295–6542* ⊕ *www.jimmymaks.com.*

OLD TOWN

BARS AND LOUNGES

Davis Street Tavern. This convivial spot in an old brick building with hardwood floors and beam ceilings offers cheerful service, late-night dining, and one of the neighborhood's most popular happy hours. It's a refreshingly refined yet friendly bar and tavern amid Old Town's many rather rowdy clubs. ⊠ *135 N.W. 5th Ave., Old Town* ☎ *503/505–5050* ⊕ *www.davisstreettavern.com.*

GAY AND LESBIAN

Fodor's Choice ★ **C.C. Slaughters Nightclub & Lounge.** The most popular gay and lesbian dance club in the city, "C.C.'s" also has a quieter cocktail bar in front called the Rainbow Room. ⊠ *219 N.W. Davis St., Old Town* ☎ *503/248–9135* ⊕ *www.ccslaughterspdx.com.*

LIVE MUSIC

Roseland Theater. This spacious theater holds 1,400 people (standing-room only except for the 21+ balcony seating area), primarily stages rock, alternative, and blues shows. Past performers have included Miles Davis, Pearl Jam, the Police, Bonnie Raitt, and Prince. ⊠ *10 N.W. 6th Ave., Old Town* ☎ *971/230–0033* ⊕ *www.roselandpdx.com.*

NOB HILL

BARS AND LOUNGES

Fodor's Choice ★ **The Fireside.** Warmed by an open fire pit and a roaring fireplace, and decorated with lots of wood and leather, this cozy campfire-chic spot on Nob Hill's retail strip offers one of the best happy hours in Northwest, wallet-friendly appetizers made from locally sourced ingredients, and well-crafted cocktails. Try the Dillicious, made with rye whiskey, semidry vermouth, dill tincture, Kümmel liqueur, and lemon zest. ⊠ *801 N.W. 23rd Ave., Nob Hill* ☎ *503/477–9505* ⊕ *www.pdxfireside.com.*

NORTH
BREWPUBS AND MICROBREWERIES
Prost! At the northern end of the hip North Mississippi retail and restaurant strip, Prost! is an airy, amber-lit, contemporary bar specializing in old-school German beers like Spaten Lager, Franziskaner Weissbier, and Erdinger Dunkel Weisse. Nosh on Bavarian pretzels and other Euro snacks or venture next door to one of the East Side's best food-cart pods, Mississippi Marketplace. ⊠ *4237 N. Mississippi Ave., North* ☎ *503/954–2674* ⊕ *www.prostportland.com.*

LIVE MUSIC
Fodor's Choice ★ **Mississippi Studios.** An intimate neighborhood music venue, with a seated balcony and old Oriental rugs covering the standing-room-only floor, Mississippi Studios offers high-quality live music performances every night of the week in a wide range of genres. Between sets, you can jump back and forth from the adjacent BarBar, a hip, comfortable bar with a delicious hamburger and a covered back patio. ⊠ *3939 N. Mississippi, Boise, North* ☎ *503/288–3895* ⊕ *www.mississippistudios.com.*

NORTHEAST
BARS AND LOUNGES
Branch Whiskey Bar. Amid Alberta Street's offbeat galleries and indie cafés, candlelit and cozy Branch Whiskey Bar serves creative cocktails like the Branchattan—a blend of rye, Vya, Angostura bitters, and orange bitters, and well-crafted food, including expansive charcuterie boards, beef tartare, and seafood ceviche. ⊠ *2926 N.E. Alberta St., Northeast* ☎ *503/206–6266* ⊕ *www.branchpdx.com.*

Fodor's Choice ★ **The Bye and Bye.** An Alberta go-to specializing in creative drinks (sample the house favorite, the Bye and Bye, a refreshing concoction of peach vodka, peach bourbon, lemon, cranberry juice, and soda served in a Mason jar) and vegan fare, Bye and Bye has a big covered patio and a festive dining room. The owners also operate two other similarly trendy bars around town, Sweet Hereafter in Southeast and Jackknife at Downtown's Sentinel Hotel. ⊠ *1011 N.E. Alberta St., Northeast* ☎ *503/281–0537* ⊕ *www.thebyeandbye.com.*

Fodor's Choice ★ **Expatriate.** Opened in 2013 by Kyle Webster and his wife, celeb-chef partner Naomi Pomeroy of Beast (across the street), this intimate, candlelit spot has quickly gained a following for its balanced, boozy cocktails and addictively delicious Asian bar snacks, like curried-potato-and-English-pea samosas. Each of the eight nightly cocktails are meticulously crafted, but the Holding Patter—a mix of Laird's Bonded Apple Brandy, Priorat Vermut Natur, Luxardo Amaro Abano liqueur, and Peychaud's and Regan's bitters—is a house favorite. ⊠ *5424 N.E. 30th Ave., Concordia, Northeast* ☎ *503/805–3750* ⊕ *www.expatriatepdx.com.*

Swift Lounge. The bird-themed Swift Lounge, an endearingly dive-y hipster hangout, offers a menu of Mason-jar cocktails inlcuding the Guilty Sparrow (citrus vodka, lemongrass, and house limoncello), the Stoned Finch (cucumber-infused vodka and house elderflower syrup), and the

Topless Robin (ginger-lemongrass-infused vodka and apricot brandy). You can order the drinks in two sizes—the 32-ounce "Fatty" or the 16-ounce "Sissy." The weekend "hangover brunch" is quite the scene. ✉ *1932 N.E. Broadway, Sullivan's Gulch, Northeast* ☎ *503/288–3333* ⊕ *www.swiftloungepdx.com.*

COFFEEHOUSES

Barista. If you're looking to test-drive a few of Portland's best beans, this dapper café with other locations in Downtown, in the Pearl, and on N.E. Alberta is a great option. You'll find Stumptown, Coava, and other fine coffees, as well as a few craft beers and a small selection of high-quality chocolates and desserts. The high-ceilinged Alberta location is the most inviting, with plenty of indoor and outdoor seating. Other locations include 529 S.W. 3rd Ave. (Downtown), 539 N.W. 13th Ave. (Pearl District), and 823 N.W. 23rd Ave. (Nob Hill). ✉ *1725 N.E. Alberta St., Alberta, Northeast* ☎ *503/274–1211* ⊕ *www.baristapdx.com.*

SOUTHEAST

BARS AND LOUNGES

Bar Avignon. Drop by this neighborhood wine bar on S.E. Division for one of the neighborhood's best happy hours, and to check out the impressive European-heavy wine selection; there are plenty of interesting bottles as well as more than 20 pours by the glass. The staff is friendly and knowledgeable, and the Northwest–French food menu consistently delivers. ✉ *2138 S.E. Division St., Hosford-Abernethy, Southeast* ☎ *503/517–0808* ⊕ *www.baravignon.com.*

Fodor's Choice ★ **Coopers Hall.** Part of the Central East Side's burgeoning wine scene, this urban winery and taproom is set inside a dramatic and spacious Quonset-hut structure, which was once home to an auto-repair shop. Order any of the outstanding wines produced on-site, or delve into the happily esoteric menu of unusual wines from all over the West Coast, with a few French varieties in the mix. The kitchen turns out seriously good food, too. ✉ *404 S.E. 6th St., Central East Side, Southeast* ☎ *503/719–7000* ⊕ *www.coopershall.com.*

Double Dragon. Drop by this festive, low-lit bar for its sassy cocktails, such as the Burnt Reynolds (bourbon, Lapsang souchong honey, lemon, and orange bitters), scene-y crowd, and Saturday-night Baby Ketten Karaoke parties. Stay for the delish Asian bar food, including the eight-hour-braised pork-belly *banh mi* sandwiches and curried-coconut ramen with chicken and pork. ✉ *1235 S.E. Division St., Hosford-Abernethy, Southeast* ☎ *503/230–8340* ⊕ *www.doubledragonpdx.com.*

Fodor's Choice ★ **Horse Brass Pub.** A laid-back beer-drinking crowd fills the venerable, dark-wood Horse Brass Pub, as good an English-style pub as you will find in Portland, with more than 50 beers on tap (including some cask-conditioned varieties). ■ TIP➔ Try the fish-and-chips. ✉ *4534 S.E. Belmont St., Sunnyside, Southeast* ☎ *503/232–2202* ⊕ *www.horsebrass.com.*

Fodor's Choice ★ **Sapphire Hotel.** In the lobby of a former brothel, the deep-red, candlelit Sapphire Hotel serves cocktails, beer, and wine with an intimate, sultry atmosphere. There's a terrific food menu, too, served late and at bargain prices during happy hour. ✉ *5008 S.E. Hawthorne Blvd., Hawthorne District, Southeast* ☎ *503/232–6333* ⊕ *www.thesapphirehotel.com.*

Fodor'sChoice ★ **Southeast Wine Collective.** This hive of boutique wine-making has an inviting tasting room–cum–wine bar in which you can sample the vinos of several up-and-coming producers. It's open until 10 most evenings, and the energy shifts from low-key tasting space to scene-y wine bar after about 5 pm. You could carve out a full meal from the extensive menu's tapas, salads, baguette sandwiches, and cheese and meats plates. ⊠ 2425 S.E. 35th Pl., Richmond, Southeast ☎ 503/208–2061 ⊕ www. sewinecollective.com.

Fodor'sChoice ★ **Victory Bar.** As beloved for its hefty venison burgers, chorizo spaetzle, and other stick-to-your-ribs bar victuals as for its impressive drinks selection, this dark corner bar with a pressed-tin ceiling is the definitive East Side hipster hangout, retaining a happily unfussy—almost dive-y— ambience in the face of Division Street's rapid transformation into a snazzy row of contemporary condos and A-list restaurants. ⊠ 3652 S.E. Division St., Richmond, Southeast ☎ 503/236–8755 ⊕ www. thevictorybar.com.

BREWPUBS AND MICROBREWERIES

Cascade Brewing. This laid-back brewpub and pioneer of the Northwest sour-beer movement is a good place for friends and sour-beer lovers to share tart flights of several varieties, including Blackcap Raspberry, Kriek, and potent (9.8% ABV) Sang Noir. You'll find 18 rotating taps, small plates and sandwiches to complement the sour beers, and ample outdoor seating. ⊠ 939 S.E. Belmont St., Central East Side, Southeast ☎ 503/265–8603 ⊕ www.cascadebrewingbarrelhouse.com.

Commons Brewery. This small, artisanal brewery, born in brewer Mike Wright's garage, maintained its small-batch, hands-on approach as it rapidly outgrew its first and second homes and even more rapidly earned a big reputation for exceptionally flavorful farmhouse-style ales. Wright's brews—inspired by European brewing traditions and crafted with local ingredients—have garnered many accolades; the fruit-forward Flemish Kiss and potent Bourbon Little Brother (aged in Heaven Hill bourbon barrels) are especially popular. Commons moved to this larger space, with a much-expanded tasting room, in early 2015. ⊠ 628 S.E. Belmont St., Central East Side, Southeast ☎ 503/343–5501 ⊕ www.commonsbrewery.com.

Hopworks Urban Brewery. A bicycle-themed microbrewery with deftly crafted beer, sandwiches, and pizzas, Hopworks Urban Brewery (HUB for short) occupies an industrial lodge-inspired building that's 100% renewably powered and water neutral. Hopworks BikeBar, located on the bike highway of North Williams, offers similar fare with the same bikey, eco-friendly vibe. ⊠ 2944 S.E. Powell Blvd., Creston-Kenilworth, Southeast ☎ 503/232–4677 ⊕ www.hopworksbeer.com ⊠ 3947 N. Williams Ave., Boise, Northeast ☎ 503/287–6258 ⊕ www. hopworksbeer.com.

COFFEEHOUSES

Fodor'sChoice ★ **Coava Coffee Roasters.** Located next door to the roastery, the light and open, bamboo wood–filled Coava Coffee Roasters offers some of the highest-quality single-origin, pour-over coffees in the city. A second branch opened in Hawthorne in 2014. ⊠ 1300 S.E. Grand Ave.,

Buckman, Southeast ☎ *503/894–8134* ⊕ *coavacoffee.com* ✉ *2631 S.E.*
Hawthorne Blvd., Hawthorne District, Southeast ☎ *503/894–8134*
⊕ *coavacoffee.com.*

Stumptown Coffee Roasters. Stumptown Coffee Roasters has three cafés
on the east side. At the original site (S.E. Division), organic beans are
still roasted on a regular basis. At The Annex (S.E. Salmon), patrons can
participate in "cuppings," or tastings, at 3 pm each day. ✉ *4525 S.E.*
Division St., Richmond, Southeast ☎ *503/230–7702* ⊕ *stumptowncoffee.*
com ✉ *100 S.E. Salmon St, Buckman, Southeast* ☎ *503/467–4123*
⊕ *stumptowncoffee.com.* ✉ *3356 S.E. Belmont St., Sunnyside, South-*
east ☎ *503/232–8889* ⊕ *stumptowncoffee.com*

Tao of Tea. With soft music and the sound of running water in the background, the Tao of Tea serves more than 80 loose-leaf teas as well as
vegetarian snacks and sweets. The company also operates the tearoom
inside Old Town's Lan Su Chinese Garden. ✉ *3430 S.E. Belmont St.,*
Belmont District, Southeast ☎ *503/736–0119* ⊕ *www.taooftea.com.*

Fodor's Choice **Water Avenue Coffee.** Java aficionados serious about single-origin coffee
★ favor this Central East Side roastery that sources its beans from top
growers in Colombia, Ethiopa, and Indonesia, roasts on custom-built
machines, and provides its house-roasted coffees to many restaurants
and cafés around town. ✉ *1028 S.E. Water Ave., Central East Side,*
Southeast ☎ *503/808–7084* ⊕ *www.wateravenuecoffee.com.*

DANCE CLUBS

Branx/Rotture. Legions of club goers of all styles and persuasions pour
into these adjoining Central East Side nightclubs for arguably the best
gay party in town—Blow Pony (fourth Saturday of each month), frequent live performances and shows by visiting DJs, and a variety of
other parties and gatherings, most with a decided hipster vibe. Rot-
ture (pronounced roh-TUR-ay) is on the upper level, and Branx is
downstairs. ✉ *320 S.E. 2nd Ave., Southeast* ☎ *503/234–5683* ⊕ *www.*
branxpdx.com.

GAY AND LESBIAN

Crush. A favorite gay hangout in Southeast, Crush serves up tasty food,
strong cocktails, and DJ-fueled dance parties. The front section is mellow and good for conversation, while the back area contains a small
but lively dance floor. ✉ *1400 S.E. Morrison St., Buckman, Southeast*
☎ *503/235–8150* ⊕ *www.crushbar.com* ☾ *Closed Mon.*

LIVE MUSIC

Fodor's Choice **Doug Fir Lounge.** Part retro diner and part log cabin, the Doug Fir serves
★ food and booze and hosts DJs and live rock shows from both up-and-
coming and established bands most nights of the week. It adjoins the
trendy Hotel Jupiter. ✉ *830 E. Burnside St., Central East Side, South-*
east ☎ *503/231–9663* ⊕ *www.dougfirlounge.com.*

PERFORMING ARTS

For a city of this size, there is truly an impressive—and accessible—
scope of talent from visual artists, performance artists, and musicians.
The arts are alive, with outdoor sculptural works strewn around the

city, ongoing festivals, and premieres of traveling Broadway shows. Top-named international acts, such as David Byrne, Arcade Fire, Joan Baez, and Mumford and Sons regularly include Portland in their world-wide stops.

PERFORMANCE VENUES

Fodor's Choice ★ **Arlene Schnitzer Concert Hall.** The 2,776-seat Arlene Schnitzer Concert Hall, built in 1928 in an Italian rococo revival style, hosts rock concerts, choral groups, lectures, and concerts by the Oregon Symphony and others. ⊠ *Portland Center for the Performing Arts, 1037 S.W. Broadway, Downtown* ☎ *503/248-4335* ⊕ *www.portland5.com.*

Keller Auditorium. With 3,000 seats and outstanding acoustics, Keller Auditorium hosts performances by the Portland Opera and Oregon Ballet Theater, as well as country and rock concerts and touring Broadway shows. ⊠ *222 S.W. Clay St., Downtown* ☎ *503/248–4335* ⊕ *www. portland5.com.*

Portland'5 Centers for the Arts. The city's top performing arts complex hosts opera, ballet, rock shows, symphony performances, lectures, and Broadway musicals in its five venues (⇨ *Downtown in Exploring Portland).* ⊠ *1111 S.W. Broadway, Downtown* ☎ *503/248–4335* ⊕ *www. portland5.com.*

Moda Center. This 21,000-seat facility, formerly known as the Rose Garden, is home to the Portland Trail Blazers basketball team and the site of other sporting events and rock concerts. It's right on the MAX light-rail line, just across from Downtown. ⊠ *Rose Quarter, 1 Center Ct., Lloyd District, Northeast* ☎ *503/797–9619* ⊕ *www.rosequarter.com.*

CLASSICAL MUSIC

The Oregon Symphony, established in 1896, is Portland's largest classical group—and one of the largest orchestras in the country.

CHAMBER MUSIC

Chamber Music Northwest. Some of the most sought-after soloists, chamber musicians, and recording artists from the Portland area and abroad perform here during the five-week summer concert series; performances take place at Reed College's Kaul Auditorium and the Lincoln Performance Hall at Portland State University. ☎ *503/294–6400* ⊕ *www.cmnw.org.*

OPERA

Portland Opera. This well-respected opera company performs five productions a year at Keller Auditorium. ⊠ *Keller Auditorium, 222 S.W. Clay St., Downtown* ☎ *503/241–1802, 866/739–6737* ⊕ *www. portlandopera.org.*

ORCHESTRAS

FAMILY
Fodor's Choice ★ **Oregon Symphony.** Established in 1896, the symphony is Portland's largest classical group—and one of the largest orchestras in the country. Its season officially starts in September and ends in May, with concerts held at Arlene Schnitzer Concert Hall, but throughout the summer the orchestra and its smaller ensembles can be seen at Waterfront Park and Washington Park for special outdoor summer performances. It also presents about 40 classical, pop, children's, and family concerts each year. ☎ *503/228–1353, 800/228–7343* ⊕ *www.orsymphony.org.*

DANCE

Portland has a wonderful variety of both progressive and traditional dance companies. As part of their productions, many of these companies bring in international talent for choreography and guest performances.

BodyVox. Led by Emmy Award-winning choreographers, Body Vox performs energetic contemporary dance–theater works at its state-of-the-art space in the Pearl District. ⊠ *1201 N.W. 17th Ave., Pearl District* ☎ *503/229–0627* ⊕ *www.bodyvox.com.*

Fodor's Choice **Northwest Dance Project.** Founded in 2004, this first-rate contemporary-★ dance company performs several shows—typically including a world premier or two—each season at different venues around town, including the Newmark Theatre and PSU's Lincoln Hall. ☎ *503/421–7434* ⊕ *www.nwdanceproject.org.*

Oregon Ballet Theatre. This respected company produces several classical and contemporary works a year, including a much-loved holiday *Nutcracker.* Most performances are at Keller Auditorium and the Portland Center for the Arts' Newmark Theatre. ☎ *503/222–5538, 888/922–5538* ⊕ *www.obt.org.*

FILM

The McMenimans "brew theaters" are a great place to catch a flick while chowing down and sipping on local beer. They are not-to-be-missed Portland landmarks when it comes to movie viewing in uniquely renovated buildings that avoid any hint of corporate streamlining.

If you're a film buff, be sure to check out the Northwest Film Center's calendar of events for special screenings and film festivals, with genres that include international, LGBT, and animation.

Fodor's Choice **Bagdad Theater.** Built in 1927, the stunningly restored, eminently quirky ★ Bagdad Theater shows first-run Hollywood films on a huge screen and serves pizza, burgers, sandwiches, and McMenamins ales. The Bagdad is a local favorite. ⊠ *3702 S.E. Hawthorne Blvd., Hawthorne District, Southeast* ☎ *503/249–7474* ⊕ *www.mcmenamins.com.*

Hollywood Theatre. A landmark movie theater that showed silent films when it opened in 1926, the not-for-profit Hollywood Theatre screens everything from obscure foreign art films to old American classics and second-run Hollywood hits, and hosts an annual Academy Awards viewing party. ⊠ *4122 N.E. Sandy Blvd., Hollywood District, Southeast* ☎ *503/281–4215* ⊕ *www.hollywoodtheatre.org.*

Kennedy School Theater. Furnished with couches and end tables, the Kennedy School Theater, which is located in a renovated elementary school that also contains a hotel, a restaurant, several bars, and a soaking pool, screens second-run and occasional Indie movies. ⊠ *5736 N.E. 33rd Ave., Concordia, Northeast* ☎ *503/249–3983* ⊕ *www.mcmenamins.com.*

Laurelhurst Theater. With a classic neon sign out front, the historic Laurelhurst Theater serves beer and pizza and shows excellent second-run features and cult classics for only $4. ⊠ *2735 E. Burnside St., Kerns, Northeast* ☎ *503/232–5511* ⊕ *www.laurelhursttheater.com.*

Living Room Theater. The sleek, upscale cinema, which has a lobby restaurant with a full bar, shows 3-D blockbuster, foreign, and independent films in cozy theaters furnished with spacious seats and moveable couches and tables. You can dine and drink from your seat. ✉ *341 S.W. 10th Ave., West End, Downtown* ⊕ *pdx.livingroomtheaters.com.*

Fodor's Choice ★ **Northwest Film Center.** Located adjacent to and operated by the Portland Art Museum, the Northwest Film Center screens art films, documentaries, and independent features, and presents the three-week Portland International Film Festival every February. Films are shown at the Whitsell Auditorium, next to the museum. ✉ *1219 S.W. Park Ave., Downtown* ☎ *503/221–1156* ⊕ *www.nwfilm.org.*

THEATER

From the largest of productions to the smallest of venues, theater comes to life in Portland year-round.

Artists Repertory Theatre. The theater company performs seven to nine productions a year including regional premieres, occasional commissioned works, and classics. ✉ *1515 S.W. Morrison St., Downtown* ☎ *503/241–1278* ⊕ *www.artistsrep.org.*

Imago Theatre. One of Portland's most outstanding innovative theater companies, the Imago specializes in movement-based work for both young and old. ✉ *17 S.E. 8th Ave., Buckman, Southeast* ☎ *503/231–9581* ⊕ *www.imagotheatre.com.*

FAMILY Fodor's Choice ★ **Northwest Children's Theater.** This long-running company presents four shows during its fall–spring season, geared to both the toddler and teen set. Performances are staged in the handsome Northwest Neighborhood Cultural Center in Nob Hill. ✉ *1819 N.W. Everett St., Nob Hill* ☎ *503/222–4480.*

FAMILY **Oregon Children's Theatre.** This kid-centric company puts on four to five shows a year for school groups and families at Downtown's Newmark and Winningstad theaters. ✉ *1111 S.W. Broadway, Downtown* ☎ *503/228–9571* ⊕ *www.octc.org.*

Fodor's Choice ★ **Portland Center Stage.** Housed in a handsomely restored 1891 armory, Portland Center Stage puts on contemporary and classical works in the LEED-certified green building between September and June. ✉ *Gerding Theater at the Armory, 128 N.W. 11th Ave., Pearl District* ☎ *503/445–3700* ⊕ *www.pcs.org.*

SPORTS AND THE OUTDOORS

Portlanders avidly gravitate to the outdoors and they're well acclimated to the elements year-round—including winter's wind, rain, and cold. Once the sun starts to shine in spring and into summer, the city fills with hikers, joggers, and mountain bikers, who flock to Portland's hundreds of miles of parks, paths, and trails. The Willamette and Columbia rivers are popular for boating and water sports. Locals also have access to a playground for fishing, camping, skiing, and snowboarding all the way through June, thanks to the proximity of Mt. Hood.

As for competitive sports, Portland is home to the Timbers, a major league soccer team with a devout local fan base, and NBA basketball's beloved Trail Blazers, who play at the Moda Center (aka Rose Quarter) arena, just across the Willamette River from Downtown.

PARTICIPANT SPORTS

BIKING

Biking is a cultural phenomenon in Portland—likely the most beloved mode of transportation in the city. Besides the sheer numbers of cyclists you see on roads and pathways, you'll find well-marked bike lanes and signs reminding motorists to yield to cyclists.

There are more than 320 miles of bicycle boulevards, lanes, and off-street paths in Portland. Accessible maps, specialized tours, parking capacity (including lockers and sheltered racks Downtown), and bicycle-only traffic signals at confusing intersections make biking in most neighborhoods easy. Cyclists can find the best routes by following green direction-and-distance signs that point the way around town, and the corresponding white dots on the street surface.

Cycling in Portland has evolved into a medium for progressive politics and public service. Several bike co-ops in the city are devoted to providing used bikes at decent prices, as well as to teaching bike maintenance and the economic and environmental benefits of becoming a two-wheel commuter. Check out the helpful Bike Portland (⊕ www.bikeportland. org) website for information on regularly scheduled bike events, cycling-related local news and advice, and referrals to reliable bike rental, sales, and repair shops.

BIKE RENTALS

Fat Tire Farm. For treks in Forest Park, rent mountain bikes at Fat Tire Farm, which is close to the park's Leif Erikson trailhead. The staff here really knows their stuff, from repair and maintenance help to advice on the best trails and routes. ⊠ 2714 N.W. Thurman St., Nob Hill ☎ 503/222–3276 ⊕ www.fattirefarm.com.

Waterfront Bicycle Rentals. For jaunts along the Willamette River, Waterfront Bicycles has everything a visiting bicyclist needs. There is a variety of styles and sizes of bikes to outfit the entire family, including balance bikes for the little rider. Reservations can be made online at least 48 hours ahead. Guided bike tours are offered as well. ⊠ 10 S.W. Ash St., Suite 100, Downtown ☎ 503/227–1719 ⊕ www.waterfrontbikes.com.

BIKE ROUTES

If you're a social rider, group rides set out from several local shops. Check the events pages of **Bike Gallery** (⊕ www.bikegallery.com), **River City Bicycles** (⊕ www.rivercitybicycles.com), and **Bike Portland** (⊕ www. bikeportland.org).

Bike paths line both sides of the **Willamette River** through Downtown, so you can easily make a mild, several-mile loop through Waterfront Park via the Steel, Hawthorne, or Sellwood bridges.

Though much of **Forest Park's** 70-plus miles of trails are reserved for hiking and nonbiking activities, there are 28 miles of single track mountain-biking trails and fire lanes open to biking, including Leif Erikson Drive, an 11-mile ride whose dense canopy occasionally gives way to river views. Along the park's trails you may come across old-growth forest as well as some of the park's more than 100 species of animals and birds. To reach the Leif Erikson trailhead, bike up steep Thurman Street or shuttle there via TriMet Bus 15. Maps and information on the trails can be found at ⊕ *www.forestparkconservancy.org.*

Department of Transportation. For information on bike routes and resources in and around Portland, visit the Department of Transportation website (look for the Active Transportation tab). You can download and view maps and learn about upcoming bike-related events and group rides. ☎ *503/823–5490* ⊕ *www.portlandoregon.gov/transportation.*

PARKS

The variety of Portland's parks ensures that there's something for just about everyone, from the world's smallest park (Mill Ends) to one of the largest urban natural areas in the country (Forest Park).

Fodor's Choice ★ **Cathedral Park.** Whether it's the view of the imposing and stunning Gothic St. John's Bridge, which rises some 400 feet above the Willamette River, or the historic significance of Lewis and Clark having camped here in 1806, this park is divine. Though there's no church, the park gets its name from the picturesque arches supporting the bridge. It's rumored that the ghost of a young girl haunts the bridge, and that may be true, but if you're told that it was designed by the same man who envisioned the Golden Gate Bridge, that's just a popular misconception. Dog lovers, or those who aren't, should take note of the off-leash area. ⊠ *N. Edison St. and Pittsburg Ave., St. John's, North* ⊕ *www. portlandoregon.gov/parks.*

Council Crest Park. The highest point in Portland, at 1,073 feet, this 43-acre bluff-top patch of greenery is a superb spot to take in sunsets and sunrises. Along with nearly 180-degree views of the Portland metro area, a clear day also affords views of the surrounding peaks—Mt. Hood, Mt. St. Helens, Mt. Adams, Mt. Jefferson, and Mt. Rainier. A bronze fountain depicting a mother and child has been erected in the park twice; first in the 1950s and the second in the 1990s. The peaceful piece was stolen in the 1980s, uncovered in a narcotics bust 10 years later, and then returned to the park. Trails connect Council Crest with Marquam Nature Park and Washington Park. ■TIP➔ **It's quite busy on weekends so visit on a weekday, if possible.** ⊠ *3400 Council Crest Dr., West Hills* ⊕ *www.portlandoregon.gov/parks.*

Peninsula Park & Rose Garden. The "City of Roses" moniker started here, at this park that harks back to another time. The city's oldest (1909) public rose garden (and the only sunken one) houses about 5,000 plantings of roses. The daunting task of deadheading all these flowers is covered in classes taught to volunteers twice a season. The bandstand is a historic landmark, and the last of its kind in the city. This 16-acre North Portland park also contains a 100-year-old fountain, Italian villa–inspired community center, playground, wading pool, tennis and volleyball courts, and picnic tables. ⊠ *700 N. Rosa Parks Way, Piedmont, North* ⊕ *www.portlandoregon.gov/parks.*

Fodor's Choice ★ **Sauvie Island.** If it's a day to take advantage of gorgeous weather, then drive about a half hour northwest of Downtown to Sauvie Island. The

Walkers crossing the Hawthorne Bridge

island has a wildlife refuge, three beaches (including Collins Beach, which is clothing-optional), superb biking and hiking trails, and several farms offering "u-pick" bounty. To get to the beaches, take U.S. 30 north to Sauvie Island Bridge, and turn right; follow N.W. Sauvie Island Road to Reeder Road and follow signs. There's plenty of parking at the beaches, but a permit is required ($7 for a one-day permit, available at the general store at the base of the bridge). ⊠ *N.W. Sauvie Island Rd., across Sauvie Island bridge at U.S. 30, Sauvie Island* ⊕ *www.sauvieisland.org.*

FAMILY **Tryon Creek State Natural Area.** Portland is chock-full of parks, but this is the only state park within city limits. And at 670 acres, there's plenty of room for all its admirers. The area was logged starting in the 1880s, and the natural regrowth has produced red alder, Douglas fir, big leaf maple, and western red cedar, giving home to more than 50 bird species. The eastern edge has a paved trail, in addition to 14 miles of trails for bikes, hikers, and horses. Before heading to the trails, stop by the nature center to check out the exhibits and topographical relief map. ⊠ *11321 S.W. Terwilliger Blvd., Collins View, Southwest* ☎ *503/636–4398* ⊕ *www. tryonfriends.org* ◷ *Daily 7 am–8 pm, Nature Center 9–4.*

SPECTATOR SPORTS

Since Portland isn't home to a large national football or baseball team, fans tend to show a lot of support for the NBA's Portland Trail Blazers and MLS's Portland Timbers.

BASKETBALL

Portland Trail Blazers. The NBA's Portland Trail Blazers play their 82-game season in the Moda Center (aka Rose Garden Arena), which can hold up to 20,000 spectators. The MAX train pulls up just a couple of blocks from the arena's front door. ⊠ *Moda Center, 1 N. Center Ct., Rose Quarter, North* ☎ *503/797–9600* ⊕ *www.nba.com/blazers.*

SOCCER

Portland Timbers. Portland's major-league soccer team plays their 34-game season at the Downtown Jeld-Wen Field from March through October. The city has many ardent soccer fans known as the Timbers Army. Sitting near this group means a raucous time with drumming, chanting, and cheers. The MAX stops right by the stadium. ⊠ *Jeld-Wen Field, 1844 S.W. Morrison St., Downtown* ☎ *503/553–5555* ⊕ *www. portlandtimbers.com.*

SHOPPING

The shopping landscape in Portland has changed significantly in recent years, perhaps not quite as dramatically as the much-buzzed-about culinary scene, but in similar (pardon the pun) fashion. Specifically, those same hip and indie-spirited neighborhoods around the city that have become hot spots for food and drink—areas like the Pearl District, Downtown West End, Alberta, North Mississippi, and Central East Side—are also enjoying a steady influx of distinctive, well-curated boutiques specializing in edgy fashion and jewelry, handcrafted home accessories and household goods, and artisanal foods.

The city's longstanding shopping hubs, including the Downtown core, Nob Hill, and the Hawthorne District continue to support a number of both established and up-and-coming retailers, too. Generally speaking, you'll find more of Portland's nationally known chain stores in these traditional commercial districts, especially around Downtown's Pioneer Courthouse Square, the Pearl District (particularly the lower half of the neighborhood, nearest Burnside Street), and along the lower blocks of Nob Hill's N.W. 23rd Avenue. Additionally, on the East Side, the prosaic but convenient Lloyd Center Mall and surrounding neighborhood has plenty of chain stores.

DOWNTOWN

CLOTHING

Fodor's Choice ★ **Frances May.** Located in the hip West End section of Downtown, this grandmother-and-granddaughter-owned clothing store is a favorite of stylish local men and women who come for that cool, understated, high-quality look (casual to dressy) that Portlanders are known for. You'll find made-in-America labels like Steven Alan and Rachel Comey as well as European faves like Acne and APC. The Alex Mill cashmere beanies and Carven women's pullovers and sweaters are especially popular during Portland's cool winters. ⊠ *1013 S.W. Washington St., Downtown* ☎ *503/227–3402* ⊕ *www.francesmay.com.*

Mario's. Portland's best store for fine men's and women's clothing, Mario's carries designer lines by Prada, Dolce & Gabbana, Etro, and Loro Piana—among others. The store's buyers make regular trips to Italy in search of the latest fashions and trends. There's a *huge* shoe department, too. ⊠ *833 S.W. Broadway, Downtown* ☎ *503/227–3477* ⊕ *www.marios.com.*

Nike Portland. It's safe to assume that Nike's flagship retail store, just a short drive from the company's mammoth HQ campus in Beaverton, has the latest and greatest in swoosh-adorned products. The high-tech setting has athlete profiles, photos, and interactive displays. ⊠ *638 S.W. 5th Ave., Downtown* ☎ *503/221–6453* ⊕ *www.nike.com.*

FOOD

Cacao. Chocolate fiends and sweet-tooths get their fix at this inviting storefront shop and café in the West End, which also has a branch inside Downtown's natty Heathman Hotel. Browse the huge selection of ultrafine, single-origin, artisanal chocolates from around the world, or order a cup of luscious and satisfying house-made drinking chocolate. ⊠ *414 S.W. 13th Ave., Downtown* ☎ *503/241–0656* ⊕ *www.cacaodrinkchocolate.com.*

FAMILY
Fodor's Choice
★
Portland Farmers' Market. Running on Saturday mornings and early afternoons from March through December, this astoundingly large and diverse farmers' market carries not only Oregon's bounty of flowers and produce (look especially for berries in summer and stone fruits in fall) but also hazelnuts, cheese, delectable baked goods, wines and ciders, and other goodies. It's great for people-watching and souvenir shopping, and several stalls sell great food to eat on-site—be sure to come hungry. If you can't make the Saturday market, check the website for locations of smaller but still very popular versions of the market, held most days during the warmer months at various locations around town. ⊠ *South Park Blocks at S.W. Park Ave. and Montgomery St., Downtown* ☎ *503/241–0032* ⊕ *www.portlandfarmersmarket.org.*

GIFTS

Made in Oregon. This eclectic retail tribute to the Beaver State sells books, smoked salmon, artisanal chocolates, local wines, Pendleton woolen goods, carvings made of myrtle wood, and other products made in the state. There are numerous branches around the area, including Portland International Airport and all the larger shopping malls. ⊠ *Pioneer Place Mall, 340 S.W. Morrison St., Downtown* ☎ *503/241–3630, 866/257–0938* ⊕ *www.madeinoregon.com.*

HOUSEHOLD GOODS AND FURNITURE

Boys Fort. If the name of this colorful Downtown emporium brings back memories of hanging out with friends in a rad basement rec room, you'll likely love this offbeat store curated by designers R. Rolfe and Jake France. They've stocked this high-ceilinged shop with a mix of artful items for the hip dude's urban nest, including earthy-hued terra-cotta planters, model sailboats, and mounted wooden faux deer heads, plus old posters and games. ⊠ *902 S.W. Morrison St., Downtown* ☎ *503/567–1015* ⊕ *www.boysfort.com.*

Fodor's Choice ★ **Canoe.** Form meets function at this stylish, contemporary boutique with a carefully curated selection of clean-lined, modern goods and gifts for every room in the home. You'll find curvy thick-glass bowls, modern lamps with sheer paper shades, polished-stone trays, Bigelow natural-bristle toothbrushes, and Chemex coffee kettles, with some goods produced locally and exclusively for Canoe, and others imported from Asia and northern Europe. ⊠ *1136 S.W. Alder St., West End, Downtown* ☎ *503/889–8545* ⊕ *www.canoeonline.net.*

JEWELRY

The Real Mother Goose. Selling mostly handcrafted, unique artistic pieces, current collections can include woodworking, furniture, blown glass and jewelry. Dangling earrings that incorporate copper wire wrapped around brilliant, colored glass are a customer favorite. The clothing store next door, Changes Designs to Wear, is part of The Real Mother Goose as well. ⊠ *901 S.W. Yamhill St., Downtown* ☎ *503/223–9510* ⊕ *www.therealmothergoose.com.*

MALLS AND DEPARTMENT STORES

Fodor's Choice ★ **Union Way.** A modern take on an old-fashioned European shopping arcade, this indoor alley—which opened in 2013—spans one block from Stark to Burnside streets (right across the street from Powell's Books) and contains about a dozen diverting boutiques, plus a branch of Little T Bakery and the trendy Asian restaurant Boxer Ramen. Most of these shops specialize in apparel and accessories, including Will Leather Goods, Steven Alan eyewear, and Danner sports and outerwear, but you'll also find Quin Candy shop and Spruce Apothecary. ⊠ *1022 W. Burnside St., West End, Downtown* ☎ *503/922–0056.*

TOYS

Finnegan's Toys and Gifts. Downtown Portland's largest toy store, Finnegan's stocks artistic, creative, educational, and other types of toys. ⊠ *820 S.W. Washington St., Downtown* ☎ *503/221–0306* ⊕ *www.finneganstoys.com.*

OLD TOWN/CHINATOWN

GIFTS

Hand-Eye Supply. One of a handful of intriguing shops that have opened in Old Town in recent years, Hand-Eye specializes in work wear, studio supplies, tools, and books. But before you write this place off as a purely utilitarian resource, you should know that the buyers here have a keen eye for beautifully designed goods. This is first and foremost an emporium of cool lifestyle goods, including natty, gray, linen-cotton work aprons, wood-handle Midori Hamono paring knives, bright-red Feuerhand camp lanterns, and other stylish curiosities. ⊠ *427 N.W. Broadway, Old Town/ Chinatown* ☎ *503/575–9769* ⊕ *www.handeyesupply.com.*

MARKETS

Fodor's Choice ★ **Portland Saturday Market.** The open-air Portland Saturday Market, which has been going strong since 1976 and runs from March to December on weekends (including Sunday, despite the name), is a favorite place to find one-of-a-kind, handcrafted home, garden, and clothing

Farmers' markets in Portland offer fresh produce and other local goodies.

items—everything from T-shirts and souvenirs to high-quality sculptures and housewares. An impressive new pavilion, part of it covered, houses the more than 300 artisans. ■TIP→ **Don't confuse this crafts-oriented market with the equally popular Portland Farmers' Market, which takes place on Saturday on the campus of Portland State University.** ⊠ *Tom McCall Waterfront Park, 2 S.W. Naito Pkwy., adjacent to Burnside Bridge, Old Town/Chinatown* ☎ *503/222–6072* ⊕ *www. portlandsaturdaymarket.org.*

PEARL DISTRICT

BOOKS

Oblation Papers. Employing antique presses and old-world processes, this dapper shop in the Pearl District houses a paper mill, letterpress shop, and retail store where you can find one-of-a-kind cards, stationery, albums, and journals. The quality, handcrafted cards featuring vintage posters or images of local wildlife make wonderful keepsakes and gifts. ⊠ *516 N.W. 12th Ave., Pearl District* ☎ *503/223–1093* ⊕ *www. oblationpapers.com.*

Fodor'sChoice ★ **Powell's City of Books.** The largest retail store of used and new books in the world (with more than 1.5 million volumes) covers an entire city block and rises three stories on the edge of the Pearl District. A local legend, and rightfully so, Powell's also carries rare and collectible books and contains a popular coffeehouse, World Cup. There are also branches in Portland International Airport as well as a large outpost in the heart of the Hawthorne District, with its own coffeehouse, Fresh

Pot. ⊠ *1005 W. Burnside St., Pearl District* ☎ *503/228–4651* ⊕ *www. powells.com.*

CLOTHING

Lizard Lounge. Shop until your caffeine levels drop at this expansive men's and women's fashion source in the Pearl, where staff will pour you a complimentary cup of Stumptown coffee as you browse that particularly Portland mix of hip and hipster chic. Lizard Lounge carries everything from major midrange brands like Levi's and Timberland to higher-end clubbing labels, like G-Star, Nudie Jeans, and Fetch Eyewear. There's also a good selection of gifts and household items, like Mast Brothers Chocolate and Portland-based Maak Soap Lab bath products. ⊠ *1323 N.W. Irving St., Pearl District* ☎ *503/416–7476* ⊕ *www. lizardloungepdx.com.*

Fodor'sChoice **Mabel & Zora.** The owner of this chic Pearl destination for elegant
★ ready-to-wear fashion, Tiffany Bean, carries her eponymous, widely acclaimed, and locally produced label as well as clothing, accessories, and jewelry from designers including Nic + Zoe, Lily Pulitzer, Trina Turk, and Michael Stars. If you're gearing up for a big night on the town, look no further. ⊠ *748 N.W. 11th Ave., Pearl District* ☎ *503/241–5696* ⊕ *www.mabelandzora.com.*

FOOD

Fodor'sChoice **Smith Teamaker.** Tea drinkers rejoice: you don't have to resort to coffee
★ just because you're in Portland. Proprietor and legendary tea guru Steve Smith launched two renowned companies, Stash Tea and Tazo, before opening his own company inside a former blacksmith shop on the northwestern edge of the Pearl District. At this handsome tea shop, you can see how the tea is made and packaged, shop teas and accessories, and then sample different varieties at a small tasting bar. Select a tea flight from a menu, try a tea latte, or work your way through an oxidation spectrum—from white to black. The sturdy, pastel-hued boxes in which Smith packages his exquisite, carefully sourced teas make great gifts. ⊠ *1626 N.W. Thurman St., Pearl District* ☎ *503/719–8752* ⊕ *www.smithtea.com.*

GALLERIES

Fodor'sChoice **First Thursday.** This gallery walk the first Thursday of every month gives
★ art appreciators a chance to check out new exhibits while enjoying music and wine. Typically, the galleries, which are largely located in the Pearl District, are open in the evening from 6 to 9, but hours vary. Be prepared for a lively scene including throngs of people, street musicians, and local art vendors, with much of the action along N.W. 13th Avenue between Hoyt and Kearney streets, which is pedestrian only during this event. ⊠ *Pearl District* ☎ *503/227–8519* ⊕ *www.explorethepearl.com.*

Quintana Galleries. The only Native American art gallery in Portland, Quintana focuses on Pacific Northwest Coast, Navajo, and Hopi art, pottery, and jewelry. ⊠ *124 N.W. 9th Ave., Pearl District* ☎ *503/223– 1729, 800/321–1729* ⊕ *www.quintanagalleries.com.*

NOB HILL

CLOTHING

Sloan Boutique. Set among the several fine clothiers on the 700 and 800 blocks of N.W. 23rd Avenue, Sloan Boutique carries a good mix of affordable women's casual and fashion brands, including Kensie, Free People, Kut, and Franco Sarto. The boutique's adjoining space—PlaT-form—carries a good selection of trendy shoes and accessories. Sloan has a second branch across the river in Hawthorne. ⊠ *738 N.W. 23rd Ave., Nob Hill* ☎ *503/222–6666* ⊕ *www.sloanpdx.com.*

GALLERIES

Laura Russo Gallery. A longtime staple of the Portland arts scene, the Laura Russo Gallery displays contemporary Northwest work of all styles, including landscapes and abstract expressionism. ⊠ *805 N.W. 21st Ave., Nob Hill* ☎ *503/226–2754* ⊕ *www.laurarusso.com.*

Twist. This huge space in Nob Hill is well stocked with contemporary American ceramics, glass, furniture, sculpture, and handcrafted jewelry often with a whimsical touch. ⊠ *30 N.W. 23rd Pl., Nob Hill* ☎ *503/224–0334* ⊕ *www.twistonline.com.*

GIFTS

Moonstruck Chocolate Cafe. Even without getting a nod from Oprah in her magazine, Moonstruck would still be known as a chocolatier extraordinaire. There are five cafés in the Portland metro area, including Downtown locations at Pioneer Place Mall and at S.W. Alder Street. All offer made-to-order hot chocolate, cocoa, shakes, and mochas, as well as truffles, chocolate bars, and dynamic holiday treats. ⊠ *526 N.W. 23rd Ave., Nob Hill* ☎ *503/542–3400* ⊕ *www.moonstruckchocolate.com.*

Stella's on 21st. At this colorful neighborhood shop, you'll find eccentric, artsy items for the home, including lamps, candles, and decorations, as well as jewelry. ⊠ *1108 N.W. 21st Ave., Nob Hill* ☎ *503/295–5930* ⊕ *www.stellason21st.com.*

JEWELRY

Gilt. Portland's premier estate and vintage jewelry destination occupies a dapper Craftsman bungalow along a fashionable stretch of Nob Hill's Northwest 23rd. Inside you'll find an ever-changing inventory of radiant gold and silver rings, bracelets, earrings, and necklaces, many inlaid with dazzling gems. The antique wedding and engagement rings are especially popular. Gilt's owner, Paula Bixel, is especially fond of Georgian and Victorian pieces. ⊠ *720 N.W. 23rd Ave., Nob Hill* ☎ *503/226–0629* ⊕ *www.giltjewelry.com.*

NORTH

FOOD

Fodor's Choice
★

The Meadow. Food writer Mark Bitterman knows a thing or two about salt—he's written two popular books on the subject, and he's the owner of this tiny purveyor of gourmet finishing salts, some of them smoked or infused with unusual flavors, like cherry and plums, or saffron. At this flagship location (there's a second Meadow in Nob Hill, and a third in

Manhattan's West Village) you can also purchase the additional magical touches you might need to create the perfect dinner party, from Oregon and European wines and vermouths, to fresh-cut flowers, aromatic cocktail bitters, and high-quality, single-origin chocolates. ⊠ *3731 N. Mississippi Ave., North* ☎ *503/288–4633* ⊕ *www.atthemeadow.com.*

HOUSEHOLD GOODS AND FURNITURE

Fodor'sChoice   **Beam & Anchor.** Set on a busy street corner several blocks from the North
★   Side's trendy North Mississippi strip, this once-dilapidated warehouse houses an upstairs workshop for makers of artisanal goods and an inspiring downstairs retail space where proprietors Robert and Jocelyn Rahm sell a carefully curated selection of lifestyle goods for every room in the home, many of them produced locally—some as local as upstairs. Among the hipster treasures, look for warm and soft camp blankets and Navajo rugs with vibrant prints, women's jewelry in a variety of simple-but-beautiful styles, Portland Apothecary bath salts and soaps, and quite a few larger pieces of distinctive furniture. ⊠ *2710 N. Interstate Ave., Eliot, North* ☎ *503/367–3230* ⊕ *www.beamandanchor.com.*

TOYS

Fodor'sChoice   **Paxton Gate.** Here, science and biology mix with whimsy and imagina-
★   tion. You'll find everything from taxidermied scorpions and baby goats to ostrich eggs and ceramic chimes. It's a fascinating and strangely beguiling mix of goods, and not for the faint of heart. ⊠ *4204 N. Mississippi Ave., Boise, North* ☎ *503/719–4508* ⊕ *www.paxtongate.com.*

NORTHEAST

GALLERIES

Ampersand Gallery & Fine Books. Part art gallery, part store, this minimalist white-wall space on Alberta Street has monthly shows featuring edgy, contemporary art, and stocks a fascinating trove of photography and art books, vintage travel brochures, curious photography, pulp-fiction novels, and other printed materials of the sort you might find in a chest in a mysterious neighbor's attic. The owners also operate the cute Cord boutique next door, which stocks artfully designed household goods, from handcrafted soaps to aerodynamic coffeepots. ⊠ *2916 N.E. Alberta St., Alberta, Northeast* ☎ *503/805–5458* ⊕ *www. ampersandgallerypdx.com.*

FAMILY   **Last Thursday Arts Walk.** The Alberta Arts District hosts an arts walk
Fodor'sChoice   on the last Thursday of each month. This quirky procession along 15
★   blocks of one of the city's favorite thoroughfares for browsing art galleries, distinctive boutiques, and hipster bars and restaurants features street performers and buskers, crafts makers, and food vendors. The street is closed to traffic from 6 to 9:30 pm. ⊠ *N.E. Alberta St., Alberta Arts District, Northeast* ⊕ *www.lastthursdayonalberta.com.*

MUSIC

Fodor'sChoice   **Music Millennium.** The oldest record store in the Pacific Northwest, Music
★   Millennium stocks a huge selection of new and used music in every possible category, including local punk groups. The store also hosts a number of in-store performances, often by top-name artists like Lucinda

Williams, Richard Thompson, Matthew Sweet, Sheryl Crow, and Randy Newman. ⊠ *3158 E. Burnside St., Laurelhurst, Southeast* ☎ *503/231–8926* ⊕ *www.musicmillennium.com.*

SOUTHEAST

CLOTHING

Herbivore Clothing. An animal-rights-minded shop in the Central East Side, Herbivore is a terrific resource if you're seeking clothing and accessories—from cotton-rayon tees and sweaters to braided canvas belts and wallets fashioned out of reclaimed bike and truck tubes—that have been created without the harm or use of animals. There's also a great selection of books on veganism, plus food, health-care products, and gifts. ⊠ *1211 S.E. Stark St., Central East Side, Southeast* ☎ *503/281–8638* ⊕ *www.herbivoreclothing.com.*

Fodor'sChoice ★ **Machus.** This small, somewhat under-the-radar, upscale, men's clothier carries arguably the best selection of fashion-forward, emerging labels in the city. In addition to Machus's own private-label dress shirts and tees, check out the form-fitting, refreshingly unadorned Naked and Famous skinny jeans, stylish sportswear by Knomadik, and edgy, urbane bomber jackets and hoodies from ADYN. You won't find many—or any—pastels or bright prints in here; expect clean classics, with lots of blacks, grays, and whites. ⊠ *542 E. Burnside St., Central East Side, Southeast* ☎ *503/206–8626* ⊕ *www.machusonline.com.*

Fodor'sChoice ★ **Mag-Big.** A tiny but impressively stocked boutique in a charming, old, Craftsman-style house that also houses the excellent Hazel Room café, Mag-Big is devoted to decorative items, fashion, jewelry, and crafts made by Portlanders. The selection is eclectic and fun—everything from handcrafted soaps made with local beer to geometric-shape brass necklaces. Clothing at Mag-Big is geared mostly to women. ⊠ *3279 S.E. Hawthorne Blvd., Hawthorne District, Southeast* ☎ *503/236–6120* ⊕ *www.magbig.com.*

Union Rose. For distinctive women's fashion and accessories designed and made in Portland, check out this boutique in up-and-coming Montavilla. Though there are scores of dresses for any season, including a very good selection of dresses and skirts in plus sizes, there's also plenty of everyday wear, like hoodies and hats. ⊠ *7909 S.E. Stark St., Montavilla, Southeast* ☎ *503/287–4242* ⊕ *www.unionrosepdx.com.*

GIFTS

Pastaworks. Fine charcuterie and cheeses, organic produce, and an exceptional selection of Italian wines, cookware, and fresh-made pastas and sauces are all sold at this spacious market in Hawthorne, adjoining Powell's Books for Home and Garden. There's a second location in Nob Hill. ⊠ *3735 S.E. Hawthorne Blvd., Hawthorne District, Southeast* ☎ *503/232–1010* ⊕ *www.pastaworks.com.*

HOUSEHOLD GIFTS AND FURNITURE

House of Vintage. This mammoth 13,000-square-foot shop, just down the street from one of the better Goodwill shops in the city, is de rigueur among vintage aficionados. Inside, you can rifle through the wares of some 55 dealers; bell-bottom jeans and plaid blazers are a big draw, but this time capsule also brims with kitschy ceramic ashtrays, Naugahyde couches, '50s magazines, old-school lunchboxes, and pretty much anything else you might recall from your childhood. ✉ *3315 S.E. Hawthorne Blvd., Southeast* ☎ *503/236–1991* ⊕ *www.houseofvintageportland.com.*

Tilde. With wares that could work just as well in an urban loft as in a cozy country cottage, this compact storefront space is filled with a mix of eye-catching lifestyle goods and functional artwork, including Matt & Nat wallets and bags, lacy steel-and-silver earrings, ceramic bowls and vases, and stylish Nixon watches in bright colors. ✉ *7919 S.E. 13th Ave., Sellwood, Southeast* ☎ *503/234–9600* ⊕ *www.tildeshop.com.*

OUTDOOR SUPPLIES

Next Adventure Sports. It's all about the gear here. Next Adventure Sports carries new and used sporting goods, including camping gear, snowboards, kayaks, and mountaineering supplies. Kayak classes and Outdoor School provide plenty of opportunities to get out and enjoy Oregon like a local. They also operate The Paddle Sports Center, just a few blocks southeast at 624 S.E. 7th Avenue. ✉ *426 S.E. Grand Ave., Central East Side, Southeast* ☎ *503/233–0706* ⊕ *www.nextadventure.net.*

TOYS

FAMILY

Fodor's Choice

★

Cloud Cap Games. There's more than just run-of-the-mill board games at Cloud Cap. For children and grown-ups alike, the games here challenge the mind and provide hours of entertainment. There's a room with tables to play or try out a game. The knowledgable owners and staff may sit down and join in the fun and are always happy to answer questions and offer sugestions. ✉ *1226 S.E. Lexington St., Sellwood, Southeast* ☎ *503/505–9344* ⊕ *www.cloudcapgames.com.*

THE OREGON COAST

WELCOME TO THE OREGON COAST

TOP REASONS TO GO

★ **Enjoy the beaches:** The Oregon Coast has breathtaking beaches, from romantic stretches perfect for linking fingers with loved ones to creature-teeming tide pools great for exploring with kids. Hikers delight in the rugged trails that traverse the lush woodlands and stunning cliffs that flank many of the beaches.

★ **Shop for blown glass:** Artisanal glass shops dot the coastline—at some, you can even craft your own colorful creations.

★ **Explore the dunes:** Whether you're screaming in a dune buggy or scrambling over them on foot, southern Oregon's mountainous sand dunes bring out the kid in anyone who traverses them.

★ **Wine and dine:** You don't have to spend a lot to enjoy creatively prepared seafood, artisanal microbrews, and local wines. There's a nice balance between affordable no-frills fish shacks and increasingly sophisticated farm-to-table bistros.

1 North Coast. As the primary gateway for both Portlanders and those visiting from neighboring Washington, the north coast is the busiest stretch of Oregon coastline, although it's still rife with secluded coves and funky seaside hamlets. Its lighthouse-dotted shoreline stretches from the mouth of the Columbia River south to Pacific City. The 90-mile region includes the historic working-class fishing town of Astoria and its recent influx of hip cafés and restored hotels; family-friendly Seaside with its touristy but bustling boardwalk; art-fueled and refined Cannon Beach; laid-back and stunningly situated Manzanita Beach; and tiny Pacific City, where a colorful fleet of dories dots the wide, deep beach.

2 Central Coast. The 75-mile stretch from Lincoln City to Florence offers whale-watching, incomparable seafood, shell-covered beaches, candy confections, and close-up views of undersea life. At the north end, in Lincoln City visitors can indulge in gaming, shopping, golfing, and beachcombing. The harbor town of Depoe Bay is a center for whale-watching, and nearby Newport offers a stellar aquarium and science center. It's also home to one of Oregon's largest fishing fleets. The less-developed town of Yachats is a true seaside gem with astounding coastal views, where the only demands are to relax and enjoy. The cute town of Florence and its bustling downtown hugs the Siuslaw River—it's also the northern access point for the Oregon dunes.

3 South Coast. From the heart of Oregon dunes country in Reedsport to the southernmost Oregon town of Brookings, the 134-mile stretch of U.S. 101 is less touristy than points north, but still abundant with mesmerizing beaches, headlands, and coastal rain forests. Coos Bay and adjacent North Bend make up the region's largest population center. The beach town of Bandon is a world-class golfing destination that's also popular for beach-combing and lighthouse gazing. Ruggedly situated and low-key Port Orford has gorgeous beach landscapes and a growing arts scene, while Gold Beach, farther south, bathes in sunshine.

GETTING ORIENTED

Oregon's coastline begins in the north in the town of Astoria, which lies at the mouth of the Columbia River on the Washington state line. It's a slow-going but spectacular 363-mile drive south along U.S. Highway 101 to the small town of Brookings at Oregon's southwestern corner, several miles from the California border. The rugged Coast Range flanks the entire coast to the east, providing a picturesque barrier between the ocean and the lush Willamette, Umpqua, and Rogue valleys, where you'll find Oregon's larger communities, including Portland and Eugene.

Columbia River
Astoria
Seaside
Tillamook Head
Cannon Beach
Manzanita
Nehalem Bay
Tillamook Bay
Tillamook
Pacific City
Nestucca Bay
Otis
Lincoln City
Depoe Bay
Cape Foulweather
Yaquina Head
Newport
Yachats
Heceta Head
Mapleton
Florence
Dunes City
Reedsport
North Bend
Coos Bay
Bandon
Coquille
Langlois
Cape Blanco
Port Orford
Port Orford Head
Nesika Beach
Gold Beach
Pistol River
Brookings

Westport
Mist
McMinnville
SALEM
Toledo
Corvallis
Eugene
Curtin
Yoncalla
Roseburg
Dillard
Canyonville
Grants Pass
Medford
Ashland

WA

COAST RANGES

PACIFIC OCEAN

CALIFORNIA

0 — 40 mi
0 — 40 km

EXPLORING OREGON'S BEST BEACHES

Oregon's 300 miles of public coastline is the backdrop for thrills, serenity, rejuvenation, and romance. From yawning expanses of sand dotted with beach chairs to tiny patches bounded by surf-shaped cliffs, the state's shoreline often draws comparisons to New Zealand.

(above) Surfing the Oregon Coast; (opposite page, top) Oregon Dunes National Recreation Area; (opposite page, bottom) Cannon Beach Sandcastle Contest

Most awe-inspiring are the massive rock formations just offshore in the northern and southern sections of the coast, breaking up the Pacific horizon. Beaches along the north coast, from Astoria to Pacific City, are perfect for romantic strolls on the sands. The central-coast beaches, from Lincoln City to Florence, are long and wide, providing perfect conditions for sunbathers, children, clam diggers, horseback riders, and surfers. The southern-coast beaches from Reedsport to Brookings are less populated, ideal for getting away from it all.

In late July and August the climate is kind to sun worshipers. During the shoulder months, keep layers of clothing handy for the unpredictable temperature swings. Winter can be downright blustery, a time that many seaside inns optimistically call "storm-watching season."

GLASS FLOATS: FINDERS KEEPERS

Since 1997, between mid-October and Memorial Day, more than 2,000 handcrafted glass floats made by local artists have been hidden along Lincoln City's 7½-mile public beach. If you happen to come upon one, call the local tourism office (📞 800/452–2151) to register it, and find out which artist made it. While antique glass floats are extremely rare, these new versions make great souvenirs.

THE OREGON COAST'S BEST BEACHES

Cannon Beach. In the shadow of glorious **Haystack Rock,** this beach is wide, flat, and perfect for bird-watching, exploring tide pools, building sand castles, and romantic walks in the sea mist. Each June the city holds a **sand-castle contest,** drawing artists and thousands of visitors. The rest of the year the beach is far less populated. The dapper beachfront town has several of the region's swankiest hotels and finest restaurants, as well as spots for surfing, hiking, and beachcombing.

Pacific City. This beach is postcard perfect, with its colorful fleet of dories sitting on the sand. Dozens of them lie tilted in between early-morning fishing excursions to catch lingcod, surf perch, and rockfish. Like Cannon Beach, this town also has a huge (less famous) Haystack Rock that provides the perfect scenic backdrop for horseback riders, beach strollers, and people with shovels chasing sand-covered clams. With safe beach breaks that are ideal for beginners and larger peaks a bit to the south, this is also a great spot for surfers. Winterstorm-watchers love Pacific City, where winds exceeding 75 mph twist Sitka spruce, and tides deposit driftwood and logs on the beach.

Winchester Bay. One reason the Pacific Northwest isn't known for its

amusement parks is because nature hurls more thrills than any rattling contraption could ever provide. This certainly is true at **Oregon Dunes National Recreation Area.** Here riders of all-terrain vehicles (ATVs) will encounter some of the most radical slips, dips, hills, and chills in the nation. It is the largest expanse of coastal sand dunes in North America, extending for 40 miles, from Florence to Coos Bay. More than 1.5 million people visit the dunes each year. For those who just want to swim, relax, hike, and marvel at the amazing expanse of dunes against the ocean, there are spaces off-limits to motorized vehicles. Overlooking the beach is the gorgeous **Umpqua River Lighthouse.**

Samuel H. Boardman State Scenic Corridor. It doesn't get any wilder than this—or more spectacular. The 12-mile strip of forested, rugged coastline is dotted with smaller sand beaches, some more accessible than others. Here visitors will find the amazing **Arch Rock** and **Natural Bridges** and can hike 27 miles of the **Oregon Coast Trail.** Beach highlights include **Whaleshead Beach, Secret Beach,** and **Thunder Rock Cove,** where you might spot migrating gray whales. From the 345-foot-high **Thomas Creek Bridge** you can take a moderately difficult hike down to admire the gorgeous, jagged rocks off **China Beach.**

Updated
by Andrew
Collins

If you aren't from the Pacific Northwest, Oregon's spectacular coastline might still be a secret: it's less visited and talked about than California's coast, but certainly no less beautiful. But in recent decades, the state's reputation for scenic drives and splendid hikes, reasonably priced oceanfront hotels and vacation rentals, low-key towns with friendly, creative vibes, and consistently fresh and well-prepared seafood has garnered increased attention. The true draw here is the beaches, where nature lovers delight at their first sight of a migrating whale or a baby harbor seal sitting on a rock.

Oregon's coastline is open to all; not a grain of its 300 miles of white-sand beaches is privately owned. The coast's midsize towns and small villages (you won't find any large cities) are linked by U.S. 101, which runs the length of the state. It winds past sea-tortured rocks, brooding headlands, hidden beaches, historic lighthouses, and tiny ports. This is one of the most picturesque driving routes in the country, and it should not be missed. Embracing it is the vast, gunmetal-gray Pacific Ocean, which presents a range of moods with the seasons. On summer evenings it might be glassy, and reflect a romantic sunset. In winter the ocean might throw a thrilling tantrum for storm watchers sitting snug and safe in a beachfront cabin.

Active visitors indulge in thrills from racing up a sand dune in a buggy to making par at Bandon Dunes, one of the nation's finest links-style golf courses. Bicyclists pedal along misty coastline vistas, cruising past historic lighthouses. Hikers enjoy breezy, open trails along the sea as well as lush, evergreen-studded treks into the adjoining Coast Range. Boaters explore southern-coast rivers on jet boats while the more adventuresome among them shoot rapids on guided raft trips. If the weather turns, don't overlook indoor venues like the Oregon Coast Aquarium and Columbia River Maritime Museum.

Shoppers appreciate the several art galleries in Newport and Cannon Beach; for more family-oriented shopping fun, giggle in the souvenir shops of Lincoln City and Seaside while eating fistfuls of caramel corn or chewing saltwater taffy.

THE OREGON COAST PLANNER

WHEN TO GO

December through June are generally rainy months, but once the fair weather comes, coastal Oregon is one of the most gorgeous places on earth. July through September offer wonderful, dry days for beachgoers. Autumn is also a great time to visit, as the warm-enough weather is perfect for crisp beachcombing walks followed by hearty harvest meals paired with local ales.

Even with the rain, coastal winter and spring do have quite a following. Many hotels are perfectly situated for storm watching, and provide a romantic experience. Think of a toasty fire, sweet music, a smooth Oregon Pinot, and your loved one, settled in to watch the waves dance upon a jagged rocky stage.

FESTIVALS

If you're looking for one time of year to experience what friendly frivolity can be found on the coast, check out the **Cannon Beach Sandcastle Contest** in June—if you can find a room or a parking spot. Fans of opera and classical works flock to the increasingly popular **Astoria Music Festival** during the last two weeks of June. The **Newport Seafood and Wine Festival** occurs the last full weekend in February, and bills itself the premier seafood and wine event of the Oregon Coast. Dozens of wineries are represented at this expansive celebration, which also features myriad crafts and eateries. In Bandon each September the **Cranberry Festival** comprises a fair and parade.

GETTING HERE AND AROUND

By far the most practical way to reach and to explore the coast is by car. There's only one small regional airport with commercial service, the regional bus lines provide fairly slow and infrequent service from other parts of the state, and there's zero train service. Several two-lane state highways connect the central and northern sections of the coast with the state's two largest cities, Portland and Eugene; the southern portion of the coast is more remote and requires a longer drive.

AIR TRAVEL

From Portland, which has Oregon's largest airport, the drive is about two hours to Astoria and Cannon Beach, and 2½ hours to Lincoln City and Newport. If you're headed farther south, you have a few other options, including flying into the regional airport in Eugene, which is served by most major airlines and is a 90-minute drive from Florence; flying into the tiny Southwest Oregon Regional Airport in the coast town of North Bend, which is an hour south of Florence and 2½ hours north of Brookings; flying into Rogue Valley International Airport in Medford, which is a 2½-hour drive from Brookings and a three-hour drive from Bandon; and flying into Del Norte County

Airport in Crescent City, California, which is just a 30-minute drive south of Brookings.

Southwest Oregon Regional Airport has flights to Portland on SeaPort Airlines and to San Francisco on United Express. The airport has Hertz and Enterprise car-rental agencies as well as cab companies serving the area, including Coos Bay and Bandon.

There are a few shuttle services connecting the airports in Portland and Eugene to the coast, but these tend to be far less economical than renting a car. Caravan Airport Transportation runs a daily shuttle service from Portland International Airport to Lincoln City and on down to Yachats. OmniShuttle provides door-to-door van service from the Eugene airport to the central coast, from Florence down to around Bandon.

Contacts Caravan Airport Transportation ☎ 503/288–5102 ⊕ www. caravanairporttransportation.com. **OmniShuttle** ☎ 541/461–7959, 800/741– 5097 ⊕ www.omnishuttle.com. **SeaPort Airlines** ☎ 888/573–2767 ⊕ www. seaportair.com. **Southwest Oregon Regional Airport** ⊠ 1100 Airport La., North Bend ☎ 541/756–8531 ⊕ www.flyoth.com.

BUS TRAVEL

There is bus travel to the coast from Portland and Eugene, but this is a fairly slow and cumbersome way to explore the area. North by Northwest Connector is a nonprofit organization that coordinates travel among five rural transit services in the northwestern corner of the state. From its website, you can plan and book trips from Portland to Astoria, with connecting service between the two along the coast, stopping in Seaside, Cannon Beach, Manzanita, and other communities. Additionally, Northwest Point, operated by MTR Western bus line, has twice-daily bus service from Portland to Cannon Beach, and then up the coast to Astoria; Greyhound handles the company's reservations and ticketing. Porter Stage Lines connects Florence, Coos Bay, and Reedsport with Eugene every day except Saturday.

Contacts North by Northwest Connector ⊕ www.nworegontransit.org. **Northwest Point** ☎ 800/231–2222 ticketing through Greyhound, 541/484– 4100 information ⊕ www.northwest-point.com. **Porter Stage Lines** ☎ 541/269– 7183 ⊕ www.porterstageline.com.

CAR TRAVEL

Beautiful U.S. 101 hugs the entire Oregon coastline from Brookings near the California border in the south to Astoria on the Columbia River in the north. The road can be slow in places, especially where it passes through towns and curves over headlands and around coves. In theory, you could drive the entire 345-mile Oregon stretch of U.S 101 in a little under eight hours, but that's without stopping—and, of course, the whole point of driving the coast is stopping regularly to enjoy it. If you want to do a full road trip of the Oregon Coast, give yourself at least three days and two nights; that's enough time to see a few key attractions along the way, enjoy the many scenic viewpoints, and stop to eat and overnight in some small towns along the route.

Several two-lane roads connect key towns on the coast (Astoria, Cannon Beach, Tillamook, Lincoln City, Newport, Waldport, Florence,

Reedsport, and Bandon) with the major towns in the Willamette and Rogue valleys (Portland, Eugene, Roseburg). All these roads climb over the Coast Range, meaning the drives tend to be winding and hilly but quite picturesque. Keep in mind that winter storms in the mountains occasionally create slick conditions and even road closures. Always use numbered, paved state roads when crossing the mountains from the valley to the coast, especially in winter; what might appear to be a scenic alternative or shortcut on a map or GPS device is likely an unmaintained logging or forest road that leads through a secluded part of the mountains, without cell service.

RESTAURANTS

Deciding which restaurant has the best clam chowder is just one of the culinary fact-finding expeditions you can embark upon along the Oregon Coast. Chefs here take full advantage of the wealth of sturgeon, chinook, steelhead, and trout that abound in coastal rivers as well as the fresh rockfish, halibut, albacore, and lingcod caught in the Pacific. Fresh mussels, bay shrimp, and oysters are also standard fare in many establishments. Newport's bounty is its Dungeness crab. Razor clams also appear as a succulent addition to many restaurant menus along the coast. You'll find relatively few upscale dining options here, with most of these being in resorts, but quite a few midpriced urbane bistros emphasizing local seafood and seasonal produce have opened in recent years. They still tend to be casual, but with fine service, art-filled dining rooms, and prices more similar to what you'll find in Portland or Eugene. Most other restaurants tend to be low-key and affordable, many of them catering to both kids and adults. There are plenty of cozy brewpubs and clam shacks, and tasty fish-and-chips are easy to come by. In addition, many Oregon Coast restaurants focus heavily on locally produced wines, beers, and even spirits.

HOTELS

Compared with other coastal destinations in the United States, the Oregon Coast offers a pretty good value, although during high season in July and August, rates can get fairly steep at some higher-end inns and resorts, especially along the northern stretch of the coastline. Still, you can typically find clean but basic motels and rustic inns, often with beachfront locations, that have nightly rates well below $150, even in high season. Spring and fall rates often drop by 20% to 30%, and in winter—especially on weekdays—a hotel room that costs $250 in July might go for as little as $99. There are plenty of budget- and midpriced chains in larger towns, but for the most part, the lodging landscape is dominated by family-owned or independent motels and hotels, vacation rentals, and a smattering of distinctive B&Bs.

Properties in much of the north and central coast fill up fast in the summer, so book in advance. Many lodgings require a minimum two-night stay on a summer weekend. *Hotel reviews have been shortened. For full information, visit Fodors.com.*

WHAT IT COSTS IN U.S. DOLLARS			
	$	**$$**	**$$$**	**$$$$**
Restaurants	Under $17	$17–$23	$24–$30	Over $30
Hotels	Under $151	$151–$200	$201–$250	Over $250

Restaurant prices are the average cost of a main course at dinner, or if dinner is not served, at lunch. Hotel prices are the lowest cost of a standard double room in high season.

VISITOR INFORMATION
Central Oregon Coast Association ☎ *541/265–2064, 800/767–2064* ⊕ *www.coastvisitor.com.* **Eugene, Cascades & Coast Visitor Center** ✉ *3312 Gateway St., Springfield* ☎ *541/484–5307, 800/547–5445* ⊕ *www. travellanecounty.org.* **Oregon Coast Visitors Association** ☎ *541/574–2679, 888/628–2101* ⊕ *www.visittheoregoncoast.com.*

NORTH COAST

This is the primary beach playground for residents of Portland, and in recent years, several sophisticated cafés and wine bars, colorful art galleries and boutiques, and smartly restored boutique hotels have opened along this stretch of the Oregon Coast. What distinguishes the region historically from other areas of the coast are its forts, its graveyard of shipwrecks, historic sites related to Lewis and Clark's early visit, and a town—Astoria—that is closer in look and misty temperament to Monterey, California, than any other city in the West. Just south, Cannon Beach and its several high-end hotels feels a bit swankier than any other town in the area.

Every winter Astoria celebrates fisherman poets: hardworking men and women who bare their souls as to what makes their relationship to Oregon's north-coast waters so magical. It's easy to understand their inspiration, whether in the incredibly tempestuous ocean or the romantic beaches.

ASTORIA

96 miles northwest of Portland.

The mighty Columbia River meets the Pacific at Astoria, the oldest city west of the Rockies and a bustling riverfront getaway with a creative spirit and urbane vibe. It is named for John Jacob Astor, owner of the Pacific Fur Company, whose members arrived in 1811 and established Fort Astoria. In its early days, Astoria was a placid amalgamation of small town and hardworking port city. With rivers rich with salmon, the city relied on its fishing and canning industries. Settlers built sprawling Victorian houses on the flanks of Coxcomb Hill; many of the homes have since been restored and used as backdrops in movies or been converted into bed-and-breakfast inns. In recent years the city itself has awakened, with a greater variety of trendy dining and lodging options, as well as a superb museum dedicated to the Columbia River.

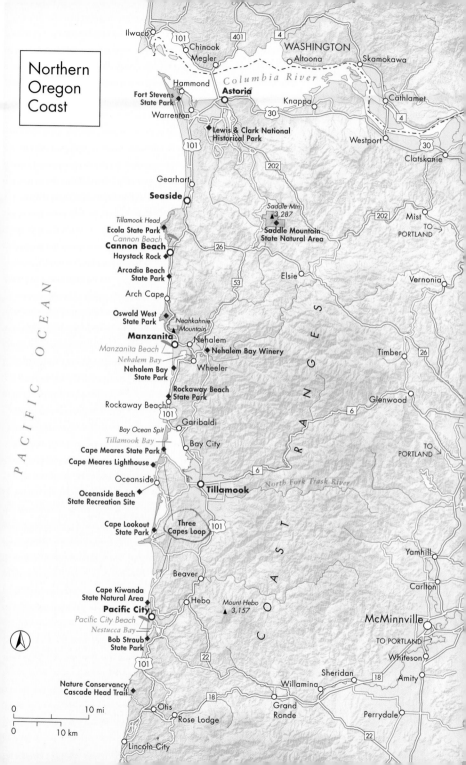

Northern Oregon Coast

WASHINGTON

101   Chinook
Ilwaco
401   4
Megler
Altoona   Skamokawa
Columbia River
Hammond
Fort Stevens   **Astoria**
State Park   Knappa   Cathlamet
Warrenton   30
101   Westport   30
◆ Lewis & Clark National   Clatskanie
Historical Park
202
Gearhart
Seaside   *Saddle Mtn*
▲ *3,287*   Mist
Tillamook Head   Saddle Mountain   202   TO
Ecola State Park ◆   State Natural Area   PORTLAND
Cannon Beach
Cannon Beach ◆   26
Haystack Rock ◆
Arcadia Beach ◆   Elsie   Vernonia
State Park   53
Arch Cape
Oswald West ◆   C   O
State Park   *Neahkahnie*   A
Mountain ▲   S   Timber   26
Manzanita ◆   Nehalem   T
Manzanita Beach   ◆ Nehalem Bay Winery
Nehalem Bay   Wheeler   R
Nehalem Bay ◆   A   Glenwood
State Park   N
Rockaway Beach ◆   G   6
State Park   E
Rockaway Beach   S
101   Garibaldi   6   TO
Bay Ocean Spit   PORTLAND
Tillamook Bay   Bay City
Cape Meares State Park ◆   6
Cape Meares Lighthouse ◆   *North Fork Trask River*
Oceanside   **Tillamook**
Oceanside Beach ◆
State Recreation Site   C
Cape Lookout ◆   Three   O   Yamhill
State Park   Capes Loop   101   A
S   Carlton
Beaver   T
Cape Kiwanda ◆   Hebo   *Mount Hebo*   R
State Natural Area   ▲ *3,157*   A   **McMinnville**
Pacific City ◆   N
Pacific City Beach   G   TO PORTLAND
Nestucca Bay   E   Whiteson
Bob Straub ◆   22   S
State Park   Sheridan   Amity
101   18
Willamina   18
Nature Conservancy ◆
Cascade Head Trail   Grand   Perrydale
Otis   Ronde
18
Rose Lodge   22

PACIFIC OCEAN

0   10 mi
0   10 km

Lincoln City

But Astoria still retains the soul of a fisherman's town, celebrated each February during its FisherPoets Gathering. The town of about 9,500 also has wonderful views from most areas and a richly forested backdrop to the east, yet it remains a working waterfront. There is little public beach access in the town proper; to reach the Pacific, you have to drive a few miles west to Fort Stevens in Warrenton.

GETTING HERE AND AROUND
The northernmost town on the Oregon Coast, Astoria is just across the Columbia River from southwestern Washington via U.S. 101 (over the stunning Astoria-Megler Bridge) and a two-hour drive from Portland on U.S. 30. It only takes about 20 extra minutes to get here from Portland via the more scenic route of U.S. 101 south and U.S. 26 east.

ESSENTIALS
Visitor Information Astoria-Warrenton Area Chamber of Commerce ⊠ *111 W. Marine Dr.* ☎ *503/325–6311, 800/875–6807* ⊕ *www.oldoregon.com.*

EXPLORING
TOP ATTRACTIONS
Astoria Column. For the best view of the city, the Coast Range, volcanic Mt. Helens, and the Pacific Ocean, scamper up the 164 spiral stairs to the top of the Astoria Column. When you get to the top, you can throw a small wooden plane and watch it glide to earth; each year some 35,000 gliders are tossed. The 125-foot-high structure sits atop Coxcomb Hill, and was patterned after Trajan's Column in Rome. There are little platforms to rest on if you get winded, or, if you don't want to climb, the column's 500 feet of artwork, depicting important Pacific Northwest historical milestones, are well worth a study. ⊠ *16th St. S* ☎ *503/325–2963* ⊕ *www.astoriacolumn.org* ⊡ *$2 per car* ☉ *Weekdays 9–5:30, weekends 9–5.*

FAMILY
Fodor's Choice
★

Columbia River Maritime Museum. One of Oregon's best coastal attractions illuminates the maritime history of the Pacific Northwest and provides visitors with a sense of the perils of guiding ships into the mouth of the Columbia River. Vivid exhibits recount what it was like to pilot a tugboat and participate in a Coast Guard rescue on the Columbia River Bar. You can tour the actual bridge of a World War II–era U.S. Navy destroyer and the U.S. Coast Guard lightship *Columbia*. Also on display is a 44-foot Coast Guard motor lifeboat, artifacts from the region's illustrious riverboat heyday, and details about Astoria's seafood-canning history. One especially captivating exhibit displays the personal belongings of some of the ill-fated passengers of the 2,000 ships that have foundered here since the early 19th century. In addition, the theater shows an excellent documentary about the river's heritage as well as rotating 3-D films about sea life. At the east end of the property, the city's former railroad depot now houses the museum's Barbey Maritime Center, which offers classes and workshops on maritime culture and wooden boatbuilding. ⊠ *1792 Marine Dr.* ☎ *503/325–2323* ⊕ *www. crmm.org* ⊡ *$12* ☉ *Daily 9:30–5.*

Flavel House. The Queen Anne–style mansion helps visitors imagine what life was like for the wealthy in late-19th-century Astoria. It rests on parklike grounds covering an entire city block and has been gorgeously restored, with its three-story octagon tower visible from throughout town. It was built for George Flavel, an influential Columbia River bar pilot and businessman who was one of the area's first millionaires. Visits start in the Carriage House interpretive center. ⊠ *441 8th St.* ☎ *503/325–2203* ⊕ *www.cumtux.org* ⊠ *$6* ☉ *May–Sept., daily 10–5; Oct.–Apr., daily 11–4.*

FAMILY
Fodor's Choice
★

Fort Clatsop at Lewis and Clark National Historical Park. See where the 30-member Lewis and Clark Expedition endured a rain-soaked winter in 1805–06, hunting, gathering food, making salt, and trading with the local Clatsops, Chinooks, and Tillamooks. This memorial is part of the 3,200-acre Lewis and Clark National Historical Park and is a faithful replica of the log fort depicted in Clark's journal. The fort lies within a forested wonderland, with an exhibit hall, gift shop, film, and trails. Park rangers dress in period garb during the summer and perform such early-19th-century tasks as making fire with flint and steel. Hikers enjoy the easy 1½-mile Netul Landing trail and the more strenuous but still fairly flat 6½-mile Fort to Sea trail. ⊠ *92343 Fort Clatsop Rd., 6 miles southwest of downtown Astoria* ☎ *503/861–2471* ⊕ *www.nps.gov/ lewi* ⊠ *$3* ☉ *Mid-Jun.–Labor Day, daily 9–6; Labor Day–mid-Jun., daily 9–5.*

WORTH NOTING

Bumble Bee Cannery Museum. Drive or walk over the rickety (but actually completely sturdy) bridge onto historic Pier 39, which juts out into the Columbia River on the east side of downtown, to visit this small but interesting museum that occupies the oldest extant cannery building in Astoria. It was once operated by Bumble Bee Seafood, and some 30,000 cans of salmon were processed here annually during the plant's late-19th-century heyday. Exhibits and artifacts, including three vintage gill-net boats, some wonderful old photos, and equipment and cans tell the story of the town's—and facility's—canning history. Also on the pier is Coffee Girl café and Rogue Ales tavern. ⊠ *100 39th St.* ☎ *503/325–2502* ⊕ *www.canneryworker.org* ⊠ *Free* ☉ *Daily 9–6.*

NEED A
BREAK?

Coffee Girl. This cozy café inside a 19th-century cannery building on historic Pier 39 has big windows overlooking the river—you can always take your well-crafted espresso or latte with you for a stroll around the pier. Open until 4 pm each day, Coffee Girl also serves tasty quiches, pastries, soups, and grilled panini sandwiches. ⊠ *100 39th St.* ☎ *503/325–6900* ⊕ *www.thecoffeegirl.com.*

FAMILY

Fort Stevens State Park. This earthen fort at Oregon's northwestern tip was built during the Civil War to guard the Columbia River against attack. None came until World War II, when a Japanese submarine fired upon it. The fort still has cannons and an underground gun battery, of which tours are available in summer (call for details). The park has year-round camping, with full hookup sites and 15 yurts. There are also bike paths, boating, swimming, hiking trails, and a short walk to a gorgeous, wide beach where the corroded skeleton—or the tiny bit that remains of it—of the *Peter Iredale* pokes up through the sand. This century-old English four-master shipwreck is a reminder of the nearly

2,000 vessels claimed by these treacherous waters. ⊠ *100 Peter Iredale Rd., 9 miles west of Astoria* ☎ *503/861–3170, 800/452–5687* ⊕ *www. oregonstateparks.org* 🖃 *Day use $5 per vehicle* ☉ *Daily.*

FAMILY   **Oregon Film Museum.** Housed in the old Clatsop County Jail, this small but engaging museum celebrates Oregon's long history of filmmaking and contains artifacts from and displays about prior productions. The location is apt because it was featured prominently in the famous cult film *The Goonies.* The state's film productions date back to 1908 for *The Fisherman's Bride.* Since then, Oregon has helped give birth to such classics as *The General, The Great Race, One Flew Over the Cuckoo's Nest, Paint Your Wagon, Animal House,* and *Twilight,* leading some to call the state Hollywood North. *Kindergarten Cop, The Ring II, Free Willy I* and *II,* and *Short Circuit* are among those filmed in Astoria. You can download an audio tour of filmed sites (or buy a tour CD for $2) from the Astoria-Warrenton Chamber of Commerce—it's a fun way to see the city's oft-unsung landmarks, especially during the annual Goonies festival, held in June. ⊠ *732 Duane St.* ☎ *503/325–2203* ⊕ *www.oregonfilmmuseum.org* 🖃 *$6* ☉ *May–Sept. daily 10–5; Oct.–Apr. daily 11–4.*

WHERE TO EAT

$ ✕ **Astoria Coffeehouse & Bistro.** A source of fine coffee drinks and baked
ECLECTIC   goods, this cheerful storefront café has both sidewalk seating and a
Fodor'sChoice   living-room-like interior decorated with old photos. The always-bus-
★   tling restaurant serves consistently well-prepared food, a mix of American classics and international treats. Try the decadent Monte Cristo sandwich at breakfast. Later in the day, highlights include tuna *poke* (salad) with mango and avocado, slow-roasted-beet salad with chèvre and apples, local-rockfish tacos with tomatillo salsa, and pad thai with fresh salmon. The fine drink selection makes this a favorite nightlife option, too. ⑤ *Average main: $15* ⊠ *243 11th St.* ☎ *503/325–1787* ⊕ *www.astoriacoffeehouse.com.*

$ ✕ **Blue Scorcher Bakery Café.** "Joyful work, delicious food, and strong
CAFÉ   community" is this family-friendly café's rallying cry. It serves up every-
FAMILY   thing from *huevos scorcheros* (poached eggs with rice, beans, cheese, and salsa) and organic, handcrafted breads to a variety of foods using local, fair trade, and organic ingredients. The offerings change with the seasons, but there's always a vegan or gluten-free option. There's also a Pie-of-the-Month Club. Big windows overlook downtown and the Columbia River in the distance, and there's a children's play area. ⑤ *Average main: $8* ⊠ *1493 Duane St.* ☎ *503/338–7473* ⊕ *www. bluescorcher.com* ☉ *No dinner.*

$$ ✕ **Bridgewater Bistro.** In the same complex as the Cannery Pier Hotel, this
PACIFIC   stylish restaurant has great views of the river and bridge to Washington.
NORTHWEST   Inside, high ceilings are supported by ancient fir timbers, and an extensive menu is strong on creative seafood and meat grills, including roasted spice-encrusted duck breast with cranberry-blackberry demi-glace, and seared wild local salmon with an arugula-strawberry salad and a star anise–balsamic vinaigrette. You'll also find more affordable burgers, pastas, and vegetarian options. There's a much-celebrated brunch on Sunday. ⑤ *Average main: $22* ⊠ *20 Basin St., Suite A* ☎ *503/325–6777* ⊕ *www.bridgewaterbistro.com.*

$$ ✕**Clemente's.** Serving some of the best seafood on the northern Oregon
SEAFOOD   Coast, chefs Gordon and Lisa Clement have played a big role in Asto-
Fodor'sChoice   ria's steady growth into a legitimate dining destination. Grounded in
★   the Mediterranean culinary traditions of Italy and the Adriatic Coast,
Clemente's inventive specials feature the freshest catches of that day,
from a succulent pan-seared local halibut with truffle salt and red-
pepper coulis to a hearty cioppino—all served up for reasonable prices.
Dungeness crab cakes stuffed with crab rather than breading, and wild
scallop fish-and-chips liven up a varied menu. The Clements have a
strong commitment to locally sourced ingredients and environmen-
tally friendly practices. ⑤ *Average main: $22* ✉ *1198 Commercial St.*
☎ *503/325–1067* ⊕ *www.clementesrestaurant.com* ⊗ *No lunch Mon.*

$$ ✕**Columbian Cafe.** Locals love this unpretentious diner that defies cat-
ECLECTIC   egorization by offering inventive, fresh seafood, spicy vegetarian dishes,
and meats cured and smoked on the premises. Located next to the
quirky Voodoo Room bar and historic Columbian Theater, the café
serves simple food, such as crepes with broccoli, cheese, and homemade
salsa for lunch; grilled salmon and pasta with a lemon-cream sauce for
dinner. Colorful owner-chef Uriah Hulsey is usually on hand. Be sure
to come early as this place always draws a crowd. ⑤ *Average main: $23*
✉ *1114 Marine Dr.* ☎ *503/325–2233* ⊕ *www.columbianvoodoo.com/*
cafe ▭ *No credit cards* ⊗ *Closed Mon. and Tues.*

WHERE TO STAY

$$$$ ⬚**Cannery Pier Hotel.** From every room in this captivating property
HOTEL   there's a gorgeous view of the mighty Columbia River flowing toward
Fodor'sChoice   the Pacific Ocean, and it's almost hypnotic to watch the tugboats shep-
★   herding barges to and fro. **Pros:** amazing river views; great in-room
amenities; hotel hot tub and day spa. **Cons:** pricey; a bit of a walk
from downtown. ⑤ *Rooms from: $279* ✉ *10 Basin St.* ☎ *503/325–*
4996, 888/325–4996 ⊕ *www.cannerypierhotel.com* ↴ *46 rooms, 8*
suites ¶○¶ *Breakfast.*

$ ⬚**Clementine's B& B.** This painstakingly restored 1888 Italianate Vic-
B&B/INN   torian home is just a couple of blocks up the hill from Flavel House
Museum and a short walk from several fine restaurants and shops. **Pros:**
superb, multicourse breakfast included; handy downtown location.
Cons: the traditional lacy room decor isn't for everyone. ⑤ *Rooms from:*
$109 ✉ *847 Exchange St.* ☎ *503/325–2005* ⊕ *www.clementines-bb.*
com ↴ *4 rooms, 1 suite* ¶○¶ *Breakfast.*

$ ⬚**Commodore Hotel.** An economical but stylish downtown boutique
HOTEL   hotel, the Commodore has become a favorite with young and artsy
Fodor'sChoice   souls from Portland and Seattle thanks to its vintage-chic aesthetic, large
★   wall murals and photos, and hip café off the lobby. **Pros:** hip ambience;
wallet-friendly rates; excellent Street 14 Coffee café on-site. **Cons:** least
expensive rooms share a bath; simple decor. ⑤ *Rooms from: $79* ✉ *258*
14th St. ☎ *503/325–4747* ⊕ *www.commodoreastoria.com* ↴ *18 rooms,*
10 with shared bath ¶○¶ *No meals.*

$ ⬚**Hotel Elliott.** This atmospheric, five-story hotel stands in the heart of
HOTEL   Astoria's historic district and retains the elegance of yesteryear, updated
with modern comforts like cozy underfloor heating in the bathrooms.
Pros: captures the city's historic ambience beautifully; every effort

made to infuse the rooms with upscale amenities; popular wine bar. **Cons:** some areas have a lingering smell of cigar smoke; no on-site dining. $ *Rooms from: $149* ☒ *357 12th St.* ☎ *503/325–2222* ⊕ *www. hotelelliott.com* ↪ *21 rooms, 11 suites* ⊚ *Breakfast.*

NIGHTLIFE

Fodor's Choice
★

Fort George Brewery. The spacious taproom and brewery set in a former 1920s auto showroom has plenty of indoor and outdoor seating where you can sample some of the best craft beers on the coast, including the Belgian-style Quick Wit or the oatmeal-infused Sunrise OPA, a light American pale ale. Plenty of seasonal brews appear on the menu as well, along with tasty pub fare. ☒ *1483 Duane St.* ☎ *503/325–7468* ⊕ *www.fortgeorgebrewery.com.*

SHOPPING

Josephson's. One of the Oregon Coast's oldest commercial smokehouses, Josephson's uses alder for all processing and specializes in Pacific Northwest chinook and coho salmon. The mouthwatering fish that's smoked on the premises includes hot smoked pepper or wine-maple salmon, as well as smoked halibut, sturgeon, tuna, oysters, mussels, scallops, and prawns by the pound or in sealed gift packs. ☒ *106 Marine Dr.* ☎ *503/325–2190* ⊕ *www.josephsons.com.*

SEASIDE

12 miles south of Astoria on U.S. 101.

As a resort town, Seaside has somewhat spruced up its kitschy, arcade-filled reputation and now supports a bustling tourist trade, with hotels, condominiums, and restaurants lining a traditional promenade. It still has fun games and plenty of carny noise to appeal to young people, but it has added plenty of classy getaways for adults, as well as some of the more affordable lodging options on this stretch of the coast. Only 90 miles from Portland, Seaside is often crowded, so it's not the place to come if you crave solitude. Peak times include mid- to late March, when hordes of teenagers descend on the town during spring break; and late June, when the annual Miss Oregon Pageant is in full swing. Just south of town, waves draw surfers to the Cove, a spot jealously guarded by locals.

GETTING HERE AND AROUND

Seaside is about a 90-minute drive from Portland via U.S 26 and a 20-minute drive south of Astoria on coastal U.S. 101.

VISITOR INFORMATION

Seaside Visitors Bureau ☒ *7 N. Roosevelt Ave.* ☎ *503/738–3097, 888/306–2326* ⊕ *www.seasideor.com.*

WHERE TO EAT AND STAY

$
DINER

✕ **Firehouse Grill.** This bustling diner-style café in a former firehouse in downtown Seaside hits the mark with its hearty breakfast fare, including fluffy biscuits with gravy, cinnamon French toast, meat-loaf scrambles, and a couple of lighter options, such as house-made granola with fresh fruit. The excellent Sleepy Monk coffee from Cannon Beach is served, too, as are eye-opening Bloody Marys. Open only until early afternoon, the restaurant also turns out excellent burgers, panfried oysters, and halibut tacos at lunch. $ *Average main: $10* ⊠ *841 Broadway* ☎ *503/717–5502* ⊘ *Closed Tues. and Wed. No dinner.*

$$ 🏨 **McMenamins Gearhart Hotel.** The quirky McMenamins group, which
HOTEL   operates several historic and offbeat hotels around the state, opened this
18-room boutique inn on the upper floor of the Cape Cod–style Kelly
House in 2012. **Pros:** short walk from beach; rooms have distinctive and
arty flair; excellent 18-hole golf course. **Cons:** ocean view is blocked by
condos across the street; not within walking distance of shopping and
dining; restaurant on-site is just so-so. $ *Rooms from: $195* ⊠ *1157
N. Marion Ave., 4 miles north of Seaside, Gearhart* ☎ *503/717–8159,
855/846–7583* ⊕ *www.mcmenamins.com/gearharthotel* ➫ *18 rooms*
⊙ *No meals.*

$$ 🏨 **Rivertide Suites.** Although it's not right on the beach, the Rivertide's
HOTEL   splendid accommodations are within walking distance of the town's
FAMILY   best cuisine, shopping, and beach activities. **Pros:** contemporary;
clean; near plenty of shopping and boardwalk activities. **Cons:** it's on
a city river instead of the beach; rooms on lower floors have less of a
view. $ *Rooms from: $169* ⊠ *102 N. Holladay Dr.* ☎ *503/717–1100,
877/871–8433* ⊕ *www.rivertidesuites.com* ➫ *70 rooms* ⊙ *Breakfast.*

$ 🏨 **Sandy Cove Inn.** This small, nicely maintained motel is fun and color-
HOTEL   fully decorated, and it's just a block away from Seaside's promenade.
Pros: near plenty of restaurants; distinctive room themes. **Cons:** not
directly on the beach; funky rooms don't suit every taste. $ *Rooms
from: $89* ⊠ *241 Ave. U* ☎ *503/738–7473* ⊕ *www.sandycoveinn.net*
➫ *13 rooms, 2 suites* ⊙ *No meals.*

SPORTS AND THE OUTDOORS

HIKING

Saddle Mountain State Natural Area. One of the most accessible mountain
peaks in the Coast Range, 3,283-foot Saddle Mountain is reached via
a challenging but beautiful 2½-mile climb, with a 1,603-foot elevation
gain—the reward, on clear days, is a view of the ocean to the west and
the Cascade peaks far to the east. Wear sturdy shoes, and be prepared
for sections with steep upgrades. There's a zippy change in the altitude
as you climb higher, but the wildflowers make it all worthwhile. The
trailhead is well signed off of U.S. 26, the main highway from Portland
to Cannon Beach and Seaside. ⊠ *Saddle Mountain Rd., off U.S. 26, 20
miles east of Seaside and 70 miles west of Portland* ☎ *800/551–6649,
503/368–5943* ⊕ *www.oregonstateparks.org.*

CANNON BEACH

25 miles south of Astoria.

Cannon Beach is a mellow but relatively affluent town where locals
and part-time residents—many of the latter reside in Portland—come
to enjoy shopping and dining, the sea air, and the chance to explore
the spectacular state parks at either end of the area: Ecola to the north
and Oswald West to the south. Shops and galleries selling surfing gear,
upscale clothing, local art, wine, coffee, and candies line Hemlock
Street, Cannon Beach's main thoroughfare. In late June the town hosts
the Cannon Beach Sandcastle Contest, for which thousands throng

the beach to view imaginative and often startling works in this most transient of art forms. On the downside, this so-called Carmel of the Oregon Coast can be more expensive and crowded than other towns along U.S. 101.

GETTING HERE AND AROUND

It's a 90-minute drive east from Portland on U.S. 26 to reach Cannon Beach, which is a 10-minute drive south of Seaside. To make a scenic loop, consider returning to Portland by way of Astoria and U.S. 30 (about 2¼ hours) or Tillamook and Highway 6 (about 2½ hours).

ESSENTIALS

Visitor Information Cannon Beach Chamber of Commerce ⊠ *207 N. Spruce St., Cannon Beach* ☎ *503/436–2623* ⊕ *www.cannonbeach.org.*

EXPLORING

Haystack Rock. Towering over the broad, sandy beach is a gorgeous, 235-foot-high dome that is one of the most photographed natural wonders on the Oregon Coast. For safety and to protect birding habitats, people are not allowed to climb on the rock, but you can walk right up to its base at low tide. ⊠ *Cannon Beach.*

WHERE TO EAT

$$
IRISH

✕ **Irish Table.** Adjacent to the Sleepy Monk café, this cozy restaurant with a timber-beam ceiling and warm lighting serves seasonal food with an Irish twist, such as potato-kale soup and its heralded Irish lamb stew. Other offerings include a perfect steak or delicate fresh halibut. Start with chicken-bacon chowder or the curried mussels, and soak up the sauce with slices of piping-hot soda bread. Naturally, there's a rich assortment of drinks, including Irish whiskey, and the wine list features plenty of noted Oregon options. It's a popular place, so be prepared to wait in summer and on weekends—reservations are available only for parties of four or more. ⑤ *Average main: $18* ⊠ *1235 S. Hemlock St.* ☎ *503/436–0708* ⊕ *www.theirishtablerestaurant.com* ⊘ *Closed Wed. and Jan. No lunch.*

$
CAFÉ
Fodor's Choice
★

✕ **Sleepy Monk.** In a region renowned for artisan coffee, this small roaster brews some of the best espresso and coffee drinks in the state. Sleepy Monk attracts java aficionados on caffeine pilgrimages from near and far eager to sample its certified-organic, fair-trade beans. Local, fresh pastries are stacked high and there's also a good selection of herbal and green teas. The Irish Table restaurant next door is under the same management. ⑤ *Average main: $5* ⊠ *1235 S. Hemlock St.* ☎ *503/436–2796* ⊕ *www.sleepymonkcoffee.com* ⊘ *Closed Wed. and Thurs. No dinner.*

$$$$
PACIFIC
NORTHWEST
Fodor's Choice
★

✕ **Stephanie Inn Dining Room.** As diners enjoy a romantic view of Haystack Rock, this luxe hotel's sophisticated, supremely romantic dining room prepares a new menu nightly, crafting exquisite dinners using fresh, local ingredients. Diners can expect dishes such as butternut squash risotto, cedar plank–roasted salmon, savory duck confit, and a lemon-curd tart with wild berry sauce. You can order a la carte or opt for the four-course prix-fixe, with or without wine pairings. There's an extensive regional and international wine list. The view, cuisine, and attentive service combine to make it one of the finest dining experiences in the Pacific Northwest. ⑤ *Average main: $43* ⊠ *2740 S. Pacific St.*

☎ *503/436–2221, 800/633–3466* ⊕ *www.stephanie-inn.com* ✍ *Reservations essential* ☾ *No lunch.*

$$$ ✕ **Wayfarer Restaurant.** The dazzling beach and ocean views, especially
AMERICAN at sunset, are just part of the story at this casually elegant restaurant
at the Surfsand Resort; it's also the top destination in town for a leisurely meal of tasty American food, including plenty of local seafood
options, such as sesame-breaded Pacific razor clams with jalapeño-lime
jelly, and Oregon-hazelnut-seared sole with a berry beurre blanc. If fish
isn't your game, consider the prodigious 22-ounce "tomahawk" rib-
eye steak with a Cabernet butter. There's a nice list of Oregon wines,
and breakfast—featuring several delicious Benedicts and omelets—is
offered daily. ⑤ *Average main: $29* ⊠ *1190 Pacific Dr.* ☎ *503/436–1108*
⊕ *www.wayfarer-restaurant.com.*

WHERE TO STAY

$ ☷ **Ecola Creek Lodge.** With a quiet, shady courtyard just off the main
HOTEL road leading into the north side of town, this small, reasonably priced
1940s hotel offers 22 suites and rooms with a mix of configurations,
from two-bedroom units with kitchens to cozy standard rooms. **Pros:**
quiet setting; rooms come in wide range of layouts; good value. **Cons:**
not on the beach; slight walk from downtown shopping. ⑤ *Rooms
from: $124* ⊠ *208 5th St.* ☎ *503/436–2776, 800/873–2749* ⊕ *www.
ecolacreeklodge.com* ⤳ *9 rooms, 13 suites* �ℿ *No meals.*

$$$$ ☷ **Ocean Lodge.** Designed to capture the feel of a 1940s beach resort, this
RESORT rustic but upscale lodge is perfect for special occasions and romantic get-
aways. **Pros:** beachfront location; spacious rooms; warm cookies deliv-
ered to rooms. **Cons:** expensive; balconies are shared with neighboring
rooms. ⑤ *Rooms from: $259* ⊠ *2864 S. Pacific St.* ☎ *503/436–2241,
888/777–4047* ⊕ *www.theoceanlodge.com* ⤳ *45 rooms* �ℿ *Breakfast.*

$$$$ ☷ **Stephanie Inn.** One of the coastline's most beautiful views is paired
RESORT with one of its most splendid hotels, where the focus is firmly on
Fodor's Choice romance, superior service, and luxurious rooms. **Pros:** incredibly plush
★ accommodations; lots of little extras included; top-notch service. **Cons:**
among the highest rates of any hotel in the state; not for families with
younger children; some minimum-night stay requirements. ⑤ *Rooms
from: $479* ⊠ *2740 S. Pacific St.* ☎ *503/436–2221, 800/633–3466*
⊕ *www.stephanie-inn.com* ⤳ *27 rooms, 14 suites* ⍿ *Breakfast.*

$ ☷ **Tolovana Inn.** Set on the beach at the quieter southern end of town, the
HOTEL large, rambling Tolovana Inn is one of the better-priced options in this
FAMILY tony seaside community, especially considering that most rooms enjoy
partial or full views of the Pacific. **Pros:** panoramic beach views; good mix
of layouts and room sizes; some units have kitchens. **Cons:** a 10-minute
drive from downtown shops; some rooms are relatively small. ⑤ *Rooms
from: $134* ⊠ *3400 S. Hemlock St.* ☎ *503/436–2211, 800/333–8890*
⊕ *www.tolovanainn.com* ⤳ *74 rooms, 103 suites* ⍿ *No meals.*

SHOPPING

Cannon Beach Art Galleries. The numerous art galleries that line Can-
non Beach's Hemlock Street are an essential part of the town's spirit
and beauty. A group of about a dozen galleries featuring beautifully
innovative works in ceramic, bronze, photography, painting, and other

mediums have collaborated to form the Cannon Beach Gallery Group. You'll find information about exhibits and special events on the website. ✉ *Hemlock St.* ⊕ *cbgallerygroup.com.*

SPORTS AND THE OUTDOORS

BEACHES

FAMILY

Fodor's Choice

★

Cannon Beach and Ecola State Park. Beachcombers love Cannon Beach for its often low foamy waves and the wide stretch of sand that wraps the quaint community, making it ideal for fair-weather play or for hunting down a cup of coffee and strolling in winter. This stretch can get feisty in storms, however, which also makes Cannon Beach a good place to curl up indoors and watch the show. Haystack Rock rises 253 feet over the beach on the south side of downtown, one of 1,853 protected rocks that's part of the Oregon Ocean Island Wildlife Refuge, providing a nesting habitat for birds. Continue south past Tolovana Park—a playground located in the flood plain—to find the quiet side of Cannon Beach with a bevy of tide pools and few other souls. To the north of town, the beach gives way to Ecola State Park, a breathtakingly beautiful series of coves and rocky headlands where William Clark spotted a beached whale in 1806 and visitors still come to view them offshore during the twice-yearly migrations. From here, Sitka spruce and barbecues feature along the sands. There are a few excellent trails that hug the sometimes steep cliffs that rise above sand, including a 6-mile trail first traced by Lewis and Clark that runs from this spot all the way to Seaside. **Amenities:** parking; toilets. **Best for:** partiers; sunset; walking. ✉ *Ocean Ave.* ☎ *503/436–2844, 800/551–6949* ⊕ *www.cannon-beach. net* ✉ *Ecola State Park day use $5 per vehicle.*

MANZANITA

20 miles south of Cannon Beach.

Manzanita is a secluded and gorgeously situated seaside community with only a few more than 500 full-time residents—but a growing following among weekenders from the Willamette Valley means there's one of the highest number of vacation rentals along the northern Oregon Coast here. The village is on a sandy peninsula, peppered with tufts of grass, on the northwestern side of Nehalem Bay, a noted windsurfing destination. It's a fairly laid-back town, but its growing crop of notable restaurants and boutiques has made it increasingly popular with visitors, as has its proximity to beautiful Oswald West State Park.

GETTING HERE AND AROUND

Tiny Manzanita is an easy and picturesque 20-minute drive south of Cannon Beach on coastal U.S. 101; from Portland, it takes just under two hours to get here.

WHERE TO EAT AND STAY

$$$

MODERN AMERICAN

✗ **Blackbird.** Laid-back and decidedly causal downtown Manzanita received a significant culinary boost with the 2014 opening of this sophisticated, locavore-driven bistro. The menu changes often but might feature a salad of local greens, balsamic-soaked cherries, and smoked duck breast; roasted free-range chicken with kale, carrots, and spaetzle; or tender beef tenderloin with potato gratin, sautéed Swiss chard, and red-wine jus—the fresh, uncomplicated food is attractively presented and sings with flavor. Save room for the rich dark-chocolate pot de crème topped with sea salt and caramel. Reservations are a good idea during busy times, as this intimate space has just a handful of tables plus several stools at the bar. ⑤ *Average main: $25* ✉ *503 Laneda Ave.* ☎ *503/368–7708* ⊕ *www.blackbirdmanzanita.com* ⊗ *Closed Sun. No lunch.*

$ ✕ **Bread and Ocean Bakery.** This small bakery with a handful of tables
CAFÉ inside and several more on the sunny patio is hugely popular for breakfast and lunch with the many folks who rent cottages in the friendly beach town; if it's crowded, consider taking your food to go—the beach is just a few blocks away. Start the morning with a slice of quiche or breakfast frittata. At lunchtime, tuck into a hefty deli sandwich, such as turkey with pear-apple compote and Gorgonzola on house-baked ciabatta. Fresh-baked breads, daily rotating side salads, decadent cinnamon rolls, Sleepy Monk coffee, gourmet sodas, craft beers, and local wines are sold, too. ⑤ *Average main: $9* ✉ *154 Laneda Ave.* ☎ *503/368–5823* ⊕ *www.breadandocean.com* ▭ *No credit cards* ⊗ *Closed Mon. and Tues. No dinner.*

$ ✕ **San Dune Pub.** Once just a neighborhood dive bar, this 1930s pub has
AMERICAN upped its game over the years and become a local magnet for delicious seafood, burgers, sweet-potato fries, grilled-cod tacos, oyster po'boys, and, on Tuesday, baby back ribs. Desserts are worth saving room for here—a few different fresh-fruit and cream pies are always featured. There are 17 beers on tap, regular live music ($5 cover charge), and a 50-inch screen for sports, so it's a one-stop shop. Patio seating on nicer days is a bonus, particularly if you've brought the dog along. ⑤ *Average main: $14* ✉ *127 Laneda Ave.* ☎ *503/368–5080* ⊕ *www.sandunepub.com.*

$$$ ⌂ **Inn at Manzanita.** Shore pines around this 1987 Scandinavian struc-
B&B/INN ture give upper-floor patios a treehouse feel, and it's just half a block
FAMILY from the beach. **Pros:** tranquil ambience with a Japanese garden atmosphere; very light and clean; several rooms good for families. **Cons:** two-night minimum stay on weekends; can book up fast in summer. ⑤ *Rooms from: $179* ✉ *67 Laneda Ave.* ☎ *503/368–6754* ⊕ *www.innatmanzanita.com* ⊅ *13 rooms, 1 suite* ⦿ *No meals.*

SPORTS AND THE OUTDOORS

BEACHES

Manzanita Beach and Nehalem Bay State Park. The long stretch of white sand that separates the Pacific Ocean from the town of Manzanita is as loved a stretch of coastline as the next, its north side reaching into the shadows of Neahkanie Mountain, right where the mountain puts its foot in the ocean (the mountain itself, which makes for a great hike, lies within Oswald West State Park). The beach is frequented by vacationers, day-trippers, kite flyers, and dogs on its north end, but it extends a breezy 7 miles to the tip of Nehalem Bay State Park, which is accessible on foot over sand or by car along the road. At the south end of the park's parking lot, a dirt horse trail leads all the way to a peninsula's tip, a flat walk behind grassy dunes—you can book horseback rides from **Oregon Beach Rides** (☎ *971/237–6653* ⊕ *www.*

oregonbeachrides.com) which has a stable inside the park. Cross to the right for a secluded patch of windy sand on the ocean, or to the left for a quiet, sunny place in the sun on Nehalem Bay, out of the wind. **Amenities:** toilets. **Best for:** sunset; walking. ⊠ *Foot of Laneda Ave.* ☎ *503/368–5154, 800/551–6949* ⊕ *www.oregonstateparks.org* 🖃 *Nehalem Bay State Park day use $5 per vehicle.*

RECREATIONAL AREAS

Fodor's Choice
★

Oswald West State Park. Adventurous travelers will enjoy a sojourn at one of the best-kept secrets on the Pacific coast, at the base of Neahkahnie Mountain. Park in one of the two free lots on U.S. 101 and hike a half-mile trail to dramatic Short Sand Beach, aka "Shorty's," one of the top spots along the Oregon Coast for surfing. It's a spectacular beach with caves and tidal pools. There are several trails from the beach, all offering dazzling scenery; the relatively easy 2½-mile trail to Cape Falcon overlook joins with the Oregon Coast Trail and offers impressive views back toward Shorty's Beach. The arduous 5½-mile trail to the 1,680-foot summit of Neahkahnie Mountain (access the trailhead about 2 miles south of the parking lots marked only by a "hikers" sign, or get there via Short Sand Beach) provides dazzling views south for many miles toward the surf, sand, and mountains fringing Manzanita and, in the distance, Tillamook. Come in December or March and you might spot pods of gray whales. ⊠ *U.S. 101, 5 miles north of downtown Manzanita, Arch Cape* ☎ *800/551–6949* ⊕ *www.oregonstateparks.org* 🖃 *Free* ☉ *Daily dawn–dusk.*

HORSEBACK RIDING

FAMILY

Oregon Beach Rides. Saddle up for horseback rides at Nehalem Bay State Park, available Memorial Day through Labor Day weekends. Guides take you on a journey along the beach in Manzanita, and reserved rides can last from one to several hours. There's even a romantic sunset trot. It's appropriate for ages six and up. ⊠ *Nehalem Bay State Park, 9500 Sandpiper La., Nehalem* ☎ *971/237–6653* ⊕ *www.oregonbeachrides.com.*

TILLAMOOK

27 miles south of Manzanita.

More than 100 inches of annual rainfall and the confluence of three rivers contribute to the lush green pastures around Tillamook, probably best known for its thriving dairy industry and cheese factory. The Tillamook County Cheese Factory ships about 40 million pounds of cheese around the world every year. The town itself lies several miles inland from the ocean and doesn't offer much in the way of attractions, but it is the best jumping-off point for driving the dramatic Three Capes Loop, which passes over Cape Meares, Cape Lookout, and Cape Kiwanda and offers spectacular views of the ocean and coastline. The small village of Oceanside, just north of Cape Lookout, has several cute restaurants and shops.

GETTING HERE AND AROUND

Tillamook is a 90-minute drive from Portland on U.S. 26 to Highway 6. It's a winding, pretty, 45-minute drive south of Cannon Beach on U.S. 101, and a one-hour drive north of Lincoln City along the same coastal highway.

ESSENTIALS

VISITOR INFORMATION

Tillamook Chamber of Commerce ☎ *503/842–7525* ⊕ *www.GoTillamook. com.*

EXPLORING

FAMILY **Tillamook Cheese Factory.** In high season, hundreds of visitors stop by the largest cheese-making plant on the West Coast to watch the cheese-making process, enjoy free samples, and order delicious ice cream (try the marionberry) from the on-site parlor. Here the rich milk from the area's thousands of Holstein and brown Swiss cows becomes ice cream, butter, and cheddar and Monterey Jack cheeses. The self-guided cheese-making tours don't allow much interaction—you view the operations from a glassed-in mezzanine, but they're free. The store carries a variety of other specialty-food products, including smoked meats, chocolates, jams, and honeys. ⊠ *4175 U.S. 101 N* ☎ *503/815–1300, 800/542–7290* ⊕ *www.tillamookcheese.com* ⌦ *Free* ☉ *Labor Day–mid-June, daily 8–6; mid-June–Labor Day, daily 8–8.*

WHERE TO EAT

$$ ✗ **Roseanna's Cafe.** In a rustic 1915 building on the beach, this café is
SEAFOOD right opposite Three Arch Rock, a favorite resting spot for sea lions and puffins. The calm of the beach is complemented in the evening by candlelight and fresh flowers. The menu includes halibut or salmon cooked half a dozen ways, baked oysters, and Gorgonzola seafood pasta, and the meal's not complete without marionberry cobbler. ⑤ *Average main: $21* ⊠ *1490 Pacific Ave., Oceanside* ☎ *503/842–7351* ⊕ *www.roseannascafe.com.*

SPORTS AND THE OUTDOORS

The **Three Capes Loop**, an enchanting 35-mile byway off U.S. 101, winds along the coast between Tillamook and Pacific City, passing three distinctive headlands—Cape Meares, Cape Lookout, and Cape Kiwanda. Bayocean Road heading west from Tillamook passes what was the thriving resort town of Bayocean, which washed into the sea more than 30 years ago. A road still crosses the levee to Bayocean, and along the beach on the other side you can find the remnants of an old hotel to the north. The panoramic views from the north end of the peninsula are worth the walk. A warm and windless road returns hikers on the bay side.

Cape Kiwanda State Natural Area. Huge waves pound the jagged sandstone cliffs and caves here, and the much-photographed, 327-foot-high **Haystack Rock** (not to be confused with the 235-foot-tall rock of the same name up in Cannon Beach) juts out of the Pacific Ocean to the south. Surfers ride some of the longest waves on the coast, hang gliders soar above the shore, and beachcombers explore tidal pools and take in unparalleled ocean views. ⊠ *Cape Kiwanda Dr., 1 mile north* *of Pacific City, Pacific City* ☎ *503/842–3182* ⊕ *www.oregonstateparks. org* ✉ *Free* ⊙ *Daily sunrise–sunset.*

Fodor's Choice ★ **Cape Lookout State Park.** Located about 8 miles south of the beach town Netarts, this park includes a moderately easy (though often muddy) 2-mile trail—marked on the highway as "wildlife viewing area"—that leads through giant spruces, western red cedars, and hemlocks, and ends with views of Cascade Head to the south and Cape Meares to the north. Wildflowers, more than 150 species of birds, and occasional whales throughout the summer months make this trail a favorite with nature lovers. The section of the park just north of the trail comprises a long, curving stretch of beach with picnic areas and campsites. ⊠ *Cape Lookout Rd. at Netarts Bay Rd.* ☎ *503/842–4981* ⊕ *www.oregonstateparks. org* ✉ *Day use $5* ⊙ *Daily dawn–dusk.*

Cape Meares State Park. On the northern tip of the Three Capes Loop is Cape Meares State Park. The restored **Cape Meares Lighthouse,** built in 1890 and open to the public April through October, provides a sweeping view over the cliff to the caves and sea lion rookery on the rocks below. A many-trunked Sitka spruce known as the Octopus Tree grows near the lighthouse parking lot. ⊠ *3500 Cape Meares Loop, 10 miles west of Tillamook, Oceanside* ☎ *503/842–3182* ⊕ *www.oregonstateparks. org* ✉ *Free* ⊙ *Park daily dawn–dusk. Lighthouse Apr.–Oct., daily 11–4.*

PACIFIC CITY

24 miles south of Tillamook.

There's a lot to like about Pacific City, not the least of which is that it's 3 miles off Oregon's busy coastal highway, U.S. 101. That means there's no backup at the town's only traffic light—a blinking-red, four-way stop in the center of town. There's just the quiet, happy ambience of a town whose 1,000-or-so residents live the good life in the midst of extraordinary beauty. There are a few notable dining and hotel options here, along with some wonderful opportunities for recreation. The beach at Pacific City is one of the few places in the state where fishing dories (flat-bottom boats with high, flaring sides) are launched directly into the surf instead of from harbors or docks. Pacific City's windy climes tend to keep even the summer months quieter than most.

GETTING HERE AND AROUND
Between Tillamook and Lincoln City, the unincorporated village of Pacific City is just off U.S. 101 on the south end of the beautiful Three Capes Loop. It is a two-hour drive from Portland on U.S. 26 to Highway 6, or a 75-minute drive from Salem via Highway 22.

ESSENTIALS
Visitor Information Pacific City-Nestucca Valley Chamber of Commerce ☎ *503/392–4340* ⊕ *www.pcnvchamber.org.*

WHERE TO EAT AND STAY

$ ✕ **Grateful Bread Bakery & Restaurant.** This airy and bright café uses
CAFÉ the cod caught by the local dories for its fish-and-chips. Everything it
FAMILY makes is fresh and from scratch, including delicious breads, pastries,

breakfasts, and pizzas. $ *Average main: $9* ✉ *34805 Brooten Rd.* ☎ *503/965–7337* ◷ *Closed Tues. and Wed. No dinner.*

$$ ✕ **Pelican Pub & Brewery.** This beer lover's favorite stands on the ocean-
AMERICAN front by Haystack Rock. The microbrewery has garnered consider-
FAMILY able kudos for its beers, including the Kiwanda Cream Ale and deep, rich Tsunami Stout, while the pub excels with creative comfort fare. Many entrées are infused with house-made beverages, such as pale-malt-crusted salmon and the root-beer float. The pub periodically hosts Brewers Dinners—splendid affairs that pair beers with Scottish, Greek, Italian, and Belgian cooking. Kids love the gourmet pizzas and children's menu. $ *Average main: $17* ✉ *33180 Cape Kiwanda Dr.* ☎ *503/965–7007* ⊕ *www.yourlittlebeachtown.com/pelican.*

$$$$ ⊞ **Cottages at Cape Kiwanda.** For a memorable resort experience with a
RENTAL glorious beach view, this complex has 18 units for rent that can sleep four or six people—perfect for families or that beach get-together with friends. **Pros:** upscale; comfortable; short walk from Pacific City eat-eries. **Cons:** the beach is lively, and tail-gating cars can be a fixture. $ *Rooms from: $299* ✉ *33000 Cape Kiwanda Dr.* ☎ *866/571–0605* ⊕ *www.kiwandacottages.com* ⤶ *18 rooms* ⦿ *No meals.*

$$$ ⊞ **Inn at Cape Kiwanda.** You won't find a weather-beaten beach cottage
RESORT here—each of the 35 deluxe, fireplace-warmed rooms has a gorgeous
FAMILY view of Haystack Rock. **Pros:** great views; light and contemporary rooms; terrific restaurants nearby. **Cons:** guests might get hit up with a sales pitch to buy a unit. $ *Rooms from: $219* ✉ *33105 Cape Kiwanda Dr.* ☎ *888/965–7001, 503/965–7001* ⊕ *www.yourlittlebeachtown.com/inn* ⤶ *33 rooms, 2 suites* ⦿ *No meals.*

SPORTS AND THE OUTDOORS

BEACHES

Fodor'sChoice **Pacific City beach.** The town's public beach sits between Cape Kiwanda
★ State Natural Area and Bob Straub State Park. Adjacent to Cape Kiwan-da's massive dune, it's a favorite for kids who often climb its bulk (by some estimates 500 feet) just for the thrill of sliding back down again. Hikers also get a thrill from the top, where the view opens on a tiny cove and tide pools below, and the walk down is infinitely easier than the climb. The beach is also popular with tailgaters—it's one of the few places on the Oregon Coast where it's legal to park your vehicle on the sand. Other parking is available off Cape Kiwanda Drive, near the Pelican Pub. For quieter outings, try the Bob Straub. **Amenities:** none. **Best for:** partiers; walking. ✉ *Cape Kiwanda Drive* ⊕ *www.pcnvchamber.org.*

RECREATIONAL AREAS

Fodor'sChoice **Bob Straub State Park.** An often sand-blasting walk along the flat white-
★ sand beach leads down to the mouth of the Nestucca River, considered by many to be the best fishing river on the north coast. The beach along the Pacific is frequently windy, but it's separated from the stiller, warmer side of the peninsula by high dunes. Multiple trails cross the dunes into a forest that leads to small beaches on the Nestucca. Relax here with a book, and easily find stillness and sunshine. It's possible to skip the Pacific stroll all together, and find trails to the Nestucca straight from the parking lot, but it's hard to resist the views from the top of the dunes

at the Bob Straub. If you choose the ocean side, pitch your beach-camp in the dunes, not the flat sand, and you'll find respite from the sometimes unrelenting wind. ⊠ *Sunset Dr., just south of where Pacific Ave. crosses river* ☎ *503/842–3182* ⊕ *www.oregonstateparks.org* ☒ *Free.*

CENTRAL COAST

This is Oregon's coastal playland, drawing families, shoppers, kite flyers, deep-sea fishing enthusiasts, surfers, and dune-shredding daredevils. Although it's a bit touristy and bisected by a rather tatty commercial stretch of U.S. 101, Lincoln City offers a wealth of shops devoted to souvenirs and knickknacks, and visitors can even blow their own glass float at a few local studios. Depoe Bay is popular for whale-watching excursions, and Newport is designated the Dungeness crab capital of the world. As you venture farther south, you'll roll through gorgeous and less developed Yachats and charming Florence to reach the iconic mountains of sand that fall within Oregon Dunes National Recreation Area. Even if you're not intent on making tracks in the sand, the dunes provide vast, unforgettable scenery.

LINCOLN CITY

16 miles south of Pacific City; 90 miles southwest of Portland.

Lincoln City is a captivating destination for families and lovers who want to share some time laughing on the beach, poking their fingers in tide pools, and trying to harness wind-bucking kites. Once a series of small villages, Lincoln City is a sprawling town without a center. But the endless tourist amenities make up for a lack of a small-coastal-town ambience. Clustered like barnacles on the offshore reefs are fast-food restaurants, gift shops, supermarkets, candy stores, antiques markets, dozens of motels and hotels, a factory-outlet mall, and a busy casino. Lincoln City is the most popular destination city on the Oregon Coast, but its only real geographic claim to fame is the 445-foot-long D River, stretching from its source in Devil's Lake to the Pacific; *Guinness World Records* lists the D as the world's shortest river.

GETTING HERE AND AROUND

Lincoln City is a two-hour drive from Portland on Highway 99W and Highway 18, and a 2½-hour drive south of Astoria along coastal U.S. 101.

ESSENTIALS

Visitor Information Lincoln City Visitors & Convention Bureau ⊠ *801 S.W. U.S. 101, Suite 401* ☎ *541/996–1274, 800/452–2151* ⊕ *www.oregoncoast.org.*

WHERE TO EAT

$$$$
PACIFIC
NORTHWEST
✕ **Bay House.** Inside a charming bungalow, this restaurant serves meals to linger over while you enjoy views across sunset-gilded Siletz Bay. The seasonal Pacific Northwest cuisine includes Dungeness crab cakes with roasted-chili chutney, fresh halibut Parmesan, and roast duckling with cranberry compote. Naturally, there's lamb, pork, and tasty fillets. There's lighter fare available in the lounge. The wine list is extensive,

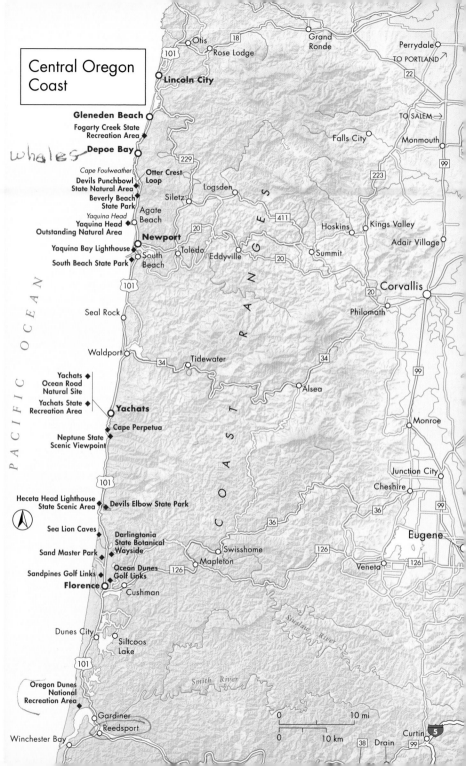

and the service impeccable. $ *Average main: $33* ✉ *5911 S.W. U.S. 101* ☎ *541/996–3222* ⊕ *www.thebayhouse.org* ⊙ *Closed Mon. and Tues. No lunch.*

$ ✕ **Beach Dog Café.** These are darn good dogs, dressed about 20 differ-
AMERICAN   ent ways. You'll find everything from Coney, Philly, and Kosher to Hot
Fodor'sChoice   Diggity. There's also a galaxy of dog photos adorning the walls of this
★   family-owned joint and its breakfasts have the morning crowds gathering. Roger and Sonja Seals offer a menu full of hearty potato dishes, scrambles, stuffed French toast, and delicious breakfast sandwiches. The apple potato pancake with sour cream and a Polish sausage is the keystone to any nutritious breakfast. $ *Average main: $9* ✉ *6042 S.E. U.S. 101* ☎ *541/996–3647* ▭ *No credit cards* ⊙ *Closed Mon. and Tues. No dinner.*

$$ ✕ **Blackfish Café.** Owner and chef Rob Pounding serves simple-but-
SEAFOOD   succulent dishes that blend fresh ingredients from local fishermen and
Fodor'sChoice   gardeners. Before starting his own restaurant in 1999, Pounding was
★   the executive chef of acclaimed Salishan Lodge for nearly 15 years, winning top national culinary awards. His skillet-roasted, "ocean trolled" chinook salmon, basted with fennel lime butter, and Oregon blue-cheese potatoes are flavorful and perfect. The Blackfish Ding Dong dessert, with mixed-berry sauce and whipped cream, is the best way to finish a meal. $ *Average main: $20* ✉ *2733 N.W. U.S. 101* ☎ *541/996–1007* ⊕ *www.blackfishcafe.com* ⊙ *Closed Tues.*

WHERE TO STAY

$ ⊡ **Coho Oceanfront Lodge.** Set on a romantic cliff, the renovated Coho is
HOTEL   a perfect hybrid of family-friendly lodging and a quiet, intimate hide-
FAMILY   away for couples. **Pros:** great value; family-friendly; lots of nice in-room
Fodor'sChoice   amenities. **Cons:** no restaurant. $ *Rooms from: $117* ✉ *1635 N.W.*
★   *Harbor Ave.* ☎ *541/994–3684* ⊕ *www.thecoholodge.com* ⤳ *33 studios, 32 suites* ⦿ *Breakfast.*

$ ⊡ **Historic Anchor Inn.** This quirky bungalow might not be for everyone,
B&B/INN   but for those who appreciate a warm, spirited inn with a decidedly inventive and whimsical touch, this is a remarkable find. **Pros:** a memorable, truly unique property; everything you need to explore Lincoln City. **Cons:** not on the beach; very quirky and rustic. $ *Rooms from: $89* ✉ *4417 S.W. U.S. 101* ☎ *541/996–3810* ⊕ *www.historicanchorinn. com* ⤳ *19 rooms* ⦿ *Breakfast.*

$$$ ⊡ **Inn at Spanish Head.** Driving up to this upscale resort hotel, you'd
RESORT   think it might be a fairly intimate place, but on further investigation you'll see that the property takes up the entire side of a bluff like a huge staircase. **Pros:** sweeping views of the ocean through floor-to-ceiling windows; good restaurant; easy beach access via elevator; great place to watch winter storms. **Cons:** pricey; isolated setting not within walking distance of many restaurants or shops. $ *Rooms from: $209* ✉ *4009 S.E. U.S. 101* ☎ *541/996–2161, 800/452–8127* ⊕ *www.spanishhead. com* ⤳ *68 rooms, 52 suites* ⦿ *Some meals.*

NIGHTLIFE

Chinook Winds Casino Resort. Oregon's only beachfront casino has a great variety of slot machines, blackjack, poker, keno, and off-track betting. The Rogue River Steakhouse serves a great fillet and terrific appetizers.

There's also the Siletz Bay Buffet, the Chinook Seafood Grill, a snack bar, and a lounge. An arcade keeps the kids busy while you are on the gambling floor. Big-name entertainers perform in the showroom. Players can take a break from the tables and enjoy a round of golf at the Chinook Winds Golf Resort next door. ☒ *1777 N.W. 44th St.* ☎ *541/996–5825, 888/244–6665* ⊕ *www.chinookwindscasino.com.*

SHOPPING

Jennifer L. Sears Glass Art Studio. Blow a glass float or make a glorious glass starfish, heart, or fluted bowl of your own design (it costs $65 for a glass float). The studio's expert artisans will guide you every step of the way. It's a fun, memorable keepsake of the coast. ☒ *4821 S.W. U.S. 101* ☎ *541/996–2569* ⊕ *www.jennifersearsglassart.com.*

Lincoln City Surf Shop. Darn right they surf on the Oregon Coast. Maybe the surfers are dressed from head to toe in wet suits, but they're riding some tasty waves just the same. At Lincoln City's oldest surf shop, there's equipment and apparel for purchase or rent. Lessons provide a great family activity, and rates include board, wet suits, hood, and booties. The shop also has a collection of kiteboards, skimboards, and skateboards. ☒ *4792 S.E. U.S. 101* ☎ *541/996–7433* ⊕ *www. lcsurfshop.com.*

SPORTS AND THE OUTDOORS

BOATING

Devil's Lake State Recreation Area. Canoeing and kayaking are popular on this small lake just inland from the coast, also loved by coots, loons, ducks, cormorants, bald eagles, and grebes. Visitors can sign up in advance for popular kayaking tours in the summer, for which bird guides are provided. A campground has tent and RV sites as well as yurts. ☒ *N.E. 6th St., just east of U.S. 101* ☎ *541/994–2002, 800/551–6949* ⊕ *www.oregonstateparks.org* ☉ *Daily.*

OFF THE
BEATEN
PATH

Nature Conservancy Cascade Head Preserve and trail. This dense, green trail winds through a rain forest where 100-inch annual rainfalls nourish 250-year-old Sitka spruces, mosses, and ferns. Emerging from the forest, hikers come upon grassy and treeless Cascade Head, an undulating maritime prairie. There are magnificent views down to the Salmon River and east to the Coast Range. Continuing along the headland, black-tailed deer often graze and turkey vultures soar in the strong winds. You need to be in fairly good shape for the first and steepest part of the hike, which can be done in about an hour (it's a little over 4 miles round-trip). The 270-acre area has been named a United Nations Biosphere Reserve. The website has detailed driving directions to reach the preserve. ☒ *Savage Rd. at Headland Circle, 9 miles north of Lincoln City via U.S. 101, Otis* ⊕ *www.nature.org* ☒ *Free* ☉ *Upper trail closed Jan.–mid-July.*

GLENEDEN BEACH

7 miles south of Lincoln City.

Gleneden Beach is a small vacation town known primarily for the famed Salishan Resort, which is perched high above placid Siletz Bay. This expensive collection of guest rooms, vacation homes, condominiums, restaurants, golf fairways, tennis courts, and covered walkways blends into a forest preserve; if not for the signs, you'd scarcely be able to find it.

GETTING HERE AND AROUND

Little Gleneden Beach is a 10-minute drive south of Lincoln City via U.S. 101.

ESSENTIALS

Visitor Information **Discover Newport** ✉ *555 S.W. Coast Hwy., Newport* ☎ *541/265–8801, 800/262–7844* ⊕ *www.discovernewport.com.*

EXPLORING

Lawrence Gallery at Salishan. The well-respected gallery has an informed staff that will guide you through the collections of work by Northwest artists, including paintings (pastels, oils, and watercolors), glassworks, bronze and metal, furniture, and ceramics and porcelain. ✉ *7755 N. U.S. 101* ☎ *541/764–2318, 800/764–2318* ⊕ *www.lawrencegallery.net.*

WHERE TO EAT AND STAY

$$$ ✕ **Side Door Café.** This dining room, set in an old brick and tile factory
PACIFIC with a high ceiling, exposed beams, a fireplace, and many windows,
NORTHWEST shares its space with Eden Hall performance venue. The menu changes often—fresh preparations have included mushroom-crusted rack of lamb and broiled swordfish with citrus-raspberry vinaigrette over coconut-ginger basmati rice. ⑤ *Average main: $27* ✉ *6675 Gleneden Beach Loop Rd.* ☎ *541/764–3825* ⊕ *www.sidedoorcafe.com* ☽ *Closed Mon. and Tues.*

$ ⬚ **Beachcombers Haven vacation rentals.** This cluster of properties is right
RENTAL off the beach, and features spacious one-, two-, or three-bedroom accommodations, some with a hot tub or in-room Jacuzzi. **Pros:** very friendly; well-furnished units with full kitchens; near the beach. **Cons:** not especially fancy; two-night minimum. ⑤ *Rooms from: $149* ✉ *7045 N.W. Glen* ☎ *541/764–2252, 800/428–5533* ⊕ *www.beachcombershaven. com* ⊐ *14 homes* ⑩ *No meals.*

$$$ ⬚ **Salishan Lodge and Golf Resort.** Secluded and refined, this upscale resort
RESORT in a hillside forest preserve has long been revered as a luxury weekend getaway as well as a destination for tony corporate retreats, with plenty of reasons to stay on the property. **Pros:** very elegant; secluded resort with a terrific golf course; plenty of activities on the property. **Cons:** ocean views are few; service a bit hit-or-miss. ⑤ *Rooms from: $209* ✉ *7760 N. U.S. 101* ☎ *541/764–3600, 800/452–2300* ⊕ *www.salishan. com* ⊐ *205 rooms* ⑩ *No meals.*

SPORTS AND THE OUTDOORS

GOLF

Salishan Golf Resort. With a layout designed by Peter Jacobsen, this par-71 course is a year-round treat for hackers and aficionados alike. The front nine holes are surrounded by a forest of old-growth timber, while the back nine holes provide old-school, links-style play. There's an expansive pro shop and a great bar and grill for relaxing after a "rough" day out on the links. ✉ *7760 N. U.S. 101* ☎ *541/764–3600, 800/452–2300* ⊕ *www.salishan.com* ⊠ *$119 on summer weekends.*

Salishan Golf Resort, Gleneden Beach

DEPOE BAY

5 miles south of Gleneden Beach.

Depoe Bay calls itself the whale-watching capital of the world. The small town was founded in the 1920s and named in honor of Charles DePoe of the Siletz tribe, who was named for his employment at a U.S. Army depot in the late 1800s. With a narrow channel and deep water, its tiny harbor is also one of the most protected on the coast. It supports a thriving fleet of commercial and charter fishing boats. The Spouting Horn, a natural cleft in the basalt cliffs on the waterfront, blasts seawater skyward during heavy weather.

GETTING HERE AND AROUND

Depoe Bay lies right between Newport and Lincoln City along U.S. 101—it's a 20-minute drive to either town.

ESSENTIALS

Visitor Information Depoe Bay Chamber of Commerce ✉ *223 S.W. U.S. 101, Suite B* ☎ *541/765–2889, 877/485–8348* ⊕ *www.depoebaychamber.org.*

WHERE TO EAT AND STAY

$$$

PACIFIC NORTHWEST

Fodor'sChoice

★

✕ **Restaurant Beck.** Immensely talented chef-owner Justin Wills presents a short but memorable menu of creatively prepared, modern, Pacific Northwest cuisine each night in this romantic, contemporary dining room at the Whale Cove Inn. The menu changes regularly, with chef Wills sourcing largely from local farms, ranches, and fisheries. You might start with jasmine-tea-cured tuna crudo with jalapeño, citrus, garlic chips, and finger lime, followed by local rockfish served beside a bed of cannellini beans and bacon with grilled-kale-and-pine-nut pesto. Save room for dessert;

it's impressive here, with the Meyer lemon–and-almond pancake with figs, Italian plums, and honey-yogurt ice cream a particular standout. There are also great views from the large windows overlooking the cove and the Pacific. $ *Average main: $29* ⊠ *Whale Cove Inn, 2345 U.S. 101* ☎ *541/765–3220* ⊕ *www.restaurantbeck.com* ⊘ *No lunch.*

$$
B&B/INN

The Harbor Lights Inn. This bed-and-breakfast overlooking tiny Depoe Bay Harbor provides a dreamy setting for watching boats and relaxing in a quaint atmosphere. **Pros:** small, quiet, and pretty; great breakfasts. **Cons:** on the water of the bay but no beach. $ *Rooms from: $139* ⊠ *235 S.E. Bay View Ave.* ☎ *541/765–2322, 800/228–0448* ⊕ *www.theharborlightsinn.com* ↘ *13 rooms* ⧍ *Breakfast.*

$$$$
B&B/INN
Fodor's Choice
★

Whale Cove Inn. This small and exquisitely decorated inn overlooks the picturesque cove for which it's named and contains just eight spacious suites, each with a dazzling view of the water. **Pros:** astoundingly good restaurant; stunning building with cushy and spacious suites; fine ocean views. **Cons:** not a good fit for kids (only those 16 and over are permitted); quite pricey; not within walking distance of town. $ *Rooms from: $425* ⊠ *2345 U.S. 101* ☎ *541/765–4300, 800/628–3409* ⊕ *www.whalecoveinn.com* ↘ *8 suites* ⧍ *Breakfast.*

SPORTS AND THE OUTDOORS

RECREATIONAL AREAS

Fogarty Creek State Recreation Area. Bird-watching and viewing the tidal pools are the key draws here, but hiking and picnicking are also popular at this park found along U.S. 101. Wooden footbridges wind through the dense forest and tall cliffs rise above the beach. ⊠ *U.S. 101, 3 miles north of Depoe Bay* ☎ *800/551–6949, 541/265–4560* ⊕ *www.oregonstateparks.org* ⧂ *Free* ⊘ *Daily.*

NEWPORT

12 miles south of Depoe Bay.

Called the Dungeness crab capital of the world, Newport offers accessible beaches, a popular aquarium, the coast's premier performing-arts center, and a significant supply of both elegant and affordable accommodations and restaurants. Newport exists on two levels: the highway above, threading its way through the community's main business district, and the old Bayfront along Yaquina Bay below (watch for signs on U.S. 101). With its high-masted fishing fleet, well-worn buildings, seafood markets, art galleries, and touristy shops, Newport's Bayfront is an ideal place for an afternoon stroll. So many male sea lions in Yaquina Bay loiter near crab pots and bark from the waterfront piers that locals call the area the Bachelor Club. Visit the docks to buy fresh seafood or rent a kayak to explore the bay. In 2010 Newport was designated the National Oceanic and Atmospheric Administration's (NOAA) Pacific Marine Operations Center and a $38 million, 5-acre facility (and a port for four ships) opened a year later.

GETTING HERE AND AROUND

Newport is a 2½-hour drive from Portland by way of Interstate 5 south to Albany and U.S. 20 west; the town is a 40-minute drive south along U.S. 101 from Lincoln City, and a 75-minute drive north of Florence.

ESSENTIALS

Visitor Information Destination Newport ✉ *555 S.W. Coast Hwy.*
☎ *503/262–8801, 800/262–7844* ⊕ *www.discovernewport.com.*

TOURS

Marine Discovery Tours. Sealife cruises, departing throughout the day, are conducted on a 65-foot excursion boat *Discovery*, with inside seating for 49 people and two viewing levels. The cruise season is March through October. ✉ *345 S.W. Bay Blvd.* ☎ *800/903–2628, 541/265–6200* ⊕ *www.marinediscovery.com* 🎫 *From $36.*

EXPLORING

FAMILY **Hatfield Marine Science Center.** Interactive and interpretive exhibits at Oregon State University appeal to the kid in everyone. More than just showcasing sea life, the center contains exhibits and holds classes that teach the importance of scientific research in managing and sustaining coastal and marine resources. The staff regularly leads guided tours of the adjoining estuary. ✉ *2030 S. Marine Science Dr.* ☎ *541/867–0100* ⊕ *www.hmsc.oregonstate.edu* 🎫 *$5 suggested donation* ☉ *Memorial Day–Labor Day, daily 10–5; Labor Day–Memorial Day, Thurs.–Mon. 10–4.*

FAMILY **Oregon Coast Aquarium.** This 4½-acre complex brings visitors face to face with the creatures living in offshore and near-shore Pacific marine habitats: frolicking sea otters, colorful puffins, pulsating jellyfish, and even a 60-pound octopus. There's a hands-on interactive area for children, including tide pools perfect for "petting" sea anemones and urchins. The aquarium houses one of North America's largest seabird aviaries, including glowering turkey vultures. Permanent exhibits include *Passages of the Deep*, where visitors walk through a 200-foot underwater tunnel with 360-degree views of sharks, wolf eels, halibut, and a truly captivating array of sea life. Large coho salmon and sturgeon can be viewed in a naturalistic setting through a window wall 9-feet high and 20-feet wide. The sherbet-colored nettles are hypnotizing. ✉ *2820 S.E. Ferry Slip Rd.* ☎ *541/867–3474* ⊕ *www.aquarium.org* 🎫 *$19.95* ☉ *Summer, daily 9–6; winter, daily 10–5.*

FAMILY **Yaquina Head Lighthouse.** The tallest lighthouse on the Oregon Coast has been blinking its beacon since its head keeper first walked up its 114 steps to light the wicks on the evening of August 20, 1873. Next to the 93-foot tower is an interpretive center. Bring your camera and call ahead to confirm tour times. ✉ *N.W. Lighthouse Dr., off U.S. 101, 4 miles north of Newport* ☎ *541/574–3100* ⊕ *www.yaquinalights.org* 🎫 *Free. Donations suggested* ☉ *Thurs.–Tues. noon–3.*

WHERE TO EAT

$$
SEAFOOD
FAMILY
Fodor's Choice
★

✕ **Georgie's Beachside Grill.** This stand-alone restaurant for the Hallmark Inns and Resorts serves up some wonderfully innovative dishes. From the sea scallops blackened in house-mixed herbs to coconut shrimp in pineapple salsa with chili slaw, the food here lives up to the ocean view. Local ingredients are frequently mixed with tropical ones like the Dungeness crab cakes topped in mango salsa, and the plates are often layered—the bed of honey mustard-romaine is dressed apart from the blueberry barbecued salmon that lands on top. On the oceanside of Newport, Georgie's is one of few places in town with ocean views.

Oregon Coast Aquarium, Newport

Windows line a half-moon of table seating, and tiered booths mean even the back of the room has decent views. Georgie's is also extremely popular for its breakfasts. ⑤ *Average main: $19* ✉ *744 S.W. Elizabeth St.* ☎ *503/265–9800, 888/448–4449* ⊕ *www.georgiesbeachsidegrill.com.*

$$
SEAFOOD
FAMILY
Fodor's Choice
★

✕ **Local Ocean Seafoods.** At this fish market and sleek grill on picturesque Yaquina Bay, the operators purchase fish directly from more than 60 boats in the fishing fleet right outside and take the mission of locally sourced, sustainable seafood seriously. This is also one of few restaurants on the Oregon Coast that doesn't own a deep fryer—even the fish-and-chips are panfried. The menu includes such fish-lovers' fare as tuna mignon (bacon-wrapped albacore with pan-seared vegetables), panko-buttermilk-crusted oysters, and Fishwives Stew—a tomato broth stew loaded with both shell- and finfish, but come early, because it closes at 8 pm (9 in summer). From the bustling interior, there are views through windowed garage doors that roll up in summer. Those tempted to take home more than a doggie bag can dive into the fish case, where house-smoked offerings include a rare smoked black cod, and every fish comes with details about the boat that caught it. ⑤ *Average main: $20* ✉ *213 S.E. Bay Blvd.* ☎ *514/574–7959* ⊕ *www.localocean.net.*

$
CAFÉ

✕ **Panini Bakery.** The owner, who operates this local favorite bakery and espresso bar, prides himself on hearty and home-roasted meats, hand-cut breads, and friendly service. The coffee's organic, the eggs free-range, the orange juice fresh-squeezed, and just about everything is made from scratch. Take a seat inside, or, in good weather, streetside tables are a great place to view the Nye Beach scene. The café closes at 7 pm. ⑤ *Average main: $10* ✉ *232 N.W. Coast Hwy.* ☎ *541/265–5033* ▭ *No credit cards.*

WHERE TO STAY

$$$
HOTEL
Fodor's Choice
★

🏨 **Inn at Nye Beach.** With a prime beachfront location in the historic Nye Beach section of Newport, this chic, eco-friendly, boutique hotel contains 22 rooms and suites. **Pros:** direct beach access and great views; smartly furnished; contemporary rooms. **Cons:** the complimentary breakfast is very limited (a full one costs extra); views not great from some rooms. 💲 *Rooms from: $209* ✉ *729 N.W. Coast St.* ☎ *541/265–2477, 800/480–2477* ⊕ *www.innatnyebeach.com* ⤴ *6 rooms, 16 suites* ⦿|*Breakfast.*

$
B&B/INN

🏨 **Newport Belle B&B.** This fully operational stern-wheeler is permanently moored at the Newport Marina, where guests have front-row seats to all the boating activity around Yaquina Bay. **Pros:** one-of-a-kind lodging experience; great harbor views. **Cons:** not suitable for kids; need a car to get into town. 💲 *Rooms from: $150* ✉ *Dock H, 2126 S.E. Marine Science Dr.* ☎ *541/867–6290* ⊕ *www.newportbelle.com* ⤴ *5 rooms* ⊙ *Closed Nov.–early Feb.* ⦿|*Breakfast.*

$
HOTEL

🏨 **Sylvia Beach Hotel.** Make reservations far in advance for this 1913-vintage beachfront hotel, where reading, writing, and conversation eclipse technological hotel-room isolation. **Pros:** distinctive decor; great place to disconnect. **Cons:** no TV, telephone, or Internet access; sharing tables with other guests at mealtimes doesn't suit everyone; least expensive rooms don't have ocean views. 💲 *Rooms from: $115* ✉ *267 N.W. Cliff St.* ☎ *541/265–5428, 888/795–8422* ⊕ *www.sylviabeachhotel.com* ⤴ *20 rooms* ⦿|*Breakfast.*

NIGHTLIFE AND THE PERFORMING ARTS

Fodor's Choice
★

Newport Symphony Orchestra. The only year-round, professional symphony orchestra on the Oregon Coast plays at the 400-seat Newport Performing Arts Center, just a few steps away from the seashore in Nye Beach. Adam Flatt is the music director and conductor, and actor and narrator David Ogden Stiers serves as associate conductor. The orchestra performs a popular series of concerts in the Newport Performing Arts Center September through May, and special events in the summer, including its popular free community concert every July 4. ✉ *777 W. Olive St.* ☎ *541/574–0614* ⊕ *www.newportsymphony.org.*

SPORTS AND THE OUTDOORS

RECREATIONAL AREAS

Beverly Beach State Park. Seven miles north of Newport, this beachfront park extends from Yaquina Head, where you can see the lighthouse, to the headlands of Otter Rock. It's a great place to fly a kite, surf the waves, or hunt for fossils. The campground is well equipped, with a wind-protected picnic area and a yurt meeting hall. ✉ *N.E. Beverly Dr., off U.S. 101, 6 miles north of Newport* ☎ *541/265–9278, 800/551–6949* ⊕ *www.oregonstateparks.org* ▦ *Free* ⊙ *Daily.*

Devil's Punchbowl State Natural Area. A rocky shoreline separates the day-use area from the surf. It's a popular whale-watching site and has excellent tidal pools. ✉ *1st St., off U.S. 101, 8 miles north of Newport, Otter Rock* ☎ *541/265–4560, 800/551–6949* ⊕ *www.oregonstateparks.org* ▦ *Free* ⊙ *Daily.*

Yaquina Head Outstanding Natural Area. Thousands of birds—cormorants, gulls, common murres, pigeon guillemots—make their home just beyond shore on Pinnacle and Colony rocks, and nature trails wind through fields of sea grass and wildflowers, leading to spectacular views. There is also an interpretive center and the historic Yaquina Head Lighthouse. ✉ *750 N.W. Lighthouse Dr.* ☎ *541/574–3100* ⊕ *www.yaquinalights. org* 🕮 *Free; donations suggested* ⊙ *Interpretive center June–early Sept., daily 9–4:30; mid-Sept.–May, daily 10–4:30.*

YACHATS

24 miles south of Newport.

The small town of Yachats (pronounced "yah-*hots*") is at the mouth of the Yachats River, and from its rocky shoreline, which includes the highest point on the Oregon Coast, trails lead to beaches and dozens of tidal pools. A relaxed alternative to the more touristy communities to the north, Yachats has all the coastal pleasures without the traffic: B&Bs and oceanfront hotels, some terrific restaurants, deserted beaches, tidal pools, surf-pounded crags, fishing, and crabbing.

GETTING HERE AND AROUND

Yachats lies between Newport and Florence on coastal U.S. 101—it's a 40-minute drive from either town, and a three-hour drive via Interstate 5 and Highway 34 from Portland.

ESSENTIALS

Visitor Information Yachats Visitors Center ✉ *241 U.S. 101* ☎ *800/929–0477* ⊕ *www.yachats.org.*

WHERE TO EAT

$ 　✕ **Bread and Roses Baking.** Artisan breads are handmade in small batches
BAKERY 　here, along with pastries, muffins, scones, cookies, cinnamon rolls, and desserts. In the bright, yellow-cottage bakery you can also try the daily soup and sandwiches at lunchtime, or just while away the morning with pastries and good coffee. It's a couple of blocks from Yachats State Recreation Area and across the road from Yachats Commons Park. ■TIP➜ Let the kids out to play in the park, then settle in here for lunch. ⑤ *Average main: $10* ✉ *238 4th St.* ☎ *541/547–4454* ⊙ *No dinner.*

$$ 　✕ **The Drift Inn.** This restaurant is a terrific find, with the best fresh razor
SEAFOOD 　clams on the coast. Each night a musician plays to the crowd that sits
Fodor'sChoice 　below a ceiling full of umbrellas, with views of the Yachats River where
★ 　it meets the ocean. Family-friendly and lively, the Drift Inn features fresh seafood, juicy steaks, and other local meats and produce. The bar stools are usually crowded, and there's a great selection of Oregon craft brews and wines. ⑤ *Average main: $18* ✉ *124 U.S. 101 N* ☎ *541/547–4477* ⊕ *www.the-drift-inn.com.*

$ 　✕ **Luna Sea Fish House.** The freshest Dungeness crab around is one of the
SEAFOOD 　seasonal attractions in this small weathered restaurant, coming straight from owner Robert Anthony's boat—he catches much of the fish served here using sustainable hook-and-kind methods for salmon, cod, and albacore tuna. And in season, he pots the crab seen bubbling in outdoor

kettles. Diners often eat family style here, bellied up to a few colorful tables. Fish-and-chips of all stripes, including clam and salmon, are served, but the fish tacos and a sinful dish called slumgullion—chowder baked with cheese and bay shrimp—are the most popular choices. The house special adds three cheeses to a bowl of thick, rich clam chowder, then tops it off with bay shrimp. You can also buy fresh fish here. ⑤ *Average main: $12 ⊠ 153 N.W. U.S. 101 ☎ 541/547–4794, 888/547–4794 ⊕ www.lunaseafishhouse.com.*

WHERE TO STAY

$$

HOTEL

Fodor'sChoice

★

🛏 **Overleaf Lodge.** On a rocky shoreline at the north end of Yachats, this is a romantic place to enjoy a spectacular sunset in splendid comfort. **Pros:** best hotel in one of the coast's best communities; on-site full-service spa. **Cons:** no restaurant; exercise room is small; a bit of a walk from the action. ⑤ *Rooms from: $200 ⊠ 280 Overleaf Lodge La. ☎ 541/547–4885, 800/338–0507 ⊕ www.overleaflodge.com ⇦ 54 rooms, 4 suites ⦿ Breakfast.*

SPORTS AND THE OUTDOORS

RECREATIONAL AREAS

Cape Perpetua Scenic Area. The highest lookout point on the Oregon Coast, Cape Perpetua towers 800 feet above the rocky shoreline. Named by Captain Cook on St. Perpetua's Day in 1778, the cape is part of a 2,700-acre scenic area popular with hikers, campers, beachcombers, and naturalists. General information and a map of several trails are available at the **Cape Perpetua Visitors Center,** on the east side of the highway, 2 miles south of Devil's Churn. The easy 1-mile **Giant Spruce Trail** passes through a fern-filled rain forest to an enormous 500-year-old Sitka spruce. Easier still is the marked Auto Tour; it begins about 2 miles north of the visitor center and winds through Siuslaw National Forest to the ¼-mile **Whispering Spruce Trail.** Views from the rustic rock shelter here extend 50 miles north to south, and some 40 miles out to sea. The **Cape Perpetua Interpretive Center,** in the visitor center, has educational movies and exhibits about the natural forces that shaped Cape Perpetua. ⊠ *2400 U.S. 101, 3 miles south of Yachats ☎ 541/547–3289 ⊕ www.fs.usda.gov/siuslaw ☒ Parking fee $5 ⊗ Visitors Center: summer, daily 10–5; winter, daily 10–4.*

Neptune State Scenic Viewpoint. Visitors have fun searching for animals, watching the surf, or hunting for agates. The benches set above the beach on the cliff provide a great view of Cumming Creek. It's also a terrific spot for whale-watching. At low tide, beachcombers have access to a natural cave and tidal pools. ⊠ *U.S. 101, 4 miles south of Yachats ☎ 800/551–6949, 541/547–3416 ⊕ www.oregonstateparks. org ☒ Free ⊗ Daily.*

Yachats State Recreation Area. The public beach in Yachats is more like the surface of the moon than most other places, and certainly most beaches. A wooden platform overlooks the coastline, where the waves roll in sideways and spash over the rocks at high tide. As is the case throughout most of the town, the beach itself is paralleled by an upland walking trail and dotted with picnic tables, benches, and interpretive signs. Visit to spot the sea lions that frequent this stretch of coast. Or join the intrepid beachcombers who climb the rocks for a closer look at tide pools populated by sea urchins, hermit crabs, barnacles, snails, and sea stars. **Amenities:** parking; toilets. **Best for:** walking; sunset. ⊠ *Ocean View Dr., off 2nd St. and U.S. 101* ☎ *800/551–6949, 541/867–7451* ⊕ *www.oregonstateparks.org.*

FLORENCE

25 miles south of Yachats; 64 miles west of Eugene.

Tourists and retirees have been flocking to Florence in ever-greater numbers in recent years. The restored riverfront Old Town has restaurants, antiques stores, fish markets, and other diversions, but what really makes the town so appealing is its proximity to remarkable stretches of coastline. Seventy-five creeks and rivers empty into the Pacific Ocean in and around Florence, and the Siuslaw River flows right through town. When the numerous nearby lakes are added to the mix, it makes for one of the richest fishing areas in Oregon. Salmon, rainbow trout, bass, perch, crabs, and clams are among the water's treasures. Fishing boats and pleasure crafts moor in Florence's harbor, forming a pleasant backdrop for the town's restored buildings. South of town, miles of white sand dunes lend themselves to everything from solitary hikes to rides aboard all-terrain vehicles.

GETTING HERE AND AROUND

It's a 75-minute drive west to Florence on Highway 126 from Eugene and a 40-minute drive south on U.S. 101 from Yachats. It takes about an hour to drive U.S. 101 south to Coos Bay, a stretch that takes in all of Oregon Dunes National Recreation Area.

ESSENTIALS

Visitor Information Florence Area Chamber of Commerce ⊠ *290 U.S. 101* ☎ *541/997–3128* ⊕ *www.florencechamber.com.*

EXPLORING

FAMILY   **Sea Lion Caves.** In 1880 a sea captain named Cox rowed a small skiff into a fissure in a 300-foot-high sea cliff. Inside, he was startled to discover a vaulted chamber in the rock, 125 feet high and 2 acres in size. Hundreds of massive sea lions—the largest bulls weighing 2,000 pounds or more—covered every available surface. Cox's discovery would become one of the Oregon Coast's premier attractions, if something of a tourist trap. An elevator near the cliff-top ticket office descends to the floor of the cavern, near sea level, where vast numbers of Steller's and California sea lions relax on rocks and swim about (their cute, fuzzy pups can be viewed from behind a wire fence). This is the only known hauling-out area and rookery for wild sea lions on the mainland in the Lower 48, and it's an awesome sight and sound. In spring and summer the mammals usually stay on the rocky ledges outside the cave; in fall and winter they move inside. You'll also see several species of seabirds here, including migratory pigeon guillemots, cormorants, and three varieties of gulls. Gray whales are visible during their northern and southern migrations, October–December and March–May. The gift shop has tasty fudge—try the jalapeño. ⊠ *91560 U.S. 101, 10 miles north of* *downtown Florence* ☎ *541/547–3111* ⊕ *www.sealioncaves.com* ⌲ *$12* ☉ *Daily 9–5.*

NEED A BREAK? **Siuslaw River Coffee Roasters.** This small, homey business serves cups of drip-on-demand coffee—you select the roast and they grind and brew it on the spot. Beans are roasted on-site, muffins and breads are freshly baked, and a view of the namesake river can be savored from the deck out back. It closes at 5 pm. ⊠ *1240 Bay St.* ☎ *541/997–3443* ⊕ *www.coffeeoregon.com.*

WHERE TO EAT AND STAY

$$
SEAFOOD
✕ **Bridgewater Fishhouse.** Freshly caught seafood—20 to 25 choices nightly—is the mainstay of this creaky-floored, Victorian-era restaurant in Florence's Old Town. Whether you opt for patio dining during summer or lounge seating in winter, the eclectic fare of pastas, burgers, salads, and seafood-packed stews is consistently well-prepared. A live jazz band provides some foot-tapping fun many evenings, and the sounds otherwise trend toward reggae and southern influence. For a light snack, try the peel-and-eat shrimp and a cup of chowder in the restaurant's stylish Zebra Lounge. ⑤ *Average main: $18* ⊠ *1297 Bay St.* ☎ *541/997–1133* ⊕ *www.bridgewaterfishhouse.com* ☉ *Closed Tues.*

$$
MODERN
AMERICAN
✕ **Homegrown Public House.** This bustling, intimate gastropub in Old Town Florence—a couple of blocks north of the riverfront—specializes in locally sourced, creatively prepared American fare and offers a well-chosen list of Oregon beers on tap, plus local spirits, iced teas, and kombucha. Stop by for lunch to enjoy the lightly battered albacore fish and hand-cut fries with tartar sauce, or a cheeseburger topped with Rogue blue and served with marinated vegetables and local greens. More substantial dinner options include grilled Carlton Farms pork loin over Parmesan polenta, and market fish of the day grilled over a bed of red quinoa, fennel, and arugula. An excellent brunch is served on Sunday. ⑤ *Average main: $17* ⊠ *294 Laurel St.* ☎ *541/997–4886* ⊕ *www.homegrownpub.com* ☉ *Closed Mon.*

$$
SEAFOOD
✕ **Waterfront Depot Restaurant and Bar.** The detailed chalkboard menu says it all: from the fresh, crab-encrusted halibut to Bill's Flaming Spanish Coffee, this is a place serious about fresh food and fine flavors. Located in the old Mapleton train station, the atmospheric tavern has a great view of the Siuslaw River and the Siuslaw River Bridge. In the summer diners can enjoy patio seating right at the water's edge and chomp on the nice variety of tapas plates. ⑤ *Average main: $17* ⊠ *1252 Bay St.* ☎ *541/902–9100* ⊕ *www.thewaterfrontdepot.com* ☉ *No lunch.*

$$$
B&B/INN
Fodor's Choice
★
📷 **Heceta Head Lighthouse B&B.** On a windswept promontory, this unusual late-Victorian property is one of Oregon's most remarkable bed-and-breakfasts, owned by the U.S. Forest Service and managed by two certified executive chefs. **Pros:** unique property with a magical setting; exceptionally good food. **Cons:** remote location; some rooms share a bath. ⑤ *Rooms from: $209* ⊠ *92072 U.S. 101, 12 miles north of Florence* ☎ *541/547–3696, 866/547–3696* ⊕ *www.hecetalighthouse. com* ⌲ *6 rooms, 4 with bath* ❍ *Breakfast.*

$
B&B/INN
📷 **River House Inn.** On the beautiful Siuslaw River, this property has terrific accommodations and is near quaint shops and restaurants in

Florence's Old Town. **Pros:** spacious rooms; great views from most rooms; close proximity to dining and shopping. **Cons:** not on the beach; interior style is a bit bland. ⑤ *Rooms from: $119* ✉ *1202 Bay St.* ☎ *541/997–3933, 888/824-2750* ⊕ *www.riverhouseflorence.com* ⇰ *40 rooms* �‖ *Breakfast.*

SPORTS AND THE OUTDOORS

RECREATIONAL AREAS

Fodor'sChoice
★
Heceta Head Lighthouse State Scenic Area. A ½-mile trail from the beachside parking lot leads to the oft-photographed Heceta Head Lighthouse built in 1894, whose beacon, visible for more than 21 miles, is the most powerful on the Oregon Coast. More than 7 miles of trails traverse the rocky landscape north and south of the lighthouse, which rises some 200 feet above the ocean. For a mesmerizing view of the lighthouse and Heceta Head, pull over at the scenic viewpoint just north of Sea Lion Caves. ✉ *U.S. 101, 11 miles north of Florence, Yachats* ☎ *541/547–3416, 800/551–6949* ⊕ *www.oregonstateparks.org* �️ *Day use $5, lighthouse tours free* ⊙ *Lighthouse tours daily 11–3.*

FAMILY
Fodor'sChoice
★
Oregon Dunes National Recreation Area. The Oregon Dunes National Recreation Area is the largest expanse of coastal sand dunes in North America, extending for 40 miles, from Florence to Coos Bay. The area contains some of the best ATV riding in the United States and encompasses some 31,500 acres. More than 1.5 million people visit the dunes each year, and about 350,000 are ATV users. Honeyman Memorial State Park, 522 acres within the recreation area, is a base camp for dune-buggy enthusiasts, mountain bikers, hikers, boaters, horseback riders, and dogsledders (the sandy hills are an excellent training ground). There's a campground, too. The dunes are a vast playground for children, particularly the slopes surrounding cool **Cleawox Lake.** If you have time for just a quick scamper in the sand, stop by the Oregon Dunes Overlook off U.S. 101, 11 miles south of Florence and 11 miles north of Reedsport—it's on the west side of the road, just north of Perkins Lake. ✉ *855 U.S. 101 (office), at Hwy. 38, Reedsport* ☎ *541/271–6000* ⊕ *www.fs.usda.gov/recarea/ siuslaw/recreation* �️ *Day use $5* ⊙ *Office hours Sept.–May, weekdays 8–4:30; Jun.–Aug., Mon.–Sat. 8–4:30.*

FAMILY
Fodor'sChoice
★
Sandland Adventures. This outfitter provides everything you need to get the whole family together for the ride of their lives. Start off with a heart-racing dune-buggy ride with a professional that will take you careening up, over, down, and around some of the steepest sand in the Oregon Dunes National Recreation Area. After you're done screaming and smiling, Sandland's park has bumper boats, a go-kart track, a miniature golf course, and a small railroad. ✉ *85366 U.S. 101* ☎ *541/997-8087* ⊕ *www.sandland.com.*

GOLF

Ocean Dunes Golf Links. A favorite of locals year-round, this course operated by Three Rivers Casino & Hotel is a straightforward 18 holes that reward great shots and penalize the poor ones. You won't find many sand bunkers, because the narrow course is surrounded by sand dunes. Instead, you'll encounter fairways winding about dunes lined with ball-swallowing gorse, heather, shore pines, and native sea grasses. Pot bunkers guard small greens, and play can get pretty frisky if the

Umpqua Sand Dunes in Oregon Dunes National Recreation Area

frequent wind picks up. However, the course is well drained and play-able—even under the wettest conditions. ⊠ *3345 Munsel Lake Rd.* ☎ *541/997–3232, 877/374–8377* ⊕ *www.threeriverscasino.com/golf* ✉ *Summer green fees $99.*

Sandpines Golf Links. This Scottish Links–style course is playable year-round. Designed by Rees Jones, the outward nine is cut out of pine forest and near blue lakes; and the inward nine provides some undulating fun, with the rolling dunes at the forefront from tee to green. While challenging, the course is generous enough to provide a great day on the links for beginners and more polished players. Sandpines has a fully equipped practice area with a driving range, bunkers, and putting greens. ⊠ *1201 35th St.* ☎ *800/917–4653, 541/997–1940* ⊕ *www.sandpines.com* ✉ *Summer greens fees $79.*

HORSEBACK RIDING

C & M Stables. Ride year-round along the Oregon Dunes National Recreation Area. The area is rich with marine life, including sea lions, whales, and coastal birds. Sharp-eyed riders also might spot bald eagles, red-tailed fox, and deer. Rides range from hour-long trots to half-day adventures. Children must be at least eight years old for the beach ride or six years old for the dune trail rides. ⊠ *90241 U.S. 101 N* ☎ *541/997–7540* ⊕ *www.oregonhorsebackriding.com* ✉ *From $60.*

SANDBOARDING

Sand Master Park. Everything you need to sandboard the park's private dunes is right here: board rental, wax, eyewear, clothing, and instruction. The staff is exceptionally helpful, and will get beginners off on their sandboarding adventure with enthusiasm. However, what must be surfed, must first be hiked up, and so on. ✉ *5351 U.S. 101* ☎ *541/997–6006* ⊕ *www.sandmasterpark.com.*

SOUTHERN COAST

Outdoors enthusiasts find a natural amusement park along this gorgeous stretch of coast from Reedsport to Brookings. The northern portion has a continuation of the Oregon Dunes National Recreation Area, and is the location of its visitor center. The Umpqua Discovery Center is a perfect trip with (or without) the kids, to learn about the region's history and animals. In Bandon golfers flock to one of the most celebrated clusters of courses in the nation at Bandon Dunes. Lovers of lighthouses, sailing, fishing, crabbing, elk viewing, camping, and water sports may wonder why they didn't venture south sooner.

BAY AREA: COOS BAY AND NORTH BEND

27 miles south of Reedsport on U.S. 101.

The Coos Bay–Charleston–North Bend metropolitan area, collectively known as the Bay Area (population 27,000), is the gateway to rewarding recreational experiences. The town of Coos Bay lies next to the largest natural harbor between San Francisco Bay and Seattle's Puget Sound. A century ago, vast quantities of lumber cut from the Coast Range were milled in Coos Bay and shipped around the world. Coos Bay still has a reputation as a rough-and-ready port city, but with mill closures and dwindling lumber reserves it is looking to tourism and other industries for economic growth.

To see the best of the Bay Area, head west from Coos Bay on Newmark Avenue for about 7 miles to **Charleston.** Though it's a Bay Area community, this quiet fishing village at the mouth of Coos Bay is a world unto itself. As it loops into town, the road becomes the Cape Arago Highway and leads to several stunning oceanfront parks.

GETTING HERE AND AROUND
The area lies along a slightly inland stretch of U.S. 101 that's a 40-minute drive south of Reedsport and a 30-minute drive north of Bandon; from the Umpqua Valley and Interstate 5 corridor, Coos Bay is just under two hours' drive west from Roseburg on Highway 42.

Southwest Oregon Regional Airport in North Bend has commercial flights from Portland and San Francisco.

ESSENTIALS
Visitor Information Coos Bay–North Bend Visitors & Convention Bureau ✉ *50 Central Ave.* ☎ *541/269–0215, 800/824–8486* ⊕ *www.oregonsadventurecoast.com.*

EXPLORING
Cape Arago Lighthouse. On a rock island just offshore from Charleston near Sunset Bay State Park, this lighthouse has had several iterations; the first lighthouse was built here in 1866, but it was destroyed by storms and erosion. A second, built in 1908, suffered the same fate. The current white tower, built in 1934, is 44 feet tall and towers 100

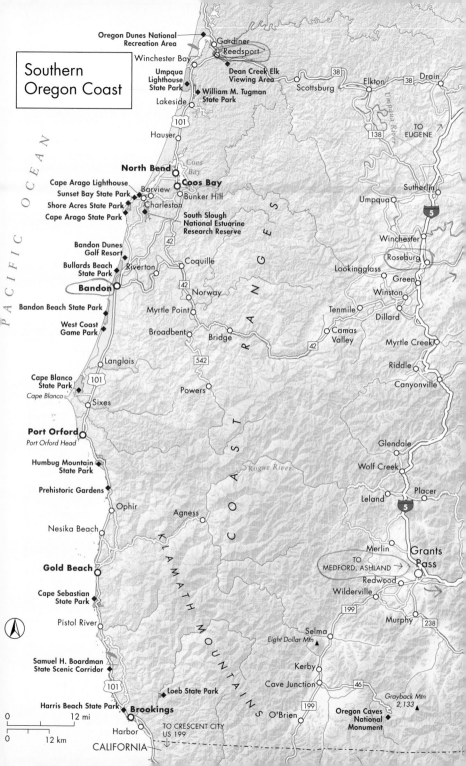

Southern Oregon Coast

PACIFIC OCEAN

Oregon Dunes National Recreation Area
Gardiner
Reedsport
Winchester Bay
Umpqua Lighthouse State Park
Dean Creek Elk Viewing Area
Scottsburg
William M. Tugman State Park
Lakeside
101
Hauser

Coos Bay

North Bend
Cape Arago Lighthouse
Sunset Bay State Park
Shore Acres State Park
Cape Arago State Park
Barview
Coos Bay
Bunker Hill
Charleston
South Slough National Estuarine Research Reserve

Bandon Dunes Golf Resort
Bullards Beach State Park
Riverton
42
Coquille

Bandon
42
Norway
Bandon Beach State Park
West Coast Game Park
Myrtle Point
Broadbent
Bridge
Langlois
542

Cape Blanco State Park
Cape Blanco
Sixes
Powers

Port Orford
Port Orford Head
Humbug Mountain State Park
Prehistoric Gardens
Ophir
Agness
Nesika Beach

Gold Beach
Cape Sebastian State Park
Pistol River

Samuel H. Boardman State Scenic Corridor
101
Loeb State Park
Harris Beach State Park
Brookings
Harbor

CALIFORNIA

TO CRESCENT CITY US 199

COAST RANGES

KLAMATH MOUNTAINS

Rogue River

Elkton
38
38
Drain

138
TO EUGENE

Sutherlin
Umpqua
5
Winchester
Roseburg
Lookingglass
Green
Winston
Tenmile
Dillard
Camas Valley
Myrtle Creek
Riddle
Canyonville

Glendale
Wolf Creek
Placer
Leland
5

Merlin
Grants Pass
TO MEDFORD, ASHLAND
Redwood
Wilderville
199
Murphy
238

Selma
Eight Dollar Mtn
Kerby
Cave Junction
46
Grayback Mtn 2,133
O'Brien
199
Oregon Caves National Monument

0   12 mi
0   12 km

feet above the ocean. If you're here on a foggy day, listen for its unique foghorn. The lighthouse is connected to the mainland by a bridge. Neither is open to the public, but there's an excellent spot to view this lonely guardian and much of the coastline. From U.S. 101, take Cape Arago Highway to Gregory Point, where it ends at a turnaround, and follow the short trail. ⊠ *Cape Arago Highway, just north of Sunset Bay State Park, Charleston.*

Charleston Marina Complex. At this bustling marina 8 miles west of Coos Bay, there's a launch ramp, a store with tackle and marine supplies, a 110-space RV park, a motel, restaurants, and gift shops. Fishing charters also set out from here. ⊠ *4535 Kingfisher Dr., Charleston* ☎ *541/888–2548* ⊕ *www.charlestonmarina.com.*

Coos History Museum & Maritime Collection. The highlight here is a 1922 steam locomotive used in Coos County logging. On display are a formal 1900 parlor, a pioneer kitchen, and exhibits on Native American history, agriculture, and industry such as logging, shipping, and mining. As of this writing, the museum is in the midst of moving into a new 11,000-square-foot facility on the waterfront in downtown Coos Bay—it's expected to be completed by early 2015. ⊠ *N. Front St., just north of Marshfield Sun Printing Museum* ☎ *541/756–6320* ⊕ *www. cooshistory.org* 🏷 *$5* ☾ *Tues.–Sat. 10–5.*

South Slough National Estuarine Research Reserve. The reserve's fragile ecosystem supports everything from algae to bald eagles and black bears. More than 300 species of birds have been sighted at the reserve, which has an interpretive center with interesting nature exhibits, guided walks (summer only), and nature trails that give you a chance to see things up close. ⊠ *61907 Seven Devils Rd., 4 miles south of Charleston* ☎ *541/888–5558* ⊕ *www.oregon.gov/dsl/ssnerr* 🏷 *Free* ☾ *Trails daily dawn–dusk; interpretive center daily 10–4:30.*

WHERE TO EAT AND STAY

$ ╳ **Blue Heron Bistro.** The specialty at this bustling downtown bistro is
GERMAN   hearty German fare, but you'll also find a number of local seafood items, as well as sandwiches and lighter dishes, from panfried oysters to meatball sandwiches. The skylit, tile-floor dining room seats about 70 amid natural wood and blue linen. The seating area outside has blue awnings and colorful Bavarian window boxes that add a festive touch. Eighteen microbrews are available. ⑤ *Average main: $14* ⊠ *100 W. Commercial St., Coos Bay* ☎ *541/267–3933* ⊕ *www.blueheronbistro. com.*

$ ╳ **Miller's at the Cove.** Often packed with local fishing and dock workers
SEAFOOD   as well as tourists en route to and from Sunset Bay and nearby state parks, this lively and fun—if at times raucous—sports bar and tavern makes a great dinner or lunch stop for fresh seafood, pitchers of craft beer, and watching a game on TV. Favorites here include the fish-and-chips (available with local snapper or cod), oyster burgers, Dungeness crab melts, meatball subs, clam chowder, and Baja-style fish or crab tacos. ⑤ *Average main: $10* ⊠ *63346 Boat Basin Rd., Charleston* ☎ *541/808–2404* ⊕ *www.millersatthecove.com.*

$ ⚇ **Coos Bay Manor.** Built in 1912 on a quiet residential street, this
B&B/INN 15-room Colonial Revival manor is listed on the National Register of
Historic Places. **Pros:** very nicely kept and decorated; family-friendly.
Cons: in busy downtown Coos Bay; a 15-minute drive from the ocean.
⟨$⟩ *Rooms from: $145* ⊠ *955 S. 5th St.* ☎ *541/269–1224, 800/269–1224*
⊕ *www.coosbaymanor.com* ⇆ *5 rooms, 1 suite* ⦿ *Breakfast.*

$ ⚇ **Mill Casino Hotel.** Even if you're not a big fan of gambling, this attrac-
RESORT tive hotel near the waterfront in North Bend (a short distance north
of downtown Coos Bay) makes a handy and fairly economical base
for exploring this stretch of the coast. **Pros:** attractive, contemporary
rooms; location close to downtown dining and shopping; nice views
from rooms in tower. **Cons:** casino can be noisy and smoky. ⟨$⟩ *Rooms
from: $109* ⊠ *3201 Tremont Ave., North Bend* ☎ *541/756–8800,
800/953–4800* ⊕ *www.themillcasino.com* ⇆ *207 rooms, 10 suites*
⦿ *No meals.*

SPORTS AND THE OUTDOORS

RECREATIONAL AREAS

Cape Arago State Park. The distant barking of sea lions echoes in the air
at a trio of coves connected by short but steep trails. The park overlooks
the **Oregon Islands National Wildlife Refuge,** where offshore rocks,
beaches, islands, and reefs provide breeding grounds for seabirds and
marine mammals, including seal pups (the trail is closed in spring to
protect them). ⊠ *End of Cape Arago Hwy., 1 mile south of Shore Acres
State Park* ☎ *800/551–6949, 541/888–3778* ⊕ *www.oregonstateparks.
org* ⌕ *Free* ⊙ *Daily dawn–dusk. Trail closed Mar.–June.*

Fodor's Choice **Shore Acres State Park.** An observation building on a grassy bluff over-
★ looking the Pacific marks the site that held the mansion of lumber
baron Louis J. Simpson. The view over the rugged wave-smashed cliffs
is splendid, but the real glory of Shore Acres lies a few hundred yards
to the south, where an entrance gate leads into what was Simpson's
private garden. Beautifully landscaped and meticulously maintained, the
gardens incorporate formal English and Japanese designs. From March
to mid-October the grounds are ablaze with blossoming daffodils, rho-
dodendrons, azaleas, roses, and dahlias. In December the garden is
decked out with a dazzling display of holiday lights. ⊠ *89526 Cape
Arago Hwy., 1 mile south of Sunset Bay State Park* ☎ *800/551–6949,
541/888–2472 info center, 541/888–3732* ⊕ *www.oregonstateparks.
org* ⌕ *$5 per vehicle day-use fee* ⊙ *Daily 8–dusk.*

BANDON

25 miles south of Coos Bay.

Referred to by some who cherish its romantic lure as Bandon-by-the-
Sea, Bandon is both a harbor town and a popular vacation spot, famous
for its cranberry products and its artists' colony, complete with galleries
and shops. Two national wildlife refuges, Oregon Islands and Bandon
Marsh, are within the town limits. The Bandon Dunes links-style golf
courses are a worldwide attraction, often ranked among the top courses
in the nation.

Tiny Bandon bills itself as Oregon's cranberry capital—10 miles north of town you'll find acres of bogs and irrigated fields where tons of the tart berries are harvested every year. Each October there's the Cranberry Festival, featuring a parade and a fair.

GETTING HERE AND AROUND

Bandon, on U.S. 101, is a half-hour drive south of Coos Bay and North Bend, and a two-hour drive north up the coast from the California border; allow 4½ hours to get here from Portland.

ESSENTIALS

Visitor Information **Bandon Chamber of Commerce** ✉ *300 2nd St.* ☎ *541/347–9616* ⊕ *www.bandon.com.*

EXPLORING

Bandon Historical Society Museum. In the old city hall building, this museum depicts the area's early history, including Native American artifacts, logging, fishing, cranberry farming, and the disastrous 1936 fire that destroyed the city. The well-stocked gift shop has books, knickknacks, jewelry, myrtlewood, and other little treasures. ✉ *270 Fillmore St.* ☎ *541/347–2164* ⊕ *www.bandonhistoricalmuseum.org* ⌑ *$3* ⊙ *Daily 10–4.*

FAMILY

Fodor's Choice

★

Oregon Islands National Wildlife Refuge. Each of the colossal rocks jutting from the ocean between Bandon and Brookings is protected as part of this refuge, in total comprising a string of 1,853 rocks, reefs, islands, and two headland areas spanning 320 miles. Thirteen species of seabirds, totalling 1.2 million birds, nest here, and harbor seals, California sea lions, Steller sea lions, and Northern elephant seals also breed within the refuge. Coquille Point, a mainland unit of Oregon Islands Refuge, is one of many places to observe seabirds and harbor seals. The point overlooks a series of offshore rocks, and a paved trail that winds over the headland ends in stairways to the beach on both sides, allowing for a loop across the sand when tides permit. Visitors are encouraged to steer clear of harbor seals and avoid touching seal pups. A complete list of viewpoints and trails is available online. ✉ *11th St. W and Portland Ave. SW, drive west to road's end for Coquille Point and parking* ☎ *541/347–1470* ⊕ *www.fws.gov/oregoncoast/oregonislands.*

West Coast Game Park Safari. The "walk-through safari" on 21 acres has free-roaming wildlife (it's the visitors who are behind fences); more than 450 animals and about 75 species, including lions, tigers, snow leopards, lemurs, bears, chimps, cougars, and camels, make it one of the largest wild-animal petting parks in the United States. The big attractions here are the young animals: bear cubs, tiger cubs, whatever is suitable for actual handling. ✉ *46914 U.S. 101, 8 miles south of Bandon on U.S. 101* ☎ *541/347–3106* ⊕ *www.westcoastgameparksafari. com* ⌑ *$17.50* ⊙ *Mar.–Nov. and last week Dec., weekdays 9:30–5, weekends 9:30–5:30; Jan. and Feb., weekends 9:30–5.*

WHERE TO EAT

$$

SEAFOOD

✕ **Edgewaters Restaurant.** This second-story bar above Edgewaters Restaurant has some of the best west-facing views of the ocean from Bandon, and is among few properties in Old Town that don't face north toward the Coquille River. You can sometimes see whales from this spot during whale-watching season. It makes a great happy-hour stop with its tall ceilings, warm fireplace, and many windows. Downstairs, the main dining room also has large windows with views of the river. The menu features fresh seafood, pastas, creative salads, and even a sushi dish or two. ⑤ *Average main: $18* ✉ *480 1st St.* ☎ *541/347–8500* ⊕ *www.edgewaters.net* ☾ *Closed Mon. No lunch Tues.–Thurs.*

$$$
PACIFIC
NORTHWEST
Fodor's Choice
★

✕ **The Loft Restaurant & Bar.** This hip eatery in Bandon's Old Town is notable for chef-owner Kali Fieger's innovative, modern spin on French basics. On the second floor of an old Port of Bandon property, The Loft's vaulted, wood-trimmed ceilings, three-sided view of the Coquille River, and classic wooden tables are all ingredients for an enjoyable meal. Every dish on the menu is as intentional as the next, prepared with thoughtful sauces, delicate chopping, and artful presentation, often combining unexpected flavors into single servings with fantastic results. You might start with grilled baby octopus with capers and chimichurri sauce, followed either by pan-seared sea scallops with shaved fennel, brown-butter hollandaise, and crisp root vegetables, or braised pork cheeks in an aromatic red-wine sauce. There's a deli, gourmet market, and wineshop on the ground floor, handy options for planning a beach picnic. ⑤ *Average main: $25* ✉ *315 1st St.* ☎ *541/329–0535* ⊕ *www. theloftofbandon.com* ⇗ *0* ☾ *Closed Mon.–Wed. No lunch.*

$$$
MODERN
AMERICAN
Fodor's Choice
★

✕ **Lord Bennett's.** His lordship has a lot going for him: a cliff-top setting, a comfortable and spacious dining area in a dramatic contemporary building, sunsets visible through picture windows overlooking Face Rock Beach, and occasional live music on weekends. The modern American menu features plenty of local seafood; try the nut-crusted halibut, blackened red snapper with potato-horseradish crust, or wild prawns with garlic butter and sherry. Steaks and chops are offered, too. The weekend brunch is a big hit—consider reserving a table for this. ⑤ *Average main: $25* ✉ *1695 Beach Loop Rd.* ☎ *541/347–3663* ⊕ *www.lordbennett.com* ☾ *No lunch Mon.–Thurs.*

$
SEAFOOD

✕ **Tony's Crab Shack & Seafood Grill.** Started in 1989 as a bait and tackle shop, Tony's Crab Shack has since become a staple of the Bandon boardwalk, popular with locals and visitors for its crab cakes, fish tacos, crab and bay shrimp sandwich, and smoked Alaskan sockeye. Open only until 6 pm, it's a reliable bet for lunch or perhaps very early dinner. ⑤ *Average main: $14* ✉ *155 1st St.* ☎ *541/347–2875* ⊕ *tonyscrabshack.com.*

WHERE TO STAY

$
HOTEL
Fodor's Choice
★

🏠 **Bandon Beach Motel.** As its owners like to proclaim, it's all about the view at this low-frills, exceptionally well-kept seaside motel set high on a bluff on Coquille Point and overlooking the smooth beach and rugged offshore rock formations below. **Pros:** terrific value; gorgeous beach views; run by a friendly and helpful family. **Cons:** basic rooms with few bells and whistles; 20-minute walk to downtown; often books up weeks in advance in summer. ⑤ *Rooms from: $105* ✉ *1090 Portland Ave. SW* ☎ *541/347–9451, 866/945–0133* ⊕ *www.bandonbeachmotel. com* ⇗ *20 rooms* ⦿ *No meals.*

$$$
RESORT
Fodor'sChoice
★

⌅ Bandon Dunes Golf Resort. This golfing lodge provides a comfortable place to relax after a day on the links, with accommodations ranging from single rooms to four-bedroom condos, many with beautiful views of the famous golf course. **Pros:** if you're a golfer, this adds to an incredible overall experience; if not, you'll have a wonderful stay anyway. **Cons:** the weather can be wet and wild in the shoulder-season months. ⑨ *Rooms from: $230 ⊠ 57744 Round Lake Dr. ☎ 541/347–4380, 888/345–6008 ⊕ www.bandondunesgolf.com ⇥ 186 rooms ⦿⧈ Some meals.*

SPORTS AND THE OUTDOORS

RECREATIONAL AREA

Bullards Beach State Park. At this rugged park along the north bank of the Coquille River (just across from downtown Bandon but reached via a 3½-mile drive up U.S. 101), you can tour the octagonal **Coquille Lighthouse,** built in 1896 and no longer in use. From turnoff from U.S. 101, the meandering 2-mile drive to reach it passes through the Bandon Marsh, a prime bird-watching and picnicking area. The beach beside the lighthouse is a good place to search for jasper, agate, and driftwood—the firm sand is also popular for mountain biking. There's a campground with a wide variety of tent and RV sites. ⊠ *52470 U.S. 101, 2 miles north of Bandon ☎ 800/452–5687, 541/347–2209 ⊕ www. oregonstateparks.org ⧈ Free ⊙ Lighthouse: May–mid-Oct., daily 11–5.*

GOLF

Fodor'sChoice
★

Bandon Dunes Golf Resort. This playland for the nation's golfing elite is no stranger to well-heeled athletes flying in to North Bend on private jets to play on the resort's four distinct courses, including the Old Macdonald course. The expectations at Bandon Dunes are that you will walk the course with a caddy—adding another refined, traditional touch. Greens fees range, according to season and other factors, from $245 to $310 a round from May to October, $75 to $220 other months. Caddy fees are determined by the player, but suggested fees are $80 to $100 per bag, per round. ⊠ *57744 Round Lake Dr. ☎ 541/347–4380, 888/345–6008 ⊕ www.bandondunesgolf.com.*

PORT ORFORD

30 miles south of Bandon.

The westernmost incorporated community in the contiguous United States, Port Orford is surrounded by forests, rivers, lakes, and beaches. The jetty at Port Orford offers little protection from storms, so every night the fishing boats are lifted out and stored on the docks. Commercial fishing boats search for crab, tuna, snapper, and salmon in the waters out of Port Orford, and diving boats gather sea urchins for Japanese markets. Visitors can fish off the Port Orford dock or the jetty for smelt, sardine, herring, lingcod, and halibut. Dock Beach provides beach fishing. The area is a favorite spot for sport divers because of the near-shore, protected reef, and for whale-watchers in fall and early spring.

GETTING HERE AND AROUND

Port Orford is a 30-minute drive south of Bandon and a one-hour drive north of Brookings along U.S. 101.

ESSENTIALS

Visitor Information **Port Orford Visitors Center** ⊠ *520 Jefferson St.*
☏ *541/332–4106* ⊕ *www.portorford.org.*

EXPLORING

OFF THE BEATEN PATH

Prehistoric Gardens. As you round a bend between Port Orford and Gold Beach, you'll see one of those sights that make grown-ups groan and kids squeal with delight: a huge, open-jawed tyrannosaurus rex, with a green brontosaurus peering out from the forest beside it. You can view 23 other life-size dinosaur replicas on the trail that runs through the property. ⊠ *36848 U.S. 101* ☏ *541/332–4463* ⊕ *www. prehistoricgardens.com* 🖾 *$12* ☺ *Summer, daily 9–6; call for winter hrs.*

WHERE TO EAT AND STAY

$
SEAFOOD
FAMILY

✗ **Crazy Norwegians Fish and Chips.** This quirky and casual hole-in-the-wall in Port Orford excels at what they do: good old-fashioned fish-and-chips. With everything from shrimp to cod to halibut paired with fries, the Crazy Norwegians serve it up with a side of pasta salad or coleslaw. Dine in at wooden tables with the mostly family crowd or take it to go to nearby Battle Rock Park. ⑤ *Average main: $12* ⊠ *259 6th St.* ☏ *541/332–8601* ☺ *Closed Mon. and Tues.*

$$$
MODERN
AMERICAN
Fodor's Choice
★

✗ **Redfish.** Two walls of windows allow diners at the stylish Redfish in downtown Port Orford spectacular ocean views, but the views inside are pretty inviting, too, from the modern artwork provided by sister establishment Hawthorne Gallery to the artfully presented and globally influenced food. Start with the Manila clams in lemongrass-coconut red-curry broth or the daily ceviche, before graduating to cedar-plank chinook salmon with mushroom risotto, or organic chicken with truffle grits, garlic-tomato marmalade, and broccoli rabe. The good-size portions make it possible to enjoy a moderately priced dinner here by ordering a couple of smaller plates. Weekend brunch items include crab cakes Benedict and a lingcod sandwich with spicy-pickle-tarragon aioli. ⑤ *Average main: $25* ⊠ *517 Jefferson St.* ☏ *541/366–2200* ⊕ *www. redfishportorford.com.*

$
HOTEL
FAMILY

⌂ **Castaway by the Sea.** This old-school motel operated by friendly proprietor Rockne Berge offers fantastic views from nearly every room, most of which have enclosed sun porches—the simplest and least expensive rooms open to an enclosed breezeway that takes in these same views. **Pros:** within walking distance of local restaurants; panoramic ocean views; reasonable rates. **Cons:** decor is a bit dated; not actually on the beach. ⑤ *Rooms from: $95* ⊠ *545 5th St.* ☏ *541/332–4502* ⊕ *www. castawaybythesea.com* ⇄ *9 rooms, 4 suites* ⦿ *No meals.*

$$$$
RESORT
Fodor's Choice
★

⌂ **WildSpring Guest Habitat.** This rustic outpost in the woods above Port Orford blends all the comforts and privacy of a vacation rental with the services of a resort. **Pros:** relaxing, secluded, and private; gorgeous rooms; eco-conscious management. **Cons:** need to drive to the beach and stores. ⑤ *Rooms from: $288* ⊠ *92978 Cemetery Loop Rd.* ☏ *541/332–0977, 866/333–9453* ⊕ *www.wildspring.com* ⇄ *5 cabins* ⦿ *Breakfast.*

SPORTS AND THE OUTDOORS

RECREATIONAL AREAS

FAMILY **Battle Rock Park and Port Orford Heads State Park.** Stroll the mocha-colored sand and admire pristine Battle Rock right in the heart of downtown Port Orford. Named for a battle between white settlers and the Dene Tsut Dah that took place here in 1850, this spot sits just below Port Orford Heads State Park. Atop the bluff that is Port Orford Heads, a trail loops the rocky outcropping between the Pacific and the Port Orford Lifeboat Station, taking in the hillside below, from which crews once mounted daring rescues on the fierce sea. The lifeboat station and adjoining museum is open for tours Wednesday–Monday, 10–3:30. Their motto? "You have to go out; you don't have to come back." ⊠ *Port Orford Hwy.; follow signs from U.S. 101* ☎ *800/551–6949, 541/332–6774* ⊕ *www.oregonstateparks.org* ⊑ *Free.*

> **THE FAB 50**
>
> U.S. 101 between Port Orford and Brookings, often referred to as the "fabulous 50 miles," soars up green headlands, some of them hundreds of feet high, and past a seascape of cliffs and sea stacks. The ocean is bluer and clearer—though not appreciably warmer—than it is farther north, and the coastal countryside is dotted with farms, grazing cattle, and small rural communities.

Cape Blanco State Park. Said to be the westernmost point in Oregon and perhaps the windiest—gusts clocked at speeds as high as 184 mph have twisted and battered the Sitka spruces along the 6-mile road from U.S. 101 to the **Cape Blanco Lighthouse.** The lighthouse, atop a 245-foot headland, has been in continuous use since 1870, longer than any other in Oregon. No one knows why the Spaniards sailing past these reddish bluffs in 1603 called them *blanco* (white). One theory is that the name refers to the fossilized shells that glint in the cliff face. Campsites at the 1,880-acre park are available on a first-come, first-served basis. Four cabins are available for reservation. ⊠ *91814 Cape Blanco Rd., off U.S. 101, 6 miles north of Port Orford, Sixes* ☎ *541/332–2973, 800/551–6949* ⊕ *www.oregonstateparks.org* ⊑ *Day use and Hughes House tour free; lighthouse tour $2* ⊗ *Park daily; lighthouse and Hughes House Apr.–Oct., Wed.–Mon. 10–3:30.*

Humbug Mountain State Park. This secluded, 1,850-acre park, especially popular with campers, usually has warm weather, thanks to the nearby mountains that shelter it from ocean breezes. A 6-mile loop leads to the top of 1,756-foot Humbug Mountain, one the highest points along the state's coastline. It's a pretty, moderately challenging hike, but the summit is fairly overgrown and doesn't provide especially panoramic views. The campground has tent and RV sites. ⊠ *U.S. 101, 6 miles south of Port Orford* ☎ *541/332–6774, 800/551–6949* ⊕ *www.oregonstateparks.org.*

GOLD BEACH

28 miles south of Port Orford.

The fabled Rogue River is one of about 150 U.S. rivers to merit Wild and Scenic status from the federal government. From spring to late fall an estimated 50,000 visitors descend on the town to take one of the daily jet-boat excursions that roar upstream from Wedderburn, Gold Beach's sister city across the bay, into the Rogue River Wilderness Area. Black bears, otters, beavers, ospreys, egrets, and bald eagles are seen regularly on these trips.

Gold Beach is very much a seasonal town, thriving in summer and nearly deserted the rest of the year because of its remote location. It marks the entrance to Oregon's banana belt, where mild, California-like temperatures take the sting out of winter and encourage a blossoming trade in lilies and daffodils.

GETTING HERE AND AROUND
It's a 90-minute drive south along U.S. 101 from Coos Bay and North Bend to reach Gold Beach, which is a one-hour drive north of the California border.

ESSENTIALS
Visitor Information Gold Beach Visitors Center ✉ *94080 Shirley La.* ☎ *541/247–7526, 800/525–2334* ⊕ *www.goldbeach.org.*

WHERE TO EAT

$$

MODERN
AMERICAN

✕ **Anna's by the Sea.** Dining at Anna's by the Sea is like stepping into one man's artisan universe: bowed and wood-trimmed ceilings, hand-made cheeses, and blackberry honey lemonade, even a hydroponic herb garden, crafted by owner/head cook Peter Dower. The enchanting, intimate eatery seats only 18, six of those seats stools with a view into the kitchen. Diners get a dash of personality with their meal service, which offers such choices as wild shrimp in black truffle oil and seared albacore and chicken thighs in chanterelle gravy. A former wine retailer, Dower also stocks nearly 100 well-chosen wines and an Oregon Spirits Collection that's a menu standout. Dower is as much entertainer as curator of the restaurant, so drop in ready for the performance and the bistro's buoyant atmosphere. ⑤ *Average main: $20* ✉ *29672 Stewart St.* ☎ *514/247–2100* ⊕ *www.annasbythesea.com* ☉ *No lunch.*

$

AMERICAN
FAMILY

✕ **The Port Hole Café.** A local staple in the old cannery building at the Port of Gold Beach since 1995, this family business has been passed down a generation, and many of the employees are friends and relations who have been tied to it for years. This is a great place to experience local life in Gold Beach, and enjoy standard lunch or dinner fare by the sea. The café overlooks the mouth of the Rogue River, an area with great views but too blustery for outdoor dining. The bright interior is furnished with casual wooden tables and there are—you guessed it—portholes. Try the panko-breaded fish-and-chips and the blueberry pie, made from berries picked locally by a family friend. Beers from the town's excellent Arch Rock Brewing are served. ⑤ *Average main: $13* ✉ *29975 Harbor Way* ☎ *541/247–7411* ⊕ *www.portholecafe.com.*

WHERE TO STAY

$

HOTEL
FAMILY

⊡ **Pacific Reef and Resort.** This resort offers a little something for everyone: from comfy, clean, no-frills lodging in the original renovated 1950s hotel to modern two-story condos with expansive ocean views, king-size beds, full kitchens, and outdoor patios. **Pros:** luxurious condos; full kitchens. **Cons:** rocky beach; on a busy road. ⑤ *Rooms from: $89*

✉ *29362 Ellensburg Hwy. (U.S. 101)* ☎ *541/247–6658, 800/808–7263* ⊕ *www.pacificreefresort.com* ⇆ *39 units* ♨ *Breakfast.*

$$$$
RESORT
Fodor's Choice
★

♨ **Tu Tu' Tun Lodge.** Pronounced "too-*too*-tin," this renowned and rather lavish resort is a slice of heaven on the Rogue River, and owner Kyle Ringer is intent on providing his guests with a singular Northwest experience. **Pros:** luxurious, beautifully outfitted rooms; exceptional dining; peaceful location overlooking river. **Cons:** no TV; not well suited for young kids; 15-minute drive from downtown. ⑤ *Rooms from: $255* ✉ *96550 N. Bank Rogue River Rd., 7 miles east of Gold Beach* ☎ *541/247–6664, 800/864–6357* ⊕ *www.tututun.com* ⇆ *16 rooms, 2 suites, 2 cottages* ♨ *Breakfast.*

SPORTS AND THE OUTDOORS

BOATING

Jerry's Rogue Jets. These jet boats operate from May through September in the most rugged section of the Wild and Scenic Rogue River, offering 64, 81, and 104-mile tours. Whether visitors choose a shorter, 6-hour lower Rogue scenic trip or an 8-hour white-water trip, folks have a rollicking good time. Its largest vessels are 40-feet long and can hold 75 passengers. The smaller, white-water boats are 32-feet long and can hold 42 passengers. ✉ *29985 Harbor Way* ☎ *541/247–4571, 800/451–3645* ⊕ *www.roguejets.com.*

FISHING

Five Star Charters. Fishing charter trips range from a 4-hour bottom-fish outing to a full-day salmon, steelhead, or halibut charter. They offer all the tackle needed, and customers don't even need experience—they'll take beginners and experts. The outfit has four riverboats, including two drift boats and two powerboats, as well as two ocean boats. They operate year-round. ✉ *29957 Harbor Way* ☎ *541/247–0217, 888/301–6480* ⊕ *www.goldbeachadventures.com.*

RECREATIONAL AREAS

Cape Sebastian State Park. The parking lots at this scenic area are more than 200 feet above sea level. At the south parking vista you can see up to 43 miles north to Humbug Mountain. Looking south, you can see nearly 50 miles toward Crescent City, California, and the Point Saint George Lighthouse. A deep forest of Sitka spruce covers most of the park. There's a 1½-mile walking trail. ✉ *U.S. 101, 6 miles south of Gold Beach* ☎ *541/469–2021, 800/551–6949* ⊕ *www.oregonstateparks.org.*

EN ROUTE
Between Gold Beach and Brookings you'll cross Thomas Creek Bridge, the highest span in Oregon. Take advantage of the off-road coastal viewing points along the 10-mile-long **Samuel H. Boardman State Scenic Corridor**—especially in summer, when highway traffic becomes heavy and rubbernecking can be dangerous.

Samuel H. Boardman State Scenic Corridor. This 12-mile corridor through beach forests and alongside rocky promontories and windswept beaches contains some of Oregon's most spectacular stretches of coastline, though seeing some of them up close sometimes requires a little effort. About 27 miles of the Oregon Coast Trail weaves its way through this area, a reach dominated by Sitka spruce trees that stretch up to 300 feet and by rocky coast interspersed with sandy beaches. Starting from the north, walk a short path from the highway turnoff to view Arch Rock. The path travels a meadow that blooms in spring time. Down the road, find **Secret Beach**—hardly a secret—where trails run from two parking lots into three separate beaches below. Visit at low tide to make your way through all three, including through a cave that connects to the third beach close to Thunder Rock. At **Thunder Rock,** just north of milepost 345 on U.S. 101, walk west for a 1-mile loop that traces inlets and headlands, edging right up to steep drops. Find the highest bridge in Oregon just south—the **Thomas Creek Bridge**—from which a moderately difficult trail extends to wide, sandy **China Beach.** Find some sun on China Beach, or continue south to walk the unusual sculpted sandstone at **Indian Sands.** Easy beach access is had at Whaleshead Beach, where shaded picnic tables shelter the view. From farther south at **Lone Ranch,** climb the grassy hillside to the top of **Cape Ferrelo** for a sweeping view of the rugged coastline, also a great spot for whale-watching in fall and summer. ⌧ *U.S. 101 between Gold Beach and Brookings* ☎ *800/551–6949, 541/469–2021* ⊕ *www.oregonstateparks.org* ⌧ *Free.*

BROOKINGS

27 miles south of Gold Beach on U.S. 101.

A startling 90% of the pot lilies grown in the United States come from a 500-acre area inland from Brookings. Mild temperatures along this coastal plain provide ideal conditions for flowering plants of all kinds—even a few palm trees, a rare sight in Oregon.

The town is equally famous as a commercial and sportfishing port at the mouth of the turquoise-blue Chetco River. Salmon and steelhead weighing 20 pounds or more swim here.

GETTING HERE AND AROUND
Brookings is the southernmost town on Oregon's coastal 101, just 10 miles north of the California border and a half-hour drive from Crescent City; it's a 2½-hour drive south on U.S. 101 from the Coos Bay and North Bend area. Allow about six hours to get here from Portland via Interstate 5 to Grants Pass and U.S. 199 to Crescent City.

VISITOR INFORMATION
Brookings Harbor Chamber of Commerce ⌧ *16330 Lower Harbor Rd.* ☎ *541/469–3181, 800/535–9469* ⊕ *www.brookingsharborchamber. com.*

WHERE TO EAT AND STAY

$
AMERICAN
✕ **Superfly Martini Bar & Grill.** The unusual name of this stylish little bar and grill has nothing to do with the Curtis Mayfield '70s funk anthem—rather, owner Ryan Webster named this establishment, which is also an artisanal-vodka distillery, after a fishing fly. Appropriately, the bar serves first-rate cocktails, including a refreshing lemon-basil martini. But the food is tasty, too; consider the rare-seared yellowfin tuna over yakisoba noodles with lemon-zest wasabi, or the pulled-pork sandwich. The restaurant's breakfast is a good time to sample the Bloody Marys and a "monster" burrito with eggs, chorizo, and cheese.

$ *Average main: $12* ✉ *623 Memory La.* ☎ *530/520–8005* ⊕ *www. superflybooze.com.*

$ ✕ **Vista Pub.** An affordable, friendly, and attractive family-run tavern in
AMERICAN   downtown Brookings, Vista Pub is known both for its extensive selection of rotating craft beers and tasty but simple comfort food, including hefty bacon-cheddar burgers, beer-cheese soup in a bread bowl, thick-cut fries sprinkled with sea salt, fried locally grown zucchini, and smoked-salmon chowder with bacon. The dining area has a long polished-wood bar and several wooden tables, and walls decorated with eclectic artwork and mounted fish. $ *Average main: $11* ✉ *1009 Chetco Ave.* ☎ *541/813–1638* ☉ *Closed Mon.*

$$ 🛏 **Best Western Plus Beachfront Inn.** This spotlessly clean three-story Best
HOTEL   Western across the street from the Brookings boat basin has direct beach access and ocean views, making it one of the best-maintained and most appealingly located lodging options along the southern coast. **Pros:** fantastic ocean views; quiet location away from busy U.S. 101; very well kept. **Cons:** rooms don't have much personality; not many restaurants within walking distance. $ *Rooms from: $169* ✉ *16008 Boat Basin Rd.* ☎ *541/469–7779* ⊕ *www.bestwesternoregon.com* ⇗ *102 rooms* ❘⊚❘ *Breakfast.*

SPORTS AND THE OUTDOORS

RECREATIONAL AREAS

Fodor's Choice   **Harris Beach State Park.** The views from the parking areas, oceanfront
★   trails, and beaches at this popular tract of craggy rock formations and evergreen forest are some of the prettiest along the southern Oregon Coast. The proximity to downtown Brookings makes this an easy place to head for morning beachcombing or a sunset stroll. You might see gray whales migrate in spring and winter. Just offshore, Bird Island, also called Goat Island, is a National Wildlife Sanctuary and a breeding site for rare birds. The campground here, with tent and RV sites, is very popular. ✉ *1655 Old U.S. 101* ☎ *541/469–2021, 800/551–6949* ⊕ *www.oregonstateparks.org* ✉ *Free* ☉ *Daily.*

THE WILLAMETTE VALLEY AND WINE COUNTRY

WELCOME TO THE WILLAMETTE VALLEY AND WINE COUNTRY

Forest Grove

TOP REASONS TO GO

★ **Swirl and sip:** Each region in the Willamette Valley offers some of the finest vintages and dining experiences found anywhere.

★ **Soar through the air:** Newberg's hot-air balloons will give you a bird's-eye view of Yamhill's wine country.

★ **Run rapids:** Feel the bouncing exhilaration and the cold spray of white-water rafting on the wild, winding McKenzie River outside Eugene.

★ **Walk on the wild side:** Hillsboro's Jackson Bottom Nature Preserve gives walkers a chance to view otters, beavers, herons, and eagles.

★ **Back the Beavers or Ducks:** Nothing gets the blood pumping like an Oregon State Beaver or University of Oregon Ducks football game.

1 **North Willamette Valley.** Most visitors begin their journey into wine country here, an area rich with upscale dining, shopping, the arts, and wineries. Close to Portland, North Willamette's communities provide all the amenities of urban life with a whole lot less concrete. Wine enthusiasts will relish the excellent vineyards in Beaverton, Hillsboro, and Forest Grove.

2 **Yamhill County.** This part of the state has undergone a renaissance in the past 20 years, as the world has beaten a path to its door, seeking the perfect Pinot. Many of the Willamette's highest-rated wineries are here. There are gorgeous inns, wine bars, and unforgettable restaurants providing a complete vacation experience.

3 **Mid-Willamette Valley.** Agriculture is the mainstay of this region; roadsides are dotted with fruit and veggie stands, and towns boast farmers' markets. The flat terrain is ideal for bicycle trips and hikes. The state capitol is Salem, and Oregon State University is in Corvallis.

4 **South Willamette Valley.** Here visitors soak in natural hot springs, hike in dense forest, run the rapids. Eugene, home to the University of Oregon, has a friendly, youthful vibe, which is enhanced by the natural splendor of the region.

GETTING ORIENTED

The Willamette Valley is a fertile mix of urban, rural, and wild stretching from Portland at the north to Cottage Grove at the south. It is bordered by the Cascade Range to the east and the Coast Range to the west. The Calapooya Mountains border it to the south and the mighty Columbia River runs along the north. Running north and south, Interstate 5 connects communities throughout the valley. In the mid-1800s the Willamette Valley was the destination of emigrants on the Oregon Trail, and today is home to about two-thirds of the state's population. The Willamette Valley is 150 miles long and up to 60 miles wide, which makes it Oregon's largest wine-growing region.

Updated
by Dave
Sandage

The Willamette (pronounced "wil-*lam*-it") Valley has become a wine lover's Shangri-La, particularly in the northern Yamhill and Washington counties between Interstate 5 and the Oregon Coast, a region that is not only carpeted with vineyards but encompasses small hotels and inns, cozy restaurants, and casual wine bars.

The valley divides two mountain ranges (the Cascade and Coast), and contains more than 200 wineries. The huge wine region is made up of six sub-appellations: Chehalem Mountains, Ribbon Ridge, Dundee Hills, Yamhill-Carlton, Eola-Amity Hills, and McMinnville. With its incredibly rich soil perfect for growing Pinot Noir, Pinot Gris, Chardonnay, and Riesling, the valley has received worldwide acclaim for its vintages. The region's farms are famous for producing quality fruits, vegetables, and cheeses that are savored in area restaurants. During spring and summer there are many roadside stands dotting the country lanes, and farmers' markets appear in most of the valley's towns. Also delicious are the locally raised lamb, pork, chicken, and beef. The valley also is a huge exporter of plants and flowers for nurseries, with a large number of farms growing ornamental trees, bulbs, and plants.

The valley definitely has an artsy, expressive, and fun side, with its wine and beer festivals, theater, music, crafts, and even ballooning. Many residents and visitors are serious runners and bicyclists, particularly in Corvallis and Eugene, so pay attention while driving.

The entire state is riveted by the collegiate rivalry between the Willamette Valley–based Oregon State Beavers in Corvallis and University of Oregon Ducks in Eugene. In these towns businesses think nothing of closing for the home football games, and getting a ticket to the "Civil War" game between the two is a feat in itself.

THE WILLAMETTE VALLEY AND WINE COUNTRY PLANNER

WHEN TO GO

July to October are the best times to wander the country roads in the Willamette Valley, exploring the grounds of its many wineries. Fall is spectacular, with leaves at their colorful peak in late October. Winters are usually mild, but they can be relentlessly overcast and downright rainy. Visitors not disturbed by dampness or chill will find excellent deals on lodging. In the spring rains continue, but the wildflowers begin to bloom, which pays off at the many gardens and nature parks throughout the valley.

FESTIVALS

International Pinot Noir Celebration. During the International Pinot Noir Celebration in late July and early August, wine lovers flock to McMinnville to sample fine regional vintages along with Pinot Noir from around the world. ⊠ *P.O. Box 1310800, McMinnville* ☎ *800/775–4762* ⊕ *www.ipnc.org.*

Oregon Bach Festival. Eugene hosts the world-class Oregon Bach Festival, with 18 summer days of classical music performances. ⊠ *1257 University of Oregon, Eugene* ☎ *541/346–5666, 800/457–1486* ⊕ *oregonbachfestival.com.*

Oregon State Fair. In late August and early September the Oregon State Fair in Salem has 8,000 things to do, see, and taste, ranging from carnival rides, top-name concert performances, animals, carnival-style games, and bodacious rides. ⊠ *2330 17th St. NE, Salem* ☎ *503/947–3247* ⊕ *oregonstatefair.org.*

Tigard Festival of Balloons. Look high in the sky for evidence of the colorful Tigard Festival of Balloons in June—hot-air balloons soar above the town throughout the weekend, launching from Cook Park. ⊠ *19600 S.W. Cipole Rd., Tualatin* ☎ *503/612–8213* ⊕ *www.tigardballoon.org.*

GETTING HERE AND AROUND

AIR TRAVEL

Portland's airport is an hour's drive east of the northern Willamette Valley. The **Aloha Express Airport Shuttle** and the **Beaverton Airporter** provide shuttle service. **Eugene Airport** is more convenient if you're exploring the region's southern end. It's served by Delta, Alaska/Horizon, American, and United/United Express. The flight from Portland to Eugene is 40 minutes. Smaller airports for private aircraft are scattered throughout the valley.

Rental cars are available at the Eugene airport from Budget, Enterprise, and Hertz. Taxis and airport shuttles will transport you to downtown Eugene for about $22. **Omni Shuttle** will provide shuttle service to and from the Eugene airport from anywhere in Oregon.

Air Contacts Aloha Express Airport Shuttle ☎ *503/356–8848* ⊕ *www.alohaexpressshuttle.com.* **Beaverton Airporter** ☎ *503/760–6565, 866/665–6965* ⊕ *www.beavertonairporter.com.* **Omni Shuttle** ☎ *541/461–7959, 800/741–5097* ⊕ *www.omnishuttle.com.*

BUS TRAVEL

Buses operated by Portland's **TriMet** network connect Forest Grove, Hillsboro, Beaverton, Tigard, Lake Oswego, and Oregon City with Portland and each other; light-rail trains operated by MAX run between Portland and Hillsboro. Many of the **Lane Transit District** buses will make a few stops to the outskirts of Lane County, such as McKenzie Bridge. All buses have bike racks. **Yamhill County Transit Area** (*YCTA* ☎ *503/472–0457* ⊕ *www.yctransitarea.org*) provides bus service for Yamhill County, with links to Hillsboro/MAX, Sherwood/TriMet, and Salem/SAMT.

Bus Contacts Lane Transit District (*LTD*). ☎ *541/682–6100* ⊕ *www.ltd.org.*

CAR TRAVEL

Interstate 5 runs north–south the length of the Willamette Valley. Many Willamette Valley attractions lie not too far east or west of Interstate 5. Highway 22 travels west from the Willamette National Forest through Salem to the coast. Highway 99 travels parallel to Interstate 5 through much of the Willamette Valley. Highway 34 leaves Interstate 5 just south of Albany and heads west, past Corvallis and into the Coast Range, where it follows the Alsea River. Highway 126 heads east from Eugene toward the Willamette National Forest; it travels west from town to the coast. U.S. 20 travels west from Corvallis. Rental cars are available from Budget (Beaverton), Enterprise, and Hertz (both Beaverton, Salem).

RESTAURANTS

The buzzwords associated with fine dining in this region are "sustainable," "farm-to-table," and "local." Fresh salmon, Dungeness crab, mussels, shrimp, and oysters are harvested just a couple of hours away on the Oregon Coast. Lamb, pork, and beef are local and plentiful, and seasonal game appears on many menus. Desserts made with local blueberries, huckleberries, raspberries, and marionberries should not be missed. But what really sets the offerings apart are the splendid local wines that receive worldwide acclaim.

Restaurants in the Willamette Valley are low-key and unpretentious. Expensive doesn't necessarily mean better, and locals have a pretty good nose for good value. Reasonably priced Mexican, Indian, Japanese, and Italian do very well. Food carts in the cities are a growing phenomenon. But there's still nothing like a great, sit-down meal at a cozy bistro for some fresh fish or lamb, washed down with a stellar Pinot Noir.

HOTELS

One of the great pleasures of touring the Willamette Valley is the incredible selection of small, ornate bed-and-breakfast hotels sprinkled throughout Oregon's wine country. In the summer and fall they can fill up quickly, as visitors come from around the world to enjoy wine tastings at the hundreds of large and small wineries. Many of these have exquisite restaurants right on the premises, with home-baked goods available day and night. There are plenty of larger properties located closer to urban areas and shopping centers, including upscale resorts with expansive spas, as well as national chains that are perfect for travelers who just need a place to lay their heads. *Hotel reviews have been shortened. For full information, visit Fodors.com.*

WHAT IT COSTS IN U.S. DOLLARS				
	$	$$	$$$	$$$$
Restaurants	Under $17	$17–$24	$25–$30	Over $30
Hotels	Under $150	$150–$200	$201–$250	Over $250

Restaurant prices are the average cost of a main course at dinner or, if dinner is not served, at lunch. Hotel prices are the lowest cost of a standard double room in high season.

TOURS

Oregon Wine Tours and **EcoTours of Oregon** provide informative guided outings across the Willamette Valley wine country.

Contacts EcoTours of Oregon ☎ *503/475–0226, 888/868–7733* ⊕ *www. ecotours-of-oregon.com.* **Oregon Wine Tours** ☎ *503/681–9463* ⊕ *www. orwinetours.com.*

VISITOR INFORMATION

Contacts Chehalem Valley Chamber of Commerce ✉ *115 N. College St., Newberg* ☎ *503/538–2014* ⊕ *www.chehalemvalley.org.* **Oregon Wine Country/ Willamette Valley Visitors Association** ☎ *866/548–5018* ⊕ *www.oregonwinecountry.org.* **Travel Lane County** ✉ *754 Olive St., Eugene* ☎ *541/484–5307, 800/547–5445* ⊕ *www.eugenecascadescoast.org.* **Washington County Visitors Association** ✉ *12725 S.W. Millikan Way, Suite 210, Beaverton* ☎ *503/644–5555, 800/537–3149* ⊕ *www.oregonswashingtoncounty. com.*

NORTH WILLAMETTE VALLEY

Just outside Portland the suburban areas of Tigard, Hillsboro, and Forest Grove have gorgeous wineries, wetlands, rivers, and nature preserves. The area has a wealth of golfing, biking, and trails for running and hiking, and, appropriately, is home to the headquarters of Nike. From wetlands to residential neighborhoods, it's not unusual to spot red-tail hawks, beavers, and ducks on your route. Shopping, fine dining, and proximity to Portland make this a great area in which to begin your exploration of the Willamette Valley and the wine country.

EN ROUTE

Vineyard and Valley Scenic Tour. A 60-mile driving route through the lush Tualatin Valley runs between the city of Sherwood in the southern part of the valley and Helvetia at the northern end. The rural drive showcases much of Washington County's agricultural bounty, including many of the county's wineries and farms (some with stands offering seasonal fresh produce and/or U-pick), along with pioneer and historic sites, wildlife refuges, and scenic viewpoints of the Cascade Mountains. For more information, contact the **Washington County Visitors Association** (⊕ *www.oregonswashingtoncounty. com*). ⊕ *www.oregonswashingtoncounty.com/Discover-Wine-Country/ Scenic-Tour-Route.*

North Willamette Valley and Yamhill County

WASHINGTON

Vancouver

Portland

Hillsboro

Forest Grove

Yamhill

Carlton

Dundee

Newberg

McMinnville

David Hill Vineyards & Winery
Elk Cove Vineyards
Utopia Vineyard
Carlton Winemakers Studio
Domaine Drouhin
Anne Amie Vineyards
Domaine Serene Winery
Lafayette
Eyrie Vineyards
Vista Hills Vineyard
Aramenta Cellars
Adelsheim Vineyard
Bergstrom Vineyard
Raptor Ridge Winery
Erath Vineyard and Winery
Torii Mor Winery
Archery Summit Winery
Sokol-Blosser Winery
Argyle Winery
Rex Hill Vineyards
Ponzi Vineyards
Cooper Mountain Vineyards
Jackson Bolton Wetlands Preserve

Trask River

Banks
Gaston
Whiteson
Amity
Perrydale
Sheridan
Willamina
Dayton
Donald
Hubbard
Woodburn
Gervais
Mount Angel
Aurora
Barlow
Canby
Wilsonville
Sherwood
Tualatin
King City
Tigard
Beaverton
Rockcreek
Rockwood
Gresham
Hemlock
Camas
Lake Oswego
Johnson City
Oregon City
Molalla
Estacada
Sandy

Willamette Mission State Park

15 mi
15 km

99W
99E
47
8
8
26
30
84
205
405
5
5
26
213
224
219
221
18

HILLSBORO

20 miles southwest of Portland.

Hillsboro offers a wealth of eclectic shops, preserves, restaurants, and proximity to the valley's fine wineries. In the past 20 years Hillsboro has experienced rapid growth associated with the Silicon Forest, where high-tech business found ample sprawling room. Several of Intel's industrial campuses are in Hillsboro, as are the facilities of other leading electronics manufacturers. Businesses related to the town's original agricultural roots remain a significant part of Hillsboro's culture and economy. Alpaca ranches, nurseries, berry farms, nut and fruit orchards, and numerous wineries are among the area's most active agricultural businesses.

GETTING HERE AND AROUND

Hillsboro is about a 45-minute drive west from Portland International Airport. The **Aloha Express Airport Shuttle** (☎ *503/356–8848* ⊕ *www. alohaexpressshuttle.com*) and the **Beaverton Airporter** (☎ *503/760–6565* ⊕ *www.beavertonairporter.com*) provide shuttle service.

From Downtown Portland it's a short 20-minute car ride, or visitors can ride the MAX light rail. The TriMet Bus Service connects to the MAX light rail in Hillsboro, with connections to Beaverton, Aloha, and other commercial areas.

EXPLORING

Hillsboro Saturday Market. Fresh local produce—some from booths, some from the backs of trucks—as well as local arts and crafts are on sale Saturdays from May through October. Live music is played throughout the day. The market is just a block from the light-rail line. ⊠ *Main St. between 1st and 3rd Aves.* ☎ *503/844–6685* ⊕ *www.hillsboromarkets. org.*

Fodor's Choice ★ **Ponzi Vineyards.** One of the founding families of Willamette Valley wine, Dick and Nancy Ponzi planted their original estate vineyard in 1970. While you can still visit the historic estate that looks out over these old vines, your best bet is to drop in at their new visitors facility at the winery just 12 miles south of Hillsboro. Here you'll find red and white flights of the current releases, as well as the occasional older vintage from the library. Enjoy tableside wine service indoors around the fireplace, or out on the covered terrace. Antipasti plates are a nice accompaniment to the wine. Pictures on the walls and displays provide a wonderful visual history of this winery that is still family owned and operated. The Ponzi family also launched the BridgePort Brewing Company in 1984, and runs a wine bar and restaurant in Dundee (⇨ *Dundee Bistro in Dundee*). ⊠ *19500 S.W. Mountain Home Rd., Sherwood* ☎ *503/628–1227* ⊕ *www.ponziwines.com* ☉ *Daily 11–5:30.*

FAMILY **Rice Northwest Museum of Rocks and Minerals.** Richard and Helen Rice began collecting beach agates in 1938, and over the years they developed one of the largest private mineral collections in the United States. The most popular item here is the Alma Rose rhodochrosite, a 4-inch red crystal. The museum (in a ranch-style home) also displays petrified wood from all over the world and a gallery of Northwest minerals—including specimens of rare crystallized gold. Tours are offered Saturdays at 2 pm. ✉ *26385 N.W. Groveland Dr.* ☎ *503/647–2418* ⊕ *www.ricenorthwestmuseum.org* 🔖 *$8* ⊗ *Wed.–Sun. 1–5.*

Washington County Museum and Historical Society. This impressive space on the second floor of the Hillsboro Civic Center houses a range of exhibits focusing on the history and culture of the area. Most of the exhibits include activities for children. ✉ *120 E. Main St.* ☎ *503/645–5353* ⊕ *www.washingtoncountymuseum.org* 🔖 *$6* ⊗ *Wed.–Sat. 10–5.*

WHERE TO EAT

$

MEXICAN

✕ **Mazatlan Mexican Restaurant.** Though this popular spot is hidden away in a small shopping mall, once you're inside and surrounded by stunning murals and ceramica you'll feel like you're in a charming village. Try the Mazatlan Dinner, a house specialty with sirloin, a chile relleno, and an enchilada, or *arroz con camarones,* prawns sautéed with vegetables. Save room for the flan or the *sopapillas* (fried dough). The kids' menu is a good value. ⑤ *Average main: $13* ✉ *20413 S.W. TV Hwy., Aloha* ☎ *503/591–9536* ⊕ *www.mazatlanmexicanrestaurant.com.*

$

JAPANESE

✕ **Syun Izakaya.** A large assortment of sushi and sashimi, soups, and salads are served in quiet surroundings in the basement of the old Hillsboro Library. Wonderful grilled and fried meats and vegetables are also available, accompanied by a vast sake selection. Be sure to look for the daily specials for superfresh and sometimes unusual selections. A nice assortment of small plates is served during happy hour, between 5 and 6 pm and from 9 to close. ⑤ *Average main: $13* ✉ *209 N.E. Lincoln St.* ☎ *503/640–3131* ⊕ *www.syun-izakaya.com* ⊗ *No lunch Sun.*

SPORTS AND THE OUTDOORS

The Tualatin, a slow, meandering river, flows into Hillsboro and along its length offers fantastic opportunities for paddlers who are new to the sport, as well those who are experienced.

RECREATIONAL AREAS

Cook Park. On the banks of the Tualatin River in Tigard, east of Hillsboro, this 79-acre park is where local suburbanites gather to enjoy a variety of outdoor activities, and plays host to the annual Festival of Balloons in June. The park has horseshoe pits, a fishing dock, small boat ramp, picnic shelters, and several walking trails and bike paths. Wildlife includes great blue herons and river otters. ✉ *17005 S.W. 92nd Ave., Tigard* ☎ *503/718–2641* ⊕ *www.tigard-or.gov.*

Jackson Bottom Wetlands Preserve. Several miles of trails in this 710-acre floodplain and woods are home to thousands of ducks and geese, deer, otters, beavers, herons, and eagles. Walking trails allow birders and other animal watchers to explore the wetlands for a chance to catch a glimpse of indigenous and migrating creatures in their own habitats. The **Education Center** has several hands-on exhibits, as well as a real bald eagle's nest that was rescued from the wild, and completely preserved (and sanitized) for public display. No dogs or bicycles are allowed. ✉ *2600 S.W. Hillsboro Hwy.* ☎ *503/681–6206* ⊕ *www. jacksonbottom.org* 🔖 *$2 suggested donation* ⊗ *Trails daily dawn–dusk, Education Center daily 10–4.*

FAMILY **L.L. "Stub" Stewart State Park.** This 1,654-acre, full-service park has hiking, biking, and horseback riding trails for day use or overnight camping. There are full hookup sites, tent sites, small cabins, and even a horse camp. Lush rolling hills, forests, and deep canyons are terrific for bird-watching, wildflower walks, and other relaxing pursuits. An 18-hole disc golf course winds its way through a dense forest. In case you don't know, in disc golf players throw a disc at a target and attempt to complete the course with the fewest throws. ⊠ *30380 N.W. Hwy. 47, Buxton* ☎ *503/324–0606* ⊕ *www.oregonstateparks.org* ⊠ *$5 for day use permit.*

Tualatin River Wildlife Refuge. This sanctuary for indigenous and migrating birds, waterfowl, and mammals is in Sherwood (about 18 miles south of Hillsboro). It is one of only a handful of national urban refuges in the United States and has restored much of the natural landscape common to western Oregon prior to human settlement. The refuge is home to nearly 200 species of birds, 50 species of mammals, 25 species of reptiles and amphibians, and a variety of insects, fish, and plants. It features an interpretive center, a gift shop, photography blinds, and restrooms. This restoration has attracted animals back to the area in great numbers, and with a keen eye, birders and animal watchers can catch a glimpse of these creatures year-round. In May the refuge hosts its Migratory Songbird Festival. ⊠ *19255 S.W. Pacific Hwy., Tigard* ☎ *503/625–5944* ⊕ *www.fws.gov/tualatinriver* ☾ *Daily dawn–dusk; Wildlife Center, Tues.–Sun. 10–4.*

FOREST GROVE

24 miles west of Portland on Hwy. 8.

This small town is surrounded by stands of Douglas firs and giant sequoia, including the largest giant sequoia in the state. There are nearby wetlands, birding, the Hagg Lake Recreation Area, a new outdoor adventure park, and numerous wineries and tasting rooms. To get to many of the wineries, head south from Forest Grove on Highway 47 and watch for the blue road signs between Forest Grove, Gaston, and Yamhill. To the west of town, you'll find some of the oldest Pinot Noir vines in the valley at David Hill Winery.

GETTING HERE AND AROUND

Forest Grove is about an hour's drive west from Portland International Airport. The **Aloha Express Airport Shuttle** (☎ *503/356–8848* ⊕ *www. alohaexpressshuttle.com*) and the **Beaverton Airporter** (☎ *503/760–6565* ⊕ *www.beavertonairporter.com*) provide shuttle service.

From Downtown Portland it's a short 35-minute car ride with only a few traffic lights during the entire trip. TriMet Bus Service provides bus service to and from Forest Grove every 15 minutes, connecting to the MAX light rail 6 miles east in Hillsboro, which continues into Portland. Buses travel to Cornelius, Hillsboro, Aloha, and Beaverton.

ESSENTIALS

Forest Grove Chamber of Commerce ⊠ *2417 Pacific Ave.* ☎ *503/357–3006* ⊕ *www.visitforestgrove.com.*

David Hill Vineyards and Winery, Forest Grove

EXPLORING

David Hill Vineyards and Winery. In 1965 Charles Coury came to Oregon from California and planted some of the Willamette Valley's first Pinot Noir vines on the site of what is now the David Hill Winery. The original farmhouse serves as the tasting room and offers splendid views of the Tualatin Valley. They produce Pinot Noir, some of which comes from the original vines planted by Coury, along with Chardonnay, Gewürztraminer, Merlot, Tempranillo, Pinot Gris, and Riesling. The wines are well made and pleasant, especially the eclectic blend called Farmhouse Red and the estate Riesling. ⊠ *46350 N.W. David Hill Rd.* ☎ *503/992–8545* ⊕ *www.davidhillwinery.com* ⊙ *Daily 11–5.*

Elk Cove Vineyard. Founded in 1974 by Pat and Joe Campbell, this well-established winery covers 600 acres on four separate vineyard sites. The tasting room is set in the beautiful rolling hills at the foot of the Coast Range overlooking the vines. The focus is on Willamette Valley Pinot Noir, Pinot Gris, and Pinot Blanc. Be sure to also try the limited bottling of their Pinot Noir Rosé if they're pouring it. ⊠ *27751 N.W. Olson Rd., Gaston* ☎ *503/985–7760, 877/355–2683* ⊕ *www.elkcove. com* ▭ *$10* ⊙ *Daily 10–5.*

Montinore Estate. Locals chuckle at visitors who try to show off their French savvy when they pronounce it "Mont-in-or-ay." The estate, originally a ranch, was established by a tycoon who'd made his money in the Montana mines before he retired to Oregon; he decided to call his estate "Montana in Oregon." Montinore (no "ay" at the end) has 232 acres of vineyards, and its wines reflect the high-quality soil and fruit. Highlights include a crisp Gewürztraminer, a light Müller-Thurgau, an off-dry Riesling, several lush Pinot Noirs, and a delightful white blend called Borealis that's a perfect partner for Northwest seafood. The tasting-room staff is among the friendliest and most knowledgeable in Oregon wine country. ⊠ *3663 S.W. Dilley Rd.* ☎ *503/359–5012, 888/359–5012* ⊕ *www.montinore.com* ⊙ *Daily 11–5.*

Pacific University. Founded in 1849, this is one of the oldest educational institutions in the western United States. Concerts and special events are held on the shady campus in the Taylor-Meade Performing Arts Center. ⊠ *2043 College Way* ☎ *503/352–6151, 877/722–8648* ⊕ *www. pacificu.edu.*

SakéOne. After the founders realized that the country's best water supply for sake was in the Pacific Northwest, they built their brewery in Forest Grove in 1997. It's one of only six sake brewing facilities in America and produces award-winning sake under three labels, in addition to importing from partners in Japan. The tasting room offers three different flights, including one with a food pairing. Be sure to catch one of the tours, offered daily, where your guide will walk you through every phase of the sake-making process, from milling the rice to final filtration and bottling. ⊠ *820 Elm St.* ☎ *503/357–7056, 800/550–7253* ⊕ *www. sakeone.com* ⌦ *Free* ⊙ *Daily 11–5.*

WHERE TO STAY

$ ⚔ **McMenamins Grand Lodge.** On 13 acres of pastoral countryside, this
HOTEL converted Masonic rest home has accommodations that run from bunk-bed rooms to a three-room fireplace suite, with some nice period antiques in all. **Pros:** relaxed, friendly brewpub atmosphere. **Cons:** not as refined as some tourists would like; most rooms have shared bathrooms. ⑤ *Rooms from: $60* ⊠ *3505 Pacific Ave.* ☎ *503/992–9533, 877/992–9533* ⊕ *www.mcmenamins.com/grandlodge* ⟳ *77 rooms* ⍓ *No meals.*

SPORTS AND THE OUTDOORS
RECREATIONAL AREAS

Scoggin Valley Park and Henry Hagg Lake. This beautiful area in the Coast Range foothills has a 15-mile-long hiking trail that surrounds the lake. Bird-watching is best in spring. Recreational activities include fishing, boating, waterskiing, picnicking, and hiking, and a 10 -mile, well-marked bicycle lane parallels the park's perimeter road. ⊠ *50250 S.W. Scoggins Valley Rd., Gaston* ☎ *503/846–8715* ⊕ *www.co.washington. or.us/hagglake* ⌦ *$6* ⊙ *Mar.–Nov., daily sunrise–sunset.*

Tree to Tree Adventure Park. At the first public aerial adventure park in the Pacific Northwest—and only the second of its kind in the United States—the aerial adventure course features 19 zip lines and more than 60 treetop elements and obstacles. You can experience the thrills of moving from platform to platform (tree to tree) via wobbly bridges, tight ropes, Tarzan swings, and more. The courses range from beginner to extreme, with certified and trained instructors providing guidance to adventurers. "Woody's Ziptastic Voyage" zip-line tour features six extreme zip lines (including one that is 1,280 feet long), a bridge, and a 40-foot rappell. Harnesses and helmets are provided, and no open-toed shoes are allowed. Reservations are required. ⊠ *2975 S.W. Nelson*

Rd., Gaston ☎ *503/357–0109* ⊕ *tree2treeadventurepark.com* ✉ *Aerial park $48, zip tour $75* ⊙ *Mar.–mid Nov., daily 9–3 hrs before sunset.*

YAMHILL COUNTY

Yamhill County, at the northern end of the Willamette Valley, has a fortunate confluence of perfect soils, a benign climate, and talented winemakers who craft world-class vintages. In recent years several new wineries have been built in Yamhill County's hills, as well as on its flatlands. While vineyards flourished in the northern Willamette Valley in the 19th century, viticulture didn't arrive in Yamhill County until the 1960s and 1970s, with such pioneers as Dick Erath (Erath Vineyards Winery), David and Ginny Adelsheim (Adelsheim Vineyard), and David and Diana Lett (The Eyrie Vineyards). The focus of much of the county's enthusiasm lies in the Red Hills of Dundee, where the farming towns of Newberg, Dundee, Yamhill, and Carlton have made room for upscale bed-and-breakfasts, spas, wine bars, and tourists seeking that perfect swirl and sip.

The Yamhill County wineries are only a short drive from Portland, and the roads, especially Route 99W and Route 18, can be crowded on weekends—that's because these roads link suburban Portland communities to the popular Oregon Coast.

NEWBERG

24 miles south of Portland on Hwy. 99W.

Newberg sits in the Chehalem Valley, known as one of Oregon's most fertile wine-growing locations, and is called the Gateway to Oregon Wine Country. Many of Newberg's early settlers were Quakers from the Midwest, who founded the school that has become George Fox University. Newberg's most famous resident, likewise a Quaker, was Herbert Hoover, the 31st president of the United States. For about five years during his adolescence, he lived with an aunt and uncle at the Hoover-Minthorn House, now a museum listed on the National Register of Historic Places. Now the town is on the map for the nearby wineries, fine-dining establishments, and a spacious, spectacular resort, the Allison. St. Paul, a historic town with a population of about 325, is about 8 miles south of Newberg, and every July holds a professional rodeo.

GETTING HERE AND AROUND

Newberg is just under an hour's drive from Portland International Airport; **Caravan Airport Transportation** (☎ *541/994–9645* ⊕ *www. caravanairporttransportation.com*) provides shuttle service. The best way to visit Newberg and the Yamhill County vineyards is by car. Situated on Highway 99W, Newberg is 90 minutes from Lincoln City, on the Oregon Coast. Greyhound provides bus service to McMinnville.

EXPLORING

TOP ATTRACTIONS

Fodor'sChoice
★

Adelsheim Vineyard. David Adelsheim is the knight in shining armor of the Oregon wine industry—tirelessly promoting Oregon wines abroad, and always willing to share the knowledge he has gained from his long viticultural experience. He and Ginny Adelsheim founded their pioneer winery in 1971. They make their wines from grapes picked on their 230 acres of estate vineyards, as well as from grapes they've purchased. Their Pinot Noir, Pinot Gris, Pinot Blanc, and Chardonnay all conform to the Adelsheim house style of rich, balanced fruit and long, clean finishes. They also make a spicy cool-climate Syrah from grapes grown just outside the beautiful tasting room. Tours are available by appointment. ⊠ *16800 N.E. Calkins La.* ☎ *503/538–3652* ⊕ *www.adelsheim. com* 🍷 *$15* ⊙ *Daily 11-4.*

Bergstrom Winery. Focusing on classic Oregon Pinot Noir and Chardonnay, this family-owned winery produces elegant and refined wines that represent some of the best the Willamette Valley has to offer. The tasting room is surrounded by the Silice vineyard, and offers beautiful views of several neighboring vineyards as well. French-trained winemaker Josh Bergstrom sources fruit from his estate vineyards and from several other local sites to produce a wide range of single-vineyard Pinots. Enjoy your tasting on the deck on a warm summer day. ⊠ *18215 N.E. Calkins La.* ☎ *503/554–0468* ⊕ *www.bergstromwines.com* 🍷 *$20* ⊙ *Daily 10–4.*

Penner-Ash Wine Cellars. Lynn Penner-Ash brings years of experience working in Napa and as Rex Hill's winemaker to the winery that she and her husband Ron started in 1998. Although focused primarily on silky Pinot Noir, Penner-Ash also produces very good Syrah, Viognier, and Riesling. From its hilltop perch in the middle of the Dussin vineyard, this state-of-the-art gravity-flow winery and tasting room offers commanding views of the valley below. ⊠ *15771 N.E. Ribbon Ridge Rd.* ☎ *503/554–5545* ⊕ *www.pennerash.com* ⊙ *Daily 11–5.*

Rex Hill Vineyards. A few hundred feet off the busy highway, surrounded by conifers and overlooked by vineyards, Rex Hill seems to exist in a world of its own. The winery opened in 1982, after owners Paul Hart and Jan Jacobsen converted a former nut-drying facility. It produces first-class Pinot Noir, Pinot Gris, Chardonnay, Sauvignon Blanc, and Riesling from both estate-grown and purchased grapes. The tasting room has a massive fireplace, elegant antiques, and an absorbing collection of modern art. Another highlight is the beautifully landscaped garden, perfect for picnicking. ⊠ *30835 N. Hwy. 99W* ☎ *503/538–0666, 800/739–4455* ⊕ *www.rexhill.com* 🍷 *$10* ⊙ *Daily 10–5.*

WORTH NOTING

Aramenta Cellars. Owners Ed and Darlene Looney have been farming this land for more than 40 years. In 2000, they planted grape vines after keeping cattle on the property. The winery and tasting room are built on the foundation of the old barn, and Ed makes the wine while Darlene runs the tasting room. Of the 27 acres planted in vines, 20 acres are leased to Archrey Summit for their Looney Vineyard Pinot Noir, and the Looneys farm 7 acres for their own wines which have very limited distribution. If you're looking for a break from all the Pinot Noir, try the Tillie Claret—a smooth Bordeaux blend made with grapes from eastern Washington and southern Oregon. Aramenta offers a great opportunity to interact with farmers who have worked the land for several generations and to taste some great small production wine. ⊠ *17979 N.E. Lewis Rogers La.* ☎ *503/538–7230* ⊕ *www.aramentacellars.com* ☉ *Daily 10–4.*

Champoeg State Heritage Area. Pronounced "sham-*poo*-ee," this 615-acre state park on the south bank of the Willamette River is on the site of a Hudson's Bay Company trading post, granary, and warehouse that was built in 1813. This was the seat of the first provisional government in the Northwest. The settlement was abandoned after a catastrophic flood in 1861, then rebuilt and abandoned again after the flood of 1890. The park's wide-open spaces, groves of oak and fir, modern visitor center, museum, and historic buildings provide vivid insight into pioneer life. Tepees and wagons are displayed here, and there are 10 miles of hiking and cycle trails. ⊠ *8239 Champoeg Rd. NE, St. Paul* ☎ *503/678–1251* ⊕ *www.oregonstateparks.org* ⌦ *$5 per vehicle*

Fox Farm Vineyards. Conveniently located in downtown Newberg, this tasting room is a fun and easy stop if you're interested in trying fine wines from small producers that you won't likely find anywhere else. Winemaker Joe Dobbes produces small lots of Pinot Noir, Pinot Gris, Pinot Blanc, and Syrah. In addition to showcasing Fox Farm's own small-production wines, the tasting room will often pour an extra wine from one of several other boutique wineries in the area. Check the website for a schedule of live music and movie nights at the tasting room. ⊠ *606 E. 1st St.* ☎ *503/538–8466* ⊕ *www.foxfarmvineyards. com* ☉ *Daily noon–8.*

Hoover-Minthorn House Museum. In 1885 Dr. Henry Minthorn invited his orphan nephew Herbert "Bertie" Hoover to come west and join the Minthorn family in Newberg. Built in 1881, the restored frame house, the oldest and most significant of Newberg's original structures, still has many of its original furnishings, including the president's boyhood bed and dresser. Hoover maintained his connection to Newberg, and visited several times after his presidency. ⊠ *115 S. River St.* ☎ *503/538–6629* ⊕ *www.thehoover-minthornhousemuseum.org* ⌦ *$3* ☉ *Mar.–Nov., Wed.–Sun. 1–4; Dec. and Feb., weekends 1–4.*

Raptor Ridge Winery. The huge windows in the new tasting room look out over the vines of their estate vineyard on the northeast slope of the Chehalem Mountains. If you keep a sharp eye, you may even catch a glimpse of the many raptors (red-tail hawks, sharp-shinned hawks, and kestrels) that give this small winery its name. Raptor Ridge specializes in single-vineyard Pinot Noirs that capture the sense of place of their estate vineyard as well as several other vineyards throughout the Willamette Valley. They also produce Chardonnay, Pinot Gris, and a very nice Tempranillo. During the summer, enjoy your tasting at a table on the outside deck that overlooks the vineyards. Tours of the wine-making facility are available by appointment. ⊠ *18700 S.W. Hillsboro Hwy* ☎ *503/628–8463* ⊕ *www.raptoridge.com* ☉ *Mid-Jan.–mid May* *and mid-Oct.–mid-Dec., Thurs.–Mon. 11–4; mid-May–mid-Oct., daily 11–4; mid-Dec.–mid-Jan., by appointment.*

Utopia Vineyard. Take a trip back in time to when the Oregon wine industry was much smaller and more intimate. Utopia owner and winemaker Daniel Warnhius moved north from California looking for a vineyard site that would produce world-class Pinot Noir, and he found this location with the right combination of location, climate, and soil structure. In the tasting room, you're likely to be served by Daniel himself. In addition to several great Pinot Noirs, they also produce a bright, crisp Chardonnay, and a Pinot Noir Rosé. ⊠ *17445 N.E. Ribbon Ridge Rd.* ☎ *503/687–1671* ⊕ *utopiawine.com* 🎫 *$10* 🕘 *May–Nov,. daily 11–6; Dec. –Apr., Sat. & Sun. 11-6.*

4

Vercingetorix. This small winery south of Newberg, which produces only Pinot Gris, Pinot Blanc, and Pinot Noir, is part of Willamette Farms, a grower of hazelnuts, trees, and wine grapes. The crisp, fruity Pinot Gris is especially worth seeking out. The winery has a half mile of Willamette River frontage, so you can claim a picnic table and keep your eyes peeled for wildlife (beavers, deer, ducks, geese, and raptors). ⊠ *8000 N.E. Parrish Rd.* ☎ *503/537–0799* ⊕ *www.vxvineyardwine. com* 🕘 *May–Nov., weekends 11–5.*

WHERE TO EAT AND STAY

$$$$

MODERN AMERICAN

✕ **Jory.** This exquisite hotel dining room is named after one of the soils in the Oregon wine country. Chef Sunny Jin sources the majority of his ingredients locally, many from the on-site garden. The menu changes according to season, but always features fresh seafood (usually salmon and halibut), local lamb and pork, and an abundance of local veggies. Ask for a seat at the counter overlooking the open kitchen if you want to see the chefs in action. Naturally, the restaurant has an expansive wine list focused on Oregon wines. ⑤ *Average main: $35* ⊠ *The Allison Inn, 2525 Allison La.* ☎ *503/554–2525, 877/294-2525* ⊕ *www.theallison. com* 🕘 *No lunch Sun.*

$$$$

RESORT

Fodor's Choice

★

🛏 **The Allison Inn & Spa.** At this luxurious, relaxing base for exploring the region's 200 wineries, each bright, comfortable room includes a gas fireplace, original works of art, a soaking tub, impressive furnishings, bay-window seats, and views of the vineyards from the terrace or balcony. **Pros:** outstanding on-site restaurant; excellent gym and spa facilities; located in the middle of wine country. **Cons:** not many nearby off-property activities other than wine tasting. ⑤ *Rooms from: $350* ⊠ *2525 Allison La.* ☎ *503/554–2525, 877/294-2525* ⊕ *www.theallison. com* 🍴 *65 rooms, 20 suites.*

$$$

B&B/INN

🛏 **Le Puy, A Wine Valley Inn.** This beautiful wine country retreat caters to wine enthusiasts with amenities that include wine bars in each individually decorated room, along with hot tubs and gas fireplaces in some. **Pros:** beautiful surroundings; lots of nice architectural and decorative touches. **Cons:** a distance from sights other than wineries. ⑤ *Rooms from: $225* ⊠ *20300 N.E. Hwy. 240* ☎ *503/554–9528* ⊕ *lepuy-inn. com* 🍴 *8 Rooms* 🍽 *Breakfast.*

NIGHTLIFE AND THE ARTS

99W Drive-in. Ted Francis built this drive-in in 1953, and operated it until his death at 98; the business is now run by his grandson. The first film begins at dusk. ✉ *3110 Portland Rd. (Hwy. 99W)* ☎ *503/538–2738* ⊕ *www.99w.com* ✉ *$8, vehicles with single occupant $12* ⊙ *Fri.–Sun.*

SPORTS AND THE OUTDOORS

BALLOONING

Hot-air balloon rides are nothing less than a spectacular, breathtaking thrill—particularly over Oregon's beautiful Yamhill County.

Vista Balloon Adventures. Enjoy floating gently above beautiful Oregon wine country as the sun rises behind the vines. Your FAA-licensed pilot will take the balloon up about 1,500 feet and can often steer the craft down to skim the water, then up to view hawk's nests. A brunch is served upon returning to the ground. ✉ *1055 Commerce Pkwy.* ☎ *503/625–7385, 800/622–2309* ⊕ *www.vistaballoon.com* ✉ *$199 per person* ⊙ *Apr.–Sept., Fri.–Mon.*

DUNDEE

3 miles southwest of Newberg on Hwy. 99W.

Dundee used to be known for growing the lion's share (more than 90%) of the U.S. hazelnut crop. Today, some of Oregon's top-rated wineries are just outside Dundee, and the area is now best known for wine tourism and wine bars, bed-and-breakfast inns, and restaurants.

GETTING HERE AND AROUND

Dundee is just under an hour's drive from Portland International Airport; **Caravan Airport Transportation** (☎ *541/994–9645* ⊕ *www.caravanairporttransportation.com*) provides shuttle service.

What used to be a pleasant drive through quaint Dundee on Highway 99W now can be a traffic hassle, as it serves as the main artery from Lincoln City on the Oregon Coast to suburban Portland. Others will enjoy wandering along the 25 miles of Highway 18 between Dundee and Grande Ronde, in the Coast Range, which goes through the heart of the Yamhill Valley wine country.

EXPLORING

TOP ATTRACTIONS

Fodor's Choice ★ **Archery Summit Winery.** The winery that Gary and Nancy Andrus, owners of Pine Ridge winery in Napa Valley, founded in the 1990s has become synonomous with premium Oregon Pinot Noir. Because they believed that great wines are made in the vineyard, they adopted such innovative techniques as narrow spacing and vertical trellis systems, which give the fruit a great concentration of flavors. In addition to the standard flight of Pinot Noirs in the tasting room, you can call ahead and reserve a private seated tasting or a tasting paired with small bites or a tour of the winery and, weather permitting, a walk out to the vineyard. You're welcome to bring a picnic, and as at many Oregon wineries, you can bring your dog, too. ✉ *18599 N.E. Archery Summit Rd., Dayton* ☎ *503/864–4300* ⊕ *www.archerysummit.com* ⊙ *Daily 10–4.*

Argyle Winery. A beautiful establishment, Argyle has its tasting room in a Victorian farmhouse set amid gorgeous gardens. The winery is tucked into a former hazelnut processing plant—which explains the Nuthouse label on its reserve wines. Since Argyle opened in 1987, it has consistently produced sparkling wines that are crisp on the palate, with an aromatic, lingering finish and bubbles that seem to last forever. And these sparklers cost about a third of their counterparts from California. The winery also produces Chardonnay, dry Riesling, Pinot Gris, and Pinot Noir. ✉ *691 Hwy. 99W* ☎ *503/538–8520, 888/427–4953* ⊕ *www. argylewinery.com* ⊙ *Daily 11–5.*

Fodor'sChoice
★

Domaine Drouhin Oregon. When the French winery magnate Robert Drouhin ("the Sebastiani of France") planted a vineyard and built a winery in the Red Hills of Dundee back in 1987, he set local oenophiles abuzz. His daughter Veronique is now the winemaker and produces silky and elegant Pinot Noir and Chardonnay. Ninety acres of the 225-acre estate have been planted on a hillside to take advantage of the natural coolness of the earth and to establish a gravity-flow winery. No appointment is needed to taste the Oregon wines, but if you can plan ahead for the tour (reservations required), you can taste Oregon and Burgundy side-by-side. ✉ *6750 N.E. Breyman Orchards Rd., Dayton* ☎ *503/864–2700* ⊕ *www.domainedrouhin.com* ⊙ *June–Sept.: daily 11–4; Oct.–May: Wed.–Sun. 11–4. Tours by appointment only.*

Winderlea. The tasting room looks over the acclaimed former Goldschmidt vineyard, first planted in 1974, and the view can be enjoyed on the outside deck on a warm summer day. Winemaker Robert Brittan crafts lush Pinot Noir and Chardonnay from several nearby vineyards in both single-vineyard offerings and blends from multiple vineyards. Proceeds from the tasting fee are donated to Salud, a partnership between Oregon winemakers and local medical professionals to provide healthcare services for Oregon's seasonal vineyard workers and their families. ✉ *8905 N.E. Worden Hill Rd.* ☎ *503/554–5900* ⊕ *www.winderlea.com* ⊙ *Daily 11–4.*

WORTH NOTING

Dobbes Family Estate. Joe Dobbes makes a lot of wine, but he's definitly not a bulk winemaker. He provides custom wine-making services to many Oregon wineries that are too small to have their own winery or winemaker. But he also makes several lines of his own wine, ranging from his everyday "Wine By Joe" label to the premium Dobbes Family Estate label featuring great Pinot Noir, Syrah, Sauvignon Blanc, Viognier, and Grenache Blanc. In addition to a few single vineyard Pinot Noir bottlings, Dobbes focuses on blends from multiple vineyards to provide consistent, balanced, and interesting wines. Two different tasting fights are available in the tasting room, and seated tastings and tours can be arranged by appointment. ✉ *240 S.E. 5th St.* ☎ *503/538–1141* ⊕ *www.joedobbeswines.com* ⊙ *Daily 11–6.*

Domaine Serene. This world-class winery in Dundee's Red Hills is a well-regarded producer of Oregon Pinot Noir and Chardonnay. Bring a picnic and enjoy the beautiful grounds of the estate. As an alternative to the standard drop-in tasting in the high-ceiling tasting room, call ahead

Continued on page 194

The Willamette Valley is Oregon's premier wine region. With a milder climate than any growing area in California, cool-climate grapes like Pinot Noir and Pinot Gris thrive here, and are being transformed into world-class wines.

There may be fewer and smaller wineries than in Napa, but the experience is often more intimate. The winemaker himself may even pour you wine.

Touring is easy, as most wineries are well marked, and have tasting rooms with regular hours. Whether you're taking a day trip from Portland, or staying for a couple of days, here's how to get the most out of your sipping experience.

By Dave Sandage and John Doerper

Above and right, Willamette Valley

Wine Tasting
in the
Willamette
Valley

OREGON'S WINES: THEN AND NOW

Rex Hill Vineyards

THE EARLY YEARS

The French made wine first—French Canadians, that is. In the 1830s, retired fur trappers from the Hudson's Bay Company started to colonize the Willamette Valley and planted grapes on the south-facing buttes. They were followed by American settlers who made wine.

Although wine-making in the region-languished after these early efforts, it never quite vanished. A few wineries hung on, producing wines mainly for Oregonians of European descent.

It wasn't until the 1970s that the state's wine industry finally took off. Only after a group of young California winemakers started making vinifera wines in the Umpqua and Willamette Valleys and gained international acclaim for them, did Oregon's wines really take hold.

WINEMAKING TODAY

Today, Oregon's wine industry is racing ahead. Here the most prolific white and red grapes are Pinot Gris and Pinot Noir, respectively. Other prominent varietals include Riesling, Gewürztraminer, Viognier, Chardonnay, Carbernet Franc, and Syrah.

The wine industry in Oregon is still largely dominated by family and boutique wineries that pay close attention to quality and are often keen to experiment. That makes traveling and tasting at the source an always-interesting experience.

OREGON CERTIFIED SUSTAINABLE WINE

The latest trend in Oregon winemaking is a dedication to responsible grape growing and winemaking. When you see the Oregon Certified Sustainable Wine (OCSW) logo on the back of a wine bottle, it means the winery ensures accountable agricultural and winemaking practices (in conjunction with agencies such as USDA Organic, Demeter Biodynamic, the Food Alliance, Salmon-Safe, and Low Input Viticulture and Enology) through independent third-party certification. For more information on Oregon Certified Sustainable wines and participating wineries, check ⊕ *www.ocsw.org.*

WINE TASTING PRIMER

Ordering and tasting wine—whether at a winery, bar, or restaurant—is easy once you master a few simple steps.

LOOK AND NOTE

Hold your glass by the stem and look at the wine in the glass. Note its color, depth, and clarity.

For whites, is it greenish, yellow, or gold? For reds, is it purplish, ruby, or garnet? Is the wine's color pale or deep? Is the liquid clear or cloudy?

SWIRL AND SNIFF

Swirl the wine gently in the glass to intensify the scents, then sniff over the rim of the glass. What do you smell? Try to identify aromas like:

- **Fruits**—citrus, peaches, berries, figs, melon

- **Flowers**—orange blossoms, honey, perfume

- **Spices**—baking spices, pungent, herbal notes

- **Vegetables**—fresh or cooked, herbal notes

- **Minerals**—earth, steely notes, wet stones

- **Dairy**—butter, cream, cheese, yogurt

- **Oak**—toast, vanilla, coconut, tobacco

- **Animal**—leathery, meaty notes

Are there any unpleasant notes, like mildew or wet dog, that might indicate that the wine is "off?"

SIP AND SAVOR

Prime your palate with a sip, swishing the wine in your mouth. Then spit in a bucket or swallow.

Take another sip and think about the wine's attributes. Sweetness is detected on the tip of the tongue, acidity on the sides of the tongue, and tannins (a mouth-drying sensation) on the gums. Consider the body—does the wine feel light in the mouth, or is there a rich sensation? Are the flavors consistent with the aromas? If you like the wine, try to pinpoint what you like about it, and vice versa if you don't like it.

Take time to savor the wine as you're sipping it—the tasting experience may seem a bit scientific, but the end goal is your enjoyment.

4

IN FOCUS WINE TASTING IN THE WILLAMETTE VALLEY

WINE TOURING AND TASTING

Wine tasting at Argyle and Rex Hill

WHEN TO GO

In high season (June through October) and on weekends and holidays during much of the year, wine-country roads can be busy and tasting rooms are often crowded. If you prefer a more intimate tasting experience, plan your visit for a weekday.

To avoid the frustration of a fruitless drive, confirm in advance that wineries of interest will be open when you plan to visit.

Choose a designated driver for the day: Willamette wine-country roads are often narrow and curvy, and you may be sharing the road with bicyclists and wildlife as well as other wine tourists.

IN THE TASTING ROOM

Tasting rooms are designed to introduce newcomers to the pleasures of wine and to the wines made at the winery. At popular wineries you'll sometimes have to pay for your tasting, anything from a nominal $2 fee to $30 and up for a tasting that might include a glass you can take home. This fee is often deducted if you buy wine before leaving.

WHAT'S AN AVA?

AVAs (American Viticultural Areas) are geographic winegrowing regions that vaguely reflect the French concept of terroir, or "sense of place." The vineyards within a given AVA have similar characteristics such as climate, soil types, and/or elevation, which impart shared characteristics to the wines made from grapes grown in that area. AVAs are strictly geographic boundaries distinct from city or county designations. AVAs can also be subdivided into sub-AVAs; each of the AVAs mentioned here is actually part of the larger Willamette Valley AVA.

Each taste consists of an ounce or two. Feel free to pour whatever you don't finish into one of the dump buckets on the bar. If you like, rinse your glass between pours with a little water. Remember, those sips add up, so pace yourself. If you plan to visit several wineries, try just a few wines at each so you won't suffer from palate fatigue, when your mouth can no longer distinguish subtleties. It's also a good idea to bring a picnic lunch, which you can enjoy on the deck of a winery, taking in the surrounding wine country vistas.

FALL FOLIAGE

In autumn, Willamette Valley vineyards are particularly stunning as the leaves
change color.

DAY TRIP FROM PORTLAND

With nearly 150 vineyards, the Chehalem Mountain and Ribbon Ridge AVAs offer widely varied soil types and diverse Pinot Noirs. The region is less than an hour away from Portland.

Ponzi Vineyards

CHEHALEM MOUNTAIN AND RIBBON RIDGE AVAS

➊ PONZI VINEYARDS

First planted in 1970, Ponzi has some of Oregon's oldest Pinot Noir vines. In addition to current releases, the tasting room sometimes offers older library wines. **Try:** *Arneis, a crisp Italian white varietal.*

✉ 19500 SW Mountain Home Rd., Sherwood

☎ 503/628–1227

⊕ www.ponziwines.com

➋ REX HILL VINEYARDS

Before grapevines, the Willamette Valley was widely planted with fruits and nuts. Enjoy classic Oregon Pinot Noir in this tasting room built around an old fruit and nut drying facility. **Try:** *dark and spicy Dundee Hills Pinot Noir.*

✉ 30835 N. Hwy. 99W, Newberg

☎ 800/739–4455

⊕ www.rexhill.com

➌ VERCINGETORIX (VX) VINEYARD

This 10-acre vineyard sits in the middle of a 210-acre farm near the Willamette River. The tasting room is in one of the barns; a relaxed, friendly atmosphere for sampling. **Try:** *crisp and refreshing Pinot Blanc.*

✉ 8000 N.E. Parrish Rd., Newberg

☎ 503/538–9895

⊕ www.vxvineyard.com

➍ FOX FARM VINEYARDS TASTING ROOM

In addition to offering their own wines, this multi-winery tasting room in downtown Newberg features samples from several small local producers. The menu changes periodically.

✉ 606 E. First St., Newberg

☎ 503/538–8466

⊕ www.foxfarmvineyards.com

➎ UTOPIA VINEYARD

The tasting room at this small Oregon winery is quite intimate—you'll likely be served by the winemaker himself. **Try:** *light and slightly sweet Rosé.*

✉ 17445 N.E. Ribbon Ridge Rd., Newberg

☎ 503/298–7841

⊕ www.utopiawine.com

Vercingetorix (VX) Vineyard

Adelsheim Vineyard

Rex Hill

Pinot Gris grapes

219
Scholls Ferry Rd.
Winery La.
Scholls
❶
15.7 mi

219
Scholls Sherwood Blvd.

TO PORTLAND ↗
Beef Bend Rd.

CHEHALEM
MOUNTAINS

LeBeau Rd.
99W

Edy Rd.

Bell Rd.
○ Sherwood
Sunset Blvd.

ell Rd. 23 mi
❾
Quarry Rd.

Pleasant Hill Rd.

❷
21.1 mi
Haugen Rd.
Ladd Hill

❿
○ Newberg
Corral Cr.

KEY	
❶	*Driving distance*
00 mi	*from Portland*

99W
23.9 mi
❹

219

Parrish Rd.
Wilsonville Rd.
5th St
❸
25.8 mi
Ladd Hill

❽ ARAMENTA CELLARS

A small, family-run operation that offers tastings in its winery, built on the foundation of an old barn. The on-site vineyard grows primarily Pinot Noir and Chardonnay. **Try:** *smooth and structured Tillie Claret.*

✉ 17979 N.E. Lewis Rogers La., Newberg
☎ 503-538-7230
⊕ www.aramentacellars.com

STOP FOR A BITE

❾ JORY RESTAURANT

Located within the luxurious Allison Inn and Spa, Jory serves creative dishes that highlight the bounty of the Willamette Valley.

✉ 2525 Allison La., Newberg
☎ 503-554-2526
⊕ www.theallison.com

❿ SUBTERRA

Casual fine dining in a wine cellar atmosphere underneath the Dark Horse wine bar. The menu features global cuisine and a good selection of local wines.

✉ 1505 Portland Rd., Newberg
☎ 503-538-6060
⊕ www.subterrarestaurant.com

❻ ADELSHEIM VINEYARD

One of Oregon's older Pinot Noir producers, Adelsheim has just opened a new tasting room inside its modern winery, with friendly, knowledgeable employees. **Try:** *dark and smoky Elizabeth's Reserve Pinot Noir.*

✉ 16800 N.E. Calkins La., Newberg
☎ 503-538-3652
⊕ www.adelsheim.com

❼ BERGSTROM WINERY

A beautiful tasting room, but the real high point here is the classic Oregon Pinot Noir sourced from several of its estate vineyards as well as other local sites. **Try:** *earthy Bergstrom Pinot Noir.*

✉ 18215 N.E. Calkins La., Newberg
☎ 503-554-0468
⊕ www.bergstromwines.com

TWO DAYS IN WINE COUNTRY

DAY 1
DUNDEE HILLS AVA

The Dundee Hills AVA is home to some of Oregon's best known Pinot Noir producers. Start your tour in the town of Dundee, about 30 miles southwest of Portland, then drive up into the red hills and enjoy the valley views from many wineries.

❶ ARGYLE WINERY

If you don't want to drive off the beaten path, this winery is right on Highway 99W in Dundee. They specialize in sparkling wines, but also make very nice still wines. **Try:** *crisp Brut Rosé.*

✉ 691 Hwy. 99 W, Dundee
☎ 503/538–8520
🌐 www.argylewinery.com

❷ PONZI WINE BAR

This tasting room close to Argyle has a nice selection of local wines. It's a good choice for those who want to sample a large selection side-by-side. **Try:** *bright and fruity Ponzi Pinot Gris.*

✉ 100 S.W. 7th St., Dundee
☎ 503/554–1500
🌐 www.ponziwines.com

❸ ARCHERY SUMMIT

An Oregon Pinot Noir pioneer, Archery Summit features memorable wines and equally pleasing views. Call in advance to schedule a tour of the winery and aging caves. **Try:** *dark and rich Premier Cuvée Pinot Noir.*

✉ 18599 NE Archery Summit Rd., Dayton
☎ 503/864–4300
🌐 www.archerysummit.com

❹ DOMAINE DROUHIN OREGON

Started in the late 1980s by the Drouhin family of Burgundy fame, this winery makes notable Oregon Pinot Noir, as well as Chardonnay. **Try:** *smooth and earthy Willamette Valley Pinot Noir.*

✉ 6750 Breyman Orchards Rd., Dayton
☎ 503/864–2700
🌐 www.domainedrouhin.com

❺ VISTA HILLS VINEYARD

The so-called Treehouse is arguably the most stunning tasting room in Oregon. Sample wine made from estate fruit on a deck that overlooks the vineyards of the Dundee Hills. **Try:** *fruity Treehouse Pinot Noir.*

✉ 6475 N.E. Hilltop La., Dayton
☎ 503/864–3200
🌐 www.vistahillsvineyard.com

DAY 2
YAMHILL-CARLTON AVA

To the west of the Dundee Hills AVA is the horseshoe-shaped Yamhill-Carlton AVA. Vineyards here are found on the slopes that surround the towns of Yamhill and Carlton. Carlton has become a center of wine tourism, and you could easily spend a day visiting tasting rooms in town.

❻ PENNER-ASH WINE CELLARS

This state-of-the-art winery and tasting room is atop a hill with an excellent view of the valley below. **Try:** *smooth and dark Shea Vineyard Pinot Noir.*

✉ 15771 N.E. Ribbon Ridge Rd., Newberg
☎ 503/554–5545
🌐 www.pennerash.com

In map:

RIBBON RIDG
Yamhill
47
35.2 mi
Woodland Loop
240
30.3 mi
6
Ribbon Ridge Rd.
Laughlin Rd.
Blackburn Rd.
Yamhill Rd.
Stag Hollow Rd.
YAMHILL-CARLTON
33.7 mi
7
Hendricks Rd.
Pine St.
35.8 mi
8
11
Malo St.
9
35.9 mi
Oak Spring Farm Rd.
Abbey Rd.
31.2
Hilltop La.
5
34 mi
Mineral Springs Rd.

KEY
🍷 Driving distance
00 mi from Portland

10
47

Penner-Ash Wine Cellars

Ponzi Wine Bar

TO ↗
NEWBERG,
PORTLAND

Red Hill Rd.

Fox Farm Rd.

99W

**UNDEE
HILLS**

Fairview

26.5 mi
7th St.
9th St.

5th St.

⑫
②   ①   26.4 mi
⑬

O Dundee

29.4 mi

③

Albert St.

Archery Summit Rd.

Orchards Rd.

STOP FOR A BITE

**⑪ THE HORSERADISH
WINE AND CHEESE BAR**
Located in downtown Carlton,
The Horseradish offers a wide
selection of local wines as
well as cheese from around
the world. The sandwiches and
small plates make for a great
quick lunch.
- ✉ 211 W. Main St., Carlton
- ☎ 503/852–6656
- ⊕ www.thehorseradish.com

⑫ DUNDEE BISTRO
A favorite of winemakers,
Dundee Bistro serves seasonal
local ingredients paired with
Willamette Valley wines. Enjoy
outdoor seating, or watch chefs
work in the open kitchen inside.
- ✉ 100-A S.W. 7th St., Dundee
- ☎ 503/554–1650
- ⊕ www.dundeebistro.com

⑬ TINA'S
The warm and intimate Tina's
features dishes made with seasonal ingredients, organic vegetables, and free-range meats.
Stop by for lunch Tuesday–Friday, or nightly dinner.
- ✉ 760 Hwy. 99 W, Dundee
- ☎ 503/538–8880
- ⊕ www.tinasdundee.com

---

⑦ LEMELSON VINEYARDS
Although it specializes in
single-vineyard Pinot Noir,
Lemelson also makes several
crisp white wines. The deck
overlooking the vineyards is
perfect for picnics. **Try:** *crisp
and fruity Riesling.*
- ✉ 12020 N.E. Stag Hollow Rd.,
  Carlton
- ☎ 503/852–6619
- ⊕ www.lemelsonvineyards.com

⑧ TYRUS EVAN WINE
Well-known winemaker Ken
Wright's second label features
big reds. The tasting room is
in the historic Carlton train
station. **Try:** *bold and spicy Del
Rio Claret.*
- ✉ 120 N. Pine St., Carlton
- ☎ 503/852–7070
- ⊕ www.tyrusevanwine.com

⑨ SCOTT PAUL WINES
In addition to making Oregon Pinot Noir, Scott Paul
Wines also runs a Burgundy
import company, allowing
you to taste locally grown
Pinot Noir alongside some
of the best Burgundies.
Try: *structured and elegant
La Paulée Pinot Noir.*
- ✉ 128 S. Pine St., Carlton
- ☎ 503/852–7300
- ⊕ www.scottpaul.com

⑩ LENNÉ ESTATE
Lenné specializes in highly
regarded Pinot Noir,
although it's often pouring
a couple of non-Pinot wines
from other wineries as
well. The tasting room in a
small stone building overlooks the vineyards.
Try: *complex and earthy
Estate Pinot Noir.*
- ✉ 18760 Laughlin Rd.,
  Yamhill
- ☎ 503/956–2256
- ⊕ www.lenneestate.com

4

IN FOCUS WINE TASTING IN THE WILLAMETTE VALLEY

to reserve a tour or private seated tasting, which includes an extended flight of rare wines. ⊠ *6555 N.E. Hilltop La., Dayton* ☎ *503/864–4600, 866/864-6555* ⊕ *www.domaineserene.com* ⊗ *Daily 11–4.*

Erath Vineyards Winery. When Dick Erath opened one of Oregon's pioneer wineries more than a quarter century ago, he focused on producing distinctive Pinot Noir from grapes he'd been growing in the Red Hills since 1972—as well as full-flavored Pinot Gris, Pinot Blanc, Chardonnay, Riesling, and late-harvest Gewürztraminer. The wines are excellent and reasonably priced. In 2006 the winery was sold to Washington State's giant conglomerate Ste. Michelle Wine Estate. The tasting room is in the middle of the vineyards, high in the hills, with views in nearly every direction; the hazelnut trees that covered the slopes not so long ago have been replaced with vines. The tasting-room terrace, which overlooks the winery and the hills, is a choice spot for picnicking. Crabtree Park, next to the winery, is a good place to stretch your legs after a tasting. ⊠ *9409 N.E. Worden Hill Rd.* ☎ *503/538–3318, 800/539–9463* ⊕ *www.erath.com* ⊗ *Daily 11–5.*

Ponzi Wine Bar. Located right on the main highway between Portland and wine country, the Ponzi Wine Bar offers the opportunity to sample wines from both the Ponzi family and small local producers without straying far from the beaten path. The tasting menu features current releases of Ponzi wines, as well as a rotating selection of other local wines. If you've had enough wine for a while, you can also get snacks, Italian coffee, or a craft beer to enjoy in the comfortable tasting room. ⊠ *100 S.W. 7th St.* ☎ *503/554–1500* ⊕ *ponziwines.com/our-locations/ wine-bar-dundee* ⊗ *Daily 11–5.*

Sokol Blosser. One of Yamhill County's oldest wineries (it was established in 1971) makes consistently excellent wines and sells them at reasonable prices. Set on a gently sloping south-facing hillside and surrounded by vineyards, lush lawns, and shade trees, it's a splendid place to learn about wine. A demonstration vineyard with several rows of vines contains the main grape varieties and shows what happens to them as the seasons unfold. Winery tours are available by reservation as well as vineyard hikes and ATV tours during the summer. ⊠ *5000 Sokol Blosser La., 3 miles west of Dundee off Hwy. 99W* ☎ *503/864–2282, 800/582–6668* ⊕ *www.sokolblosser.com* ⊗ *Daily 10–4.*

Torii Mor Winery. Established in 1993, this winery makes small quantities of handcrafted Pinot Noir, Pinot Gris, and Chardonnay and is set amid Japanese gardens with breathtaking views of the Willamette Valley. The gardens were designed by Takuma Tono, the same architect who designed the renowned Portland Japanese Garden. The owners, who love all things Japanese, named their winery after the distinctive Japanese gate of Shinto religious significance; they added a Scandinavian *mor*, signifying "earth," to create an east-west combo: "earth gate." Jacques Tardy, a native of Nuits Saint Georges, in Burgundy, France, is the current winemaker. Under his guidance Torii Mor wines have become more Burgundian in style. ⊠ *18323 N.E. Fairview Dr.* ☎ *800/839–5004* ⊕ *www.toriimorwinery.com* ⊗ *Daily 11–5.*

Vista Hills Vineyard. The Treehouse tasting room here is arguably the most beautiful in Oregon. Step out onto the deck and enjoy the view from underneath the towering trees. Vista Hills is a bit different from its neighbors in that there is no winery but several well-known local wine-makers create wine from the vineyard grapes to sell under the Vista Hills label. The result is a range of distinctive wine styles, all made from the same vineyard. Also available are Hawaiian chocolate and coffee from their sister farm in Kona. ⊠ *6475 Hilltop Ln., Dayton* ☏ *503/864–3200* ⊕ *www.vistahillsvineyard.com* ⊘ *Daily noon–5.*

White Rose Estate. Like many of its better-known neighbors in the Dundee Hills, White Rose Estate produces elegant Pinot Noir that reflects the land where it is grown. In addition to their own estate vineyard, they purchase grapes from several highly regarded vineyards around the Willamette Valley. They describe their wines as "neo-classical," using traditional techniques in the vineyard, and state-of-the-art equipment and handling in the winery. Somewhat unusual for Oregon, most of the wines have a fairly high percentage of whole clusters included during fermentation, giving the wines more complexity and a bit of spice. ⊠ *6250 N.E. Hilltop La., Dayton* ☏ *503/864–2328* ⊕ *www.whiteroseestate.com* ⊘ *Daily 11–5.*

WHERE TO EAT

$$ ✕ **Babica Hen.** Breakfast is the headliner and is served until 2 pm at this
PACIFIC second location of a popular Portland-area eatery. But don't worry: you
NORTHWEST can get a great lunch and dinner, too. They use fresh eggs from local pasture-raised chickens, and serve local pork, beef, and dairy products, and even produce from their own garden. The dinner menu changes frequently to reflect seasonal ingredients, and usually features local seafood and meats, along with a few familiar comfort dishes like meat loaf or chicken and dumplings. Ⓢ *Average main: $18* ⊠ *1410 N. Hwy. 99W* ☏ *503/538-7970* ⊕ *babicahencafe.com.*

$$$ ✕ **Dundee Bistro.** The Ponzi wine family are capable restaurateurs as
CONTEMPORARY well and use Northwest organic foods such as Draper Valley chicken, Carlton Farms pork, and locally produced wines, fruits, vegetables, nuts, mushrooms, fish, and meats. Vaulted ceilings provide an open feeling inside, warmed by abundant fresh flowers and the works of local Oregon artists. Ⓢ *Average main: $25* ⊠ *100-A S.W. 7th St.* ☏ *503/554–1650* ⊕ *www.dundeebistro.com.*

$ ✕ **Red Hills Market.** Serving great sandwiches, salads, and pizza, this is the
PACIFIC perfect stop for a quick lunch in the middle of a day of wine tasting, or
NORTHWEST a casual no-frills dinner at the end of the day. Many of the sandwiches feature locally made charcuterie and cheeses, and the pizzas range from traditional Margherita to a spicy chorizo, blue cheese, and arugula. In addition to wine, there are cocktails and a great selection of local and imported craft beers. There's also a market where you can stock up on snacks to keep you going for the rest of the day, and many of the menu items are available to go. Ⓢ *Average main: $12* ⊠ *155 S.W. 7th St.* ☏ *971/832–8414* ⊕ *www.redhillsmarket.com.*

$$$ ✕ **Tina's.** Chef–proprietors Tina and David Bergen bring a powerful one-
FRENCH   two punch to this Dundee favorite that often lures Portlanders away
Fodor'sChoice   from their own restaurant scene. The couple shares cooking duties—
★   Tina does the baking and is often on hand to greet you, and David
brings his experience as a former caterer and employee of nearby Sokol
Blosser Winery to the table, ensuring that you have the right glass of
wine to match your course. Fish and game vie for attention on the
country-French menu: entrées might include grilled Oregon salmon or
Alaskan halibut, or a braised rabbit, local lamb, or tenderloin. Avail
yourself of any special soups, particularly if there's corn chowder in the
house. The lunch menu includes soup, sandwiches, and creative salads
with local, seasonal ingredients. Service is as intimate and laid-back as
the interior. A double fireplace divides the dining room, with heavy glass
brick shrouded by bushes on the highway side, so you're not bothered
by the traffic on Highway 99. ⑤ *Average main: $30* ⊠ *760 Hwy. 99W*
☎ *503/538–8880* ⊕ *www.tinasdundee.com* ☯ *No lunch Sat.–Mon.*

WHERE TO STAY

$$ ⏛ **Dundee Manor Bed and Breakfast.** This 1908-built traditional home
B&B/INN   on expansive grounds is filled with treasures and collectibles that add
Fodor'sChoice   intrigue to each themed room: African, Asian, European, and North
★   American. **Pros:** terrific amenities; lots of activities; attentive staff.
Cons: few rooms. ⑤ *Rooms from: $200* ⊠ *8380 N.E. Worden Hill
Rd.* ☎ *503/554–1945, 888/262–1133* ⊕ *www.dundeemanor.com* ⤵ *4
rooms* ⑧ *Breakfast.*

$$ ⏛ **The Inn at Red Hills.** These spacious and extremely comfortable rooms,
HOTEL   each with its own layout, offer plenty of local flavor, from the materials
in the building, the wines served, and the ingredients used in the kitchen.
Pros: contemporary, stylish surroundings; close to many wineries. **Cons:**
located on the main highway through town rather than the country.
⑤ *Rooms from: $179* ⊠ *1410 N. Hwy. 99W* ☎ *503/538–7666* ⊕ *www.
innatredhills.com* ⤵ *18 rooms, 2 suites* ⑧ *No meals.*

YAMHILL-CARLTON

14 miles west of Dundee.

Just outside the small towns of Carlton and Yamhill are neatly combed
benchlands and hillsides, an American Viticultural Area (AVA) estab-
lished in 2004, and home to some of the finest Pinot Noir vineyards in
the world. Carlton has exploded with many small tasting rooms in the
past few years, and you could easily spend an entire day tasting wine
within three or four blocks. The area is a gorgeous quilt of nurseries,
grain fields, and orchards. Come here for the wine tasting, but don't
expect to find too much else to do.

GETTING HERE AND AROUND

Having your own car is the best way to explore this rural region of
Yamhill County, located a little more than an hour's drive from Portland
International Airport. The towns of Yamhill and Carlton are about an
hour's drive from Downtown Portland, traveling through Tigard, to
Newberg and west on Highway 240.

EXPLORING

TOP ATTRACTIONS

Lemelson Vineyards. This winery was designed from the ground up to be a no-compromises Pinor Noir production facility with an eye to Willamette Valley aesthetics, and the highlight is a diverse range of single-vineyard Pinot Noirs. But don't neglect the bright Pinot Gris and Riesling, perfect with seafood or spicy fare. The spacious high-ceiling tasting room is a great place to relax and take in the view through the floor-to-ceiling windows, or bring a picnic and enjoy the deck on a warm summer day. ⊠ *12020 N.E. Stag Hollow Rd., Carlton* ☎ *503/852–6619* ⊕ *www.lemelsonvineyards.com* ⊗ *Thurs.–Mon. 11–4.*

Lenné Estate. The small stone building that houses the tasting room is surrounded by the estate vineyard and looks like something right out of Burgundy. Steve Lutz was looking for the perfect site to grow Pinot Noir and bought the property in 2000. In addition to offering his own rich and elegant estate Pinot Noirs for tasting, he often pours other varietals from other wineries. ⊠ *18760 N.E. Laughlin Rd., Yamhill* ☎ *503/956–2256* ⊕ *www.lenneestate.com* ⊟ *$10* ⊗ *Thurs.-Fri. 12:30–5, Sat.–Sun. 12–5.*

WORTH NOTING

Anne Amie Vineyards. Early wine country adopters Fred and Mary Benoit established this hilltop winery as Chateau Benoit in 1979. When the winery changed hands in 1999, it was renamed Anne Amie and has been concentrating on Pinot Blanc, Pinot Gris, and Pinot Noir, but still makes a dry Riesling. In addition, they also make Syrah and a Bordeaux blend from eastern Washington grapes. Both the tasting room and the picnic area have spectacular views across the hills and valleys of Yamhill County. ⊠ *6580 N.E. Mineral Springs Rd., Carlton* ☎ *503/864–2991* ⊕ *www.anneamie.com* ⊗ *Open Mar.–Dec., daily 10–5; Jan.–Feb., Fri.–Sun. 10–5 or by appointment.*

Carlton Winemakers Studio. Oregon's first cooperative winery was specifically designed to house multiple small premium wine producers. This gravity-flow winery has up-to-date wine-making equipment as well as multiple cellars for storing the different makers' wines. You can taste and purchase bottles from the different member wineries: Andrew Rich, Asilda, Bachelder, Dukes Family Vineyard, Hamacher Wines, Lazy River Vineyard, Merriman Wines, Mad Violets, Omero, Retour Wine Co., Trout Lily Ranch, Utopia Vineyard, and Wahle Vineyards and Cellars. The emphasis is on Pinot Noir, but more than a dozen other types of wines are poured, from Cabernet Franc to Gewürztraminer to Mourvèdre on a rotating basis. The selection of wines available to taste changes every few days. ⊠ *801 N. Scott St., Carlton* ☎ *503/852–6100* ⊕ *www.winemakersstudio.com* ⊗ *Daily 11–5.*

Ken Wright Cellars Tasting Room. Carlton's former train depot is now the tasting room for Ken Wright Cellars and his warm-climate label, Tyrus Evan. The winery specializes in single-vineyard Pinot Noirs, each subtly different from the next depending on the soil types and grape clones. The wines are poured side by side, giving you an opportunity to go back and forth to compare them. The Tyrus Evan wines are quite different from the Ken Wright Pinots: they are warm-climate varieties like Cabernet Franc, Malbec, Syrah, and red Bordeaux blends, from grapes Wright buys from vineyards in eastern Washington and southern Oregon. You can also pick up cheeses and other picnic supplies, as well as wine country gifts and souvenirs. ⊠ *120 N. Pine St., Carlton* ☎ *503/852–7010* ⊕ *www.kenwrightcellars.com* ⊗ *Daily 11–5.*

Scott Paul Tasting Room and Winery. Pinot Noir fans, listen up: this small spot in the center of Carlton not only makes Pinot Noir from Oregon grapes, but it also imports and sells Pinot Noirs from Burgundy (as well as grower Champagne). The mainstay Pinot Noirs made from local grapes are Audrey, the finest wine of the vintage, and La Paulée, a selection of the best lots of each vintage. In addition, they'll make several other Pinots customized to the widely variable growing conditions each year in Oregon. All are splendid examples of the wines that can be made from this great, challenging grape. The tasting room, a quaint redbrick building, is across the street from the winery. Tours are by appointment only. Wine seminars are offered periodically, and private guided tastings are available by appointment. ⊠ *128 S. Pine St., Carlton* ☎ *503/852–7300* ⊕ *www.scottpaul.com* ⊗ *Sat. noon–5.*

MCMINNVILLE

11 miles south of Yamhill on Hwy. 99W.

The Yamhill County seat, McMinnville lies in the center of Oregon's thriving wine industry. There is a larger concentration of wineries in Yamhill County than in any other area of the state. Among the varieties are Chardonnay, Pinot Noir, and Pinot Gris. Most of the wineries in the area offer tours and tastings. McMinnville's downtown area, with a pleasantly disproportionate number of bookstores and art galleries for its size, is well worth exploring; many of the historic district buildings, erected 1890–1915, are still standing, and are remarkably well maintained.

GETTING HERE AND AROUND

McMinnville is a little more than an hour's drive from Downtown Portland; **Caravan Airport Transportation** (☎ *541/994–9645* ⊕ *www.caravanairporttransportation.com*) provides shuttle service to Portland International Airport. McMinnville is just 70 minutes from Lincoln City on the Oregon Coast, and 27 miles west of Salem.

ESSENTIALS

Visitor Information McMinnville Chamber of Commerce ⊠ *417 N.W. Adams St.* ☎ *503/472–6196* ⊕ *www.mcminnville.org.*

EXPLORING

FAMILY

Fodor's Choice

★

Evergreen Aviation and Space Museum. Howard Hughes' *Spruce Goose,* the largest plane ever built and constructed entirely of wood, is on permanent display, but if you can take your eyes off the giant you will also see more than 45 historic planes and replicas from the early years of flight and World War II, as well as the postwar and modern eras. Across the parking lot from the aviation museum is the space museum with artifacts that include a German V-2 rocket and a Titan missile, complete with silo and launch control room. A water park (separate admission) has 10 waterslides, including one that starts at a Boeing 747-100 that sits on *top* of the building. The IMAX theater is open daily and features several different films each day. There's a museum store and two cafés, as well as ongoing educational programs and special events. ⊠ *500 N.E. Michael King Smith Way* ☎ *503/434–4185* ⊕ *www.evergreenmuseum. org* 🖾 *$25, includes IMAX movie* ⊙ *Daily 9–5, closed holidays.*

The Eyrie Vineyards. When David Lett planted the first Pinot Noir vines in the Willamette Valley in 1965, he was setting in motion a series of events that has caused Willamette Valley Pinot Noir to be recognized as among the best in the world. Affectionately known as Papa Pinot, Lett, along with several other pioneering winemakers nurtured the Oregon wine industry to what it is today. Today David's son Jason Lett is now the winemaker and vineyard manager, and continues to make Pinot Noir, Pinot Gris, and Chadonnay that reflect the gentle touch that has always characterized Eyrie wines. In recent years, many small wineries have sprung up in the neighborhood around this historic winery. ⊠ *935 N.E. 10th Ave.* ☎ *503/472–6315, 888/440–4970* ⊕ *www.eyrievineyards.com* ⊙ *Daily noon–5.*

NEED A BREAK?

Serendipity Ice Cream. Historic Cook's Hotel, built in 1886, is the setting for a true, old-fashioned ice-cream parlor experience. Try a sundae, and take home cookies made from scratch. If you don't feel like ice cream, the homemade soup is a great choice on a rainy day. ⊠ *502 N.E. 3rd St.* ☎ *503/474–9189* ⊕ *serendipityicecream.com.*

WHERE TO EAT AND STAY

$$$$
CONTEMPORARY

✕ **Joel Palmer House.** Wild mushrooms and truffles are the stars at this 1857 home, named after an Oregon pioneer, that is now on the National Register of Historic Places. There are three small dining rooms, each seating about 15 people. A popular starter is Heidi's three-mushroom tart, and while the menu changes seasonally, the mushroom tart, Joe's wild mushroom soup, and wild mushroom risotto with Oregon truffle oil are traditions that are always available. The standard dinner is a 3 course prix-fixe menu, but if you really, really like mushrooms, have your entire table order Chef Christopher's Mushroom Madness Menu, a six-course extravaganza. ⑤ *Average main: $50* ⊠ *600 Ferry St., Dayton* ☎ *503/864–2995* ⊕ *www.joelpalmerhouse.com* ⊙ *Closed Sun. and Mon. No lunch.*

$$$
ITALIAN

✕ **Nick's Italian Cafe.** Famed for serving Oregon's wine country enthusiasts, this fine-dining venue is a destination for a special evening or lunch. Modestly furnished but with a voluminous wine cellar, Nick's serves spirited and simple food, reflecting the owner's northern Italian heritage. A five-course prix-fixe menu changes nightly with optional wine pairings. À la carte options are also available. ⑤ *Average main: $26* ⊠ *521 N.E. 3rd St.* ☎ *503/434–4471* ⊕ *www.nicksitaliancafe.com* ⌖ *Reservations essential.*

$
HOTEL

▤ **Hotel Oregon.** Rooms in the former Elberton Hotel, built in 1905, have tall ceilings and high windows, are outfitted in late-Victorian furnishings, and filled with whimsical art—sometimes serene, often bizarre—as well as photos and sayings scribbled on the walls. **Pros:** inexpensive; casual and lively; plenty of food and drink on the premises. **Cons:** shared baths for most rooms; those seeking upscale ambience should look elsewhere. $ *Rooms from: $60* ⊠ *310 N.E. Evans St.* ☎ *503/472–8427, 888/472–8427* ⊕ *www.mcmenamins.com* ⬎ *42 rooms* ⊺⊙⊺ *No meals.*

$$

B&B/INN

Fodor'sChoice

★

⊞ **Joseph Mattey House Bed & Breakfast.** The four upstairs rooms in this Queen Anne Victorian mansion are whimsically named after locally grown grape varieties and are decorated in keeping with the character of those wines: crisp white furnishings in the Chardonnay Room, dark-wood pieces and reddish wine accents in the Pinot Noir room. **Pros:** refined bed-and-breakfast atmosphere. **Cons:** not many modern amenities in the rooms. $ *Rooms from: $170* ⊠ *10221 N.E. Mattey La., off Hwy. 99W, ¼ mile south of Lafayette* ☎ *503/434–5058* ⊕ *www. matteyhouse.com* ⬎ *4 rooms* ⊺⊙⊺ *Breakfast.*

NIGHTLIFE AND THE ARTS

Spirit Mountain Casino and Lodge. Located 24 miles southwest of McMinnville on Highway 18, this popular gambling getaway is owned and operated by the Confederated Tribes of the Grande Ronde Community of Oregon. The 90,000-square-foot casino has more than a thousand slots, as well as poker and blackjack tables, roulette, craps, Pai Gow poker, keno, bingo, and off-track betting. Big-name comedians and rock and country musicians perform in the 1,700-seat concert hall, and there's an arcade for the kids. Complimentary shuttle service from Portland and Salem is available. Dining options include an all-you-can-eat buffet, a deli, and a café. ⊠ *27100 S.W. Salmon River Hwy., Grand Ronde* ☎ *503/879–2350, 800/760–7977* ⊕ *spiritmountain.com.*

MID-WILLAMETTE VALLEY

While most of the wineries are concentrated in Washington and Yamhill counties, there are several finds in the Mid-Willamette Valley that warrant extending a wine enthusiast's journey. There are also flower, hops, berries, and seed gardens scattered throughout Salem, Albany, and Corvallis. The huge number of company stores concentrated on Interstate 5 will have you thinking about some new Nikes, and Oregon State University will have you wearing orange and black long after Halloween is over. Be aware that many communities in this region are little more than wide spots in the road. In these tiny towns you might find only a gas station, a grocery store, a church or two, and a school. Watch out for any "School Crossing" signs: Oregon strictly enforces its speed-limit laws.

SALEM

24 miles from McMinnville, south on Hwy. 99W and east on Hwy. 22; 45 miles south of Portland on I–5.

The state capital has a rich pioneer history, but before that it was the home of the Calapooia Indians, who called it Chemeketa, which means "place of rest." Salem is said to have been renamed by missionaries.

Although trappers and farmers preceded them in the Willamette Valley, the Methodist missionaries had come in 1834 to minister to Native Americans, and they are credited with the founding of Salem. In 1842 they established the first academic institution west of the Rockies, which is now known as Willamette University. Salem became the capital when Oregon achieved statehood in 1859 (Oregon City was the capital of the Oregon Territory). Salem serves as the seat to Marion County as well as the home of the state fairgrounds. Government ranks as a major industry here, while the city's setting in the heart of the fertile Willamette Valley stimulates rich agricultural and food-processing industries. More than a dozen wineries are in or near Salem. The main attractions in Salem are west of Interstate 5 in and around the Capitol Mall.

GETTING HERE AND AROUND

Salem is located on Interstate 5 with easy access to Portland, Albany, and Eugene. **Hut Portland Airport Shuttle** (☏ *503/364–4444* ⊕ *www.portlandairportshuttle.com*) provides transportation to Portland International Airport, which is one hour and 15 minutes away. Salem's McNary Field no longer has commercial airline service, but serves general aviation aircraft.

Bus transportation throughout Salem is provided by **Cherriot's** (⊕ *www.cherriots.org*). Amtrak operates regularly, and its train station is located at ✉ *500 13th Street SE.*

ESSENTIALS

Visitor Information Salem Convention & Visitors Center ✉ *181 High St. NE* ☏ *503/581–4325, 800/874–7012* ⊕ *www.travelsalem.com.*

EXPLORING
TOP ATTRACTIONS

Oregon Garden. Just outside the town of Silverton is a gardener's oasis, showcasing the amazing botanical diversity of the Willamette Valley and Pacific Northwest. Open 365 days a year, the 80-acre garden features themed plots ranging from a conifer forest to medicinal plants. There is also a whimsical children's garden complete with a model train, and another garden featuring the agricultural bounty of the area. A free narrated tram tour operates from April to October, allowing visitors an overview of the garden before exploring on their own. ✉ *879 W. Main St., Silverton* ☏ *503/874–8100, 877/674–2733* ⊕ *www.oregongarden.org* ⌨ *$11* ☉ *May–Sept., daily 9–6; Oct.–Apr., daily 10–4.*

Willamette Heritage Center at The Mill. Take a trip back in time and experience the story of Oregon's early pioneers and the industrial revolution. The **Thomas Kay Woolen Mill Museum** complex (circa 1889), complete with working waterwheels and millstream, looks as if the workers have just stepped away for a lunch break. Teasel gigging, napper flock bins, and the patented Furber double-acting napper are but a few of the machines and processes on display. The **Jason Lee House,** the **John D. Boon Home,** and the **Methodist Parsonage** are also part of the village. There is nothing grandiose about these early pioneer homes, the oldest frame structures in the Northwest, but they reveal a great deal about domestic life in the wilds of Oregon in the 1840s.

Mid-Willamette
Valley and
South Willamette
Valley

0   15 mi

0   15 km

Willamette Mission
State Park
Bethel Heights
Winery
Witness Tree
Vineyard
Keizer
Salem
Hayesville
Four Corners
Dallas
Monmouth
Turner
Aumsville
Stayton
Jefferson
Scio
Millersburg
North Albany
Albany
OSU
Corvallis
Tangent
Shedd
Halsey
Brownsville
Monroe
Harrisburg
Junction City
Cheshire
Coburg
Santa Clara
River Road
Eugene
Springfield
Cascades
Raptor Center
Sweet Cheeks
Winery
Creswell
King Estate
Winery
Cottage Grove

Mount
Angel
Scotts
Mills
Silverton
Oregon
Garden
Silver Falls
State Park
Lyons
Gates
Mill
City
Detroit
Detroit
Lake
Green Peter
Lake
Foster
Cascadia
Sweet Home
Holley
Waterloo
Lebanon
Crabtree
Marcola
Vida
Blue River
Dam
Blue River
McKenzie
Bridge
Cougar Dam
Cougar
Reservoir
Leaburg
McKenzie River
Highway
Terwilliger Hot Springs
Walterville
Mt. Pisgah
Arboretum
Lowell

C A S C A D E S

22
99W
213
214
226
34
99W
58
5
5
20
20
126
126
58
58

✉ *1313 Mill St. SE* ☎ *503/585–7012* ⊕ *www.willametteheritage.org* 🎟 *$6* ⊙ *Mon.–Sat. 10–5.*

Witness Tree Vineyard. Named for the ancient oak that towers over the vineyard (it was used as a surveyor's landmark in the 1850s), this winery produces premium Pinot Noir made entirely from grapes grown on its 100-acre estate nestled in the Eola Hills northwest of Salem. The vineyard also produces limited quantities of estate Chardonnay, Viognier, Pinot Blanc, Dolcetto, and a sweet dessert wine called Sweet Signé. Tours are available by appointment. ✉ *7111 Spring Valley Rd. NW* ☎ *503/585–7874* ⊕ *www.witnesstreevineyard.com* ⊙ *May–Oct., Tues.–Sun. 11–5; Mar.–Apr. and Nov.–mid-Dec., Thurs.–Sun. 11–5.*

WORTH NOTING

FAMILY **Gilbert House Children's Museum.** This is a different kind of kids' museum; an amazing place to let the imagination run wild. Celebrating the life and the inventions of A.C. Gilbert, a Salem native who became a toy manufacturer and inventor, the historic houses included many themed interactive rooms along with a huge outdoor play structure. In addition to the children's activities, many beloved toys created by A.C. Gilbert are on display, including Erector sets and American Flyer trains. The wide range of indoor and outdoor interactive exhibits will appeal to children (and adults) of all ages. ✉ *116 Marion St. NE* ☎ *503/371–3631* ⊕ *www.acgilbert.org* 🎟 *$8* ⊙ *Mon.–Sat. 10–5, Sun. noon–5.*

Bethel Heights Vineyard. Founded in 1977, Bethel Heights was one of the first vineyards planted in the Eola Hills region of the Willamette Valley. It produces Pinot Noir, Chardonnay, Pinot Blanc, and Pinot Gris. The tasting room has one of the most glorious panoramic views of any winery in the state; its terrace and picnic area overlook the surrounding vineyards, the valley below, and Mount Jefferson in the distance. ✉ *6060 Bethel Heights Rd. NW* ☎ *503/581–2262* ⊕ *www. bethelheights.com* ⊙ *Feb.–Nov., Tues.–Sun. 11–5; Dec.–Jan., weekends 11–4.*

Bush's Pasture Park. These 105 acres of rolling lawn and formal English gardens include the remarkably well-preserved Bush House, an 1878 Italianate mansion at the park's far-western boundary. It has 10 marble fireplaces and virtually all of its original furnishings, and can be visited only on informative tours. Bush Barn Art Center, behind the house, exhibits the work of Northwest artists and has a sales gallery. ✉ *600 Mission St. SE* ☎ *503/363–4714* ⊕ *www.salemart.org* 🎟 *House $4* ⊙ *Gorunds: daily, dawn–midnight; house: Mar.–Dec. 23, Wed.–Sun., tours at 1, 2, 3, and 4.*

Elsinore Theatre. This flamboyant Tudor Gothic vaudeville house opened on May 28, 1926, with Edgar Bergen in attendance. Clark Gable (who lived in nearby Silverton) and Gregory Peck performed on stage. The theater was designed to look like a castle, with a false-stone front, chandeliers, ironwork, and stained-glass windows. It's now a lively performing arts center with a busy schedule of bookings, and there are concerts on its Wurlitzer pipe organ. ✉ *170 High St. SE* ☎ *503/375–3574* ⊕ *www.elsinoretheatre.com.*

Oregon Capitol building in Salem

Mount Angel Abbey. This Benedictine monastery on a 300-foot-high butte was founded in 1882 and is the site of one of two Modernist buildings in the United States designed by Finnish architect Alvar Aalto. A masterpiece of serene and thoughtful design, Aalto's library opened its doors in 1970, and has become a place of pilgrimage for students and aficionados of modern architecture. ⊠ *1 Abbey Dr., St. Benedict* ⊹ *18 miles from Salem; east on Hwy. 213 and north on Hwy. 214* ☎ *503/845–3030* ⊕ *www.mountangelabbey.org* ⊠ *Free* ⊗ *Mon.–Sat. 9–4:30.*

Oregon Capitol. A brightly gilded bronze statue of the *Oregon Pioneer* stands atop the 140-foot-high Capitol dome, looking north across the Capitol Mall. Built in 1939 with blocks of gray Vermont marble, Oregon's Capitol has an elegant yet austere neoclassical feel. East and west wings were added in 1978. Relief sculptures and deft historical murals soften the interior. Tours of the rotunda, the House and Senate chambers, and the governor's office leave from the information center under the dome. ⊠ *900 Court St. NE* ☎ *503/986–1388* ⊕ *www.leg.state.or.us* ⊠ *Free* ⊗ *Weekdays 8–5.*

WHERE TO EAT AND STAY

$$
ITALIAN
Fodor'sChoice
★

✕ **DaVinci.** Salem politicos flock to this two-story downtown gathering spot for Italian-inspired dishes cooked in a wood-burning oven. No shortcuts are taken in the preparation, so don't come if you're in a rush. But if you're in the mood to linger over seafood and fresh pasta that's made on the premises, this may be your place. The wine list features a wide selection from the Northwest and Italy, and includes a good selection of wines by the glass. The staff is courteous and extremely professional, and there's live music most evenings. Ⓢ *Average main:*

$24 ⊠ 180 High St. SE ☎ 503/399–1413 ⊕ www.davincisofsalem.com ⊗ No lunch.

$ ⚏ **Grand Hotel in Salem.** Large rooms, with comfortable and luxurious

HOTEL furnishings, are the best in town, a good base for guests attending shows and meetings at Salem Conference Center or touring the region. **Pros:** spacious rooms; centrally located. **Cons:** some street noise; not a lot of character. *⑤ Rooms from: $139 ⊠ 201 Liberty St. SE ☎ 503/540–7800, 877/540–7800 ⊕ www.grandhotelsalem.com ⤳ 143 rooms, 50 suites �◉| Breakfast.*

$ ⚏ **Oregon Garden Resort.** Bright, spacious, and tastefully decorated

RESORT rooms, each with a fireplace and a private landscaped patio or balcony, neighbor the Oregon Garden (admission is included in the rates). **Pros:** gorgeous grounds; luxurious rooms; pool and plenty of other amenities. **Cons:** a distance from other activities. *⑤ Rooms from: $110 ⊠ 895 W. Main St., Silverton ☎ 503/874–2500 ⊕ www.oregongardenresort.com ⤳ 103 rooms ◉| Breakfast.*

SHOPPING

Reed Opera House. These days the 1869 opera house in downtown Salem contains an eclectic collection of locally owned stores, shops, restaurants, bars, and bakeries, everything from art galleries to tattoo parlors. Its Trinity Ballroom hosts special events and celebrations. *⊠ 189 Liberty St. NE ☎ 503/391–4481 ⊕ www.reedoperahouse.com.*

Woodburn Company Stores. Located 18 miles north of Salem on Interstate 5 are more than 100 brand-name outlet stores, including Nike, Calvin Klein, Bose, Gymboree, OshKosh B'Gosh, Ann Taylor, Levi's, Chico's, Fossil, Forever 21, Polo, and Columbia Sportswear, and plenty of places to eat. Chances are that someone in your traveling party would enjoy burning an hour or three perusing these famous outlet stores. *⊠ 1001 Arney Rd., Woodburn ☎ 503/981–1900, 888/664–7467 ⊕ www.woodburncompanystores.com ⊗ Mon.–Sat. 10–9, Sun. 10–7.*

SPORTS AND THE OUTDOORS

RECREATIONAL AREAS

Silver Falls State Park. Hidden amid old-growth Douglas firs in the foothills of the Cascades, this is the largest state park in Oregon (8,700 acres). South Falls, roaring over the lip of a mossy basalt bowl into a deep pool 177 feet below, is the main attraction here, but 13 other waterfalls—half of them more than 100 feet high—are accessible to hikers. The best time to visit is in the fall, when vine maples blaze with brilliant color, or early spring, when the forest floor is carpeted with trilliums and yellow violets. There are picnic facilities and a day lodge; in winter you can cross-country ski. Camping facilities include tent and trailer sites, cabins, and a horse camp. *⊠ 20024 Silver Falls Hwy. SE, Sublimity ☎ 503/873–8681, 800/551–6949 ⊕ www.oregonstateparks. org ⌦ $5 per vehicle ⊗ Daily 8am–dusk.*

Willamette Mission State Park. Along pastoral lowlands by the Willamette River, this serene park holds the largest black cottonwood tree in the United States. A thick-barked behemoth by a small pond, the 275-year-old tree has upraised arms that bring to mind J.R.R. Tolkien's fictional Ents. Site of Reverend Jason Lee's 1834 pioneer mission, the park also offers quiet strolling and picnicking in an old orchard and along the river. The Wheatland Ferry, at the north end of the park, began carrying covered wagons across the Willamette in 1844 and is still in operation today. ⊠ *Wheatland Rd., 8 miles north of Salem, I–5 Exit 263* ☎ *503/393–1172, 800/551–6949* ⊕ *www.oregonstateparks.org* ⊠ *$5 per vehicle* ⊙ *Daily 8–5.*

ALBANY

20 miles from Salem, south on I–5 and west on U.S. 20.

Known as the grass-seed capital of the world, Albany has some of the most historic buildings in Oregon. Some 700 buildings, scattered over a 100-block area in three districts, include every major architectural style developed in the United States since 1850. The area is listed on the National Register of Historic Places. Eight covered bridges can also be seen on a half-hour drive from Albany. Oregon has the largest collection of covered bridges in the western United States, and the Willamette Valley has more than 34 of the wooden structures.

GETTING HERE AND AROUND

Albany is located on Interstate 5 with easy access to Portland, Salem, and Eugene. Portland International Airport is one hour, 40 minutes away, and the Eugene airport is one hour away to the south. Several shuttle services are available from both airports.

Albany Transit System provides two routes for intercity travel. The Linn-Benton loop system provides for transportation between Albany and Corvallis. Albany is served by Amtrak.

ESSENTIALS

Visitor Information Albany Visitors Association ⊠ *110 3rd Ave. SE* ☎ *541/928–0911, 800/526–2256* ⊕ *www.albanyvisitors.com.*

EXPLORING

Albany Historic Carousel and Museum. It's not often that you get to watch a carousel being built, but that's exactly what's happening here. Craftsmen and volunteers from the Albany area have come together to contribute thousands of hours to carving and painting a huge array of whimsical carousel creatures ranging from traditional horses to giant frogs and dragons. They hope to have the carousel in operation in 2016, but in the meantime you can enjoy watching the creations come together, as well as viewing many historical carousel artifacts in the museum. ⊠ *503 1st Ave. W* ☎ *541/791–3340* ⊕ *albanycarousel.com* ⊙ *Thurs.–Tues. 10–4, Wed. 10–9.*

WHERE TO EAT

$ ╳ **Novak's Hungarian.** Since 1984, the Novak family has been a delight-
HUNGARIAN ful fixture in Albany's dining scene. Whether you're ordering Hungarian hash and eggs in the morning or chicken paprika served over homemade Hungarian pearl noodles for dinner, you can't go wrong in this establishment. There's a huge assortment of desserts as well. On Sunday they serve brunch. ⑤ *Average main: $14* ⊠ *2306 Heritage Way SE* ☎ *541/967–9488* ⊕ *www.novakshungarian.com* ⊙ *No breakfast Mon.–Tues.*

$$ ✕ **Sybaris.** A rotating menu at this fine bistro in Albany's historic down-
ECLECTIC town changes monthly and features flavorful cuisine at reasonable
Fodors Choice prices. The restaurant strives to ensure that most of the ingredients,
★ including the lamb, eggs, and vegetables, are raised within 10 miles.
Even the huckleberries in the ice cream are gathered in secret locations
by the restaurant's mushroom picker. The wine list includes worldwide
classics, but is strong on local Oregon wines, too. $ *Average main: $20*
⊠ *442 1st Ave. W* ☎ *541/928–8157* ⊕ *www.sybarisbistro.com* ⊗ *Closed
Sun.–Mon. No lunch.*

CORVALLIS

10 miles southwest of Albany on U.S. 20.

To some, Corvallis is a brief stopping place along the way to Salem or
Portland. To others, it's a small town that gives you a chance to escape
the bigger cities. To still others, it's an academic and sports center, home
to Oregon State University and its Beavers. Driving the area's economy
are a growing engineering and high-tech industry, a burgeoning wine
industry, and more traditional local agricultural crops, such as grass
and legume seeds. The town and its environs offer plenty of outdoor
activities as well as scenic attractions, from covered bridges to winer-
ies and gardens.

GETTING HERE AND AROUND

Corvallis Transit System (CTS) operates eight bus routes throughout
the city. **Hut Shuttle** (☎ *503/364–4444* ⊕ *www.portlandairportshuttle.
com*) provides transportation between Corvallis and the Portland air-
port, located one hour, 53 minutes away. **OmniShuttle** (☎ *541/461–7959*
⊕ *www.omnishuttle.com*) provides transportation between Corvallis
and the Eugene airport, 50 minutes away. Corvallis Municipal Airport
is a public airport 4 miles south of the city.

ESSENTIALS

Visitor Information Corvallis Tourism ⊠ *420 N.W. 2nd St.* ☎ *541/757–1544,
800/334–8118* ⊕ *www.visitcorvallis.com.*

EXPLORING

Oregon State University. It's a thrill to be on campus on game day, when
students are a sea of orange and black cheering on their beloved Bea-
vers. This 400-acre campus, west of the city center, was established as
a land-grant institution in 1868. OSU has more than 26,000 students,
many of them studying the university's nationally recognized programs
in conservation biology, agricultural sciences, nuclear engineering, for-
estry, fisheries and wildlife management, community health, pharmacy,
and zoology. ⊠ *15th and Jefferson Sts.* ☎ *541/737–1000* ⊕ *oregonstate.
edu.*

WHERE TO EAT AND STAY

$$$ ✕ **Del Alma.** This multilevel waterfront eatery gives every table a nice
LATIN AMERICAN view of the river and puts a modern spin on tapas, bringing unex-
pected flavors and textures to classic Latin food. The menu features
both tapas and larger dishes, with a strong emphasis on seafood and
beef. If you're not in the mood for meat, the chile relleno marries a mild

poblano pepper with goat cheese and an amazing smoky salsa. They pride themselves on creative, Latin-inspired cocktails, and there's an extensive list of wines by the glass. $ *Average main: $28* ⊠ *136 S.W. Washington Ave.* ☎ *541/753–2222* ⊕ *delalmarestaurant.com* ⊗ *Closed Sun. No lunch.*

$$$ ✕ **Gathering Together Farm.** When spring arrives, it means that the organic
MODERN farmers outside Philomath are serving their bounty. Fresh vegetables,
AMERICAN pizzas, local lamb, pork, and halibut are frequent highlights on a menu
Fodor'sChoice that features simple fresh ingredients impeccably prepared. Local wines
★ and tempting desserts make the evening perfect. If you don't see coppa
(cured pork from the shoulder of the pig) on the menu, ask your server
if the chef has any available. They can often add it to a dish, and it's
fantastic. $ *Average main: $25* ⊠ *25159 Grange Hall Rd., Philomath*
☎ *541/929–4270* ⊕ *www.gatheringtogetherfarm.com* ⌖ *Reservations essential* ⊗ *Closed Sun.–Mon. No breakfast Tues.–Fri., no lunch Sat., no dinner Tues., Wed., or Sat.*

$ ⊞ **Hanson Country Inn.** On a knoll overlooking the Willamette Valley, this
B&B/INN 7,100-square-foot 1928 Dutch Colonial that was once headquarters of
a poultry-breeding business now has a massive fireplace in the living
room, many sitting areas, tall windows, and a sunporch with stained-
glass windows and rattan furniture. **Pros:** flexible breakfast schedule;
close to town. **Cons:** needs paint touch-up and minor maintenance.
$ *Rooms from: $135* ⊠ *795 S.W. Hanson St.* ☎ *541/752–2919* ⊕ *www. hcinn.com* ⌖ *5 suites, 1 cottage* ¶⊙¶ *Breakfast.*

SPORTS AND THE OUTDOORS

RECREATIONAL AREAS

Fodor'sChoice **Siuslaw National Forest.** The forest, starting just 2 miles from Corvallis
★ and extending to the coast, includes the Oregon Dunes National Rec-
reation Area and the Cape Perpetua Interpretive Center. Within the
park is the highest point in the Coast Range, Mary's Peak (4,097 feet),
offering panoramic views of the Cascades, the Willamette Valley, and
the rest of the Coast Range. On a clear day you can see as far as the
Pacific Ocean. There are several picnicking areas, more than 10 miles
of hiking trails, and a small campground, as well as stands of noble fir
and alpine meadows. You can access Mary's Peak from Highway 34
between Corvallis and Newport and the central coast. Several other
major highways (Highways 26, 6, 18, 26, and 126) also run through the
forest between the Willamette Valley and the coast, providing access to
recreation areas. ⊠ *Forest office, 3200 S.W. Jefferson Way* ☎ *541/750–
7000* ⊕ *www.fs.fed.us/r6/siuslaw* ⌖ *$5 per vehicle at some recreation sites* ⊗ *Daily dawn–dusk.*

SWIMMING

Osborn Aquatic Center. This is not your ordinary lap pool. There are
waterslides, a water channel, water cannons, and floor geysers. The
indoor pools are open all year. ⊠ *1940 N.W. Highland Dr.* ☎ *541/766–
7946* ⌖ *$5* ⊗ *Daily, hours vary.*

SOUTH WILLAMETTE VALLEY

Lane County rests at the southern end of the Willamette Valley, encompassing Eugene, Springfield, Drain, McKenzie Bridge, and Cottage Grove. Visitors can enjoy a wide range of outdoor activities such as running, fishing, swimming, white-water rafting, and deep-woods hiking along the McKenzie River, while Eugene offers great food, shopping, and the arts. There are plenty of wineries to enjoy, too, as well as cheering on the Oregon Ducks. To the west lies the Oregon Dunes Recreation Area, and to the east are the beautiful central Oregon communities of Sisters, Bend, and Redmond.

EUGENE

63 miles south of Corvallis on I–5.

Eugene was founded in 1846, when Eugene Skinner staked the first federal land-grant claim for pioneers. Eugene is consistently given high marks for its "livability." As the home of the University of Oregon, a large student and former-student population lends Eugene a youthful vitality and countercultural edge. Full of parks and oriented to the outdoors, Eugene is a place where bike paths are used, pedestrians *always* have the right-of-way, and joggers are so plentiful that the city is known as the Running Capital of the World. Shopping and commercial streets surround the Eugene Hilton and the Hult Center for the Performing Arts, the two most prominent downtown buildings. During football season you can count on the U of O Ducks being the primary topic of most conversations.

GETTING HERE AND AROUND

Eugene's airport has rental cars, cabs, and shuttles that make the 15-minute trip to Eugene's city center. By train, Amtrak stops in the heart of downtown. Getting around Lane County's communities is easy with **Lane Transit District** (*LTD* ☎ *541/687–5555* ⊕ *www.ltd.org*) public transportation. Eugene is very bicycle-friendly.

ESSENTIALS

Visitor Information Eugene, Cascades and Coast Adventure Center ✉ *3312 Gateway St., Springfield* ☎ *541/484–5307, 800/547–5445* ⊕ *www. eugenecascadescoast.org.*

EXPLORING
TOP ATTRACTIONS

FAMILY **Cascades Raptor Center.** This birds-of-prey nature center and hospital hosts more than 30 species of birds. A visit is a great outing for kids, who can learn what owls eat, why and where birds migrate, and all sorts of other raptor facts. Some of the full-time residents include turkey vultures, bald eagles, owls, hawks, falcons, and kites. ✉ *32275 Fox Hollow Rd.* ☎ *541/485–1320* ⊕ *www.eraptors.org* ☐ *$8* ☉ *Apr.–Oct., Tues.–Sun. 10–6, Nov.–Mar., Tues.–Sun. 10–4.*

King Estate Winery. One of Oregon's largest producers is known for their crisp Pinot Gris and silky Pinot Noir and boasts the world's largest organic vineyard. The visitor center offers wine tasting and production tours, and the restaurant highlights local meats and organic produce grown in the estate gardens. ⊠ *80854 Territorial Rd.* ☎ *541/942–9874* ⊕ *www.kingestate.com* ⊙ *Daily 11–8.*

Ninkasi Brewing Company. Named after the Sumerian goddess of fermentation, Ninkasi has grown from a little startup in 2006 to a major supplier of craft beer. Its flagship beer, Total Domination IPA, is signature Northwest, with bold flavor and lots of hops. Visit the tasting room and enjoy a tasting flight or a pint, either indoors or on the patio. The beer menu changes often and includes a few hard-to-find limited-production beers. If you'd like a little food to go with your beer, you'll usually find one of Eugene's many food carts right there on the patio. Free brewery tours are offered daily. ⊠ *272 Van Buren St.* ☎ *541/344–2739* ⊕ *www. ninkasibrewing.com* ⊙ *Daily noon–10 pm.*

WORTH NOTING

5th Street Public Market. A former chicken-processing plant is the site of this popular shopping mall, filled with small crafts, art, and gifts stores. Dining includes sit-down restaurants, a wine bar, and the international diversity of the second-floor food esplanade. ⊠ *296 E. 5th Ave.* ☎ *541/484–0383* ⊕ *www.5stmarket.com* ⊙ *Shops Mon.–Sat. 10–7, Sun. 11–6.*

Alton Baker Park. This parcel of open land on the banks of the Willamette River is named after the late publisher of Eugene's newspaper, the *Register-Guard,* and is the site of many community events. Live music is performed in summer at the Cuthbert Amphitheater. There's fine hiking and biking on a footpath that runs along the river for the length of the park, and an 18-hole disc golf course. Also worth seeing is the Whilamut Natural Area, an open space with 13 "talking stones," each with an inscription. ⊠ *200 Day Island Rd.* ☎ *541/682–4906* ⊕ *www. altonbakerpark.com/.*

Jordan Schnitzer Museum of Art. Works from the 20th and 21st centuries are a specialty in these handsome galleries on the University of Oregon campus. They feature works by many leading Pacific Northwest artists, and European, Korean, Chinese, and Japanese works are also on view, as are 300 works commissioned by the Works Progress Administration in the 1930s and '40s. You can also view an ever-changing collection of important works from private collections by internationally recognized artists through the museum's Masterworks On Loan program. ⊠ *1430 Johnson La.* ☎ *541/346–3027* ⊕ *jsma.uoregon.edu* ⬙ *$5* ⊙ *Tues.–Sun. 11–5, Wed. 11–8.*

FAMILY **Mount Pisgah Arboretum.** This beautiful nature preserve near southeast Eugene includes extensive all-weather trails, educational programs for all ages, and facilities for special events. Its visitor center holds workshops and features native amphibian and reptile terraria; microscopes for exploring tiny seeds, bugs, feathers, and snakeskins; "touch me" exhibits; reference books; and a working viewable beehive. ⊠ *34901 Frank Parrish Rd.* ☎ *541/747–3817* ⊕ *www.mountpisgaharboretum. org* ⬙ *Parking $4* ⊙ *Park, daily dawn–dusk; visitor center, hours vary.*

FAMILY **Science Factory.** Formerly the Willamette Science and Technology Center (WISTEC), and still known to locals by its former name, Eugene's imaginative, hands-on museum assembles rotating exhibits designed for curious young minds. The adjacent **planetarium,** one of the largest in the Pacific Northwest, presents star shows and entertainment events. ✉ *2300 Leo Harris Pkwy.* ☎ *541/682–7888* ⊕ *www.sciencefactory.org* ⬚ *$4 for exhibit hall or planetarium, $7 for both* ⊙ *Exhibit hall, Wed.– Sun. 10–4; planetarium, Sat.–Sun., shows at 10:30 and on the hour until 3; closed Oregon Ducks home football games.*

Sweet Cheeks Winery. This estate vineyard lies on a prime sloping hillside in the heart of the Willamette Valley appellation. It also supplies grapes to several award-winning wineries. Bring a picnic and enjoy the amazing view from the lawn outside the tasting room, or take advantage of the food available for purchase. Friday-night tastings are embellished with cheese pairings and live music. ✉ *27007 Briggs Hill Rd.* ☎ *541/349– 9463, 877/309–9463* ⊕ *www.sweetcheekswinery.com* ⊙ *Sat.–Thurs. noon–6, Fri. noon–9.*

University of Oregon. The true heart of Eugene lies southeast of the city center at its university. Several fine old buildings can be seen on the 250-acre campus; **Deady Hall,** built in 1876, is the oldest. More than 400 varieties of trees grace the bucolic grounds, along with outdoor sculptures that include *The Pioneer* and *The Pioneer Mother.* The two bronze figures by Alexander Phimster Proctor were dedicated to the men and women who settled the Oregon Territory and less than a generation later founded the university. ✉ *1585 E. 13th Ave.* ☎ *541/346–1000* ⊕ *www.uoregon.edu.*

University of Oregon Museum of Natural and Cultural History. Relics on display are devoted to Pacific Northwest anthropology and the natural sciences. Highlights include the fossil collection of Thomas Condon, Oregon's first geologist, and a pair of 9,000-year-old sandals made of sagebrush. ✉ *1680 E. 15th Ave.* ☎ *541/346–3024* ⊕ *natural-history. uoregon.edu* ⬚ *$5* ⊙ *Tues.–Sun. 11–5.*

WHERE TO EAT

$$
MODERN
AMERICAN
✕ **Café 440.** Putting a modern twist on classic comfort food, this airy, industrial-chic space features locally grown ingredients and a great local beer list. Along with updated classics like mac and cheese, burgers, and fish-and-chips, you'll find innovative versions of ahi *poke* (salad) and salmon cakes. Be sure and save room for one of the house-made dessert classics like crème brûlée or bread pudding. Enjoy live music every other Tuesday night, or try the wine-tasting flight on Wednesday nights. ⑤ *Average main: $21* ✉ *440 Coburg Rd.* ☎ *541/505–8493* ⊕ *cafe440eugene. com* ⊙ *No dinner Sun.*

$$
PACIFIC
NORTHWEST
✕ **Grit Kitchen and Wine.** You know you're in for local, seasonal ingredients when the chalkboard in this intimate place right across the street from the Ninkasi Brewery in Eugene's eccentric Whiteaker neighborhood lists nearly 20 local farmers and purveyors who are suppliers. The menu changes often, depending on what's in season. Eat inside and take advantage of the open kitchen to watch the chefs at work, or enjoy a pleasant outdoor dining experience on either of the two decks. The food is quintessential Northwest, featuring complex and unexpected flavors and a wide range of textures. You can order à la carte, or

Fresh produce from Hey Bayles! Farm at the Lane County Farmers' Market in Eugene.

choose the Fixed Four, the weekly changing four-course feast; optional wine pairings are available. $ *Average main: $21* ✉ *1080 W. 3rd St.* ☎ *541/343–0501* ⊕ *gritkitchen.com* ☾ *Closed Sun. and Mon. No lunch.*

$$$
FRENCH
✕ **Marché.** The name translates into "market," which is appropriate given the location in the bustling 5th Street Market, but also because this renowned Eugene restaurant works with more than a dozen local farmers to bring fresh, local organic food to the table. Specialties include salmon, halibut, sturgeon, and beef tenderloin, braised pork shoulders, and outstanding local oysters. The extensive wine list puts an emphasis on Oregon and France. There's also a Sunday brunch that offers amazing warm beignets. $ *Average main: $30* ✉ *296 E. 5th Ave.* ☎ *541/342–3612* ⊕ *www.marcherestaurant.com.*

$$$
ITALIAN
✕ **Ristorante Italiano.** The chef uses fresh local produce from the restaurant's own farm, but this bistro-style café across from the University of Oregon is best known for its authentic Italian cuisine, with a heavy emphasis on fresh local seafood. The menu changes according to the season, but staples include delicious salads and soups, ravioli, grilled chicken, pizza, and sandwiches. At dinner they feature daily lamb and seafood specials that are well worth asking about. The dining room, shaded by blossoming cherry trees in the spring, has a quiet, understated European feel, and there's outdoor seating on the patio in good weather. Breakfast and Sunday brunch are served. $ *Average main: $26* ✉ *754 E. 13th Ave.* ☎ *541/342–6963, 800/321–6963* ☾ *No lunch Sat.*

WHERE TO STAY

$ **Campbell House.** One of the oldest structures in Eugene, built in 1892,
B&B/INN combines architectural details and a mixture of century-old antiques and reproductions to lend each of the rooms a distinctive personality. **Pros:** classic architecture; comfortable rooms; well-kept grounds. **Cons:** rooms lack some of the amenities of nearby hotels. *$ Rooms from: $129 ⊠ 252 Pearl St.* ☎ *541/343–1119, 800/264–2519 ⊕ www.campbellhouse.com ⤴ 12 rooms, 6 suites ⏐◎⏐ Breakfast.*

$$ **C'est la Vie Inn.** Listed on the National Register of Historic Places,
B&B/INN this 1891 Queen Anne Victorian bed-and-breakfast provides old-world
Fodor's Choice comfort and modern-day amenities in its luxurious and romantic guest
★ rooms. **Pros:** outstanding service and value. **Cons:** few rooms. *$ Rooms from: $150 ⊠ 1006 Taylor St.* ⊕ *cestlavieinn.com ⤴ 3 rooms, 1 suite ⏐◎⏐ Breakfast.*

$ **Excelsior Inn.** Quiet sophistication, attention to architectural detail,
B&B/INN and rooms furnished in a refreshingly understated manner, each with
Fodor's Choice a marble-and-tile bath and some with fireplaces, suggest a European
★ inn. **Pros:** romantic accommodations; excellent service and restaurant. **Cons:** formal in a casual town. *$ Rooms from: $135 ⊠ 754 E. 13th Ave.* ☎ *541/342–6963, 800/321–6963 ⊕ www.excelsiorinn.com ⤴ 14 rooms ⏐◎⏐ Breakfast.*

$$ **Valley River Inn.** At this sprawling inn on the banks of the Willamette
HOTEL River, some rooms have an outdoor patio or balcony, some have river or pool views, and concierge rooms have access to a private lounge. **Pros:** location on the river; lots of amenities; **Cons:** basic and fairly banal room decor, mediocre restaurant. *$ Rooms from: $159 ⊠ 1000 Valley River Way* ☎ *541/743–1000, 800/543–8266 ⊕ www.valleyriverinn.com ⤴ 257 rooms.*

NIGHTLIFE AND THE ARTS

Hult Center for the Performing Arts. This is the locus of Eugene's cultural life. Renowned for the quality of its acoustics, the center has two theaters that are home to Eugene's symphony and opera. ⊠ *1 Eugene Center* ☎ *541/682–5087 Administration, 541/682–5000 Tickets ⊕ www.hultcenter.org.*

Oregon Bach Festival. Conductor Helmuth Rilling leads the internationally known Oregon Bach Festival every summer. Concerts, chamber music, and social events—held mainly in Eugene at the Hult Center and the University of Oregon School of Music but also in Corvallis and Florence—are part of this three-week event. ⊠ *1787 Agate St.* ☎ *541/682–5000 for tickets, 800/457–1486 for information ⊕ oregonbachfestival.com.*

SPORTS AND THE OUTDOORS

BIKING AND JOGGING

The **River Bank Bike Path**, originating in Alton Baker Park on the Willamette's north bank, is a level and leisurely introduction to Eugene's topography. It's one of 120 miles of trails in the area. **Prefontaine Trail,** used by area runners, travels through level fields and forests for 1½ miles.

RECREATIONAL AREAS

FAMILY **Skinner Butte Park.** Rising from the south bank of the Willamette River, this forested enclave provides the best views of any of the city's parks; it also has the greatest historic cachet, since it was here that Eugene Skinner staked the claim that put Eugene on the map. Children can scale a replica of Skinner Butte, uncover fossils, and cool off under a rain circle. Skinner Butte Loop leads to the top of Skinner Butte, traversing sometimes difficult terrain through a mixed-conifer forest. ⊠ *248 Cheshire Ave.* ☎ *541/682–4800* ⌑ *Free* ⊙ *Dawn–dusk.*

SKIING

Willamette Pass. With a summit 6,683 feet high in the Cascade Range, this pass packs an annual average snowfall of 430 inches and has access to 29 ski runs with a vertical drop of 1,563 feet. Four triple chairs and one six-person detachable service the downhill ski areas, and 13 miles of Nordic trails lace the pass. Facilities include a ski shop; day care; a bar and restaurant; and Nordic and downhill rentals, repairs, and instruction. ⊠ *Hwy. 58, 69 miles southeast of Eugene* ☎ *541/345–7669* ⊕ *www.willamettepass.com* ⊙ *Wed.–Sun. 9–4 during ski season.*

SWIMMING

OFF THE
BEATEN
PATH

Waldo Lake. Nestled in old-growth forest, this mountain lake is famed as being remarkably clean and pristine. The lake is accessible only after a short hike, so bring comfortable shoes. ⊠ *Off Hwy. 58* ✛ *From Eugene, take Hwy. 58 to Oakridge and continue toward Willamette Pass; take Forest Road 5897 north 8 miles to the southern part of the lake, or 14 miles to the north portion.*

SHOPPING

Tourists coming to the Willamette Valley, especially to Eugene, can't escape without experiencing the **5th Street Public Market** in downtown Eugene. There are plenty of small crafts shops, and the food mall offers many cuisines, including vegetarian, pizza, and seafood.

Valley River Center. The largest shopping center between Portland and San Francisco has five department stores, including Macy's and JCPenney, plus 130 specialty shops and a food court. ⊠ *293 Valley River Center* ☎ *541/683–5513* ⊕ *www.valleyrivercenter.com.*

MCKENZIE BRIDGE

58 miles east of Eugene on Hwy. 126.

On the beautiful McKenzie River, lakes, waterfalls, and covered bridges surround the town of McKenzie Bridge and wilderness trails in the Cascades. Fishing, skiing, backpacking, and rafting are among the most popular activities in the area.

GETTING HERE AND AROUND

McKenzie Bridge is about an hour from Eugene, on Highway 126. It is just 38 miles from Hoodoo Ski Area, but its proximity can be deceiving if the snow is heavy. Bend also is close at 64 miles to the east.

EXPLORING

McKenzie River Highway. Highway 126, as it heads east from Eugene, is known as the McKenzie River Highway. Following the curves of the river, it passes grazing lands, fruit and nut orchards, and the small riverside hamlets of the McKenzie Valley. From the highway you can glimpse the bouncing, bubbling, blue-green McKenzie River, one of Oregon's top fishing, boating, and white-water rafting spots, against a backdrop of densely forested mountains, splashing waterfalls, and jet-black lava beds. The small town of McKenzie Bridge marks the end of the McKenzie River Highway and the beginning of the 26-mile McKenzie River National Recreation Trail, which heads north through the Willamette National Forest along portions of the Old Santiam Wagon Road.

OFF THE BEATEN PATH

McKenzie Pass. Just beyond McKenzie Bridge, Highway 242 begins a steep, 22-mile eastward climb to McKenzie Pass in the Cascade Range. The scenic highway, which passes through the Mt. Washington Wilderness Area and continues to the town of Sisters (⇨ *Central Oregon*), is generally closed November through June because of heavy snow. Novice motorists take note, this is not a drive for the timid: it's a challenging exercise in negotiating tight curves at quickly fluctuating, often slow speeds—the skid marks on virtually every turn attest to hasty braking—so take it slow, and don't be intimidated by cars on your tail itching to take the turns more quickly. The route is closed to trucks and large trailers and motor homes.

WHERE TO EAT AND STAY

$ ✕ **Takoda's Restaurant.** A popular roadside café serves burgers, sandwiches, great soups, salads, pizza, and daily specials. The burger selection includes not only beef, but seafood, chicken, turkey, and veggie options. If the weather is nice, sit outside in their beautiful garden area out back. A video game room keeps kids happy. $ *Average main: $10* ⊠ *91806 Mill Creek Rd., Milepost 47.5 McKenzie Hwy., Blue River* ☎ *541/822–1153* ⊕ *www.takodasrainbow.com.*

AMERICAN
FAMILY

$ ▦ **Belknap Hot Springs Resort.** A pleasant lodge, with comfortable though not luxurious rooms, and a campground with both tent and trailer sites, are nestled onto the banks of the beautiful McKenzie River. **Pros:** hot springs; wooded location. **Cons:** 14-day cancellation policy; two-night minimum on weekends; trailers and motor homes detract from the rustic atmosphere. $ *Rooms from: $120* ⊠ *59296 Belknap Springs Rd.* ☎ *541/822–3512* ⊕ *www.belknaphotsprings.com* ⤢ *19 rooms, 7 cabins* ¶⊙¶ *Breakfast.*

RESORT

$ ▦ **Eagle Rock Lodge.** These wood-paneled rooms filled with quilts and antiques are surprisingly luxurious and provide a romantic, relaxing retreat in the woods. **Pros:** great location on the McKenzie River; comfortable atmosphere. **Cons:** a distance from non-outdoor activities. $ *Rooms from: $130* ⊠ *49198 McKenzie Hwy., Vida* ☎ *541/822–3630, 888/773–4333* ⊕ *www.eaglerocklodge.com* ⤢ *8 rooms* ¶⊙¶ *Breakfast.*

B&B/INN

4

SPORTS AND THE OUTDOORS

GOLF

Tokatee Golf Club. Ranked one of the best golf courses in Oregon by *Golf Digest*, this 18-hole beauty is tucked away near the McKenzie River with views of the Three Sisters Mountains, native ponds, and streams. *Tokatee* is a Chinook word meaning "a place of restful beauty." The course offers a practice range, carts, lessons, rentals, a coffee shop and snack bar, and Wi-Fi. ✉ *54947 McKenzie Hwy.* ☎ *541/822–3220, 800/452–6376* ⊕ *www.tokatee.com* ⛳ *18 holes $47; 9 holes $27.*

RECREATIONAL AREAS

Cougar Dam and Lake. Four miles outside McKenzie Bridge is the highest embankment dam ever built by the Army Corps of Engineers—452 feet above the streambed. The resulting reservoir, on the South Fork McKenzie River, covers 1,280 acres. The dam generates 25 megawatts of power, and includes a fish collection and sorting facility, and a temperature control tower to keep the downstream water at a suitable temperature for spawning. The public recreation areas are in the Willamette National Forest. You can visit the dam year-round, but some campgrounds are open only from April to September. ✉ *Forest Rd. 19, Willamette National Forest* ☎ *541/822–3381* ⛳ *Free* ☉ *June–Sept., daily.*

Terwilliger Hot Springs (Cougar Hot Springs). Bring a towel and enjoy the soaking pools in this natural hot-springs area. Located an hour east of Eugene off Highway 126, the pools are a short hike from the parking area, and include a changing area. Soaking aficionados will find Terwilliger to be rustic, which many regard as an advantage, though the popularity of this beautiful spot can be a drawback. The pools are in a forest of old-growth firs and cedars, and just downstream is a beautiful lagoon complete with waterfall that is also suitable for swimming. Clothing is optional. ✉ *Off Forest Rd. 19, Blue River* ☎ *541/822–3381* ⛳ *$6* ☉ *Dawn–dusk.*

Willamette National Forest. Stretching 110 miles along the western slopes of the Cascade Range, this forest boasts boundless recreation opportunities, including camping, hiking, boating, ATV riding, and winter sports. It extends from the Mt. Jefferson area east of Salem to the Calapooya Mountains northeast of Roseburg, encompassing 1,675,407 acres. ✉ *3106 Pierce Pkwy., Suite D, Springfield* ☎ *541/225–6300* ⊕ *www.fs.usda.gov/willamette.*

WHITE-WATER RAFTING

FAMILY
Fodor's Choice
★

High Country Expeditions. Raft the white waters of the McKenzie River on a guided full- or half-day tour. You'll bounce through rapids, admire old-growth forest, and watch osprey and blue herons fishing. The outfit provides life jackets, splash gear, wet suits, booties (if requested), boating equipment, paddling instructions, river safety talk, a three-course riverside meal, and shuttle service back to your vehicle. Full day trips are $90, half-day trips $60. ✉ *Belknap Hot Springs Resort, 59296 Belknap Springs Rd.* ☎ *541/822–8288, 888/461–7238* ⊕ *www. highcountryexpeditions.com.*

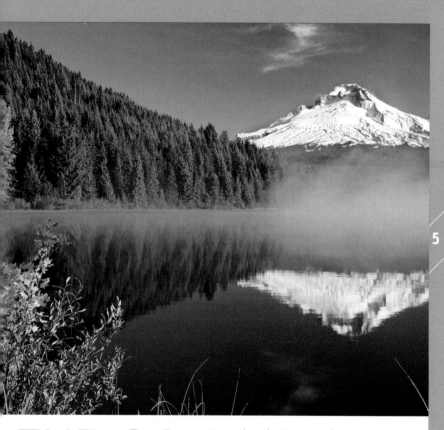

THE COLUMBIA RIVER GORGE AND MT. HOOD

WELCOME TO THE COLUMBIA RIVER GORGE AND MT. HOOD

TOP REASONS TO GO

★ **Outdoor rec mecca:** From kiteboarding in the Columbia River to mountain biking the slopes of Mt. Hood to hiking among the roaring waterfalls of the Gorge, this is a region tailor-made for adventure junkies.

★ **Historico-luxe:** Grand, distinctive landmarks like Timberline Lodge and the Columbia Gorge Hotel exude history and architectural distinction, offering some of the most memorable lodgings in the Northwest.

★ **Road-tripping:** This is a perfect region for backcountry driving through spectacular scenery—from Portland, you can make a full 250-mile loop through the Gorge out to Goldendale, Washington, returning to Hood River and then circling Mt. Hood to the south.

★ **Hop havens:** Oregon is the national seat of craft beer brewing, and the Gorge/Hood area has a fast-growing proliferation of taprooms, from Stevenson's tiny Walking Man Brewing to Pfriem, in Hood River.

1 Columbia River Gorge. The dams of the early 20th century transformed the Columbia River from the raging torrent that vexed Lewis and Clark in 1805 to the breathtaking but comparatively docile waterway that hosts kiteboarders and windsurfers today. Auto visitors have been scoping out the Gorge's picturesque bluffs and waterfalls for quite a while now—the road between Troutdale and The Dalles, on which construction began in 1913, was the country's first planned scenic highway.

2 Mt. Hood. Visible from 100 miles away, Mt. Hood (or simply "the Mountain," as some Portlanders call it) is the kind of rock that commands respect. It's holy ground for mountaineers, more than 10,000 of whom make a summit bid each year. Sightseers are often shocked by the summer snows, but skiers rejoice, keeping the mountain's resorts busy year-round. Mingle with laid-back powderhounds and other outdoorsy types in the hospitality villas of Welches and Government Camp.

Carson

Stevenson

Columbia River Gorge National Scenic Area

North Bonneville

Cascade Locks

Oneonta Gorge

Multnomah Falls

84

30

TO PORTLAND

Wahtum Lake

Lost L.

Mt. Hood National Forest

Brightwood

26

Mount Hood Village

Rhododendron

Salmon River

224

Timothy Lake

0   10 mi

0   10 km

5

GETTING ORIENTED

The mighty Columbia River flows west through the Cascade Range, past the Mt. Hood Wilderness Area, to Astoria. It's a natural border between Oregon and Washington to the north, and bridges link roads on both sides of the Gorge at Biggs Junction, The Dalles, Hood River, and Cascade Locks. The Gorge's watery recreation corridor stretches from Portland's easternmost suburbs past Hood River and The Dalles out to Maryhill and Goldendale, Washington. For portions of that drive, snowcapped Mt. Hood looms to the southwest. While the massive peak feels remote, the snowcapped heights are just 60 miles east of Portland. Hood River drains the mountain's north side, emptying into the Columbia at its namesake town. Follow the river upstream and you'll trade the warm, low-elevation climes of the Gorge for the high country's tall pines and late-season snows.

Updated
by Andrew
Collins

Volcanoes, lava flows, Ice Age floodwaters, and glaciers were Nature's tools of choice when carving a breathtaking, nearly 100-mile landscape now called the Columbia River Gorge. Proof of human civilization here reaches back 31,000 years, and excavations near The Dalles have uncovered evidence that salmon fishing is a 10,000-year-old tradition in these parts. In 1805 Lewis and Clark discovered the Columbia River, the only major waterway that leads to the Pacific. Their first expedition was a treacherous route through wild, plunging rapids, but their successful navigation set a new exodus in motion.

Today the river has been tamed by a comprehensive system of hydroelectric dams and locks, and the towns in these parts are laid-back recreation hamlets whose residents harbor a fierce pride in their shared natural resources. Sightseers, hikers, and skiers have long found contentment in this robust region, officially labeled a National Scenic Area in 1986. They're joined these days by epicures scouring the Columbia's banks in search of farm-to-table cuisine, artisanal hop houses, and top-shelf vino. Highlights of the Columbia River Gorge include Multnomah Falls, Bonneville Dam, the rich orchard and vineyard land of Hood River, and Maryhill Museum of Art. Sailboaters, windsurfers, and kiteboarders take advantage of the blustery Gorge winds in the summer, their colorful sails decorating the waterway like windswept confetti.

To the south of Hood River are all the alpine attractions of the 11,250-foot-high Mt. Hood. With more than 2.2 million people living just up the road in greater Portland, you'd think this mountain playground would be overrun, but it's still easy to find solitude in the 300,000-acre wilderness surrounding the peak. Some of the world's best skiers take advantage of the powder on Hood, and they stick around in summertime for the longest ski season in North America at Palmer Snowfield, above Timberline Lodge.

THE COLUMBIA RIVER GORGE AND MT. HOOD PLANNER

WHEN TO GO

Winter weather in the Mt. Hood area is much more severe than in Portland and the Willamette Valley, and occasionally rough conditions permeate the Gorge, too. Rarely, Interstate 84 closes because of snow and ice. If you're planning a winter visit, be sure to carry plenty of warm clothes. High winds and single-digit temps are par for the course around 6,000 feet—the elevation of Timberline Lodge on Mt. Hood—in January. Note that chains are sometimes required for traveling over mountain passes.

Temperatures in the Gorge are mild year-round, rarely dipping below 30°F in winter and hovering in the high 70s in midsummer. As throughout Oregon, however, elevation is often a more significant factor than season, and an hour-long drive to Mt. Hood's Timberline Lodge can reduce those midsummer temps by 20–30 degrees. Don't forget that the higher reaches of Mt. Hood retain snow year-round.

In early fall, look for maple, tamarack, and aspen trees around the Gorge, bursting with brilliant red and gold color. No matter the season, the basalt cliffs, the acres of lush forest, and that glorious expanse of water make the Gorge one of the West's great scenic wonders.

FESTIVALS

Columbia Gorge Bluegrass Festival. One of the premier bluegrass fests in the West takes place in Stevenson, Washington, every fourth weekend in July. ⊕ *www.columbiagorgebluegrass.net.*

Hood River Hops Fest. In late September, beer lovers have the chance to sample some 60 hop-intensive beers in Hood River, which has become one of the top small towns in Oregon for craft brewing. ⊕ *www.hoodriver.org.*

Maryhill Winery Concert Series. About 20 minutes east of The Dalles on the Washington side of the Gorge, Maryhill Winery hosts summer concerts, drawing some nationally renowned rock and pop acts, in a cozy, 4,000-person amphitheater. ⊕ *www.maryhillwinery.com.*

Nicky USA's Wild About Game. This meat-centric food festival held in early September on Mt. Hood at Timberline Lodge features a competition among four top chefs each from Portland and Seattle. Guests can sample and vote on each dish and nibble and sip from a large marketplace of top Oregon purveyors, including cheese makers, charcuterie producers, wineries, and breweries. ⊕ *www.nickyusa.com/wag.*

Timberline Lodge Mountain Music Fest. This free single-day gathering at iconic Timberline Lodge takes place over Labor Day weekend and showcases top-name bluegrass bands from around the country. ⊕ *www.timberlinelodge.com/mountain-music-festival.*

GETTING HERE AND AROUND

The Columbia Gorge, which is easily accessed from Portland, is best explored by car. The same is generally true for the Mt. Hood area, but in season, the area ski resorts do have shuttle services from Portland and the airport. Even light exploring of the region, however, requires an automobile—take heart that the driving in these parts is scenic and relatively free of traffic. Just keep in mind that winter storms can result in road closures around Mt. Hood and, occasionally, even in the Gorge. It's just a 20-minute drive east of Portland to reach the beginning of the Columbia Gorge, in Troutdale. From Portland it's a one-hour drive to Hood River, a 90-minute drive to Mt. Hood, and a two-hour drive to Goldendale, Washington *(the farthest-away point covered in this chapter)*.

CAR TRAVEL

Interstate 84 is the main east–west route into the Columbia River Gorge, although you can also reach the area on the Washington side via slower but quite scenic Highway 14, which skirts the north side of the river. U.S. 26, which leads east from Portland, is the main route into the Mt. Hood area.

The scenic Historic Columbia River Highway (U.S. 30) from Troutdale to just east of Oneonta Gorge passes Crown Point State Park and Multnomah Falls. Interstate 84/U.S. 30 continues on to The Dalles. Highway 35 heads south from Hood River to the Mt. Hood area, intersecting with U.S. 26 near Government Camp. From Portland, the Columbia Gorge–Mt. Hood Scenic Loop is the easiest way to fully explore the Gorge and the mountain. Take Interstate 84 east to Troutdale and then follow U.S. 26 east to Mt. Hood, then take Highway 35 north to Hood River and Interstate 84 back to Portland. Or make the loop in reverse.

RESTAURANTS

A prominent locavore mentality pervades western Oregon generally, and low elevations around the Gorge mean long growing seasons for dozens of local producers. Fresh foods grown, caught, and harvested in the Northwest dominate menus in the increasingly sophisticated restaurants in the Gorge, especially in the charming town of Hood River, and up around Mt. Hood. Columbia River salmon is big, fruit orchards proliferate around Hood River, delicious huckleberries flourish in Mt. Hood National Forest, and the Gorge nurtures a glut of excellent vineyards. Additionally, even the smallest towns around the region have their own lively brewpubs with consistently tasty pub fare and tap after tap of craft ales. In keeping with the region's green and laid-back vibe, outdoor dining is highly popular.

HOTELS

The region is close enough that you could spend a day or two exploring the Gorge and Mt. Hood, using Portland hotels as your base. The best way to fully appreciate the Gorge, however, is to spend a night or two—look to Hood River and The Dalles for the largest selections of lodging options, although you'll also find some noteworthy resorts, motels, and B&Bs in some of the towns between Portland and Hood River, on both sides of the river. There are a couple of run-of-the-mill motels in Goldendale, but otherwise, you won't find any accommodations in the region east of The Dalles. The slopes of Mt. Hood are dotted with smart ski resorts, and towns like Government Camp and Welches have a mix of rustic and contemporary vacation rentals. The closer you are to Mt. Hood in any season, the earlier you'll want to reserve. With ski country working ever harder to attract summer patrons, Mt. Hood resorts like Timberline Lodge and Mt. Hood Skibowl offer some worthwhile seasonal specials. *Hotel reviews have been shortened. For full information, visit Fodors.com.*

WHAT IT COSTS IN U.S. DOLLARS				
	$	$$	$$$	$$$$
Restaurants	Under $17	$17–$23	$24–$30	Over $30
Hotels	Under $151	$151–$200	$201–$250	Over $250

Restaurant prices are the average cost of a main course at dinner or, if dinner is not served, at lunch. Hotel prices are the lowest cost of a standard double room in high season.

TOURS

EverGreen Escapes. The energetic crew at this highly respected tour operator provides both regularly scheduled and customizable tours of the Gorge (with themes that range from wine to hiking) and Mt. Hood, where options include hiking and snowshoeing. ☎ *503/252–1931, 866/203–7603* ⊕ *www.evergreenescapes.com* ✉ *From $135.*

Explore the Gorge. Customizable tours of the Gorge, Mt. Hood, and the Hood River Valley explore everything from the Lewis and Clark Trail to the region's microbreweries. ☎ *800/899–5676* ⊕ *www.explorethegorge.com* ✉ *From $180.*

Martin's Gorge Tours. Wine tours, waterfall hikes, and spring wildflower tours are among the popular trips offered by this Portland-based guide. ☎ *503/349–1323* ⊕ *www.martinsgorgetours.com* ✉ *From $49.*

Mt. Hood Adventure. The only outfitter on Mt. Hood that rents snowmobiles and offers snowmobile tours is also a well-respected tour company for snowshoe treks and sleigh rides in winter, and mountain hikes, biking trips, and boat excursions on area rivers—the shop is also a good place to buy gear and ask for advice on outdoorsy activities in the area. ✉ *88335 Government Camp Loop Rd., Government Camp* ☎ *503/715–2175* ⊕ *www.mthoodadventure.com* ✉ *Snowmobile tours from $189.*

VISITOR INFORMATION

Columbia River Gorge Visitors Association ☎ *509/427–8911* ⊕ *www.crgva.org.*

Mt. Hood Territory ☎ *800/424–3002* ⊕ *www.mthoodterritory.com.*

COLUMBIA RIVER GORGE

When glacial floods carved out most of the Columbia River Gorge at the end of the last Ice Age, they left behind massive, looming cliffs where the river bisects the Cascade mountain range. The size of the canyon and the wildly varying elevations make this small stretch of Oregon as ecologically diverse as anyplace in the state. In a few days along the Gorge you can mountain bike through dry canyons near The Dalles, hike through temperate rain forest in Oneonta Gorge, and take a woodland wildflower stroll just outside Hood River. At night you'll be rewarded with historic lodging and good food in one of a half-dozen mellow river towns. The country's second federally designated National Scenic Area remains exceptionally inviting.

HISTORIC COLUMBIA RIVER HIGHWAY

U.S. 30, paralleling I–84 for 22 miles between Troutdale and interstate Exit 35.

The oldest scenic highway in the United States is a construction marvel that integrates asphalt path with cliff, river, and forest landscapes. Paralleling the interstate, U.S. 30 climbs to forested riverside bluffs, passes half a dozen waterfalls, and provides access to hiking trails leading to still more falls and scenic overlooks. Completed in 1922, the serpentine highway was the first paved road in the Gorge built expressly for automotive sightseers. Technically, the Historic Columbia River Highway extends some 74 miles to The Dalles, but much of that is along modern Interstate 84—the 22-mile western segment is the real draw.

GETTING HERE AND AROUND

U.S. 30 heads east out of downtown Troutdale, but you can also access the route from Interstate 84 along the way, via Exit 22 near Corbett, Exit 28 near Bridal Veil Falls, Exit 31 at Multnomah Falls, and Exit 35, where it rejoins the interstate.

ESSENTIALS

Visitor Information **Multnomah Falls Visitor Center** ⊠ *53000 E. Historic Columbia River Hwy., Exit 31 off I-84, 15 miles east of Troutdale, Bridal Veil* ☎ *503/695–2372* ⊕ *www.multnomahfallslodge.com.*

EXPLORING

FAMILY

Fodor'sChoice

★

Multnomah Falls. A 620-foot-high double-decker torrent, the second-highest year-round waterfall in the nation, Multnomah is by far the most spectacular of the Gorge cataracts east of Troutdale. You can access the falls and Multnomah Lodge via a parking lot at Exit 31 off I-84, or via the Historic Columbia River Highway; from the parking area, a paved path winds to a bridge over the lower falls. A much steeper, though paved, 1.1-mile trail climbs to a viewing point overlooking the upper falls, and from here, unpaved but well-groomed trails join with others, allowing for as much as a full day of hiking in the mountains above the Gorge, if you're up for some serious but scenic trekking. Even the paved ramble to the top is fairly strenuous, but worth it to avoid the crowds that swarm the lower falls area in every season.

Columbia River Gorge

WASHINGTON

Goldendale Observatory State Park
Goldendale
Blockhouse
Centerville
Klickitat
Husum
141
Carson
Stevenson
Columbia Gorge Interpretive Center
Bridge of the Gods
Cascade Locks
Bonneville Dam and Fish Hatchery
North Bonneville
Ainsworth State Park
Oneonta Gorge
Multnomah Falls
Beacon Rock State Park
Washougal
Rooster Rock State Park
Camas
Troutdale
Vista House at Crown Point
Historic Columbia River Hwy.
GREATER PORTLAND

Cliffs
Rufus
Maryhill
Maryhill Museum
Biggs
Wishram
84
Celilo Park
Dallesport
Dalles Lock and Dam
Columbia Gorge Discovery Center
14
Mosier
Lyle
Mayer State Park
Syncline Winery
Bingen
White Salmon
84
Gorge White House
Glassometry Studio
Chenoweth
Fort Dalles Museum
The Dalles
AniChe Cellars
Hood
Hood River
Hood River Lavender Farm
Odell
Dee
281
Mt. Hood Railroad
Parkdale
35
Columbia River Gorge National Scenic Area
Hood River
Columbia River

TO PENDLETON
Moro
Grass Valley
197
Dufur
197
Tygh Valley
Wamic
Maupin
197
Wapinitia
216
216
TO BEND
26
Warm Springs Indian Res.
Mt. Hood
see detail map
Mt. Hood
Columbia Gorge–Mt. Hood Scenic Highway
35
Timberline Lodge
Government Camp
Pacific Coast Trail
Salmon River
Timothy Lake
26
Rhododendron
Mount Hood Village
Brightwood
Mt. Hood National Forest
Lost Lake
Pacific Coast Trail
Wahtum Lake
Middle Fork
224
26
Estacada
Sandy
Boring
26
224

TO FALL CREEK FALLS

10 mi
10 km

N

Columbia River

✉ *53000 E. Historic Columbia River Hwy., 15 miles east of Troutdale, Bridal Veil* ☏ *503/695–2376* ⊕ *www.multnomahfallslodge.com.*

Fodor's Choice
★

Vista House at Crown Point. A two-tier octagonal structure perched on the edge of this 730-foot-high cliff offers unparalleled 30-mile views up and down the Columbia River Gorge. The building dates to 1917, its rotunda and lower level filled with displays about the Gorge and the highway. Vista House's architect Edgar Lazarus was the brother of Emma Lazarus, author of the poem displayed at the base of the Statue of Liberty. The property is part of the Crown Point State Scenic Corridor, which is administered by the Oregon State Parks office. ✉ *40700 E. Historic Columbia River Hwy., 10 miles east of Troutdale, Corbett* ☏ *503/695–2230, 800/551–6949* ⊕ *www.vistahouse.com* 🖅 *Free* ☽ *Daily 9–6.*

WHERE TO EAT AND STAY

$$
AMERICAN

✕ **Multnomah Falls Lodge.** Vaulted ceilings, stone fireplaces, and exquisite views of Multnomah Falls are complemented by friendly service and reliably good American fare at this landmark restaurant, which is listed on the National Register of Historic Places. Consider the smoked salmon starter with apple-huckleberry compote, cod fish-and-chips, or the elk burger with aged Tillamook cheddar and garlic-sesame mayo. Breakfast favorites include the Hang Town fry oyster frittata with bacon, and the pancakes, available with marionberries, blueberries, or huckleberries. A particular pleaser for out-of-town guests, the champagne Sunday brunch is held 8–2. For a treat during warmer months, sit on the patio and get close to the falls without feeling a drop. $ *Average main: $20* ✉ *53000 Historic Columbia River Hwy., Exit 31 off I–84, 15 miles east of Troutdale, Bridal Veil* ☏ *503/695–2376* ⊕ *www.multnomahfallslodge.com.*

$
RESORT
Fodor's Choice
★

🏨 **McMenamins Edgefield.** Set in 74 acres of gardens, murals, orchards, and vineyards, this Georgian Revival manor that once housed the county poor farm is now operated by Northwest brewers and hospitality innovators par excellence Mike and Brian McMenamin. **Pros:** plenty of eating and drinking choices; large variety of rooms and prices; great spa; on-site movie theater (only $3); live music events. **Cons:** this busy place can get pretty crowded; no TVs, phones, or air-conditioning in the rooms; most rooms share baths. $ *Rooms from: $115* ✉ *2126 S.W. Halsey St.* ☏ *503/669–8610, 800/669–8610* ⊕ *www.mcmenamins.com* 🛏 *114 rooms, 20 with bath* ☽ *No meals.*

SPORTS AND THE OUTDOORS

RECREATIONAL AREAS

Rooster Rock State Park. The most famous beach lining the Columbia River is right below Crown Point. Three miles of sandy beaches, panoramic cascades, and a large swimming area makes this a popular spot. True naturists appreciate that one of Oregon's two designated nude beaches is at the east end of Rooster Rock, and that it's not visible to conventional sunbathers—the area is especially popular with Portland's LGBT community. Rooster Rock is 9 miles east of Troutdale, and it's accessible only via the interstate. ✉ *I–84, Exit 25, 9 miles east*

*of Troutdale, Corbett ☎ 503/695–2261 ⊕ www.oregonstateparks.org
🎫 Day use $5 per vehicle ⊙ Daily 7–dusk.*

CASCADE LOCKS

*7 miles east of Oneonta Gorge on Historic Columbia River Hwy. and
I–84; 30 miles east of Troutdale on I–84.*

In pioneer days, boats needing to pass the bedeviling rapids near the
town of Whiskey Flats had to portage around them. The locks that gave
the town its new name were completed in 1896, allowing waterborne
passage for the first time. In 1938 they were submerged beneath the
new Lake Bonneville when the Bonneville Lock and Dam became one
of the most massive Corps of Engineers projects to come out of the
New Deal. The town of Cascade Locks hung on to its name, though. A
historic stern-wheeler still leads excursions from the town's port district,
and the region's Native American tribes still practice traditional dip-net
fishing near the current locks.

GETTING HERE AND AROUND

Cascade Locks is 45 miles east of Portland and 20 miles west of Hood
River on Interstate 84. The town is also home to Bridge of the Gods ($1
toll), which is the only auto bridge crossing the Columbia River (it connects with Stevenson, Washington) between Portland and Hood River.

EXPLORING

FAMILY **Bonneville Dam.** President Franklin D. Roosevelt dedicated the first federal dam to span the Columbia in 1937. Its generators (visible from
a balcony on a self-guided tour or up close during free guided tours
offered daily in summer and on weekends the rest of the year) have a
capacity of more than a million kilowatts, enough to supply power to
more than 200,000 single-family homes. There's an extensive visitor
center on Bradford Island, complete with underwater windows where
gaggles of kids watch migrating salmon and steelhead as they struggle up
fish ladders. The best viewing times are between April and October. In
recent years the dwindling runs of wild Columbia salmon have made the
dam a subject of much environmental controversy. ⊠ *Exit 40 from I–84,
follow signs 1 mile to visitor center, Cascade Locks* ☎ *541/374–8820
⊕ www.nwp.usace.army.mil/Locations/ColumbiaRiver/Bonneville
🎫 Free ⊙ Visitor center daily 9–5; powerhouse tours mid-June–Aug.,
daily at 11, 1, and 3; Sept.–mid-June, weekends at 11, 1, and 3.*

Cascade Locks Marine Park. This riverfront park is the home port of the
500-passenger stern-wheeler *Columbia Gorge*, which churns upriver,
then back again, on one- and two-hour excursions through some of
the Columbia River Gorge's most impressive scenery, mid-May to early
October; brunch and dinner cruises are also available. The ship's captain
discusses the Gorge's fascinating 40-million-year geology and pioneering spirits and legends, such as Lewis and Clark, who once triumphed
over this very same river. The park itself, which includes a pedestrian
bridge to leafy and tranquil Thunder Island, is a lovely spot for picnicking, and Thunder Island Brewing—at the north end of the park—serves
first-rate craft beers. ⊠ *Marine Park, S.W. Portage Rd., Cascade Locks*

☎ *541/224–3900, 800/224–3901* ⊕ *www.portlandspirit.com* ✉ *Cruises from $23* ⚲ *Reservations essential* ⊙ *Park open daily dawn–dusk; cruises May–Oct.*

WHERE TO EAT

$ ╳ **Thunder Island Brewing.** Hikers, boaters, and others exploring the
AMERICAN Gorge gather at this laid-back, funky brewpub with several tables inside, as well as a large patio with picnic tables overlooking the Columbia River, Marine Park, and the little island for which the brewery is named. Order a glass of hoppy Pacific Crest Trail Pale Ale or malty Scotch Porter, and enjoy it with one of the light dishes from the short menu—the spinach-and-feta pasty, chicken-salad sandwich, and charcuterie, cheese, and smoked-fish plate are all excellent. Wine and hard cider are also served. ⑤ *Average main: $8* ⊠ *515 S.W. Portage Rd., Cascade Locks* ☎ *971/231–4599* ⊕ *www.thunderislandbrewing.com.*

SPORTS AND THE OUTDOORS

HIKING

Pacific Crest Trail. Cascade Locks bustles with grubby thru-hikers refueling along the 2,650-mile Canada-to-Mexico Pacific Crest Trail. Check out a scenic and strenuous portion of it, heading south from the trailhead at Herman Creek Horse Camp, just east of town. The route heads up into the Cascades, showing off monster views of the Gorge. Backpackers out for a longer trek will find idyllic campsites at Wahtum Lake, 14 miles south. You can also access the trail from the free parking area at Toll House Park, by the Bridge of the Gods. ⊠ *Off N.W. Forest La., 1 mile east of downtown, Cascade Locks* ☎ *541/308–1700* ⊕ *www.pcta.org.*

STEVENSON, WASHINGTON

Across the river from Cascade Locks via the Bridge of the Gods and 1 mile east on Hwy. 14.

With the Bridge of the Gods toll bridge spanning the Columbia River above the Bonneville Dam, Stevenson acts as a sort of "twin city" to Cascade Locks on the Oregon side. Tribal legends and the geologic record tell of the original Bridge of the Gods, a substantial landslide that occurred here sometime between AD 1000 and 1760, briefly linking the two sides of the Gorge before the river swept away the debris. The landslide's steel namesake now leads to tiny Stevenson, where vacationers traverse quiet Main Street, which has a few casual eateries and shops. Washington's Highway 14 runs through the middle of town, and since the cliffs on the Oregon side are more dramatic, driving this two-lane highway actually offers better views.

GETTING HERE AND AROUND

From the Oregon side of the Gorge, cross the Columbia River at the Bridge of the Gods ($1 toll).

ESSENTIALS

Visitor Information Skamania County Chamber of Commerce ⊠ *167 N.W. 2nd St., Stevenson* ☎ *509/427–8911, 800/989–9178* ⊕ *www.skamania.org.*

Dog Mountain Trail, Columbia River Gorge National Scenic Area

EXPLORING

FAMILY **Columbia Gorge Interpretive Center Museum.** A petroglyph whose eyes seem to look straight at you, "She Who Watches" or "Tsagaglalal" is the logo for this museum. Sitting among the dramatic basaltic cliffs on the north bank of the Columbia River Gorge, the museum explores the life of the Gorge: its history, culture, architecture, legends, and much more. Younger guests enjoy the reenactment of the Gorge's formation in the Creation Theatre, and the 37-foot-high fish wheel, a device like a mill wheel equipped with baskets for catching fish, from the 19th century. Historians appreciate studying the water route of the Lewis and Clark Expedition. There's also an eye-opening exhibit that examines current environmental impacts on the area. ⊠ *990 S.W. Rock Creek Dr.* ☎ *509/427–8211, 800/991–2338* ⊕ *www.columbiagorge.org* ✉ *$10* ⊙ *Daily 10–5.*

WHERE TO EAT AND STAY

$ ✕ **Big River Grill.** A tradition with hikers, bikers, fishermen, and scenic
AMERICAN drivers out exploring the Gorge, especially for weekend breakfast but also at lunch and dinnertime, this colorful roadhouse in the center of town is festooned with license plates, vintage signs, and kitschy artwork. Grab a seat at the counter or in one of the high-back wooden booths, and tuck into grilled wild salmon sandwich, chicken-fried chicken with eggs, home-style meat loaf with buttermilk-garlic mashed potatoes, and other hearty, reasonably priced fare. ⑤ *Average main: $14* ⊠ *192 S.W. 2nd St.* ☎ *509/427–4888* ⊕ *www.thebigrivergrill.com.*

$$ ✕ **Cascade Room at Skamania Lodge.** At Skamania Lodge's signature res-
PACIFIC taurant, with its stunning views of sky, river, and cliff scapes, chef
NORTHWEST Mark Henry, draws on local seafood and regionally sourced meats and
Fodor's Choice produce, turning out dandy dishes like a Dungeness crab tower with
★ avocado, beet coulis, and basil oil; and braised lamb shank with an
aromatic Merlot sauce and buttermilk-mashed potatoes. There are sev-
eral lighter and less-pricey items, too, from burgers to wild-mushroom
risotto. The lavish Sunday Champagne brunch buffet draws patrons
from miles around. Henry also oversees the kitchen at the resort's sim-
pler and more casual River Rock café, which has both indoor and
outdoor seating with the same smashing views. $ *Average main: $23*
✉ *Skamania Lodge, 1131 S. W. Skamania Lodge Way* ☎ *509/427–7700*
⊕ *www.skamania.com.*

$$$ ⬚ **Bonneville Hot Springs Resort and Spa.** At this modern resort on a
RESORT wooded tract just west of Stevenson, spacious rooms with upscale fur-
nishings allow guests to enjoy historic mineral springs and glorious
grounds. **Pros:** impressive architectural detail; the Pacific Crest Trail
passes directly through the property. **Cons:** the dull, boxy exterior
belies what's inside; rooms and public areas could use some updat-
ing. $ *Rooms from: $209* ✉ *1252 E. Cascade Dr., North Bonneville*
☎ *509/427–7767, 866/459–1678* ⊕ *www.bonnevilleresort.com* ⌂ *78
rooms* ⦿ *No meals.*

$$$ ⬚ **Skamania Lodge.** This warm, woodsy lodge on an expansive, verdant
RESORT swath of forest and meadows impresses with a multitude of windows
FAMILY overlooking the surrounding mountains and Gorge, an outstanding
Fodor's Choice array of recreational facilities, and handsome, Pacific Northwest–chic
★ accommodations, many with fireplaces and all with views. **Pros:** Just a
45-minute drive from Portland but feels secluded and totally relaxing;
plenty of fun outdoorsy activities; first-rate spa and dining facilities.
Cons: expensive for a large family; can get crowded—sometimes there's
a wait for a table in the dining room. $ *Rooms from: $205* ✉ *1131
S. W. Skamania Lodge Way* ☎ *509/427–7700, 800/221–7117* ⊕ *www.
skamania.com* ⌂ *254 rooms* ⦿ *No meals.*

NIGHTLIFE AND THE ARTS

Walking Man Brewing. This sunshiny patio and cozy interior are great
spots for creative pizzas and sampling the dozen-or-so craft ales. After
a couple of pints of the strong Homo Erectus IPA and Knuckle Drag-
ger Pale Ale, you may go a little ape. Live music on summer weekends
skews twangy and upbeat. ✉ *240 S. W. 1st St.* ☎ *509/427–5520* ⊕ *www.
walkingmanbeer.com* ⦿ *Closed Mon. and Tues.*

SPORTS AND THE OUTDOORS

RECREATIONAL AREA

Fodor's Choice **Beacon Rock State Park.** For several hundred years this 848-foot rock was
★ a landmark for river travelers, including Native Americans, who rec-
ognized this point as the last rapids of the Columbia River. Lewis and
Clark are thought to have been the first white men to see the volcanic
remnant. Even most casual hikers can make the steep but safe trek up
to the top of the rock—allow about 45–60 minutes round-trip. More
serious hikers should head to the trailhead for Hamilton Mountain,

5

which is reached via a beautiful, though arduous, 8-mile ramble over a roaring waterfall, through dense temperate rain forest, and finally up to a 2,400-foot summit with breathtaking views up and down the Gorge. ✉ *34841 Hwy. 14, 7 miles west of Bridge of the Gods, Skamania* ☎ *509/427–8265* ⊕ *www.parks.wa.gov* ✉ *$10 day pass.*

HOOD RIVER

20 miles east of Cascade Locks and 60 miles east of Portland on I–84.

This picturesque riverside community of about 7,200 residents affords visitors spectacular views both of the Columbia River and snowcapped Mt. Hood. More than 40 civic and commercial buildings date from 1893 to the 1930s, some of which are listed in the National Register of Historic Places.

Hood River is the dining and lodging hub of the Gorge, with an increasingly respected bounty of urbane farm-to-table restaurants, up-and-coming craft breweries and wine-tasting rooms, and diverting shops and art galleries. Little wonder this is one of the most popular weekend getaways among Portlanders, all the more so since the surrounding countryside abounds with orchards and vineyards, making it a favorite destination for fans of U-pick farmsteads and tasting rooms. Hood River wineries grow a broader range of grapes than Oregon's more famous Willamette Valley, and wine touring has become a favorite activity in the area.

GETTING HERE AND AROUND

Reach Hood River from Portland by driving 60 miles east on Interstate 84, or from Mt. Hood by heading 40 miles north on Highway 35.

ESSENTIALS

Visitor Information Hood River County Chamber of Commerce ✉ *720 E. Port Marina Dr.* ☎ *541/386–2000, 800/366–3530* ⊕ *www.hoodriver.org.*

EXPLORING

Glassometry Studios. Artist and teacher Laurel Marie Hagner operates this colorful gallery and sculpture garden just off the Hood River Fruit Loop, near the village of Odell. You can admire the larger-than-life, riotously vibrant glass sculptures with a walk through the garden, watch live glass-blowing demonstrations (and take classes) in the studio, and browse the fanciful yet absolutely functional vases, bowls, drinking glasses, decanters, and decorative glass art in the studio. ✉ *3015 Lower Mill Dr.* ☎ *541/354–3015* ⊕ *www.glassometry.com* ✉ *Free* ☉ *Wed.–Sun. 11–5.*

Fodor'sChoice
★ **Gorge White House.** You'll find pretty much everything the Hood River Valley is famous for growing and being produced at this picturesque, century-old farm anchored by a Dutch Colonial farmhouse and surrounded by acres of U-pick flowers, apple and peach trees, and blackberry and blueberry bushes. After strolling through the farm fields, stop inside the main house to sample wines—the tasting room carries one of the largest selections of Columbia River wines in the region. Out back, there's a farm store, another tasting room serving local craft beer and cider, and a garden patio with seating and a food-truck-style

Vineyards in the Hood River Valley

café serving delicious strawberry salads, pulled-pork sandwiches, pear pizzas, and other light fare. ⊠ *2265 Hwy. 35* ☎ *541/386–2828* ⊕ *www. thegorgewhitehouse.com* ⊗ *June–Sept., daily 10–7; Apr., May, and Oct., Fri.–Mon. 10–7.*

Fodor'sChoice
★

Marchesi Vineyards. Somewhat unusual for the Pacific Northwest, this boutique winery with a small, airy tasting room and a verdant garden patio specializes in Italian varietals—Moscato, Primitivo, Dolcetto, Sangiovese, Barbera, Nebbiolo, and a few others. Owner Franco Marchesi hails from Italy's Piemonte regoin, and he's earned serious kudos for his finesse as a winemaker. ⊠ *3955 Belmont Dr.* ☎ *541/386–1800* ⊕ *www. marchesivineyards.com* ⊗ *June–late Nov., daily 11–6; late Nov.–May, Fri.–Sun. 11–6.*

Mt. Hood Railroad. Scenic passenger excursions along a small rail line established in 1906 offer a picturesque and relaxing way to survey Mt. Hood and the Hood River Valley. Chug alongside the Hood River through vast fruit orchards before climbing up steep forested canyons, glimpsing Mt. Hood along the way. There are several trip options, from $30: a four-hour excursion (serves light concessions), dinner, brunch, and several themed trips, like murder-mysteries and Old West robberies. Exceptional service is as impressive as the scenery. ⊠ *110 Railroad Ave.* ☎ *541/386–3556, 800/872–4661* ⊕ *www.mthoodrr.com* ⊗ *Mid-Apr.–late Oct.*

Viento Wines. Focused more on whites than most of the winemakers in the Gorge region, Viento has a stunning tasting room with vaulted ceilings, soaring windows, and a large patio overlooking the on-site vineyard of Riesling grapes. This is a lovely space for tasting and chatting with fellow oenophiles. Notable wines here include a crisp Grüner Velt-liner, a food-friendly Brut Rosé, and one of the better Oregon Pinot Noirs you'll find in the Hood River region. ⊠ *301 Country Club Rd.* ☎ *541/386–3026* ⊕ *www.vientowines.com* ☾ *Daily 11–5.*

NEED A BREAK?

Doppio Coffee + Lounge. Sunshine fills the small dining room and outdoor seating area of this high-ceilinged, contemporary downtown coffee bar that serves fine espresso drinks as well as local wines and craft beers. It's great for light snacking—there's a nice selection of baked goods and fine chocolates—but there are also substantial grilled panini sandwiches, salads, and soups. ⊠ *310 Oak St.* ☎ *541/386–3000* ⊕ *www. doppiohoodriver.com* ☾ *No dinner.*

Western Antique Aeroplane and Automobile Museum. Housed at Hood River's tiny airport (general aviation only), the museum's impressive, meticulously restored, propeller-driven planes are all still in flying condition. The antique steam cars, Model Ts, and sleek Depression-era sedans are road-worthy, too. Periodic car shows and an annual fly-in draw thousands of history buffs and spectators. ⊠ *1600 Air Museum Rd., off Hwy. 281* ☎ *541/308–1600* ⊕ *www.waaamuseum.org* ▧ *$14* ☾ *Daily 9–5.*

WHERE TO EAT

$$$

PACIFIC NORTHWEST

✕ **Celilo Restaurant.** Refined and relaxing, this high-ceilinged restaurant in a contemporary downtown building is popular both for dinner and enjoying a glass of local wine in the bar, which has both indoor and outdoor seating on colorful Oak Street. Chef Ben Stenn presents a seasonally changing menu of deftly crafted Pacific Northwest fare—order the cast-iron-skillet seafood-and-chorizo roast if it's on the menu, and also keep an eye out for house-preserved duck-leg confit with pickled green beans, pork-belly lardons, and organic greens. ⑤ *Average main: $24* ⊠ *16 Oak St.* ☎ *541/386–5710* ⊕ *www.celilorestaurant.com.*

$$

ECLECTIC

Fodor'sChoice ★

✕ **Nora's Table.** Chef Kathy Watson brings bold, world-beat flavors to this unpretentious but sophisticated downtown bistro that's also well regarded for its Northwest-focused wine list. Mussels simmered in Goan-style curry, local salmon with cannellini beans and Italian salsa verde, and New Mexico–style veggie enchiladas reflect the menu's varied approach. Nora's doesn't serve lunch, but is justly popular for breakfast, served only Friday–Sunday, and featuring the likes of Bombay-town fry with curried potatoes and vegetables, fried oysters, and poached eggs, and Louisiana-style eggs Benedict with tasso ham and grits. ⑤ *Average main: $18* ⊠ *110 5th St.* ☎ *541/387–4000* ⊕ *www.norastable.com* ☾ *No lunch.*

$$

PIZZA

✕ **Solstice Wood Fire Cafe.** It can be hard to score a table on weekends in this snazzy space along the Hood River waterfront. What's all the fuss? Wood-fire-grilled pizzas with unusual toppings—such as the Cherry Girl, layered with local cherries, spicy chorizo, goat cheese, mozzarella, and marinara sauce—plus bountiful salads, wood-fired mac-and-cheese, and juicy burgers. The wood-fire oven comes into play for dessert, too, with classic s'mores. ⑤ *Average main: $17* ⊠ *501 Portway Ave.* ☎ *541/436–0800* ⊕ *www.solsticewoodfirecafe.com.*

$$ ⚔ **Stonehedge Gardens.** It's not just the cuisine that's out of this world,
AMERICAN
Fodor'sChoice
★

this Columbia Gorge institution is of another time and place, surrounded by 7 acres of lush English-style gardens that gracefully frame its multitude of stone terraces and trickling fountains. There's a *petanque* (lawn bowling) court for quick predinner activity, and music on Wednesday nights in summer draws a full house. Each of the four dining rooms in the restored 1898 home has a distinct personality, from cozy to verdant to elegant, but the tiered patio is where summer diners gather. The kitchen tends toward the traditional side, specializing in classics like steak Diane and filet mignon. Just when you think your meal is complete, along comes the Flaming Bread Pudding. $ *Average main: $23* ⊠ *3405 Cascade Ave.* ☎ *541/386–3940* ⊕ *www.stonehedgeweddings. com* ☾ *No lunch*.

WHERE TO STAY

$$ ☷ **Best Western Plus Hood River Inn.** This low-slung, rambling hotel beside
HOTEL
the Hood River Bridge offers some of the best river views of any hotel in the Gorge, and many units have private balconies or patios on the water; the deluxe accommodations have full kitchens, fireplaces, and Jacuzzi tubs. **Pros:** riverfront location with great views; good restaurant and lounge. **Cons:** tends to be a little pricey in summer; downtown shopping and dining isn't within walking distance. $ *Rooms from: $169* ⊠ *1108 E. Marina Way* ☎ *541/386–2200, 800/828–7873* ⊕ *www. hoodriverinn.com* ↰ *194 rooms* � *Breakfast.*

$$$ ☷ **Columbia Cliff Villas Hotel.** This elegant condo-style compound on a
HOTEL
FAMILY
Fodor'sChoice
★

sheer cliff overlooking the Columbia River contains some of the plushest accommodations in the region—units have one to three bedrooms, fireplaces, terraces or patios, stone-and-tile bathrooms, and fine linens. **Pros:** private apartment-style accommodations; great river views; sophisticated decor and top-flight amenities. **Cons:** no restaurants or fitness center on-site; pricey. $ *Rooms from: $205* ⊠ *3880 Westcliff Dr.* ☎ *541/490–8081, 866/912–8366* ⊕ *www.columbiacliffvillas.com* ↰ *37 suites* ⊐ *No meals.*

$ ☷ **Hood River Hotel.** In the heart of the lively and hip business district,
HOTEL
steps from great restaurants and shops, this handsomely restored building has a grand, Old West facade, behind which are simple rooms with tasteful period-style antiques and a few larger suites that have kitchenettes and large sitting rooms. **Pros:** excellent downtown location; several available adventure and romance packages; antiques-heavy interiors have feel of a European inn. **Cons:** smallish rooms; no king-size beds; rooms in back have great river views but tend to receive some freeway noise. $ *Rooms from: $129* ⊠ *102 Oak St.* ☎ *541/386–1900, 800/386–1859* ⊕ *www.hoodriverhotel.com* ↰ *32 rooms, 9 suites* ⊐ *Breakfast.*

$$ ☷ **Sakura Ridge.** The five warm but sleekly furnished rooms of this con-
B&B/INN
Fodor'sChoice
★

temporary lodge-style B&B on a 72-acre farm on the south side of town offer magical panoramas of Mt. Hood amid a welcome absence of clutter. **Pros:** spectacular mountain views; rustic yet urbane decor; lush gardens and orchards on the grounds. **Cons:** secluded location is a 15-minute drive from downtown. $ *Rooms from: $170* ⊠ *5601 York Hill Rd.* ☎ *541/386–2636, 877/472–5872* ⊕ *www.sakuraridge. com* ↰ *5 rooms* ⊐ *Breakfast.*

5

$$
B&B/INN

☂ **Villa Columbia B&B.** The five guest rooms in this handsomely maintained 1911 Craftsman-style bed-and-breakfast are a tasteful but eclectic mix of older and newer pieces; all are named for famous Oregon rivers, and from the Columbia River room you're actually treated to a fine view of the Gorge. **Pros:** helpful, knowledgeable innkeepers; proximity to downtown galleries, restaurants, and brewpubs; decor is upscale but unfussy. **Cons:** river views are somewhat obstructed by trees and other houses; on a busy street. $\boxed{S}$ *Rooms from: $159* ⊠ *902 Oak St.* ☎ *541/386–6670* ⊕ *www.villacolumbia.com* ⤴ *5 rooms* ⦿❙ *Breakfast.*

NIGHTLIFE AND THE ARTS

Brian's Pourhouse. A cute downtown cottage with a spacious deck serves excellent, eclectic food, but is even better known as a later-in-the-evening spot. It's the favored place in town to enjoy a cocktail or glass of wine and perhaps a sweet nosh—the Dutch apple pie with caramel sauce, whipped cream, and ice cream is memorable. ⊠ *606 Oak St.* ☎ *541/387–4344* ⊕ *www.brianspourhouse.com.*

Pfriem Family Brewers. Inside a striking new building on the Columbia River, Pfriem (pronounced "freem") is all about the marriage of Belgium's brewing traditions and Oregon's decidedly hoppy style. The brewery has quickly vaulted to the top echelon of Northwest craft beer makers, earning accolades for its heady Belgian Strong Blonde and one of the best IPAs in the state. The on-site restaurant serves stellar pub fare, too, including mussels and fries, vegan Moroccan stew, and house-made bratwurst. ⊠ *707 Portway Ave.* ☎ *541/321–0490* ⊕ *www. pfriembeer.com.*

SPORTS AND THE OUTDOORS
KAYAKING
Columbia Gorge Kayak School. Whether you want to practice your Eskimo roll in the safety of a pool, run the Klickitat River in an inflatable kayak, or try out a stand-up paddleboard on the Columbia, the Gorge's premier kayak guides can arrange the trip. Book online, by phone, or at the Kayak Shed downtown. ⊠ *6 Oak St.* ☎ *541/806–4190* ⊕ *www. gorgekayaker.com.*

WHITE SALMON, WASHINGTON

5 miles north of Hood River on Hwy. 14.

Tiny White Salmon, which sits on a bluff with commanding views of the Columbia River as well as the town of Hood River, is a good base for exploring the Washington side of the eastern end of the Gorge. A few noteworthy restaurants and shops in the village center cater to hikers, kayakers, and wine- and beer-tasting aficionados checking out this quieter but similar scenic counterpart to Hood River. Several first-rate wineries have opened in the rural communities just west and east of White Salmon along Highway 14.

GETTING HERE AND AROUND

You reach White Salmon by driving across the Hood River Bridge (toll $1), turning east onto Highway 14, and then north in the small village of Bingen onto Highway 141—it's just a 10-minute drive from Hood River.

ESSENTIALS

Mt. Adams Chamber of Commerce ✉ *1 Heritage Plaza, off Hwy. 14, just west of Hood River Bridge* ☎ *509/493–3630* ⊕ *www.mtadamschamber. com.*

EXPLORING

Aniche Cellars. This friendly boutique winery has one of the prettiest tasting-room settings in the area—it's high on Underwood Mountain, with outdoor seating that affords spectacular views looking east toward Hood River and deep into the Gorge. The cleverly named wines here—Puck, an Albarino–Pinot Gris blend; Three Witches, a Rhône-style blend of Cinsault, Carignan, and Counoise—are paired with little amuse-bouche-style nibbles, typically chocolate, prosciutto, or fruit. The winery is a 10-minute drive west of White Salmon. ✉ *71 Little Buck Creek Rd., Underwood* ☎ *360/624–6531* ⊕ *www.anichecellars. com* ☉ *Wed.–Sun. noon–6.*

Fodor'sChoice ★ **Syncline Wines.** The focus at this intimate winery is predominantly on elegant, full-bodied Rhône-style wines. The friendly, knowledgeable tasting-room has garnered plenty of awards for its aromatic Cuvée Elena Grenache-Syrah-Mourvedre blend, as well as a first-rate stand-alone Syrah, and several racy, dry whites—Picpoul, Grenache Blanc, Gruner Veltliner—that seem tailor-made for the Gorge's warm summer nights. Note that three other outstanding small wineries—Domaine Pouillon, Memaloose, and COR Cellars—are in the same rural town, 10 miles east of White Salmon. ✉ *111 Balch Rd., Lyle* ☎ *509/365–4361* ⊕ *www.synclinewine.com* ☉ *Thurs.–Sun. 11–6.*

WHERE TO EAT

$$
PACIFIC
NORTHWEST
Fodor'sChoice ★
✕ **Henni's Kitchen & Bar.** It's well worth venturing across the Columbia from Hood River to this jewel of a neighborhood tavern, which serves well-priced, creatively prepared international fare with a decided Northwest focus—think kale fritters with romesco sauce, Thai red curry with local flat-iron steak, and classic fish-and-chips. This is hearty comfort food, but with healthy and fresh ingredients. The bar serves terrific, innovative cocktails, and food prices during the weekday evening (5–6 pm) happy hour represent one of the best deals around. ⑤ *Average main: $18* ✉ *120 E. Jewett Blvd.* ☎ *509/493–1555* ⊕ *www. henniskitchenandbar.com* ☉ *No lunch.*

NIGHTLIFE

Everybody's Brewing. Head to this festive downtown brewpub for seriously impressive beers, with the potent Big Brother Imperial IPA (7.7% ABV) and orange-peel-enhanced Daily Bread Common Ale leading the way. There's live music many evenings, and tasty pub fare, too. ✉ *151 E. Jewett Blvd.* ☎ *509/637–2774* ⊕ *www.everybodysbrewing.com.*

SPORTS AND THE OUTDOORS

Wet Planet Whitewater. This outfitter just outside White Salmon offers half- and full-day white-water rafting trips on the White Salmon, Wind, Klickitat, Hood, and Tieton Rivers, which rank among some of the top waterways for this activity in the region. The Wind and Hood Rivers contain stretches of hairy Class IV–Class V rapids (previous experience is required), but the other trips are suitable for beginners. The company also offers kayaking instruction and trips. ⊠ *860 Hwy. 141, Husum* ☎ *509/493–8989, 877/390–9445* ⊕ *www.wetplanetwhitewater.com.*

THE DALLES

20 miles east of Hood River on I–84.

The Dalles lies on a crescent bend of the Columbia River where it narrows and once spilled over a series of rapids, creating a flagstone effect. French voyagers christened it *dalle,* or "flagstone." The Dalles is the seat of Wasco County and the trading hub of north-central Oregon. It gained fame early in the region's history as the town where the Oregon Trail branched, with some pioneers departing to travel over Mt. Hood on Barlow Road and the others continuing down the Columbia River. This may account for the small-town, Old West feeling that still permeates the area. Several historic Oregon moments as they relate to The Dalles' past are magnificently illustrated on eight murals painted by renowned Northwest artists, located downtown within short walking distance of one another.

GETTING HERE AND AROUND

From Hood River, it's a 22-mile drive east on Interstate 84 to reach The Dalles. Alternatively, you can take the slightly slower and more scenic Highway 14, on the Washington side of the Columbia, from White Salmon to U.S. 197, which leads you into town via The Dalles Bridge.

ESSENTIALS

Visitor Information The Dalles Area Chamber of Commerce ⊠ *404 W. 2nd St.* ☎ *541/296–2231, 800/255–3385* ⊕ *www.thedalleschamber.com.*

EXPLORING

FAMILY **Columbia Gorge Discovery Center–Wasco County Historical Museum.** Exhibits and artwork at this expansive, contemporary museum just off I–84 as you approach The Dalles from the west highlight the geological history of the Columbia Gorge, back 40 million years when volcanoes, landslides, and floods carved out the area. History exhibits focus on 10,000 years of Native American life and exploration of the region by white settlers, from Lewis and Clark to the early-20th-century engineers who developed the Historic Columbia River Highway. ⊠ *5000 Discovery Dr.* ☎ *541/296–8600* ⊕ *www.gorgediscovery.org* ⊠ *$9* ⊙ *Daily 9–5.*

Sunshine Mill Winery. You won't find many wineries situated in more unusual buildings than Quenett, which operates out of an early-1900s flour mill with huge grain elevators that soar over the southern end of The Dalles's downtown. Inside this dramatic old structure that nearly fell to the wrecking ball before winemakers James and Molli Martin bought it, you'll find the tasting room for Quenett, which produces first-rate Malbec, Viognier, Barbera, and a Chardonnay-Viognier-Sauvignon Blanc-Semillon blend. You can also order cheese boards and other snacks, and sample wines from the company's other line, Copa Di Vino, an inexpensive brand of single-serving table wines sold throughout the country. ⊠ *901 E. 2nd St.* ☎ *541/298–8900* ⊕ *www.sunshinemill. com* ⊘ *May–Oct., Sat.–Thurs. noon–6; Fri.–noon–7; call for winter hrs.*

WHERE TO EAT AND STAY

$ ✕ **Petite Provence.** This popular downtown bistro-bakery-dessertery,
CAFÉ which also has branches in Portland, serves delicious eggs, crepes, and croissants for breakfast; hot and cold sandwiches and salads for lunch; and fresh-baked pastries and breads (you can take a loaf home). For lunch, consider the Columbia River steelhead fillet with hazelnut-crust, served over sautéed leeks and roasted artichokes. The sparkling display case tempts with a goodly selection of napoleons, éclairs, tarts, and mousses. A good variety of local and French wines are available, too. $ *Average main: $8* ⊠ *408 E. 2nd St.* ☎ *541/506–0037* ⊕ *www. provencepdx.com* ⊘ *No dinner.*

$ 🛏 **Celilo Inn.** A prototypical retro motor lodge gone high-design, with
HOTEL exterior-entry rooms and a '50s light-up motel sign that disguise a
Fodor'sChoice slick, boutique feel, commands a hilltop overlooking the Columbia
★ River and Dalles Dam. **Pros:** sexy design; terrific wine-touring packages; most rooms have great views. **Cons:** not all rooms have views; those on the far end feel very away from the front desk. $ *Rooms from: $119* ⊠ *3550 E. 2nd St.* ☎ *541/769–0001* ⊕ *www.celiloinn.com* ⟿ *46 rooms* ⦿*| No meals.*

$ 🛏 **Fairfield Inn & Suites.** Although it's part of Marriott's midrange brand,
HOTEL this four-story hotel a couple of blocks from Interstate 84 does have the brightest and most up-to-date rooms in the eastern end of the Gorge, with spacious work areas, comfy bedding, mini-refrigerators, microwaves, and marble-accent bathrooms. **Pros:** upscale rooms at reasonable prices; nice indoor pool and fitness center. **Cons:** bland location on the west side of town that's a bit of a long walk from downtown. $ *Rooms from: $107* ⊠ *2014 W. 7th St.* ☎ *541/769–0753, 800/306–1665* ⊕ *www.marriott.com* ⟿ *57 rooms, 23 suites* ⦿*| Breakfast.*

SPORTS AND THE OUTDOORS

RECREATIONAL AREAS

Mayer State Park. Views from atop the park's Rowena Crest bluff are knockout, especially during the March and April wildflower season, and there are a couple of fairly short and scenic hikes that lead from the bluff parking lot (off U.S. 30, 13 miles west of The Dalles, and 6 miles east of Mosier). The 3.5-mile (round-trip) trek up to McCall Point being especially scenic—it affords great views of Mt. Hood. The lower part of the park hugs the Columbia River and is accessed from I–84; here the activities include swimming, boating, fishing, and picnicking. ⊠ *Lower Mayer State Park access, Exit 76 off I–84* ☎ *800/551–6949* ⊕ *www.oregonstateparks.org* 🎫 *Day use $5 per vehicle* ⊘ *Daily.*

GOLDENDALE, WASHINGTON

34 miles northeast of The Dalles via Hwy. 14 and U.S. 97.

Although the actual town of Goldendale lies about 12 miles north of the Columbia River, this easygoing community is a good base for exploring the eastern end of the Gorge. It's home to one of the only notable restaurants in this vast but sparsely populated section of the Columbia River Valley, and it also has a couple of basic motels, a small downtown with a few funky cafés and shops, and the small but excellent Goldendale Observatory State Park. Views on the drive to Goldendale and in town itself are some of the most dramatic in the drier, eastern reaches of the Gorge—you'll see soaring white wind turbines lining the grassy bluffs and cliffs on both sides of the river, and along U.S. 97 as it leads into Goldendale, you can see the snowcapped summit of Washington's 12,281-foot Mt. Adams, which receives a little less attention than its southerly twin, Mt. Hood, but is actually taller and every bit as dramatic.

GETTING HERE AND AROUND

Although it's quickest to drive east along Interstate 84 and then north on U.S. 97 to reach Goldendale (a total of 34 miles) and the attractions around Maryhill, it takes only a few extra minutes and is far more scenic to cross the Columbia via The Dalles Bridge into Washington and drive east on Highway 14 to U.S. 97.

ESSENTIALS

Greater Goldendale Chamber of Commerce ✉ *903 E. Broadway St.* ☎ *509/773–3400* ⊕ *www.goldendalechamber.org.*

EXPLORING

FAMILY **Goldendale Observatory State Park.** This 5-acre park on a 2,100-foot-elevation bluff just north of Goldendale's compact downtown contains one of the nation's largest public telescopes, and the town's remote location, far from the lights of any cities, is ideal. Fascinating astronomy programs and sky-watching events are held during the day and evening, year-round. ✉ *1602 Observatory Dr.* ☎ *509/773–3141* ⊕ *www.goldendaleobservatory.com* ✉ *$10 day pass* ☉ *Observatory, Apr.–Sept., Wed.–Sun. 1–11:30 pm; Oct.–Mar., Fri.–Sun. 1–9 pm.*

Fodor's Choice **Maryhill Museum of Art.** A wonderfully eclectic mix of artworks, including
★ the largest assemblage of Rodin works outside France; posters, glasswork, and ephemera related to the modern-dance pioneer Loïe Fuller; an impressive cache of Native American artifacts; furniture and art that belonged to another Hill companion, Queen Marie of Romania; an art nouveau glass collection; and a large collection of mostly Victorian-era European and American landscape paintings: they're all housed within the walls of a grandiose mansion built rather improbably in the middle of nowhere by Sam Hill, the man who spearheaded the development of a scenic highway through the Columbia Gorge. The main Beaux-Arts building dates to 1914, and a daring, beautifully executed, LEED-certified modern wing, opened in 2012, extends from the back, with a terraced slope overlooking the Columbia River—it contains the museum café, a lovely spot for lunch. The extensive, harmoniously

landscaped grounds include a sculpture garden and pathways along the Gorge rim. ✉ *35 Maryhill Museum of Art Dr., off Hwy. 14, 3 miles west of junction with U.S. 97* ☎ *509/773–3733* ⊕ *www.maryhillmuseum.org* 🎫 *$9* ⊗ *Mid-Mar.–mid-Nov., daily 10–5.*

Maryhill Winery. Just down the road from Maryhill Museum, this large winery enjoys the same phenomenal views up and down the Gorge. The largest tasting room in the Gorge has a good-size gift shop as well as a market selling cheese, charcuterie, and other gourmet goodies. Maryhill produces dozens of wines at a variety of prices—the reserves, including stellar Cabernet Franc, Cabernet Sauvignon, Malbec, and Chardonnay, tend to earn most acclaim. In summer, the outdoor amphitheater on the grounds hosts a series of pop concerts—recent performers have included Jethro Tull, Peter Frampton, Styx, and Foreigner. ✉ *9774 Hwy. 14* ☎ *509/773–1976* ⊕ *www.maryhillwinery.com* ⊗ *Daily 10–6.*

Stonehenge Memorial. Built by Maryhill Museum founder Sam Hill, this full-scale replica of England's legendary Neolithic stone creation was constructed in 1918 as the nation's first memorial to servicemen who perished in World War I. The memorial is a five-minute drive east of the museum, on a promontory overlooking the Columbia River. ✉ *Stonehenge Dr., off Hwy. 14, just east of U.S. 97* ☎ *509/773–3733* ⊕ *www. maryhillmuseum.org* 🎫 *Free* ⊗ *Daily 7 am–dusk.*

WHERE TO EAT

$ ✕ **Glass Onion.** Visitors to small, unpretentious Goldendale will be surprised to find one of the culinary gems of the Columbia Gorge in the center of town, set within a cozy, beautifully restored house hung with local artwork. Chef Matt McGowan sources seasonal ingredients from local farms and purveyors, serves a great selection of local beers and wines, and keeps the price of everything on his menu at least $10 below what you'd pay in Hood River or Portland. Recent dishes from the regularly changing menu have included charcoal-grilled pork tenderloin with tomato jam and whole-grain mustard, and crispy Korean chicken wings with sweet-and-sour sauce and sesame seeds. Chocolate pot de crème with fresh blueberries and cream makes for a perfect ending. $ *Average main: $13* ✉ *604 S. Columbus Ave.* ☎ *509/773–4928* ⊕ *www.theglassonionrestaurant.com* ⊗ *Closed Sun.–Tues.*

MODERN
AMERICAN
Fodor's Choice
★

MT. HOOD

The Multnomah tribe call Mt. Hood "Wy'East," named, according to popular legend, for a jealous lover who once sparred over a woman with his rival, Klickitat. When their fighting caught the Great Spirit's attention, Wy'East and Klickitat were transformed into two angry, smoke-bellowing mountains—one became Washington's Mt. Adams, the other became Mt. Hood. Wy'East has mellowed out a bit since then, but the mountain is still technically an active volcano, and it's had very minor, lava-free eruptive events as recently as the mid-1800s.

Today Mt. Hood is better known for the challenge it poses to climbers, its deep winter snows, and a dozen glaciers and snowfields that make skiing possible nearly year-round. Resort towns and colorful hospitality

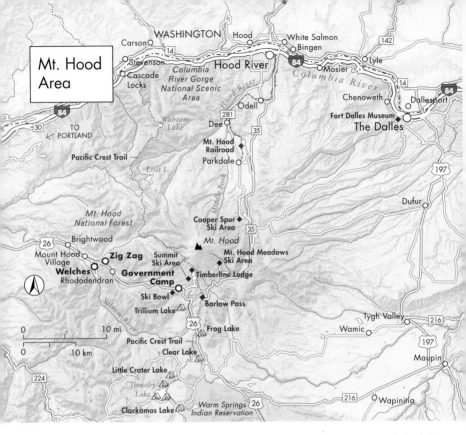

villages are arranged in a semicircle around the mountain, full of ski bars and rental cabins that host hordes of fun-loving Portlanders each weekend. In every direction from the postcard-perfect peak, the million-acre Mt. Hood National Forest spreads out like a big green blanket, and more than 300,000 acres of that are designated wilderness. Mule deer, black bears, elk, and the occasional cougar share the space with humans who come to hike, camp, and fish in the Pacific Northwest's quintessential wild ecosystem.

AROUND THE MOUNTAIN

About 60 miles east of Portland on I–84 and U.S. 26, and 42 miles south of Hood River via Hwy. 35 and U.S. 26.

Majestically towering 11,245 feet above sea level, Mt. Hood is what remains of the original north wall and rim of a volatile crater. Although the peak no longer spews ash or fire, active vents regularly release steam high on the mountain. The mountain took its modern moniker in 1792, when a crew of the British Royal Navy, the first recorded Caucasians sailing up the Columbia River, spotted it and named it after a famed British naval officer by the name of—you guessed it—Hood.

A snowboarder catches some air on Mt. Hood.

Mt. Hood offers the longest ski season in North America, with three major ski areas and some 30 lifts, as well as extensive areas for cross-country skiing and snowboarding. Many of the ski runs turn into mountain-bike trails in summer. The mountain is also popular with climbers and hikers. In fact, some hikes follow parts of the Oregon Trail, and signs of the pioneers' passing are still evident.

GETTING HERE AND AROUND
From Portland, U.S. 26 heads east into the heart of Mt. Hood National Forest, while Highway 35 runs south from Hood River along the mountain's east face. The roads meet 60 miles east of Portland, near Government Camp, forming an oblong loop with Interstate 84 and the Historic Columbia Gorge Highway. It's about a 75-minute drive from Downtown Portland to Government Camp via U.S. 26. Sea to Summit—call for timetables and pickup and drop-off sites—offers shuttle service from Portland International Airport and Downtown Portland hotels to all of the Mt. Hood resorts; the fare is $50 each way, with discounted lift-ticket and ski-rental packages available. Additionally, the **Mt. Hood Express** bus line operates daily and links the villages along the corridor—including Welches, Government Camp, and Timberline Lodge—to the Portland suburb of Sandy, which you can get to via TriMet commuter bus. This option is slower (it takes 2½ to 3 hours each way from the airport or Downtown to Timberline Lodge, for example) than a direct shuttle but costs just $2, plus $2.50 for TriMet bus fare to Sandy.

Contacts Mt. Hood Express ☎ 503/668–3466 ⊕ www.mthoodexpress.com. **Sea to Summit** ☎ 503/286–9333 ⊕ www.seatosummit.net.

ESSENTIALS

Visitor Information Mt. Hood Area Chamber of Commerce ☎ *503/622–3017* ⊕ *www.mthood.org.* **Mt. Hood National Forest Headquarters** ✉ *16400 Champion Way, Sandy* ☎ *503/668–1700* ⊕ *www.fs.usda.gov/mthood.*

EXPLORING

Fodor's Choice   **Mt. Hood National Forest.** The highest spot in Oregon and the fourth-
★   highest peak in the Cascades, "the Mountain" is a focal point of the 1.1-million-acre forest, an all-season playground attracting around 3 million visitors annually. Beginning 20 miles southeast of Portland, it extends south from the Columbia River Gorge for more than 60 miles and includes more than 311,000 acres of designated wilderness. These woods are perfect for hikers, horseback riders, mountain climbers, and cyclists. Within the forest are more than 80 campgrounds and 50 lakes stocked with brown, rainbow, cutthroat, brook, and steelhead trout. The Sandy, Salmon, Clackamas, and other rivers are known for their fishing, rafting, canoeing, and swimming. Both forest and mountain are crossed by an extensive trail system for hikers, cyclists, and horseback riders. The **Pacific Crest Trail,** which begins in British Columbia and ends in Mexico, crosses at the 4,157-foot-high Barlow Pass. As with most other mountain destinations within Oregon, weather can be temperamental, and snow and ice may affect driving conditions as early as October and as late as June. Bring tire chains and warm clothes as a precaution.

Since this forest is close to the Portland metro area, campgrounds and trails are potentially crowded over the summer months, especially on weekends. If you're planning to camp, get info and permits from the Mt. Hood National Forest Headquarters. Campgrounds are managed by the U.S. Forest Service and a few private concessionaires, and standouts include a string of neighboring campgrounds on the south side of Mt. Hood: Trillium Lake, Still Creek, Timothy Lake, Little Crater Lake, Clackamas Lake, Summit Lake, Clear Lake, and Frog Lake. Each varies in what it offers and in price. The mountain overflows with day-use areas. From mid-November through April, all designated Winter Recreation Areas require a Sno-Park permit, available from the U.S. Forest Service and many local resorts and sporting goods stores. ✉ *Headquarters, 16400 Champion Way, Sandy* ☎ *503/668-1700* ⊕ *www.fs.usda.gov/mthood* 🖼 *day pass $5–$7.*

WHERE TO EAT AND STAY

$$$$ ✕ **Cascade Dining Room.** Vaulted wooden beams and a wood-plank floor,
PACIFIC   handcrafted furniture, hand-woven drapes, and a lion-size stone fire-
NORTHWEST   place set the scene in Timberline Lodge's esteemed restaurant, from which views of neighboring mountains are enjoyed, except when snow drifts cover the windows. The atmosphere is traditional and historic, but chef Jason Stoller Smith is a former wine-country *wunderkind* whose résumé includes orchestrating a salmon bake at the White House. The dinner menu's local/organic emphasis embraces, for example, cedar-plank steelhead with artichoke-polenta cake and saffron-tomato jus. The daily Taste of Oregon lunch buffet is itself worth the drive up— it highlights different seasonal ingredients and purveyors each week,

from Dungeness crab to local hazelnuts to Oregon cherries. Pick up a few culinary tips by attending a chef demonstration. $ *Average main: $34* ⊠ *27500 E. Timberline Rd., Timberline Lodge* ☎ *503/272–3104* ⊕ *www.timberlinelodge.com* ⟟ *Reservations essential.*

$$
RESORT
FAMILY
Fodor'sChoice
★

Timberline Lodge. Guest rooms are simple, rustic, and charming, but don't expect a cushy experience—the reason for staying here is the location and setting. **Pros:** a thrill to stay on the mountain itself; great proximity to all snow activity; amazing architecture. **Cons:** rooms are small and the least expensive ones have shared bathrooms; views from rooms are often completely blocked by snow in winter; carloads of tourists. $ *Rooms from: $155* ⊠ *27500 E. Timberline Rd., Timberline Lodge* ☎ *503/272–3311, 800/547–1406* ⊕ *www.timberlinelodge.com* ⟟ *70 rooms, 60 with bath* ⟟ *Some meals.*

SPORTS AND THE OUTDOORS
DOWNHILL SKIING

Timberline Lodge & Ski Area. The longest ski season in North America unfolds at this full-service ski area, where the U.S. ski team conducts summer training. Thanks to the omnipresent Palmer Snowfield, it's the closest thing to a year-round ski area in the Lower 48 (it's typically closed for just a few weeks in September). Timberline is famous for its Palmer chairlift, which takes skiers and snowboarders to the high glacier for summer skiing. There are five high-speed quad chairs, one triple chair, and one double. The top elevation is 8,500 feet, with a 3,700-foot vertical drop, and the longest run is 3 miles. Facilities include a day lodge with fast food and a ski shop; lessons and equipment rental and repair are available. Parking requires a Sno-Park permit. The Palmer and Magic Mile lifts are popular with both skiers and sightseers. Timberline's long-awaited mountain-biking park is slated to open by summer 2015. ⊠ *27500 E. Timberline Rd., Timberline Lodge* ☎ *503/272–3311* ⊕ *www.timberlinelodge.com.*

5

GOVERNMENT CAMP

54 miles east of Portland on I–84 and U.S. 26, and 42 miles south of Hood River via Hwy. 35 and U.S. 26.

This alpine resort village with a bohemian vibe has several hotels and restaurants popular with visitors exploring Mt. Hood's ski areas and mountain-biking and hiking trails. "Govy" is also just a 12-mile drive up the hill from Welches, which also has restaurants and lodging.

WHERE TO EAT AND STAY

$
AMERICAN

✕ **Charlie's Mountain View.** Old and new ski swag plasters the walls, lift chairs function as furniture, and photos of famous (and locally famous) skiers and other memorabilia are as abundant as the menu selections. Open-flame-grilled steaks and hamburgers are worthy here, and the happy hour crowd shares plates piled high with waffle fries. When they're in season, try the apple dumplings. Charlie's is a local institution for powder hounds, and the fun, divey bar in back stays busy with ski bums and other lively degenerates. Live music packs them in on Friday and Saturday nights. $ *Average main: $9* ⊠ *88462 E. Government Camp Loop* ☎ *503/272–3333* ⊕ *www.charliesmountainview.com.*

$$ ✕ **Glacier Haus Bistro.** This lively, family-operated spot in the center of
EASTERN Government Camp is a good bet for a simple snack and espresso drink
EUROPEAN or a full meal. Pizzas and sandwiches are an option, but locals especially
love the Eastern European standards, such as Hungarian beef goulash,
Wiener schnitzel, and Bavarian sausages with sauerkraut and garlic-
mashed potatoes—the kind of cooking that'll provide you warmth and
comfort after a long day of skiing or hiking on the mountain. ⑤ *Average
main: $17* ✉ *88817 E. Government Camp Loop Rd.* ☎ *503/272–3471*
⊕ *www.glacierhaus.com* ☾ *Closed Mon.*

$ ✕ **Mt. Hood Brewing.** Producing finely crafted beers—Multorporter
AMERICAN Smoked Porter, Ice Axe IPA, Highland Meadow Blond Ale, and oth-
ers—since the early '90s, this casual brewpub with stone walls, a fire-
place, and both booth and table seating buzzes in the early evening
for après-ski dining and drinking. It's popular for its creative comfort
food, including poutine with fontina cheese and peppercorn demi-glace,
cast-iron-skillet-baked fondue, Alsatian pizza topped with smoked ham
and crème fraîche, barbecue pulled-pork-and-porter sandwiches. Fin-
ish things off with a Tillamook Ice Cream root-beer or beer float—it's
especially good with the Hogsback Oatmeal Stout. ⑤ *Average main:
$13* ✉ *87304 E. Government Camp Loop* ☎ *503/272–3172* ⊕ *www.
mthoodbrewing.com.*

$$ ⏨ **Collins Lake Resort.** Comprising 66 poshly furnished chalets with
RESORT fireplaces and dozens of other amenities, scattered around an alpine
FAMILY lake, this contemporary, 28-acre compound is the cushiest accommo-
Fodor's Choice dations option in the Mt. Hood area. **Pros:** within walking distance of
★ Government Camp restaurants and bars; spacious layouts are ideal for
groups and families. **Cons:** steepest rates in town. ⑤ *Rooms from: $189*
✉ *88149 E. Creek Ridge Rd.* ☎ *503/928–3498, 800/234–6288* ⊕ *www.
collinslakeresort.com* ⇗ *66 condos* ⏃ *No meals.*

SPORTS AND THE OUTDOORS
DOWNHILL SKIING

Fodor's Choice **Mt. Hood Meadows Ski Resort.** The mountain's largest resort has more
★ than 2,100 skiable acres, 85 runs, five double chairs, six high-speed
quads, a top elevation of 9,000 feet, a vertical drop of 2,777 feet, and
a longest run of 3 miles. If you're seeking varied, scenic terrain with
plenty of trails for all skiing abilities, this is your best choice among the
region's ski areas. Facilities include a day lodge, nine restaurants, two
lounges, a ski-and-snowboard school, a children's learning center with
daycar, and two ski shops with equipment rentals. ✉ *Hwy. 35, 10 miles
east of Government Camp* ☎ *503/337–2222* ⊕ *www.skihood.com.*

FAMILY **Mt. Hood Skibowl.** The ski area closest to Portland is also known as
"America's largest night ski area," with 34 runs lighted each evening.
It has 960 skiable acres serviced by four double chairs and five surface
tows, a top elevation of 5,100 feet, a vertical drop of 1,500 feet, and a
longest run of 3½ miles. You can take advantage of two-day lodges, a
midmountain warming hut, four restaurants, and two lounges. Sleigh
rides are conducted, weather permitting, and a hugely popular tubing
and adventure park has several tubing hills, plus music, LED lights, and
a laser show. In summer the resort morphs into the Adventure Park at
Skibowl, with mountain biking, zip lines, bungee jumping, a five-story

free-fall Tarzan Swing, disc golf, and kid-friendly tubing and alpine slides. ⊠ *87000 E. U.S. 26* ☎ *503/272–3206* ⊕ *www.skibowl.com.*

SHOPPING

Govy General Store. Good thing this is a really nice grocery store, because it's the only one for miles around. Govy General stocks all the staples, plus a nice selection of gourmet treats like cheeses and chocolates. It's also a full-service liquor store and your one-stop shop for Mt. Hood sweatshirts, postcards, and other keepsake tchotchkes. Grab your Sno-Park permit here in winter. ⊠ *30521 E. Meldrum St.* ☎ *541/272–3107* ⊕ *www.govygeneralstore.com* ⊗ *Daily 7 am–8 pm.*

WELCHES AND ZIGZAG

12 miles west of Government Camp and 40 miles east of Portland.

One of a string of small communities known as the Villages at Mt. Hood, Welches's claim to fame is that it was the site of Oregon's first golf course, built at the base of Mt. Hood in 1928. Another golf course is still going strong today, and summer vacationers hover around both towns for access to basic services like gas, groceries, and dining. Others come to pull a few trout out of the scenic Zigzag River or to access trails and streams in the adjacent Salmon–Huckleberry Wilderness.

GETTING HERE AND AROUND

Most of Welches is found just off U.S. 26, often called the Mt. Hood Corridor here, about 45 miles east of Portland.

WHERE TO EAT AND STAY

$$$
MODERN
AMERICAN
✕ **Altitude.** The flagship restaurant at the Resort at The Mountain aims for a sleek, modernist look in its glitzy—for the rustic Mt. Hood region at least—dining room with recessed lighting and contemporary art. Ask for a table by the row of large windows looking out over the resort's greenery. The kitchen ably handles standards like bacon-wrapped beef tenderloin with huckleberry sauce and hazelnut-crusted baked halibut, along with a few adventurous dishes like braised pork cheek with pickled shallots and pan-seared polenta. The adjacent lounge has fun, lighter fare (fish-and-chips, black-bean burgers), along with a few good specialty cocktails. ⑤ *Average main: $30* ⊠ *68010 E. Fairway Ave., Welches* ☎ *503/622–2214* ⊕ *www.altituderestaurant.com* ⊗ *No lunch.*

$$
AMERICAN
Fodor'sChoice
★
✕ **The Rendezvous Grill & Tap Room.** "Serious food in a not-so-serious place" is the slogan of this casual roadhouse with surprisingly sophisticated food—it's been a locals' favorite since it opened back in mid-'90s. For a joint many miles from the coast, the 'Vous sure does a nice job with seafood, turning out appetizing plates of sautéed shrimp, Willapa Bay oysters, Dungeness crab, and char-grilled wild salmon with roasted tomatoes and artichoke hash—steaks, burgers, and salads round out the menu. Grab a seat on the leafy patio in warm weather. In the adjacent taproom, ask about the seasonal, house-infused vodkas. ⑤ *Average main: $21* ⊠ *67149 E. U.S. 26, Welches* ☎ *503/622–6837* ⊕ *www. rendezvousgrill.net.*

$
RENTAL
▦ **The Cabins Creekside at Welches.** Affordability, accessibility to recreational activities, and wonderful hosts make these cabins with

knotty-pine vaulted ceilings, log furnishings, and full-size kitchens a great lodging choice in the Mt. Hood area. **Pros:** Family-run; quiet, off-highway location; anglers will benefit from the Thurmans' fly-fishing savvy. **Cons:** No dining within walking distance; no cabin-side parking; simple but clean, functional furnishings. $⑤$ *Rooms from: $94* ⊠ *25086 E. Welches Rd., Welches* ☎ *503/622–4275* ⊕ *www.mthoodcabins.com* ⥸ *10 cabins* ⑩ *No meals.*

$$
RENTAL

⚏ **Mt. Hood Vacation Rentals.** Doggedly determined to ensure a great time for the two and four-pawed vacationer alike, this company welcomes the family pet into the majority of its homes/cabins/condos, yet the properties are still on the upscale side: you'll find fireplaces/wood-burning stoves, hot tubs, river views, and full kitchens. **Pros:** knowledgeable, hospitable staff; gorgeous homes nestled throughout the Mt. Hood area; many secluded sites; family- and pet-friendly. **Cons:** bring your own shampoo; two to five-night minimum. $⑤$ *Rooms from: $185* ⊠ *67898 E. Hwy. 26, Welches* ☎ *866/921–1757* ⊕ *www.mthoodrentals. com* ⥸ *32 units* ⑩ *No meals.*

$$
RESORT

⚏ **Resort at The Mountain.** In the evergreen-forest foothills of Mt. Hood, this expansive resort is popular year-round both with outdoorsy sorts and couples seeking romantic hideaways. **Pros:** every sport available; plenty of choices in room size. **Cons:** there will be crowds; may not appeal to those who are not fans of golf; grounds seem more designed for golf carts than pedestrians. $⑤$ *Rooms from: $179* ⊠ *68010 E. Fairway Ave., Welches* ☎ *503/622–3101, 877/439–6774* ⊕ *www.theresort. com* ⥸ *157 rooms* ⑩ *No meals.*

SPORTS AND THE OUTDOORS

GOLF

The Courses. The three 9-hole tracks at the Resort at the Mountain include the Pine Cone Nine, Oregon's oldest golf course, built on a rented hayfield in 1928—you can mix any combination of the three courses to complete a full 18-hole round. There's also a lighted 18-hole putting course that's popular with families and adults working on their short game. Check the website to review the club's dress code, or cover that T-shirt with a collared shirt from the pro shop. ⊠ *68010 E. Fairway Ave., Welches* ☎ *503/622–3151, 877/439–6674* ⊕ *www.theresortcourses.com* ⛳ *Pine Cone: 9 holes. 3299 yds. Par 36. Foxglove: 9 holes. 3106 yds. Par 36. Thistle: 9 holes. 2956 yds. Par 34. Greens fee: $60 for 18 holes.*

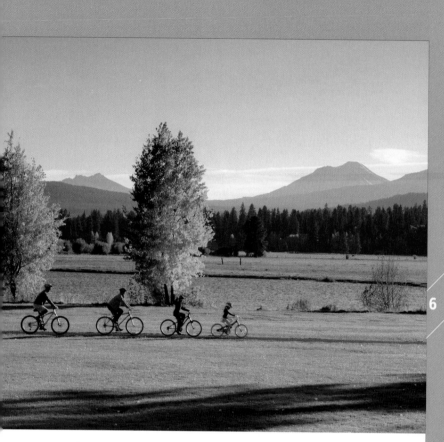

CENTRAL
OREGON

WELCOME TO CENTRAL OREGON

TOP REASONS TO GO

★ **Become one with nature:** Central Oregonians live on the flanks of the Cascade Range and are bracketed by rock formations, rivers, lakes, forests, ancient lava flows, and desert badlands. Bring your golf clubs, carabiners, snowboard, or camera, and explore deeper.

★ **Visit Bend:** Downtown Bend is lively and walkable, with a variety of appealing restaurants, galleries, and stores.

★ **Kick back at Sunriver:** This family-oriented resort has bike paths, river trails, an airstrip, horse stables, tennis courts, a golf course, and several restaurants.

★ **Check out the craft-brewing scene:** With two dozen breweries—and more on the horizon—you can discover nearly any type of beer that fits your tastes.

★ **Discover the Old West:** Cowboy towns, such as Sisters and Prineville, offer a glimpse into what life was like when the West was wild.

1 **West Central Oregon.** The western portion of central Oregon ranges from lush and green in the Cascades to dry and full of conifers down to the Deschutes River. It's the side with the ski areas, the high mountain lakes, most of the resorts, and the rushing waters. The region's largest town is Bend, and it straddles the forested west and the harshly beautiful east.

2 **East Central Oregon.** East of the Deschutes River this land is marked by rugged buttes, tough junipers, and bristly sagebrush. It's a place that still hugs the edge of the wilderness, with weathered barns, painted desert hills, a caldera holding two popular lakes, and some world-class rock climbing.

GETTING ORIENTED

Central Oregon provides a natural meeting place between the urban west side and the rural east side. It nestles neatly below the Columbia River basin and is drained by the Deschutes River, which flows from south to north. Skiers and snowboarders flock to winter sports areas on the western edge, anglers head to the Deschutes, the Metolius, and the Cascade Lakes, and climbers, campers, rockhounds, and wanderers explore the arid landscapes on the east side. Bend, the largest town for more than 120 miles in any direction, sits roughly in the center of this region.

6

Updated by Kimberly Bowker

After a day on the Sunriver bike paths, a first-time visitor from Europe shook her head. "This place is paradise," she declared. It's easy to see why she thought so. Central Oregon has snowfields so white they sharpen the edges of the mountains; canyons so deep and sudden as to induce vertigo; air so crisp that it fills the senses; water that ripples in mountain lakes so clear that boaters can see to the bottom, or rushes through turbulent rapids favored by rafters.

A region born of volcanic tumult is now a powerful lure for the adventurous, the beauty-seeking, and even the urbane—Bend has grown into a sophisticated city of 80,000-plus, a magnet for people retreating from larger, noisier city centers. For most visitors Bend is the sunny face of central Oregon, a haven for hikers, athletes, and aesthetes, but with the charm and elegance of much larger cities.

From Bend it's easy to launch to the attractions that surround it. To the northwest, Camp Sherman is a stunning place to fish for rainbow trout or kokanee. The Smith Rocks formation to the north draws climbers and boulderers, and, to the south, Lava Lands and the Lava River Caves fascinate visitors more than 6,000 years after they were chiseled out of the earth. The Oregon Badlands Wilderness to the east draws hikers and horseback riders wanting to connect with the untamed landscape. Lake Billy Chinook to the north is a startling oasis, where summer visitors drift in houseboats beneath the high walls of the Deschutes River canyon. The Deschutes River itself carries rafters of all descriptions, from young families to solo adventurers.

The area's natural beauty has brought it a diverse cluster of resorts, whether situated on the shores of high mountain lakes or cradling golf courses of startling green. They dot the landscape from the dry terrain around Warm Springs to the high road to Mt. Bachelor.

CENTRAL OREGON PLANNER

WHEN TO GO

Central Oregon is a popular destination year-round. Skiers and snow-boarders come from mid-December through March, when the powder is deepest and driest. During this time, guests flock to the hotels and resorts along Century Drive, which leads from Bend to Mt. Bachelor. In summer, when temperatures reach the upper 80s, travelers are more likely to spread throughout the region. But temperatures fall as the elevation rises, so take a jacket if you're heading out for an evening at the high lakes or Newberry Crater.

You'll pay a premium at the mountain resorts during ski season, and Sunriver and other family and golf resorts are busiest in summer. It's best to make reservations as far in advance as possible; six months in advance is not too early.

FESTIVALS

Bend Film Festival. This popular local film festival takes place in October. ⊠ *1000 N.W. Wall St., Suite 260, Bend* ☎ *541/388–3378* ⊕ *www.bendfilm.org.*

Bend Summer and Fall Festival. Downtown Bend is blocked off with food, crafts, art booths, and music in July and September. ⊠ *Box 1424, Bend* ☎ *541/508–4280* ⊕ *www.bendfestivals.com.*

Oregon Winterfest. February brings music, food, brews, wine, ice carving, and other winter sports to Bend's Old Mill District. ⊠ *Bend* ⊕ *www.oregonwinterfest.com.*

Sisters Rodeo. Multiple rodeo and community events, held annually for more than 70 years, take place over a weekend in June. ⊠ *67637 U.S. 20, south of Sisters* ☎ *541/549–0121, 800/827–7522* ⊕ *www.sistersrodeo.com.*

GETTING HERE AND AROUND

AIR TRAVEL

Visitors fly into **Redmond Municipal Airport–Roberts Field** (RDM), about 17 miles north of downtown Bend. Rental cars are available for pickup at the airport from several national agencies. The **Redmond Airport Shuttle** provides transportation throughout the region (reservations requested); a ride from the airport to downtown Bend costs about $35. Taxis are available at curbside, or can be summoned from the call board inside the airport. Portland's airport is 160 miles northwest of Bend.

Air Contacts Redmond Airport Shuttle ⊠ *Redmond* ☎ *541/382–1687, 888/664–8449* ⊕ *www.redmondairportshuttle.net.* **Redmond Municipal Airport–Roberts Field** (*RDM*). ⊠ *2522 S.E. Jesse Butler Circle, Redmond* ☎ *541/548–0646* ⊕ *www.flyrdm.com.*

BUS TRAVEL

The **Central Oregon Breeze,** a regional carrier, runs one bus a day each way between Portland and Bend, with stops in Redmond and Madras. **Cascades East Transit** is Bend's intercity bus service, and connects Redmond, La Pine, Madras, Prineville, Bend, and Sisters. Trips from the airport require reservations. **Greyhound** also serves the area with a shuttle that runs between Salem and Bend.

Bus Contacts Cascades East Transit ✉ *334 Hawthorn Ave., Bend* ☎ *541/385-8680, 866/385-8680* ⊕ *www.cascadeseasttransit.com.* **Central Oregon Breeze** ✉ *2045 N.E. Hwy. 20, Bend* ☎ *541/389-7469, 800/847-0157* ⊕ *www.cobreeze. com.* **Greyhound Bend** ✉ *334 N.E. Hawthorne Ave., Bend* ☎ *541/923-1732* ⊕ *www.greyhound.com.*

CAR TRAVEL

U.S. 20 heads west from Idaho and east from the coastal town of Newport into central Oregon. U.S. 26 goes southeast from Portland to Prineville, where it heads northeast into the Ochoco National Forest. U.S. 97 heads north from California and south from Washington to Bend. Highway 126 travels east from Eugene to Prineville; it connects with U.S. 20 heading south (to Bend) at Sisters. Major roads throughout central Oregon are well maintained and open throughout the winter season, although it's always advisable to have tire chains in the car. Some roads are closed by snow during winter, including Oregon 242. Check the **Oregon Department of Transportation's TripCheck** (⊕ *www.tripcheck. com*) or call **ODOT** (☎ *800/977–ODOT*).

RESTAURANTS

The center of culinary ambition is in downtown Bend, but good-to-excellent restaurants also serve diners in Sisters, Redmond, Prineville, and the major resorts. Styles vary, but many hew to the Northwest preference for fresh foods grown, caught, and harvested in the region.

Central Oregon also has many down-home places and family-friendly brewpubs, and authentic Mexican restaurants have emerged to win faithful followings in Prineville, Redmond, Madras, and Bend.

HOTELS

Central Oregon has lodging for every taste, from upscale resort lodges to an in-town brewpub village, eclectic bed-and-breakfasts, rustic Western inns, and a range of independent and chain hotels and motels. If you're drawn to the rivers, stay in a pastoral fishing cabin along the Metolius near Camp Sherman. If you came for the powder, you'll want a ski-snowboard condo closer to the mountain. For soaking up the atmosphere, you might favor one of downtown Bend's luxurious hotels, or Old St. Francis, the Catholic school–turned-brewpub village. *Hotel reviews have been shortened. For full information, visit Fodors.com.*

WHAT IT COSTS IN U.S. DOLLARS			
$	$$	$$$	$$$$
Restaurants	Under $17	$17–$24	$25–$30	Over $30
Hotels	Under $150	$150–$200	$201–$250	Over $250

Restaurant prices are the average cost of a main course at dinner, or if dinner is not served, at lunch. Hotel prices are the lowest cost of a standard double room in high season.

TOURS

Cog Wild. Bicycle tours are offered for people of all skill levels and interests. ✉ *255 Century Dr., Ste. 201, Bend* ☎ *541/385–7002* ⊕ *www. cogwild.com.*

Sun Country Tours. A longtime provider of raft and tube trips on central Oregon rivers offers rafting excursions that range from two hours to full days May through September. ☎ *541/382–6277* ⊕ *www. suncountrytours.com.*

Wanderlust Tours. Popular and family-friendly half-day or evening excursions are offered around Bend, Sisters, and Sunriver. Options include kayaking, canoeing, snowshoeing, and caving. ☎ *541/389–8359* ⊕ *www.wanderlusttours.com.*

VISITOR INFORMATION

Central Oregon Visitors Association ✉ *705 S. W. Bonnett Way, Suite 1000, Bend* ☎ *541/389–8799, 800/800–8334* ⊕ *www.visitcentraloregon.com.*

WEST CENTRAL OREGON

Sunshine, crisp pines, pure air, rushing waters, world-class skiing and snowboarding at Mt. Bachelor, destination golf resorts, a touch of the frontier West at Sisters, an air of sophistication in Bend—the forested side of central Oregon serves up many recreational flavors. The area draws young couples, seniors, families, athletes, and adventurers, all of whom arrive with a certain sense of purpose, but also with an appreciation for the natural world. Travelers will have no problem filling a week in central Oregon's western half with memorable activities, from rafting to enjoying some sensational meals.

BEND

160 miles southeast of Portland.

Bend, Oregon's largest city east of the Cascades, is once more one of the fastest-growing cities in the state, recovering abundantly from the hard-hitting recession. Construction has renewed and new businesses seem to open every day. The people of Bend continue to enjoy an enviable climate, proximity to skiing, dynamic lifestyle, and a reputation as a playground and recreational escape. At times it seems that everybody in Bend is an athlete or a brewer, but it remains a tolerant, welcoming town, conscious of making a good first impression. Bend's heart is an area of about four square blocks, centered on Wall and Bond streets. Here you'll find boutique stores, galleries, independent coffee shops, brewpubs, fine restaurants, lively nightlife establishments, and historic landmarks such as the Tower Theatre, built in 1940. A few traditional barbershops and taverns are also spread around, keeping it real.

Neighboring Mt. Bachelor, though hardly a giant among the Cascades at 9,065 feet, is blessed by an advantage over its taller siblings—by virtue of its location, it's the first to get snowfall, and the last to see it go. Inland air collides with the Pacific's damp influence, creating skiing

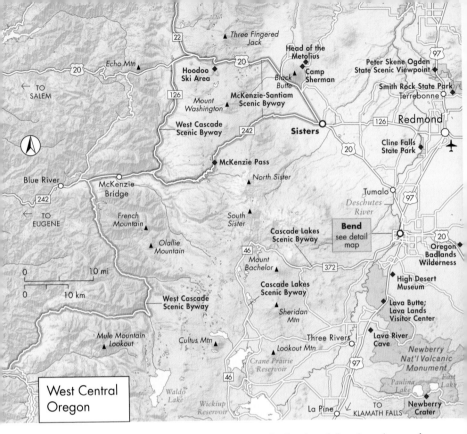

West Central
Oregon

conditions immortalized in songs by local rock bands and raves from the ski press.

GETTING HERE AND AROUND

Portlanders arrive via car on U.S. 20 or U.S. 26, and folks from the mid-Willamette Valley cross the mountains on Oregon 126. Redmond Municipal Airport, 17 miles to the north, is an efficient hub for air travelers, who can rent a car or take a shuttle or cab into town. **Greyhound** also serves the area with a shuttle from Salem. The **Central Oregon Breeze**, a privately operated regional carrier, runs daily between Portland and Bend, with stops in Redmond and Madras. Bend is served by a citywide bus system called **Cascades East Transit**, which also connects to Redmond, La Pine, Sisters, Prineville, and Madras. To take a Cascades East bus between cities in central Oregon, reservations are not required but recommended. *For more on bus travel to and from Bend, see Getting Here and Around in the Central Oregon Planner.*

If you're trying to head out of or into Bend on a major highway during the morning or 5 pm rush, especially on U.S. 97, you may hit congestion. Parking in downtown Bend is free for the first two hours (three hours at the centrally located parking garage), or park for free in the residential neighborhoods just west of downtown. In addition to the car-rental counters at the airport, Avis, Budget, Enterprise, and Hertz also have rental locations in Bend.

ESSENTIALS

Visitor Information Bend Chamber of Commerce ✉ *777 N.W. Wall St., Ste. 200* ☎ *541/382–3221* ⊕ *www.bendchamber.org.* **Visit Bend/Bend Visitor Center** ✉ *750 N.W. Lava Rd.* ☎ *541/382–8048, 877/245–8484* ⊕ *www.visitbend. com.*

EXPLORING

FAMILY **Des Chutes Historical Museum.** Originally built as a schoolhouse in 1914 from locally quarried volcanic tuff, the museum is operated by the Deschutes County Historical Society. Exhibits depict historical life in the area, including a pioneer schoolroom, native artifacts, and relics from the logging, ranching, homesteading, and railroading eras. Outdoor heritage walks are conducted in the summer. ✉ *129 N.W. Idaho Ave.* ☎ *541/389–1813* ⊕ *www.deschuteshistory.org* ☎ *$5* ⊙ *Tues.–Sat. 10–4:30.*

Drake Park and Mirror Pond. At its western edge, downtown Bend slopes down to these 13 acres of manicured greensward and trees lining the edge of the Deschutes, attracting flocks of Canada geese as well as strollers from downtown. Various events, such as music festivals, occur in the park during the summer months. Note the 11-foot high wheel log skidder, harkening back to Bend's logging industry in the early 20th century, when four draft horses pulled the wheel to move heavy logs. ✉ *Bounded on the west by N.W. Brooks St. and Drake Park; N.W. Lava Rd on the east; N.W. Franklin Ave. to the south; and N.W. Greenwood Ave. to the north* ⊕ *www.downtownbend.org.*

FAMILY **High Desert Museum.** The West was actually wild, and this combo
Fodor'sChoice museum/zoo proves it. Kids will love the up-close-and-personal
★ encounters with gila monsters, snakes, porcupines, birds of prey, Vivi the bobcat, and Snowshoe the lynx. Characters in costume take part in the Living History series, where you can chat with stagecoach drivers, boomtown widows, pioneers, homesteaders, and sawmill operators. Peruse the 110,000-square-feet of indoor and outdoor exhibits, such as Spirit of the West and a historic family ranch, to experience how the past can truly come alive. ✉ *59800 S. Hwy. 97, 7 miles south of downtown Bend* ☎ *541/382–4754* ⊕ *www.highdesertmuseum.org* ☎ *$15 May–Oct., $12 Nov.–Apr.* ⊙ *May–Oct., daily 9–5; Nov.–Apr., daily 10–4.*

Newberry National Volcanic Monument and Lava Lands. The last time hot lava flowed from Newberry Volcano was about 13 centuries ago. The north end of the monument has several large basalt flows, as well as the 500-foot **Lava Butte** cinder cone—a coal-black and scorched-red, symmetrical mound thrust from the depths 7,000 years ago. The cone is now home to the **Lava Lands Visitor Center**, which features interpretive exhibits that explain the volcanic and early human history of the area. **Lava River Cave**, a 1-mile-long lava tube, takes about 90 minutes to explore on your own with a lantern (available for rent, $4-$6). On the south end of the monument, an unpaved road leads to beautiful views from **Paulina Peak**. Along the shores of **Paulina Lake** and **East**

6

Restaurants ▼

10 Barrel
Brewing Co. **9**

Deschutes
Brewery &
Public House ... **5**

Jackson's
Corner **10**

Joolz **4**

McKay Cottage
Restaurant **3**

Pine Tavern **2**

Pizza Mondo **7**

Spork **1**

The Victorian
Café **8**

Zydeco Kitchen +
Cocktails **6**

Hotels ▼

Lara House
Lodge **3**

Old St. Francis
School **2**

The Oxford
Hotel **1**

Sunriver
Resort **4**

Bend

KEY

❶ *Restaurants*

① *Hotels*

Lake, you can hike, fish, camp, or stay at the rustic resorts. The monument offers 100 miles of summer trails, and may be accessible during winter months, depending on snowmelt, for snowmobiling, snowshoeing, and skiing. ✉ *58201 S. Hwy. 97* ☎ *541/593–2421* ⊕ *www.fs.usda. gov/centraloregon* 💰 *$5 per vehicle* ☉ *Mid-May–mid-Oct., daily 9–5.*

EN
ROUTE

Cascade Lakes Scenic Byway. For about 90 miles, this forest-highway loop beginning and ending in Bend meanders past a series of high mountain lakes and is good for fishing, hiking, and camping in the summer months. (Much of the road is closed by snow during the colder months.) To find, take Century Drive/Oregon 372 out of Bend and follow it around Mt. Bachelor, and then U.S. 97 at La Pine to return. ⊕ *www. visitbend.com.*

WHERE TO EAT

$ ✕ **10 Barrel Brewing Co.** Attracting locals and travelers alike, this trendy
AMERICAN brewpub supplies good beer and compatible food. Pizzas are hand tossed daily, salads are fresh, and sandwiches are varied. This is a popular place, so expect to wait during busy meal hours. Grab a table or stool in the bar for a cozier setting, and enjoy the windowed-garage doors that open to the Central Oregon sun on summer days and to patio fires on crisp winter nights. ⑤ *Average main: $12* ✉ *1135 N.W. Galveston Ave.* ☎ *541/678–5228* ⊕ *www.10barrel.com.*

Paulina and East Lakes in Newberry National Volcanic Monument

$ ✕ **Deschutes Brewery & Public House.** Bendites are fiercely loyal to their
AMERICAN city's original brewpub, established in 1988. Not only does the Brewery
bake its own bread and pizza dough (adding in its own spent grain),
it makes its sausages, sauces, mustards, dressings, soups, etc. House
favorites include the elk burger and fish-and-chips. Though the always-
popular Black Butte Porter is a Public House classic, Deschutes brews
a diverse lineup of craft beers, including such seasonals as Jubelale
(winter holidays) and Twilight Ale (summer). It is almost always hopping, and you may find yourself waiting to be seated, as there are
no reservations. However, time flies as you sip one of 19 Deschutes
beers on tap and people-watch the boisterous crowd while you wait.
⑤ *Average main: $12* ✉ *1044 N.W. Bond St.* ☎ *541/382–9242* ⊕ *www.*
deschutesbrewery.com.

$ ✕ **Jackson's Corner.** This family-friendly community restaurant is housed
AMERICAN in an unassuming vintage building tucked into a neighborhood near
FAMILY downtown. The open, inviting space is a great place for casual gatherings, with live music Friday nights. The eclectic menu leans heavily on
locally grown and organic dishes. Order seasonal market salads, house-
made pasta dishes, or brick-oven pizza and sandwiches at the counter
to be served at your table. ⑤ *Average main: $12* ✉ *845 N.W. Delaware*
Ave. ☎ *541/647–2198* ⊕ *www.jacksonscornerbendor.com.*

$$ ✕ **Joolz.** "An insider's treasure," as one diner called it, serves vibrant
MIDDLE EASTERN Middle Eastern food with an Oregon flair. The chef, raised in Beirut,
is son of a Lebanese father and Oregonian mother (who is rumored to
still make the family's melt-in-your-mouth spiced date cake). Enjoy the
intimate and authentic ambience, including colorful drapes, while din-
ing on small dishes such as Oregon lamb meatballs, tabbouleh salad,

CLOSE UP

Central Oregon Brewery Boom

Central Oregon is not only home to gorgeous views and exciting outdoor activities, but a recent boom in breweries has turned the high desert into a haven for craft-beer lovers. With two-dozen breweries and counting, central Oregon only hit the map as a beer travel destination in recent years. Since the first microbrewery opened its doors in 1988 (Deschutes Brewery in downtown Bend), the industry has continued to grow and expand. Each brewery and brewpub approaches craft beer in an original manner, often supported by locals and a combination of live music, good food, unique marketing, experimental brews, and good ole standbys that keep pint glasses and growlers filled.

Residents may buoy the industry, but breweries in turn support the community. Local artists design labels, many beer proceeds go to neighborhood causes, and brews are continually concocted with local events and culture in mind.

BEND ALE TRAIL
Pick up a Bend Ale Trail brochure, or download the app, to guide you through Bend's 14 breweries. Stop at each brewery, have a taste or a pint, and receive a stamp in your passport. Once your passport is complete, drop by the Bend Visitor Center to receive your prize: a commemorative pint glass.

and cauliflower with tahini dipping sauce, or main plates such as a local free-range longhorn beef burger or Pacific seafood tagine. $ *Average main: $17* ⊠ *916 N.W. Wall St.* ☎ *541/388–5094* ⊕ *www.joolzbend. com* ⊙ *No lunch.*

$ ✕ **McKay Cottage Restaurant.** This breakfast and lunch spot is housed
AMERICAN in a 1916 pioneer cottage that was home to a former state senator. Locals relax throughout its cozy rooms and spill over onto the porch and patio below. The menu is long on comfort food, including fresh scones and sticky buns, and servers are friendly and attentive. On your way out, you can pick up baked goods and coffee drinks at the to-go bakery. $ *Average main: $12* ⊠ *62910 O.B. Riley Rd.* ☎ *541/383–2697* ⊕ *www.themckaycottage.com* ⊙ *No dinner.*

$$ ✕ **Pine Tavern.** Named for the Ponderosa pine tree growing through the
AMERICAN back dining room, this locally loved restaurant has been dishing up high-end meals in the heart of downtown Bend since 1936. Specialties include steaks, prime rib, pot pie, and other traditional American cuisine. Longtime regulars share the dining room with out-of-towners. In summertime, seek a spot on the patio—named Best Patio in Bend for multiple years—overlooking Mirror Pond and Drake Park. $ *Average main: $21* ⊠ *967 N.W. Brooks St.* ☎ *541/382–5581* ⊕ *www.pinetavern. com.*

$ ✕ **Spork.** Bend's favorite food cart–turned-restaurant offers a globally
INTERNATIONAL inspired and healthy menu with an intimate and trendy decor. Try Peruvian stir-fry, Thai steak salad, coconut green curry, or organic tofu tacos. Ingredients are local and fresh, and practices are eco-conscious. $ *Average main: $10* ⊠ *937 N.W. Newport Ave.* ☎ *541/390–0946* ⊕ *www.sporkbend.com.*

$ **✕ The Victorian Café.** In a renovated house on the west side of Bend, this
AMERICAN breakfast and lunch place offers a wide selection of surprising combi-
Fodor'sChoice nations of eggs Benedict, such as the Caribbean Benedict with Cuban
★ seasoned ham, mango, and black beans. Weekly mouthwatering specials may include deep-fried graham cracker–crusted Texas toast filled
with mascarpone. With local accolades for Best Breakfast in Bend for
many years, the restaurant is also known for its homemade applesauce
and scones. There's often a long wait on weekends, so order a Bloody
Mary or a "Man-mosa" (a mimosa in a pint glass) and enjoy around
the outdoor fireplace. $ *Average main: $16* ✉ *1404 N.W. Galveston
Ave.* ☎ *541/382–6411* ⊕ *www.victoriancafebend.com* ☽ *No dinner.*

$$ **✕ Zydeco Kitchen & Cocktails.** The blended menu of Northwest special-
AMERICAN ties and Cajun influences has made this restaurant (named after a
Fodor'sChoice style of Creole music) a very popular spot. On the menu, fillet medal-
★ lions, chicken, and pasta sit alongside jambalaya and redfish dishes.
The owners emphasize the preparation of fresh, organic foods and
provide a gluten-free selection. The bar is trendy, but welcoming. In
warm weather, ask to sit on the patio. Bonus: Kids eat free on Sunday.
$ *Average main: $23* ✉ *919 N.W. Bond St.* ☎ *541/312–2899* ⊕ *www.
zydecokitchen.com* ☽ *No lunch weekends.*

OFF THE **Cowboy Dinner Tree.** Seventy miles south of Sunriver you'll find an
BEATEN authentic barbecue cook firing up a genuine taste of the Old West for
PATH dinner. Oregonians will tell you that the "true cowboy cut" 30-ounce
steak or whole chicken over an open flame, plus all the fixings, is more
than worth the trip. Don't expect to plug in your laptop: there's no
electricity, nor is alcohol served, nor credit cards accepted. If you are
making a day out of it, detour to Fort Rock State Natural Area to hike
around a prehistoric volcanic tuff emerging from the flat horizon, and
explore a nearby cave home to the oldest sandals ever discovered. If you
journey from afar, lodging is available in rustic buckaroo bunkhouses.
Plates are $28.00 per adult, $10.25 for kids 7–13; kids 6 and under
free. Reservations required. ✉ *County Rd. 4-12/Forest Service Rd. 28,
Silver Lake* ☎ *541/576–2426* ⊕ *www.cowboydinnertree.net.*

WHERE TO STAY

$$ **Lara House Lodge.** Located in a manicured residential neighborhood
B&B/INN across from Drake Park, guests will feel at home at this historically
grand and cherished Bend house. **Pros:** clean lines and an uncluttered
feel; downtown is a short walk away; wine hour every night. **Cons:** no
pets or kids; can be crowded during peak travel times; check-in only
4–6 or by prior arrangement. $ *Rooms from: $195* ✉ *640 N.W. Congress St.* ☎ *541/388–4064, 800/766–4064* ⊕ *www.larahouse.com* ➥ *6
rooms* ⦿ *Breakfast.*

$$ **Old St. Francis School.** This charming and fun outpost in a restored
RESORT 1936 Catholic schoolhouse has classrooms turned into lodging quarters,
restaurant and bars, a brewery, a stage, a mosaic-tile soaking pool, and
a movie theater with couches and food service. **Pros:** a self-contained
destination village, yet only footsteps from downtown Bend and Drake
Park; kids and pets welcome. **Cons:** few modern appliances. $ *Rooms
from: $155* ✉ *700 N.W. Bond St.* ☎ *541/382–5174, 877/661–4228*
⊕ *www.mcmenamins.com* ➥ *19 rooms* ⦿ *No meals.*

6

$$$$
HOTEL
Fodor'sChoice
★
🖵 **The Oxford Hotel.** Stepping into the sleek, high-ceilinged lobby tells you you've found a new kind of accommodations in central Oregon, with stylish Northwest interiors and elegantly spacious rooms. **Pros:** generous and environmentally sustainable amenities; luxurious spa and fitness room; loaner bikes, iPods, and Breedlove guitars; exceptional service. **Cons:** on the exterior, property appears inconspicuously wedged into a half block on the edge of downtown. ⑤ *Rooms from: $279* ⊠ *10 N.W. Minnesota Ave.* ☎ *877/440–8436* ⊕ *www.oxfordhotelbend.com* ⇥ *59 rooms* ⦿ *No meals.*

$$$
RESORT
FAMILY
Fodor'sChoice
★
🖵 **Sunriver Resort.** Central Oregon's premier family playground and luxurious destination resort encapsulates so many things that are distinctive about central Oregon, from the mountain views and winding river, to the biking, rafting, golfing, skiing, and family or romantic getaways that live up to the resort's tagline of "the start of something unforgettable." **Pros:** many activities for kids and adults; much pampering in elegant lodge facilities; close to The Village at Sunriver. **Cons:** when visitors throng the shops, restaurants, and bike paths, it can feel as if an entire city has relocated here. ⑤ *Rooms from: $229* ⊠ *17600 Center Dr., 15 miles south of Bend on Hwy. 97, Sunriver* ☎ *800/801–8765* ⊕ *www.sunriver-resort.com* ⇥ *245 rooms, 284 houses* ⦿ *No meals.*

NIGHTLIFE

900 Wall Restaurant and Bar. In a historic corner brick building on a downtown Bend crossroads, this sophisticated restaurant and bar serves hundreds of bottles and about 50 different wines by the glass, earning it the Wine Spectator Award of Excellence. ⊠ *900 N.W. Wall St.* ☎ *541/323–6295* ⊕ *www.900wall.com.*

Bend Brewing Company. Another local brewery, founded in 1995, BBC (as it is affectionately called by locals) offers about 10 different types of beers on tap. It's located on the second floor above the brewpub, where diners and drinkers can look up through windows to the tanks above. Since space is limited for brewing, BBC focuses not on the quantity of beer, but the quality. Tours are available by appointment only. ⊠ *1019 N.W. Brooks St.* ☎ *541/383–1599* ⊕ *www.bendbrewingco.com.*

Deschutes Brewery. Central Oregon's first and most famous brewery produces and bottles its beer in this facility separate from the popular brewpub. Built in 1993 and expanded in 2004, it now distributes beer to more than half the country, as well to Canada. Take a free tour between 1 and 4 pm every day; be sure to make reservations online or by phone since groups fill quickly. The tour ends in the tasting room and gift shop, where participants get to try samples of the fresh beer. ⊠ *901 S.W. Simpson Ave.* ☎ *541/385–8606* ⊕ *www.deschutesbrewery.com.*

Level 2. After a day of shopping, or before concert-going at the ampiteater, sip on a perfectly mixed cocktail at this trendy Old Mill District urban-esque lounge. The rich chai martini is a delectable winter treat. ⊠ *360 S.W. Powerhouse Dr.* ☎ *541/323–5382* ⊕ *www.bendlevel2.com.*

Sunriver Resort

SPORTS AND THE OUTDOORS

BIKING

U.S. 97 north to the Crooked River Gorge and Smith Rock and the route along the **Cascade Lakes Highway** out of Bend provide bikers with memorable scenery and a good workout. **Sunriver** has more than 30 miles of paved bike paths.

Hutch's Bicycles. Road, mountain, and kids' bikes can be rented at this shop as well as a location at 725 N.W. Columbia St. ✉ *820 N.E. 3rd St.* ☎ *541/382–6248 3rd St. shop, 541/382–9253 Columbia St. shop* ⊕ *www.hutchsbicycles.com.*

BOATING

A popular summer activity is floating the Deschutes River at your own pace.

Riverbend Park. In Bend, rent an inner tube at Riverbend Park from a kiosk operated from Memorial Day to Labor Day by **Sun Country Tours** (⇨ *see Tours in the Central Oregon Planner)* and float an hour and a half downriver to Drake Park, where you can catch a shuttle back for a minimal cash fee. ✉ *799 S.W. Columbia St.* ☎ *541/389–7275* ⊕ *www.bendparksandrec.org.*

Tumalo Creek Kayak & Canoe. Rent a kayak or stand-up paddleboard and enter the river from the store's backyard, but be prepared to paddle upriver before a leisurely float downstream. ✉ *805 S.W. Industrial Way* ☎ *541/317–9407* ⊕ *tumalocreek.com.*

RECREATIONAL AREAS

Deschutes National Forest. This 1½-million-acre forest has 20 peaks higher than 7,000 feet, including three of Oregon's five highest mountains, more than 150 lakes, and 500 miles of streams. If you want to park your car at a trailhead, some of the sites require a Northwest Forest Pass; day-use passes are also needed May through September at many locations for boating and picnicking. Campgrounds (fees payable) are operated by a camp host. ⊠ *63095 Deschutes Market Rd.* ☏ *541/383–5300* ⊕ *www.fs.usda.gov/centraloregon* ⊠ *Park pass $5.*

SKIING

Many Nordic trails—more than 165 miles of them—wind through the Deschutes National Forest.

FAMILY **Mt. Bachelor.** This alpine resort area has 60 percent of downhill runs that are rated advanced or expert, with the rest geared for beginner and intermediate skiers and snowboarders. One of 10 lifts takes skiers all the way to the mountain's 9,065-foot summit. One run has a vertical drop of 3,265 feet for thrill-seekers, and the longest of the 88 runs is 4 miles. Facilities and services include equipment rental and repair, a ski school, retail shop, and day care; you can enjoy seven restaurants, three bars, and six lodges. Other activities include cross-country skiing, a tubing park, sled-dog rides, snowshoeing, and in summer, hiking, biking, disc golfing, and chairlift rides. The 35 miles of trails at the **Mt. Bachelor Nordic Center** are for all abilities.

During the offseason, the lift to the **Pine Marten Lodge** provides sightseeing, stunning views, and fine sunset dining. Visitors can play disc golf on a downhill course that starts near the lodge. At the base of the mountain, take dry-land dog sled rides with four-time Iditarod musher Rachael Scdoris. ⊠ *13000 S.W. Century Dr.* ☏ *541/382–7888, 800/829–2442* ⊕ *www.mtbachelor.com* ⊠ *Lift tickets $47–$79 per day; kids 5 and under free* ☉ *Nov.–May, daily 9–4, or as weather allows.*

SHOPPING

In addition to Bend's compact downtown, the Old Mill District draws shoppers from throughout the region. Chain stores and franchise restaurants have filled in along the approaches to town, especially along U.S. 20 and U.S. 97.

Cowgirl Cash. This funky western outfitter buys and sells vintage boots and western apparel. You never know exactly what you'll find, but you can expect a fair share of leather, turquoise, silver, and, always, boots. It's a quirky and welcome feature of the downtown scene but closed Thursday–Sunday in the winter. ⊠ *924 N.W. Brooks St.* ☏ *541/678–5162* ⊕ *www.cowgirlcashbend.com.*

Dudley's BookShop Café. This independent bookseller offers Wi-Fi, a small café, and seating areas that attract interesting people who meet amidst new and used books to participate in all kinds of activites, from tango classes to philosophical debates. ⊠ *135 N.W. Minnesota Ave.* ☏ *541/749–2010* ⊕ *www.dudleysbookshopcafe.com.*

Goody's. If the aroma of fresh waffle cones causes a pause on your downtown stroll, you've probably hit one of Central Oregon's favorite soda fountain and candy shops. Try the Oreo cookie ice cream, a local favorite, or the homemade chocolate. If you purchase a stuffed toy animal that calls the store home, expect for it to smell sweetly for weeks to come. ✉ *957 N.W. Wall St.* ☎ *541/389–5185* ⊕ *www. goodyschocolates.com.*

Newport Avenue Market. In business for more than 20 years, this culinary mecca not only offers a large selection of organic and gourmet foods, but also sells items such as high-end kitchen supplies and humorous gifts. Pick up a pair of squirrel underwear—it's as small as you might expect. ✉ *1121 N.W. Newport Ave.* ☎ *541/382–3940* ⊕ *www. newportavemarket.com.*

Old Mill District. Bend was once the site of one of the world's largest sawmill operations, with a sprawling industrial complex along the banks of the Deschutes. In recent years the abandoned shells of the old factory buildings have been transformed into an attractive shopping center, a project honored with national environmental awards. National chain retailers can be found here, along with restaurants, boutiques, a 16-screen multiplex and IMAX movie theater, and the Les Schwab Amphitheater that attracts nationally renowned artists, local bands, and summer festivals. ✉ *450 S.W. Powerhouse Dr.* ☎ *541/312–0131* ⊕ *www.theoldmill.com.*

SISTERS

21 miles northwest of Bend.

If Sisters looks as if you've stumbled into the Old West, that's entirely by design. The town fathers—or perhaps we should say "sisters"—strictly enforce an 1800s-style architecture. Rustic cabins border ranches on the edge of town, and you won't find a stoplight on any street. Western storefronts give way to galleries, the century-old hotel now houses a restaurant and bar, and a bakery occupies the former general store. Although its population is just a little more than 2,000, Sisters increasingly attracts visitors as well as urban runaways who appreciate its tranquillity and charm. If you're driving over from the Willamette Valley, note how the weather seems to change to sunshine when you cross the Cascades at the Santiam Pass and begin descending toward the town.

Black Butte, a perfectly conical cinder cone, rises to the northwest. The Metolius River/Camp Sherman area to the west is a special find for fly-fishermen and abounds with springtime wildflowers.

GETTING HERE AND AROUND

Travelers from Portland and the west come to Sisters over the Santiam Pass on Oregon 126. This is also the route for visitors who fly into Redmond Municipal Airport, rent a car, and drive 20 miles west. Those coming from Bend drive 21 miles northwest on U.S. 20. **Cascades East,** a regional bus carrier, runs routes between Sisters and the Redmond airport by reservation.

ESSENTIALS

Visitor Information Sisters Chamber of Commerce ✉ *291 E. Main Ave.* ☎ *541/549–0251* ⊕ www.sisterscountry.com.

EXPLORING

Camp Sherman. Surrounded by groves of whispering yellow-bellied ponderosa pines, larch, fir, and cedars and miles of streamside forest trails, this small, peaceful resort community of about 250 full-time residents (plus a few stray cats and dogs) is part of a designated conservation area. The area's beauty and natural resources are the big draw: the spring-fed Metolius River prominently glides through the community. In the early 1900s Sherman County wheat farmers escaped the dry summer heat by migrating here to fish and rest in the cool river environment, making Camp Sherman one of the first destination resorts in central Oregon. As legend has it, to help guide fellow farmers to the spot, devotees nailed a shoebox top with the name "camp sherman" to a tree at a fork in the road. Several original buildings still stand from the early days, including some cabins, a schoolhouse, and a tiny railroad chapel. The "action" is at the Camp Sherman Store & Fly Shop, built in 1918, adjacent to the post office. ☒ *25451 S.W. Forest Service Rd. 1419, 10 miles northwest of Sisters on U.S. 20, 5 miles north on Hwy. 14.* ☎ *541/595–6711* ⊕ *www.campshermanstore.com* ☉ *June–Aug., Mon.–Thurs. 8–7, Fri.–Sat. 8–8, Sun. 8–6; Sept. hours vary; Oct.–May, Fri.–Sat. 9–5, Sun. 9–4.*

NEED A BREAK?

Sisters Bakery. In a rustic Western-looking former general store built in 1925, Sisters Bakery turns out high-quality pastries, doughnuts, and specialty breads from 5 am–5 pm. The bakery serves Bend's Strictly Organic coffee, and harkens back to a time when doughnuts were simple and tasty. Cash and checks only. ☒ *251 E. Cascade St.* ☎ *541/549–0361* ⊕ *www. sistersbakery.com.*

WHERE TO EAT

$ × **The Depot Café.** A railroad theme prevails at this main-street rustic café. A miniature train circles above as the kitchen dishes out sandwiches, salads, and dinner specials. Sit inside next to the rough-wood walls or out back on the deck. ⑤ *Average main: $15* ☒ *250 W. Cascade St.* ☎ *541/549–2572* ⊕ *www.sistersdepot.com* ☉ *Closed Tues.; no breakfast weekdays.*

AMERICAN

$$$ × **Jen's Garden.** "Everything is beautiful and delicious" one diner said about this top-class restaurant that offers a three-course prix-fixe option, as well as traditional five-course meal in an intimate cottage setting. In keeping with the European custom of small servings, the courses are deliberately integrated so that the flavors complement each other in a vibrant and sometimes daring manner. The menu changes often to incorporate seasonal specialites and fresh products, with choices for each course: summer vegetable and wild mushroom gnocchi, basil-scented Oregon bay shrimp and chilled corn soup, braised beef cheek ragout, olive oil cake with mascarpone icing. If one particular dish tantalizes the senses, ordering à la carte is also an option. ⑤ *Average main: $27* ☒ *403 E. Hood Ave.* ☎ *541/549–2699* ⊕ *www.intimatecottagecuisine. com* ⌘ *Reservations essential* ☉ *No lunch* ☉ *Closed Mon. and Tues. in fall and spring, and for a few weeks around Thanksgiving and after Valentine's Day.*

FRENCH
Fodor's Choice
★

$$$
AMERICAN
Fodor'sChoice
★

✕**Kokanee Café.** The remarkable restaurant near the banks of the Metolius River draws diners from across the mountains to sample artful Northwest dishes at this homey hideaway with a paneled dining room and warm-weather porch. Local lamb, fresh fish, and vegetarian options are presented with creative elegance. As if brilliant appetizers, entrées and full bar weren't enough, sample the house-made desserts. ⑤ *Average main: $25* ✉ *25545 S.W. Forest Service Rd. 1419, Camp Sherman* ☎ *541/595–6420* ⊕ *www.kokaneecafe.com* ⬥ *Reservations essential* ⊘ *Closed Nov.–Apr. No lunch.*

$
ITALIAN

✕**The Open Door.** Serving simple and light Italian fare, such as panini and flatbread pizzas, this quaint and cozy restaurant offers a different homemade pasta dish every night for dinner. The interior is an eclectic mix of mismatched tables and chairs, the restaurant and wine bar opens into Clearwater Gallery & Framing, which displays Northwest artwork. An outdoor patio is open in the summer, but since the indoor eating space is small and fills quickly, come early for lunch or try to make reservations for dinner. If the place is busy on a winter's eve, you may find yourself eating in the gallery among paintings and pottery. ⑤ *Average main: $12* ✉ *303 W. Hood Ave.* ☎ *541/549–4994* ⊕ *www. theclearwatergallery.com* ⊘ *Closed Tues. in fall and winter.*

$
AMERICAN

✕**Sno Cap Drive In.** Since 1945, this burger joint has been serving iconic burgers, sandwiches, fries, milk shakes, and ice cream to residents and visitors. Be prepared for long lines out the doors, as travelers driving across the mountain often plan to stop here for lunch. Inside there are a few tables and checkered curtains, and outdoor seating with umbrellas is available. ⑤ *Average main: $8* ✉ *380 W. Cascade Ave.* ☎ *541/549–6151.*

WHERE TO STAY

$$
RESORT
Fodor'sChoice
★

🏨 **FivePine Lodge.** At this authentic, luxury, Western-style resort resembling a forest lodge, high-end furnishings were built by Amish craftsmen. **Pros:** top-quality amenities, like the Kohler waterfall tubs; peaceful atmosphere, but conviently located on the fringes of downtown Sister; every detail and pleasure is considered, including the softest sheets and towels seemingly available. **Cons:** only slightly set back from U.S. 20, where traffic is sometimes heavy; some cabins are close to neighbors. ⑤ *Rooms from: $189* ✉ *1021 Desperado Trail* ☎ *541/549–5900, 866/974–5900* ⊕ *www.fivepinelodge.com* ⬎ *8 rooms, 24 cabins* ⦿| *Breakfast.*

$$$$
RESORT

🏨 **The Lodge at Suttle Lake.** Presiding over the eastern side of Suttle Lake, with supersized wooden architecture and whimsical charm, this Grand Cascadian style getaway offers 11 lodge rooms that are big on luxury, with fireplaces and glorious lake or forest views, and six waterfront cabins. **Pros:** peaceful setting in luxurious accomodations; accessibility to varied sports in all seasons; various rooms and prices. **Cons:** no air-conditioning in summer; cell reception is spotty. ⑤ *Rooms from: $263* ✉ *13300 U.S. Hwy. 20, 13 miles northwest of Sisters* ☎ *541/595–2628* ⊕ *www.thelodgeatsuttlelake.com* ⬎ *11 rooms, 14 cabins* ⦿| *No meals.*

$$$$
RENTAL

🏨 **Metolius River Resort.** Each of the immaculate, individually owned cabins that nestle amid the pines and aspen at this peaceful resort has splendid views of the sparkling Metolius River, decks furnished with

6

Adirondack chairs, a full kitchen, and a fireplace. **Pros:** privacy; cabins feel like home—a very luxurious home; fall asleep and wake up to the sound of the river. **Cons:** no additional people (even visitors) allowed; no cell-phone service; bring supplies on winter weekdays when Camp Sherman closes down. ⑤ *Rooms from: $265* ✉ *25551 S.W. Forest Service Rd. 1419, Camp Sherman* ✛ *Off U.S. 20, northeast 10 miles from Sisters, turn north on Camp Sherman Rd., stay to left at fork (1419), and then turn right at the only stop sign* ☎ *800/818–7688, 541/595–6281* ⊕ *www.metoliusriverresort.com* ⌂ *11 cabins* ¡⊙¡ *No meals.*

NIGHTLIFE AND THE ARTS

Bronco Billy's Ranch Grill and Saloon. Pass through the swinging saloon doors into this Old West watering hole, originally built more than a century ago as the Hotel Sisters. Head to the bar, which is decorated with a mural of cancan dancers, weathered saddles hanging on the wall, and a mounted stuffed buffalo head. The saloon beckons to both residents and travelers alike. ✉ *190 E. Cascade Ave.* ☎ *541/549–7427* ⊕ *www.broncobillysranchgrill.com.*

Three Creeks Brewing Co. Currently Sisters' only brewery, Three Creeks offers a selection of beers at its brewing facility and brewpub that play on Northwest culture and the outdoor lifestyle. It's currently in the middle of an expansion project and plans to start canning its beers to further promote a convenient relationship between craft beer and the great outdoors. The brewery is visible from the brewpub and tours are available by appointment, although plans are in motion to formalize a touring schedule. The brewpub, with 10 of its beers on tap, also serves a wide range of food. Order a frothing pint of the popular Knotty Blonde, or the clever Stonefly Rye, and perhaps even sign up for in-house educational classes to learn more about beers. ✉ *721 Desperado Ct.* ☎ *541/549–1963* ⊕ *www.threecreeksbrewing.com.*

SHOPPING

Don Terra Artworks. This gallery represents local artists and craftspeople. You'll find stone sculptures, pottery, jewelry, glass, paintings, and photography. ✉ *103 E. Hood Ave.* ☎ *541/549–1299* ⊕ *www.donterra.com* ⊗ *Closed Tues.–Thurs. Jan.–Mar.*

Paulina Springs Books. Select a book from the discounted staff recommendation table, or from categories such as history, outdoor recreation, field guides, regional, science, and fiction. Sisters' leading independent bookstore also sells toys and games, and has a substantial young readers section. ✉ *252 W. Hood Ave.* ☎ *541/549–0866* ⊕ *www. paulinasprings.com.*

Stitchin' Post. Owned by a mother and daughter team, the famous knitting, sewing, and quilting store opened its doors in 1975. The spacious store not only inspires the senses with colorful fabric, patterns and yarns, but also conducts classes throughout the year. The Sisters Outdoor Quilt Show, annually held the second Saturday of July, is the largest in the world and intertwines its origins with the store's early years. ✉ *311 W. Cascade St.* ☎ *541/549–6061* ⊕ *www.stitchinpost.com.*

SPORTS AND THE OUTDOORS

FISHING

Fly-fishing the Metolius River attracts anglers who seek a challenge.

Camp Sherman Store & Fly Shop. This local institution, center of life in the riverside community, sells gear and provides information about where and how best to fish. ✉ *25451 Forest Service Rd.1419, Camp Sherman* ☎ *541/595–6711* ⊕ *www.campshermanstore.com.*

Fly and Field Outfitters. This large supplier of gear also sets anglers up with expert guides. ✉ *35 S.W. Century Dr., Bend* ☎ *866/800–2818* ⊕ *www. flyandfield.com.*

RECREATIONAL AREAS

Metolius Recreation Area. On the eastern slope of the Cascades and within the 1.6-million-acre Deschutes National Forest, this bounty of recreational wilderness is drier and sunnier than the western side of the mountains, giving way to bountiful natural history, outdoor activities, and wildlife. There are spectacular views of jagged, 10,000-foot snow-capped Cascade peaks, looming high above the basin of an expansive evergreen valley clothed in pine.

Five miles south of **Camp Sherman** (⇨ *See Exploring listings*), (two miles to head waters) the dark and perfectly shaped cinder cone of **Black Butte** rises 6,400 feet. At its base the **Metolius River** springs forth. Witness the birth of this "instant" river by walking a short paved path embedded in ponderosa forest, eventually reaching a viewpoint with the dramatic snow-covered peak of **Mt. Jefferson** on the horizon. At this point, water gurgles to the ground's surface and pours into a wide trickling creek cascading over moss-covered rocks. Within feet it funnels outward, expanding its northerly flow; becomes a full-size river; and meanders east alongside grassy banks and a dense pine forest to join the Deschutes River downstream. Within the 4,600-acre area of the Metolius and along the river, there are ample resources for camping, hiking, biking, and floating. Enjoy fly-fishing for rainbow, brown, and bull trout in perhaps the best spot within the Cascades. ✉ *Off Hwy. 20, 9 miles northwest of Sisters, Camp Sherman* ⊕ *www.metoliusriver.org.*

SKIING

Hoodoo Ski Area. On a 5,703-foot summit, this winter sports area has more than 800 acres of skiable terrain. With 32 runs and five lifts, skiers of all levels will find suitable thrills. Upper and lower Nordic trails are surrounded by silence, and an inner-tube run and night skiing round out the range of activites. At a 60,000-square-foot lodge at the mountain's base you can take in the view, grab a bite, shop, or rest your weary feet. The ski area has kids' activities and child-care services available. Lift tickets range from $10 to $51, depending on the type and day. ✉ *U.S. 20, 20 miles northwest of Sisters* ☎ *541/822–3799* ⊕ *www.hoodoo.com.*

6

EAST CENTRAL OREGON

East of the Cascades, central Oregon changes to desert. The land is austere, covered mostly in sage and juniper, with a few hardy rivers and great extrusions of lava, which flowed or was blasted across the prehistoric landscape. In recent years resorts have emerged to draw west-side residents weary of the rain. They come over to bask in the sun and to soak up the feeling of the frontier, reinforced by ranches and resilient towns like Redmond and Prineville. They also come to fish and boat on the man-made lakes near Culver and Prineville.

REDMOND

20 miles east of Sisters, 17 miles northeast of Bend.

Redmond sits at the western end of Oregon's high desert, a handful of miles from the Deschutes River and within minutes of several lakes. It is a place where desert ranches meet runways, as it serves as the regional hub for air travel. It is the town nearest to Eagle Crest Resort and Smith Rock, a magnet for rock climbers. As with Deschutes County, Redmond has experienced rapid growth in the state during the past 10 years, largely owing to a dry and mild climate and year-round downhill and cross-country skiing, fishing, hiking, mountain biking, and rockhounding. Still, this is no gentrified resort town à la Bend, as a stroll through the compact and historic downtown will attest. A few blocks of vintage buildings remain, but north–south traffic hustles through the city core, with most residents in neighborhoods strung out to the west. Centennial Park is a small but attractive open space with fountains and an expansive lawn, aspen trees, flowers, and a kiosk selling drinks and ice cream. The park is a great place for the kids to play in the splash fountain on a hot summer's day. A clock tower contains a time capsule buried in 2010, marking the centennial celebration of Redmond's founding.

GETTING HERE AND AROUND

A couple of highways—U.S. 97 and Oregon 126—cross in Redmond. U.S. 97 carries travelers north and south to Washington and California, and Highway 126 runs between Sisters in the west to Prineville in the east. If you're driving on U.S. 26 from Portland, stop at **The Museum at Warm Springs** (☎ *541/553–3331* ⊕ *www.museumatwarmsprings.org*) at the Confederated Tribes of Warm Springs Reservation for a look at Native American artifacts and history. Taxis and the **Redmond Airport Shuttle** ferry travelers to the Redmond Municipal Airport. Two bus lines, the **Central Oregon Breeze** and **Cascades East Transit**, serve Redmond. The Central Oregon Breeze links Bend, Redmond, Madras, and Portland, and Cascades East runs buses to and from Redmond and Madras, Prineville, and Bend. Passengers should call to ensure a ride.

ESSENTIALS

Visitor Information Redmond Chamber of Commerce and Convention Visitor's Bureau ✉ *446 S.W. 7th St.* ☎ *541/923–5191* ⊕ *www. visitredmondoregon.com.*

EXPLORING

OFF THE
BEATEN
PATH

The Cove Palisades State Park. Many people who drive through this part of north central Oregon are more intent on their distant destinations than on the arid landscape they're passing through. But venture down the two-lane roads to this mini Grand Canyon of red-rock cliffs and gorges 14 miles west of small-town Madras. On a clear day a column of snow-capped Cascades peaks lines the horizon during the drive from town. Lake Billy Chinook, a glittering oasis amid the rocks, snakes through the park. It's formed by the Deschutes, Metolius, and Crooked rivers.

The park is accessible year-round, but high season is summertime, when families camp on the lakeshore and houseboats drift unhurriedly from cliff to cleft. The lake is renowned for its wildlife, from the lake's bull trout to turkey vultures that fill the sky with their cries. Nature lovers also flock to the park in February for the annual eagle watch. The Crooked River Day Use Area is the most immediately accessible part of the park, a great place to cast a line into the water, launch a boat, or raid your picnic basket. Nearby is the Cove Palisades Marina, where you can rent fishing and houseboats, clean fish, and buy sandwiches and boat supplies, including kids' water toys.

In addition to 10 miles of hiking trails, the Cove Palisades has a driving loop around its craggy rim. Near the Ship Rock formation, you may

Rock climbing in Smith Rock State Park

see petroglyphs carved into a boulder by indigenous people who moved through the area centuries ago.

Two full-service campgrounds have full hookups, electrical sites with water, and tent sites, boat slips, and cabins. ⊠ *7300 Jordan Rd., Off U.S. 97, 27 miles north of Redmond, Culver* ☏ *541/546–3412, 800/551–6949, 800/452–5687* ⊕ *www.oregonstateparks.org* ▱ *Day use $5 per vehicle.*

Peter Skene Ogden Scenic Viewpoint. Even the most seasoned traveler may develop vertigo peering from the cliff top into a deep river canyon. It is a view that gives insight into why Oregon's high desert looks the way it does, with sheer drops and austere landscapes. You'll want to take pictures, but hang on to your camera. ⊠ *U.S. 97 N, 9 miles north of Redmond* ☏ *800/551–6949* ⊕ *www.oregonstateparks.org.*

WHERE TO EAT AND STAY

$$$
STEAKHOUSE
✕ **Brickhouse.** An elegant dining experience in Redmond can be found at this wood-tables and brick-wall restaurant, which specializes in steaks and chops but also offers attractive plates of seafood, especially shellfish. You can get lost in the list of cocktails and wines from Oregon and around the world. ⑤ *Average main: $30* ⊠ *412 S.W. 6th St.* ☏ *541/526–1782* ⊕ *www.brickhousesteakhouse.com* ⊘ *Closed Sun. and Mon. No lunch.*

$$
MEXICAN FUSION
✕ **Diego's Spirited Kitchen.** Near the "Redmond Est. 1910" sign that straddles downtown 6th Street, this fusion restaurant serves both Mexican and classic American dishes. Answer to "senorita" and "senor" as the bartender hand-squeezes limes for fresh margaritas while considering the good ol' five-way grilled ham and cheese sandwich, or the more

adventurous pork carnitas raviolis. ⑤ *Average main: $20* ✉ *447 S.W. 6th St.* ☎ *541/316–2002.*

$$ ✕ **Terrebonne Depot.** An old train depot is the setting for a meal that can
AMERICAN match the stunning views of the Smith Rock cliffs. Offering an array of reasonably priced, tasty dishes, the kitchen plays it straight down the middle with nicely seasoned salmon, chicken, and pasta. You can also get lunch baskets to take with you on the climb. Service is friendly, and the menu is a cut above what you'd expect in this off-the-beaten-track location. The view allows you to reflect on the climb you've just made— or will inspire you to embark on one. ⑤ *Average main: $18* ✉ *400 N.W. Smith Rock Way* ☎ *541/548–5030* ⊕ *www.terrebonnedepot.com* ☽ *Closed Tues. year-round and Mon. Labor Day–Memorial Day.*

$ ⌂ **Eagle Crest Resort.** On high-desert grounds covered with juniper and
RESORT sagebrush, accommodations include vacation rental houses as well as
FAMILY rooms and suites, some with fireplaces, clustered in a single building. **Pros:** a full-service resort with a spa, three 18-hole golf courses, restaurants; great for kids; pet-friendly. **Cons:** there can be crowds, kids, and pets; clean but not luxurious. ⑤ *Rooms from: $129* ✉ *1522 Cline Falls Hwy., 5 miles west of Redmond* ☎ *541/923–2453, 888/306–9643* ⊕ *www.eagle-crest.com* ⇋ *100 rooms, 70 town houses* �ฺ⊙ฺ *No meals.*

NIGHTLIFE

Wild Ride Brewing Co. One of Redmond's newer breweries, Wild Ride is located on a block at the edge of downtown; you might spot the food carts first, where patrons can grab a bite to eat and then enjoy their meal in the brewery's taproom or the outdoor seating area. As you sample a beer, look at the pint glass and read the tag line: "What's Your Wild Ride?" The brewery focuses its theme on various "wild rides"—from motorcycles to skiing to rock climbing. In warmer months, the garage doors to the brewery open and expose the shining steel tanks inside. A full day of tours is offered once a month, or individual tours are available by appointment. ✉ *332 S.W. 5th St.* ☎ *541/516–8544* ⊕ *www. wildridebrew.com.*

SPORTS AND THE OUTDOORS

RECREATIONAL AREAS

Cline Falls State Park. Picnicking and fishing are popular at this nine-acre rest area commanding scenic views on the Deschutes River. You'll feel free from civilization here. ✉ *Hwy. 126, 4 miles west of Redmond* ☎ *800/551–6949* ⊕ *www.oregonstateparks.org.*

ROCK CLIMBING

Fodor'sChoice **Smith Rock State Park.** Eight miles north of Redmond, this park is world
★ famous for rock climbing, with hundreds of routes of all levels of difficulty. A network of trails serves both climbers and families dropping in for the scenery. In addition to the stunning rock formations, the Crooked River, which helped shape these features, loops through the park. You might spot golden eagles, prairie falcons, mule deer, river otters, and beavers. Due to the environmental sensitivity of the region, the animal leash law is strongly enforced. It can get quite hot in midsummer, so most prefer to climb in the spring and fall. The stunning scenery—specifically, a view of the river curving through the high

rocks—was adopted by Deschutes Brewery for its Twilight Summer Ale label. ✉ *9241 N.E. Crooked River Dr., Off U.S. 97* ☎ *541/548–7501, 800/551–6949* ⊕ *www.oregonstateparks.org* ☑ *Day use $5 per vehicle.*

Smith Rock Climbing Guides. Professionals with emergency medical training take visitors to the Smith Rock formation for climbs of all levels of difficulty; they also supply equipment. Guided climbs—you meet at Smith Rock—can run a half day or full day, and are priced according to the number of people. ✉ *Smith Rock State Park, Terrebonne* ☎ *541/788–6225* ⊕ *www.smithrockclimbingguides.com.*

PRINEVILLE

18 miles east of Redmond.

Prineville is the oldest town in central Oregon, and the only incorporated city in Crook County. Tire entrepreneur Les Schwab founded his regional empire here, and it remains a key hub for the company. Recently, Facebook and Apple chose Prineville as the location for new data centers. Surrounded by verdant ranch lands and the purplish hills of the Ochoco National Forest, Prineville will likely interest you chiefly as a jumping-off point for some of the region's more secluded outdoor adventures. The area attracts thousands of anglers, boaters, sightseers, and rockhounds to its nearby streams, reservoirs, and mountains. Rimrocks nearly encircle Prineville, and geology nuts dig for free agates, limb casts, jasper, and thunder eggs. Downtown Prineville consists of a handful of small buildings along a quiet strip of Highway 26, dominated by the Crook County Courthouse, built in 1909. Shopping and dining opportunities are mostly on the basic side.

GETTING HERE AND AROUND

Travelers approaching Prineville from the west on Oregon 126 descend like a marble circling a funnel, dropping into a tidy grid of a town from a high desert plain. It's an unfailingly dramatic way to enter the seat of Crook County, dominated by the courthouse on Northeast Third Street, aka Highway 26, the main drag. Prineville is 19 miles east of Redmond Municipal Airport. If you're coming to Prineville from the airport, it's easiest to rent a car and drive. However, two bus lines, **Central Oregon Breeze** and **Cascades East Transit,** run routes.

ESSENTIALS

Visitor Information Ochoco National Forest Office ✉ *3160 N.E. 3rd St.* ☎ *541/416–6500* ⊕ *www.fs.usda.gov/centraloregon.* **Prineville-Crook County Chamber of Commerce and Visitor Center** ✉ *185 N.E. 10th St.* ☎ *541/447–6304* ⊕ *www.visitprineville.org.*

EXPLORING

A.R. Bowman Memorial Museum. A tough little stone building (it was once a bank, and banks out here needed to be solid) is the site of the museum of the Crook County Historical Society. The 1910 edifice is on the National Register of Historic Places, with the inside vault and teller cages seemingly untouched. Prominent in the museum are old guns, relics from the lumber mills, and Native American artifacts that define early Prineville. A recent expansion houses a research library and life-size representations of an Old West street. ⊠ *246 N. Main St.* ☎ *541/447–3715* ⊕ *www.bowmanmuseum.org* ⊠ *Free* ☉ *Memorial Day–Labor Day, weekdays 10–5, weekends 11–4; Labor Day–Dec. and Feb.–Memorial Day, Tues.–Fri. 10–5, Sat. 11–4. Closed Jan.*

Ochoco Viewpoint. This is a truly fantastic scenic overlook that commands a sweeping view of the city, including the prominent Crook County Courthouse built in 1909, and the hills, ridges, and buttes beyond. ⊠ *U.S. Hwy. 126, ½ mile west of Prineville.*

WHERE TO EAT AND STAY

$$
STEAKHOUSE

✕ **Barney Prine's Steakhouse & Saloon.** Prineville is home to a startlingly appealing restaurant and saloon named after one of the town's founders. It's a good place to get a filet mignon, pepper steak, slow-smoked prime rib, 1-pound ribeye steak, or other cuts. Chicken, pasta, seafood, and sometimes wild game are also on the menu. The waitstaff is cheerful and attentive, and the ambience is part frontier western, part contemporary. $ *Average main: $18* ⊠ *389 N.W. 4th St.* ☎ *541/362–1272* ⊕ *www.barneyprines.com* ☉ *No lunch.*

$
DINER

✕ **Tastee Treet.** Open since 1957, this local establishment is renowned for its traditional burgers, hand-cut french fries, and milk shakes. Saunter up to the horseshoe-shaped counter to sit on swiveling stools and chat with locals, or talk with out-of-towners, some of whom never miss a chance to drop by while passing through. Claim a red-and-white leather booth for the family, a table on the patio, or pick up an order from the drive-through. Hearty breakfast plates, such as hamburger steak and eggs, are available until 11 am, when the menu switches to sandwiches, burgers, chili cheese fries, and other "Tastee Eats." $ *Average main: $9* ⊠ *493 N.E. 3rd St.* ☎ *541/447–4165.*

$$$
RESORT
Fodor'sChoice
★

▦ **Brasada Ranch.** Enjoy a luxurious guest-ranch resort with spacious suites and cabins with fireplaces and decks, all offering authentic Western experiences and pristine modern amenities in the midst of exquisite views on 1,800 acres. **Pros:** extremely helpful staff help to make nearly anything possible; superb range of on-site facilities and activities; serene beauty and stunning mountain horizons. **Cons:** not all units have hot tubs; morning light seeps through wood-slatted shades. $ *Rooms from: $249* ⊠ *16986 S.W. Brasada Ranch Rd., Powell Butte* ☎ *866/373–4882* ⊕ *www.brasada.com* ⤳ *8 suites, 63 cabins* ⦿ *No meals.*

SPORTS AND THE OUTDOORS

FISHING

It's a good idea to check the **Oregon Department of Fish and Wildlife**'s (⊕ *ww.dfw.state.or.us*) recreation report before you head out.

Ochoco Reservoir. This lake is annually stocked with fingerling trout, and you might also find a rainbow, bass, or brown bullhead tugging on your line. ⊠ *Hwy. 26, 6 miles east of Prineville* ☎ *541/447–1209* ⊕ *www. ccprd.org* ⊠ *Campsites $16.*

HIKING

Pick up maps at the Ochoco National Forest office for trails through the nearly 5,400-acre **Bridge Creek Wilderness** and the demanding Black Canyon Trail (11½ miles one way with a hazardous river crossing in spring) in the **Black Canyon Wilderness.** The 1½-mile **Ponderosa Loop Trail** follows an old logging road through ponderosa pines growing on hills. In early summer wildflowers take over the open meadows. The trailhead begins at Bandit Springs Rest Area, 29 miles east of Prineville on U.S. 26. A 2-mile, one-way trail winds through old-growth forest and mountain meadows to **Steins Pillar**, a giant lava column with panoramic views; be prepared for a workout on the trail's poorly maintained second half, and allow at least three hours for the hike. To get to the trailhead, drive east 9 miles from Prineville on U.S. 26, head north (to the left) for 6½ miles on Mill Creek Road (also signed as Forest Service Road 33), and head east (to the right) on Forest Service Road 500.

RECREATIONAL AREAS

Ochoco National Forest. Twenty-five miles east of the flat, juniper-dotted countryside around Prineville, the landscape changes to forested ridges covered with tall ponderosa pines and Douglas firs. Sheltered by the diminutive Ochoco Mountains and with only about a foot of rain each year, the national forest, established in 1906 by President Theodore Roosevelt, manages to lay a blanket of green across the dry, high desert of central Oregon. This arid landscape—marked by deep canyons, towering volcanic plugs, and sharp ridges—goes largely unnoticed except for the annual influx of hunters during the fall. The Ochoco, part of the old Blue Mountain Forest Reserve, is a great place for camping, hiking, biking, and fishing in relative solitude. In its three wilderness areas—Mill Creek, Bridge Creek, and Black Canyon—it's possible to see elk, wild horses, eagles, and even cougars. ⊠ *Office, 3160 N.E. 3rd St. (U.S. 26)* ☎ *541/416–6500* ⊕ *www.fs.usda.gov/recmain/ochoco* ⊙ *Daily; office open weekdays 8–4:30.*

Oregon Badlands Wilderness. This 29,000-acre swath of Oregon's high desert was designated a national wilderness in 2009, following the longtime advocacy of Oregonians enamored by its harshly beautiful landscape riven by ancient lava flows and home to sage grouse, pronghorn antelope, and elk. Motorized vehicles are prohibited, but visitors can ride horses on designated trails and low-impact hikers are welcome. Bring a camera to capture the jagged rock formations, birds, and wildflowers. ⊠ *BLM Office, 3050 N.E. 3rd St. (U.S. 26)* ☎ *541/416–6700* ⊕ *www.blm.gov/or/wilderness/badlands.*

Prineville Reservoir State Park. Mountain streams flow out of the Ochoco Mountains and join together to create the Crooked River, which is dammed near Prineville. Bowman Dam on the river forms this park, where recreational activities include boating, swimming, fishing, hiking, and camping. Some anglers return here year after year, although temperatures can get uncomfortably hot and water levels relatively low by late summer. The reservoir is known for its bass, trout and crappie, with fly-fishing available on the Crooked River below Bowman Dam. ⊠ *19020 S.E. Parkland Dr.* ☎ *541/447–4363, 800/452–5687* ⊕ *www. oregonstateparks.org* ◁ *Campsites $21–$31.*

SKIING

Bandit Springs Rest Area. A network of cross-country trails starts here. Designed for all levels of skiers, the trails traverse areas near the Ochoco Divide and have great views. ⊠ *U.S. 26, 29 miles east of Prineville.*

CRATER LAKE
NATIONAL PARK

WELCOME TO CRATER LAKE NATIONAL PARK

TOP REASONS TO GO

★ **The lake:** Cruise inside the caldera basin and gaze into the extraordinary sapphire-blue water of the country's deepest lake.

★ **Native land:** Enjoy the rare luxury of interacting with totally unspoiled terrain.

★ **The night sky:** Billions of stars glisten in the pitch-black darkness of an unpolluted sky.

★ **Splendid hikes:** Accessible trails spool off the main roads and wind past colorful bursts of wildflowers and cascading waterfalls.

★ **Camping at its best:** Pitch a tent or pull up a motor home at Mazama Campground, a beautifully situated, guest-friendly, and well-maintained campground.

1 Crater Lake. The focal point of the park is this nonrecreational, scenic lake known for its deep-blue hue.

2 Wizard Island. Visitors can take boat rides to this protruding landmass rising from the western section of Crater Lake; it's a great place for a hike or a picnic.

3 Mazama Village. This is your best bet for stocking up on snacks, beverages, and fuel in the park; it's about 5 miles from Rim Drive.

4 Cleetwood Cove Trail. The only safe, designated trail to hike down the caldera and reach the lake's edge is on the rim's north side off Rim Drive.

GETTING ORIENTED

Crater Lake National Park covers 183,224 acres. Located in southern Oregon less than 100 miles from the California border, it's surrounded by several Cascade Range forests, including the Winema and Rogue River national forests. Of the nearby towns, Klamath Falls is closest at 60 miles south of the park; Ashland and Medford, to the southwest, are approximately 80 miles and 90 miles from the lake, respectively, with Roseburg the farthest away at 110 miles northwest of the park.

KEY
🏠 Ranger Station
⚠ Campground
🌲 Picnic Area
🍴 Restaurant
🏨 Lodge
🚶 Trailhead
🚻 Restrooms
⚘ Scenic Viewpoint
------ Walking/Hiking Trails

TO
ROSEBURG

PCT Parking

North Entrance Station

TO →
BEND

Boundary Springs

North Entrance Rd.

Pacific Crest National Scenic Trail

*Pumice
Desert*

Cleetwood
Cove Trail

4

North Junction

*Steel
Bay*

*Cleetwood
Cove*

Rim Dr.

Scott Bluffs

Rim Trail
The Watchman
8,013 ft

Deepest point
below lake surface:
-1,943 ft

*Grotto
Cove*

*Watchman
Trail*

Wizard
Island

2

1 *Crater
Lake*

*Cloudcap
Bay*

Cloudcap Overlook

Mount Scott
8,929 ft

Pacific Crest Trail

Discovery Point
Rim Village

*Danger
Bay*

**Crater Lake
Lodge**

Phantom Ship
Overlook

*Mount Scott
Trail*

TO
MEDFORD
AND ASHLAND

Sun
Notch

Steel Visitor Center

Vidae
Falls

Rim Dr.

*Grayback Dr.
(one way)*

Lost
Creek

Annie Spring
Entrance Station

3

*Grayback
Ridge*

Mazama Village

Crater Peak

Pinnacles
Overlook

*Pumice
Flat*

TO
KLAMATH FALLS ↓

0   3 mi

0   3 km

7

Updated
by Christine
Vovakes

The pure, crystalline blue of Crater Lake astounds visitors at first sight. More than 5 miles wide and ringed by cliffs almost 2,000 feet high, the lake was created approximately 7,700 years ago, following Mt. Mazama's fiery explosion. Days after the eruption, the mountain collapsed on an underground chamber emptied of lava. Rain and snowmelt filled the caldera, creating a sapphire-blue lake so clear that sunlight penetrates to a depth of 400 feet (the lake's depth is 1,943 feet). Today it's both the clearest and deepest lake in the United States—and the ninth deepest in the world.

CRATER LAKE PLANNER

WHEN TO GO

The park's high season is July and August. September and early October tend to draw smaller crowds. From October through June, the entire park virtually closes due to heavy snowfall. The road is kept open just to the rim in winter, except during severe weather.

FESTIVALS

Oregon Shakespeare Festival. More than 400,000 Bard lovers descend on Ashland (90 miles from Crater Lake) for the annual Oregon Shakespeare Festival. Plays run from February to November in three theaters; peak season is July, August, and September. ☎ *541/482–4331* ⊕ *www. osfashland.org*.

PLANNING YOUR TIME

CRATER LAKE IN ONE DAY

Begin at **Steel Visitor Center,** where interpretive displays and a short video introduce you to the story of the lake's formation and its unique characteristics. Then circle the crater's rim by heading northeast on **Rim Drive,** allowing an hour to stop at overlooks—check out the Phantom

Ship rock formation in the lake—before you reach **Cleetwood Cove Trail** trailhead, the only safe and legal access to the lake. If you're up to the strenuous challenge, hike down the trail to reach the dock, and hop aboard one of the **tour boats** for a two-hour lake tour with a park ranger as your guide. If you have time, add on a trip to **Wizard Island** for a picnic lunch.

Back on Rim Drive, continue around the lake, stopping at the **Watchman Trail** for a short but steep hike to this peak above the rim, which affords not only a splendid view of the lake, but a broad vista of the surrounding southern Cascades. Wind up your visit at **Crater Lake Lodge**—allow time to wander the lobby of the 1915 structure perched on the rim. Dinner at the lodge restaurant, overlooking the lake and the Cascade sunset, caps the day.

GETTING HERE AND AROUND

Most of the park is accessible only in late June or early July through mid-October. The rest of the year, snow blocks all park roadways and entrances except Highway 62 and the access road to Rim Village from Mazama Village. Rim Drive is typically closed because of heavy snowfall from mid-October to mid-June and sometimes as late as early July; you could encounter icy conditions any month of the year, particularly in early morning.

PARK ESSENTIALS

PARK FEES AND PERMITS

Admission to the park, good for seven days, is $10 per car, or $5 per motorcycle, bicycle, or pedestrian. Backcountry campers and hikers must obtain a free wilderness permit at Rim Visitor Center or Steel Visitor Center for all overnight trips.

PARK HOURS

Crater Lake National Park is open 24 hours a day year-round; however, snow closes most park roadways October through June. Lodging and dining facilities usually are open from late May to mid-October. The park is in the Pacific time zone.

CELL-PHONE RECEPTION

Cell-phone reception in the park is unreliable. You'll find public telephones at Crater Lake Lodge and outside the Mazama Village Camper Store.

RESTAURANTS

There are a few casual eateries and convenience stores within the park. For fantastic upscale dining on the caldera's rim, head to the Crater Lake Lodge.

HOTELS

Crater Lake's summer season is relatively brief, and the park's main lodge is generally booked with guest reservations a year in advance. If you don't snag one, check availability as your trip approaches—cancellations are always possible. Outside the park are options in Prospect, Klamath Falls, Roseburg, Medford, and Ashland. *Hotel reviews have been shortened. For full information, visit Fodors.com.*

WHAT IT COSTS IN U.S. DOLLARS			
	$	**$$**	**$$$**	**$$$$**
Restaurants	Under $13	$13–$20	$21–$30	Over $30
Hotels	Under $101	$101–$150	$151–$200	Over $200

Restaurant prices are the average cost of a main course at dinner, or if dinner is not served, at lunch. Hotel prices are the lowest cost of a standard double room in high season.

VISITOR INFORMATION

PARK CONTACT INFORMATION

Crater Lake National Park ☎ *541/594–3000* ⊕ *www.nps.gov/crla.*

VISITOR CENTERS

Rim Visitor Center. In summer you can obtain park information here, take a ranger-led tour, or stop into the nearby Sinnott Memorial, with a small museum and a 900-foot view down to the lake's surface. In winter, snowshoe walks are offered on weekends and holidays. The Rim Village Gift Store and cafeteria are the only services open in winter. ⊠ *Rim Dr. on the south side of the lake, 7 miles north of Annie Spring entrance station* ☎ *541/594–3090* ⊕ *www.nps.gov/crla* ☉ *Late May–late-Sept., daily 9:30–5.*

Steel Visitor Center. Open year-round, the information center is part of the park's headquarters; you'll find restrooms and a first-aid station here. There's also a small post office and a shop that sells books, maps, and postcards. In the auditorium, a 22-minute film, *Crater Lake: Into the Deep*, describes the lake's formation and geology, and explores the area's cultural history. ⊠ *Rim Dr., 4 miles north of Annie Spring entrance station* ☎ *541/594–3100* ⊕ *www.nps.gov/crla* ☉ *Early Apr.– early Nov., daily 9–5; mid-Nov.–early Apr., daily 10–4.*

EXPLORING

For most visitors, the star attractions of Crater Lake are the lake itself and the breathtakingly situated Crater Lake Lodge. Other park highlights include the natural, unspoiled beauty of the forest and the geological marvels that you can access along the Rim Drive.

SCENIC DRIVES

Fodor's Choice ★ **Rim Drive.** Take this 33-mile scenic loop for views of the lake and its cliffs from every conceivable angle. The drive alone is at least two hours long; frequent stops at overlooks and short hikes can easily stretch this to a half day. Be aware that Rim Drive is typically closed due to heavy snowfall from mid-October to mid-June, and icy conditions can be encountered any month of the year, particularly in early morning. ⊠ *Drive begins at Rim Village, 7 miles from Annie Spring entrance station along Munson Valley Rd.* ⊹ *To get to Rim Dr. from the park's north entrance, access the north entrance road via either Rte. 230 or Hwy. 138, and follow it for about 10 miles.* ⊕ *www.nps.gov/crla.*

HISTORIC SITES

Fodor'sChoice **Crater Lake Lodge.** First built in 1915, this classic log-and-stone struc-
★ ture still boasts the original lodgepole-pine pillars, beams, and stone
fireplaces. The lobby, fondly referred to as the Great Hall, serves as a
warm, welcoming gathering place where you can play games, socialize
with a cocktail, or gaze out of the many windows to view spectacular
sunrises and sunsets by a crackling fire. ⊠ *Rim Village, just east of Rim
Visitor Center* ⊕ *www.craterlakelodges.com.*

SCENIC STOPS

Cloudcap Overlook. The highest road-access overlook on the Crater Lake
rim, Cloudcap has a westward view across the lake to Wizard Island
and an eastward view of Mt. Scott, the volcanic cone that is the park's
highest point, just 2 miles away. ⊠ *2 miles off Rim Dr., 13 miles northeast of Steel Visitor Center* ⊕ *www.nps.gov/crla.*

Discovery Point. This overlook marks the spot at which prospectors first
spied the lake in 1853. Wizard Island is just northeast, close to shore.
⊠ *Rim Dr., 1½ miles north of Rim Village* ⊕ *www.nps.gov/crla.*

Mazama Village. In summer a campground, motor inn, amphitheater,
gas station, post office, and small store are open here. No gasoline is
available in the park from mid-October to mid-May. Snowfall deter-
mines when the village and its facilities open and close for the season.
⊠ *Mazama Village Rd., off Hwy. 62, near Annie Spring entrance station*
☎ *541/594–2255, 888/774–2728* ⊕ *www.craterlakelodges.com* ☽ *Mid-
to late-May and late Sept.–mid-Oct., daily 10–5; June–early Sept., daily
7 am–9 pm; early Sept.–late Sept., daily 8–8.*

Phantom Ship Overlook. From this point you can get a close look at Phantom Ship, a rock formation that resembles a schooner with furled masts
and looks ghostly in fog. ⊠ *Rim Dr., 7 miles northeast of Steel Visitor
Center* ⊕ *www.nps.gov/crla.*

Pinnacles Overlook. Ascending from the banks of Sand and Wheeler
creeks, unearthly spires of eroded ash resemble the peaks of fairy-tale
castles. Once upon a time, the road continued east to a former entrance.
A path now replaces the old road and follows the rim of Sand Creek
(affording more views of pinnacles) to where the entrance arch still
stands. ⊠ *5 miles northeast of Steel Visitor Center, then 7 miles east on
Pinnacles Spur Rd.* ⊕ *www.nps.gov/crla.*

Sun Notch. It's a moderate ¼-mile hike through wildflowers and dry
meadow to this overlook, which has views of Crater Lake and Phantom
Ship. Mind the cliff edges. ⊠ *Rim Dr., 4.4 miles east of Steel Visitor
Center, east side of the lake* ⊕ *www.nps.gov/crla.*

Wizard Island. To get here, hike down the steep Cleetwood Cove Trail
(and back up on your return) and board the tour boat (⇨ *Educational
Offerings*) for a two-hour ride ($52) with the option of a half or full
day stay on the island. Bring a picnic. If you're in top shape, take the
very strenuous 2-mile hike that begins at the boat dock and steeply
ascends over rock-strewn terrain to Wizard Summit and a path around
the 90-foot-deep crater at the top. A more moderate hike is the 1.8-mile

Wildlife in Crater Lake

Two primary types of fish swim beneath the surface of Crater Lake: kokanee salmon and rainbow trout. It's estimated that hundreds of thousands of kokanee inhabit the lake, but because boating and recreational access is so limited they elude many would-be sportsman. Kokanees average about 8 inches in length, but they can grow to nearly 18 inches. Rainbow trout are larger than the kokanee but are less abundant in Crater Lake. Trout—including bull, Eastern brook, rainbow, and German brown—swim in the park's many streams and rivers; they usually remain elusive because these waterways flow near inaccessibly steep canyons.

Remote canyons shelter the park's elk and deer populations, which can sometimes be seen at dusk and dawn feeding at forest's edge. Black bears and pine martens—cousins of the short-tailed weasel—also call Crater Lake home. Birds such as hairy woodpeckers, California gulls, red-tailed hawks, and great horned owls are more commonly seen in summer in forests below the lake.

trek on a rocky trail along the shore of the island. ⊠ *Via Cleetwood Cove Trail to Wizard Island dock* ☎ *541/594–2255, 888/774–2728* ⊕ *www.craterlakelodges.com* ☯ *Daily late June–mid-Sept.*

EDUCATIONAL OFFERINGS

RANGER PROGRAMS

FAMILY **Boat Tours.** The most extensively used guided tours in Crater Lake are on the water, aboard launches that carry 37 passengers on a two-hour tour accompanied by a ranger. The boats circle the lake; two of the eight daily boats stop at Wizard Island, where you can get off and reboard a minimum of three hours later, or six hours later if you catch the morning boat. The first tour leaves the dock at 9:30 am; the last departs at 3:30 pm. To get to the dock you must hike down Cleetwood Cove Trail, a strenuous 1.1-mile walk that drops 700 feet; only those in excellent physical shape should attempt the hike. Bring adequate water with you. Purchase boat-tour tickets at Crater Lake Lodge, at the top of the trail or through advance reservations. Restrooms are available at the top and bottom of the trail. ⊠ *Cleetwood Cove Trail, off Rim Dr., 11 miles north of Rim Village on the north side of the lake* ☎ *541/594–2255, 888/774–2728* ⊕ *www.craterlakelodges.com* ☒ *$37; $52 with island drop-off* ☯ *Late June–mid-Sept., daily.*

FAMILY **Junior Ranger Program.** Kids ages 6–12 learn about Crater Lake while earning either a Junior Ranger patch or badge in daily sessions during summer months at the Rim Visitor Center, and year-round at the Steel Visitor Center. Pick up free activity booklets at either visitor center. ☎ *541/594–3100* ⊕ *www.nps.gov/crla.*

SPORTS AND THE OUTDOORS

FISHING

Fishing is allowed in the lake, but you may find the experience frustrating—in such a massive body of water, the problem is finding the fish. Try your luck near the Cleetwood Cove boat dock, or take poles on the boat tour and fish off Wizard Island. Rainbow trout and kokanee salmon lurk in Crater Lake's aquamarine depths, and some grow to enormous sizes. You don't need a state fishing license, but to protect the lake's pristine waters, use only artificial bait as opposed to live worms. Private boats are prohibited on the lake.

HIKING

EASY

Castle Crest Wildflower Trail. This short half-mile loop that passes through a spring-fed meadow is one of the park's flatter hikes. Wildflowers burst into full bloom here in July. *Easy.* ⊠ *Across the street from Steel Visitor Center parking lot, East Rim Dr.* ⊕ *www.nps.gov/crla.*

Godfrey Glen Trail. This 1-mile loop trail is an easy stroll through an old-growth forest with canyon views. Its dirt path is accessible to wheelchairs with assistance. *Easy.* ⊠ *2.4 miles south of Steel Visitor Center* ⊕ *www.nps.gov/crla.*

MODERATE

Annie Creek Canyon Trail. This somewhat strenuous 1.7-mile hike loops through a deep stream-cut canyon, providing views of the narrow cleft scarred by volcanic activity. This is a good area to look for flowers and deer. *Moderate.* ⊠ *Mazama Campground, behind ampitheater, between D&E campground loops; Mazama Village Rd., near Annie Spring entrance station* ⊕ *www.nps.gov/crla.*

Boundary Springs Trail. If you feel like sleuthing, take this moderate 5-mile round-trip hike to the headwaters of the Rogue River. The trail isn't always well marked, so a detailed trail guide is necessary. You'll see streams, forests, and wildflowers along the way before discovering Boundary Springs pouring out of the side of a low ridge. *Moderate.* ⊠ *Pullout on Hwy. 230, near milepost 19, about 5 miles west of the junction with Hwy. 138* ⊕ *www.nps.gov/crla.*

Watchman Peak Trail. This is one of the best hikes in the park. Though it's less than a mile each way, the trail climbs more than 400 feet—not counting the steps up to the actual lookout, which has great views of Wizard Island and the lake. *Moderate.* ⊠ *Watchman Overlook, 3.8 miles northwest of Rim Village on Rim Dr., west side of the lake* ⊕ *www.nps.gov/crla.*

DIFFICULT

Cleetwood Cove Trail. This strenuous 2.2-mile round-trip hike descends 700 feet down nearly vertical cliffs along the lake to the boat dock. Be in top shape before you take this one. *Difficult.* ⊠ *Cleetwood Cove*

7

trailhead, Rim Dr., 11 miles north of Rim Village, north side of the lake ⊕ www.nps.gov/crla.

Fodor'sChoice **Mt. Scott Trail.** This strenuous 5-mile ★ round-trip trail takes you to the park's highest point—the top of Mt. Scott, the oldest volcanic cone of Mt. Mazama, at 8,929 feet. The average hiker needs 90 minutes to make the steep uphill trek—and nearly 60 minutes to get down. The trail starts at an elevation of about 7,450 feet, so the climb is not extreme but does get steep in spots. Views of the lake and the broad Klamath Basin are spectacular. *Difficult.* ⊠ *14 miles east of Steel Visitor Center on Rim Dr., east side of the lake, across from the road to Cloudcap Overlook ⊕ www.nps.gov/crla.*

SERIOUS SAFETY

There's only one safe way to reach Crater Lake's edge: the Cleetwood Cove Trail from the north rim. The rest of the inner caldera is steep and composed of loose gravel, basalt, and pumice—extremely dangerous, in other words. That's why all hiking and climbing are strictly prohibited inside the rim, and rangers will issue citations for violations.

Pacific Crest Trail. You can hike a portion of the Pacific Crest Trail, which extends from Mexico to Canada and winds through the park for 33 miles. For this prime backcountry experience, catch the trail off Highway 138 about a mile east of the north entrance, where it heads south and then toward the west rim of the lake and circles it for about 6 miles, then descends down Dutton Creek to the Mazama Village area. You'll need a detailed map for this hike; check online or with the PCT association. *Difficult.* ⊠ *Pacific Crest Trail parking lot, north access road off Hwy. 138, 2 miles east of the Hwy. 138–north entrance road junction ⊕ www.nps.gov/crla.*

SKIING

There are no maintained ski trails in the park, although some backcountry trails are marked with blue diamonds or snow poles. Most cross-country skiers park at Rim Village and follow a portion of West Rim Drive toward Wizard Island Overlook (4 miles). The road is plowed to Rim Village, but it may be closed temporarily due to severe storms. Snow tires and chains are essential. The park's online brochure (available at ⊕ *www.nps.gov/crla*) lists additional trails and their length and difficulty.

SWIMMING

Swimming is allowed in the lake, but it's not advised. Made up entirely of snowmelt, Crater Lake is very cold—about 45°F to 56°F in summer. The lagoons on Wizard Island and at Cleetwood Cove are your best choices—but only when the air temperature rises above 80°F, which is rare. If you're able to brave the cold, though, you can say that you've taken a dip in the deepest lake in the United States.

WHERE TO EAT

$$ ✕ **Annie Creek Restaurant.** At this
AMERICAN family-friendly dining spot you'll
FAMILY find pizza and pasta along with
chicken, beef, and fish entrées. Less
expensive sandwich selections are
available, plus a breakfast menu.
The outdoor seating area is sur-
rounded by towering pine trees.
$ *Average main: $16* ✉ *Mazama
Village Rd., near Annie Spring
entrance station* ☎ *541/594–2255*
⊕ *www.craterlakelodges.com*
☾ *Closed mid-Sept.–late May.*

$$$ ✕ **Dining Room at Crater Lake Lodge.**
AMERICAN Virtually the only place where you
Fodor'sChoice can dine well once you're in the park, the lodge emphasizes fresh,
★ regional Northwest cuisine. The dining room is magnificent, with a
large stone fireplace and views of Crater Lake's clear-blue waters. Breakfast and lunch are enjoyable here, but the evening menu is the main
attraction, with tempting delights such as wild Alaskan salmon, pork
loin with apple compote, steak, and vegetarian offerings. An extensive
wine list tops off the gourmet experience. No reservations accepted for
breakfast and lunch, but they're essential for dinner. $ *Average main:
$30* ✉ *Crater Lake Lodge, 1 Lodge Loop Rd., Rim Village* ☎ *541/594–
2255* ⊕ *www.craterlakelodges.com* ⟿ *Reservations essential* ☾ *Closed
mid-Oct.–late May.*

> **PEST ALERT**
>
> Early summer snowmelt often creates watery breeding areas for large groups of mosquitoes. Bring lots of insect repellent in June and July, and expect mosquito swarms in the early morning and at sunset. They can also be a problem later in the summer in campgrounds and on the Cleet-wood Cove Trail, so pack repellent if you plan on camping or hiking.

PICNIC AREAS

Rim Drive. About a half-dozen picnic-area turnouts encircle the lake; all
have good views, but they can get very windy. Most have pit toilets, and
a few have fire grills, but none have running water. ✉ *Rim Dr.*

Rim Village. This is the only park picnic area with running water. The
tables are set behind the visitor center, and most have a view of the lake
below. There are flush toilets inside the visitor center. ✉ *Rim Dr. on the
south side of the lake, 7 miles north of Annie Spring entrance station.*

Wizard Island. The park's best picnic venue is on Wizard Island; pack a
lunch and book yourself on one of the early-morning boat tour depar-
tures, reserving space on an afternoon return. There are no formal
picnic areas and just pit toilets, but you'll discover plenty of sunny,
protected spots where you can have a quiet meal and appreciate the
astounding scene that surrounds you. The island is accessible by boat
tour only (⇨ *Educational Offerings*). ✉ *Wizard Island, Crater Lake.*

WHERE TO STAY

$$ ⊡ **The Cabins at Mazama Village.** In a wooded area 7 miles south of the
HOTEL lake, this complex is made up of several A-frame buildings and has
mostly modest rooms with two queen beds and a private bath. **Pros:** clean

Best Campgrounds in Crater Lake

Both tent campers and RV enthusiasts will enjoy the heavily wooded and well-equipped setting of Mazama Campground. Drinking water, showers, and laundry facilities help ensure that you don't have to rough it too much. Lost Creek Campground is much smaller, with minimal amenities and a more "rustic" Crater Lake experience.

Lost Creek Campground. The 16 small, remote tent sites here are usually available on a daily basis from late May to early October, depending on snow; in July and August arrive early to secure a spot. ⊠ 3 miles *south of Rim Rd. on Pinnacles Spur Rd. at Grayback Dr.* ☎ 541/594–3100.

Mazama Campground. This campground is set well below the lake caldera in the pine and fir forest of the Cascades not far from the main access road (Highway 62). About half the spaces are pull-throughs, some with electricity; no hookups are available. The best tent spots are on some of the outer loops above Annie Creek Canyon. ⊠ *Mazama Village, near Annie Spring entrance station* ☎ 541/594–2255, 888/774–2728 ⊕ *www.craterlakelodges.com.*

and well-kept facility. **Cons:** lots of traffic into adjacent campground. ⑤ *Rooms from: $144* ⊠ *Mazama Village, near Annie Spring entrance station* ☎ *541/594–2255, 888/774–2728* ⊕ *www.craterlakelodges.com* ⟿ *40 rooms* ⊗ *Closed mid-Oct.–late May* ❌ *No meals.*

$$$
HOTEL
📷 **Crater Lake Lodge.** The period feel of this 1915 lodge on the caldera's rim is reflected in its lodgepole-pine columns, gleaming wood floors, and stone fireplaces in the common areas. **Pros:** ideal location for watching sunrise and sunset reflected on the lake. **Cons:** very difficult to reserve rooms; some rooms have tubs only, no shower. ⑤ *Rooms from: $167* ⊠ *Rim Village, east of Rim Visitor Center, 1 Lodge Loop Rd., Crater Lake* ☎ *541/594–2255, 888/774–2728* ⊕ *www.craterlakelodges.com* ⟿ *71 rooms* ⊗ *Closed mid-Oct.–mid-May* ❌ *No meals.*

8

SOUTHERN
OREGON

WELCOME TO SOUTHERN OREGON

TOP REASONS TO GO

★ **Discover the other wine regions:** The underrated Umpqua and Rogue River wine regions offer picturesque pastoral views and numerous tasting rooms.

★ **Go underground:** Explore deep into mysterious underground chambers and marble caves at Oregon Caves National Monument.

★ **Savor Shakespeare:** The acclaimed Oregon Shakespeare Festival draws drama lovers to Ashland nine months a year, presenting a wide variety of both classic and contemporary theater.

★ **Enjoy quaint towns:** Southern Oregon's own throwback to the Old West, Jacksonville abounds with well-preserved buildings while Ashland claims one of the prettiest downtowns in the state.

★ **Get wet and wild:** Each fall more than 1 million waterfowl descend upon Klamath Basin National Wildlife Refuge Complex. The Rogue River is Oregon's white-water-rafting capital, and the entire region is laced with stunning hiking trails.

1 Umpqua Valley. Known increasingly for its up-and-coming wineries, including award-winning Abacela, this valley is home to historic Oakland, Roseburg and its family-friendly Wildlife Safari park, and the Umpqua River Scenic Byway, a particularly scenic route to Crater Lake.

2 Rogue Valley. This fertile, mild-temperature region that extends from Grants Pass southeast through Medford and down to Ashland takes in the most populous communities in the area—it's also the gateway for reaching Klamath Falls, to the east, and the remote but fascinating Oregon Caves National Monument to the southwest. The Oregon Shakespeare Festival and an abundance of historic buildings have turned Ashland into a hub of arts, culture, and fine bed-and-breakfasts. Grants Pass, which also has a lively downtown dining and shopping district, is the launch point for some of the best white-water rafting around, while Medford and historic Jacksonville are surrounded by vineyards and farms that produce some of the state's tastiest local edibles, from pears to Pinot Gris.

GETTING ORIENTED

To locals, southern Oregon really refers to the southwestern corner of the state, encompassing the Rogue and several other river valleys that lie between the Coast and Cascade mountain ranges, from a little north of Roseburg down to the California border. The area is due south of Eugene and the Willamette Valley, and has a lush, hilly, and fertile terrain that lends itself perfectly to agriculture and wine-making. Towns in the valleys, such as Ashland and Roseburg, have elevations ranging from about 500 to 2,000 feet, while peaks to the east, in the Cascade Range, rise as high as 9,000 feet. This area is also the gateway to Crater Lake National Park—many visitors to that park overnight in Medford or Ashland, which are about 85 miles away.

8

Updated by Andrew Collins

Southern Oregon begins where the verdant lowlands of the Willamette Valley give way to a complex collision of mountains, rivers, and ravines. The intricate geography of the "Land of Umpqua," as the area around Roseburg is somewhat romantically known, signals that this is territory distinct from neighboring regions to the north, east, and west.

Wild rivers—the Rogue and the Umpqua are legendary for fishing and boating—and twisting mountain roads venture through the landscape that saw Oregon's most violent Indian wars and became the territory of a self-reliant breed. "Don't-Tread-on-Me" southern Oregonians see themselves as markedly different from fellow citizens of the Pacific Wonderland. In fact, several early-20th-century attempts to secede from Oregon (in combination with Northern California) and proclaim a "state of Jefferson" survive in local folklore and culture. That being said, Ashland and parts of the surrounding area have gradually become more progressive and urbane in recent decades, as wineries, art galleries, and stylish restaurants continue to proliferate. The mix of folks from all different political, social, and stylistic bents is a big part of what makes southern Oregon so interesting—and appealing.

Some locals describe this sun-kissed, sometimes surprisingly hot landscape as Mediterranean; others refer to it as Oregon's banana belt. It's a climate built for slow-paced pursuits and a leisurely outlook on life, not to mention agriculture—the region's orchards, farms, and increasingly acclaimed vineyards have lately helped give southern Oregon cachet among food and wine aficionados. The restaurant scene has grown partly thanks to a pair of big cultural draws, Ashland's Oregon Shakespeare Festival and Jacksonville's open-air, picnic-friendly Britt Festivals concert series.

Roseburg, Medford, and Klamath Falls are also all popular bases for visiting iconic Crater Lake National Park (⇨ *see Chapter 7)*, which lies at the region's eastern edge, about two hours away by car. Formed nearly 8,000 years ago by the cataclysmic eruption of Mt. Mazama, this stunningly clear-blue lake is North America's deepest.

SOUTHERN OREGON PLANNER

WHEN TO GO

Southern Oregon's population centers, which all lie chiefly in the valleys, tend to be warmer and quite a bit sunnier than Eugene and Portland to the north, receiving almost no snow in winter and only 2 to 3 inches of rain per month. In summer, temperatures regularly climb into the 90s, but the low humidity makes for a generally comfortable climate. This makes most of the region quite pleasant to visit year-round, with spring and fall generally offering the best balance of sunny and mild weather.

The exceptions, during the colder months, are southern Oregon's mountainous areas to the east and west, which are covered with snow from fall through spring. Some of the roads leading from the Umpqua and Rogue Valleys up to Crater Lake are closed because of snow from mid-October through June, making summer the prime time to visit.

FESTIVALS

Fodor's Choice ★ **Oregon Shakespeare Festival.** From mid-February to early November, more than 100,000 Bard-loving fans descend on Ashland for some of the finest Shakespearean productions you're likely to see outside of Stratford-upon-Avon—plus works by Ibsen, Williams, and contemporary playwrights. Between June and October plays are staged in the 1,200-seat Elizabethan Theatre, an atmospheric re-creation of the Fortune Theatre in London; the 600-seat Angus Bowmer Theatre, a state-of-the-art facility typically used for five different productions in a single season; and the 350-seat New Theater, which mostly hosts productions of new or experimental work. The festival generally operates close to capacity, so it's important to book ahead. ⊠ 15 S. Pioneer St., Ashland ☎ 541/482–4331 ⊕ www.osfashland.org.

Winter Wings Festival. Each February nature enthusiasts flock to the Klamath Basin for the Winter Wings Festival, the nation's oldest birding festival. ⊠ Box 354, Klamath Falls ☎ 877/541–2473 ⊕ winterwingsfest.org.

GETTING HERE AND AROUND

AIR TRAVEL

Medford's Rogue Valley International Airport (MFR) is the state's third-largest facility, with direct flights to Denver, Los Angeles, Phoenix, Portland, Salt Lake City, San Francisco, and Seattle, and service by Allegiant, Alaska, Delta, and United. Most national car-rental branches are at the airport. A few taxi and shuttle companies provide transportation from the airport to other towns in the area; these are used mostly by locals, as a car is the only practical way to explore this relatively rural part of Oregon. The one exception is Ashland, where many attractions, restaurants, and accommodations are within walking distance. Cascade Airport Shuttle offers door-to-door service from the airport to Ashland for about $30 to $35. Among taxi companies, Valley Cab serves the Rogue Valley region, with fares costing $3 base per trip, plus $2.50 per mile thereafter.

Roseburg is a 75-mile drive from Oregon's second-largest airport, in Eugene (EUG). Ashland is about 300 miles south of the state's largest airport, in Portland, and 350 miles north of San Francisco. Although it's often cheaper to fly into these larger airports than it is to Medford, what you lose in gas costs, time, and inconvenience will likely outweigh any savings.

Contacts Cascade Airport Shuttle ☎ *541/488–1998, 888/760–7433* ⊕ *www. cascadeshuttle.com.* **Rogue Valley International Airport** ☎ *541/772–8068* ⊕ *www.jacksoncountyor.org/airport.* **Valley Cab** ☎ *541/772–1818* ⊕ *www. myvalleycab.com.*

CAR TRAVEL

Unquestionably, your best way to explore the region is by car, although most of Ashland's key attractions, hotels, and dining are downtown and within walking distance of one another. Interstate 5 runs north–south the length of the Umpqua and Rogue River Valleys, linking Roseburg, Grants Pass, Medford, and Ashland. Many regional attractions lie not too far east or west of Interstate 5. Jacksonville is a short drive due west from Medford. Highway 138 winds scenically along the Umpqua River east of Roseburg to the less-visited northern end of Crater Lake National Park. Highway 140 leads from Medford east to Klamath Falls, which you can reach from Bend via U.S. 97.

RESTAURANTS

Southern Oregon's dining scene varies greatly from region to region, with the more tourism-driven and upscale communities of Ashland, Jacksonville, and Grants Pass leading the way in terms of sophisticated farm-to-table restaurants, hip coffeehouses, and noteworthy bakeries and wine bars. Other larger towns in the valleys, including Roseburg and Medford, have grown in culinary stature and variety of late, while Klamath Falls and Cave Junction have few dining options of note. In the former communities you'll find chefs emphasizing Oregon-produced foods; Oregon wines, including many from the Rogue and Umqua Valleys, also find their way onto many menus.

HOTELS

Ashland has the region's greatest variety of distinctive lodgings, from the usual low- to midpriced chain properties to plush B&Bs set in restored Arts and Crafts and Victorian houses. Nearby Jacksonville also has several fine, upscale inns. Beyond that, in nearly every town in southern Oregon you'll find two or three interesting B&Bs or small hotels, and in any of the communities along Interstate 5—including Roseburg, Grants Pass, and Medford—a wide variety of chain motels and hotels. Rooms in this part of the state book up earliest in summer, especially on weekends. If you're coming to Ashland or Jacksonville, try to book at least a week or two ahead. Elsewhere, you can usually find a room in a suitable chain property on less than a day's notice. *Hotel reviews have been shortened. For full information, visit Fodors.com.*

WHAT IT COSTS IN U.S. DOLLARS			
$	$$	$$$	$$$$
Restaurants	Under $17	$17–$23	$24–$30	Over $30
Hotels	Under $151	$151–$200	$201–$250	Over $250

Restaurant prices are the average cost of a main course at dinner or, if dinner is not served, at lunch. Hotel prices are the lowest cost of a standard double room in high season.

TOURS

Hellgate Jetboat Excursions. You'll see some of Oregon's most magnificent scenery on these excursions, which depart from the Riverside Inn in Grants Pass. The 36-mile round-trip runs through Hellgate Canyon and takes two hours. There is also a five-hour, 75-mile round-trip from Grants Pass to Grave Creek, with a stop for a meal on an open-air deck (cost of meal not included). Trips are available May through September, conditions permitting. ☎ *541/479–7204, 800/648–4874* ⊕ *www. hellgate.com* ✉ *From $40.*

Wine Hopper Tours. Getting to know the region's more than 125 wineries can be a challenge to visitors, especially when you factor in having to drive from tasting room to tasting room. This outfitter with knowledgeable guides leads seven-hour tours leaving daily from Ashland, Medford, and Jacksonville—the day includes a tour of a winery, picnic lunch, and tasting at a few of the area's top producers. ☎ *541/476–9463, 855/550–9463* ⊕ *www.winehoppertours.com* ✉ *From $79.*

VISITOR INFORMATION

Southern Oregon Visitors Association ⊕ *www.southernoregon.org.*

UMPQUA VALLEY

The northernmost part of southern Oregon, beginning about 40 miles south of Eugene and the Willamette Valley, the rural and sparsely populated Umpqua Valley is the gateway to this part of the state's sunny and relatively dry climate. As you drive down Interstate 5 you'll descend through twisting valleys and climb up over scenic highlands. In summer you can follow the dramatic Umpqua River Scenic Byway (Highway 138) east over the Cascades to access Crater Lake from the north—it's the prettiest route to the lake. Within the Umpqua Valley, attractions are relatively few, but this area has several excellent wineries, some of the best river fishing in the Northwest, and one of the region's top draws for animal lovers, the Wildlife Safari park.

ROSEBURG

73 miles south of Eugene on Interstate 5.

Fishermen the world over hold the name Roseburg sacred. The timber town on the Umpqua River attracts anglers in search of a dozen popular fish species, including bass, brown and brook trout, and chinook, coho, and sockeye salmon. The native steelhead, which makes its run to the sea in the summer, is king of them all.

The north and south branches of the Umpqua River meet up just north of Roseburg. The roads that run parallel to this river provide spectacular views of the falls, and the North Umpqua route also provides access to trails, hot springs, and the Winchester fish ladder. White-water rafting is also popular here, although not to the degree that it is farther south in the Rogue Valley.

About 80 miles west of the northern gateway to Crater Lake National Park and in the Hundred Valleys of the Umpqua, Roseburg produces innovative, well-regarded wines. Wineries are sprouting up throughout the mild, gorgeous farm country around town, mostly within easy reach of Interstate 5.

GETTING HERE AND AROUND

Roseburg is the first large town you'll reach driving south from Eugene on Interstate 5. It's also a main access point into southern Oregon via Highway 138 if you're approaching from the east, either by way of Crater Lake or U.S. 97, which leads down from Bend. And from the North Bend–Coos Bay region of the Oregon Coast, windy but picturesque Highway 42 leads to just south of Roseburg. It's a 75-mile drive north to Eugene's airport, and a 95-mile drive south to Rogue Valley Airport in Medford. Attractions in the region are spread over a large area—a car is a must.

ESSENTIALS

Visitor Information Roseburg Visitors & Convention Bureau ⊠ *410 S.E. Spruce St.* ☎ *541/672–9731, 800/444–9584* ⊕ *www.visitroseburg.com.*

EXPLORING

Fodor's Choice ★ **Abacela Vineyards and Winery.** The name derives from an archaic Spanish word meaning "to plant grapevines," and that's exactly what this winery's husband-wife team did not so very long ago. Abacela released its first wine in 1999 and has steadily established itself as one of the state's most acclaimed producers—one of the best outside the Willamette Valley. Hot-blooded Spanish Tempranillo is Abacela's pride and joy, though inky Malbec and torrid Sangiovese also highlight a repertoire heavy on Mediterranean varietals. ⊠ *12500 Lookingglass Rd.* ☎ *541/679–6642* ⊕ *www.abacela.com* ☉ *June–Oct., daily 11–6; Nov.–May, daily 11–5.*

Douglas County Museum. One of the best county museums in the state surveys 8,000 years of human activity in the region. The fossil collection is worth a stop, as is the state's second-largest photo collection, numbering more than 24,000 images, some dating to the 1840s. ⊠ *123 Museum Dr.* ☎ *541/957–7007* ⊕ *www.umpquavalleymuseums. org* ☞ *$5* ☉ *Tues.–Sat. 10–5.*

FAMILY Fodor's Choice ★ **Wildlife Safari.** Come face-to-face with some 500 free-roaming animals at the 600-acre drive-through wildlife park. Inhabitants include alligators, bobcats, cougars, gibbons, lions, giraffes, grizzly bears, Tibetan yaks, cheetahs, Siberian tigers, and more than 100 additional species. There's also a petting zoo, a miniature train, and elephant rides. The admission price includes two same-day drive-throughs. This nonprofit

Wine production in southern Oregon

zoological park is a respected research facility with full accreditation from the American Zoo and Aquarium Assocation, with a mission to conserve and protect endangered species through education and breeding programs. ⊠ *1790 Safari Rd., Winston* 🕾 *541/679–6761* ⊕ *www.wildlifesafari.net* ⊠ *$18* ⊘ *Mid-Mar.–Oct., daily 9–5; Nov.–mid-Mar., daily 10–4.*

WHERE TO EAT AND STAY

$$
AMERICAN
✕ **Brix 527.** This handsome downtown American bistro with exposed-brick walls, curving leather banquettes, and high ceilings serves reasonably priced breakfast and lunch fare daily, and somewhat more upscale dinners. There's also a convivial lounge, and an impressive wine, beer, and cocktail list available in either space. Start the day with blueberry–lemon zest pancakes or eggs Benedict topped with wild salmon. Highlights from the evening menu include the fusion-y chicken artichoke-spinach nachos, and blackened, rare-seared ahi tuna steak. Several more affordable sandwiches, burgers, and salads are available, too. ⑤ *Average main: $20* ⊠ *527 S.E. Jackson St.* 🕾 *541/440–4901* ⊕ *www.brix527.com* ⊘ *No dinner Sun.*

$$
B&B/INN
Fodor's Choice
★
🛏 **The Steamboat Inn.** The world's top fly-fishermen converge at this secluded forest inn, high in the Cascades above the emerald North Umpqua River; others come simply to relax in the reading nooks or on the broad decks of the riverside guest cabins nestled below soaring fir trees and surrounded by verdant gardens. **Pros:** good option if en route to Crater Lake; access to some of the best fishing in the West; great escape. **Cons:** extremely far from civilization. ⑤ *Rooms from: $195* ⊠ *42705 N. Umpqua Hwy., 38 miles east of Roseburg on Hwy. 138,*

near Steamboat Creek, Idleyld Park ☎ *541/498–2230, 800/840–8825* ⊕ *www.thesteamboatinn.com* ⤷ *8 cabins, 5 cottages, 2 suites, 5 houses* ⦿*No meals.*

SPORTS AND THE OUTDOORS

FISHING

You'll find some of the best river fishing in Oregon along the Umpqua, with smallmouth bass, shad, steelhead, salmon (coho, chinook, and sockeye), and sturgeon—the biggest reaching 10 feet in length—among the most prized catches. In addition to the Steamboat Inn, several out-fitters in the region provide full guide services, which typically include all gear, boats, and expert leaders. There's good fishing in this region year-round, with sturgeon and steelhead at their best during the colder months, chinook and coho salmon thriving in the fall, and most other species prolific in spring and summer.

Big K Guest Ranch. Set along a 10-mile span of the upper Umpqua River near Elkton (about 35 miles north of Roseburg), Big K is a pasto-ral 2,500-acre guest ranch. The accommodations are geared primarily to groups and corporate retreats, but the ranch offers individual fish-ing packages starting at $400 per person, per day (meals and lodging included), with three- and four-night deals available at a better rate. Adventures include fly-fishing for smallmouth bass and summer steel-head, as well as spin-casting and drift-boat fishing. ⊠ *20029 Hwy. 138 W., Elkton* ☎ *541/584–2295* ⊕ *www.big-k.com.*

Oregon Angler. One of the state's most respected and knowledgeable guides, Todd Hannah, specializes in jet-boat and drift-boat fishing excursions along the famed "Umpqua Loop," an 18-mile span of river that's long been lauded for exceptional fishing. Full-day trips start at $200 per person. ⊠ *1037 Maupin Rd., Elkton* ☎ *800/428–8585* ⊕ *www.theoregonangler.com.*

RAFTING

There's thrilling Class III and higher white-water rafting along the North Umpqua River, with several outfitters providing trips ranging from a few hours to a few days throughout the year.

North Umpqua Outfitters. Since 1987, this trusted provider has offered both half- and full-day rafting and kayaking trips along the frothy North Umpqua. ⊠ *P.O. Box 158, Idleyd Park* ☎ *888/454–9696* ⊕ *www.nuorafting.com.*

ROGUE VALLEY

Encompassing the broad, curving, southeasterly swath of towns from Grants Pass through Medford down to Ashland, the mild and sun-kissed Rogue Valley is southern Oregon's main population center, and also where you'll find the bulk of the region's lodging, dining, shop-ping, and recreation.

Interstate 5 cuts through the valley en route to Northern California, but venture away from the main thoroughfare to see what makes this part of Oregon so special, including the superb—if underrated—wineries.

Kayaking Rainey Falls on the Rogue River

With warmer temperatures, this area is conducive to many more varietals than the Willamette Valley—from reds like Syrah, Tempranillo, and Cabernet Sauvignon to increasingly well-known old-world whites like Viognier and Pinot Gris. Foodies are drawn to the region's abundance of local food producers, from nationally acclaimed cheese makers and chocolatiers to farms growing juicy pears, blackberries, and cherries. Access to excellent food has helped turn the small but artsy city of Ashland into one of Oregon's top restaurant destinations, with nearby communities also growing in culinary cachet. Additionally, the area's reputation for performing arts, which manifests itself in the famed Oregon Shakespeare Festival in Ashland and Britt Music Festival in historic Jacksonville, continues to grow.

Flanked by 1.8-million-acre Rogue–Siskiyou National Forest, which has rangers' offices near Grants Pass and Medford, the Rogue Valley is a hub of outdoor recreation, from fishing and white-water rafting along its clear rivers to mountain biking, hiking, and even skiing in the higher elevations—peaks in the Cascade Range, to the east, rise to nearly 10,000 feet. Klamath Falls lies technically a bit east of the Rogue Valley but shares the region's abundance of unspoiled wilderness and opportunities for getting in touch with nature.

GRANTS PASS

70 miles south of Roseburg on I–5.

"It's the Climate!" So says a confident 1950s vintage neon sign presiding over Josephine County's downtown. Grants Pass bills itself as Oregon's white-water capital: the Rogue River, preserved by Congress in 1968 as a National Wild and Scenic River, runs right through town. Downtown Grants Pass is a National Historic District, a stately little enclave of 19th-century brick storefronts housing a mix of folksy businesses harking back to the 1950s and newer, trendier cafés and boutiques. It's all that white water, however, that compels most visitors—and not a few moviemakers (*The River Wild* and *Rooster Cogburn* were both filmed here). If the river alone doesn't serve up enough natural drama, the sheer rock walls of nearby Hellgate Canyon rise 250 feet.

GETTING HERE AND AROUND

Grants Pass is easily reached from elsewhere in the region via Interstate 5, and it's also where U.S. 199 cuts southwest toward Oregon Caves National Monument and, eventually, the northernmost section of California's coast (as well as the northern sections of Redwood National Park). Many visitors to the southern Oregon coastline backtrack inland up U.S. 199 to create a scenic loop drive, ultimately intersecting with Interstate 5 at Grants Pass. Medford's airport is a 30-mile drive south.

ESSENTIALS

Visitor Information Grants Pass Tourism ✉ *198 S.W. G St.* ☎ *800/547–5927, 541/450–6180* ⊕ *www.visitgrantspass.org.*

EXPLORING

Fodor'sChoice ★ **Troon Vineyards.** Few winemakers in southern Oregon have generated more buzz than Troon, whose swank tasting room and winery is patterned after a French country villa. Troon produces relatively small yields of exceptional wines more typical of Sonoma than Oregon (Cabernet Sauvignon, Zinfandel, and Syrah are the heavy hitters), but they also plant less typical U.S. varietals, such as Viognier and Cabernet Franc. The winery is 14 miles southeast of downtown Grants Pass, in the northern edge of the Applegate Valley. ✉ *1475 Kubli Rd.* ☎ *541/846–9900* ⊕ *www.troonvineyard.com* ☾ *Late May–early Sept., daily 11–6; early Sept.–late May, daily 11–5.*

WHERE TO EAT

$ AMERICAN Fodor'sChoice ★ ✕ **Ma Mosa's.** Sustainability is the name of the game at this lively café spot in downtown Grants Pass, with a cozy dining room of colorfully painted tables and mismatched chairs, and a large adjacent patio with picnic tables and lush landscaping—it's pet-friendly out here, too. The kitchen sources from local farms and purveyors to create beer-battered fried chicken and waffles, kale Caesar salads, and line-caught-fish tacos with seasonal slaw and housemade salsa. Mimosa's are, as you might guess, a favorite drink throughout the day, and beer lover's will always find a few rotating taps of mostly Oregon craft brews. $ *Average main: $10* ✉ *118 N.W. E St.* ☎ *541/479–0236* ⊕ *www.mamosas. com* ☾ *Closed Mon. No dinner Tues.*

$$ MODERN AMERICAN ✕ **Roux 26.** Set in the handsome, vintage Grants Pass Steam Laundry building—a brick-red beauty with a light-filled, solarium-style dining room—this casually upscale neighborhood bistro and bar offers an extensive and eclectic menu of well-crafted modern American fare. Start things off, perhaps, with an order of the addictively good garlic truffle fries or the citrus-shrimp salad with heirloom cherry tomatoes, avocado, and cotija cheese. Worthy main dishes include several thin-crust pizzas, fettucine with spicy habanero chilis and smoked chicken, and the classic Southern favorite, shrimp-and-grits with tomato-corn salsa and house-chili oil. $ *Average main: $17* ✉ *234 S.W. 5th St.* ☎ *541/507–1234* ⊕ *www.roux26.com* ☾ *Closed Sun. and Mon.*

$ WINE BAR ✕ **Twisted Cork Wine Bar.** With a mission to showcase southern Oregon's fast-growing reputation for acclaimed vino, this dapper, art-filled space has lent a bit of urbane sophistication to downtown Grants Pass. In addition to pouring varietals from throughout the Umpqua and Rogue Valleys, Twisted Cork carries wines from more than 115 wineries throughout the Northwest, along with a few from California. The menu focuses on small plates ideal for sharing—fruit-and-cheese plates, cured meats—as well as creative and quite affordable larger plates, including pomegranate-cinnamon flank steak, ginger-glazed salmon, and wild-mushroom flatbread with butternut-mint hummus. There's a nice list of local ports, too. $ *Average main: $15* ✉ *210 S.W. 6th St.* ☎ *541/295–3094* ⊕ *www.thetwistedcorkgrantspass.com* ☾ *Closed Sun. and Mon.*

WHERE TO STAY

$ HOTEL **Lodge at Riverside.** The pool and many rooms overlook the Rogue River as it passes through downtown, and all but a few rooms, furnished with stylish country house–inspired armoires, plush beds, and

8

oil paintings, have private balconies or patios; suites have river-rock fireplaces and Jacuzzi tubs. **Pros:** central location; beautiful modern furnishings; attractively landscaped pool overlooks Rogue River. **Cons:** among the highest rates in town; no restaurant on-site. $ *Rooms from: $145* ✉ *955 S.E. 7th St.* ☎ *541/955–0600, 877/955–0600* ⊕ *www. thelodgeatriverside.com* ⟿ *29 rooms, 4 suites* ❙◎❙ *Breakfast.*

$$$ 🏨 **Weasku Inn.** Pacific Northwest–inspired art, handmade furnishings,
B&B/INN   and fine fabrics fill a rambling timber-frame home overlooking the
Fodor'sChoice   Rogue River, 11 handsomely outfitted cabins, and an A-frame bunga-
★   low to create the most luxurious accommodations between Ashland and Eugene. **Pros:** set directly on the Rogue River; impeccably decorated; fireplaces in many rooms. **Cons:** it's a 10-minute drive east of downtown; among the highest rates in the region. $ *Rooms from: $202* ✉ *5560 Rogue River Hwy.* ☎ *541/471–8000, 800/493–2758* ⊕ *www. weaskuinn.com* ⟿ *5 rooms, 12 cabins* ❙◎❙ *Breakfast.*

SPORTS AND THE OUTDOORS

RAFTING

Fodor'sChoice   More than a dozen outfitters guide white-water rafting trips along the
★   Rogue River in and around Grants Pass. In fact, this stretch of Class III rapids ranks among the best in the West. The rafting season lasts from about July through August and often into September, and the stretch of river running south from Grants Pass, with some 80 frothy rapids, is exciting but not treacherous, making it ideal for novices, families, and others looking simply to give this enthralling activity a try.

Orange Torpedo Trips. One of the most reliable operators on the Rogue River offers half-day to several-day trips, as well as relaxed dinner-and-wine float trips along a calmer stretch of river. ✉ *210 Merlin Rd., Merlin* ☎ *541/479–5061, 866/479–5061* ⊕ *www.orangetorpedo.com.*

Rogue River Raft Trips. If you're up for an adventure that combines rafting with overnight accommodations, consider booking one of these exciting excursions that run along a 44-mile stretch of the Rogue River. They last for four days and three nights, with options for both lodge and camping stays along the way. ✉ *8500 Galice Rd., Merlin* ☎ *800/826–1963, 541/476–3825* ⊕ *www.rogueriverraft.com.*

RECREATIONAL AREAS

Rogue River–Siskiyou National Forests, Grants Pass. In the Klamath Mountains and the Coast Range of southwestern Oregon, the 1.8-million-acre forest contains the 35-mile-long Wild and Scenic section of the Rogue River, which races through the Wild Rogue Wilderness Area, and the Illinois and Chetco Wild and Scenic Rivers, which run through the 180,000-acre Kalmiopsis Wilderness Area. Activities include white-water rafting, camping, and hiking, but many hiking areas require trail-park passes. ✉ *Off U.S. 199* ☎ *541/618–2200* ⊕ *www.fs.fed.us/r6/rogue-siskiyou.*

Valley of the Rogue State Park. A 1¼-mile hiking trail follows the bank of the Rogue, the river made famous by novelist and fisherman Zane Grey. There's a campground along 3 miles of shoreline with full RV hookups as well as yurts. There are picnic tables, walking trails, playgrounds, and restrooms. The park is 12 miles east of downtown Grants

Pass. ✉ *3792 N. River Rd., Gold Hill* ☎ *541/582–1118, 800/551–6949* ⊕ *www.oregonstateparks.org* ⊗ *Daily.*

MEDFORD

30 miles southeast of Grants Pass on I–5.

Medford is the professional, retail, trade, and service center for eight counties in southern Oregon and Northern California. As such, it offers more professional and cultural venues than might be expected for a city of its size (with a population of about 80,000). The workaday downtown has shown signs of gentrification and rejuvenation in recent years, and in the outskirts you'll find several major shopping centers and the famed fruit and gourmet-food mail-order company Harry & David.

Lodging tends to be cheaper in Medford than in nearby (and easily accessible) Ashland or Jacksonville, although cookie-cutter chain properties dominate the hotel landscape. It's also 71 miles southwest of Crater Lake and 80 miles northeast of the Oregon Caves, making it an affordable and convenient base for visiting either.

GETTING HERE AND AROUND

Medford is in the heart of the Rogue Valley on I–5, and is home to the state's third-largest airport, Rogue Valley International. A car is your best way to get around the city and surrounding area.

ESSENTIALS

Visitor Information Medford Visitors & Convention Bureau ✉ *1314 Center Dr.* ☎ *541/776–4021, 800/469–6307* ⊕ *www.visitmedford.org.*

EXPLORING

Butte Creek Mill. This 1872 water-powered gristmill, which is 12 miiles north of Medford, is listed in the National Historic Register and still produces whole-grain food products, which you can buy at the country store here. There's also a modest display of antiques. ✉ *402 Royal Ave. N, Central Point* ☎ *541/826–3531* ⊕ *www.buttecreekmill.com* ✎ *Free* ⊗ *Mon.–Sat. 9–5, Sun. 11–5.*

Crater Rock Museum. Jackson County's natural history and collections of the Roxy Ann Gem and Mineral Society are on display at this quirky, 12,000-square-foot museum in Central Point (6 miles northwest of Medford). Fossils, petrified wood, fluorescent rocks, and precious minerals from throughout Oregon and elsewhere in the West are included, plus works of glass by renowned artist Dale Chihuly. ✉ *2002 Scenic Ave., Central Point* ☎ *541/664–6081* ⊕ *www.craterrock.com* ✎ *$5* ⊗ *Tues.–Sat. 10–4.*

EdenVale Winery. Four miles southwest of downtown Medford amid a bucolic patch of fruit orchards, this winery and tasting room, called the Rogue Valley Wine Center, adjoins a rather grand 19th-century white-clapboard farmhouse surrounded by flower beds and vegetable gardens. Inside the tasting room you can sample and buy not only EdenVale's noted reds and late-harvest whites but also other respected labels from vineyards throughout the region. ✉ *2310 Voorhies Rd.* ☎ *541/512–2955* ⊕ *www.edenvalewines.com* ⊗ *Mar.–Oct., Mon.–Thurs. 11–6,*

Fri.–Sat. 11–7, Sun. 11–5; Nov.–Feb., Mon.–Thurs. 11–5, Fri.–Sat. noon–6, Sun. noon–4.

WHERE TO EAT AND STAY

$$
TAPAS

✗ **Elements Tapas Bar.** A touch of urbane sophistication and a taste of impressively authentic Spanish fare—these are the draws of this handsome tapas restaurant in downtown Medford's turn-of-the-20th-century "Goldy" building. Owner Chris Dennett set out to create a space that's fun for groups of friends, where sharing and conversation are encouraged. Pass around plates of mussels in romesco sauce, apricot-braised-pork empanadas, chorizo-studded Andalucian paella, and lamb-sausage flatbread, while sampling selections from the lengthy beer and cocktail menus. Food is served till at least 11 nightly, and there's a great Sunday brunch. ⓢ *Average main: $20* ✉ *101 E. Main St.* ☎ *541/779–0135* ⊕ *www.elementsmedford.com* ⊘ *No lunch.*

$
BURGER

✗ **Jaspers Cafe.** This cute road-house-style building a few miles northwest of downtown Medford has made a name for itself serving obscenely large, decadently topped, and deliciously crafted burgers. Polish off the Jasperado, wth chorizo, salsa verde, and a fried egg, and you probably won't be experiencing any hunger pains for the rest of the day—especially if you add a side of sweet potato fries or pork pot stickers. Veggie and game (from lamb to antelope to kangaroo) burgers are offered, too. Although potentially a dinner option, keep in mind that Jaspers closes between 6 and 8 pm, depending on the night of week. ⓢ *Average main: $7* ✉ *2739 N. Pacific Hwy.* ☎ *541/776–5307* ⊕ *www.jasperscafe.com.*

$
HOTEL

⌂ **Best Western Horizon Inn.** Convenient to downtown, Bear Creek Park, and the freeway, this midpriced, comfortable Best Western motel is set around a large outdoor pool and contains 122 rooms with tasteful blond-wood furniture, tan armchairs with ottomans, and decent-quality—if run-of-the-mill—bedding and towels. **Pros:** nice pool and fitness center for a midrange motel; central location; clean and updated room. **Cons:** cookie-cutter decor; on a busy road. ⓢ *Rooms from: $89* ✉ *1154 E. Barnett Rd.* ☎ *541/779–5085, 800/452–2255* ⊕ *www.bestwesternoregon.com* ⇆ *122 rooms* ⦿| *Breakfast.*

$
HOTEL

⌂ **Rodeway Inn–Medford.** If you're on a budget and seeking a simple and immaculately clean base camp, check into this friendly, family-run '50s vintage motor court on the city's south side. **Pros:** vintage charm; convenient to sights in Medford as well as Jacksonville and Ashland. **Cons:** few amenities and luxuries; rather dated (though that's part of the charm). ⓢ *Rooms from: $60* ✉ *901 S. Riverside Ave.* ☎ *541/776–9194, 877/424–6423* ⊕ *www.rodewayinn.com* ⇆ *40 rooms* ⦿| *Breakfast.*

NIGHTLIFE AND THE ARTS

Jefferson Spirits. This hip newcomer is helping to spur downtown Medford's ongoing renaissance by creating a sophisticated, stylish environment for hobnobbing and enjoying creative craft cocktails, like the locally inspired Rogue Pear, with whiskey, pear, and a splash of lemon juice. The owners have plans to develop their own microdistillery and will continue to carry a fine selection of premium booze, local and international wines, and mostly Oregon beers. ✉ *404 E. Main St.* ☎ *541/622–8190* ⊕ *www.jeffersonspirits.com.*

SPORTS AND THE OUTDOORS

FISHING

With close access to some of the best freshwater fishing venues in the Northwest, Medford has several companies that lead tours and provide gear.

Carson's Guide Service. Based 22 miles north of Medford along Highway 62 (going toward Crater Lake), Carson's provides expert instruction and knowledge of many of the area's rivers, including the Rogue, Umpqua, Coquille, Elk, and Chetco, as well as several lakes. Steelhead, salmon, shad, and smallmouth bass are the most common catches. ⊠ *595 Ragsdale Rd., Trail* ☎ *541/261–3279* ⊕ *www.fishwithcarson.com.*

HIKING

Fodor's Choice
★

Table Rock. One of the best venues for hiking in the Rogue Valley comprises a pair of monolithic rock formations that rise some 700 to 800 feet above the valley floor about 10 miles north of Medford and just a couple of miles north of TouVelle State Park. Operated by a partnership between the Bureau of Land Management and the Nature Conservancy, the Table Rock formations and surrounding 4,864 acres of wilderness afford panoramic valley views from their summits. You reach Lower Table Rock by way of a moderately challenging 2-mile trail, and Upper Table Rock via a shorter (1-mile) and less-steep route. The trailheads to these formations are a couple of miles apart—just follow the road signs from Table Rock Road, north of TouVelle State Park (reached from Exit 33 of Interstate 5). ⊠ *Off Table Rock Rd., Central Point* ☎ *541/618–2200* ⊕ *www.blm.gov.*

RAFTING

Medford is close to a number of the region's great white-water-rafting rivers, including the famed Rogue River. Both overnight and day trips are offered by several outfitters.

Rogue Klamath River Adventures. This popular outfitter for guided whitewater rafting trips as well as fishing adventures (for salmon and steelhead) throughout the area also offers boating excursions on inflatable kayaks. The company visits a great variety of waterways, from fairly gentle but scenic Class II rivers to wild and exciting Class V rapids. ☎ *541/779–3708, 800/231–0769* ⊕ *www.rogueklamath.com.*

RECREATIONAL AREAS

Rogue River–Siskiyou National Forest, Medford. Covering 2 million acres, this immense tract of wilderness woodland has fishing, swimming, hiking, and skiing. Motorized vehicles and equipment—even bicycles—are prohibited in the 113,000-acre Sky Lakes Wilderness, south of Crater Lake National Park. Its highest point is the 9,495-foot Mt. McLoughlin. Access to most of the forest is free, but there are fees at some trailheads. ⊠ *Off Hwy. 140* ☎ *541/618–2200* ⊕ *www.fs.fed.us/r6/rogue-siskiyou.*

OFF THE
BEATEN
PATH

Rogue River Views. Nature lovers who want to see the Rogue River at its loveliest can take a side trip to the Avenue of the Boulders, Mill Creek Falls, and Barr Creek Falls, off Highway 62, near Prospect, which is about 45 miles northeast of Medford—it's a scenic one-hour drive, and it's on the way to Crater Lake. Here the wild waters of the upper Rogue foam past volcanic boulders and the dense greenery of the Rogue River National Forest. ⊠ *Hwy. 62, Prospect.*

FAMILY   **Rogue Valley Family Fun Center.** You'll find an impressive array of kids' games and recreation at this complex just off Exit 33 of Interstate 5 (about 5 miles north of Medford). Miniature golf, batting cages, a golf driving range, bumper boats, and go-karts are among the offerings, and there's also a video arcade and game room. ⊠ *1A Peninger Rd., Central Point* ☎ *541/664–4263* ⊕ *www.rvfamilyfuncenter.com.*

SHOPPING

Harry & David. Famous for their holiday gift baskets, Harry & David is based in Medford and offers hour-long tours of its huge facility on weekdays at 9:15, 10:30, 12:30, and 1:45. The tours cost $5 per person, but the fee is refunded if you spend a minimum of $40 in the mammoth Harry & David store, great for snagging picnic supplies to carry with you on any winery tour. Reservations are recommended, as space is limited. ⊠ *1314 Center Dr.* ☎ *541/864–2278, 877/322–8000* ⊕ *www. harryanddavid.com.*

Fodor'sChoice   **Lillie Belle Farms.** Next door to Rogue River Creamery, this artisan choc-
★   olatier handcrafts outstanding chocolates using local, often organic ingredients. A favorite treat is the Smokey Blue Cheese ganache made with Rogue River blue, but don't overlook the dark-chocolate–mari-onberry bonbons (made with organic marionberries grown on-site) or the delectable hazelnut chews. Most unusual, however, is the chocolate-covered bacon. Yes, you read that correctly—the bacon is coated in chipotle and brown sugar, hand-dipped in chocolate, and sprinkled with sea salt. ⊠ *211 N. Front St., Central Point* ☎ *541/664–2815* ⊕ *www. lilliebellefarms.com.*

Fodor'sChoice   **Rogue Creamery.** Just a few miles up the road from Medford in the little
★   town of Central Point, you'll find one of the nation's most respected cheese makers, started in 1935 by Italian immigrants. Current owners Cary Bryant and David Gremmels bought the company in 2002, and promptly won one of the highest honors for cheese making, the London World Cheese Award. You can purchase any of the company's stellar cheeses here, from Smokey Blue to a lavender-infused cheddar, and you can watch the production through a window on most days. There's a wine-tasting room that carries vintages by a few local vineyards; the best nearby place to enjoy a picnic is the small neighborhood park a few blocks north at Laurel and North 6th streets. ⊠ *311 N. Front St., Central Point* ☎ *541/664–1537, 866/396–4704* ⊕ *www.roguecreamery.com.*

JACKSONVILLE

5 miles west of Medford on Hwy. 238.

This perfectly preserved town founded in the frenzy of the 1851 gold rush has served as the backdrop for several western flicks. It's easy to see why. Jacksonville is one of only eight towns corralled into the National Register of Historic Places lock, stock, and barrel. These days, living-history exhibits offering a glimpse of pioneer life and the world-renowned Britt Festivals of classical, jazz, and pop music are the draw, rather than gold. Trails winding up from the town's center lead to the festival amphitheater, mid-19th-century gardens, exotic madrona groves, and an intriguing pioneer cemetery.

GETTING HERE AND AROUND

Most visitors to Jacksonville come by way of Medford, 5 miles east, on Highway 238—it's a scenic drive over hilly farmland and past vineyards. Alternatively, you can reach the town coming the other way on Highway 238, driving southeast from Grants Pass. This similarly beautiful drive through the Applegate Valley takes about 45 minutes.

ESSENTIALS

Visitor Information Jacksonville Visitor Center ⌂ *185 N. Oregon St.* ☎ *541/899–8118* ⊕ *www.jacksonvilleoregon.org.*

EXPLORING

FAMILY

Fodor'sChoice

★

Jacksonville Cemetery. A trip up the winding road—or, better yet, a hike via the old cart track marked Catholic access—leads to the resting place of the clans (the Britts, the Beekmans, and the Orths) that built Jacksonville. You'll also get a fascinating, if sometimes unattractive, view of the social dynamics of the Old West: older graves (the cemetery is still in use) are strictly segregated, Irish Catholics from Jews from Protestants. A somber granite plinth marks the pauper's field, where those who found themselves on the losing end of gold-rush economics entered eternity anonymously. The cemetery closes at sundown. ⌂ *Oregon St., follow signs from downtown* ☎ *541/826–9939* ⊕ *www. friendsjvillecemetery.org.*

Valley View Vineyard. Perched on a bench in the scenic Applegate Valley, you can sample acclaimed Chardonnay, Viognier, Rousanne, Merlot, Tempranillo, Pinot Noir, and Cabernet Franc while soaking up some of the best views in southern Oregon. The valley's especially sunny, warm climate produces highly acclaimed vintages. Founded in the 1850s by pioneer Peter Britt, the vineyard was reestablished in 1972. A restored pole barn houses the winery and tasting room. ⌂ *1000 Upper Applegate Rd., 10 miles southwest of downtown* ☎ *541/899–8468, 800/781–9463* ⊕ *www.valleyviewwinery.com* ⊙ *Daily 11–5.*

WHERE TO EAT AND STAY

$$

SOUTHERN

✕**Back Porch Bar & Grill.** For an excellent, midpriced alternative to Jacksonville's more upscale eateries, head to this roadhouse-style clapboard building six blocks northeast of the town's historic main drag. Authentic central Texas–style barbecue is served here: char-grilled red-hot sausage, slow-cooked pork ribs, chicken-fried steak, and ½-pound burgers, plus a few dishes to remind you that you're in Oregon, including wild local salmon baked with Cajun spices. ⑤ *Average main: $18* ⌂ *605 N. 5th St.* ☎ *541/899–8821* ⊕ *www.backporchbbqinc.com.*

$$

PACIFIC

NORTHWEST

✕**Déjà Vu Bistro.** This classy but unpretentious wine bar and bistro resides inside downtown Jacksonville's historic McCully House Gardens inn. Chef Bill Prahl is a strong adherent of using seasonal ingredients. Some notable dishes that reflect his talent and philosophy include a summertime starter of pan-roasted Brussels sprouts, heirloom cherry tomatoes, crumbled goat cheese, and balsamic, and the entrée of coffee-rubbed flat-iron steak with local green beans, roasted red potatoes, and stone-ground mustard sauce. The natty wine bar makes an inviting spot for a pre-dinner sip. $ *Average main: $20* ✉ *240 E. California St.* ☎ *541/899–1942* ⊕ *www.dejavubistrowinebar.com* ⊗ *Closed Mon. and Tues. No lunch.*

$$$ ✕ **Gogi's.** Many visitors overlook this small, low-key restaurant just
ECLECTIC   down the hill from Britt Gardens—it's a favorite of foodies and locals,
Fodor'sChoice   and word is out about the artful presentation and innovative style of
★   chef-owner Gabriel Murphy's sophisticated international cuisine. The menu changes regularly, but has featured a tower of roasted beets and chèvre topped with toasted walnuts and a balsamic-truffle reduction, followed by prosciutto-wrapped quail with cauliflower, asparagus, and roasted mushrooms. The wine list is small but discerning. If you're in town on a Sunday, do not miss the super brunch. $ *Average main: $26* ✉ *235 W. Main St.* ☎ *541/899–8699* ⊕ *www.gogisrestaurant.com* ⊗ *Closed Mon. and Tues. No lunch Wed.–Sat.*

$$ ⌂ **Jacksonville Inn.** The spotless pioneer period antiques and the wealth
B&B/INN   of well-chosen amenities (fireplaces, saunas, whirlpool tubs, double steam showers) at this 1861-vintage inn evoke what the Wild West might have been had Martha Stewart been in charge. **Pros:** in heart of downtown historic district; one of the town's most historically significant buildings; very good restaurant on-site. **Cons:** rather old-fashioned decor for some tastes. $ *Rooms from: $159* ✉ *175 E. California St.* ☎ *541/899–1900, 800/321–9344* ⊕ *www.jacksonvilleinn.com* ⇋ *8 rooms, 4 cottages* ❧ *Breakfast.*

$ ⌂ **TouVelle House B&B.** This six-bedroom inn set inside a grand 1916
B&B/INN   Craftsman-style home a few blocks north of Jacksonville's tiny com-
Fodor'sChoice   mercial strip manages that tricky balance between exquisite and comfy.
★   **Pros:** situated on a gentle bluff surrounded by beautiful gardens; downtown dining is a 5-minute walk away; knowledgeable and friendly hosts. **Cons:** a couple of rooms require climbing two flights of stairs to third floor. $ *Rooms from: $135* ✉ *455 N. Oregon St.* ☎ *541/899–8938, 800/846–8422* ⊕ *www.touvellehouse.com* ⇋ *6 rooms* ❧ *Breakfast.*

SHOPPING

Jacksonville's historic downtown has several engaging galleries, boutiques, and gift shops. It's best just to stroll along California Street and its cross streets to get a sense of the retail scene.

Jacksonville Barn Co. This colorful shop specializes in both antiques and contemporary home decor, from Victorian pieces that have come from many nearby estates to modern garden accessories and country-house furnishings. ✉ *150 S. Oregon St.* ☎ *541/702–0307* ⊕ *www.jacksonvillebarnco.com.*

Jacksonville Mercantile. The racks of this gourmet-food store abound with sauces, oils, vinegars, jams, and tapenades. Watch for Lillie Belle Farms lavender–sea salt caramels, and the shop's own private-label Merlot-wine jelly. ✉ *120 E. California St.* ☎ *541/899–1047* ⊕ *www.jacksonvillemercantile.com.*

Ashland's Main Street

ASHLAND

20 miles southeast of Jacksonville and 14 miles southeast of Medford on I–5.

As you walk Ashland's twisting hillside streets, it seems like every house is a restored Victorian operating as an upscale B&B, though that's not nearly all there is to this town: the Oregon Shakespeare Festival attracts thousands of theater lovers to the Rogue Valley every year, from late February to early November (though tourists don't start showing up en masse until June). That influx means that Ashland is more geared toward the arts, more eccentric, and more expensive than its size (about 21,000 people) might suggest. The mix of well-heeled theater tourists, bohemian students from Southern Oregon University, and dramatic show folk imbues the town with some one-of-a-kind cultural frissons. The stage isn't the only show in town—skiing at Mt. Ashland and the town's reputation as a secluded getaway and growing culinary destination keep things hopping year-round.

GETTING HERE AND AROUND

Ashland is the first town you'll reach on Interstate 5 if driving north from California, and it's the southernmost community in this region. You can also get here from Klamath Falls by driving west on winding but dramatic Highway 66. Cascade Airport Shuttle offers door-to-door service from the airport to Ashland for about $30 to $35. A car isn't necessary to explore downtown and to get among many of the inns and restaurants, but it is helpful if you're planning to venture farther afield or visit more than one town, which most visitors do.

ESSENTIALS

Visitor Information **Ashland Chamber of Commerce and Visitors Informa-tion Center** ⊠ *110 E. Main St.* ☏ *541/482–3486* ⊕ *www.ashlandchamber.com.*

EXPLORING

Fodor'sChoice **Lithia Park.** The Elizabethan Theatre overlooks this park, a 93-acre jewel
★ that is Ashland's physical and psychological anchor. The park is named for the town's mineral springs, which supply a water fountain by the band shell as well as a fountain on the town plaza—be warned that the slightly bubbly water has a strong and rather disagreeable taste. Whether thronged with colorful hippie folk and picnickers on a summer evening or buzzing with joggers and dog walkers in the morning, Lithia is a well-used, well-loved, and well-tended spot. On summer weekend mornings the park plays host to a '60s-ish artisans' market. Each June the Oregon Shakespeare Festival opens its outdoor season by hosting the Feast of Will in the park, with music, dancing, bagpipes, and food. Tickets ($15) are available through the festival box office (☏ *541/482–4331* ⊕ *www.osfashland.org*). ⊠ *W. Fork and S. Pioneer Sts.* ⊕ *www.ashland.or.us.*

Schneider Museum of Art. At the edge of the Southern Oregon University campus, this museum includes a light-filled gallery devoted to special exhibits by Oregon, West Coast, and international artists. The permanent collection has grown considerably over the years, and includes pre-Columbian ceramics and works by such notables as Alexander Calder, George Inness, and David Alfaro Siqueiros. Hallways and galleries throughout the rest of the 66,000-square-foot complex display many works by students and faculty. ⊠ *1250 Siskiyou Blvd.* ☏ *541/552–6245* ⊕ *www.sou.edu/sma* ⊡ *$5* ⊙ *Mon.–Sat. 10–4.*

Weisinger's Winery. Although downtown Ashland has wine bars and tasting rooms, the only major winery of note here is Weisinger's, which set up shop in 1988 and is set a few miles south of town on a hilltop with broad views of the surrounding mountains. Specialties here include a fine Cabernet Franc, a well-respected Petit Blanc, and a nicely balanced Tempranillo. ⊠ *3150 Siskiyou Blvd.* ☏ *541/488–5989, 800/551–9463* ⊕ *www.weisingers.com* ⊙ *May–Sept., daily 11–6; Oct.–Apr., Wed.–Sun. 11–5.*

WHERE TO EAT

$$$ ✕ **Alchemy.** Meticulous attention to detail, with regard both to prepa-
PACIFIC ration and presentation, are hallmarks of this refined contemporary
NORTHWEST Pacific Northwest restaurant inside the plush Winchester Inn, just a
Fodor'sChoice few blocks from the Shakespeare Festival theaters. Typically artful cre-
★ ations from the seasonal menu include a starter of goat cheese gnocchi seared in brown butter with chorizo and mint-compressed apricots, and a tender 14-day dry-aged Oregon filet mignon cooked *sous vide* and sunchoke purée, sautéed root vegetables, and a radish–watercress–Serrano ham salad. Alchemy serves only dinner and a well-attended Sunday brunch, where you might try a hash of duck confit, sunnyside-up egg, crispy fingerling potatoes, and cranberry-citrus cream sauce. Additionally, lighter fare—flatbread pizzas, pork-belly burgers, baked Brie with onion-fennel jam and bourbon-orange marmalade—are offered in the more casual bistro. ⑤ *Average main: $28* ⊠ *Winchester Inn, 35 S. 2nd*

St. ☎ 541/488–1115 ⊕ *www.alchemyashland.com* ⊙ *Closed Mon.–Tues. No lunch Wed.–Sat.*

$$$
ECLECTIC
Fodor's Choice
★

✕**Amuse.** Northwest-driven French cuisine here is infused with seasonal, organic meat and produce. Chef-owners Erik Brown and Jamie North prepare a daily-changing menu. You might sample braised cheek and grilled tenderloin of pork with herb spaetzle, Savoy cabbage, and pomegranate molasses, or truffle-roasted game hen with kale and tarragon jus. Try your best to save room for the warm hazelnut crepes filled with banana ganache and topped with brandy whipped cream. If you're craving pastries during the day, stop by the sister establishment, Mix Sweet Shop, a few blocks away on North Main Street. ⓢ *Average main: $28* ⊠ *15 N. 1st St.* ☎ 541/488–9000 ⊕ *www.amuserestaurant. com* ⊙ *Closed Mon. and Tues. No lunch.*

$
AMERICAN
Fodor's Choice
★

✕**Morning Glory.** Breakfast reaches new heights in an eclectically furnished, blue Craftsman-style bungalow across the street from Southern Oregon University. The extraordinarily good food emphasizes breakfast fare—omelets filled with crab, artichokes, Parmesan, and smoked-garlic cream; Tandoori tofu scrambles with cherry-cranberry chutney; lemon-poppy waffles with seasonal berries; and cranberry-hazelnut French toast with lemon butter. Expect a wait on weekend mornings, especially for a table on the good-weather patio; it's first-come, first-served. ⓢ *Average main: $11* ⊠ *1149 Siskiyou Blvd.* ☎ 541/488–8636 ⌔ *Reservations not accepted* ⊙ *No dinner.*

$$
MODERN
AMERICAN

✕**Peerless Restaurant & Bar.** This cosmopolitan, neighborhood bistro and wine bar anchors the up-and-coming Railroad District, on the north side of downtown, just a few blocks from Main Street and the Shakespeare theaters. It's adjacent to the Peerless Hotel, a stylish little property with the same creative spirit and hipster vibe of the restaurant. Regulars here come as much for the well-crafted cocktails and thoughtful wine list as for the consistently tasty locally sourced American food. Start with the Manila clams in a broth of pernod, garlic confit, and smoked bacon, before tucking into a plate of sage-rubbed roast chicken, or baked ziti with sweet corn, chunks of lobster, and three cheeses. Desserts are the one spendy item on the menu, but they're delicious, too. ⓢ *Average main: $19* ⊠ *265 4th St.* ☎ 541/488–6067 ⊕ *www.peerlesshotel.com* ⊙ *Closed Sun. and Mon. No lunch.*

WHERE TO STAY

The Oregon Shakespeare Festival has stimulated one of the most extensive networks of B&Bs in the Northwest—more than 25 in all. High season for Ashland-area bed-and-breakfasts is between June and October.

Ashland B&B Network. The network provides referrals and has an online booking system for about two dozen of the town's top inns. ⊕ *www.stayashland.com.*

$$$
B&B/INN

▢ **Ashland Creek Inn.** Every plush suite in this converted mill has a geographic theme—the Normandy is outfitted with rustic country French prints and furniture, while Moroccan, Danish, and New Mexican motifs are among the designs in other units—and each sitting room–bedroom combo has its own entrance, a full kitchen or kitchenette, and a deck just inches from burbling Ashland Creek. **Pros:** exceptionally good breakfasts; peaceful but central location; enormous suites. **Cons:** spendy for this part of the state; limited common areas. ⑤ *Rooms from: $245 ✉ 70 Water St.* ☎ *541/482–3315* ⊕ *www.ashlandcreekinn.com* ➟ *10 suites* ¦⊙¦ *Breakfast.*

$$
HOTEL
🏨 **Ashland Springs Hotel.** Ashland's stately 1925 landmark hotel towers seven stories over the center of downtown, with 70 rooms done with a preponderance of gentle fall colors and unconventional decor—think French-inspired botanical-print quilts and lampshades with leaf designs. **Pros:** rich with history; upper floors have dazzling mountain views; the excellent Larks restaurant is on-site. **Cons:** central location translates to some street noise and bustle; some rooms are on the small side. ⑤ *Rooms from: $199 ✉ 212 E. Main St.* ☎ *541/488–1700, 888/795–4545* ⊕ *www.ashlandspringshotel.com* ➟ *70 rooms* ¦⊙¦ *Breakfast.*

$$
B&B/INN
Fodor's Choice
★
🏨 **Chanticleer Inn.** At this courtly, 1920 Craftsman-style bed-and-breakfast, owner Ellen Campbell has given the rooms a tasteful, contemporary flair with muted, nature-inspired colors and Arts and Crafts furnishings and patterns. **Pros:** rooms all have expansive views of the Cascade Mountains; only eco-friendly products are used. **Cons:** it's intimate and homey, so fans of larger and more anonymous lodgings may prefer a bigger inn or hotel. ⑤ *Rooms from: $160 ✉ 120 Gresham St.* ☎ *541/482–1919, 800/898–1950* ⊕ *www.ashland-bed-breakfast.com* ➟ *6 rooms* ¦⊙¦ *Breakfast.*

$$$
B&B/INN
FAMILY
🏨 **The Winchester Inn.** These rooms and suites have character and restful charm—some have fireplaces, refrigerators, and wet bars, and private exterior entrances, and most are well-suited to having one or two children in the room. **Pros:** the adjacent Alchemy wine bar and restaurant serve outstanding international fare; one of the more child-friendly B&Bs in town; surrounded by lush gardens. **Cons:** among the more expensive lodgings in town. ⑤ *Rooms from: $225 ✉ 35 S. 2nd St.* ☎ *541/488–1113, 800/972–4991* ⊕ *www.winchesterinn.com* ➟ *11 rooms, 8 suites* ¦⊙¦ *Breakfast.*

NIGHTLIFE AND THE ARTS

With its presence of college students, theater types, and increasing numbers of tourists (many of them fans of local wine), Ashland has developed quite a festive nightlife scene. Much of the activity takes place at bars inside some of downtown's more reputable restaurants in the center of town.

Fodor's Choice
★
Caldera Tap House. In addition to operating a full-service restaurant at their brewing facility out at 590 Clover Lane, just off Interstate 5, exit 14, this highly acclaimed Ashland craft-beer maker with wide distribution throughout the Northwest also has this tap room downtown. Here you can sample the signature Hopportunity Knocks IPA, Old Growth Imperial Stout, and an extensive selection of tasty apps, burgers, and pub fare. ✉ *31 Water St.* ☎ *541/482–7468* ⊕ *www.calderabrewing.com.*

Tabu. This Nuevo Latino restaurant keeps busy with revelers into the later hours. Live comedy, reggae, salsa, and other entertainment takes place most Thursday through Saturday nights. ✉ *76 N. Pioneer St.* ☎ *541/482–3900* ⊕ *www.tabuashland.com.*

SPORTS AND THE OUTDOORS
MULTISPORT OUTFITTERS

Adventure Center. This respected Ashland company offers "mild to wild" outdoor expeditions, including white-water rafting, fishing, and bike excursions. ⊠ *40 N. Main St.* ☎ *541/488–2819, 800/444–2819* ⊕ *www. raftingtours.com.*

RAFTING

Noah's River Adventures. This long-running outfitter provides white-water rafting and wilderness fishing trips throughout the region—the company can lead single- or multiple-day adventures along the mighty Rogue River as well as just across the border, in Northern California, on the Salmon and Scott Rivers. ⊠ *53 N. Main St.* ☎ *800/858–2811* ⊕ *www.noahsrafting.com.*

SKIING

Mt. Ashland Ski Area. This winter-sports playground in the Siskiyou Mountains is halfway between San Francisco and Portland. The ski runs average more than 280 inches of snow each year. There are 23 trails, virtually all of them intermediate and advanced, in addition to chute skiing in a glacial cirque called the bowl. Two triple and two double chairlifts accommodate a vertical drop of 1,150 feet; the longest of the runs is 1 mile. Facilities include rentals, repairs, instruction, a ski shop, a restaurant, and a bar. A couple of days a week, usually Thursday and Friday, there's also lighted twilight skiing until 9 pm. Anytime of year the drive up the twisting road to the ski area is incredibly scenic, affording views of 14,162-foot Mt. Shasta, some 90 miles south in California. ⊠ *Mt. Ashland Access Rd., off Exit 6 from I–5, 18 miles southwest of downtown* ☎ *541/482–2897* ⊕ *www.mtashland. com* ⊑ *Lift ticket $46* ⊙ *Nov.–Apr., daily 9–4; twilight skiing, Jan.–mid-Mar., Thurs. and Fri. 3–9.*

SHOPPING

Dagoba Organic Chocolate. A few miles' drive south of town you'll find the retail outlet of this company that produces those small, handsomely packed, superfine chocolate bars sold in fancy-food shops and groceries throughout the country. Although Hershey Company now owns the company, Dagoba was founded in Ashland, and its operation remains here, where a small retail shop—open weekdays only—sells its goods. ⊠ *1105 Benson St.* ☎ *866/608–6944* ⊕ *www.dagobachocolate.com.*

KLAMATH FALLS

65 miles east of Ashland via Hwy. 66; 75 miles east of Medford via Hwy. 140.

Often overlooked by visitors traveling the Interstate 5 corridor, the greater Klamath Falls area is one of the most beautiful parts of Oregon. The small (about 20,000 people), if not especially exciting, city of Klamath Falls stands at an elevation of 4,100 feet, on the southern shore of Upper Klamath Lake. The highest elevation in Klamath County is the peak of Mt. Scott, at 8,926 feet. There are more than 82 lakes and streams in Klamath County, including Upper Klamath Lake, which covers 133 square miles.

The Klamath Basin, with its six national wildlife refuges, hosts the largest wintering concentration of bald eagles in the contiguous United States and the largest concentration of migratory waterfowl on the continent. Each February nature enthusiasts from around the world flock here for the Winter Wings Festival, the nation's oldest birding festival.

The Nature Conservancy has called the basin a Western Everglades, because it is the largest wetland area west of the Mississippi. But humans have significantly damaged the ecosystem through farming and development. More than 25% of vertebrate species in the area are now endangered or threatened. As recently as the 1980s, about 6 million birds used the area every year; today that number is down to 2 to 3 million. Environmental organizations are working to reverse some of the damage.

GETTING HERE AND AROUND

Klamath Falls lies along U.S. 97, one of the Northwest's main north–south routes—it's a prime stop between Bend, 140 miles north, and Weed, California, about 70 miles south. You can also get here from the Rogue Valley, either by way of Highway 66 from Ashland or Highway 140 from Medford, which is home to the nearest airport (about a 90-minute drive).

ESSENTIALS

Visitor Information Discover Klamath ⊠ *205 Riverside Dr.* ☎ *541/882–1501, 800/445–6728* ⊕ *www.discoverklamath.com.*

EXPLORING

Fodor'sChoice ★ **Klamath Basin National Wildlife Refuge Complex.** As many as 1,000 bald eagles make Klamath Basin their rest stop, amounting to the largest wintering concentration of these birds in the contiguous United States. Located along the Pacific Flyway bird migration route, the nearly 40,000 acres of freshwater wetlands in the refuge complex serve as a stopover for nearly 1 million waterfowl in the fall. Any time of year is bird-watching season; more than 400 species of birds—including about 15 types of raptors—have been spotted in the Klamath Basin. For a leisurely ramble by car take the tour routes in the Lower Klamath and Tule Lake Refuges. There's a superb bookstore at the visitor center. ⊠ *Visitor Center, 4009 Hill Rd., 27 miles south of Klamath Falls via Hwy. 39, Tulelake, California* ☎ *530/667–2231* ⊕ *www.fws.gov/refuge/ Tule_Lake* ⊡ *Free* ⊙ *Visitor center: weekdays 8–4:30, weekends 9–4.*

WHERE TO EAT AND STAY

$$
AMERICAN
✕ **Basin Martini Bar.** Although the name of this swell-elegant storefront spot in the heart of the downtown historic district suggests an option for evening cocktails, the bar is just as well regarded for its reliably tasty dinner fare—New York strip steaks, burgers topped with Crater Lake blue cheese, and bacon-wrapped scallops are among the highlights. There's seating in a handful of comfy booths or at stools along the modern bar. The creative drinks are notable, too—consider the lemon-basil martini. ⑤ *Average main: $17* ⊠ *632 Main St.* ☎ *541/884–6264* ⊙ *No lunch.*

$$
RESORT
FAMILY
⊡ **Running Y Ranch Resort.** Golfers rave about the Arnold Palmer–designed course at this 3,600-acre Holiday Inn resort situated in a juniper-and-ponderosa–shaded canyon overlooking Upper Klamath Lake. **Pros:** kids enjoy an indoor pool; walkers and joggers have 8

miles of paved trails. **Cons:** may be a bit too far off the beaten path for some. ⑤ *Rooms from: $154* ✉ *5500 Running Y Rd., 8 miles north of Klamath Falls, Klamath Falls* ☎ *541/850–5500, 800/569–0029* ⊕ *www. runningy.com* ⌁ *82 rooms, 43 houses* ⦿ *No meals.*

SPORTS AND THE OUTDOORS

MULTISPORT OUTFITTERS

The Ledge Outdoor Store. For advice, gear, clothing, books, and maps for hiking, birding, mountaineering, canoeing, camping, and fishing throughout the area, visit this extensively stocked shop in downtown Klamath Falls, which carries all kinds of equipment, and also offers guided fly-fishing trips. ✉ *369 S. 6th St.* ☎ *541/882–5586.*

BOATING

Birding & Boating. For a chance to enjoy the beauty of Klamath Lake while also observing the region's abundant birdlife, rent a sailboat, canoe, or kayak from this outfit with a prime spot on the lake and a staff that can offer expert advice on wildlife-viewing. You can also fish from a dock on the lake. ✉ *658 Front St.* ☎ *541/885–5450* ⊕ *www. birdingandboating.com.*

CAVE JUNCTION

30 miles southwest of Grants Pass via U.S. 199, 60 miles west of Jacksonville via Hwy. 238 and U.S. 199.

One of the least populated and most pristine parts of southern Oregon, the town of Cave Junction and the surrounding Illinois Valley attract outdoors enthusiasts of all kinds for hiking, backpacking, camping, fishing, and hunting. Expect rugged terrain and the chance to view some of the tallest Douglas fir trees in the state. Other than those passing through en route from Grants Pass to the Northern California coast via U.S. 199, most visitors come here to visit the Oregon Caves National Monument, one of the world's only marble caves (formed by erosion from acidic rainwater). Sleepy Cave Junction makes an engaging little base camp, its main drag lined with a handful of quirky shops, short-order restaurants, and gas stations.

GETTING HERE AND AROUND

Cave Junction lies along U.S. 199, the main road leading from Grants Pass. You can also reach Cave Junction by heading west from Jacksonville on Highway 238 to U.S. 199. From Cave Junction, head east on Highway 46 to reach Oregon Caves National Monument. Cave Junction is about a 75-minute drive southwest of Medford's regional airport. Alternatively, the small airport (served by United Airlines, with service from San Francisco) in Crescent City, California, is the same distance.

ESSENTIALS

Visitor Information Illinois Valley Chamber of Commerce ✉ *201 Caves Hwy. (Hwy. 46), just off U.S. 199* ☎ *541/592–3326* ⊕ *www.cavejunction.com.*

EXPLORING

Bridgeview Vineyard and Winery. The producers of the well-distributed and reasonably priced Blue Moon wines (known especially for Riesling, Chardonnay, Pinot Gris, and Merlot), as well as more premium vintages such as Black Beauty Syrah and a very nice reserve Pinot Noir, established the winery in 1986, and—despite considerable skepticism from observers—have gone on to tremendous success. There's a second tasting room, open summer only, in the Applegate Valley, near Grants Pass. ⊠ *4210 Holland Loop Rd.* ☎ *541/592–4688, 877/273–4843* ⊕ *www. bridgeviewwine.com* ☉ *Daily 11–4.*

Fodor'sChoice **Oregon Caves National Monument.** Marble caves, large calcite formations,
★ and huge underground rooms shape this rare adventure in geology. Guided cave tours take place on the hour in late spring and fall, and every half hour June through August. The 90-minute half-mile tour is moderately strenuous with low passageways, twisting turns, and more than 500 stairs; children must be at least 42 inches tall to go on the tour. Cave tours aren't given in winter. Aboveground, the surrounding valley holds an old-growth forest with some of the state's largest trees. ⚠ **Park officials say that GPS coordinates for the caves often direct drivers onto a mostly unpaved forest service road meant for four-wheel-drive vehicles. Instead, follow Highway 46 off U.S. 199 at Cave Junction, which is also narrow and twisty in parts; RVs or trailers over 32 feet not advised.** ⊠ *19000 Caves Hwy. (Hwy. 46), 20 miles east of U.S. 199* ☎ *541/592–2100* ⊕ *www.nps.gov/orca* ✉ *Entrance to park, free; tours $8.50* ☉ *Late Apr.–late May, and mid-Oct.–early Nov., daily 10–4; late May–early Sept., daily 9–6; early Sept.–mid-Oct., daily 9–4.*

WHERE TO STAY

$ ⊡ **Oregon Caves Chateau.** This six-story wood-frame lodge, virtually
HOTEL   unchanged since it was built in 1934, has a rustic authenticity and steep
FAMILY   gabled roofs, while the simple rooms, all with their original furnishings, have canyon or waterfall views. **Pros:** on the grounds of the national monument; historic and funky personality; wonderfully tranquil setting. **Cons:** no-frills rooms; no Internet or phones (and very limited cell reception); location well out of the way if you aren't visiting the caves. ⑤ *Rooms from: $109* ⊠ *20000 Caves Hwy.* ☎ *541/592–3400, 877/245–9022* ⊕ *www.oregoncaveschateau.com* ⇲ *23 rooms* ☉ *Closed Oct.–mid-May* ⑩ *No meals.*

$ ⊡ **Out 'n' About.** You sleep among the leaves in the tree houses of this
B&B/INN   extraordinary resort—the highest is 37 feet from the ground, one has
FAMILY   an antique claw-foot bath, and another has separate kids' quarters connected to the main room by a swinging bridge. **Pros:** kids love the Swiss Family Robinson atmosphere; it truly feels at one with the surrounding old-growth forest; amazingly quiet and peaceful. **Cons:** accommodations are extremely rustic; some units don't have bathrooms; two-night minimum during week and three-night minimum weekends during spring to fall. ⑤ *Rooms from: $120* ⊠ *300 Page Creek Rd.* ☎ *541/592–2208* ⊕ *www.treehouses.com* ⇲ *15 tree houses, 1 cabin* ⑩ *Breakfast.*

EASTERN
OREGON

WELCOME TO EASTERN OREGON

TOP REASONS TO GO

★ **Wallowa wonder:** The usually snowcapped peaks of the Wallowa Range ornament one of the West's most overlooked alpine playgrounds, with Wallowa Lake resting at its base and Hells Canyon beckoning nearby.

★ **Time travel:** See architecture from Oregon's mining-era heyday in Baker City's authentically restored downtown, where a short walking tour takes you past more than 100 historic buildings, many of which now contain indie boutiques and cafés.

★ **For the birds:** Visit countless feathered friends at the ruggedly idyllic Malheur National Wildlife Refuge.

★ **Let 'er buck:** Pendleton's famous rodeo attracts 50,000 people every September, but the cowboy mystique sticks around all year.

★ **Rugged seclusion:** Oregon doesn't get more remote than around stunning Steens Mountain.

1 East Gorge. Near the majestic Colombia River Gorge, the high plains around Umatilla and Pendleton are the heart of Oregon's ranching and agricultural communities. "Let 'er buck!" is the rallying cry at the hugely popular Pendleton Round-Up rodeo, a phrase that sets the tone for the whole region's rootin', tootin' vibe.

2 Northeast Oregon. The superlative Wallowa and Blue Mountains dominate this corner of the state. Both ranges attract bands of hikers, mountain bikers, and other adventure types. In former frontier towns like Joseph and Baker City, old-school ranchers and cowboys mingle with a swelling population of artisans, foodies, and creative spirits.

3 Southeast Oregon. The sprawling, scrubby ranchlands of Oregon's high desert country have a beauty all their own, and give way when you least expect it to majestic river canyons and stunning vistas. Food and lodging can be scarce out here, but outdoor enthusiasts and adventurous family travelers will be rewarded with scenic backcountry roads, serene hot springs, and small-town hospitality.

GETTING ORIENTED

At its eastern end, Oregon begins in a high, sage-scented desert plateau that covers nearly two-thirds of the state's 96,000 square miles. To the north, the border with Washington follows the Colombia River, then stretches eastward across the Colombia River Plateau to meet the Snake River, itself forming much of the state's eastern border with Idaho. East-central Oregon is carved out by the forks and tributaries of the John Day River, the country's third-largest undammed waterway. Its north–south course to the Columbia marks an invisible line extending southward, separating eastern Oregon from central Oregon's high plateaus and Cascade foothills. To the south, the Nevada border is an invisible line slicing through a high, desolate region sometimes known as the Oregon outback—it's one of the most sparsely settled areas in the Lower 48 states.

WASHINGTON Umatilla
NWR
Umatilla
Hat Rock
State Park
Boardman
Echo
Hermiston
Walla Walla
Milton-
Freewater
Umatilla
National
Forest
3
11
204
Pendleton
82
84
BLUE MOUNTAINS
2
82
Wallowa
Imnaha
Biggs
84
TO PORTLAND
Heppner
74
74
La Grande
244
395
Island
City
Elgin
Lostine
Enterprise
Joseph
WALLOWA MTS.
Wallowa Whitman
National Forest
39
Kent
206
206
Condon
97
19
207
North
Powder
203
30
Halfway
86
Antelope
Clarno
Fossil
218
Umatilla
National
Forest
Granite
Sumpter
Baker
City
7
John Day Fossil Beds
National Monument
Long Creek
Painted
Hills
Mitchell
Sheep
Rock
Dayville
Prairie
City
245
84
30
IDAHO
26
Ochoco
National
Forest
19
Mt.
Vernon
John Day
26
TO
BOISE
Snake R.
380
Paulina
Malheur
National Forest
395
20
Ontario
Yale
← TO
BEND
Ochoco
National
Forest
20
Riley
Burns
Crane
3
Lake
Owyhee
Leslie
Gulch
Owyhee R.
9
Malheur
Lake
New
Princeton
78
Turnbull
Lake Bed
Summer
Lake
395
Harney
Lake
Malheur National
Wildlife Refuge
Frenchglen
Diamond
Jordan
Valley
95
Owyhee
Canyon
Overlook
Lake
Abert
31
Hart Mtn.
National
Antlope
Refuge
205
Steens Mtn.
Alvord
Desert
Burns
Junction
Owyhee R.
Fremont-
Winema
National
Forest
Valley Falls
Andrews
95
Lakeview
140
Fields
0   40 miles
0   40 kilometers
CALIFORNIA
NEVADA

Columbia R.
John Day R.
John Day R.

Updated
by Andrew
Collins

Travel east from The Dalles, Bend, or any of the foothill communities blossoming in the shade of the Cascades, and you'll find a very different side of Oregon. The air is drier, clearer, and often pungent with the smell of juniper. The vast landscape of sharply folded hills, wheat fields, and mountains shimmering in the distance evokes the mythic Old West. There is a lonely grandeur in eastern Oregon, a plainspoken, independent spirit that can startle, surprise, and enthrall.

Much of eastern Oregon consists of national forest and wilderness, and the population runs the gamut from spur-janglin' cowboys to conservationists and urban expats. This is a world of ranches and rodeos, pickup trucks and country-western music. For the outdoor-adventure crowd, it's one of the West's last comparatively undiscovered playgrounds.

Some of the most important moments in Oregon's history took place in the towns of northeastern Oregon. The Oregon Trail passed through this corner of the state, winding through the Grande Ronde Valley between the Wallowa and Blue mountain ranges. The discovery of gold in the region in the 1860s sparked a second invasion of settlers, eventually leading to the displacement of the Native American Nez Perce and Paiute tribes. Pendleton, La Grande, and Baker City were all beneficiaries of the gold fever that swept through the area. Yet signs of even earlier times have survived, from the John Day Fossil Beds, with fragments of saber-toothed tigers, giant pigs, and three-toed horses, to Native American writings in the secluded mountains and deserts of vast and enormous Malheur County, which at 9,930 square miles is larger than Connecticut, Rhode Island, and Delaware combined.

Recreation and tourism are gaining a foothold in eastern Oregon today, but the region still sees only a fraction of the visitors that drop in on Mt. Hood or the coast each year. For off-the-beaten-path types, eastern Oregon's mountains and high desert country are as breathtaking as any landscape in the West, and you'd be pretty hard-pressed to get farther from the noise and distractions of city life.

EASTERN OREGON PLANNER

WHEN TO GO

Though skiers and snowboarders appreciate the Blues and the Wallowas in winter, summer is eastern Oregon's primary travel season. It comes late in the state's northeast corner, where snow can remain on the mountains until July, and May flurries aren't uncommon at lower elevations. July and August are the best months for wildflowers in the high northeast, and they're also the only months when many remote-but-scenic Forest Service roads are guaranteed to be open. For visitors in the southeast, though, midsummer is often uncomfortably hot and dry, and avian action along the Pacific Flyway tends to peak around April and September.

Summer temps in northeast Oregon generally level out in the 80s around July and August. In midwinter, 20-degree days are the norm. The deserts of southeastern Oregon are a bit warmer. Midsummer sees highs in the upper 90s, while January and February can remain in the 40s in the low country. Bear in mind: elevation varies greatly in eastern Oregon, and this can render seasonal averages pretty meaningless. It's not uncommon to gain or lose several thousand feet during the course of an hour's drive, and for much of the year this can mean the difference between flip-flops and snow boots.

FESTIVALS

Bronze, Blues & Brews. Fans of music, ale, and bronze sculptures are drawn to the artsy and outdoorsy mountain town of Joseph in mid-August for the Bronze, Blues & Brews Festival. ⊕ *www.bronzebluesbrews.com.*

Miner's Jubilee. The third weekend in July, Baker City salutes its mining heritage during the Miner's Jubilee, with a rodeo, beer gardens, outdoor music, and the state championship gold-panning competition. ☎ *541/523–5855* ⊕ *www.visitbaker.com.*

GETTING HERE AND AROUND

AIR TRAVEL

Eastern Oregon Regional Airport at Pendleton has service daily (except Saturday) from Portland on SeaPort Airlines; there's a Hertz car-rental agency on-site. Across the Washington border, Tri-Cities Airport is just 35 miles from Hermiston and 70 miles from Pendleton and has service on Allegiant, Delta, Alaska/Horizon, and United Express from several major cities in the West. If visiting Baker City or other communities in the eastern edge of the region, your best bet is flying into Boise, which is about a two-hour drive from Baker City. To reach the John Day region, it's easiest to fly into Bend, which is 2½ to 3 hours away.

Contacts Eastern Oregon Regional Airport at Pendleton ☎ *541/276–7754* ⊕ *www.pendleton.or.us/pendleton-airport.* **Tri-Cities Airport** ☎ *509/547–6352* ⊕ *www.portofpasco.org.*

BUS TRAVEL

The major Greyhound route travels along I–84, passing through Pendleton, La Grande, Baker City, and Ontario, but buses are an extremely impractical way to get around the vast distances of this part of the state.

Contacts Greyhound ☏ *800/231–2222* ⊕ *www.greyhound.com.*

CAR TRAVEL

Virtually all visitors to eastern Oregon get around by car. Interstate 84 runs east along the Columbia River and dips down to Pendleton, La Grande, Baker City, and Ontario. U.S. 26 heads east from Prineville through the Ochoco National Forest, passing the three units of the John Day Fossil Beds. U.S. 20 travels southeast from Bend in central Oregon to Burns. U.S. 20 and U.S. 26 both head west into Oregon from Idaho.

In all these areas, equip yourself with chains for winter driving. Four-wheel drive is beneficial on a lot of eastern Oregon's designated Scenic Byways. Plan ahead for gas, since service stations can be few and far between. They often close early in small towns, and because drivers in Oregon can't legally pump their own gas, you'll be out of luck until morning.

RESTAURANTS

Chef-driven restaurants serving anything beyond traditional pub fare and hearty steaks are rare on the eastern Oregon range, but it's not hard to find a tasty, authentic meal if you know where to look. Restaurants around the Wallowas, in particular, have a burgeoning locavore-organic ethos: locally grown produce abounds, farmers' markets are a big draw, and the rural county even has its own Slow Food chapter. A few noteworthy brewpubs have also cropped up around Pendleton, the Wallowas, and Baker City.

Elsewhere in the high desert, an entrenched ranching culture means big eating: farm-boy breakfasts and steak house after spur-jangling steak house. Generations of *braceros* (Hispanic laborers) have left their mark on the region's culinary scene as well, and excellent taquerias can be found in even the dustiest ranch towns. Pack a lunch if you're touring the southeasternmost corner of the state—towns are few and far between.

HOTELS

Chain hotels are easy to find in the gorge and in bigger towns like Baker City and Pendleton, but elsewhere, small motels and bed-and-breakfasts are more typical. Properties described as "rustic" or "historic" aren't kidding around—a lot of the region's lodging hasn't seen a major renovation since the Eisenhower administration.

Triple-digit rates are an anomaly in eastern Oregon, and you'd have to work pretty hard to spend more than $150 on a night's lodging. In summer, book early in no-stoplight towns like Diamond and Frenchglen, where the few hotel rooms fill up fast. Much of eastern Oregon shuts down in the off-season, so don't count on winter lodging without calling first. *Hotel reviews have been shortened. For full information, visit Fodors.com.*

WHAT IT COSTS IN U.S. DOLLARS			
$	$$	$$$	$$$$
Restaurants	Under $16	$16–$23	$24–$30	Over $30
Hotels	Under $125	$125–$175	$176–$250	Over $250

Restaurant prices are the average cost of a main course at dinner, or if dinner is not served, at lunch. Hotel prices are the lowest cost of a standard double room in high season.

TOURS

Hells Canyon Adventures. From April through September, Hells Canyon Adventures leads full- and half-day jet-boat tours of the country's deepest gorge. ☎ *800/422–358, 541/785–3352* ⊕ *www.hellscanyonadventures. com* ✉ *From $60.*

Jenkins Historical Tours. Operating out of the Round Barn Visitor Center in Diamond, this knowledgeable company provides chatty, full-day van tours to the Steens Mountain and the Malheur National Wildlife Refuge areas. ☎ *541/493–2070* ⊕ *www.roundbarn.net* ✉ *From $150.*

VISITOR INFORMATION

Eastern Oregon Visitors Association ☎ *800/332–1843* ⊕ *www. visiteasternoregon.com.*

EAST GORGE

Heading east along the interstate through the beige flats and mono-culture croplands between Hermiston and Pendleton, you could be forgiven for supposing that the most interesting part of Oregon was behind you. But just off the beaten path in the East Gorge country are seasonal wetlands chock-full of avian wildlife, roadside relics of the Old West, and dusty frontier towns undergoing commercial rebirths. Parks like Hat Rock State Park offer boaters and anglers access to the vast Columbia River Gorge, one of the country's most impressive waterways. A few dozen miles away in Pendleton, one of the world's largest and oldest rodeos anchors a town with an unexpectedly hip dining and shopping scene. Look south and east to where the river plateau gives way to the forested foothills of the Blue Mountains.

HERMISTON

188 miles east of Portland, 30 miles west of Pendleton.

Although its population is just over 17,000, Hermiston is the urban service center for nearly three times that many people in the expansive and productive agricultural industry that surrounds it. Irrigated farmlands and ranch lands produce livestock and crops, including alfalfa, potatoes, corn, and wheat. But the most popular export is the watermelons: the confluence of sandy loam soil, dry days, and cool nights creates the sugary magic that makes for the Hermiston brand of extraordinarily tasty fruit. Named for Robert Louis Stevenson's unfinished novel, *The Weir of Hermiston*, the city has more than 75 acres of parks, with the

Columbia River just 6 miles to the north and the Umatilla River and Blue Mountains nearby.

GETTING HERE

Nearly all visitors arrive by car, but commercial flights do land at the Tri-Cities Airport in Pasco, Washington, 37 miles north, and at Pendleton's Eastern Oregon Regional Airport, 26 miles southeast. From Portland, it's a three-hour drive on Interstate 84.

VISITOR INFORMATION

Hermiston Chamber of Commerce ⊠ *415 S. U.S. 395* ☎ *541/567–6151* ⊕ *www.hermistonchamber.com.*

EXPLORING

Echo. Ten miles south of Hermiston, just off I–84, lies a little town at the intersection of the Oregon Trail and the transcontinental railroad. On the short walking tour of downtown, approximately an hour, mounted plaques tell the story of the town's historic buildings, including the Chinese House/ON&R Railroad Museum (now filled with railroad artifacts) and 10 sites on the National Register of Historic Places. Other draws include a fun pub, the Wheat and Barley, and a small winery, Sno Road. ⊠ *Oregon Trail Rd. at N. Thielson St., 1 mile south of I–84 at Exit 188* ☎ *541/376–8411* ⊕ *www.echo-oregon.com*

WHERE TO EAT AND STAY

$$ ✕ **Walker's Farm Kitchen.** In this rich agricultural region, it makes sense

PACIFIC that downtown Hermiston is home to a restaurant with a strong

NORTHWEST farm-to-table ethos, along with a great list of regional craft beers

Fodor'sChoice and wines. Chefs Larry and Cynthia rotate their menu regularly, but

★ recent dishes have included ruby red trout with butternut squash, potato-and-apple hash, and sautéed haricot verts, and hearty chili with three kinds of pork (ground, loin, and belly) with poblano chilis and local "tongues of fire" beans. The restaurant occupies a simple gray Craftsman bungalow with a charming dining room that befits the unpretentious cuisine. ⑤ *Average main: $21* ✉ *920 S.E. 4th St.* ☎ *541/289–3333* ⊕ *www.walkersfarmkitchen.com* ✆ *Closed Sun. and Mon. No dinner Tues. and Wed.*

$ ✕ **Wheat and Barley Pub.** This dapper pub in a historic brick storefront

MODERN in downtown Echo gives visitors—and fans of creative American com-

AMERICAN fort fare and local beer, wines, and craft cocktails—a good reason to hang out in the charming village after sundown. Creations from the kitchen include sausage slow-cooked in the pub's alderwood smoker, smoked scallop ceviche with candied jalapeños and cherry tomatoes, and house-made gnocchi with duck confit. Desserts are every bit as impressive; try the blackberry pie when it's in season. ⑤ *Average main: $12* ✉ *201 W. Main St., Echo* ☎ *541/376–5053* ✆ *Closed Sun.–Tues. No lunch.*

$ ⌂ **Oxford Suites Hermiston.** The region's most attractive and best-main-

HOTEL tained hotel, this relatively upscale (for the area) chain property has spacious rooms, all with large sitting areas with work desks and sofas. **Pros:** complimentary breakfast and evening snacks; convenient location. **Cons:** most of the "suites" are really just large rooms with sitting areas; cookie-cutter decor. ⑤ *Rooms from: $109* ✉ *1050 N. 1st St.* ☎ *541/564–8000, 888/545–7848* ⊕ *www.oxfordsuiteshermiston.com* ⇱ *114 rooms, 12 suites* ❚⊙❚ *Breakfast.*

SPORTS AND THE OUTDOORS

FAMILY **Hat Rock State Park.** On the south shore of Lake Wallula, a 70-foot basalt rock is the first major landmark that Lewis and Clark passed on their expedition down the Columbia. In his notations, William Clark called it "Hat Rock," and the name stuck. Standing tall amid rolling sagebrush hills, it overlooks Lake Wallula, a popular spot for jet skiing, swimming, boating, and fishing for rainbow trout, walleye, and sturgeon. In addition to water sports, the park provides scenic picnic spots and expansive views of the stark, desertlike landscape. But because it abuts an upscale lakeside housing development that's visible from some portions of the park, it might be a challenge to pretend you're back in the days of Lewis and Clark. ✉ *82375 C St., off U.S. 730, 9 miles east of Hermiston* ☎ *800/551–6949, 541/983–2277* ⊕ *www.oregonstateparks. org* ⇱ *Free* ✆ *Daily dawn–dusk.*

Umatilla National Wildlife Refuge. The 23,555-acre refuge includes marsh, woodland, and wetland habitats that make it vital to migrating waterfowl and bald eagles in addition to myriad species of resident wildlife. Although there are numerous routes to access portions of the refuge, the best and easiest way to view wildlife in ponds and wetlands is to

9

drive along the McCormick Auto Tour Route, accessible from Paterson Ferry Road, off U.S. 730, 19 miles west of Hermiston. ⊠ *Stretches from Boardman, 20 miles west of Umatilla, to Irrigon, 9 miles west of Umatilla, north of I–84 along Columbia River, Umatilla* ☎ *509/546–8300* ⊕ *www.fws.gov/refuge/umatilla* ⊠ *Free* ⊙ *Daily dawn–dusk on designated roadways only.*

PENDLETON

200 miles east of Portland, 130 miles east of the Dalles.

At the foot of the Blue Mountains amid waving wheat fields and cattle ranches, Pendleton is a quintessential Western town with a rip-snorting history. It was originally acquired in a swap for a couple of horses, and the town's history of wild behavior was evident from the first city ordinance, which outlawed public drunkenness, fights, and shooting off one's guns within the city limits. But Pendleton is also the land of the Umatilla Tribe—the herds of wild horses that once thundered across this rolling landscape were at the center of the area's early Native American culture (today the tribe operates the shimmering and modern Wildhorse Resort & Casino). Later Pendleton became an important pioneer junction and home to a sizable Chinese community. The current cityscape still carries the vestiges of yesteryear, with many of its century-old homes still standing, from simple farmhouses to stately Queen Anne Victorians.

Given its raucous past teeming with cattle rustlers, saloons, and bordellos, the largest city in eastern Oregon (population 17,000) looks unusually sedate. But all that changes in September when the **Pendleton Round-Up** (⇨ *Sports and the Outdoors)* draws thousands.

GETTING HERE

Pendleton has the region's only airport, the Eastern Oregon Regional Airport, which has daily service on SeaPort Air to Portland. Nevertheless, Pendleton is located right on I–84 and most visitors arrive by car.

VISITOR INFORMATION

Pendleton Chamber of Commerce ⊠ *501 S. Main St.* ☎ *541/246–7411, 800/547–9811* ⊕ *www.pendletonchamber.com.*

EXPLORING

Fodor's Choice **Pendleton Underground Tours.** This 90-minute tour transports you below
★ ground and back through Pendleton's history of gambling, girls, and gold. The Underground Tours depict town life from more than a century ago (when 32 saloons and 18 brothels were operating in full swing) to the 1953 closure of the Cozy Rooms, the best-known bordello in town. The Underground Tour eventually resurfaces, climbing the "31 Steps to Heaven" to those Cozy Rooms where madam Stella Darby reigned. The secret gambling lairs, opium dens, and bathhouses that lie directly below the pavement will give you a whole new perspective of the streets of Pendleton. Reservations are required. ⊠ *31 S.W. Emigrant Ave.* ☎ *541/276–0730* ⊕ *www.pendletonundergroundtours.org* ⊠ *$15* ⊙ *Daily; call for schedule.*

Pendleton Underground Tours

Pendleton Woolen Mills. Pendleton's most significant source of name-recognition in the country comes from this mill, home of the trademark wool plaid shirts and colorful woolen Indian blankets. This location is the company's blanket mill; there's also a weaving mill in the Columbia Gorge town of Washougal, Washington, near Portland and about three hours west of Pendleton. If you want to know more about the production process, the company gives 20-minute tours on weekdays (call for tour times). The mill's retail store stocks blankets and clothing with good bargains on factory seconds. ⊠ *1307 S.E. Court Pl.* ☎ *541/276–6911, 800/568–3156* ⊕ *www.pendleton-usa.com* ⊗ *Mon.–Sat. 8–6, Sun. 9–5; tours weekdays.*

FAMILY **Round-Up Hall of Fame Museum.** The museum's collection spans the rodeo's history since 1910, with photographs—including glamorous glossies of prior Rodeo Queens and the Happy Canyon Princesses (all Native American)—as well as saddles, guns, and costumes. A taxidermied championship bronco named War Paint is the museum's cool-if-slightly-creepy prize artifact. ⊠ *1114 S.W. Court Ave., across from Round-Up grounds* ☎ *541/278–0815* ⊕ *www.pendletonhalloffame.com* ⊠ *$5* ⊗ *Mon.–Sat. 10–4.*

FAMILY **Tamástslikt Cultural Institute.** Located at the Wildhorse Resort and Casino, this impressive 45,000-square-foot interpretive center depicts history from the perspective of the Cayuse, Umatilla, and Walla Walla tribes (*Tamástslikt* means "interpret" in the Walla Walla native language). An art gallery showcases the work of local and regional tribal artists, and on Saturdays in summer you can visit the adjacent Living Culture Village, Naami Nishaycht, and watch a variety of talks and demonstrations on everything from teepee-building to traditional community games. There's also a museum gift shop, a theater showing a short film about the tribe's heritage, and a café. ✉ *47106 Wildhorse Blvd.* ☎ *541/966–9748* ⊕ *www.tamastslikt.org* ✉ *$10* ⊙ *Mon.–Sat. 10–5; Living Culture Village, late May–early Sept., Sat. 10–3.*

WHERE TO EAT

$
CAFÉ
✕**Great Pacific Wine.** Set in a stately 1880s former Masonic lodge in downtown Pendleton, what began as a coffeehouse and wine bar has expanded over the years into a full restaurant serving reasonably priced salads, sandwiches, soups, pizzas, and appetizers. The food tends toward traditional American café fare, with focaccia topped with Kalamata olives and chevre, smoked-salmon Caesar salads, and barbecue-pork pizzas among the favorites. A wide variety of flavored espresso drinks is also available, along with a great selection of both international and local wines as well as a mix of bottled and draft beers. Live music is presented many evenings in this warmly lit spot with exposed-brick walls and light-wood tables. ⑤ *Average main: $9* ✉ *403 S. Main St.* ☎ *541/276–1350* ⊕ *www.greatpacific.biz* ⊙ *Closed Sun.*

$$$
STEAKHOUSE
✕**Hamley Steakhouse.** A large downtown complex of Western-style brick and log cabin–style buildings holds a steak house, café, and saloon, and captures Pendleton's cowboy heritage with its stunningly ornate interior—note the pressed-tin ceilings, 19th-century mahogany bar, and the opulent custom woodwork and Old West memorabilia throughout. Whether it's prime rib, country-fried steaks, or peppercorn-crusted top sirloin Hamley's USDA prime hand-cut beef, this place will leave even the most ferocious carnivores satisfied. Burgers, fire-roasted salmon, and balsamic-cherry-glazed pork loin are among the other favorites. The swanky steak house is open for dinner only, the saloon serves a lighter bar menu (and produces its own whiskey), and the café serves breakfast and lunch. ⑤ *Average main: $28* ✉ *8 S.E. Court St.* ☎ *541/278–1100* ⊕ *www.hamleysteakhouse.com.*

$
AMERICAN
✕**The Prodigal Son.** A cavernous and historic former car dealership houses this hip brewpub, complete with leather couches, tabletop Pac-Man, and a mini-library. Since it opened in 2010, it's become known for its nicely crafted beers, including the heady Max Power IPA, faintly tart Huckleberry Wheat beer, and robust Bruce/Lee Porter. The kitchen serves tasty pub-food. Calamari tacos, Tillamook cheeseburgers, beer-battered cod fish-and-chips, and Scotch eggs are among the favorites. ⑤ *Average main: $12* ✉ *230 S.E. Court Ave.* ☎ *541/276–6090* ⊕ *www.prodigalsonbrewery.com* ⊙ *Closed Mon.*

WHERE TO STAY

$$
B&B/INN
Fodor's Choice
★
The Pendleton House Bed & Breakfast. This gorgeous, 6,000 square-foot pink stucco home in Pendleton's North Hill neighborhood dates to 1917 and abounds with handsome decorative details, including Chinese silk wallpaper and custom woodwork; it's a grand reminder that the Old West had its share of wealth and worldly sophistication. **Pros:** glorious home with lavishly decorated rooms; small pets allowed; quiet location just across the river from downtown. **Cons:** most rooms share a bath. ⑤ *Rooms from: $135* ✉ *311 N. Main St.*

☎ *541/276–8581* ⊕ *www.pendletonhousebnb.com* ⤺ *5 rooms, 4 with shared bath* ⦿ *Breakfast.*

$ 🏨 **Wildhorse Resort & Casino.** Situated on a sweeping mesa 6 miles south-
RESORT east of downtown Pendleton, this contemporary hotel at Wildhorse Resort (operated by the Umatilla tribe) offers plenty of perks even if you're not a gamer. **Pros:** great views and stylish decor in tower hotel; lots of amenities and dining options on-site; scenic location outside town. **Cons:** casino can be noisy and crowded; a 15-minute drive from downtown restaurants; rooms in courtyard building feel a bit dated, and some still allow smoking. ⑤ *Rooms from: $95* ⊠ *46510 Wildhorse Blvd.* ☎ *800/654–9453* ⊕ *www.wildhorseresort.com* ⤺ *300 rooms* ⦿ *No meals.*

$ 🏨 **Working Girls Hotel.** From boarding house to bordello to affordable
B&B/INN and historic inn, this refurbished 1890s edifice owned and operated by Pendleton Underground Tours advertises its "Old West Comfort" with a large vertical sign hanging from the side of the build-
ing. **Pros:** centrally located in downtown Pendleton; fun decor; very affordable. **Cons:** bathrooms are down the hall; not suitable for children. ⑤ *Rooms from: $85* ⊠ *17 S.W. Emigrant Ave.* ☎ *541/276–0730* ⊕ *www.pendletonundergroundtours.org* ⤺ *4 rooms with 2 shared baths, 1 suite* ⦿ *Breakfast.*

SPORTS AND THE OUTDOORS

FISHING

Blue Mountain Anglers and Fly Shop. Oregon's largest full-service fly shop east of the Cascades also has a fishing school and information about angling in the area; the focus here is on fishing in the Umatilla River for steelhead trout and salmon. ⊠ *1847 Westgate Pl.* ☎ *541/966–8770* ⊕ *www.bluemountainanglers.com.*

RODEO

FAMILY **Pendleton Round-Up.** More than 50,000 people roll into town during the
Fodor's Choice second full week in September for one of the oldest and most promi-
★ nent rodeos in the United States. With its famous slogan of "Let 'er buck," the Round-Up features eight days of parades, races, beauty con-
tests, and children's rodeos, culminating in four days of rodeo events. Vendors line the length of Court Avenue and Main Street, selling beadwork and curios, while country bands twang in the background. ⊠ *1205 S.W. Court Ave.* ☎ *541/276–2553, 800/457–6336* ⊕ *www. pendletonroundup.com.*

SHOPPING

Hamley & Co. Western Store & Custom Saddlery. On-site craftspeople at this Western superstore fashion hand-tooled saddles considered among the best in the world. You'll also find authentic cowboy/cowgirl gear and quality leather products, plus gifts and art. The store is next to Hamley's massive—and gorgeous—steak house, saloon, and café. ⊠ *30 S.E. Court Ave.* ☎ *541/278–1100* ⊕ *www.hamleyco.com.*

9

NORTHEAST OREGON

No part of eastern Oregon repudiates the region's reputation for flat and barren landscapes quite like its lush and mountainous northeast corner. The Wallowa Mountains are among the most underrated outdoor recreation hot spots in the Rockies, with 565 square miles of backpacker-friendly wilderness, abundant wildlife, and proximity to Hells Canyon, North America's deepest gorge. The nearby Blue Mountains are no slouches either, home to some of the state's best alpine and Nordic skiing. Towns like Baker City, Enterprise, Joseph, and La Grande have transitioned more thoroughly than much of the region from pastoral and extractive economies to hospitality and recreation, making them eastern Oregon's de facto capitals of art, food, and culture. Each city has a vibrant downtown with a growing number of sophisticated galleries and boutiques, and you'll find locals swapping fish stories and trail tales in one of the area's excellent brewpubs. Baker City in particular has maintained its mining-era integrity—the restored Geiser Grand Hotel is a must-visit, especially for history buffs.

LA GRANDE

52 miles southeast of Pendleton.

La Grande started life in the late 1800s as a farming community. It grew slowly while most towns along the Blue Mountains were booming or busting in the violent throes of gold-fueled stampedes. When the railroad companies were deciding where to lay their tracks through the valley, a clever local farmer donated 150 acres to ensure that the Iron Horse would run through La Grande. With steam power fueling a new boom, the town quickly outgrew its neighbors, took the title of county seat from fading Union City (Union City claims it "was robbed"), and with its current population of 13,000 sits at the center of the Grand Ronde Valley. Though you can appreciate it for its own charms, La Grande is a convenient stop if you're heading to the nearby Wallowa Mountains.

GETTING HERE

La Grande sits at the intersection of Interstate 84 and Highway 82, the primary route through the Wallowa Valley to Joseph and Enterprise. It's a four-hour drive from Portland and 2½ hours from Boise, Idaho.

VISITOR INFORMATION

La Grande Visitor Center ⊠ *207 Depot St.* ☎ *541/963–8588, 800/848–9969* ⊕ *www.visitlagrande.com.*

WHERE TO EAT AND STAY

$
CAFÉ
✕ **Joe and Sugar's.** If you want to remain an anonymous tourist, don't visit Joe and Sugar's. You can't avoid being chatted up by the funny, friendly, and helpful owner of this sweet-smelling café and coffee shop that's popular for breakfast, lunch, and light snacks. ⑤ *Average main: $6* ⊠ *1119 Adams Ave.* ☎ *541/975–5282.*

$$
AMERICAN
✕ **Ten Depot Street.** In a stylish historic brick building, Ten Depot Street serves an eclectic menu of classic American favorites, everything from burgers to hearty steak and seafood dishes, with favorites like marinated local-lamb kebabs, filet mignon with sautéed mushrooms, and grilled wild Alaskan salmon with a cucumber-dill sauce. With dark wood throughout accented by plum tablecloths and teal plates and napkins, it's a relatively elegant spot for this dressed-down part of the world. Start off your evening with a drink at the adjoining bar—there's a very nice wine list. ⑤ *Average main: $23* ⊠ *10 Depot St.* ☎ *541/963–8766* ⊕ *www.tendepotstreet.com* ⊘ *Closed Sun. No lunch.*

$
HOTEL
⬚ **Historic Union Hotel.** Cast-iron Victorian lampposts frame the entrance to this funky three-story, redbrick hotel about 15 miles south of La Grande. **Pros:** bargain rates; atmospheric old building in a historic town; owners are very friendly and helpful. **Cons:** no TV or phones in rooms; property is a bit dated; front view of a trailer park doesn't impress. ⑤ *Rooms from: $89* ⊠ *326 N. Main St.* ☎ *541/562–1200* ⊕ *www.theunionhotel.com* ⇆ *15 rooms* ⦿⊙ *Breakfast.*

9

ENTERPRISE

64 miles east of La Grande, 108 miles east of Pendleton.

The seat of Oregon's northeasternmost county, Enterprise is surrounded by some of the region's most rugged natural beauty. Though the town itself is pretty quiet, it's a locus for outdoor activities in winter and summer, and one of the only places in rural Wallowa County to catch a movie or sit in a coffee shop. To the south and west lie the Eagle Cap Wilderness, the craggy Wallowa Mountains, and pristine Wallowa Lake; to the east is the Hells Canyon Wilderness and National Recreation Area.

GETTING HERE

A car is by far the most practical way to reach and explore Enterprise and the region. It's a 5½-hour drive from Portland, and a three-hour drive from the Tri-Cities in Washington.

Shuttle Bus. In the summer a shuttle bus runs throughout the day between Enterprise and nearby Joseph and Wallowa Lake. ☎ *541/426–3840.*

Wallowa Link Bus. The Wallowa Link Bus runs twice a week between La Grande and Joseph, stopping in Enterprise. ☎ *541/963–2877* ⊕ *www. neotransit.org.*

VISITOR INFORMATION

Wallowa County Chamber of Commerce ⊠ *309 S. River St.* ☎ *541/426– 2622, 800/585–4121* ⊕ *www.wallowacountychamber.com.*

WHERE TO EAT

$
AMERICAN
Fodor'sChoice
★

× **Red Rooster Cafe.** A convivial and homey downtown joint serving delicious breakfast and lunch fare, the Red Rooster draws a mix of locals and tourists to its sunny dining room, where you can grab a seat at a table or the horseshoe-shaped counter. Start the day off with a biscuit sandwich, or organic-cornmeal johnnycakes with honey-cured bacon, sharp cheddar, clover honey, and honey butter. Lunch favorites include grilled tri-tip steak sandwiches and turkey salad with raisins, walnuts, and feta. Owner Kim Morris bakes famously delectable cinnamon rolls and fruit pies. ⑤ *Average main: $9* ⊠ *309 W. Main St.* ☎ *541/426–2233* ⊕ *www.red-rooster-cafe.com* ☯ *No dinner.*

$
AMERICAN
Fodor'sChoice
★

× **Terminal Gravity Brew Pub.** Beer connoisseurs from across the state and just about all the locals rave about the India Pale Ale at this small microbrewery in a canary-yellow house on the outskirts of town. (The name "Terminal Gravity" is a brewers' term for the specific gravity that occurs to beer after fermentation is done.) Aspens wave on a front yard dotted with picnic tables, and kids and dogs lounge on the wooden front porch. Between the indoor customers strumming guitars and outdoor customers playing volleyball, it isn't just about the hops at this friendly local hangout. The menu is short and simple, with creative comfort fare such as spicy Asian beef salad with wasabi-ginger dressing, and a seared sockeye salmon sandwich with lime-cilantro aioli. There's a rotating selection of house-brewed beers on tap, complete with seasonals. The brews stack up favorably against the best craft beers around Oregon. ⑤ *Average main: $10* ⊠ *803 S.E. School St.* ☎ *541/426–3000* ⊕ *www.*

terminalgravitybrewing.com ⊘ *Closed Sun. and Mon. No lunch Wed. and Thurs.*

WHERE TO STAY

$ ▦ **1910 Historic Enterprise House B&B.** Although this elegant Edward-
B&B/INN ian house dates to 1910, it's undergone a full restoration in recent years, giving it a mix of original architectural details and comfy modern amenities, including private bathrooms for each of its three rooms and suites, luxe Tarocco bath products, Wi-Fi, and air-conditioning. **Pros:** gorgeous furnishings; delicious breakfasts; close to downtown but with quiet setting. **Cons:** floral wallpapers and ornate furnishings aren't to everyone's taste. ⑤ *Rooms from: $124* ✉ *508 1st South St.* ☎ *541/426–4238* ⊕ *www.enterprisehousebnb.com* ⟟ *3 rooms, 2 suites* ⦿ *Breakfast.*

$ ▦ **Mingo Motel.** About 16 miles west of Enterprise, the tiny town of
HOTEL Wallowa has a main street, a couple of restaurants, and a few stores, as well as this small, friendly motel and its attractive, rustic rooms with carved-wood beds, country-quilt bedspreads, and handy touches like microwaves, small refrigerators, and coffeemakers. **Pros:** good base for exploring Wallowa Mountains; attractive and well-maintained rooms; short walk to groceries and dining. **Cons:** isolated from main attractions in Joseph and Enterprise. ⑤ *Rooms from: $75* ✉ *102 N. Alder St.* ☎ *541/886–2021* ⊕ *www.mingomotel.com* ⟟ *13 rooms* ⦿ *No meals.*

$ ▦ **Rimrock Inn.** The distinctive accommodations at this secluded com-
B&B/INN pound on the edge of Wallowa-Whitman National Forest, a 30-mile drive north of downtown Enterprise, include a traditional guest room in the main house, a cute and snug 1969 Aristocrat RV, a two-bedroom loft-style apartment, and four rustic but well-outfitted canvas teepees—there are also 40 tent sites and six RV spaces. **Pros:** completely peaceful and secluded location; fun and unique accommodations; terrific on-site restaurant. **Cons:** 45-minute drive from town; teepees have shared bath facilities. ⑤ *Rooms from: $88* ✉ *83471 Lewiston Hwy.* ☎ *541/828–7769, 888/440–4161* ⊕ *www.rimrockinnor.com* ⟟ *7 units* ⦿ *Breakfast.*

SPORTS AND THE OUTDOORS

RECREATIONAL AREAS

Zumwalt Prairie Preserve. The Nature Conservancy manages these 51 square miles of rolling grasslands, where elk, deer, bears, and bobcats roam. The prairie is also a first-class habitat for several birds of prey, including golden eagles and the regal, migratory Swainson's hawk, which spends its winters in South America. A handful of short, easy trails lead to impressive vistas of the prairie and nearby canyons, and a 10-mile driving tour on gravel roads leads through the south end of the preserve, reconnecting with the highway on its eastern side. The Nature Conservancy office in Enterprise has maps and trail info; the entrance to the preserve is 22 miles north of town off Zumwalt-Buckhorn Road. ✉ *906 S. River St.* ☎ *541/426–3458* ⊕ *www.nature.org* ⦿ *Free.*

Teepees overlooking Joseph Canyon

6 miles southeast of Enterprise.

The area around Wallowa Lake was the traditional home of the Nez Perce Indians—the town of Joseph is named for Chief Joseph, their famous leader. The peaks of the Wallowa Mountains, typically snow-covered until July, tower 5,000 feet above the regional tourist hubs of the town. Joseph itself isn't much more than a nice Main Street speckled with shops, galleries, brewpubs, and cafés. Follow Main Street a mile out of town, though, to reach the gorgeous Wallowa Lake, where you'll find a whole separate hospitality village of rental cabins, outfitters, go-karts, and ice-cream stands. The busy area on the south end of the lake is also the site of two of the most popular access points for the mountains, the Wallowa Lake trailhead and the Wallowa Lake Tramway.

GETTING HERE

Highway 82 ends at Joseph, which is reachable primarily by car.

VISITOR INFORMATION

Joseph Chamber of Commerce ⊠ *Kiosk at Main St. and Joseph Ave.* ☎ *541/432–1015* ⊕ *www.josephoregon.com.*

EXPLORING

Valley Bronze of Oregon. This impressive gallery displays sculptures by the many artists who cast their work at the nearby foundry, plus quite a few international pieces. The foundry itself is a half mile away; call ahead for reservations and to confirm hours. Your tour guide will lead you there after the group has gathered at the gallery. ⊠ *18 S. Main St.* ☎ *541/432–7551* ⊕ *www.valleybronze.com* ⊠ *Gallery free, tours $15*

☉ *Gallery Mon.–Sat. 10–5, Sun. 10–3; tours May–Sept., weekdays 11 am; by appointment in winter.*

Wallowa County Farmers' Market. More than just a cluster of produce tents, Joseph's Saturday markets are the social hub of the community. Grab groceries or treats from rows of veggie vendors, specialty-food producers, and sustainable cattle ranchers, then hang around for live outdoor music and bronze-sculpture street art. The market is also held in Enterprise on Thursday afternoons (4–7 pm), on the Wallowa County Courthouse lawn. ✉ *Main St. and Joseph Ave.* ⊕ *www. wallowacountyfarmersmarket.com* ☉ *Late May–mid-Oct., Sat. 10–2.*

NEED A BREAK? **Red Horse Coffee Traders.** In this modest yellow clapboard cottage in downtown Joseph, you can sample some of the finest coffee in eastern Oregon. The owners roast carefully sourced, organic, fair-trade beans from Peru, Ethopia, Sumatra, and other top java regions. Sandwiches, breakfast burritos, and baked goods are served, too. ✉ *306 N. Main St.* ☎ *541/432-3784* ⊕ *www.redhorsecoffeetraders.com.*

Wallowa County Museum. Joseph's history museum has a small but poignant collection of artifacts and photographs chronicling the flight of the Nez Perce, a series of battles against the U.S. Army that took place in the late 1870s. Built as a bank in 1888, the building was robbed in 1896, an event commemorated by a number of the museum's artifacts, including a massive old safe and some yellowing newspaper accounts. ✉ *110 S. Main St.* ☎ *541/432–6095* ⊕ *www.co.wallowa.or.us/ community_services/museum* 🎟 *$4* ☉ *Memorial Day–3rd weekend in Sept., daily 10–4.*

Wallowa Lake Tramway. The steepest tram in North America rises 3,700 feet in 15 minutes, rushing you up to the top of 8,150-foot Mt. Howard. Vistas of mountain peaks, forest, and Wallowa Lake far below will dazzle you, both on the way up and at the summit. Early and late in the season, 2½ miles of cross-country skiing trails await at the top, and the interpretive trails are open for hiking during the snowless months of midsummer, as are mountain-bike trails. A casual lunch is available at the Summit Grill and Alpine Patio, but keep in mind that it's more about the view than the sometimes-uneven food and service. ✉ *59919 Wallowa Lake Hwy.* ☎ *541/432–5331* ⊕ *www.wallowalaketramway. com* 🎟 *$28* ☉ *May–mid-June and mid-Sept.–late Sept., daily 10–4; late June–early Sept., daily 9–5.*

EN ROUTE **Wallowa Mountain Loop.** This is a relatively easy way to take in the natural splendor of the Eagle Cap Wilderness and reach Baker City without backtracking to La Grande. The three-hour trip from Joseph to Baker City, designated the Hells Canyon Scenic Byway, winds through the national forest and part of Hells Canyon Recreation Area, passing over forested mountains, creeks, and rivers. Before you travel the loop, check with the Forest Service about road conditions; the route can be impassable when snowed over. From Joseph, take Highway 350 east for 8 miles, turn south onto Forest Service Road 39, and continue until it meets Highway 86, which winds past the town of Halfway

and then continues to Baker City. ⊠ *Begins at Hwy. 82 and Hwy. 350* ☎ *541/426–5546* ⊕ *www.fs.usda.gov/wallowa-whitman.*

WHERE TO EAT AND STAY

$
AMERICAN

✕ **Mutiny Brewing Company.** A small brewpub with a bistro feel, Mutiny churns out a few respectable microbrews (the Pi-Dog Porter is excellent), but puts an equal focus on the food. Locally sourced ingredients fill out a simple menu of creative sandwiches and knockout burgers, and locals crowd the place during weekend brunch for huevos and beer shandies. There's an expansive patio out front with excellent mountain views—the prime seating area on warm summer days. ⑤ *Average main: $11* ⊠ *600 N. Main St.* ☎ *541/432–5274* ⊕ *www.mutinybrewing.com* ⊘ *Closed Mon.*

$$
EASTERN
EUROPEAN

✕ **Vali's Alpine Restaurant.** This rustic and inviting Wallowa Lake institution serves a rotating, single-entrée menu of classic Hungarian dishes like cabbage rolls and goulash, with seatings at 5 and 7 pm. The featured dish changes according to the day of the week—schnitzel on Sundays, chicken paprikash on Thursdays, and more. Friday's dinner changes weekly and is more international in flavor—it could include anything from Hungarian hunter's platter with grilled sausages and pickled cabbage to Spanish pork skewers with couscous and vegetables. Drop in before 11 am on weekends for the out-of-this-world homemade donuts. ⑤ *Average main: $16* ⊠ *59811 Wallowa Lake Hwy.* ☎ *541/432–5691* ⊕ *www.valisrestaurant.com* ⌂ *Reservations essential* ▭ *No credit cards* ⊘ *Closed Mon. and Tues. (also Wed.–Fri. in fall and spring) and Dec.–Mar. No lunch.*

$$
B&B/INN
Fodor's Choice
★

▦ **Bronze Antler B&B.** This cozy 1920s Craftsman bungalow on the south end of downtown Joseph is along Main Street, a short walk from local shops and restaurants; it's surrounded by perennial gardens laced with pathways and containing a bocce court and picnic area. **Pros:** beautiful grounds with great mountain views; friendly and helpful innkeepers; smartly furnished rooms. **Cons:** on the slightly busy main road through town. ⑤ *Rooms from: $150* ⊠ *309 S. Main St.* ☎ *541/432–0230* ⊕ *www.bronzeantler.com* ⇘ *3 rooms, 1 suite* ⦿ *Breakfast.*

$
HOTEL

▦ **Wallowa Lake Lodge.** At this friendly 1920s lodge, handmade replicas of the structure's original furniture fill a large common area with a massive fireplace. **Pros:** affordable; a visual and historical treat; staff goes out of its way to accommodate. **Cons:** no TV, phones, or Internet; closed in winter; rooms are quite rustic and simple. ⑤ *Rooms from: $99* ⊠ *60060 Wallowa Lake Hwy.* ☎ *541/432–9821* ⊕ *www.wallowalakelodge.com* ⇘ *22 rooms, 8 cabins* ⊘ *Closed mid-Sept.–Memorial Day* ⦿ *No meals.*

SHOPPING

Fodor's Choice
★

Arrowhead Chocolates. Take a break from browsing at Joseph's several galleries and boutiques to indulge in first-rate caramels and truffles at this popular downtown shop. You'll also find rich, hot mochas that blend chocolate with Portland's Stumptown coffee. The sweets come in novel flavors, including caramels topped with alder-smoked sea salt and lavender-honey chocolate truffles. ⊠ *100 N. Main St.* ☎ *541/432–2871* ⊕ *www.arrowheadchocolates.com.*

ToZion. Check out the well-curated collection of fair-trade clothing, soaps, skin-care products, Buddha statuary, jewelry, pottery, and artwork at this colorful two-story boutique carrying both local and international goods. ⊠ *200 N. Main St.* ☎ *541/432–0745* ⊕ *www.tozion.net.*

SPORTS AND THE OUTDOORS

HORSEBACK RIDING

Eagle Cap Wilderness Pack Station. Book a short or full-day guided summer pack trip from the south end of Wallowa Lake into the Eagle Cap Wilderness. ⊠ *59761 Wallowa Lake Hwy.* ☎ *541/432–4145, 541/962–5900* ⊕ *www.eaglecapwildernesspackstation.com.*

RAFTING AND BOATING

Wallowa Lake Marina. From May to mid-September, you can rent paddleboats, motorboats, rowboats, and canoes by the hour or by the day. ⊠ *Marina La., south end of Wallowa Lake, off Hwy. 351* ☎ *541/432–9115* ⊕ *www.wallowalakemarina.com.*

Winding Waters River Expeditions. Experienced river guides at this Joseph-based company lead white-water rafting and kayaking trips, as well as fly-fishing outings, on the Snake River and the nearby Grande Ronde and Salmon Rivers. ☎ *877/426–7238, 541/432–0747* ⊕ *www.windingwatersrafting.com.*

RECREATIONAL AREAS

Eagle Cap Wilderness. At more than 360,000 acres, this is the largest wilderness area in Oregon, encompassing most of the Wallowa range with 535 miles of trails for hard-core backpackers and horseback riders. Most of the popular trailheads are along Eagle Cap's northern edge, accessible from Enterprise or Joseph, but you also can find several trailheads 20 to 30 miles southeast of La Grande along Route 203. ⚠ Some areas of the wilderness are accessible year-round, while the high-elevation areas are accessible only for a few months in summer. To park at many trailheads, you must purchase a Northwest Forest Pass for $5 per day or $30 per year. To hike into the wilderness, you also need to get a free permit that will alert rangers to your plans. ⊠ *Wallowa Mountains Ranger Office, 201 E. 2nd St.* ☎ *541/426–5546* ⊕ *www.fs.usda.gov/detail/wallowa-whitman.*

Wallowa Lake. A few miles south of Joseph proper on Highway 351 (or the Wallowa Lake Highway), sparkling, blue-green Wallowa Lake is the highest body of water in eastern Oregon (elevation 5,000 feet). Boating and fishing are popular, and the lake supports a whole vacation village on its southern end, complete with cabins, restaurants, and miniature golf. ⊠ *Wallowa Lake Hwy.*

FAMILY
Fodor's Choice
★

Wallowa Lake State Park. On the south shore of beautiful Wallowa Lake, just a 10-minute drive south of downtown Joseph, this alpine park with a highly popular campground is surrounded on three sides by 9,000-foot-tall snowcapped mountains. Popular activities include fishing and powerboating on the lake, plus hiking wilderness trails, horseback riding, and canoeing. Nearby are a marina, bumper boats, miniature golf, and the tramway to the top of Mt. Howard. ⊠ *72214 Marina La., off Hwy. 351* ☎ *541/432–4185, 800/551–6949* ⊕ *www.oregonstateparks.org* ✉ *Day use $5 per vehicle* ☉ *Daily.*

Fodor's Choice **Wallowa Mountains.** Forming a rugged U-shape fortress between Hells
★ Canyon on the Idaho border and the Blue Mountains, the Wallowas
are sometimes called the American Alps or Little Switzerland. The
granite peaks in this range are between 5,000 and 9,000 feet in height.
Dotted with crystalline alpine lakes and meadows, rushing rivers, and
thickly forested valleys that fall between the mountain ridges, the
Wallowas have a grandeur that can take your breath away. Bighorn
sheep, elk, deer, and mountain goats populate the area. Nearly all
the trails in the Wallowa Mountains are at least partially contained
within the Eagle Cap Wilderness. The offices and visitor center for
the mountains are in Joseph at the Wallowa Mountains ranger office
of Wallowa-Whitman National Forest, but you can access different parts of the range from different towns in the region, including
Enterprise, La Grande, and Baker City. ⊠ *Wallowa Mountains Ranger
Office, 201 E. 2nd St.* ☎ *541/426–5546* ⊕ *www.fs.usda.gov/detail/
wallowa-whitman.*

HELLS CANYON

30 miles northeast of Joseph; 80 miles east of Baker City.

This remote place along the Snake River is the deepest river-carved
gorge in North America (7,900 feet), with many rare and endangered
animal species. There are three different routes from which to view
and experience the canyon, though only one is accessible year-round.

GETTING HERE

Many seasonal National Forest Service roads access Hells Canyon from
Imnaha east of Joseph and the Wallowa Mountain Loop. Four-wheel
drive can be necessary on certain roads, but National Forest Road 39
is paved the entire way; check with rangers at the Wallowa Mountains
Ranger Office in Joseph for road conditions and trip-planning advice.
Even in perfect conditions, these forest roads can be slow going; allow
two to three hours, for instance, to drive the 50-mile Wallowa Mountain Loop. Most float trips originate from the Hells Canyon Creek site
below the Hells Canyon Dam.

VISITOR INFORMATION
Hells Canyon Chamber of Commerce ☎ *541/742–4222* ⊕ *www.
hellscanyonchamber.com.*

EXPLORING

Fodor's Choice **Hells Canyon.** Most travelers take a scenic peek from the overlook on
★ the 45-mile **Wallowa Mountain Loop,** which follows Route National
Forest Road 39 (part of the Hells Canyon National Scenic Byway) from
just east of Halfway on Route Highway 86 to just east of Joseph on
Route Highway 350. At the junction of Route National Forest Road
39 and National Forest Road 3965, take the 6-mile round-trip spur to
the 5,400-foot-high rim at Hells Canyon Overlook. This is the easiest
way to get a glimpse of the canyon, but be aware that National Forest
Road 39 is open only during summer and early fall. During the late fall,
winter, and spring the best way to experience Hells Canyon is to follow
a slightly more out-of-the-way route along the **Snake River Segment** of
the Wallowa Mountain Loop. Following Snake River Road north from

Oxbow, the 60-mile round-trip route winds along the edge of Hells Canyon Reservoir on the Idaho side, crossing the Snake River at Hells Canyon Dam on the Oregon-Idaho border. In some places the canyon is 10 miles wide. There's a visitor center near the dam, and hiking trails continue on into the Hells Canyon Wilderness and National Recreation Area. Be sure you have a full tank before starting out, since there are no gas stations anywhere along the route. If you're starting from Joseph, you also have the option of heading to the **Hat Point Overlook**. From Joseph, take Route Highway 350 northeast to Imnaha, a tiny town along the Imnaha River. From there, National Forest Road 4240 leads southeast to Route Highway 315, which in turn heads northeast up a steep gravel road to the overlook. This route is also open only during the summer. Carry plenty of water. ⊠ *Enterprise.*

SPORTS AND THE OUTDOORS

FISHING AND BOATING

Hells Canyon Adventures. Book a fishing trip or jet-boat excursion on the Snake River through Hells Canyon with this well-respected company that offers half- and full-day trips. ⊠ *Oxbow* ☎ *541/785–3352, 800/422–3568* ⊕ *www.hellscanyonadventures.com.*

RECREATIONAL AREAS

Hells Canyon National Recreation Area. This is the site of one of the largest elk herds in the United States, plus 422 other species, including bald eagles, bighorn sheep, mule deer, white-tailed deer, black bears, bobcats, cougars, beavers, otters, and rattlesnakes. The peregrine falcon has also been reintroduced here. Part of the area was designated as Hells Canyon Wilderness, in parts of Oregon and Idaho, with the establishment of the Hells Canyon National Recreation Area in 1975. Additional acres were added as part of the Oregon Wilderness Act of 1984, and the recreation area currently extends across more than 652,000 wild and rugged acres. Nine hundred miles of trails wind through the wilderness area, closed to all mechanized travel. If you want to visit the wilderness it must be on foot, mountain bike, or horseback. Three of its rivers (the Snake, Imnaha, and Rapid) have been designated as Wild and Scenic. Environmental groups have proposed the creation of Hells Canyon National Park to better manage the area's critical habitat. You can access the canyon from several points—see the website for an overview map. ⊠ *Wallowa Mountains Office, 201 E. 2nd St., Joseph* ☎ *541/426–5546* ⊕ *www.fs.usda.gov/ wallowa-whitman.*

HALFWAY

63 miles southeast of Joseph, 40 miles south of Hells Canyon Dam, 55 miles east of Baker City.

Halfway, the closest town to Hells Canyon, got its name because it was midway between the town of Pine and the gold mines of Cornucopia. The mines are long gone now, but this small (population just under 300), straightforward town on the southern flanks of the Wallowas has an appealing main street and a quiet rural flavor. Most visitors to

Halfway are prepping for Hells Canyon or passing through along the scenic Wallowa Mountain Loop.

GETTING HERE

Halfway is reachable by car on Highway 86, part of the Hells Canyon National Scenic Byway. Interstate 84 at Baker City is 55 miles east. The summer-only Wallowa Mountain Loop road leads to Joseph, a scenic three-hour drive through the mountains.

WHERE TO STAY

$
B&B/INN
Inn at Clear Creek Farm. Amid 170 acres of orchards, ponds, woods, and fields on the southeastern flank of the Wallowa Mountains, this 1912 Craftsman-style farmhouse is a comfortable rural retreat on a working ranch. **Pros:** glorious views; peaceful and secluded; many recreational activities available. **Cons:** not exactly on the beaten path. $ *Rooms from: $100* ✉ *48212 Clear Creek Rd., off Fish Lake Rd., 3½ miles north of Halfway* ☎ *541/742–2238* ⊕ *www.clearcreekinn. com* 🛏 *5 rooms 1 suite* ⊙ *Multiple meal plans.*

$
B&B/INN
Pine Valley Lodge. From the outside, this lodge on Main Street is constructed like many others built in eastern Oregon during the timber boom of the late 1920s, using wood from the original mines' construction. **Pros:** nicely updated rooms; recreation options close by. **Cons:** in a tiny remote town with few services and amenities. $ *Rooms from: $110* ✉ *163 N. Main St.* ☎ *541/742–2027* ⊕ *www.pvlodge.com* 🛏 *8 rooms, 5 suites, 1 cottage* ⊙ *Breakfast.*

SHOPPING

Halfway Whimsical. Look past the silly name to find a cool artists' co-op chockablock full of landscape photography, textile art, and handcrafted jewelry. Some of the gallery's more "whimsical" items are clever remixes of household materials—think lamps made of toasters and jewelry made from cutlery. ✉ *231 Gover La.* ☎ *541/742–6040* ⊕ *www. halfwaywhimsical.com.*

BAKER CITY

44 miles south of La Grande, 305 miles southeast of Portland, 114 miles south of Joseph.

During the 1860s gold rush, Baker City was the hub of the action. Many smaller towns dried up after the gold rush, but Baker City transformed itself into the seat of the regional logging and ranching industries that are still around today. Remnants of its turn-of-the-century opulence, when it was the largest city between Salt Lake and Portland, are still visible in the many restored Victorian houses and downtown storefronts, many of which now hold distinctive boutiques, design shops, and cafés.

Baker City may not have that much gold left in its surrounding hills—but what hills they are. The Wallowas and Eagle Cap, the Elkhorn Ridge of the Blue Mountains, the Umatilla National Forest, the Wallowa-Whitman, Hells Canyon, Monument Rock—the panorama almost completes a full circle. Outdoor enthusiasts flock here for the climbing, fishing, hunting, waterskiing, canoeing, hiking, cycling, and skiing. It seems Baker City's gold rush has been supplanted by the "green rush."

Historic Baker City mural in downtown Baker City

GETTING HERE

Baker City is easily accessed by I–84, a five-hour drive east of Portland and a two-hour drive west of Boise, Idaho. The city is the hub for several smaller highways as well, including scenic Highway 7 through the Blue Mountains to John Day.

VISITOR INFORMATION

Baker County Chamber of Commerce and Visitors Center ✉ *490 Campbell St.* ☎ *541/523–5855, 800/523–1235* ⊕ *www.visitbaker.com.*

EXPLORING

Baker Heritage Museum. Located in a stately brick building that once housed the community's swimming pool, Baker's history center has one of the most impressive rock collections in the West. Assembled over a lifetime by a local amateur geologist, the Cavin-Warfel Collection includes thunder eggs, glowing phosphorescent rocks, and a 950-pound hunk of quartz. Other exhibits highlight pioneering, ranching, gold mining, and antique furniture. ✉ *2480 Grove St.* ☎ *541/523–9308* ⊕ *www.bakerheritagemuseum.com* ☉ *Mid-Mar.–Oct., daily 9–4.*

Adler House Museum. The museum also operates the nearby Adler House Museum, an 1889 Italianate house that was once home to an eccentric publishing magnate and philanthropist. ✉ *2305 Main St.* 🎫 *$6* ☉ *Mid-Mar.–Oct., Fri. and Sat. 10–3:30.*

EN ROUTE **Elkhorn Drive.** This scenic 106-mile loop winds from Baker City through the Elkhorn Range of the Blue Mountains. Only white-bark pine can survive on the range's sharp ridges and peaks, which top 8,000 feet; spruce, larch, Douglas fir, and ponderosa pine thrive on the lower slopes. The route is well marked; start in Baker City on Highway 7, head west to Sumpter, turn onto County Road 24 toward Granite, turn north on Forest Road 73 and take that over Granite Pass and eventually by Anthony Lakes ski area to Haines, and then return to Baker City along U.S. 30.

Fodor's Choice
★

National Historic Oregon Trail Interpretive Center. Head 5 miles east of Baker City to this sprawling facility, containing 12,000 square feet of galleries, for a superb exploration of pioneer life in the mid-1800s. From 1841 to 1861 about 300,000 people made the 2,000-mile journey from western Missouri to the Columbia River and the Oregon Coast, looking for agricultural land in the West. A simulated section of the Oregon Trail will give you a feel for camp life and the settlers' impact on Native Americans; an indoor theater presents movies and plays. A 4-mile round-trip trail winds from the center to the actual ruts left by the wagons. ⊠ *22267 Hwy. 86* ☏ *541/523–1843* ⊕ *www.blm.gov/or/ oregontrail* ⊠ *$8* ⊘ *Apr.–mid-Oct., daily 9–6; mid-Oct.–Nov. and Mar., daily 9–4; Dec.–Feb., Thurs.–Sun. 9–4.*

Sumpter Valley Railway. Though the original track was scrapped in 1947, an all-volunteer work force has rebuilt more than 7 miles of track on the railroad's original right-of-way. Today the train operates along a 5-mile route in Sumpter. The historic trains leave from the McEwen and Sumpter stations; call ahead for departure information. A few additional fall foliage runs and Christmas trains are offered in October and December respectively. ⊠ *211 Austin St., 22 miles west of Bakery City via Hwy. 7, Sumpter* ☏ *541/894–2268, 866/894–2268* ⊕ *www. sumptervalleyrailroad.org* ⊠ *$17.50* ⊘ *Memorial Day–Sept., weekends and holidays.*

WHERE TO EAT AND STAY

$$
AMERICAN

✕ **Barley Brown's.** It's the "Cheers" of Baker City–and everyone knows owner Tyler's name. A frequent winner at American beer festivals, the "Shredders Wheat" American Wheat Ale has beaten out international contenders for a gold at the World Beer Cup. You can watch the process behind glass windows as they brew some eight different beers (for example, Hot Blonde jalapeño ale and potent Tank Slapper India pale ale). Barley Brown's also makes tasty grub, from burgers and quesadillas to spicy pastas and fish-and-chips. Tyler is committed to using local produce (the hand-cut fries are Baker County potatoes) and hormone-free beef. ⑤ *Average main: $16* ⊠ *2190 Main St.* ☏ *541/523–4266* ⊕ *www. barleybrownsbeer.com* ⊘ *Closed Sun. No lunch.*

$
MODERN
AMERICAN

✕ **Earth & Vine Art & Wine Gallery.** A chic little café on the ground-floor corner of one of Baker's numerous historic buildings, Earth & Vine sticks to sandwiches, flatbread pizza, fondue, and other simple treats. Regional varieties occupy much of the short wine list, but owner Mary Ellen Stevenson keeps many more bottles in the cellar than she prints on the menu, so ask for a recommendation. Local art, live music, and periodic sushi nights pack in the Baker City creative class, as does brunch on weekends. ⑤ *Average main: $14* ⊠ *2001 Washington Ave.* ☏ *541/523–1687* ⊘ *Closed Mon.*

$
DELI

✕ **Zephyr Bakery & Deli.** In the heart of Baker City's lively downtown shopping district, Zephyr is a fine specialty-food store proffering fine jams, cheeses, and wines as well as an urbane café serving creative breakfast and lunch fare and well-made coffee drinks. Start the morning with an artichoke frittata or a ginger scone. Popular lunch options include the chevre sandwich and kale salad with polenta croutons. $ *Average main: $7* ⊠ *1917 Main St.* ☎ *541/523–4601* ⊙ *Closed Mon.–Wed. No dinner.*

$
HOTEL

🏨 **Bridge Street Inn.** Right off Main Street, the Bridge Street Inn is one of the least expensive motels in town. **Pros:** inexpensive; centrally located. **Cons:** walls can be a little thin; no-frills decor. $ *Rooms from: $65* ⊠ *134 Bridge St.* ☎ *541/523–6571, 800/932–9220* ⊕ *www.bridgestreetinn.net* ↴ *41 rooms* ⦿ *Breakfast.*

$
HOTEL
Fodor's Choice
★

🏨 **Geiser Grand Hotel.** Built in 1889, the stately Gesier Grand sits like the dowager duchess of Main Street, her cupola clock tower cutting a sharp figure against a wide Baker City sky—the Italianate Renaissance Revival beauty was once known as the finest hotel between Portland and Salt Lake City, and it's still one of the best. **Pros:** great downtown location; fascinating history; interesting Saturday afternoon hotel tour. **Cons:** rooms, while well-appointed, are decidedly old-fashioned and not to everyone's taste. $ *Rooms from: $109* ⊠ *1996 Main St.* ☎ *541/523–1889, 888/434–7374* ⊕ *www.geisergrand.com* ↴ *30 rooms* ⦿ *No meals.*

SHOPPING

MAD Habit Boutique. Whimsical crafts and decorative goods are sold at this large downtown boutique on historic Main Street, along with jewelry and women's clothing. Be sure to say hello to the friendly shop cats, Earl and Pearl, whose images appear on the shop's own line of greeting cards. ⊠ *1798 Main St.* ☎ *541/829–3157.*

No. 1911. This hip but unpretentious lifestyle and home-accessories shop stocks an eclectic assortment of goods, from whimsical Ames Bros. T-shirts to one-of-a-kind antiques. You'll also find soaps, balms, and lotions from U.S. Apothecary, Ranch Organics, and Duke Cannon Supply Co. ⊠ *1911 Main St.* ☎ *541/523–4321.*

SPORTS AND THE OUTDOORS

FAMILY **Anthony Lakes Ski Area.** Find some of the state's best powder at this hill in the Wallowa-Whitman National Forest, along with a vertical drop of 900 feet and a top elevation of 8,000 feet. There are 21 trails, one triple chairlift, and a 30-km cross-country network. Snowboards are permitted. ⊠ *47500 Anthony Lake Hwy., 35 miles northwest of Baker City, North Powder* ☎ *541/856–3277* ⊕ *www.anthonylakes.com* 🎟 *Lift tickets $35* ⊙ *Late Nov.–early Apr. (depending on conditions), Thurs.–Sun. 9–4.*

JOHN DAY

80 miles west of Baker City, 150 miles east of Bend.

More than $26 million in gold was mined in the John Day area. The town was founded shortly after gold was discovered there in 1862. Yet John Day is better known to contemporaries for the plentiful outdoor recreation it offers and for the nearby John Day Fossil Beds. The town is also a central location for trips to the Malheur National Wildlife Refuge and the towns of Burns, Frenchglen, and Diamond to the south.

As you drive west through the dry, shimmering heat of the John Day Valley on U.S. 26, it may be hard to imagine this area as a humid subtropical forest filled with lumbering 50-ton brontosauruses and 50-foot-long crocodiles. But so it was, and the eroded hills and sharp, barren-looking ridges contain the richest concentration of prehistoric plant and animal fossils in the world.

GETTING HERE

The town is a scenic, 90-minute drive from Baker City on Highways 7 and 26. To the west, it's about a three-hour drive to Bend via U.S. 26.

VISITOR INFORMATION

Grant County Chamber of Commerce ⊠ *301 W. Main St.* ☎ *551/575–0547, 800/769–5664* ⊕ *www.gcoregonlive.com.*

EXPLORING

Grant County Historical Museum. Two miles south of John Day, Canyon City is a small town that feels as if it hasn't changed much since the Old West days. Memorabilia from the gold rush is on display at the town's small museum, along with Native American artifacts and antique musical instruments. Drop in at the neighboring pioneer jail, which the locals pilfered years ago from a nearby crumbling ghost town. ⊠ *101 S. Canyon City Blvd., Canyon City* ☎ *541/575–0362, 541/575–0509 off-season* ⊕ *www.gchistoricalmuseum.com* ⊠ *$4* ☉ *Mid-May–Sept., Mon.–Sat. 9–4:30.*

Fodor'sChoice
★
Kam Wah Chung State Heritage Site. This ramshackle building operated by the state park system was a trading post on The Dalles Military Road in 1866 and 1867, then later served as a general store, a Chinese labor exchange for the area's mines, a doctor's shop, and an opium den. Listed on the National Register of Historic Places, the museum is an extraordinary testament to the early Chinese community in Oregon. Tours are on the hour with groups limited to 10 people; if you miss it, you can always catch the 19-minute video lecture given by the curator. ⊠ *125 N.W. Canton St.* ☎ *541/575–2800, 800/551–6949* ⊕ *www. oregonstateparks.org* ⊠ *Free* ☉ *May–Oct., daily 9–5.*

WHERE TO EAT AND STAY

$
AMERICAN
✕**Outpost Pizza, Pub & Grill.** The Outpost occupies one of the sleekest spaces in town: a large building with a log-cabin exterior, a vast entry lobby, and a bright, spacious, high-ceiling dining room. The kitchen serves creative pizzas and has a lengthy menu of standard entrées including burgers, steak, seafood, salads, and quesadillas. Breakfast is also available. ⑤ *Average main: $11* ⊠ *201 W. Main St.* ☎ *541/575–0250* ⊕ *www.gooutpost.com.*

$
AMERICAN
✕**Squeeze-In Restaurant & Deck.** This casual downtown eatery serves three meals a day and has a sunny deck overlooking Canyon Creek as well as a bustling, casual dining room. Regulars pile in at breakfast for buttermilk pancakes and biscuits with sausage gravy. Hearty American fare, including burgers, rib-eye steaks, salmon pasta bowls, and smothered pork ribs are served later in the day. ⑤ *Average main: $13* ⊠ *423 W. Main St.* ☎ *541/575–1045* ⊕ *www.squeeze-in.com* ☉ *No dinner Sun.*

John Day Fossil Beds

$ **Dreamers Lodge.** The outside of this hotel is quite dated if a bit fun
HOTEL   in a retro sense, but the rooms themselves are a definite step up from
the exterior, with comfortable armchairs as well as microwaves, refrigerators, and flat-screen TVs in all the rooms. **Pros:** good value; central
location. **Cons:** very basic. $ *Rooms from: $59* ✉ *144 N. Canyon Blvd.*
☎ *541/575–0526, 800/654–2849* ⤳ *25 rooms* ⚄ *No meals.*

JOHN DAY FOSSIL BEDS NATIONAL MONUMENT

40 miles west of John Day, 150 miles south of Pendleton.

FAMILY
Fodor's Choice
★

The geological formations that compose this peculiar monument cover
hundreds of square miles and preserve a diverse record of plant and
animal life spanning more than 40 million years of the Age of Mammals. The national monument itself is divided into three units: Sheep
Rock, Painted Hills, and Clarno—each of which looks vastly different
and tells a different part of the story of Oregon's history. Each unit has
picnic areas, restrooms, visitor information, and hiking trails. The main
visitor center is in the Sheep Rock Unit, 40 miles northwest of John Day;
Painted Hills and Clarno are about 70 and 115 miles northwest of John
Day, respectively. If you only have time for one unit of the park, make
it Painted Hills, where the namesake psychedelic mounds most vividly
expose the region's unique geology.

GETTING HERE

Reach the Sheep Rock Unit of the John Day Fossil Beds Monument
driving 38 miles west of John Day on U.S. 26, then 2 miles north on
Highway 19. The Painted Hills unit is an additional 35 miles west on

U.S. 26. To reach the Clarno unit, follow Highway 19 north from the Sheep Rock Unit, 60 miles northwest to Fossil. From Fossil, drive west on Highway 218 for 20 miles to the entrance. Be prepared to stop for frequent roadside interpretive exhibits between the three units. From other towns in central and eastern Oregon, it's a two-hour drive to the Sheep Rock Unit from The Dalles and Redmond, and a two-hour drive from Bend to the Painted Hills unit.

VISITOR INFORMATION

Thomas Condon Paleontology Center ⊠ *32651 Hwy. 19, 2 miles north of U.S. 26, Kimberly* ☎ *541/987–2333* ⊕ *www.nps.gov/joda.*

EXPLORING

Clarno. The 48-million-year-old fossil beds in this small section have yielded the oldest remains in the John Day Fossil Beds National Monument. The drive to the beds traverses forests of ponderosa pines and sparsely populated valleys along the John Day River before traveling through a landscape filled with spires and outcroppings that attest to the region's volcanic past. A short trail that runs between the two parking lots contains fossilized evidence of an ancient subtropical forest. Another trail climbs ½ mile from the second parking lot to the base of the Palisades, a series of abrupt, irregular cliffs created by ancient volcanic mud flows. ⊠ *Hwy. 218, 18 miles west of Fossil* ☎ *541/763–2203* ⊕ *www.nps.gov/joda* ⊙ *Daily, during daylight hrs.*

Painted Hills. The fossils at Painted Hills, a unit of the John Day Fossil Beds National Monument, date back about 33 million years, and reveal a climate that has become noticeably drier than that of Sheep Rock's era. The eroded buff-color hills reveal striking red and green striations created by minerals in the clay. Come at dusk or just after it rains, when the colors are most vivid. If traveling in spring, the desert wildflowers are most intense between late April and early May. Take the steep, ¾-mile **Carroll Rim Trail** for a commanding view of the hills or sneak a peek from the parking lot at the trailhead, about 2 miles beyond the picnic area. A few Forest Service roads lead north toward the Spring Basin Wilderness and the town of Antelope, but these can only be managed safely by high-clearance vehicles and when dry. ⊠ *37375 Bear Creek Rd., off U.S. 26, 9 miles west of Mitchell* ☎ *541/987–2333* ⊕ *www.nps. gov/joda* ⊙ *Daily, during daylight hrs.*

Sheep Rock. The **Thomas Condon Paleontology Center** at Sheep Rock serves as the area's primary visitor center, with a museum dedicated to the fossil beds, fossils on display, in-depth informational panels, handouts, and an orientation movie. Two miles north of the visitor center on Highway 19 is the impressive **Blue Basin**, a badlands canyon with sinuous blue-green spires. Winding through this basin is the ½-mile **Island in Time Trail,** where trailside exhibits explain the area's 28-million-year-old fossils. The 3-mile Blue Basin Overlook Trail loops around the rim of the canyon, yielding some splendid views. Blue Basin is a hike with a high effort-to-reward ratio, and in summer rangers lead interpretive jaunts Friday to Sunday at 10 am. ⊠ *32651 Hwy. 19, Kimberly* ☎ *541/987–2333* ⊕ *www.nps.gov/joda*

⊙ *Daily, during daylight hrs; visitor center: Sept.–May, daily 10–5; June–Aug. daily 9–5.*

WHERE TO STAY

$ **Fish House Inn and RV Park.** One of the only places to stay near the B&B/INN Sheep Rock fossil beds is 9 miles east, in the small town of Dayville, where the piscatory touches at this lovely inn include fishing gear, nets, and framed prints of fish. **Pros:** very low rates; fun atmosphere; ground floor of main house is great for a group traveling together. **Cons:** no food service other than the small mercantile shop. ⑤ *Rooms from: $50* ✉ *110 Franklin St., Dayville* ☎ *541/987-2124* ⊕ *www.fishhouseinn.com* ⌁ *5 rooms, 2 with shared bath, 1 suite* ❑❘ *No meals.*

$ **Hotel Condon.** A popular option for visitors exploring the Clarno (35 HOTEL miles south) and Painted Hills (60 miles south) sections of John Day Fodor'sChoice Fossil Beds National Monument, this three-story 1920 redbrick hotel ★ anchors the small town of Condon, which is also fairly close to the Columbia Gorge, about 70 miles southeast of The Dalles. **Pros:** grand old small-town hotel; friendly staff; large rooms with comfy furnishings. **Cons:** few dining options in the area; remote location. ⑤ *Rooms from: $100* ✉ *202 S. Main St., Condon* ☎ *541/384-4624, 800/201-6706* ⊕ *www.hotelcondon.com* ⌁ *12 rooms, 8 suites* ❑❘ *Breakfast.*

SOUTHEAST OREGON

Oregon's outback is indeed a high and lonesome setting of sagebrush desert, one-horse towns, and acre after acre of grazing cattle. And while the region may be light-years away from cosmopolitan, southeast Oregon has historically been one of the West's more demographically diverse regions. The area's indigenous Paiute and Shoshone residents came to share the land with white pioneer families, Basque herders, Mexican *bracero* cowboys, Chinese mine workers, and a number of other groups who've helped to shape Oregon's high desert culturally. The impressively spare scenery, meanwhile, has been a constant. While the sagebrush horizon can be beautiful in its constancy, visitors need only to brave some of the region's gravel back roads to discover a collection of diverse and singular landscapes. Places like the blistering white Alvord Desert, dramatic Steens Mountain, and the sculptural rock formations of Leslie Gulch can go toe-to-toe with any national park for straight-up natural beauty, but they host a comparative sliver of visitors each year.

BURNS

76 miles south of John Day, 130 miles east of Bend.

Named after poet Robert Burns, this town was the unofficial capital of the 19th-century cattle empires that staked claims to these southeastern Oregon high-plateau grasslands. Today Burns is a working-class town of 2,800 residents, surrounded by the more than 10,000 square miles of sagebrush, rimrock, and grassy plains that compose Harney County, the 10th-largest county in the United States (it's just a bit larger than all of Vermont). As the only place in the county with basic tourist amenities,

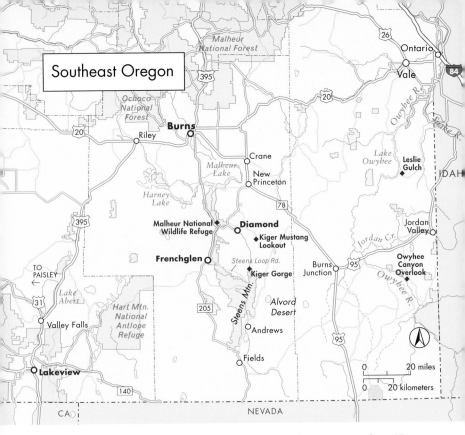

Southeast Oregon

Burns serves as a convenient stopover for many travelers. However, its usefulness as a source of modern convenience goes hand in hand with the sense that, unlike many of the region's smaller outposts, its Old West flavor has largely been lost. Rather than a final destination, think of Burns as a jumping-off point for exploring the poetry of the Malheur National Wildlife Refuge, Steens Mountain, and the Alvord Desert. Outdoor recreation includes fishing, backpacking, camping, boating, and hiking.

GETTING HERE
Bend and the nearest commercial airport are a 2½-hour drive west of Burns on U.S. 20. From John Day to the north, it's a 90-minute drive through the sagebrush scrub along U.S. 395.

VISITOR INFORMATION
Harney County Chamber of Commerce ⊠ *484 N. Broadway* ☎ *541/573–2636* ⊕ *www.harneycounty.com.*

EXPLORING

Harney County Historical Society & Museum. More like a cluttered antique superstore than a traditional museum, the county's treasure trove keeps a photo collection documenting the area's history, along with taxidermied animals, interesting rocks, old dental equipment, and all sorts of other bric-a-brac. There's a scale replica of the Liberty Bell (with the crack) made entirely of pinecones, a display of handmade quilts, and a whole lot of handmade placards exhibiting folksy Westernisms. ⊠ *18 W. D St.* ☎ *541/573–5618* ⊕ *www.hchistoricalsociety.com* ✉ *$4* ⊘ *Apr.–Sept., Tues.–Fri. 10–4, Sat. 10–3.*

WHERE TO EAT AND STAY

$ ✕ **Bella Java & Bistro.** This simple, but elegant café is in a historic store-
AMERICAN   front downtown, with high ceilings and eclectic decor. Pastries, simple sandwiches, and delicious, house-made soups anchor the small menu. Locals are in and out all day for their espresso fix, and there's local beer and wine behind the counter, too. $ *Average main: $10* ⊠ *314A N. Broadway* ☎ *541/573–3077* ⊘ *No dinner Mon. and Tues.*

$ 🛏 **Horseshoe Inn.** This no-frills motel a couple of miles outside town may
HOTEL   not be fancy, but it offers some of the best rates and cleanest rooms in the area, making it a handy and comfortable base for exploring Steens Mountain and Malheur Refuge. **Pros:** inexpensive; helpful staff; pet-friendly. **Cons:** simple decor; not within walking distance of downtown. $ *Rooms from: $59* ⊠ *30836 U.S. 20* ☎ *541/573–2034, 866/834–2034* ⊕ *www.horseshoeinn.net* ⟿ *32 rooms* ⊙ *Breakfast.*

SPORTS AND THE OUTDOORS

RECREATIONAL AREAS

Malheur National Forest. You can cut through this 1.7-million-acre forest in the Blue Mountains and Strawberry Mountains as you drive from John Day to Burns on U.S. 395. It has alpine lakes, meadows, creeks, and grasslands. Black bears, bighorn sheep, elk, and wolverines inhabit dense stands of pine, fir, and cedar. Near Burns the trees dwindle in number and the landscape changes from mountainous forest to open areas covered with sagebrush and dotted with junipers. The forest lies between U.S. 26 and U.S. 20, accessible via U.S. 395. ⊠ *Emigrant Creek Ranger District Office, 265 U.S. 20 S, Hines* ☎ *541/573–4300* ⊕ *www. fs.fed.us/r6/malheur.*

Fodor's Choice   **Malheur National Wildlife Refuge.** This unusual desert environment covers
★   187,000 acres. The squat, snow-covered summit of Steens Mountain is the only landmark in this area of alkali playas, buttes, scrubby mead-ows, and, most surprising of all, marshy lakes. It's arid and scorching hot in summer, but in the spring more than 320 species of migrating birds descend on the refuge's wetlands for their annual nesting and mating rituals. Following an ancient migratory flyway, they've been coming here for nearly a million years. The 30-mile Central Patrol Road, which runs through the heart of the refuge, is your best bet for viewing birds. But first stop at the **Malheur National Wildlife Refuge Headquarters,** where you can pick up leaflets and a free map. The staff will tell you where you're most likely to see the refuge's winged inhabitants. The refuge is a short way from local petroglyphs (ask at the headquarters); a remarkable pioneer structure called the **Round Barn** (head east from the headquarters on Narrows–Princeton Road for 9 miles; the road turns to gravel and then runs into Diamond Highway, a paved road that leads south 12 miles to the barn); and **Diamond Craters,** a series of volcanic domes, craters, and lava tubes (continue south from the barn 6 miles on Diamond Highway). Just

9

outside the refuge is a rare sagebrush lek, the spring mating grounds where clusters of gray-brown sage grouse conduct morning strutting routines with fanned-out feathers. Visit at sunrise between mid-March and mid-June to see this peculiar display (8 miles west on Foster Flat Road; ask at headquarters for more info). You'll need a car to get around Malheur National Wildlife Refuge, although the adventurous might enjoy exploring by bike or on foot. ✉ *36391 Sodhouse La., Princeton* ☎ *541/493–2612, 800/344–9453* ⊕ *www.fws.gov/malheur* ☒ *Free* ☉ *Park daily dawn–dusk; headquarters daily 8–4.*

DIAMOND

54 miles south of Burns.

Though it's tucked into a verdant little valley just east of Malheur National Wildlife Refuge, the unincorporated community of Diamond has an average year-round population of something like seven people. You could probably do your own census as you take in the undisturbed cluster of a few houses and a hotel in the midst of this wildlife-rich, wide-open country. During its heyday at the turn of the 20th century, Diamond had a population of about 50, including the McCoy family ranchers, who continue to run the town's hotel today.

GETTING HERE

Diamond Lane turns off Highway 205 about 42 miles south of Burns, heading east through the Malheur National Wildlife Refuge for 12 miles. The last few miles are unpaved but manageable for any passenger car. You can also catch up with Diamond Lane heading south from the refuge's Diamond Craters area.

WHERE TO EAT AND STAY

$ ✕ **Frazier's.** Owned by the Hotel Diamond, Frazier's is a small pub-style
AMERICAN restaurant in a renovated stone icehouse, the oldest building in Diamond and maybe the coolest little bar in southeastern Oregon. Burgers, steaks, salads, and sandwiches are served for lunch. Aside from the dinners served in the hotel, this is the only place in town to buy a meal. And as the Bureau of Land Management firefighters can tell you, it's also the only place for many miles to play a game of pool. The unmarked restaurant is found around the back of the hotel, and often looks like it might not be open, but head on in for friendly service in what feels like a subterranean speakeasy. ⑤ *Average main: $11* ✉ *Hotel Diamond, 49130 Main St.* ☎ *541/493–1898* ⊕ *www.historichoteldiamond.com* ☉ *No dinner.*

$ ⌂ **Hotel Diamond.** In the early 1900s the Hotel Diamond served the local
B&B/INN population of ranchers, Basque sheepherders, and cowhands; now it
Fodor's Choice caters to the birders, naturalists, and high-desert lovers who flock to
★   the Malheur Refuge. **Pros:** affordable; idyllic location; friendly owners. **Cons:** isolated. ⑤ *Rooms from: $81* ✉ *49130 Main St., 10 miles east of Hwy. 205* ☎ *541/493–1898* ⊕ *www.historichoteldiamond.com* ⇱ *8 rooms, 5 with shared bath* ☉ *Closed Nov.–late March* ⦿| *Breakfast.*

FRENCHGLEN

61 miles south of Burns, 30 miles southwest of Diamond.

Frenchglen, the tiny town near the base of Steens Mountain, has no more than a dozen residents, and in the off-season offers no basic services to travelers. In other words: eat first. The only lodging in town, the historic Frenchglen Hotel, is a true classic of Oregon hostelry. In the spring and summer Frenchglen's main street is crowded with birders on break from exploring the adjacent Malheur Refuge. The popular Steens Mountain Loop begins and ends here, and the town makes a nice setting-off point for adventures in the remote Alvord Desert.

GETTING HERE

Frenchglen is a one-hour drive south of Burns on Hwy. 205. It's an isolated, one-street town with minimal services, and the only gas station keeps sporadic hours. Fill up in Burns before heading down.

WHERE TO STAY

$
B&B/INN
Frenchglen Hotel. A historic example of the 1895–1930 architecture called American Foursquare, the 1920 Frenchglen Hotel is a simple white wooden house with a porch—Americana at its renovated best. **Pros:** historic round barn is on-site; close to Steens Mountain and Malheur Refuge; wonderfully historic. **Cons:** some rooms share a bathroom; no phones or TV. ⑤ *Rooms from: $75* ✉ *39184 Hwy. 205* ☎ *541/493–2825* ⊕ *www.frenchglenhotel.com* ⤳ *8 rooms, 5 with shared bath* ☾ *Closed Nov.–mid-Mar.* ⦿ *No meals.*

$
HOTEL
Steens Mountain Resort. Bordering the Malheur National Wildlife Refuge and overlooking vast prairie and mountain land, the Steens Mountain Resort has many lodging options for anyone who wants to fall asleep under the stars and wake up to an undisturbed Oregon sunrise. **Pros:** proximity to Malheur Refuge; general store on-site. **Cons:** "log cabins" are really "log trailers"—nice enough, but not particularly authentic. ⑤ *Rooms from: $75* ✉ *35678 Resort La., off North Loop Rd., 3 miles southeast of Frenchglen* ☎ *541/493–2415, 800/542–3765* ⊕ *www.steensmountainresort.com* ⤳ *9 units* ⦿ *No meals.*

SPORTS AND THE OUTDOORS

HIKING

Steens Mountain. Amid the flat landscape of southeastern Oregon, the mountain is hard to miss, although the sight of its 9,700-foot summit is more remarkable from the east. There, its sheer face rises from the flat basin of the desolate Alvord Desert, which stretches into Idaho and Nevada. On the western side, Steens Mountain slopes gently upward over a distance of about 20 miles and is less astonishing. Steens is not your average mountain—it's a huge fault block created when the ancient lava that covered this area fractured. Except for groves of aspen, juniper, and a few mountain mahogany, Steens is almost entirely devoid of trees and resembles alpine tundra. But starting in June the wildflower displays are nothing short of breathtaking, as are the views: on Steens you'll encounter some of the grandest scenery in the West.

The mountain is a great spot for hiking over untrammeled and unpopulated ground, but you can also see it by car (preferably one with

9

four-wheel drive) on the rough but passable 52-mile **Steens Loop Road,** open mid-July–October. You need to take reasonable precautions; storms can whip up out of the blue, creating hazardous conditions. On the drive up you might spot golden eagles, bighorn sheep, and deer. The view out over **Kiger Gorge,** on the southeastern rim of the mountain, includes a dramatic U-shape path carved out by a glacier. A few miles farther along the loop road, the equally stunning **East Rim viewpoint** is more than 5,000 feet above the valley floor. The view on a clear day takes in the Alvord Desert. The mountain and surrounding 669-square-mile Steens Mountain Cooperative Management and Protection Area is administered by the Bureau of Land Management, which has an office in Burns. ⊠ *Steens Mountain Loop Rd., off Hwy. 205, 10 miles southeast of Frenchglen* ☎ *541/573–4400* ⊕ *www.blm.gov/or/districts/ burns/recreation/steens-mtn.php.*

**OFF THE
BEATEN
PATH**

Alvord Desert. With the eastern face of Steens Mountain in the background, the Alvord Desert conjures up Western movie scenes of parched cowboys riding through the desert—though today you're more likely to see wind sailors scooting across these hard-packed alkali flats (the *playa*) and glider pilots using the basin as a runway. But once they go home, this desert is deserted. Snowmelt from Steens Mountain can turn it into a shallow lake until as late as mid-July. The mostly gravel Fields-Denio Road runs alongside the playa, accessing a number of rutted tracks maintained by the Bureau of Land Management. From Frenchglen, drive south on Hwy. 205 for about 50 miles, turning left near Fields onto Fields-Denio Road and following the signs. ⊠ *Fields-Denio Rd., Princeton* ⊕ *www.blm.gov/or/districts/burns/recreation/ alvord-mann.php.*

Fields Station. At the south end of the road, Fields Station pretty much *is* the town of Fields, an all-in-one post office, general store, motel, and café. The old-fashioned milk shakes at this desert outpost are themselves worth the drive, made with old-school fountain syrups and served in enormous, 24-ounce plastic cups. ⊠ *22276 Fields Dr., Fields* ☎ *541/495–2275.*

Alvord Hot Springs. Though the land is privately owned, the public is welcome to use the Alvord Hot Springs, two concrete pools taking on superheated water from the nearby springs, for a small fee. From this roadside, ramshackle soaking station, the view of Steens Mountain is superb. Be warned: although Alvord doesn't officially condone nudity, plenty who visit here go without swimwear. ⊠ *46008 Alvord Ranch La., off Fields-Denio Rd., 23 miles north of Fields, Princeton* ☎ *541/589–2282* ⊕ *www.alvordhotsprings.com* 🖃 *$5.*

LAKEVIEW

139 miles southwest of Burns, 100 miles east of Klamath Falls, and 175 miles southeast of Bend.

At 4,800 feet, Lakeview is the highest town in Oregon. For years, it had been anchored by the Old Perpetual Geyser at Hunter's Hot Springs, which erupted up to 60 feet every 90 seconds. The geyser's been dormant since 2009, however, possibly as a result of the town's digging a geothermal well nearby. The Abert Rim is still there, though, about 20 miles to the north of town, the region's best-known fault scarp. The ridge is more than 2,000 feet deep and 30 miles long. The Lakeview area is considered one of the state's best for hang gliding, rockhounding, fishing, and enjoying winter sports.

GETTING HERE

Just north of the California border, Lakeview is thoroughly remote, reachable by car from Burns (2½ hours), Klamath Falls (2 hours), and Bend (3 hours).

Lake County Chamber of Commerce ⊠ *126 N. E St.* ☎ *541/947–6040, 877/947–6040* ⊕ *www.lakecountychamber.org.*

Fremont-Winema National Forest. The 2.3-million-acre forest surrounds Lakeview, and supports small populations of cougars, bobcats, and black bears, as well as the bald eagle and the peregrine falcon. There are 600 miles of streams, as well as many lakes and reservoirs scattered throughout the forest. Anglers will find that the largemouth bass, yellow perch, black and white crappie, bullhead, and trout are plentiful. The winter recreation season, which runs from December through March, provides downhill and cross-country skiing, snowmobiling, snowshoeing, and ice fishing. In summer there's backpacking and camping. ⊠ *Headquarters, 1301 S. G St.* ☎ *541/947–2151* ⊕ *www.fs.usda.gov/ fremont-winema* ▱ *Free* ☉ *Daily.*

Paisley. People have lived in the area around Paisley, 48 miles north of Lakeview, for as long as 10,000 years. Evidence of its earlier inhabitants has been found in caves and rock paintings in the region. Over the years the Northern Paiute, Modac, and Klamath Indians settled here. Today Paisley, "Home of the Mosquito Festival" (a community fair held in late July) is a tiny, picturesque cowboy town with a general store and a restaurant. ⊠ *Hwy. 31, City Hall* ☎ *541/943–3173* ⊕ *www. cityofpaisley.net.*

WHERE TO EAT AND STAY

$
AMERICAN
✕ **Eagles Nest Food & Spirits.** Some of the finest food in the area is served here, including excellent steak, shrimp, and chicken dishes. If you're not up for a full entrée at dinner, which comes with soup, salad, potatoes, bread, and sorbet, try a Caesar salad or burger. The lounge is hopping until 2 am. ⑤ *Average main: $13* ⊠ *117 N. E St.* ☎ *541/947–4824.*

$
HOTEL
FAMILY
▦ **Fremont Inn.** The modern, well-appointed rooms in this motel in downtown Lakeview are among the brightest and most attractive in the area—the huge suites with living rooms, sleeper sofas, and full-size refrigerators are especially nice and a great option for families or friends traveling together. **Pros:** clean and contemporary rooms; several restaurants within walking distance. **Cons:** on busy main road through town. ⑤ *Rooms from: $89* ⊠ *524 N. G St.* ☎ *541/947–2060* ⊕ *www. fremontinnlakecounty.com* ⤵ *26 rooms, 6 suites* ⦿ *Breakfast.*

SPORTS AND THE OUTDOORS

Lakeview is known as the hang gliding capital of the West, and many launch spots can be found in the Fremont National Forest.

TRAVEL SMART OREGON

GETTING HERE AND AROUND

Except for Portland, you'll need a car to enjoy Oregon's cities, towns, coast, mountains, and wine country. Portland has outstanding public transportation options, such as a light rail (that goes to the airport), streetcar, buses, and taxis. This is not the case in most other towns in the state, so even if bus or train service exists between two points, you'll need a car to get around once you reach your destination.

▌ AIR TRAVEL

Flying times to Portland are about 5 hours from New York, 4 hours from Chicago, 2½ from Los Angeles, and 3¼ hours from Dallas.

AIRPORTS

Portland International Airport (PDX) is an efficient and modern airport with service to and from most major national and a handful of international destinations. It's a relatively uncrowded facility, and both check-in and security lines tend to proceed quickly. It's also easily accessible from Downtown Portland, both by car and public transit. It serves as the primary gateway to the state, with connections to a handful of smaller airports, including Bend, Coos Bay, Eugene, Medford, and Pendleton.

Airport Info Portland International Airport (PDX) (☎ 503/460–4040 or 877/739–4636 ⊕ www.portofportland.com/pdx_home.aspx).

GROUND TRANSPORTATION

PDX is just 30 minutes by car from Downtown Portland, and is served by taxi ($35–$40), light rail and bus ($2.50), and airport shuttle service ($14 one-way, $24 round-trip).

Contacts Blue Star Airporter (☎ 503/249–1837 ⊕ www.bluestarbus.com). **Broadway Cab** (☎ 503/227–1234 ⊕ www.broadwaycab. com). **Green Cab and Shuttle** (☎ 503/234–1414 or 877/853–3577 ⊕ www.greentrans. com). **New Rose City Cab** (☎ 503/282–7707 ⊕ www.newrosecitycabco.com). **Portland Shuttle Service** (☎ 503/860–5398 ⊕ www. portlandshuttles.com). **Radio Cab** (☎ 503/227–1212 ⊕ www.radiocab.net). **Portland Taxicab** (☎ 503/256–5400 ⊕ www.portlandtaxi.net).

FLIGHTS

Airline Contacts Air Canada (☎ 888/247–2262 ⊕ www.aircanada.com). **Alaska Airlines/Horizon Air** (☎ 800/252–7522 ⊕ www.alaskaair.com). **Allegiant Air** (☎ 702/505–8888 ⊕ www.allegiantair.com). **American Airlines** (☎ 800/433–7300 ⊕ www. aa.com). **Continental Airlines** (☎ 800/523–3273 ⊕ www.continental.com). **Delta Airlines** (☎ 800/221–1212 ⊕ www.delta.com). **Frontier Airlines** (☎ 800/432–1359 ⊕ www. frontierairlines.com). **Hawaiian Airlines** (☎ 800/367–5320 ⊕ www.hawaiianair.com). **jetBlue** (☎ 800/538–2583 ⊕ www.jetblue. com). **SeaPort Airlines** (☎ 888/573–2767 ⊕ www.seaportair.com). **Southwest Airlines** (☎ 800/435–9792 ⊕ www.southwest. com). **United Airlines/United Express** (☎ 800/864–8331 ⊕ www.united.com). **USAirways** (☎ 800/428–4322 800/622–1015 ⊕ www.usairways.com).

Charter Companies Express Jet (☎ 877/958–2677 ⊕ expressjet.com). **Executive Flight, Inc.** (☎ 800/762–8253 ⊕ www. execflight.com). **Premier Jets** (☎ 503/640–2927 or 800/635–8583 ⊕ premierjets.com).

▌ BOAT TRAVEL

CRUISES

From early April through early November, a few cruise lines offer excursions focused specifically on the Pacific Northwest, usually along the Columbia River, leaving from Portland. **Un-Cruise Adventures** (formerly America Safari Cruises) offers seven-day excursions (some of them wine themed) along the Columbia and Snake Rivers, calling at Richland, Clarkston–Hells Canyon, Walla Walla,

The Dalles, Hood River, Bonneville Dam, Portland, and Astoria.

American Cruise Lines runs seven-day excursions along the Columbia and Snake Rivers, departing either from Portland or Clarkston (WA), on a Victorian-style stern-wheeler, the *Queen of the West*.

American Cruise Lines ☎ *800/460–4518* ⊕ *www.americancruiselines.com.*

Un-Cruise Adventures ☎ *888/862–8881* ⊕ *www.un-cruise.com.*

∎ BUS TRAVEL

Greyhound buses travel to and within Oregon, providing frequent service to major cities, such as Portland, Eugene, and Medford.

Bus Info Greyhound Lines (☎ *800/231–2222* ⊕ *www.greyhound.com*).

In Portland, TriMet operates one of the finest mass transit systems in the country with buses connecting to MAX light rail stations, which provide faster service to the airport and suburban areas. Most buses stop every 15 minutes or so most of the day, every day. Service is less frequent outside rush hour. A single fare is $2.50, a weekly pass is $26, and a monthly, unlimited pass is $100.

TriMet Mass Transit (☎ *503/238–7433* ⊕ *trimet.org/max*).

∎ CAR TRAVEL

I–5 is the major north–south conduit for western Oregon (the most populous part of the state) and provides a straight shot at high speeds from California to Washington—provided there aren't traffic snarls due to slick conditions or summer road construction. Most of Oregon's largest cities, such as Portland, Salem, Eugene, Medford, and Ashland, are along I–5. This makes driving between the major hubs the most practical way of exploring the state, as bus and train service is limited, and once outside Portland you'll need a car to get around.

For those who have the time, traveling U.S. 101 is an attraction in itself, as it hugs the Oregon Coast the entire length of the state with its incredibly scenic road. Make sure you want to commit to the coastal drive, which may be slow going in some parts, before getting on U.S. 101, because jumping back and forth to I–5 is very time-consuming.

The Cascade Range cuts through the middle of Oregon, which means that east–west journeys often wind through mountain passes, and can be either simply breathtaking (summer) or beautiful, slow, and treacherous (winter).

I–84 is northern Oregon's major east–west artery—it enters the majestic Columbia River Gorge near Portland and continues east to Hood River, The Dalles, Pendleton, LaGrande, and Baker City. U.S. 26 provides access to Mt. Hood from Portland and eventually connects with U.S. 97, leading to Bend.

TRAVEL TIMES FROM PORTLAND BY CAR	
Bend	3½–4 hours
Crater Lake National Park	4½–5 hours
Columbia River Gorge/ Mt. Hood	1½ hours
Willamette Valley	1½–2 hours

CAR RENTALS

∎ TIP➔ **Make sure that a confirmed reservation guarantees you a car. Agencies sometimes overbook, particularly for busy weekends and holiday periods.**

Unless you only visit Portland, you will need to rent a car for at least part of your trip. It's possible to get around the big cities by public transportation and taxis, but once you go outside city limits, your options are limited.

Rates in Portland begin at $30 a day and $150 a week, not including the 17% tax. Note that summer rates can be absurd (up to $65 per day for a compact); book as far in advance as possible, and if you find a good deal, grab it. All the major agencies are represented here.

In Oregon, you must be 21 to rent a car. Non-U.S. citizens need a reservation voucher, passport, driver's license, and insurance for each driver.

GASOLINE

The first thing visitors notice in Oregon is that it is illegal for customers to pump their own gas. Gas stations are plentiful in major metropolitan areas and along major highways such as I–5. Major credit and debit cards are accepted, and stations often stay open late; except in rural areas, where you may drive long stretches without a refueling opportunity. ■**TIP➜ Keep an eye on the gauge when traveling to remote areas and off-the-beaten-path trails, particularly if you'll be heading down Forest Service roads. A good rule of thumb is to fill up before you get off (or too far away from) a major highway like I–5, U.S. 101, U.S. 97, or I–84.**

PARKING

Oregon communities offer plenty of on-street parking and pay lots. In certain urban areas, specifically Portland, there are sections of town where street parking is metered and can be hard to find, particularly during festivals and special events. Mass transit in Portland is a plentiful and efficient alternative.

ROAD CONDITIONS

Winter driving can present challenges; in coastal areas the mild, damp climate contributes to frequently wet roadways. Snowfall generally occurs only once or twice a year on the coast and in the valleys, but when snow does fall, traffic grinds to a halt and roadways become treacherous and stay that way until the snow melts.

Tire chains, studs, or snow tires are essential equipment for winter travel in mountain areas, which receive plenty of snow starting as early as October and running well into the middle of spring. If you're planning to drive into high elevations, be sure to check the weather forecast beforehand. Even the main-highway mountain passes can close because of snow conditions. In winter, state and county highway departments operate snow-advisory telephone lines that give pass conditions.

ROADSIDE EMERGENCIES

Emergency Services AAA Oregon (☎ 800/222–4357 ⊕ www.aaa.com).

Oregon State Police (☎ 503/378–3720 or 800/452–7888).

RULES OF THE ROAD

Oregon drivers tend to be fairly polite and slower going, which can be a bit maddening for those in a hurry. Bicyclists are plentiful in Oregon cities and rural highways; drivers need to be especially alert to avert accidents, including when opening the car door after parking.

Car seats are compulsory for children under four years *and* 40 pounds; older children are required to sit in booster seats until they are eight years old *and* 80 pounds.

Oregon is a hands-free state. It is illegal to talk or text on a cell phone while operating a motor vehicle, and doing so will net you a hefty fine. Use a wireless headset device if you need to stay connected.

▌ TAXI TRAVEL

Taxis in Oregon are of limited use, although Portland has several reliable companies. It can be expensive to get around town by cab, however, and you need to call for a taxi, as it's very difficult to hail them on the street. In Portland the flag-drop rate is $2.50 and then $2.60 per mile. Make sure to ask whether the driver takes credit cards, whether there's a minimum fare, and whether there are charges for extra passengers. Other charges may include waiting times and airport minimums. Other larger communities in the state have at least one or two taxi companies, but you'll generally find that a couple of cab rides per day costs about the same as a daily car-rental rate.

Portland Taxi Companies **Broadway Cab**
(📞 *503/333–3333* ⊕ *www.broadwaycab.com*).
Green Cab and Shuttle (📞 *503/234–1414*
⊕ *www.greentrans.com*). **New Rose City Cab**
(📞 *503/282–7707* ⊕ *www.newrosecitycabco.*
com).

Eugene Taxi Companies **Bio Taxi**
(📞 *541/747–2583* ⊕ *www.biotaxi.us*).
Eugene Hybrid Taxi (📞 *541/357–8294*
⊕ *eugenehybridtaxis.com*).

▌ TRAIN TRAVEL

Amtrak has daily service to the Pacific
Northwest from the Midwest and California. The *Coast Starlight* begins in Los
Angeles; makes stops throughout California, western Oregon, and Washington;
and terminates in Seattle. There are stops
in both Portland and Eugene; the 2½-hour
trip between Portland and Eugene costs
$27–$50.

Amtrak's *Cascades* begins in Vancouver,
British Columbia; makes stops in Seattle,
Tacoma, Portland, and Salem; and terminates in Eugene. The trip from Seattle
to Portland takes roughly 3½ hours and
costs $34–$44 for a coach seat; this is
a pleasant alternative to the rather dull
drive along I–5. The *Empire Builder*
begins in Chicago; makes stops in Mil-
waukee, WI; St. Paul, MN; Spokane, WA;
and other cities before arriving in Portland. The journey from Spokane to Portland is 7 hours ($70–$85), with part of
the route running through the Columbia
River Gorge.

■**TIP→** Book Amtrak tickets at least a
few days in advance, especially if you're
traveling between Seattle and Portland
on the weekend.

Train Info **Amtrak** (📞 *800/872-7245* ⊕ *www.*
amtrak.com).

ESSENTIALS

▋ ACCOMMODATIONS

The lodgings we list are the cream of the crop in each price category. We always list the facilities that are available, but we don't specify whether they cost extra; when pricing accommodations, always ask what's included and what costs extra. Properties are assigned price categories based on a standard double room in high season (excluding holidays), and excluding tax and service charges. Oregon room taxes range from 6% to 10.4%. ⇨ *For price categories, see individual chapters.*

APARTMENT AND HOUSE RENTALS

An alternative to staying in a hotel is to spread out a bit and relax in a vacation rental. There are plenty of choices, particularly along the Oregon Coast, near Mt. Hood, and in Central Oregon resort areas near Bend. Renting an apartment or a house is an especially attractive idea for long-term visitors or large groups and families.

Contacts ForGetaway (⊕ *www.forgetaway. com*). **Home Away** (⊕ *www.homeaway.com*).

BED-AND-BREAKFASTS

Oregon is renowned for its range of bed-and-breakfast options, which are found everywhere from busy urban areas to casual country farms and windswept coastal retreats. Many bed-and-breakfasts in Oregon provide full gourmet breakfasts, and some have kitchens that guests can use. Other popular amenities to ask about are fireplaces, jetted bathtubs, and outdoor hot tubs. The regional bed-and-breakfast organizations listed below can provide information on reputable establishments.

Contacts Bed & Breakfast.com (☎ *512/322–2710 or 800/462–2632* ⊕ *www. bedandbreakfast.com*). **Bed & Breakfast Inns Online** (☎ *310/280–4363 or 800/215–7365* ⊕ *www.bbonline.com*). **BnB Finder.com** (☎ *888/469–6663* ⊕ *www.bnbfinder.com*).

Oregon Bed & Breakfast Guild (☎ *800/944– 6196* ⊕ *www.obbg.org*).

CAMPING

Oregon has excellent state-run campgrounds. Half accept advance camping reservations, and the others are first come, first served. Campgrounds range from primitive tent sites to parks with yurts, cabins, and full hookups. Sites are located in and around Oregon's more spectacular natural sites, be it on the coast, the Cascade Range, or near the wine country. Privately operated campgrounds sometimes have extra amenities such as laundry rooms and swimming pools. For more information, contact the state or regional tourism department.

Campground Reservations Oregon Parks and Recreation Dept. (☎ *800/452–5687 reservations* ⊕ *www.oregon.gov/oprd/parks*).

▋ COMMUNICATIONS

INTERNET

Like the rest of the country, Oregon is well wired and virtually all hotels, most coffeehouses, and many other businesses offer Wi-Fi, which is typically free except at a handful of mostly upscale hotels that cater to business travelers.

▋ EATING OUT

The farm-to-table concept is in full bloom in Oregon. Pacific Northwest cuisine highlights regional seafood, locally raised meat, and organic produce. Farm stands are plentiful in the rural areas and are definitely worth a stop; almost all cities have at least a weekly farmers' market, and Portland has them daily most of the year.

All of Oregon's cities and prominent towns have some genuinely stellar dining options. Portland has become one of the top foodie destinations in the country, and Bend, Eugene, Ashland, Hood

River, the Willamette Valley, and several towns along the coast—most notably Astoria, Cannon Beach, and Newport—have a few superb restaurants specializing in locavore-driven cuisine. Portland has also become quite famous for its wealth of food carts.

Oregon's wines are well regarded throughout the world, particularly those produced in the Willamette Valley and, increasingly, the Rogue Valley in southern Oregon and Columbia Gorge around Hood River. It's also one of the top states in the country for craft breweries, microdistilleries, and artisan coffee roasters. Portland again leads the way when it comes to beer, booze, and beans, but Bend and Astoria also have several nationally acclaimed producers, and you'll find notable brewpubs and coffeehouses throughout the state, even in small towns. The restaurants listed in the chapters are among the best in each price category. ⇨ *For price categories, see individual chapters. For information on food-related health issues, see Health below.*

MEALS AND MEALTIMES

Unless otherwise noted, the restaurants listed in this guide are open daily for lunch and dinner. Most people eat dinner between 6 and 9 pm, although in many rural areas—including some coastal towns—some restaurants close by 8 or 8:30, especially on weeknights.

RESERVATIONS AND DRESS

Regardless of the venue, it's a good idea to inquire whether reservations are needed on a weekend evening. We only mention them specifically when reservations are essential (there's no other way you'll ever get a table) or when they are not accepted. For popular restaurants, book as far ahead as you can (often a week is more than ample), and reconfirm as soon as you arrive. (Large parties should always call ahead to check the reservations policy.) We mention dress only when men are required to wear a jacket or a jacket and

tie, although these policies are virtually unheard of in Oregon.

WINE, BEER, AND SPIRITS

Oregon's largest concentration of wineries is in the Willamette Valley between the northern Cascades and the coast, but you'll also find vibrant wine regions in the Rogue Valley and Columbia Gorge. The Oregon Wine Board maintains a helpful website, with facts, history, and information on local wineries.

Oregon has more than 150 microbreweries, with plenty of festivals and events celebrating its brews. The Oregon Brewers Guild also has links to breweries and information on events.

You must be 21 to buy alcohol in Oregon.

Contacts Oregon Brewers Guild (⊕ *www. oregonbeer.org*). **Oregon Wine Board** (⊕ *www.oregonwine.org*).

▌HOURS OF OPERATION

Oregon store hours are fairly typical compared to the rest of the United States. Major department stores or shops in the downtown areas including Portland generally follow the 10-to-6 rule, but you should always phone ahead if you have your heart set on visiting a smaller shop. Never assume that a store is open on Sunday, even in the major cities; many smaller shops have truncated Saturday hours as well. Thankfully, coffeehouses tend to keep regular and long hours, so you'll have no problem finding one to kill time in if you have to wait for a store to open.

Note that bars in Oregon close at 2 am, with last call coming as early as 1:30.

▌MONEY

Prices throughout this guide are given for adults. Substantially reduced fees are almost always available for children, students, and senior citizens.

In Portland, Downtown parking meters take credit cards.

▌PACKING

It's all about the layers here, as there's no other way to keep up with the weather, which can morph from cold and overcast to warm and sunny and back again in the course of a few hours, especially in spring and early fall. Summer days are warm and more consistent, but evenings can cool off substantially. August and September are the glorious, warm, clear months that remind Oregonians why they live there. Bring an umbrella or raincoat for unpredictable fall and winter weather. Hikers will want to bring rain gear and a hat with them, even if they're visiting in summer; insect repellent is also a good idea if you'll be hiking along mountain trails or beaches.

▌SAFETY

The greatest dangers in the Northwest are becoming lost or suffering an accident in the great outdoors. Don't hike alone, and make sure you bring enough water plus basic first-aid items. If you're not an experienced hiker, stick to tourist-friendly spots such as the well-marked trails in the national parks; if you have to drive 30 miles down a Forest Service road to reach a trail, it's possible you might be the only one hiking on it.

▌TAXES

Oregon has no sales tax, although many cities and counties levy a tax on lodging and services. Room taxes, for example, vary from 6% to 10.4%.

▌TIME

Most of Oregon is in the Pacific time zone, except for Malheur County in eastern Oregon, which is in the mountain time zone.

▌TIPPING

TIPPING GUIDELINES FOR OREGON	
Bartender	$1 to $5 per round of drinks, depending on the number of drinks
Bellhop	$1 to $5 per bag, depending on the level of the hotel
Hotel Doorman	$1–$2 if he helps you get a cab
Hotel Maid	1$–$3 a day (either daily or at the end of your stay, in cash)
Hotel Room-Service Waiter	$1 to $2 per delivery, even if a service charge has been added
Taxi Driver	15%–20%, but round up the fare to the next dollar amount
Tour Guide	10% of the cost of the tour
Valet Parking Attendant	$1–$2, but only when you get your car
Waiter	15%–20%, with 20% being the norm at high-end restaurants; nothing additional if a service charge is added to the bill
Coat Check	$1–$2 per item checked unless there is a fee, then nothing

▌VISITOR INFORMATION

Travel Oregon (☎ 503/284-4620 ⊕ www.traveloregon.com). **Travel Portland** (☎ 503/275-9750 or 800/962-3700 ⊕ www.travelportland.com).

INDEX

Z

PHOTO CREDITS

Cover credit: Front cover: Jean-Paul Azam/Hemis/Corbis [Description: Haystack Rock, Cannon Beach, Oregon]. 1, Greg Vaughn. 2, tusharkoley / Shutterstock 5, Rex Hill. Chapter 1: Experience Oregon: 8-9, zack schnepf/iStockphoto. 10, Capricornis Photographic Inc./Shutterstock. 11 (left), Aimin Tang/iStockphoto. 11 (right), Rachell Coe/Shutterstock. 14, kun0me/flickr. 15 (left), Jeremy Dunham. 15 (right), eyeliam/flickr. 16 (left), Christopher Boswell / Shutterstock. 16 (top), Lawrence Freytag/iStockphoto. 16 (bottom right), Brian Holsclaw/Flickr, [CC BY-ND 2.0]. 16 (bottom middle), Thomas Barrat / Shutterstock. 17 (top left), The High Desert Museum. 17 (top middle), James Horning/Shutterstock. 17 (right), Norman Eder/iStockphoto. 17 (bottom middle), Chuck Pefley / Alamy. 17 (bottom left), Neta Degany/iStockphoto. 18, eyeliam/flickr. 19 (left), Richard Hallman / Freelanceimaging. com. 19 (right), Xuanlu Wang/Shutterstock. 20, Eric Cable. 21 (left), Julie DeGuia/Shutterstock. 21 (right), vis-a-v./Flickr. 22, Matt McGee/Flickr. 23, Argyle Winery. 24, TFoxFoto/Shutterstock. 26, William Blacke/iStockphoto. 27, Stuart Westmorland / age fotostock. 29, Thomas Kitchin & Vict / age fotostock. 30, San Juan Safaris. Chapter 2: Portland: 31, Brian A. Ridder/Flickr. 32, --b--/Flickr. 33 (left), David Owen/Flickr. 33 (right), Michael Hashizume/Flickr. 34, Karen Massier/iStockphoto. 41 and 45, Greg Vaughn. 55, Rigucci/Shutterstock. 101, Jason Vandehey/Shutterstock. 105, Realitytimes | Dreamstime.com. Chapter 3: The Oregon Coast: 111, Greg Vaughn. 112, scaredy_kat/Flickr. 113 (top), Oksana Perkins/iStockphoto. 113 (bottom), OCVA/Flickr. 114, Tom Wald/iStockphoto. 115 (bottom), John Norris/Flickr. 115 (top), Scott Catron/wikipedia.org. 116, Pacific Northwest USCG/Flickr. 141, Greg Vaughn. 144, Oregon Coast Aquarium. 151, Greg Vaughn. Chapter 4: The Willamette Valley and Wine Country: 165, Dennis Frates / Alamy. 166, Don Hankins/Flickr. 167, Doreen L. Wynja. 168, Craig Sherod. 176, Greg Vaughn. 184, Jason Tomczak. 185, Greg Vaughn. 186, Rex Hill. 188 (left), Jason Tomczak. 188 (right), Rex Hill, 189, Doreen L. Wynja. 190 (top), Polara Studio. 190 (bottom), Rich Stanton. 191 (left), Kent Derek. 191 (center), Rex Hill. 191 (right), Norman Eder/iStockphoto. 193 (left), Andrea Johnson Photography. 193 (center), Polara Studio. 193 (right), Dundee Bistro. 204 and 212, Gerg Vaughn. Chapter 5: The Columbia River Gorge and Mt. Hood: 217, William Blacke/iStockphoto. 218, Timberline Lodge. 219 (top), Robert Crum/iStockphoto. 219 (bottom), Christian Sawicki/iStockphoto. 220, Rigucci/Shutterstock. 228, zschnepf/Shutterstock. 230 and 233, Greg Vaughn. 243, Melissa & Bryan Ripka/Flickr. Chapter 6: Central Oregon: 249, Mike Houska. 250 (bottom), Black Butte Ranch. 250 (top), Robert O. Brown Photography/iStockphoto. 251, JonDissed/Flickr. 252, Sunriver Resort. 259, Lyn Topinka/wikimedia. 263, Sunriver Resort. 272, mariachily/Flickr. Chapter 7: Crater Lake National Park: 277, William A. McConnell. 278 (bottom), Aimin Tang/iStockphoto. 278 (top left), Steve Terrill. 278 (top right), Ashok Rodrigues/iStockphoto. 279, Michael Rubin/iStockphoto. 280, Vivian Fung/Shutterstock. Chapter 8: Southern Oregon: 289, Greg Vaughn. 290, Michael Dunn~!/Flickr. 291 (top), Michael (a.k.a. moik) McCullough/wikimedia. 291 (bottom), Ellen C Campbell/Chanticleer Inn. 292, Paula C. Caudill. 297, Larry Turner. 299, nwrafting/Flickr. 309, Greg Vaughn. Chapter 9: Eastern Oregon: 317 and 318 (top), Fokket/Flickr. 318 (bottom), Jan Tik/Flickr. 319, salvez/Flickr. 320, Jeffrey T. Kreulen/iStockphoto. 327, Pendleton Underground Tours. 334, IDAK/Shutterstock. 336-37, Danny Warren/iStockphoto. 343, Cacophony/wikimedia. 347, AmySelleck/Flickr Back cover, from left to right: tusharkoley / Shutterstock; Rachell Coe / Shutterstock; Andrew Zarivny / Shutterstock. Spine: Dancestrokes / Shutterstock.

About Our Writers: All photos are courtesy of the writers except for the following: Kimberly Bowker, courtesy of Tim Gallivan; Andrew Collins, courtesy of Fernando Nocedal; Christine Vovakes, courtesy of Michael Vovakes.

NOTES

NOTES

NOTES

NOTES

NOTES

NOTES

NOTES

NOTES

NOTES

NOTES

ABOUT OUR WRITERS

 Kimberly Bowker grew up hiking and kayaking in the high desert landscape of central Oregon. She wrote for Bend's daily newspaper before pursuing a freelance writing career, focusing on the topics of travel, craft beer, and love. For more information, visit ⊕ *www.kimberlybowker.com*. She updated the Central Oregon chapter.

 Andrew Collins, a former Fodor's editor, updated Experience Oregon, Portland, Oregon Coast, Columbia River Gorge and Mt. Hood, Southern Oregon, and the Eastern Oregon chapters in this edition. A resident of Oregon who travels frequently throughout the region, he has authored more than a dozen guidebooks, is editor in chief of *The Pearl* (about Portland's hip Pearl District), and produces the website ⊕ *GayTravel.About.com*. He also writes a syndicated monthly travel column; writes about restaurants, art, and design for *Four Seasons Magazine* and travel for *New Mexico Magazine*; teaches food writing and travel writing for Gotham Writers' Workshop; and has contributed to *Travel & Leisure*, *Sunset*, and dozens of other periodicals.

 Dave Sandage is a software engineer living in the heart of Willamette Valley wine country. In his spare time he enjoys cooking, wine tasting, and making his own beer and wine. Dave wrote the Willamette Valley wine feature and updated the Willamette Valley and Wine Country chapter.

 Freelance writer **Christine Vovakes** updated the Crater Lake chapter and has also written for *Fodor's California*, *Fodor's Complete Guide to the National Parks of the West*, and *Fodor's Essential USA*. Her travel articles and photographs have appeared in many publications, including the *Washington Post*, the *Christian Science Monitor*, the *Sacramento Bee*, and the *San Francisco Chronicle*.